Let's Go

Let's Go writers travel on your budget.

"Guides that penetrate the veneer of the holiday brochures and mine the grit of real life."

—*The Economist*

"The writers seem to have experienced every rooster-packed bus and lunar-surfaced mattress about which they write."

—*The New York Times*

"All the dirt, dirt cheap."

—*People*

Great for independent travelers.

"The guides are aimed not only at young budget travelers but at the independent traveler; a sort of streetwise cookbook for traveling alone."

—*The New York Times*

"Flush with candor and irreverence, chock full of budget travel advice."

—*The Des Moines Register*

"An indispensible resource, *Let's Go*'s practical information can be used by every traveler."

—*The Chattanooga Free Press*

Let's Go is completely revised each year.

"Only *Let's Go* has the zeal to annually update every title on its list."

—*The Boston Globe*

"Unbeatable: good sightseeing advice; up-to-date info on restaurants, hotels, and inns; a commitment to money-saving travel; and a wry style that brightens nearly every page."

—*The Washington Post*

All the important information you need.

"*Let's Go* authors provide a comedic element while still providing concise information and thorough coverage of the country. Anything you need to know about budget traveling is detailed in this book."

—*The Chicago Sun-Times*

"Value-packed, unbeatable, accurate, and comprehensive."

—*Los Angeles Times*

Let's Go Publications

Let's Go: Alaska & the Pacific Northwest 2001
Let's Go: Australia 2001
Let's Go: Austria & Switzerland 2001
Let's Go: Boston 2001 **New Title!**
Let's Go: Britain & Ireland 2001
Let's Go: California 2001
Let's Go: Central America 2001
Let's Go: China 2001
Let's Go: Eastern Europe 2001
Let's Go: Europe 2001
Let's Go: France 2001
Let's Go: Germany 2001
Let's Go: Greece 2001
Let's Go: India & Nepal 2001
Let's Go: Ireland 2001
Let's Go: Israel 2001
Let's Go: Italy 2001
Let's Go: London 2001
Let's Go: Mexico 2001
Let's Go: Middle East 2001
Let's Go: New York City 2001
Let's Go: New Zealand 2001
Let's Go: Paris 2001
Let's Go: Peru, Bolivia & Ecuador 2001 **New Title!**
Let's Go: Rome 2001
Let's Go: San Francisco 2001 **New Title!**
Let's Go: South Africa 2001
Let's Go: Southeast Asia 2001
Let's Go: Spain & Portugal 2001
Let's Go: Turkey 2001
Let's Go: USA 2001
Let's Go: Washington, D.C. 2001
Let's Go: Western Europe 2001 **New Title!**

Let's Go *Map Guides*

Amsterdam
Berlin
Boston
Chicago
Florence
Hong Kong
London
Los Angeles
Madrid
New Orleans
New York City
Paris
Prague
Rome
San Francisco
Seattle
Sydney
Washington, D.C.

Coming Soon: *Dublin* and *Venice*

ISRAEL

AND THE PALESTINIAN TERRITORIES

2001

Risha Kim Lee editor
Amélie Cherlin associate editor

researcher-writers
James Colbert
Amy Levin
Rachel I. Mason
Elizabeth White

Anna L. Malsberger map editor

St. Martin's Press New York

HELPING LET'S GO If you want to share your discoveries, suggestions, or corrections, please drop us a line. We read every piece of correspondence, whether a postcard, a 10-page email, or a coconut. Please note that mail received after May 2001 may be too late for the 2002 book, but will be kept for future editions. **Address mail to:**

Let's Go: Israel and the Palestinian Territories
67 Mount Auburn Street
Cambridge, MA 02138
USA

Visit Let's Go at **http://www.letsgo.com,** or send email to:

feedback@letsgo.com
Subject: "Let's Go: Israel and the Palestinian Territories"

In addition to the invaluable travel advice our readers share with us, many are kind enough to offer their services as researchers or editors. Unfortunately, our charter enables us to employ only currently enrolled Harvard students.

Distributed outside the USA and Canada by Macmillan.

ISBN: 0-312-24680-3
First edition
10 9 8 7 6 5 4 3 2 1

Let's Go: Israel and the Palestinian Territories is written by Let's Go Publications, 67 Mount Auburn Street, Cambridge, MA 02138, USA.

Printed in the USA on recycled paper with biodegradable soy ink.

HOW TO USE THIS BOOK

And the Lord said, "Let there be *Let's Go.*"
Well. . . . not really. But biblical references are no small detail in Israel, the Holy Land for Judaism, Christianity, and Islam. Below are a few words to the wise:

Seeing the crowd mystified by the words manifest before them, we went up on the mountain, and when we sat down the disciples came to us and we opened our mouths and taught them saying,

"Blessed are those who need help in preparing for their journeys for they shall be guided by the DISCOVER section." The **Discover** section provides you with an overview of travel in Israel, including **Suggested Itineraries** that give you an idea of what sights even Moses wouldn't miss.

"Blessed are those who desire with all their heart to be knowledgeable about ISRAEL, before entering therein." The **Israel** section of the guide enlightens the traveler by expounding upon **history, cultural groups, recent news,** and **customs,** followed by a list of **festivals** and **holidays.**

"Blessed are those who have been given the ESSENTIALS section, without which no soul would have any idea how to do practical stuff." The **Essentials** section contains information on everything from buying cheap tickets to what to do when you get diarrhea. Women traveling alone, gay and lesbian travelers, and minority travelers are given separate sections with specific resources and contact groups.

"Blessed are those NIFTY BLACK TABS in the margins which denote separate regions so clearly and cleverly." The majority of this volume consists of eleven geographically arranged regional chapters, moving clockwise up the coast from **Jerusalem** and terminating in **Sinai.** The coverage of each city or town is broken down into categories, which include food, accommodations, and practical information.

"Blessed are those with discriminating TASTES." In each food and accommodations section we rank establishments according to value for money. Our favorites are denoted by the highest honor given out by *Let' s Go*, the *Let's Go* thumbs-up (☒).

"Blessed are you when people speak to you in FOREIGN TONGUES and utter all manner of strange syllables." The **appendix** contains useful conversions, a **phrasebook** of handy phrases in Hebrew and Arabic, and a **glossary** filled with cutting-edge words.

"Blessed are you who have a penchant for rectangular objects." Grayboxes at times provide wonderful cultural insight, at times simply crude humor. In any case, they're usually amusing, so enjoy. Whiteboxes, on the other hand, provide important practical information, such as warnings (☒), helpful hints and further resources (☒), and border crossing information (☒).

"Blessed are the ones who so desire to understand the dynamic of CULTURAL GROUPS." Jews in Israel, in the **Israel** section, highlights a few of the differences among distinct groups within the Jewish population.

"Blessed are those who care enough about their friends and family to TALK to them." The **phone code** appears opposite the name of each region, city, or town, and is denoted by the ☎ icon. **Phone numbers** in text are also preceded by the ☎ icon.

A NOTE TO OUR READERS The information for this book was gathered by *Let's Go* researchers from May through August of 2000. Each listing is based on one researcher's opinion, formed during his or her visit at a particular time. Those traveling at other times may have different experiences since prices, dates, hours, and conditions are always subject to change. You are urged to check the facts presented in this book beforehand to avoid inconvenience and surprises.

CONTENTS

MAPS

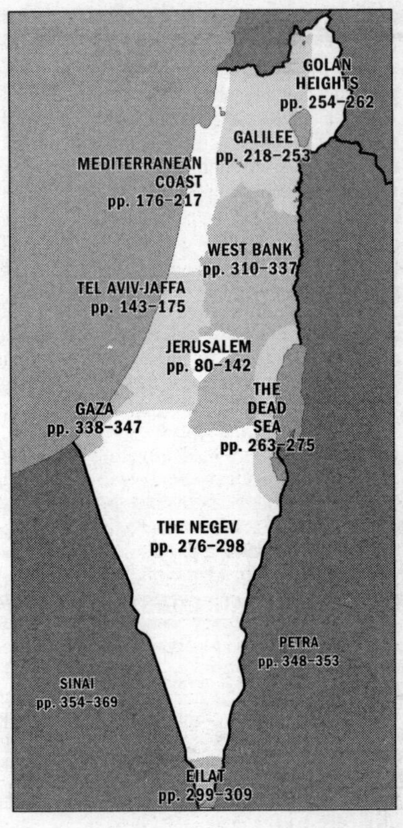

GOLAN HEIGHTS pp. 254–262
GALILEE pp. 218–253
MEDITERRANEAN COAST pp. 176–217
WEST BANK pp. 310–337
TEL AVIV-JAFFA pp. 143–175
JERUSALEM pp. 80–142
THE DEAD SEA pp. 263–275
GAZA pp. 338–347
THE NEGEV pp. 276–298
PETRA pp. 348–353
SINAI pp. 354–369
EILAT pp. 299–309

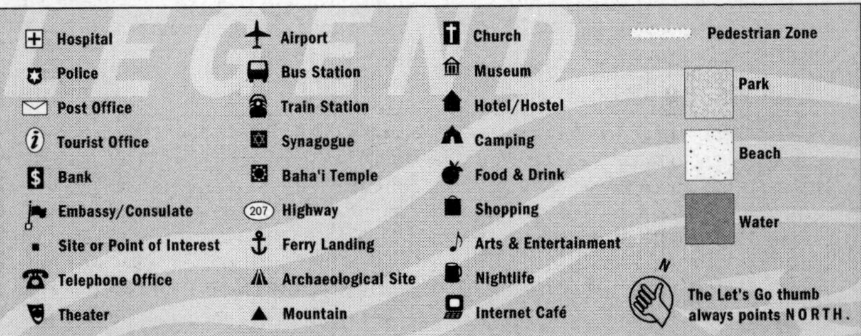

LEGEND
Hospital
Police
Post Office
Tourist Office
Bank
Embassy/Consulate
Site or Point of Interest
Telephone Office
Theater
Airport
Bus Station
Train Station
Synagogue
Baha'i Temple
207
Highway
Ferry Landing
Archaeological Site
Mountain
Church
Museum
Hotel/Hostel
Camping
Food & Drink
Shopping
Arts & Entertainment
Nightlife
Internet Café
Pedestrian Zone
Park
Beach
Water
N
The Let's Go thumb always points NORTH.

ABOUT LET'S GO

FORTY-ONE YEARS OF WISDOM

As a new millennium arrives, *Let's Go: Europe*, now in its 41st edition and translated into seven languages, reigns as the world's bestselling international travel guide. For over four decades, travelers criss-crossing the Continent have relied on *Let's Go* for inside information on the hippest backstreet cafes, the most pristine secluded beaches, and the best routes from border to border. In the last 20 years, our rugged researchers have stretched the frontiers of backpacking and expanded our coverage into Asia, Africa, Australia, and the Americas. This year, we've introduced a new city guide series with titles to San Francisco and our hometown, Boston. Now, our seven city guides feature sharp photos, more maps, and an overall more user-friendly design. We've also returned to our roots with the inaugural edition of *Let's Go: Western Europe*.

It all started in 1960 when a handful of well-traveled students at Harvard University handed out a 20-page mimeographed pamphlet offering a collection of their tips on budget travel to passengers on student charter flights to Europe. The following year, in response to the instant popularity of the first volume, students traveling to Europe researched the first full-fledged edition of *Let's Go: Europe*, a pocket-sized book featuring honest, practical advice, witty writing, and a decidedly youthful slant on the world. Throughout the 60s and 70s, our guides reflected the times. In 1969 we taught travelers how to get from Paris to Prague on "no dollars a day" by singing in the street. In the 80s and 90s, we looked beyond Europe and North America and set off to all corners of the earth. Meanwhile, we focused in on the world's most exciting urban areas to produce in-depth, fold-out map guides. Our new guides bring the total number of titles to 51, each infused with the spirit of adventure and voice of opinion that travelers around the world have come to count on. But some things never change: our guides are still researched, written, and produced entirely by students who know first-hand how to see the world on the cheap.

HOW WE DO IT

Each guide is completely revised and thoroughly updated every year by a well-traveled set of nearly 300 students. Every spring, we recruit over 200 researchers and 90 editors to overhaul every book. After several months of training, researcher-writers hit the road for seven weeks of exploration, from Anchorage to Adelaide, Estonia to El Salvador, Iceland to Indonesia. Hired for their rare combination of budget travel sense, writing ability, stamina, and courage, these adventurous travelers know that train strikes, stolen luggage, food poisoning, and marriage proposals are all part of a day's work. Back at our offices, editors work from spring to fall, massaging copy written on Himalayan bus rides into witty, informative prose. A student staff of typesetters, cartographers, publicists, and managers keeps our lively team together. In September, the collected efforts of the summer are delivered to our printer, who turns them into books in record time, so that you have the most up-to-date information available for your vacation. Even as you read this, work on next year's editions is well underway.

WHY WE DO IT

We don't think of budget travel as the last recourse of the destitute; we believe that it's the only way to travel. Living cheaply and simply brings you closer to the people and places you've been saving up to visit. Our books will ease your anxieties and answer your questions about the basics—so you can get off the beaten track and explore. Once you learn the ropes, we encourage you to put *Let's Go* down now and then to strike out on your own. You know as well as we that the best discoveries are often those you make yourself. When you find something worth sharing, please drop us a line. We're Let's Go Publications, 67 Mount Auburn St., Cambridge, MA 02138, USA (email: feedback@letsgo.com). For more info, visit our website, www.letsgo.com.

RESEARCHER-WRITERS

James Colbert *Golan Heights, Gaza, Negev, and Tzfat*

Whether riding in a hummer with Israeli soldiers, wailing with Lubavitch rabbis in Tzfat, or hiking through the slippery peaks of the Golan Heights, Jamie drank deeply of the juices of his environment. In the Negev he developed an interest in Bedouin lifestyle; in the Galilee he sat and pondered whether the Sea of Galilee was really a sea (discuss); and made friends and admirers in every city. As his editors, we are not ashamed to say that we lived vicariously through him. Once an innocent flower to Israel's charms, he emerged a strident, hitch-hiking warrior, plowing through Gaza and rarin' for more. On top of that, this witty wonder kept us in stitches. Tank you very much, Jamie.

Amy Levin *Mediterranean Coast, Dead Sea, Tel Aviv-Jaffa, and Galilee*

Proudly secular and downright sexy, Amy "Gestalt" Levin took her job a notch above and beyond the call of duty, becoming a lean, mean, detail machine. Avoiding nasty old men and emaciated hell-cats at every corner, this diamond of a researcher tackled the Mediterranean coast, extolling the virtues of every hidden, gemlike restaurant and crushing the more mundane establishments into the *Let's Go* dustbin. Our chameleon-like reporter explored all walks of life, connecting with hotel owners, hipsters, and the occasional mobster, and hitting fifteen Tel Aviv clubs in two nights in spite of a sprained ankle. At the end of her tour, this stylish heroine emerged one part American and two parts *sabra*.

Rachel I. Mason *Jerusalem, Dead Sea, and West Bank*

Ready or not here she comes. There was no stopping Rachel, a three time Let's Go veteran, who defined hard core times four. Masterminding the Jerusalem walks and playing "map-master" in every city, resisting the urge to draw in her margins and instead filling them with copious detail, she saved us from boldfacing commas at every turn. Fact checker extraordinaire, she revamped intros, corrected biblical references, and expanded history coverage at every opportunity. Drawing from her previous researching experience, she was able to give us an insider's insight as to how best to organize the book; she talked and we listened. A paragon of efficiency, Rachel barely had time to sleep let alone sit down, yet she managed to blow us away with the depth of her coverage.

Elizabeth White *Petra, Eilat, and Sinai*

As a researcher-writer for *Let's Go: Middle East 2001*, Elizabeth was known for her ability to gauge quality, sorting through kitsch to find *Let's Go* gold. In the coverage of Petra, Eilat, and Sinai, her painstaking attention to detail was apparent.

ACKNOWLEDGMENTS

Anup "Eagle Eyes" Kubal, we pledge our eternal devotion and first-born child to you for your meticulous editing and the donuts. Anna, the fastest, most organized, most efficient map editor ever, thanks for putting in the extra mile. Nazzo, you always kept us on a permanent high with your sugar highs. Turkey and Greece for depreciating our music tastes, Mindlin for dancing. Team Israel—your hard work, devotion and flexibility are what we relied on all summer. Thank you. But most importantly, to life, to life, L'Ḥaim!—**ISR Editors**

Amélie (avec l'accent), you were superb. Thanks for the summer, and making me laugh. Andrew, Alana, Ilana, Tamar, Nads, Joel, Ari, Gabe, Jesse and everyone else in ג, I thank you for your inspiration. Jessipoo, Sarah, Bethy, Yissa, Em, Toker, you have made me who I am and more. Rohit and Alex for being bad-asses. To Steph for being psychic and always believing me. To Tian, my favorite troll, for making school a home. Dylan, for pushing me and showing me who I am. Nicole, my counterpart, I can never thank you enough for your support. Michael (buh), you don't know how much I appreciate those phone conversations. Mom and Dad, thank you for your patience and love.—**RL**

Risha (with an R), thanks for accompanying me in the Britney duets, Indian-style. Thanks for all your witty, creative writing and your fabulously bad puns. Angela Carlos Daniel Baupei Kilborn-Kuo, thanks for always agreeing with me. Okay bye. Britney Spears, without you, we would be nothing. NOTHING! Roger, Elbert, Rachel, thanks for keeping me entertained. Jess and Tim, please please take your hair out of the shower drain. Oh and thanks for listening to me whine. Bathsheba Cherlin (1981-1998), born in Jerusalem's Old City, raised in New Jersey, you were an inspiration to us all. Mamie, Fernand, Maman, Papa, Grag, Blanqui: gros bisous et merci.—**AC**

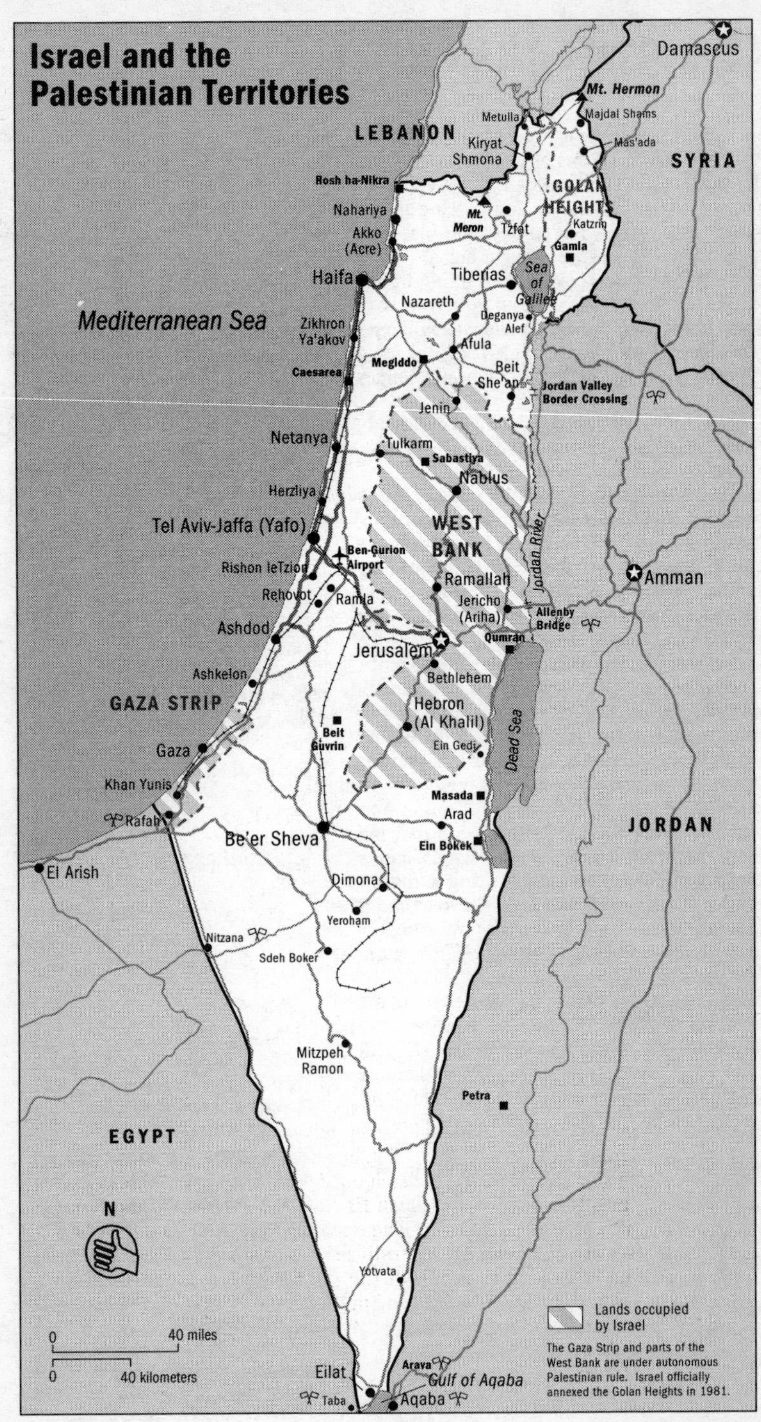

Israel and the Palestinian Territories
LEBANON
SYRIA
JORDAN
EGYPT
Damascus
Mt. Hermon
Majdal Shams
Mas'ada
Metulla
Kiryat Shmona
GOLAN HEIGHTS
Katzrin
Gamla
Rosh ha-Nikra
Nahariya
Mt. Meron
Tzfat
Akko (Acre)
Haifa
Tiberias
Sea of Galilee
Nazareth
Deganya Alef
Mediterranean Sea
Zikhron Ya'akov
Afula
Megiddo
Caesarea
Beit She'an
Jordan Valley Border Crossing
Jenin
Netanya
Tulkarm
Sabastiya
Nablus
Herzliya
WEST BANK
Tel Aviv-Jaffa (Yafo)
Ben-Gurion Airport
Jordan River
Rishon leTzion
Amman
Rehovot
Ramla
Ramallah
Jericho (Ariha)
Allenby Bridge
Ashdod
Qumran
Jerusalem
Ashkelon
Bethlehem
GAZA STRIP
Hebron (Al Khalil)
Beit Guvrin
Dead Sea
Gaza
Ein Gedi
Khan Yunis
Masada
Rafah
Arad
Be'er Sheva
Ein Bokek
El Arish
Dimona
Yeroham
Nitzana
Sdeh Boker
Mitzpeh Ramon
Petra
N
Yotvata
Lands occupied by Israel
The Gaza Strip and parts of the West Bank are under autonomous Palestinian rule. Israel officially annexed the Golan Heights in 1981.
0
40 miles
0
40 kilometers
Eilat
Arava
Gulf of Aqaba
Taba
Aqaba

DISCOVER ISRAEL AND THE PALESTINIAN TERRITORIES

Halfway through its first century, Israel has yet to resolve a psychological struggle between secularism and reverence. An inevitable sense of religion and history permeates its modern cities, where pensive philosophers and microchip millionaires sit on park benches with patriotic Zionists and day-seizing disco-goers. The nation's heterogeneity is most apparent on Friday evenings, when Tel Aviv clubs and Eilat pubs explode with revelry that can almost be heard in the reverent streets of Tzfat or in Jerusalem's Jewish Quarter. Israel has been controversial since its inception. As a result of persecution culminating in the Holocaust, Jews of all cultures came together to fashion a new kind of state and to remake themselves, sometimes at the expense of Palestinian Arabs. With the country's identity and culture in constant flux, all Israelis have their own visions of what Israel could or should be. Amos Oz, Israel's leading novelist, sees his fellow Israelis as "a warm-hearted, hot-tempered Mediterranean people that is gradually learning, through great suffering and a tumult of sound and fury, to find release both from the bloodcurdling nightmares of the past and from delusions of grandeur, both ancient and modern." Ask Israelis about their bewildering national situation, and they will tell you at length how *they* see their country—there is no lack of impassioned political or apolitical opinions. But a fundamental optimism shines through; talk with them long enough, and they will eventually smile or shrug and say, "*Yihiyeh tov*" (It will be OK).

HOLIDAY

Due to Israel's mild Mediterranean climate, seasonal factors do not play a huge role in deciding when to go, although it can get rather hot between July and August, and Jerusalem can get cold in January (see **Climate Chart,** p. 372). The traveler's primary concern is holiday season, when the country becomes jam-packed with pilgrims, hotel prices skyrocket, businesses shut down, and transportation stops running. The holidays to watch out for are mostly in October, when the country is mostly closed due to Rosh Ha-Shana, Yom Kippur and Sukkot. March and April in Jerusalem and Bethlehem are also busy due to the Orthodox Easter, but buses are still running. All festivals and holidays in Israel run from sundown the night before to nightfall the next day. For longer holidays, businesses are closed for the first day (and in the case of Passover, the last day) but remain open for the duration. For a comprehensive chart of all festivals in Israel, see **Holidays,** p. 32.

CELEBRATE

Israel is a land of great historical and religious significance. Its ancient ruins and holy sites attract visitors from around the world. There's more to do here than just tour ancient marvels, though—Israel is a modern, thriving country with a little bit of everything, from world-class scuba-diving to a Dadaist art colony. What follows are some of the best attractions and activities in Israel and the Palestinian territories. For more specific regional attractions, see the **Highlights of the Region** section at the beginning of each chapter.

LIKE A PRAYER

Jerusalem is holy to three of the world's major religions: Jews pray at the **Western Wall** (p. 112), Muslims worship at the **Dome of the Rock** (p. 111), and Christians walk the **Via Dolorosa** (p. 116). However, the spiritual richness and diversity of Israel and the Palestinian territories owe substantially to the region's many lesser-known religious and cultural centers as well. **Tzfat** (p. 234) inspired the birth of the Kabbalah, and now it and its beautiful synagogues attract seekers of spirituality to its narrow streets. The world headquarters of the Baha'i religion (p. 24) is in Haifa, and the gold-domed **Baha'i Shrine** (p. 184) and luscious surrounding gardens welcome visitors of all denominations. A visit to the village of **Daliyat al Karmel** (p. 192) offers a glimpse into the Druze way of life, hidden from the outside world for the past 1000 years (p. 24). Traditionally a nomadic people, many of Israel's Bedouin now live in villages; the **Joe Alon Bedouin Museum** (p. 283) in Be'er Sheva lends insight into their unique past and uncertain present. In 1969, the first members of the Hebrew Israelite Community (or Black Hebrews) left Chicago for Liberia, en route to the Holy Land. Forty years later, their thriving community in **Dimona** (p. 285) runs a vegan restaurant and an annual music festival.

I'M BREATHLESS

Israel's small size belies an astounding diversity in its terrain, which ranges from the arid desert of the Negev to the lush mountains of the Golan. **Makhtesh Ramon** (p. 293) is the world's largest natural crater, while **Naḥal David** (p. 270) abuts the lowest point on earth, the Dead Sea. **Har Ardon** (p. 296), in the heart of the Negev, is a challenging hike with incredible views of the desert sands. A strenuous hike to **Montfort** (p. 213), through the Galilee valley, climbs from river to hills to Crusader castle. Sinai's **Sharm esh-Sheikh** (p. 366) is renowned as the world's best scuba diving spot; **Eilat** (p. 298), at Israel's southern tip, is home to eye-catching wildlife in the sea and in the air. The rugged cliffs and cascading pools of **Naḥal Yehudiya** (p. 255) and the luminescent slopes of **Rosh Ha-Nikra** (p. 212) are a six-hour drive and worlds away.

LIVING IN A MATERIAL WORLD

While it is known more for its religious and historic sights than for its art, Israel is home to world-class museums and to burgeoning art colonies set amidst some of the country's most breathtaking landscapes. **Ein Hod** (p. 190), on the western slopes of Mt. Carmel, was founded by Dadaists and has maintained its singularly offbeat perspective. There must be something in the northern mountain air—**Tzfat** (p. 234) boasts a landscape more beautiful than the landscapes it inspires. Its winding city streets are lined with turquoise doorways and intricately painted synagogues. Sculptures by Rodin, Picasso, and others come together under the open skies in the **Billy Rose Sculpture Garden** (p. 132) of Jerusalem's Israel Museum. For a less canonical but equally illuminating experience, pay a visit to the **Hermit's House** (p. 165) in Herzliya, a one-man homage to the art of the mundane.

DON'T CRY FOR ME, ANCIENT ISRAEL

Israel and the Palestinian territories have been the stomping ground of dozens of peoples over as many centuries—the layers of civilization date back to ancient **Jericho** (p. 321), which, at 10,000 years, is the oldest known city in the world. As the sun sets over **Jerusalem** (p. 74), the remnants of fallen civilizations and startling architectural achievements shine with the city's famous gold. The hilltop fortress of **Masada** (p. 271) served as a Jewish refuge, Herod's citadel, and the site of mass martyrdom in the face of Roman conquest. **Petra** (p. 343), carved into the red cliffs of Jordan, is the country's mystical treasure. On the Mediterranean Coast, **Caesarea** (p. 197), Herod's first-century city, is remarkably intact; to the south are the hidden caves and tombs of **Beit Guvrin** (p. 173). **Nimrod's Fortress** (p. 261), an impressive crusader castle in the Golan Heights, features a secret passageway, winding stone stairways, and a magnificent view. Other highlights include **Beit She'an** (p. 229), a mound with twenty archaeologically distinct layers, and **Zippori** (p. 221), which boasts exquisite mosaics, a synagogue, and an amphitheater.

GET INTO THE GROOVE

In terms of clubs and pubs, Israel offers a lifetime supply of spandex and booze. The most hip, happening and downright sassy places can be found in **Tel Aviv** (p. 157), **Eilat** (p. 305) and (surprise, surprise) the holy city of **Jerusalem** (p. 74). Watch out for those *arsim* and *freiḥot* (your scantily-clad clubbing compadres). After your wild nights, join the slick oiled backs of the masses on a **beach** in Haifa (p. 186), Tel Aviv (p. 156), or Eilat (p. 304); don't forget to strut your stuff at night on the *tayelet*. Speaking of Eilat, use this chance to get in touch with your inner fish by **snorkeling** in the jewel-like blue-green waters. If all of the lounging liquefies your brain, sharpen your wits and your tongue by haggling at the **Shuk Ha-Pishpeshim** in Jaffa (p. 164), or the **Arab souq** in Jerusalem (p. 120).

LET'S GO PICKS

CALORIES, SHMALORIES: Let the gooey-sweet goodness of **Rukab's Ice Cream** in **Ramallah** (p. 328) dribble down your chin; gorge yourself on the sticky sweets in **Gaza City's Arafat Sweets** (p. 340); and go heavy on the heavenly chocolate syrup on your waffle from **Babette's Party** in **Jerusalem** (p. 101).

LOOK BUT DON'T FALL OFF: The **Negev** contains geological formations found nowhere else in the world. The **Makhtesh Ramon** (p. 293) crater is the closest most humans will ever come to seeing a Martian landscape. Multi-colored sand decorates the floor of nearby **Mitzpeh Ramon.** Ben-Gurion told Israelis, "Go to the desert." A visit to his tomb in **Sdeh Boker** (p. 290) on the edge of the Zin Canyon offers perhaps the most beautiful view in all of Israel.

DRINK BUT DON'T FALL DOWN:

The choice is yours: sip coffee delicately, or be a downright lush. Go for the latter at **Forum** (p. 284) in **Be'er Sheva,** and watch out for the spaceship. If you prefer the former, there's always enough time to wax intellectual at **Tmol Shilshom** (p. 102) in **Jerusalem,** which attracts readers by day and famous writers by night.

CARNIVORES BEWARE: The vegan community of **Dimona** (p. 285) in the **Negev** offers the best tofu in all of Israel, made by the Hebrew Israelites, also known as the Black Hebrews.

IF YOU GO-A, GET A BOA: Feed your shopping addiction on **Sheinken St.** with the trendiest of the trendy (Israeli trendy, that is), and stop in at the nearby **Schwartz's Fancy Feathers** (p. 157) for a fab cocktail party accessory. For a less opulent display, head on down to **Maḥaneh Yehuda** (p. 98) in Jerusalem, and bid on fresh vegetables and pita. The gargantuan **Bedouin Market** (p. 283) in **Be'er Sheva** hides a few gems amidst piles upon piles of kitsch.

SHINY, HAPPY SEA PEOPLE: Eilat is said to have some of the best scuba diving in the world (p. 305); try the **Japanese Gardens**, or, for bigger fish, take a dip at **Dolphin Reef.** The diving in **Sinai** is also extraordinary (p. 367); explore the underwater remains of the shipwreck **Yolanda** in the renowned **Ras Muhammad National Park** or **Thistlegorm**, the world's best wreck dive.

AND TO ALL A GOOD NIGHT: Israel offers all kinds of lodging in all kinds of places. **Desert Shade** (p. 294) is an eco-friendly oasis in the heart of the **Negev** with amazing views of the Ramon Crater, and **Fata Morgana** (p. 276), near the **Dead Sea**, is a secluded, bedouin-style, desert retreat. Camping out on the peak of **Mount Sinai** (p. 355), however, could be the cheapest option, and the best experience of your life.

SUGGESTED ITINERARIES

The following itineraries are meant as guidelines and generally leave 1-2 days extra for filling in the gaps. For more information on specific interests, see **Celebrate,** (p. 2) and **Let's Go Picks** (p. 4).

ITINERARY 1 (ONE WEEK) One week can be adequate for hitting Israel's highlights. Begin in **Jerusalem** (p. 75)—everyone else does—for an incredible encounter with Israel's cultural, religious, historical, and political climate. Spend at least 2 days in the **Old City** (p. 96) and another day exploring other neighborhoods. Early to bed, early to (sun)rise: catch dawn at **Masada** (p. 245), then roll around in the mineral mud and float in the therapeutic waters of the **Dead Sea** (p. 239). Visit the most oft visited pilgrimage site of the West Bank—**Bethlehem** (p. 285) is home to beautiful churches and is the closest and most easily accessible of the West Bank towns. Head north to **Tzfat** (p. 211), the birthplace of Kabbalah (Jewish mysticism) and home to an artist's colony. The stony labyrinths and bustling market of **Akko** (p. 183) are a stark contrast to Tzfat's intense serenity. For a thrill-a-minute finale, sun by day and sin by night in **Tel Aviv's** beaches, bars, and discotheques (p. 129).

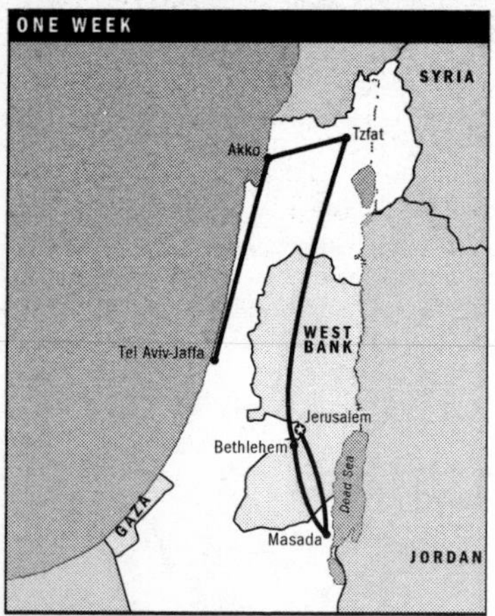

ITINERARY 2 (TWO WEEKS) Spend 4 or 5 days in **Jerusalem** (p. 75). In addition to the must-see sights, try browsing the Arab market (p. 85) or visiting some of

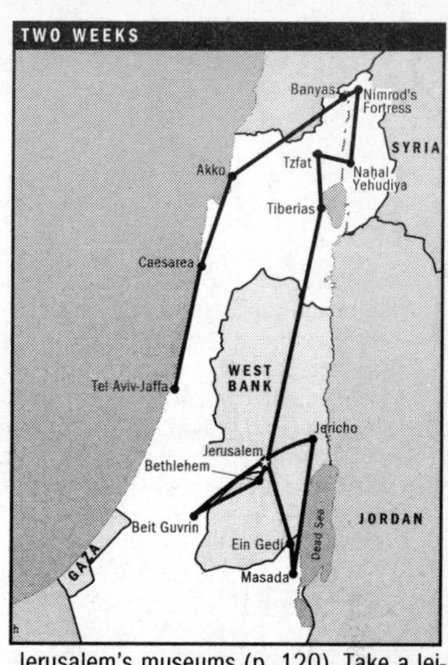

Jerusalem's museums (p. 120). Take a leisurely trip to the **Dead Sea** region: climb **Masada** (p. 245), relax at the beach, and hike **Ein Gedi's** beautiful trails (p. 243). Explore the ruins of the oldest known city in the world and experience the vibrance of modern life in **Jericho** (p. 292). The immaculately preserved underground caves and tombs of **Beit Guvrin** (p. 156) provide welcome relief from the scorching desert sun. Move on to **Bethlehem** (p. 285) via Jerusalem, and then to the **Sea of Galilee** (p. 208). Sit down to a fresh fish dinner after a day of biking around the lake and visiting historical sights. While away a peaceful day in **Tzfat** (p. 211), and continue north to the **Golan Heights** (p. 229) where lush vegetation and cascading waterfalls make for refreshing hikes. Highlights include **Naḥal Yehudiya** for hiking and splashing (p. 231), **Nimrod's Fortress** (p. 236) for ruins, and the **Banyas** (p. 236) for a combination. Cruise along the Mediterranean Coast: spend the morning in **Akko** (p. 183) and an afternoon in **Caesarea** (p. 178), Israel's premier archaeological beach town. Finish up in **Tel Aviv** (p. 129), exploring the flea market and alleyways of **Jaffa** (p. 146) before a night of club-hopping in the city.

ITINERARY 3 (THREE WEEKS) As the center of three of the world's major religions and three millennia of history, as well as a

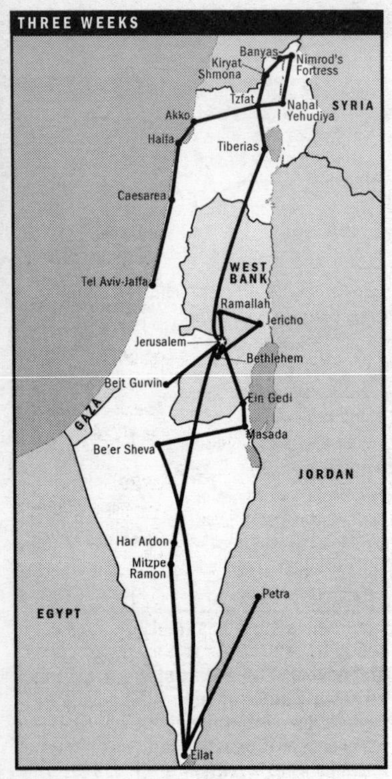

vibrant modern culture, **Jerusalem** (p. 75) warrants as much time as you can give it. **Mitzpeh Ramon** (p. 265), with the world's largest natural craters, is well worth the trip into the desert. Get glassy eyed over **Har Ardon** (p. 268), a truly magnificent hike. From there, consider a day of snorkeling and sun-bathing in **Eilat** (p. 271). Eilat is also a convenient departure-point for a trip into the rock-hewn **Petra,** Jordan (p. 313), the Nabatean city lost to historians for centuries. On the way back to Jerusalem, make a stop in **Be'er Sheva** (p. 251) for its **Bedouin market** (p. 255), then spend a couple days in the **Dead Sea** region (p. 239), including **Masada** (p. 245). From Jerusalem, **Beit Guvrin** (p. 156) makes a good day trip. Jerusalem is also a convenient base for travel to **Bethlehem** (p. 285), **Jericho** (p. 292), and **Ramallah** (p. 297), a breezy mountain town that serves as a center for Palestinian intellectual life. When you've had your fill of desert air, make your way to the **Sea of Galilee** (p. 208) and then north to **Tzfat** (p. 211) and the **Golan Heights** (p. 229). Move down the Mediterranean Coast, stopping at **Akko** (p. 183) and **Ḥaifa** (p. 159), a port city that is the world-center of the Baha'i religion and houses the stunning **Baha'i shrine** and garden (p. 165). Continuing down the coast, stop at **Caesarea's** Herodian ruins (p. 178), before heading to **Tel Aviv-Jaffa** (p. 129).

ISRAEL

HISTORY

ANCIENT HISTORY

The first true empire in world history emerged in the 24th century BCE, when a dynasty of Semitic rulers conquered all of Upper Mesopotamia, including Asia Minor and southeastern Arabia. In the land that would be Israel, the third millennium marked the end of the Early Bronze Age. Substantial urban development led to the construction of several towns that appear in the Bible. The predominantly Canaanite population spoke a language from which the language spoken in Israelite times evolved, and of which biblical Hebrew was a dialect.

An important trade route between Egypt and **Mesopotamia,** the territory that makes up modern-day Israel was periodically conquered by both civilizations, as well as by the chariot-racing Hyksos and Hittites. The Bible begins the recorded history of the area with the story of Abraham, the first of the Patriarchs. The semi-nomadic Amorite tribes' migration to the land four thousand years ago has been linked with the biblical tradition of Abraham's (Avraham in Hebrew, Ibrahim in Arabic) journey from Chaldea (Genesis 12). These Semitic-speaking people, referred to as the 'Apiru in meticulous Egyptian records, may have been the ancestors of the **Hebrews.** These semi-nomads frequently troubled Canaan's Egyptian-controlled kings, who pleaded to their overlords for help in the 14th century.

Whether or not the 'Apiru became the Israelites remains a mystery. Some theorize that the Israelites were highlanders who united in opposition to the urban, valley-dwelling Canaanite traders. Others believe that the Israelites were forced from the coastal area by invading "sea peoples" in the 13th century BCE. The invaders, now believed to be the descendants of the Myceneans of Greece, became known as the Philistines. Their cities included the ports of Gaza (see p. 334), Ashkelon (see p. 169), and Jaffa (see p. 161).

7000 BCE
Stone Age town in present-day Jericho.

1800
Nomads from Mesopotamia settle in Canaan.

1020
Israelite Monarchy established under Saul.

1000
David captures Jerusalem and makes it capital of his kingdom.

950
Solomon constructs First Temple in Jerusalem.

922
Kingdom of Israel splits after the death of King Solomon.

587
Nebuchadnezzar sacks Jerusalem and initiates the Babylonian Captivity of the Jews.

538-515
Temple in Jerusalem rebuilt

332
Alexander conquers Persians; Hellenistic rule.

THE IRON AGE (1200-586 BCE)

Whatever their origins, evidence shows that the scattered tribes of the Judean and Galilean hills began interacting around 1200 BCE. The next two centuries are known as the Period of Judges. Local leaders, Gideon and Samuel among them, united the Israelite tribes under a new god, Yahweh, to fight off the encroaching Egyptians, Canaanites, and Philistines. Despite their efforts, the Philistines triumphed in 1200 BCE and wrestled control from the Israelites. The Philistines left behind two lasting contributions: their expertise in iron work and a new name for the country—Palestine (derived from the root word Philistia). Possibly inspired by the arrival of Semitic

166-160 Maccabean revolt and beginning of Hasmonean dynasty.

163-42 Jewish autonomy under the Hasmonean monarchy.

63 Jerusalem captured by Roman general Pompey.

4 Jesus born.

66 CE Jewish revolt against the Romans.

70 Destruction of Second Temple and Jerusalem.

132-135 Bar Kokhba uprising against Rome.

638 Jerusalem becomes holy city of Islam. Dome of the Rock constructed.

969-1171 Shi'a empire controlled by Fatimids.

1099 First Crusade launched, Jerusalem occupied. Muslims and Jews massacred.

1291 Mamluk rule begins.

1517 Ottoman Turkish army defeats Mamluks.

1882 Large- scale immigration from Europe (Aliya) begins

brethren from Egypt (the Exodus), the Israelites established their own kingdom under **Saul** at the end of the 11th century BCE.

The Israelite kingdom reached its peak during the reign of Saul's successor **David,** and that of David's son, **Solomon.** The construction of the Temple of Jerusalem is considered Solomon's most formidable feat, but the cost of the Temple and other civil projects proved a heavy burden for his subjects. After Solomon's death in 922 BCE, social and political unrest split the empire into the Kingdom of Israel in the north, never very happy to be ruled by Jerusalem-centric southerners, and the Kingdom of Judah in the south. Philistia had been reduced to a small coastal strip around Gaza, though the **Phoenicians,** a sea-faring people from the area between Akko and Tartus, prospered from the decline of the Egyptian Empire.

The Assyrians conquered Phoenicia and Israel in the late 8th century BCE. The ten tribes of northern Israel were taken into captivity and never returned. Judah became a vassal state of the Assyrian empire until the Assyrians themselves were crushed by the Babylonians. The Babylonian king **Nebuchadnezzar** conquered Judah, razed the Temple, burned Jerusalem, and deported many Jews to Mesopotamia (the Babylonian Captivity or Exile) in 587 BCE. When the Persians defeated Nebuchadnezzar's successor some 50 years later, King Cyrus permitted the Jews to return to Jerusalem and build the Second Temple (completed n 515 BCE). Though small, this new Jewish community was revived by the Jewish governor Nehemiah and by the Babylonian Jew Ezra.

GREEKS & NABATEANS (332-63 BCE)

The Israelites prospered intellectually and economically under the Persians, until Alexander the Great conquered the region in 332 BCE. His heirs, the Ptolemies, succeeded him in 323 BCE when Alexander died. The Syrian-based **Seleucids** displaced the Ptolemies in 198 BCE and attempted to Hellenize the Jews. Judah Maccabee, responding to the persecutions of **Antiochus IV,** led a revolt of the Jewish lower-classes, now commemorated by the holiday of Ḥanukkah. Victorious, the **Maccabees** resanctified the Temple in 164 BCE and founded the **Hasmonean Dynasty.** In spite of potent internal conflict, the Hasmonean Dynasty ruled Palestine for over a century.

The **Nabateans,** originally a nomadic Arab tribe, moved into the area south of the Dead Sea around the 2nd century BCE, taking advantage of the enmity between the Ptolemies and Seleucids to establish their hold on those lands. They emerged as an independent kingdom by about 169 BCE. The Nabateans also interacted with the Hasmoneans, sometimes as allies, sometimes as enemies, and took control of at least a part of the Red Sea trade route, which proved to be an important source of income. With **Petra** (in modern Jordan) as its capital, the Nabatean kingdom continued to flourish, even when it became a Roman client state in the first century CE. In 106 CE, the Roman emperor **Trajan** was finally able to conquer Petra. He abolished the kingdom and reorganized its territories into a Roman province.

THE ROMANS (63 BCE-324 CE)

In 63 BCE, the Roman general **Pompey** swept in, secured much of modern-day Israel, and ruled via Herod the Great, who solidified his regal claims by a politically astute marriage with the Hasmonean princess Mariamne. The territory was made into a Roman province (Judea) in 44 CE, leading to Jerusalem's rebellion in 65-66 CE. In 70 CE the Roman general **Titus,** faced with the choice of sparing the Temple at great military cost or burning Jerusalem, chose to save his men and burned the Temple with the rest of Jerusalem. The destruction of the Second Temple led to dramatic upheaval and despair among the Jewish people. Three years later the Romans captured the last Jewish stronghold at **Masada** (see p. 271). The Romans exiled the majority of Jerusalem's population, dispersing them throughout the empire. Jewish hopes for liberation from Roman rule were raised again when an uprising broke out in 123 CE. Simon Bar Kosiba (Bar Kokhba) headed the revolt. The Jews made substantial gains in the early years of the revolt, and the tenth Roman legion was defeated and withdrew to Caesarea. In the final period, Roman troops pushed the insurgents to their fortress, Beitar, in Judea, which fell in 135 CE. In the wake of the revolt, many towns and villages in Judea were razed. Perhaps to obliterate the land's historical connection with the Jews, Hadrian bestowed on the territory the name Syria-Palestine, after the Philistines.

THE BYZANTINES (330-637)

With the division of the empire into Latin West and Byzantine East in 330 CE, Palestine came under the supervision of **Constantinople.** Although little changed administratively, the adoption of Christianity by Emperor Constantine in 331 CE created increased interest in what to many was the "Holy Land" (see p. 22). Led by pilgrim St. Eleni (Constantine's mother), worshipers and devout financiers built churches and endowed monasteries and schools. The Ghassanids, a Christian Arab client state in northern Syria, acted as a buffer between Palestine and Persia. Behind the frontier, political stability, disrupted only during the Samaritans' revolt in 529 CE and a brief Persian invasion a few decades later, fostered a new sense of prosperity in the region.

THE EARLY ARABS (636-1095)

After the death of the **Prophet Muhammad** in 632 CE (see **Islam**, p. 20), Bedouin armies, inspired by Islam and the prospect of substantial booty, ventured outside their traditional strongholds in central Arabia and, by 642, had conquered Mesopotamia, Palestine, Syria, Persia, and Egypt. The Egyptians, tired of Byzantine taxation and religious rigidity, appreciated the Arabs' relative tolerance, if not Islam itself.

1917
Balfour Declaration.

1948
State of Israel declared. War of Independence.

1949
Jerusalem divided under Israeli and Jordanian rule. Israel admitted to the UN.

1956
Sinai Campaign.

1967
Six-Day War.

1968-1970
Egypt's War of Attrition against Israel.

1970
Black September. War between Jordan and PLO.

1973
Yom Kippur War.

1978
Camp David Accords.

1979
Israel-Egypt peace treaty signed.

1985
Free Trade Agreement signed with United States.

1987
Intifada begins.

1990-91
Gulf War.

1994
Palestinian self-government in Gaza and Jericho.

ISRAEL

1995 Rabin assassinated at peace rally.

1997 Hebron Protocol signed by Israel and the Palestine Authority

2000 Israel withdraws from Lebanon

Muhammad's death gave rise to political confusion, as he had designated no successor. Amid vigorous debate as to whether the successor had to be a blood relative, **Abu Bakr** was chosen as the first successor (*khalifa*, or caliph). Ruling from 632 to 634, he was followed by Omar (634-44), Uthman (644-56), and finally Ali (656-61), all based in Medina. The election of Ali incited a civil war and produced a lasting schism in Islam between the **Sunni** (the "orthodox," who believe that the caliph should be chosen by the community of believers), and the **Shi'a** (those who supported Ali's claim and who believe that the caliph should be a direct descendant of the prophet). This division notwithstanding, the first four caliphs are known to most Muslims as the **Rashidun** (the Rightly Guided Caliphs). The advent of the **Umayyad Dynasty,** founded in 661, crushed Shi'a opposition and installed a Sunni hereditary caliphate (unrelated to the Prophet). Eighty years later, the Islamic world stretched from Narbonne to Samarkand. By 750, when the 'Abbasids overthrew the Umayyads on charges of decadence and impiety, the majority of the peasantry had converted to Islam. A mammoth bureaucracy, operating out of Baghdad and composed of everything from tax officials to scribes to Islamic jurists *(ulama)*, helped run the empire.

Successive 'Abbasid caliphs, usually based in Baghdad, were never without challenges; the rival Umayyad family had established a potentially troublesome dynasty in Spain, while various Shi'a dynasties flourished on the borders of the 'Abbasid empire. The Shi'a Fatimids, attacking eastward from their domain in Tunisia, expelled the 'Abbasids from Egypt in 969. They established Cairo as their new capital to replace the old 'Abbasid center, Fustat. By 977, the Fatimids had captured most of Palestine, controlled Jerusalem, and were prospering through trade. It was the Fatimid Caliph al-Hakim who broke the long-established trend of Muslim toleration of other faiths and destroyed the **Church of the Holy Sepulchre.**

THE CRUSADES (1095-1291)

Europe's internal violence and economic prosperity and rumors of Seljuk Muslim policies regarding the treatment of Christian pilgrims prompted western Europeans to launch a series of **Crusades** to recapture the Holy Land. Impelled by desires for land, power, and heavenly reward, the Crusaders wreaked havoc. Massacring the Muslim and Jewish inhabitants of Jerusalem in 1099, the Crusaders established a feudal kingdom under **Godfrey I** and then **Baldwin I.** Consistently outnumbered and outclassed, the members of the second and third Crusades were choked at the hands of the Zengids of Damascus and **Salah al-Din** (a Kurd), founder of the short-lived **Ayyubid** Dynasty (1171-1250). Salah al-Din dethroned the Fatimids in 1192 with an army of Turkish slaves (Mamluks). The Fourth through Seventh Crusades did little good to anyone but the Venetians, who thrived on trade with the Middle East. The Crusader States fell one by one: Edessa in 1144, Jerusalem in 1187, and Acre in 1291.

MAMLUKS & OTTOMANS (1250-1917)

Although Salah al-Din's victories over the Crusaders made him a hero among his people, his finely disciplined slave armies became a scourge for his successors. Chosen as youths, then trained and equipped by the palace, the **Mamluks** were technically property of the sultan, but their collective strength threatened the sultan's authority, which was tenuous at best. In 1250, **'Izz al-Din,** a Mamluk of the Bahri clan, resolved to dispense with formality as well as the Ayyubids and rule the sultanate directly. Chronic instability and infighting followed. Lifestyles for those at the top were still lavish, but life expectancies decreased dramatically. By 1291, Mamluks controlled all of the former Crusader outposts, including Acre, Shobak, and Montfort. They even managed to stop the Mongols at 'Ayn Jalut (1260), though the Horde had already sacked Baghdad and destroyed the 'Abbasid Caliphate (1258), as well as taken Aleppo and Damascus (both in 1260).

When the **Ottoman Empire,** expanding out from Anatolia, gained formal sovereignty over Palestine and Egypt in the early part of the 16th century, the Mamluks still retained most of their political power. Through appointments, bribery, and assassination, however, the Ottoman sultans garnered real and effective control. By manipulating their local "representatives" and playing them against one another, the Ottoman rulers enjoyed seemingly indelible authority.

When the gates of Vienna stood firm against Ottoman armies in 1683, the Ottomans began worrying about the fate of their increasingly decrepit empire. The animated ports of Palestine, Syria, and Egypt had once provided the sole access to the East; now, they were relegated to insignificance as Portuguese sailors steered their way around the Horn of Africa. Spanish discovery of the New World created opportunities for seemingly limitless economic expansion. The once-formidable Ottoman Empire became "the sick man of Europe."

ZIONISM (1882-1914)

Although small Jewish communities were present in Palestine over the 18 centuries following the Roman exile, the vast majority of the world's Jews existed in diaspora communities in Europe, the Middle East, North Africa, and, more recently, the Americas. Throughout this period, many Jews maintained the hope of someday returning to and rebuilding the ancient homeland. This became the focus of the political movement of Zionism in the late 19th and early 20th centuries. Jews in many European countries were emancipated in the 19th century. Exposed to various contemporary political movements, some Jews in European countries flocked to the banner of revolutionary socialism while others preached assimilation. A third group was inspired by nationalism and, unconvinced that European nations would accept Jews as full citizens, preached a return to Israel.

In 1882, a group of Jews made *aliya* (or "going up," the Hebrew term for Jewish immigration to Israel) to the "Old-New Land," forming agricultural settlements based on private land ownership *(moshavim)*. Many were sponsored by Parisian Baron Edmund de Rothschild. In 1896, Austrian journalist **Theodore Herzl** published a pamphlet entitled *The Jewish State*, promoting the establishment of a Jewish homeland as the answer to Jewish persecution. Settlement in *Eretz Israel* ("the land of Israel") had been proposed in such earlier works as Leo Pinsker's *Auto-Emancipation*, and spiritual Zionism had garnered substantial support among Russian and Eastern European Jews through the work of **Aḥad Ha'am**. Herzl, however, was the first Western, secular Jew to not only articulate the need for action, but to use political means to achieve that end. He initially considered Uganda and South America as sites for the Jewish state. Only Palestine, however, had the emotional lure to unite diaspora Jews.

The second *aliya* (1904-1914) witnessed the development of cooperative agricultural settlements *(kibbutzim)*, led by Jews with the socialist principles, sense of urgency, and nationalism to sustain the Zionist movement. Zionism diverged into two distinct movements: "Political Zionism," inspired by Herzl, sought to gain international support for the establishment of a Jewish state; "Practical Zionism," sparked by Aḥad Ha'am and the *ªovevei Zion*, aimed to build the Jewish community in Palestine as a source of spiritual cohesion for Diaspora Jewry.

THE BRITISH MANDATE (1914-39)

During World War I, the British government, at war with the German-allied Ottomans, conducted secret and separate negotiations with both the Arabs and the Zionists to enlist their help. To obtain Arab support, Britain pledged, in 1915-16 correspondence between Sharif Hussein of Mecca (of the Hashemite family) and the British High Commissioner in Egypt, Sir Henry McMahon, to back "the independence of the Arabs" in exchange for an Arab declaration of war against the Ottomans. The Arab revolt started in June 1916, assisted by the dynamic **Lawrence of Arabia,** who led attacks on Ottoman forces throughout what is now Jordan. At the same time, Britain sought political support from Jews worldwide by offering sympathy to the Zionist movement. Jewish military units under the flag of the Jewish Legion fought alongside British troops for the liberation of Palestine from Ottoman rule, and took part in the battle of Galipoli. The November 1917 **Balfour Declaration** stated that Britain viewed "with favour the establishment in Palestine of a national home for the Jewish people, it being clearly understood that nothing shall be done which may prejudice the civil and religious rights of existing non-Jewish communities in Palestine." Many Arabs were outraged, and Hussein's suspicions grew. The vague wording of the Balfour Declaration and the ambiguity of the boundaries agreed upon in the McMahon-Hussein correspondence complicated the situation.

Meanwhile, the British and French had made a separate deal. The **Sykes-Picot Agreement** in 1916 divided the region into zones of permanent British and French influence. At the war's end, the various promises made by Britain to the Arabs, the Jews, and the French resulted in a muddled system of mandates: the newly created **League of Nations** awarded the Western European powers control over the territories from which the Ottomans had been expelled with the stated purpose of preparing these countries for independence. Great Britain was thus given a mandate over Palestine (which included modern-day Israel, Jordan, the West Bank, and Gaza) and Iraq, while France was accorded Syria and Lebanon.

Throughout the inter-war years, rising Arab and Jewish nationalism constantly tested British and French colonial rule. In Palestine, the intervening 30 years of British rule saw institutional and economic development under the leadership of **David Ben-Gurion's** Labor Movement. Land was extensively purchased from Arab owners, many of whom resided in neighboring countries, and Jewish immigration to Palestine increased. The Arab population of Palestine grew more anxious that they were in danger of losing their clear majority, and Palestinian Arab nationalist organizations such as the Higher Arab Council were established in an effort to combat Zionist activities and influence British policy. Leaders such as the Grand Mufti of Jerusalem, Haj Amin al-Husseini, sought support abroad for the termination of the British mandate and the cessation of all Zionist activity.

The British tried various unsuccessful tactics to appease each side. With the rise of Nazism in Germany, tens of thousands of European Jews sought to enter Palestine by any means. Underground Jewish efforts to assist illegal immigration led to greater friction between the settlers and the Mandatory Government. Meanwhile, growing Arab discontent with the developing situation culminated in the Arab Revolt of 1936-39, which the British were only able to put down with considerable military force. With the outbreak of World War II, Zionist leaders patched up their relationship with the British to support the war effort against Germany—despite the notorious 1939 White Paper, which forbade any meaningful Jewish immigration to Palestine. The Arabs, discouraged by England's ambiguity, negotiated with the Germans for control of Palestine and largely supported the Nazis.

PARTITION AND WAR

THE 1948 WAR OF INDEPENDENCE. Shortly after the conclusion of World War II, an exhausted Great Britain submitted the question of Palestine to the newly formed United Nations. The UN General Assembly voted in 1947 to partition Palestine into two states, Jewish and Arab. The Jewish leadership accepted the resolution with some reluctance, while Palestinian Arab leaders and the governments of neighboring Arab states rejected the plan completely, denying the UN's authority to divide and distribute territories they considered to be Arab patrimony. As the British prepared to evacuate Palestine in accordance with the partition resolution, Jews and Arabs clashed in sporadic skirmishes, purchased arms overseas, and planned for full-scale war.

On May 14, 1948, the British mandate over Palestine ended and David Ben-Gurion declared the independence of the State of Israel. The next day, a combined army of Syrian, Iraqi, Lebanese, Saudi, Egyptian, and Jordanian troops marched in. Israel had secured not only its UN-allotted territory but also some land in the north and in the West Bank designated for Palestine by the UN. The Gaza Strip, which had also been designated for Palestine, was secured during the war by Egypt, and the West Bank and half of Jerusalem by Jordan. Thousands of Palestinian refugees crowded into camps in the West Bank, Gaza, and bordering Arab states. The dispossessed Palestinians came to bitterly remember the 1948 war as "al-Nakba," or the Catastrophe. **King Abdullah** of Jordan took control of the West Bank in 1950 and declared a unified **Hashemite Kingdom of Jordan;** this move met an icy reception from Palestinians and other Arab governments. To the Palestinians, Jordanian rule was not much different from any other foreign occupation.

THE SUEZ CRISIS AND PAN-ARABISM. Egypt, weakened by struggles between nationalists and the monarchy, fell into shambles after its 1948 loss to Israel. In 1952, following a bloody confrontation between British soldiers and Egyptian police officers, a group of young army officers, led by charismatic heartthrob **Colonel Gamal Abd al-Nasser,** seized power from the late King Fouad's corrupt son, Farouk. Drawing from the writings of countless Arab nationalists, Nasser espoused a highly emotional brand of pan-Arabism, hoping to unify the Arabic-speaking masses into one state powerful enough to resist imperial encroachments and to take control of Palestine. When Nasser forced Britain to withdraw from Egypt in 1954, many puppet Arab leaders dependent on foreign assistance became alarmed by his growing popularity.

Nasser had begun buying Soviet arms from Czechoslovakia in defiance of a 1950 West-imposed arms control deal. He also intensified the guerilla campaign against Israel from bases in the Gaza Strip. In 1956, the United States clumsily attempted to curtail Nasser's power by withdrawing its offer to finance the Aswan High Dam. Rather than yield to the snub, Nasser nationalized the previously international Suez Canal to use its revenues for the dam. On October 24, 1956, Jordan, Syria, and Egypt established a joint military command, directed against Israel.

Israel, Britain, and France devised a scheme to take the canal. Israel took the Sinai, opened its port of Eilat to international shipping, and dealt Nasser's military a major blow. The Anglo-French force entered Egypt and began to seize the canal under the pretext of separating Egyptian and Israeli combatants. The military victors, however, had not considered world reaction to their adventure. The United States and the Soviet Union, both furious, applied intense diplomatic pressure. When Israel, Britain, and France withdrew their troops to placate the U.S., Nasser was heralded as the savior of the Arab world without having won a battle.

THE 1967 SIX-DAY WAR. During the mid 1960's there was an increase in **Palestinian Liberation Organization** (PLO) -backed raids on Israel. In return, Israel hit Palestinian refugee camps. When Syria's hard-line government turned up the rhetoric, Nasser stepped in, concentrating the Egyptian army in the Sinai and successfully demanding the withdrawal of the UN buffer-zone troops stationed there since 1956. Israeli Prime Minister **Levi Eshkol** nervously warned that a blockade of the Straits of Tiran would be taken as an act of aggression. Nasser, under pressure from Syria and Saudi Arabia, initiated a blockade on May 22, 1967. Jordan, Iraq, and Syria deployed troops along Israel's borders. On June 5, 1967, Israel launched a preemptive strike against air fields in the Sinai, obliterating the Egyptian air force before it ever got off the ground. Eshkol issued a warning to **King Hussein** via the UN supervision force, but Hussein refused to heed it; he opened fire on the UN headquarters in Jerusalem and began bombarding Jewish Jerusalem. In response, Israeli forces broke through the Jordanian lines, surrounded the Old City, and advanced toward Ramallah and the Dead Sea; simultaneously, they attacked Janin in the North.

East Jerusalem and the Old City fell to Israel on June 7, and by June 9 all parties had accepted the cease-fire. Shortly afterwards, Israel annexed East Jerusalem, much to the chagrin of the United States. From Egypt, Israel had won the Sinai Peninsula (all the way to the Suez Canal) and the Gaza Strip, from Syria the Golan Heights, and from Jordan the West Bank. With the United States behind Israel and the Soviet Union behind Nasser, any local conflict raised the threat of superpower confrontation. UN Security Council Resolution 242, passed in November 1967 and accepted by all parties, stipulated "withdrawal of Israeli armed forces from territories occupied in the recent conflict." Bickering over the intentional ambiguity of the document began immediately, while the situation on the Israeli-Egyptian border (the Suez Canal) degenerated into what was known as the **War of Attrition.**

THE PLO AND JORDAN

The 1967 War created 400,000 more Palestinian refugees, most of whom went to Jordan. With this influx of Palestinians, the Jordanian government and the PLO were thrown together in a tense relationship: Hussein wanted to hold secret peace negotiations with the Israelis, while the PLO hoped to use Jordan as a base for attacks on Israeli-held territory. Responding to PLO raids, the Israeli army attacked the Jordanian town of Karameh. Though the town's resident Palestinians were defeated, the image of FATAH (Palestine National Liberation Movement) members standing together (with Jordanian support) against Israeli forces became a tremendously successful image for FATAH. Young recruits flocked, giving the PLO greater control over the camps and threatening Hussein's sovereignty.

In September 1970, Hussein's and **Yassir Arafat's** conflicting ambitions exploded. Infuriated by a hard-line PLO faction's hijacking of a number of commercial airliners (to protest the exclusion of Palestinians from negotiations between Israel, Egypt, and Jordan), Hussein declared war on the PLO. Martial law was imposed, and fighting between Jordanian and PLO troops took over 3000 lives. September 1970 became known among Palestinians as **Black September.** After Arab League mediation and Nasser's personal intervention, an agreement was forged, requiring the PLO to move its headquarters to Lebanon.

In October 1974, the Arab League declared in Rabat, Morocco that the PLO, not Jordan, was "the sole legitimate representative of the Palestinian people." This incensed King Hussein, but when the other 20 Arab nations assented to PLO representation in the League, he was forced to agree. In November 1974, the UN General Assembly granted the PLO observer status in the UN.

WAR AND PEACE: 1970-1988

WAR OF ATTRITION. In 1969, with the help of Soviet military instruction and supplies, Egypt launched the War Of Attrition against Israel. The two governments hoped to extract concessions from Israel by inflicting heavy material and human losses on the country. Within a few years, the war became too heavy a burden for Egypt to bear. In order to alleviate his country's financial crisis, Sadat sought to reopen the lucrative Suez canal and reclaim the desperately needed Sinai oil fields. In 1972, he expelled the numerous Soviet military advisors in Egypt, and, seeing little hope in negotiations, began making preparations to attack Israel.

YOM KIPPUR WAR. On October 6, 1973, when most Israelis were in synagogues for **Yom Kippur** (the Day of Atonement), the holiest day of the Jewish year, Egypt and Syria launched a surprise assault. In the war's first three days, Egyptian forces crossed the Suez Canal, swept through the Golan Heights and almost reached the Jordan River. Within a matter of days, as the Arab armies moved beyond their Soviet-supplied ground-to-air missile cover, Israel launched a series of fierce missile attacks that stopped the Arab advance. The Arab states initiated an oil embargo against the United States and Holland in retaliation against their support of Israel. Despite the success of the embargo, upheld by Western Europe, the Arab forces faced imminent military defeat.

GENEVA ACCORDS. Egypt, Jordan, and ultimately Syria, decided to participate in the Geneva Peace Conference (convened on December 21, 1973), for the settlement of the conflict under the chair of the United States and the Soviet Union. All parties finally agreed to disengage forces by May 1974 in an agreement negotiated by then-United States Secretary of State **Henry Kissinger.** The subsequent Sinai I and II agreements returned much of the Sinai to Egypt. Both sides, though, had suffered huge losses. Israeli public uproar over the government's unpreparedness prompted Prime Minister **Golda Meir** to resign in April. Israel had won, but the aura of invincibility it had earned over the years had dissipated.

Throughout the 1970s, an increasing number of Israelis began to settle in the occupied territories. On November 11, 1976, the UN Security Council condemned this West Bank policy and demanded that Israel follow the Geneva Convention's rules regarding occupied territory. Although Prime Minister **Yitzḥak Rabin** (of the left-leaning Labor Party) discouraged permanent West Bank settlement, the next government (after 1977), under Prime Minister Menaḥem Begin of the right-wing Likud bloc, invested money and effort in new settlements.

CAMP DAVID ACCORDS. Eager to regain the Sinai, Sadat decided to seek unilateral peace with Israel. In November 1977, Sadat made a historic visit to Jerusalem and was officially welcomed. By September 1978, Begin and Sadat had forged an agreement with the help of US President **Jimmy Carter** at Camp David, the presidential retreat in Maryland. The most successful and lasting stipulation was Israel's agreement to relinquish the Sinai in exchange for peace and full diplomatic relations with Egypt. However, the stipulations concerning Israel's control of the West Bank and Gaza were more muddled. Sadat returned to Cairo content that Palestinians in the occupied territories would be granted full personal and territorial sovereignty within the next five years, while Begin maintained that nothing regarding the occupied territories had been agreed upon.

After the Camp David Accords, early hopes that other Arab states would negotiate with Israel evaporated. In October 1981, in response to cracking down on fundamentalists, Sadat was assassinated and **Hosni Mubarak,** Sadat's Vice President, was sworn in. Though sticking to the terms of the 1979 Camp David peace treaty, Mubarak held Israel at arm's length, keeping the diplomatic air cool for most of the 1980s in an attempt to reintegrate Egypt with the rest of the Arab world. In 1984, Egypt restored relations with the Soviet Union and was readmitted to the Islamic Conference, and by 1988, the Arab League had invited Egypt to rejoin and dropped demands that Egypt sever ties with Israel.

THE ISRAELI INVASION OF LEBANON. On June 6, 1982, Israel invaded Lebanon. The attack, dubbed "Operation Peace for Galilee" by Defense Minister Ariel Sharon, was supposedly intended to create a protective buffer zone; it is generally accepted, however, that the attack aimed to wipe out PLO forces operating from Palestinian refugee camps that had been attacking northern Israel. The Israeli army surrounded the PLO in Beirut and began shelling the city at an enormous civilian cost, resulting in worldwide disapproval. When Lebanese Christian Phalangists began to massacre civilians at the Sabra and Shatila refugee camps within Israeli-controlled territory, the Israeli government's position eroded even further. Under an agreement negotiated by the United States, most fighting ended in 1983. Worried about the Syrian presence and active Shi'a militia in Lebanon, Israel withdrew in 1985, but maintained a strip of southern Lebanese territory as a security zone, until their recent withdrawal in May 2000.

THE INTIFADA

On December 8, 1987, an Israeli armored transport and several Arab cars collided in Gaza; four Palestinians were killed and several injured in the crash. The Palestinians' despair after 20 years of Israeli military occupation turned demonstrations at the victims' funerals into an upheaval that spread to the West Bank. The Palestinian *intifada* ("shaking off" in Arabic), was a tremendous shock to everyone, the PLO (at this point relocated to Tunis) included. At first, Israeli authorities viewed the *intifada* as a short-lived affair that would dissolve as earlier agitations had. But after Palestinians in the territories began establishing networks to coordinate their hitherto sporadic civil disobedience and strikes, the *intifada* came alive, gaining its own shadowy leadership. In the midst of all the turmoil, the world began to reconsider Israel's Palestinian policies.

In the summer of 1988, King Hussein suddenly dropped his claims to the West Bank and ceased assisting in the administration of the territories, which Jordan had been doing since 1967. Hussein's move left Israel and the United States without a negotiating partner, since they refused to negotiate with the PLO. Arafat seized the opportunity to secure a PLO role in negotiations by renouncing terrorism and recognizing Israel's right to exist. Israeli Prime Minister Yitzḥak Shamir presented his own proposal promising elections in the territories but insisted that neither the PLO nor PLO-sponsored candidates take part. When the United States and Egypt began to draw up a list of acceptable candidates, Shamir qualified his proposal by insisting that Arab residents of East Jerusalem, which had been formally annexed by Israel, be barred from participation. The PLO, local Palestinians, and Egypt could not tolerate the decades-old Israeli claim that Jerusalem, whole and undivided, was Israel's eternal capital, nor that Palestinian refugees outside the occupied territories should not be allowed to return.

Many Palestinians became convinced, by late 1989, that Arafat had weakened the position the Palestinians had gained as a result of the *intifada*. They were also worried by the growing number of Israeli settlements in the West Bank. The United States and the PLO terminated their discussions that summer.

THE GULF WAR

The Gulf Crisis began when Iraqi troops marched into Kuwait on August 2, 1990. Early on, Iraqi President **Saddam Hussein** had slyly suggested he would withdraw from Kuwait when Israel withdrew from the West Bank, Gaza, and Golan, and when Syria withdrew from Lebanon. This gesture, along with promises to liberate Palestine, won Saddam the support of Palestinians. In fighting that lasted from January 16 to February 28, 1991, a coalition formed by the United States, various European countries, Egypt, Syria, Saudi Arabia, and the other Gulf states disabled Baghdad and forced Iraq to withdraw from Kuwait. During the conflict, 39 Iraqi

SCUD missiles fell on Tel Aviv and Haifa, cheered on by Arafat and the Palestinian population. Israel, under pressure from the United States, and fearful of an Arab-Israeli conflagration and chaos in Jordan, did not retaliate.

THE PEACE PROCESS

THE MADRID CONFERENCE. When the Gulf War cease-fire was announced, hope was high that parties such as Israel and Syria—for the first time on the same side of a regional conflict—could be brought to the bargaining table. In July 1991, Syria surprised the world with the announcement that it would attend a regional peace conference. At a summit meeting in Moscow, US President George Bush and Soviet President Mikhail Gorbachev decided to host the conference jointly. A hesitant Israeli cabinet, uneasy about jeopardizing US aid, voted to attend the proposed conference provided that the PLO and residents of East Jerusalem not take part. On October 30, 1991, the Madrid peace conference was convened, with Israel carrying on separate negotiations with Syria, Lebanon, Egypt, and a joint Jordanian-Palestinian delegation. This unprecedented gathering was quickly bogged down in discussions of Resolution 242 (see p. 14), Palestinian autonomy and rights, Jerusalem, Israeli settlements, and the PLO's political scope. Subsequent sessions held in Washington, D.C. did not get much further. The Palestinian representatives, including **Faisal al-Husseini** and **Hanan Ashrawi**, were in constant contact with the PLO; the charade of PLO non-involvement was wearing thin.

THE OSLO CONFERENCE. On June 23, 1992, an Israeli election ousted Shamir's Likud (see p. 26) and brought in a Labor-led government under Yitzḥak Rabin. Rabin curtailed settlement and promised Palestinian autonomy. Optimism accompanying the first round of talks under the new Israeli government, held in November 1992, was soon undermined. **Hamas**, an Islamic socio-political movement struggling for Arab control of all of historic Palestine, carried out several terrorist attacks in Israel. In response, the Israeli government deported 415 Palestinians in December 1992. The Palestinian representatives at the negotiations refused to resume talks until the deportees, trapped in the no-man's-land between Israel and Lebanon, were allowed to return.

Almost a year later, Israel and the PLO surprised the world by announcing that representatives meeting secretly in Oslo had successfully negotiated an agreement on a framework for solving the Israeli-Palestinian conflict peacefully. The Declaration of Principles on Interim Self-Government Arrangements (the DOP—also known as the **Oslo Accord**) was signed on September 13, 1993, with President **Bill Clinton** presiding over the ceremony. The DOP provided mutual recognition between Israel and the PLO, as well as a plan for the implementation of Palestinian autonomy in the Gaza Strip and the Jericho Area, with the autonomous areas to be expanded in stages over a five-year transitional period. The DOP was followed by the negotiation and signing of several other Israeli-Palestinian agreements. The first was the Gaza/Jericho Agreement which provided the details for Israeli withdrawal from these two areas and the creation of a **Palestinian Authority (PA),** headed by Yassir Arafat and a 24-member council.

ASSASSINATION OF RABIN. Rabin's leftist politics pushed him out of favor with the right, ultimately leading to his assassination in 1995. In June 1992, Mubarak met with Rabin, the first meeting of leaders of the two countries in six years. In September, Morocco and Israel established diplomatic relations. In October, Jordan and Israel ended the state of war that had existed between them since 1948. The border between Eilat and Aqaba was opened, and Israelis were allowed into Jordan for the first time. Finally, negotiations with Syria were begun, concentrating on peace between the two countries in exchange for the withdrawal of Israeli troops from the strategic Golan Heights. Such a withdrawal is highly controversial within Israel, and the Israeli government stated that it would place any agreement negotiated with Syria on a national referendum to be decided upon by the Israeli public. On November 4, 1995, 25-year-old Yigal Amir, a Jewish right-wing university student, shot and killed Israel's Prime Minister Yitzḥak Rabin. Over one million Israelis, Arabs and Jews alike, filed by the slain leader's coffin in the days following the murder. Rabin's funeral drew over 50 world leaders to Jerusalem, including Jordan's King Hussein, Egypt's President Mubarak, and representatives from four other Arab states.

PEACE IN THE 90'S. The May 1996 election of Benjamin Netanyahu, leader of the conservative Likud party, marked a turn away from Rabin's peace-oriented politics. The change in government resulted from a bombing campaign in major population centers throughout Israel carried out by Hamas. Netanyahu's continued support of Israeli settlements in East Jerusalem prompted violent clashes. Tension was further heightened by the Palestinian Authority's enforcement of its decree which imposed a death sentence for the sale of land to Israelis.

In September 1996, the Israeli government's decision to open a tunnel entrance adjacent to the Temple Mount and to Muslim holy sites in Jerusalem sparked protests that degenerated into deadly fighting. Thirty-seven Palestinians and eleven Israelis died in the conflict as the spectacle of gunfights between Israeli soldiers and the PA's police force seemed to announce the near-collapse of the peace process. Throughout fall 1996, US President Bill Clinton met with Arafat and Netanyahu to try to salvage relations between the two groups.

Hamas dealt another blow to the peace process with the suicide bombing of a crowded Jerusalem market on July 30, 1997. The attack resulted in 16 deaths, and the Israeli government began a security crackdown of Gaza and the West Bank that caused Palestinian tempers to flare into near daily conflict with Israeli and PA authorities. On September 4, 1997, three suicide bombers simultaneously set off bombs on the Ben-Yehuda shopping promenade in Jerusalem, killing four pedestrians and wounding 200. In response, Israel cordoned off the West Bank and the Gaza Strip and arrested Palestinians. In September, Israeli forces botched an assassination attempt on the Hamas official Khalid Mishal in Jordan. The agents, detained by Jordanian security forces, were returned to Israel upon the release of Hamas founder Shaikh Yassin and others from Israeli prisons.

Israel celebrated its 50th anniversary on May 30, 1998, with aerial and naval military displays. The anniversary turned grim as Palestinians mourned the 50 years since what they call "al-Nakba," the catastrophe. Violent rioting broke out in Hebron and East Jerusalem, and Israeli soldiers fired on crowds, leaving five Palestinians dead.

Meanwhile, US Secretary of State **Madeleine Albright** managed to keep negotiations alive, though talks dragged on for months with little agreement. The US finally set a deadline in May 1998 for Netanyahu to agree to the US proposal that Israel withdraw from 13% of the West Bank, a figure that the PA accepted. Netanyahu, concerned about the surrender of territory for an intangible peace, argued that 95% of the Palestinian population was already under its own administration. He did not meet the deadline and insisted that anything over a 9% withdrawal would pose an unacceptable security risk.

RECENT NEWS

The summer of 1999 marked a tit-for-tat bombing struggle between the Israeli Army occupying South Lebanon and **Hizbullah** guerillas. In September 1999, Israeli Prime Minister Ehud Barak announced plans for a historic Israeli pullout scheduled for July 2000. Barak hoped the pullout would indicate Israeli goodwill and encourage peace talks with neighboring Syria. Escalating skirmishes through the winter, however, prompted Barak to advance the pullout to June 1, 2000. When Hizbullah attacks intensified, Barak realized that holding out an extra six days would lead to increased conflict. On May 24, when Israeli forces executed a preemptive withdrawal from all of South Lebanon, Israel's twenty-year occupation of South Lebanon came to a close.

In July 2000, Arafat and Barak met for the Camp David II summit under the auspices of the US government. These talks marked the first time that Israel was willing to consider discussing the status of Jerusalem. No progress was made, however, and at press time, no date had been set for future talks.

RELIGION

Although freedom of religion is safeguarded by the state under the 1948 Declaration of Establishment, most religious beliefs do not go unchallenged in Israel.

JUDAISM

Neither theologians nor historians can pinpoint a date for the founding of Judaism. The Israelite religion has been evolving, however, for perhaps the past four millennia. According to the Bible, **Abraham** was the first to establish a covenant with God through his self-circumcision at the ripe old age of 99. This act is symbolically repeated with each generation of Jewish males. Abraham's grandson Jacob (later renamed Israel) fathered twelve sons from whom descended twelve tribes, the nation of Israel. Abraham, his son Isaac, and his grandson Jacob are believed to be buried with their wives, Sarah, Rebecca, and Leah in the Cave of the Makhpelakh in **Hebron** (see p. 332). Because Ishmael, Abraham's other son, is believed to be the ancestor of Islam, this resting place is holy to both faiths.

The Bible says that the founding period of the Israelite nation was the generation spent wandering in the Sinai desert en route from Egypt to the Holy Land, under the leadership of Moses. It was this generation that received the Torah, the central text of Judaism, at **Mt. Sinai** (see p. 355). Historians theorize that the disparate tribes later known as the Israelites had gradually united under a common god by the third millennium BCE. This god, **Yahweh,** is thought to have been a young, warlike version of the older Canaanite deity, El (or Elyon, see Exodus 3:15). Some scholars believe Yahweh (God) was introduced to the highland Canaanites by Semitic tribes escaping from Egypt, and that he was worshiped as an alternative to the lowland storm-god, Ba'al. When the Israelites formed a kingdom, worship of God was centralized in the capital, Jerusalem. The religion became focused around the Temple, or *beit hamikdash,* where sacrifices were brought under the supervision of the priests, or *kohanim*. However, Judaism became decentralized after the destruction of the first Temple. Prayer replaced sacrifices as a significant daily ritual, taking place three times a day on weekdays, and four times a day on the sabbath and on holidays.

Historians estimate the present form of the **Torah** to be 2500 years old, although it has been continuously interpreted and re-interpreted over the centuries in an effort to maintain its vitality and applicability. The Written Torah (also known as the Pentateuch, or the Books of Moses), which consists of the first five books of the Bible, formed the template for the Oral Torah, a series of interpretations and teachings eventually codified in final form around 200 CE as the *Mishnah*. The *Gemara* then formed an additional layer of interpretation. The *Mishnah,* along with the *Gemara,* form the basis of the Babylonian and Jerusalem Talmud, finalized during the 5th century CE. The Talmud, organized as a transcribed series of discussions aimed at interpretation of the *Mishnah,* was the springboard for a new series of interpretations and teachings that continue to build upon each other. "Torah," which has come to refer to all Jewish thought and teachings, has been at the core of Jewish life through most of history.

In Judaism, faith in God is central, but the energy of Jewish life is concentrated on observing the commandments. The Torah contains 613 **mitzvot** (commandments) including directives for ritual observances and instructions concerning moral behavior. Over the ages, rabbis have interpreted and expanded these *mitzvot*. The entire set of laws is called *halakha* ("the way"). These laws are codified in intricate detail and cover every aspect of life.

HEADS UP Head coverings worn by religious Jewish men often provide a lot of information about who is wearing them. Black hats generally indicate affiliation with an ultra-Orthodox religious group, while Orthodox men with a more centrist affiliation generally wear knit *kippot*. More liberal or even hippie religious types often wear large and colorful *kippot*. The intricacies of this code are subtle and complex, often revealing possible political and social affiliations.

Much of modern Jewish life revolves around the synagogue, which plays a multifaceted role in Jewish life. The Hebrew word *(beit knesset)* means "house of assembly" and the Yiddish word *(shul)* means "school." The *aron ha-kodesh* (Holy Ark) houses the Torah scrolls and determines the orientation of the synagogue. Synagogues normally face toward Jerusalem; within Jerusalem, they face the Temple Mount. Above the *aron ha-kodesh*, a flickering *ner tamid* (eternal flame) usually hangs. The raised platform from which prayers are led is called the *bima*. Most synagogues in Israel are Orthodox and contain a *meḥitza*, a divider between men's and women's sections. Usually, the two sections have separate entrances. Men should cover their heads when entering a synagogue since head coverings symbolize a reverence for God. Often there is a box of *kippot*, or head coverings, by the entrance. Worshipers wear other items as reminders of their devotion. The *tallit*, or prayer shawl, has four *tzitzit*, sets of strings twisted and knotted to symbolize the commandments. On weekdays, worshipers wear *tefillin*, boxed scrolls wrapped around the arm and head with leather straps.

Visitors are welcome at most synagogues during prayer services. There are three prescribed prayer times every day: in the morning (the *shaḥarit* service), in the afternoon (the *minḥa* service), and in the evening (the *ma'ariv* service). Smaller synagogues, however, do not meet for every service. On Shabbat (the Jewish Sabbath) and holidays there is an additional service during the day. The *Kabbalat Shabbat* service, on Friday nights, welcomes in the Sabbath. Visitors to a synagogue should dress modestly, and nicer attire is in order on Shabbat or holi.days. Interesting times to visit are when the Torah scroll is brought out and read on Shabbat, holidays, and every Monday and Thursday morning. It is at these times when you might catch a *Bar Mitzvah* ceremony (*Bat Mitzvah* for girls), a coming of age ritual signifying the point at which a Jew becomes legally eligible to fulfill the *mitzvot*. Photographs on Shabbat and holidays are highly inappropriate.

ISLAM

The Arabic word *islam* translates, in its general sense, as "submission." The basic tenet of Islam is submission to God's will. Islam has its roots in revelations received from 610 to 622 CE by Muhammad, who was informed by the Angel Gabriel of his prophetic calling. These revelations, the **Qur'an** (recitation), form the core of Islam. Muslims believe the Arabic text to be perfect, immutable, and untranslatable—the words of God embodied in human language. Consequently, the Qur'an appears throughout the Muslim world—the majority of which is non-Arabic speaking—in Arabic. Muhammad is seen as the "seal of the prophets," the last of a chain of God's messengers that includes Jewish and Christian figures such as Abraham, Moses, and Jesus. The Qur'an incorporates many of the biblical traditions associated with these prophets.

Though Muhammad rapidly gathered followers to his faith, staunchly monotheistic Islam was met with ample opposition in polytheist Arabia. Persecuted in his native city of Mecca, Muhammad and his followers fled in 622 to the nearby city of Medina, where he was welcomed as mediator of a long-standing blood feud. This *Hijra* (flight, or emigration) marks the beginning of the Muslim community and of the Islamic calendar. For the next eight years, Muhammad and his community defended themselves against raids and later battled the Meccans and neighboring nomadic tribes. In 630, Mecca surrendered to the Muslims, and afterwards numerous Meccans converted to the new faith voluntarily. This established the pattern for **jihad** (struggle), referring first and foremost to the spiritual struggle against one's own desires, then to the struggle to make one's own Muslim community as righteous as possible, and lastly to the struggle against outsiders wishing to harm the Muslim community.

Muhammad is not believed to be divine, but rather a human messenger of God's word. His actions, however, are sanctified because God chose him to be the recipient of revelation; several verses of the Qur'an demand obedience to the Prophet. The stories and traditions surrounding the Prophet's life have been passed on as *sunna*, and those who follow the *sunna* in addition to the teachings of the Qur'an are considered to be especially devout. (In fact, the term Sunni is derived from *sunna*.) The primary source for *sunna* is the *Hadith*, a written collection of sayings attributed to Muhammad. Each *hadith* had to go through a rigorous verification process before it was accepted as truth; the tale had to be verified by several sources, preferably those who saw the action with their own eyes, and the greatest weight was given to testimony by Muhammad's close followers.

Islam continued to grow after the Prophet's death, flourishing in the "Age of Conquest" (see p. 9). The four Rightly Guided Caliphs *(Rashidun)* who succeeded Muhammad led wars against apostate nomadic tribes. Faith in Islam was the strength of the Arab armies, which defeated the once-mighty Persian empire by the year 640. The fourth Caliph, Muhammad's nephew and son-in-law Ali, was the catalyst for the major split in the Muslim world. Ali slowly lost power and was murdered in 661. The *Shi'at Ali* (Partisans of Ali or Shi'a) believe Ali, as a blood relative of the Prophet, to be the only legitimate successor to Muhammad, thus separating themselves from Sunni Muslims. Contrary to popular Western perception, Shi'ite Muslims are not fanatics, but rather Muslims with a sharp focus on divinely chosen leaders (or *Imams*) who are blood descendants of the Prophet through Ali and his wife, the Prophet's daughter Fatima.

In the 10th century, under the weight of tradition and consensus, Sunni Muslim scholars *(ulama)* proclaimed "the gates of *ijtihad* (individual judgment)" closed; new concepts and interpretations could no longer stand on their own but had to be legitimized by tradition. This proscription notwithstanding, *ijtihad* continues today, though not on the scale of the first centuries of Islam. There have been numerous reform movements throughout the Islamic world, including the Wahhabbi movement in the Arabian peninsula, the movement of the thinker Jamal al-Din al-Afghani in the Middle East, and Muhammad Iqbal in South Asia. There are four main schools of thought in the Islamic legal system, and the applicability of *sharia*, or Islamic law, is a subject of much strife in a number of Muslim countries, which have seen challenges to entrenched governments by movements carrying the banner of Islam.

The **Sufis** are a mystical movement within Islam, stressing the goal of unity with God. They are organized in orders, with a clear hierarchy from master to disciple. Different orders prescribe different ways of life in order to reach Allah; some preach total asceticism and others seem almost hedonistic in their pursuit of pleasure. Sufi *sheikhs* (masters) and saints are reputed to perform miracles, and their tombs are popular pilgrimage destinations. Jalal al-Din Rumi, the great medieval intellectual, founded the famous order of the whirling dervishes. The term "whirling dervish" derives from the joyous spinning and dancing, meant to produce a state of mind conducive to unity with Allah. Substances such as wine were often used for similar purposes, though the great poets like Rumi treat the effects of alcohol more as a metaphor for the individual's journey with God.

PILLARS OF ISLAM

Ash-hadu an la ilaha illa Allah. Ash-hadu anna Muhammadan rasul Allah. (I swear that there is no god but Allah. I swear that Muhammad is God's Messenger.) These words compose the first lines of the Islamic call to prayer *(adhan)*, which emanates hauntingly five times a day from live or recorded *muezzins* perched atop their minarets. Any person who wishes to convert to Islam may do so by repeating these lines three times, thereby completing the **first pillar** of Islam and becoming a Muslim. Enemies of Islam often memorized the lines before going into battle, thus providing themselves with an emergency survival tactic.

The second pillar is **prayer** *(salat)*, performed five times per day, preferably following the call of the *muezzin*. Prayers, preceded by ablutions, begin with a declaration of intent and consist of a set cycle of prostrations. No group or leader is necessary for prayers—they constitute a personal communication with God. The person praying must face Mecca. The word for Friday in Arabic means "the day of gathering;" on that day, communal prayer is particularly encouraged.

The third pillar is **alms** (*zakat*, or purification). Because all belongs to God, wealth is only held in trust by people, and *zakat* represents the bond between members of the community. *Zakat* has been historically administered as a tax, and the level of giving is determined as a percentage of the surplus wealth and earnings of the individual.

It is believed that Muhammad received the Qur'an during the month of **Ramadan.** Fasting during this holy month is the fourth pillar of Islam. Between dawn and sunset, Muslims are not permitted to smoke, have sexual intercourse, or let any food or water pass their lips. Exceptions are made for women who are pregnant or menstruating, the sick, and people who are traveling—they must make up the fast at a later date. As soon as the evening *adhan* is heard, Muslims break the fast and begin a night of feasting, visits to friends and relatives, and revelry.

The last pillar, required only once in a lifetime, is **pilgrimage** *(hajj)*. Only Muslims who are financially and physically able are required to fulfill this pillar by journeying to **Mecca** and **Medina** during the last month of the Muslim calendar. While *hajj* is essentially a re-creation of the actions of the Prophet Muhammad, its effects are to unite Muslims and to stress the equal status of all people who submit to the will of Allah, regardless of gender, degree of wealth, race, or nationality. All pilgrims, from Gulf princes to Cairo street-sweepers, must wrap themselves in white cloth and remove all accessories (which might indicate wealth).

CHRISTIANITY

Christianity began in Judea among the Jewish followers of **Jesus.** The most significant sources on the life of Jesus are the **Gospels.** Scholars agree that the gospels of Mark, Matthew, and Luke were written in that order some time after 70 CE, drawing on an oral tradition which recorded the words of Jesus. The Gospel of John was written in about 100 CE, but it has roots as old as those of the others. These sources provide a history influenced by the experiences of the church fathers and the belief that Jesus was the **Messiah** ("anointed one").

Various historical events date the birth of Jesus, the man regarded by millions as their savior, between 4 BCE and 6 CE. According to Matthew, **Bethlehem** is the birthplace of Jesus, and Mary and Joseph moved to **Nazareth** to protect him; in Luke, Jesus' parents are only temporarily in Bethlehem, and in Mark and John, the birth is not even mentioned. The Bible says that Jesus was born through an **Immaculate Conception;** he was conceived and brought forth by Mary, a virgin, making him a product of God's creative power and free from humanity's original sin. Afterwards, Jesus preached in the Galilee, speaking for the poor and the righteous, most notably in the Sermon on the Mount (Matthew 5-7).

After about three years of preaching, Jesus went to Jerusalem, where he was condemned to death by Pontius Pilate and the Romans at the urging of the Pharisees. The events leading up to his death are known as the **Passion**. On Good Friday, he carried his cross down the **Via Dolorosa** in Jerusalem, stopping at what became known as the Stations of the Cross, until he reached the hill of Golgotha (or Calvary), now marked by the Church of the Holy Sepulchre, where he was crucified.

According to the Gospels, three days after Jesus' crucifixion, on what is now Easter, Mary and two other women went to Jesus' tomb to anoint his body and discovered the tomb empty. An angel announced that Jesus had been resurrected; Jesus subsequently appeared to the Apostles and performed miracles. The **Resurrection** is the point of departure for the Christian faith, the beginning of a new age that the faithful believe will culminate in Christ's *parousia*, or second coming.

At first, Christianity was a sect of Judaism that accepted the Hebrew Bible. But the sect's defining tenet that Jesus was the Messiah severed it from mainstream Judaism. St. Paul (originally Saul of Tarsus), successfully adapted the faith of Christianity to meet the spiritual needs of the largest body of converts: former pagans. Paul abandoned standard Jewish practices like mandatory circumcision, further separating Christianity from Judaism. The Book of Acts documents the actions of the early Christians, and the Letters of Paul, which comprise most of the rest of the New Testament, give advice to the early Christian communities and explain the delay of the second coming. As Christianity developed, it absorbed earlier practices. The incorporation of ancient festivals such as the winter solstice helped draw the common people to the new religion, and the use of Platonic doctrines converted many intellectuals.

The Christian faith was officially legitimized by the Edict of Milan, issued by Emperor Licinius in 313 CE, which proclaimed the toleration of Christianity. In 325 CE, the **Emperor Constantine** made Christianity the official religion of the struggling Roman Empire. Constantine also summoned the first of seven Ecumenical Councils, held in Nicaea, to elaborate and unify the content of the faith. The Council of Nicaea came up with an explicit creed, declaring that Jesus Christ was of the same essence as the Father, and that there were three equal parts to God. This crucial doctrine of the **Trinity,** which is only implicitly supported in the Gospels, maintains that the Father, Son, and Holy Spirit are distinct persons yet all one God.

The Church was called "the body of Christ" and believed to be integral and indivisible. Nonetheless, the Christian community suffered many schisms. The **Egyptian (Coptic) Church** broke off in the 3rd century, when other eastern branches (including the Nestorians and Maronites) began to drift apart from western Christianity. In 1054, the **Great Schism,** caused primarily by the inflexible Cardinal Humbert, split Christendom into the western Roman Catholic Church and the Eastern Orthodox Church. Whereas Rome upheld the universal jurisdiction and infallibility of the Pope, Orthodoxy stressed the infallibility of the church as a whole. The Spirit, according to the Orthodox, proceeds through the Father, while Roman theology dictates that the Spirit proceeds from the Father and the Son. Orthodox Christians believe that God is highly personal, that each man can find God by looking within himself. In 1517, the German monk **Martin Luther** sparked the **Reformation,** which quickly split northern Europe from Roman Catholicism, and led to the development of Protestantism. **Protestantism** is composed of many sects, which generally believe in salvation through faith rather than good works. Eastern Orthodoxy, too, is divided into multiple nationalist traditions (Greek, Russian, Armenian). Only in the 18th century did these diverse churches come to speaking terms, and only in the 20th has the ecumenical movement brought extensive cooperation.

The central part of the church service for Catholics is the mass, basically a reenactment of the last supper: the priest blesses bread and wine and they are changed to Jesus' body and blood by the Holy Spirit. The congregation receives the host just as the apostles did. When visiting churches, it is inappropriate to partake in communion if not a Catholic.

OTHER FAITHS

THE DRUZE

The faith of the Druze, a staunchly independent sect of Shi'ite Muslims, centers around a hierarchy of individuals who are the sole custodians of a religious doctrine hidden from the rest of the world. Many Druze consider themselves a separate ethnicity as well as a religious group, while others consider themselves Arabs. They do not allow conversions into or out of the religion. The Druze believe that the word of God is revealed only to a divinely chosen few, and that these blessed few must be followed to the ends of the earth. The Druze generally remain loyal to their host country. Israel has a Druze population of about 85,000.

The religion was founded in 1017 by an Egyptian chieftain, al-Darazi, who drew upon various beliefs in the Muslim world at the time, especially **Shi'ism.** The Druze believe that God was incarnated in human forms, the final incarnation being the Fatimid Caliph al-Hakim (996-1021). The Druze have suffered a history of persecution and repression for their beliefs, which may partially explain the group's refusal to discuss its religion. The late 1600s was a period of prosperity, however, and under Emir Fakhir al-Din the Druze kingdom extended from Lebanon to Gaza to the Golan Heights. Sixteen villages were built from the Mediterranean Sea to the Jezreel Valley to guard the two major roads on which goods were transported. In 1830, a Druze revolt against the Egyptian pasha was crushed, along with all but two of the 14 Druze villages in the Carmel (see **Isfiya and Daliyat al-Karmel,** p. 192). In the 1860s, the Ottomans encouraged the Druze to return to the Carmel.

Because the Druze will not discuss their religion, most of what Westerners know about them comes from British "explorers" who fought their way into villages and stole holy books. Many of the Druze themselves are not completely informed. As far as outsiders know, Jethro, father-in-law of Moses, is their most revered prophet. The most important holiday falls in late April. In Israel, Druze gather in the holy village of Ḥittim, near Tiberias. Devout Druze are forbidden to smoke, drink alcohol, or eat pork, but many young Druze do not adhere strictly to these prohibitions. Some Druze believe in reincarnation and speak of their past lives. Gabriel Ben-Dor's *The Druze in Israel: A Political Study*, details their ideology, lifestyle, and political situation.

THE BAHA'I

The Baha'i religion was born in Teheran in 1863, when Mirza Hussein Ali (a son of Persian nobility) turned 46, renamed himself **Baha'ullah** ("Glory of God"), and began preaching non-violence and the unity of all religions. Baha'u'llah's arrival had been foretold in 1844 by the Persian **Siyyid Ali Muhammad** (also known as **al-Bab,** or "Gateway to God"), the first prophet of the Baha'i religion, who heralded the coming of a new religious teacher and divine messenger. Baha'ullah was imprisoned and then exiled to Palestine, where he continued to teach in the city of Acre (Akko). He is buried near the city. Al-Bab is buried in Haifa, which is now home to a large Baha'i population.

Baha'ullah's teachings fill over 100 volumes; his religion incorporates elements of major Eastern and Western religions. Baha'i believe in a Supreme Being, accepting Jesus, Buddha, Muhammad, and Baha'ullah as divine prophets. The scripture includes the Bible, the Qur'an, and the Bhagavad Gita. A central doctrine of the faith regards the Baha'i vision of the future. Instead of warning of a final Judgement Day or an end of the world (like many other religions), Baha'ullah prophesied a "flowering of humanity," an era of peace and enlightenment to come. Before this new age can arrive, however, the world must undergo dreadful events to give civilization the impetus to reform itself. The Baha'i espouse trans-racial unity, sexual equality, global disarmament, and the creation of a world community. The rapidly growing Baha'i faith currently boasts more than six million adherents, with two million converts world-wide in the last decade.

THE KARAITES

The small sect of Jews known as the Karaites dwell principally in Ashdod, Be'er Sheva, and the Tel Aviv suburb of Ramla. The community of 15,000 traces its roots to the 9th century CE. Formed out of the political and religious turmoil following the Muslim invasion, Karaites adhere strictly to the five books of the Torah, but they reject all later Jewish traditions. They are generally cohesive, and have their own religious courts. To an outsider, however, their practices appear similar to those dictated by traditional Jewish observance.

THE SAMARITANS

Currently, the Samaritan community is a tiny one, with roughly 500 adherents divided between Nablus on the West Bank and Ḥolon, a suburb of Tel Aviv. Originally the residents of Samaria, Samaritans consider themselves the original Israelites, descended from the tribes of Joseph (Manasseh and Ephraim) from whom other Israelites learned monotheism. The religion is seen by non-members as an offshoot of Judaism marked by literal interpretation of the Samaritan version of the Old Testament and the exclusion of later Jewish interpretation (i.e. the *Mishnah*, the Talmud, and all books of the Hebrew Bible after Joshua) from its canon. A gradual, centuries-long separation between the two religions culminated with the destruction of the Samaritan temple on Mt. Gerizim by the Hasmonean king John Hyrcanus in 128 BCE. The mountain is still the most holy site of the Samaritan religion. Centuries of persecution by the various rulers of Palestine and thousands of deaths in a 529 CE uprising against Byzantine rule shrank the community to its present size. While the Rabbinate does not recognize Samaritans as Jews, the Israeli government applies the Law of Return (granting settlement rights) to them.

ISRAEL TODAY

JEWS IN ISRAEL

Israel's population of 5.8 million is 80% Jewish and 15% Muslim; the remaining 5% includes Christians and Druze. Many Israeli Jews are immigrants or second generation, and are often divided along ethnic lines. Each community operates its own religious courts, funded by the Ministry of Religion, and controls its own holy sites. Every religion's days of rest are guaranteed by law.

Although Judaism is the predominant religion in Israel, by no means is it unified. The diversity of Jewish ideology in Israel is a tangible force that governs the codes of everyday interaction among its people. Beliefs held by the orthodox Jews stand in direct contradiction to those espoused by the secular, Ethiopian immigrants quibble with Russian immigrants over territory, and Islamic fundamentalists reject the notion of a Jewish state entirely. These differences lead to a society riddled with tension, where social and religious alliances are frequently of painful importance. Disputes between these groups generally hone in on the minutiae of another group's tradition, almost always distorting the already nuanced views, inflaming the community's sense of pride and too often erupting into violence.

ASHKENAZIM AND SEPHARDIM. **Sephardi** Jews (many of pre-1492 Spanish origins) come from Arab or other Mediterranean countries; **Ashkenazi** Jews have northern or eastern European origins. The rift in Israeli society is deep and wide, and goes back to the 1950s, when Sephardi Jews from Morocco and Iraq were brought to an already established, Ashkenazi-dominated state. Although Sephardim compose roughly half of the Jewish. population in Israel, Ashkenazim still fill most of the positions of power in government, the economy, the military, and academia, and Sephardim are much more likely to be poor. The last decade has brought massive immigrations from the former USSR and Ethiopia. Both immigrations have been clouded by questions concerning the religious status of immigrants claiming to be Jewish.

RELIGIOUS VS. SECULAR. About half of Israeli Jews are secular; 30% identify themselves as Orthodox and 18% as Ultra-Orthodox. The religious-secular divide forms something of a fault line in Israeli society. The religious establishment is quite powerful; the electoral system has helped Jewish religious parties to wield disproportionate power. Much to the aggravation of many secular Israelis, rabbinical courts have a state monopoly on matrimonial issues among Jews. Service in the Israeli army (mandatory for all Israelis at the age of 18) is not required for Ultra-orthodox Jews, which leads to secular resentment. Recent alterations to the **Law of Return,** which guarantees citizenship to any Jew "who has expressed his desire to settle in Israel," have excluded Jews converted by non-orthodox rabbis and further strained relationships. Outbreaks between these groups range from minor protests and demonstrations to more violent clashes.

RUSSIANS AND ETHIOPIANS. The country has experienced a wave of immigration from these two countries over the past two decades. About 50,000 **Russians** immigrate to Israel each year. Russia's continued economic problems as well as increasing anti-Semitism insures that this number will continue to rise. In 1985 and 1991 two massive operations airlifted **Ethiopian Jews** to Israel. While Russians frequently find themselves in competition with Israelis for employment and acceptance into universities, most Ethiopians remain isolated in caravans and receive a substantial amount of government aid. Because of this, Russians find themselves resentful of the attention Ethiopians receive and some skirmishes have ensued.

GOVERNMENT AND POLITICS

BASIC LAWS. The State of Israel was founded on May 14, 1948 as a parliamentary democracy. Although it was stated in the Proclamation of Independence that the first Constituent Assembly would draft a constitution for Israel, disagreement among the religious parties precluded the ratification of a written constitution at that time. In its place, a series of Basic Laws were laid out as a framework for legislation. These laws were to be incorporated into a future constitution. Fifty-two years later, that goal seems to be in sight. Several of the Basic Laws can only be amended by an absolute or special majority of the legislative body. There are 11 of these laws, which dictate everything from the organization of "The Israel Defense Forces" to the insurance of universal "Freedom of Occupation." Currently, three additional laws are under legislative consideration; one would explicitly guarantee the "Freedom of Expression and Association."

KNESSET. The Basic Laws also provide the framework for the Knesset, the Israeli parliament. Although the law defines neither the authority of the body nor its functions and regulations, it outlines general guidelines on the essence of the service, work, and immunity of the Knesset, as well as election procedures. National elections in Israel are held at least once every four years. Israelis do not directly elect candidates for seats in the Knesset; instead, they vote for political parties, fifteen of which are represented in the current Knesset. The percentage of the popular vote received by a given party is then converted to a proportion of the 120 seats of the Knesset, provided that the party receives at least 1.5% of the national vote.

As of 1996, Israelis elect their prime minister directly and vote for a parliamentary party. Intended to bolster the stability of the government by reducing the leverage of smaller parties, the current system enables the directly elected prime minister to claim a national mandate irrespective of party politics in the Knesset. A motion of no-confidence in the government can be presented only by parties not represented in the Knesset. To date, there has been only one vote of no-confidence—on March 15, 1990—that succeeded in bringing down the government.

POLITICAL PARTIES. The two major parties are **Labor** (*Avoda*, sometimes still referred to as *Ma'arakh*, or Alignment) and **Likud** (*Likud-Liberalim Leumi*, Unity-National Liberals). Labor's roots are in old-style Labor Zionism, while Likud still carries the banner of Revisionist Zionism, established by **Vladimir Jabotinsky,** who created the Jewish brigades to help the British in both world wars. The critical issue separating left and right in Israeli politics is the question of territorial compromise in exchange for peace (see **The Peace Process,** p. 17). The pressing realities of Israeli politics have generated a high degree of political awareness and participation. Seventy-nine percent of registered voters cast their votes in the 1999 elections, in which Ehud Barak (Labor) was elected.

ISRAELI DEFENSE FORCES (IDF). The state of Israel requires army service *(tzaḥal)* for all Israeli citizens at the age of 18. After a basic training program lasting several weeks, men serve for a minimum of three years, and women for two. Many Israelis who pass a rigorous physical evaluation decide to enter one of the many divisions of the army that require extra service time. These include paratroopers, *golani* (mountain soldiers), and *givati* (lowland fighting). After the termination of service, Israeli men are still required to work for *tzaḥal* for at least a month each year until the age of forty-five or fifty, unless they present one of a number of reasons for exemption (e.g. health, children, financial difficulty).

There are several controversial exemptions from the army, including Arab-Israelis, Ultra-Orthodox Jews, and National Service volunteers *(Sherut Leumi)*. These groups are all required to register their status. Arab-Israelis are automatically exempt from service; however, many choose to join. The Ultra-Orthodox are allowed to observe religious principles and study at *Yeshivot* instead of serving. A small contingent of orthodox or pacifist Israeli females can opt for two years of community service in the *Sherut Leumi*, which works on ecological projects and immigrant integration. More information on website: www.idf.il.

ECONOMY

Poor in natural resources, stymied by socialist inefficiencies, and carrying the burdens of large defense expenditures and Jewish refugee absorption, Israel for years relied upon substantial financial assistance from diaspora Jewish communities and foreign governments (especially the US). Throughout the last few years, however, the country has begun to reap the fruits of extensive privatization, free trade with the US and the European Community, and the development of a high-tech export-oriented economy of $32.5 billion.

From 1990-1996, Israel's GDP growth rate was the highest among OECD (Organization for Economic Co-Operation and Development) economies, averaging 6% per year. Its per capita GDP (approximately $16,950) is now the 21st highest in the world. Israel's trade deficit has been a persistent problem, and its reduction has been a primary goal of every Israeli government. The deficit now approaches $300 million, though it is decreasing in relative terms: exports now finance around 75% of imports, as opposed to 14% in 1950. In total, Israel's industrial exports have grown over 1550 times since 1948 and are now over $20 billion. The country's main industries are chemicals, diamond cutting and polishing, textiles, high-tech (especially bio-medical and computer) products, and military hardware. Israel is also a leader in desert agriculture and plant genetics.

Israel's economy has always suffered from high inflation. By the early 1980's, the annual inflation rate had reached three digits. In 1985, when inflation threatened to reach four digits, the government implemented an emergency stabilization program that has helped curb inflation substantially; the new Israeli shekel (NIS) has held relatively steady against the dollar for the past six years.

The two greatest burdens on Israel's economy are defense and social spending. The former has declined markedly as a result of the peace process—expenditures on defense now comprise only 10% of the GDP, as opposed to 23% in 1980. Immigration, however, continues to exert pressure on the economy. Since it attained independence, Israel has absorbed 2.6 million immigrants, four times the number of Jews living in the country in 1948. In the early 1990s alone over 800,000 immigrants, primarily from the former Soviet Union, flooded the country driving unemployment to 11.2% in 1992. Because Israel has always been committed to providing a high degree of social services, booming immigration has been a financial strain. Over 50% of public expenditure is spent on funding health care, unemployment assistance, and other social programs.

At the same time, recent immigration has flooded Israel with highly educated workers and professionals. While it took time for the economy to accommodate so many skilled individuals (horror stories abound of scientists forced to sweep streets), the net result has been a tremendous economic boom. With Israeli incomes rising and Palestinians increasingly prevented from entering Israel to work, Israel has begun importing tens of thousands of workers from Asia and Eastern Europe to work the menial jobs Israelis no longer want. Israel's newfound prosperity and the current focus of the US government on domestic issues have led many to predict that the large American foreign aid traditionally received (US$3 billion per year plus loan guarantees) will be reduced in coming years.

The peace process has contributed significantly to economic optimism as well. Increased international confidence in the stability of the area has led to a surge of foreign investment and an upgrade of Israel's international credit rating. Israeli businesses are developing profitable relationships with foreign companies that previously feared the Arab boycott. Finally, trade between Israel and its Arab neighbors makes the possibility for large-scale regional economic cooperation enormous, should real peace ensue. Plans are already in the works for major economic projects such as integrated power-grids, road networks, and a shared port.

KIBBUTZIM AND MOSHAVIM

Two percent of the Israeli population lives on about 270 **kibbutzim** (plural of *kibbutz*), somewhat socialist rural societies where production is controlled by members. The kibbutzim of today hardly resemble the fiercely ideological pioneer agricultural settlements that began 80 years ago, which were based on strong egalitarian and communal values. These days, most kibbutzim rely more on industry than on agriculture. In addition, the passion for austerity is subsiding; kibbutzniks now demand the same luxuries enjoyed by other Israelis (i.e. larger living quarters, TVs and VCRs, trips to Disney World). Most kibbutz children now live with their parents in nuclear family homes, whereas just a decade or two ago nearly all lived in separate dormitories and saw their parents only at designated times.

Today's kibbutzim face mounting problems. Labor shortages are becoming common as two-thirds of younger members leave the settlements to test their skills elsewhere. More non-member paid workers are being brought into the kibbutz to fill in labor shortages. At the same time, increasing numbers of kibbutz members are finding outside employment and giving their salaries to the kibbutz, a practice which, though financially beneficial to the kibbutz, detracts from the communal feel. In addition, billions of dollars in kibbutz debt is a daunting threat.

Approximately 3.2% of the Israeli population live on 450 **moshavim**, another type of rural settlement, which provide roughly 40% of Israel's food. *Moshavniks* typically harvest their own piece of land, though marketing is often done collectively; some have a crop that all members help cultivate. Recently, many *moshavim* near big cities have gone suburban—their members commute to the city.

SOCIALISM ROCKS! If the idea of kibbutz life gives you the warm fuzzies, be aware that the application process is long, rigorous, and highly selective. As one kibbutznik explains, "We're one big family, and you don't want just anyone in your family." Applicants first go through a series of interviews and background checks to assess the contribution they would make, both professionally and socially. Hermits need not apply. They then go through a two-year trial period, after which they must be accepted by a 2/3 majority vote of all kibbutz members. Legacies don't guarantee anything either: even kids who grew up on a kibbutz and spouses of kibbutz members must go through the same process. Get cracking on those applications, most kibbutzim don't accept anyone over 45.

LANGUAGE

The Hebrew language contains 22 characters, written from right to left. Vowels are generally left unwritten, but may appear underneath regular characters as smaller markings. The contemporary Hebrew language was created from biblical Hebrew by **Eliezer Ben-Yehuda,** who compiled the first modern dictionary in the 1920s. In a surprisingly short period, the revived biblical dialect matured into a full-fledged language, spanning from colloquial speech to poetry. While a Semitic language (like Arabic) in structure, modern Hebrew contains elements of European languages; many words for which no equivalent biblical concept exists have been lifted almost as is. Modern spoken Hebrew contains a large number of Hebraicized versions of English words that may be understandable to careful English-speaking listeners. Most Israelis speak English, and signs are usually written in English (and sometimes Russian) as well as Hebrew and Arabic, the official languages of Israel.

Today's Arabic is actually two (some say three) distinct languages, and many, many dialects. **Classical Arabic (Fusha),** was the language of pre-Islamic Arabs and the Qur'an. Its complex rules of grammar were not fully developed until the Umayyad period (see **The Early Arabs**, p. 9), when the Islamic Empire rapidly expanded to include people of non-Arab origin (i.e., Turks and Persians). Today, the intricate complexity of the Classical, rigorously taught in schools and used for Qur'anic recitation, is every student's horror. A simplified version is used for writing, public speeches, and even cartoons on television. This less rigid form of classical Arabic has been packaged and sold to Westerners as "Modern Standard Arabic." Newspapers and television broadcasts throughout the Arab world are in Modern Standard. As its name suggests, the language is a modern invention—Classical Arabic taken down a notch and updated with terms like تكسي (*taksee*, taxi). The other species of the language is the **Colloquial ('Amiyya),** the speech of daily life. Dialects are so diverse that an Iraqi and a Palestinian meeting for the first time would sound like a Monty Python sketch. Educated Arabs can always fall back on the Classical, however stilted it may sound in conversation. The **appendix** of this book contains a list of useful Hebrew and Arabic words and phrases.

MEDIA

Israelis tend to have something of an obsession with the news. Most read at least one newspaper daily, listen multiple times a day to news reports broadcasted on the radio, and watch the news on television every night. The Israeli press is far livelier than the Western norm; politics are taken seriously and opinions expressed vociferously. Accordingly, Israelis tend to have pronounced political views and expound upon them freely. The liberal *Ha'Aretz* is the most respected daily; *Ma'ariv* leans just right of center. *Yediot Aḥronot* is more tabloid-esque and therefore more widely read. *The Jerusalem Post*, the only English-language daily, tilts to the right, while the bi-weekly English-language *Jerusalem Report* has high-quality reporting and dovish editors.

FOOD AND DRINK

Some Israelis' diets are affected by *kashrut* (meaning properly prepared), the Jewish dietary laws, which require rabbinical approval for all food consumed. Observant Jews will not eat or shop in a place that carries non-kosher goods; (e.g. meat that has not been prepared in a specific way) to respect kosher clientele, the big supermarket chains in Israel carry only kosher products, and many restaurants (and most hotels) serve only kosher food. Nevertheless, observance of *kashrut* is hardly the norm in Israel—many restaurants, particularly in Haifa and Tel Aviv, are avidly *non*-kosher.

The typical Israeli eats a large breakfast, a big mid-day dinner, and a light, late supper. Because of the poor quality and high cost of beef and lamb, Israelis rely largely on chicken, dairy, and vegetable products. Popular items in the Israeli diet include **hummus** (mashed chick-peas, garlic, lemon, and *taḥina*, a sesame concoction); "salad," a finely chopped mix of tomatoes and cucumbers, garnished with oil and vinegar; *gvina levana*, soft white cheese; *schnitzel*, breaded and fried chicken breast; *chips* (french fries); and a variety of sweet dairy snacks. Many brands of yogurt vie for control of the market, making yogurt so runnily delicious that you don't need a spoon to slurp them down.

The variety of ethnic cuisines in Israel is impressive; restaurants run the gamut from Chinese to French to Moroccan to American to Yemenite. Many restaurants serve typical Middle Eastern food. Restaurants serving Eastern European Jewish food are few and very expensive. Falafel, Israel's most popular **street food,** are deep-fried ground chick-pea balls served in pita bread with vegetables and *taḥina* sauce. Other common pita-fillers are hummus and *shawarma* (chunks of roast turkey or lamb). Falafel, hummus, and *shawarma* stands always have a colorful selection of salads and toppings such as *ḥarif*, a red-hot sauce. *Burekas* (filo dough folded over a cheese, potato, spinach, or meat filling) are available at pastry and some fast-food shops. On hot summer days, street vendors sell what look like hand grenades. Not to worry—these are *sabras* (a prickly cactus fruit). The inside is edible, though the seeds give some indigestion. (*Sabra* is also a term for a native Israeli; both the fruit and the people are said to be thorny on the outside, sweet on the inside.)

Preparing your own food is cheap, especially in summer, when fresh fruits and vegetables are available in every outdoor *shuk* (market). You can buy groceries inexpensively at local *shuks*, at a *makolet* (small grocery store), or in supermarkets.

Two Israeli **beers** are the decent, deep-amber Goldstar and the lesser Maccabee lager. Goldstar is a common draft beer; Maccabee comes in bottles only. Other brews commonly available on tap are Carlsberg, Tuborg, and Heineken. Supermarkets carry a small selection of liquor; note that Nesher "black beer" is a sweet, non-alcoholic malt brew. The official drinking age (not strictly enforced) is 18.

In Arab restaurants, if you ask for **coffee** with no specifications, you'll get a small cup of strong, sweet, Arabic coffee, sometimes referred to as *turki* (Turkish). If you want something standard, ask in Hebrew for *hafukh* (mixed with milk) or *filter*. Instant coffee *(nes)* is also popular. "Black" *(shaḥor)* or "mud" *(botz)* coffee is Turkish coffee brewed in a cup; watch out for the sediment.

CRUNCH Israel has two "indigenous" snack foods that generally inspire intense love-hate reactions from tourists. One is called *bamba*, crispy peanut buttery puffs eaten as a pseudo-protein by Israeli kids. The other is *bissli;* a more complex taste to acquire as it comes in a variety of flavors ranging from falafel to pizza, as well as a variety of pasta-style shapes. Shun the *bissli* imposter *Shosh* if a storekeeper tries to pan it off as the real thing, identifiable by the bee mascot on its package. Try eating them in front of a television to get an authentically Israeli couch potato experience.

LITERATURE

The compilation of the biblical narrative was followed by the age of the *Mishnah* (200 BCE-700 CE), when *halakha* (laws derived from the Bible) and *agada* (elaboration on the Bible) were compiled. This age also saw the growth of the *piyyut* (liturgical poem). In the Middle Ages, Jewish poetry included *Megillat Antioḥus* and *Megillat Ḥanuka* (biblical texts which were not included in the old testament canon), while narrative prose focused on demonological legends.

The revival of Hebrew as a secular language in the 18th century brought a drastic shift in Hebrew literature. Josef Perl and Isaac Erter parodied Ḥasidic works in their writings. In Czarist Russia, Abraham Mapu wrote *The Hypocrite*, the first novel to portray modern Jewish social life in a fictional context. The generations that followed moved toward realism, often employing Yiddish.

At the turn of the 20th century, Hebrew was revived for literature by **Joseph Brenner,** whose hallmark character was the tragic, uprooted settler. His works are notable not only for their influence on later Israeli writers, but also for their pessimistic views of interaction between Jews and Arabs. In the 1920s and 1930s Nobel Laureate **Shmuel Yosef (Shai) Agnon** confronted the breakdown of cultural cohesion among modern Jews in *A Guest for the Night* and *The Bridal Canopy*.

Just before the creation of the State of Israel, a group of native Hebrew authors rose to prominence. Their style, characterized by concern for the landscape and the moment, is exemplified in S. Yizhar's *Efrayim Returns to Alfalfa*. Beginning in the late 1950s, writers such as Amos Oz and A. B. Yehoshua began to experiment with psychological realism, allegory, and symbolism. In the 1960s, new skepticism surfaced in Israeli literature. David Shaḥar was hailed as the Proust of Hebrew literature for his *The Palace of Shattered Vessels*, set in Jerusalem in the 1930s and 40s. Ya'akov Shabtai's *Past Continuous*, about Tel Aviv in the 1970s, is perhaps the best Israeli novel of the decade. A stunning, though initially confusing, must-read is *Arabesques*, by Anton Shammas, an Arab Israeli writing in Hebrew. The poetry of Yehuda Amichai will ensure that you never look at Jerusalem stone in the same way again. Most major Israeli works have been translated into English.

An increasingly prominent genre of Israeli literature focuses on the Israeli-Palestinian conflict by way of fiction, nonfiction, or some combination thereof. Oz's *In the Land of Israel* is a series of interviews with native Israelis and West Bank Palestinians that documents the wide range of political sentiment. His *A Perfect Peace* is a semi-allegorical account of kibbutz life just before the Six-Day War. David Grossman's *Yellow Wind* tells of one Israeli Jew's journey to the West Bank just prior to the *intifada*, while his *Sleeping on a Wire* explores the precarious predicament of Israeli Arabs. For informative Palestinian accounts, check out *The West Bank Story* by Rafik Halabi, an Israeli Druze television reporter, and Fawaz Turki's autobiographical *The Disinherited*. For a lighter note, pick up Ze'ev Chafetz's *Heroes and Hustlers, Hard Hats and Holy Men*, a hilarious satire of Israeli society and politics.

Contemporary Israeli literature is highly influenced by immigrants from vastly different cultures, tumultuous politics, and conflicts between individualism and nationalism. A cadre of young writers such as Etgar Keret and Gafi Amir highlight the disaffected and cynical outlook characteristic of what has been called the post-Zionist era.

Israel's short but tumultuous history has inspired a number of historical novels. They tend to idealize and dramatize a bit excessively, but offer an entertaining introduction to Israeli history. Consider trying Ḥayim Potok's *Wanderings*, James Michener's *The Source*, Leon Uris' *Exodus*, and Sabri Jiryis' *The Arabs in Israel*. For a more sober textbook history of the land read Barbara Tuchman's *Bible and Sword*, which chronicles Palestine from the Bronze Age to the Balfour Declaration of 1917. The elegant works of Solomon Grayzel also give historical background. Serious academic types should pick up Nadav Safran's hefty *Israel: The Embattled Ally* or Conor Cruise O'Brien's lighter *The Siege*.

MUSIC

After WWI, Jews in Palestine assembled chamber groups, a symphony orchestra, an opera company, and a choral society. During the 1930s, with the rise of Nazism in Europe, Jewish musicians fled to Israel. This influx spurred the formation of several music groups. Today seasonal music activities from October to July are held in such varied settings as the historic Crusader Castle at Akko and the modern, 3000-seat Mann Auditorium in Tel Aviv (see **Festivals,** p. 33).

Israeli **popular music** started emerging from its folk-chant origins (often echoing Russian folk melodies) in the late 1960s. Since the 1970s, Israel has been catching up with international music fashions; local bands momentarily lingered on punk, reggae, heavy metal, grunge, and even rap. **MTV** now keeps Israeli youth abreast of the goings-on in London and NYC, and Israelis expect nothing less of their own local acts. Tel Aviv is the unequivocal hub of the cutting-edge music scene in Israel, though performances occur throughout the country.

The most popular performers in Israel play music that's somewhere in between rock and a more mellow sound. Some native classics still on the performance circuit are Shlomo Artzi, Yehudit Ravitz, Rami Klinestein, and Gidi Gov. Achinoam Nini blends American rock with Middle Eastern sounds, while David Broza also throws in Latin American influences. Zahava Ben, a Sephardic Jew, is one of the more popular Israeli singers. She frequently tours in the Palestine Authority and has achieved a great deal of success in Egypt singing the songs of the legendary Umm Kulthoum. Drag queen Dana International brought Israeli pop international fame in 1998 when she won the Eurovision Song Contest. In many places Middle Eastern-style music, heavy on synthesizers and drum machines, blasts from car stereos and boomboxes: this is *muzika mizraḥit* ("oriental music"), very popular with Sephardic Jews (a good example is Avihu Medina's *mizraḥi* tunes).

FILM

Israel has a thriving film industry with numerous festivals and award ceremonies, including an Israeli version of the Academy Awards. The most recent winners of the best film award at the Israeli Academy Awards have been Zirkus Palestina (1998) and Ha-Ḥaverim Shel Yana (1999), which takes place during the Gulf War. In the award-winning Wedding in Galilee (1987) by Palestinian director Michel Khleifi, a Palestinian is granted permission to waive curfew in order to hold his son's wedding, on the condition that Israeli officers be allowed to attend. Other successful films include Clara Ha-Kedosha (Saint Clara) and Etz Ha-Domim Tafus (Under the Domim Tree, 1994) which deals with teenage survivors of the Holocaust in Israel in the 1950s.

HOLIDAYS AND FESTIVALS

Arrange your itinerary with an awareness of **holidays.** In Israel, most businesses and public facilities close Friday afternoon for **Shabbat,** the Jewish sabbath, and reopen at sundown on Saturday. They also close for Jewish holidays, which begin at sunset on the previous day. Year 2001 dates follow: **Pesaḥ,** or Passover (Apr. 8-14), celebrates the exodus of the Jews from Egypt. Observant Jews refrain from eating bread and pastries; products made with regular flour and leavening agents may be hard to come by in Jewish areas. **Shavuot** (May 28) celebrates the giving of the Torah, the Hebrew name for the first five books of the Old Testament. **Rosh Ha-Shana** (the Jewish New Year; Sept. 18-19) is only slightly less holy than **Yom Kippur** (Sept. 27), the holiest day of the Jewish calendar; observant Jews fast in atonement for their sins and Israel shuts down entirely. **Sukkot** (Oct. 2-9), the festival of the harvest, commemorates the Israelites' wilderness wanderings and culminates with **Simḥat Torah** on October 9.

In Muslim areas, most businesses close on Friday, the day of prayer. On holidays, they may close during the afternoon, but are generally open in the morning.

Holiday dates are difficult to pin down ahead of time, as Islamic holidays are based on a lunar calendar and projected dates may vary even over the course of the holiday. Approximate dates for 2000-2001 follow: **Ras al-Sana** (Mar. 26, 2001) is the Islamic New Year's Day, and **Mawlid al-Nabi** (June 4, 2001) celebrates Muhammad's birthday. The most important event and the one most likely to complicate travel is **Ramadan** (Nov. 17, 2001 to Dec. 15, 2001), the annual month-long fast during which Muslims abstain from food and drink, dawn to sunset. During this time, most restaurants close up shop until sundown. Shops may open for a few hours in the morning and a short time after *iftar*, the breaking of the fast; government services are either closed entirely or open only in the morning. It would be rude to smoke or eat in public at this time. The celebratory, three-day **Eid al-Fitr** (Dec. 27-29, 2000) feast marks the end of Ramadan. **'Eid al-Adha** (Mar. 5-8, 2001) commemorates Abraham's intended sacrifice of his son Ishmael and coincides with the *hajj* (pilgrimage) to Mecca, the fifth pillar of Islam (see **Islam,** p. 20).

Secular Israeli holidays include **Yom Ha-Sho'ah** (Holocaust Memorial Day, Apr. 19), **Yom Ha-Zikaron** (Memorial Day, Apr. 25), and **Yom Ha-Atzma'ut** (Independence Day, Apr. 26). On both Yom Ha-Sho'ah and Yom Ha-Zikaron, sirens signal moments of silence.

In addition to holidays, it would be wise to think about when everyone else in the region is vacationing. North Americans and students generally favor summer for visiting; Europeans prefer winter. The week of Passover (Apr. 8-14) brings crowds from all over. If you can manage it, off-season travel means smaller crowds, lower prices, and greater local hospitality, not to mention more falafel.

HOLIDAYS

DATE	HOLIDAY	AFFILIATION
Nov. 27, 2000	First Day of Ramadan	**Islamic**
Dec. 22-29	Ḥanukkah	**Jewish**
Dec. 25	Christmas	**Christian**
Dec. 27	'Eid al-Fitr (end of Ramadan)	**Islamic**
Mar. 6, 2001	'Eid al-Adha (Feast of the Sacrifice)	**Islamic**
Mar. 9	Purim	**Jewish**
Mar. 26	Muharram (Islamic New Year)	**Islamic**
Apr. 4	Ashoura	**Islamic**
Apr. 8-14	Passover	**Jewish**
Apr. 13	Good Friday	**Christian**
Apr. 15	Easter	**Christian**
Apr. 20	Yom Ha-Shoah	**Israeli**
Apr. 25	Yom Ha-Zikaron	**Israeli**
Apr. 28	Yom Ha-Atzma'ut	**Israeli**
May 21	Yom Yerushalayim	**Israeli**
May 28	Shavuot	**Jewish**
June 3	Pentecost	**Christian**
June 4	Eid Mawlid al-Nabi	**Islamic**
July 29	Ninth of Av (Tish'a B'av)	**Jewish**
Aug. 15	Assumption of the Virgin Mary	**Christian**
Sept. 18-19	Rosh Ha-Shanah	**Jewish**
Sept. 27	Yom Kippur	**Jewish**
Oct. 2-9	Sukkot	**Jewish**
Oct. 9	Simḥat Torah	**Jewish**
Oct. 14	Isra' and Miraj	**Islamic**
Nov. 17	First Day of Ramadan	**Islamic**
Dec. 10-17	Ḥanukkah	**Jewish**
Dec. 25	Christmas	**Christian**

FESTIVALS

DATE	FESTIVAL
Oct. 2-8	**Haifa Film Festival.** Intending to foster understanding among people of varying religions and cultures during Sukkot, this festival screens films from many of Israel's neighboring countries. (☎03 765 15 10.)
Oct. 2-8	**Ein Hod Sculpture Biennale Association.** Held once every two years during the holiday of Sukkot in an olive plantation adjacent to the Ein Hod artists' village, the Biennale includes symposia with artist seminars and a Curator's Prize Ceremony. Free admission. (☎04 984 17 79)
Oct. 2-8	**Abu Ghosh Music Festival.** This non-competitive bi-annual festival is held during the feasts of Sukkot and Shavuot. Most performances in the Ark of the Covenant and Benedictine Churches. Street performances, children's shows, exhibitions, and an arts fair. (☎02 624 20 81)
May-June	**International Student Film Festival.** Bi-annual competition held at Tel Aviv University and the Tel Aviv Cinematheque. Approximately 180 films screened over ten days. Workshops, exhibitions, and master-classes offered. (☎03 640 84 03)
May-June	**Israel Festival.** Billed as Israel's premiere international event, the festival has brought together international artists and companies in music, dance, and drama for 33 years. About 50 performances of music and light entertainment in Jerusalem Theater plaza and throughout the city streets, held over a 3 week period. (☎02 561 14 38)
May 27-29	**Abu Ghosh Music Festival,** part two. See above.
Late June-mid-July	**Jerusalem Theater Nights.** Hosted by the Palestinian National Theater in Jerusalem. A gathering of international troupes with several English-language plays. (☎02 628 09 57.)
June 13-July 8	**Caesarea International Opera Festival.** Held at the Roman Amphitheater in Caesarea, this year's program includes Verdi's "La Forza del Destino" and "Otello." Tickets range from NIS 149-325. (☎692 77 77.)
July	**Tzfat Klezmer Festival.** A three-night extravaganza, during which the city sways to the strains of everything from old-world Yiddish tunes to modern Hasidic rock. Outdoor concerts are plentiful and free. (☎692 74 85.)
July	**Jerusalem Film Festival.** Since 1984, the Jerusalem International Film Festival has screened over 140 international films over ten-day periods in July. Features professional cinema panels, exhibitions, and street performances. Films screened at the Cinematheque and in Jerusalem movie theaters. (☎02 672 41 31)
July	**Arad Festival.** Song festival encompassing all trends of Hebrew song, from classical to rock. Founded in 1982, the 3-day festival, with about 120 shows, is held every July in the town of Arad. Many Israeli popular music artists premiere here. The festival is attended by thousands of Israeli youth who flood the bazaars and street shows. (☎07 995 62 05.)
August	**Naisik Ha-Shalom Music Festival.** Two-day entertainment by the Hebrew Israelite community (see **Dimona,** p. 285). (☎05 199 63 17).
Mid-Aug.	**Jaffa Nights.** Israel's largest street-staged event, including over 70 music, theater, dance, and plastic art performances and exhibitions over a four day period. All events are free. (☎03 521 82 64.)

ESSENTIALS

FACTS FOR THE TRAVELER

DOCUMENTS AND FORMALITIES

ISRAEL'S CONSULAR SERVICES ABROAD

Australia: Embassy: 6 Turrana St., Yarralumla, Canberra ACT 2600 (☎(02) 6273 1309; fax 6273 4273). **Consulate:** 37 York St., 6th fl., **Sydney** NSW 2000 (☎(02) 9264 7933; fax 9290 2259).

Canada: Embassy: 50 O'Connor St., #1005, Ottawa, Ont. K1P 6L2 (☎(613) 567-6450, 53, or 55; fax 237-8865; email embisrott@cyberus.ca; www.israelca.org). **Consulates:** 180 Bloor St. W., #700, **Toronto,** Ont. M5S 2V6 (☎(416) 640-8500; fax 640-8555; email hasbara@idirect.com); 1155 boulevard Réné-Lévesque Ouest, #2620, **Montréal,** Québec, H3B 4S5 (☎(514) 940-8500; fax 940-8555; email cgisrmtl@videotron.net).

Ireland: Embassy: Carrisbrook House, 122 Pembrook House, Dublin 4 (☎(01) 668 0303; fax 668 0418).

New Zealand: Embassy: 13th Floor, Equinox House, 111 The Terrace, P.O. Box 2171, Wellington (☎(04) 472 2368 or 2362; fax 499 0632; email israel-ask@israel.org.nz; www.webnz.com/israel).

South Africa: Embassy: 339 Hilda St., Pretoria 001, P.O. Box 3726 (☎(12) 342 2693 or 2697; fax 342 1442; email cgijhb@global.co.za).

UK: Embassy: 2 Palace Green, London W8 4QB (☎(020) 7957 9500; fax 7957 9555; email info@israel-embassy.org.uk; www.israel-embassy.org.uk/london).

US: Embassy: 3514 International Drive NW, Washington, D.C. 20008 (☎(202) 364-5500; fax 364-5423; email ask@israelemb.org). **Consulates:** 800 2nd Ave., **New York,** NY 10017 (☎(212) 499-5410; fax 499-5425; email nycon@interport.net); 6380 Wilshire Blvd., #1700, **Los Angeles,** CA 90048 (☎(323) 852-5500; fax 852-5555; email israinfo@primenet.com). More offices in **San Francisco, Miami, Atlanta, Chicago, Boston, Philadelphia,** and **Houston.**

ENTRANCE REQUIREMENTS

Passport (see p. 36). Required for all travelers.

Visa (see p. 37). Not required for citizens of Australia, Canada, Ireland, New Zealand, South Africa, the UK, and the US.

Inoculations (see p. 45). None required.

Work Permit (see p. 37). Required for all foreigners planning to work in Israel.

Driving Permit (see p. 63). Required for all those planning to drive. International Drivers' Licenses are recommended, but licenses from many English-speaking countries are considered valid.

CONSULAR SERVICES IN ISRAEL

For more information about the following embassies and consulates see **Tel Aviv: Embassies and Consulates,** p. 146 and **Jerusalem: Consulates,** p. 89.

Australia: Embassy: Beit Europa, 37 Sha'ul Ha-Melekh Blvd., Tel Aviv 64928 (☎(03) 695 04 51; fax 696 84 04).

Canada: Embassy: 3 Nirim Beit Hasapanut, Yad Eliyahu, Tel Aviv 67060 (☎(03) 636 33 00; fax: 636 33 80; email taviv@dfait-maeci.gc.ca).

Egypt: Embassy: 54 Basel St., Tel Aviv (☎(03) 546 51 51 or 546 51 52). **Consulate:** 68 Ha-Efroni St., Eilat (☎(07) 637 68 82).

Ireland: Embassy: 3 Daniel Frisch St., 17th fl., Tel Aviv 64731 (☎(03) 696 41 66; fax 696 41 60; email ireland@inter.net.il). Honorary **Consulate:** 164 Wingate St., Herzilya Pituach, 46752 (☎(09) 950 90 55; fax 950 29 49).

Jordan: Embassy: 14 Aba Hillel, Ramat Gan, Tel Aviv (☎(03) 751 77 22).

New Zealand: The British Embassy in Tel Aviv serves New Zealanders (see below).

South Africa: Embassy: Top Tower Floor 16, 50 Reḥov Dizengoff, Tel Aviv 64332 (☎(03) 525 25 66; fax 525 32 30).

UK: Embassy: 192 Ha-Yarkon St., Tel Aviv 63405 (☎(03) 725 12 22; fax 527 15 72; email britemb@inter.net.il). **Consulates:** Migdalor Building, 6th fl., 1 Ben-Yehuda Street, Tel Aviv 63801 (☎(03) 510 01 66; fax 510 11 67); 19 Nashashibi Street, Sheikh Jarrah, P.O. Box 19690, Jerusalem 97200 (☎(02) 541 41 00; fax 532 23 68; email britain@palnet.com); 14 Tzofit Villas, Eilat (☎(07) 637 23 44).

US: Embassy: 71 Reḥov Ha-Yarkon, Tel Aviv 63903 (☎(03) 519 74 57 or 75 75; fax 510 24 44; www.israelemb.org). **Consulates:** 27 Nablus Road, East Jerusalem (☎(02) 622 72 00); 18 Agron St., West Jerusalem (☎(02) 622 72 30); 26 Ben-Gurion St., Hadar, Haifa (☎(04) 853 14 70; fax 853 14 76; email consage@netvision.net.il).

PASSPORTS

REQUIREMENTS. Citizens of Australia, Canada, Ireland, New Zealand, South Africa, the UK, and the US need valid passports to enter Israel and to re-enter their own country, but do not need visas. Israel does not allow entrance if the holder's passport expires in under six months; returning home with an expired passport is illegal and may result in a fine. Typically, countries which have unfriendly relations with Israel (Syria, Lebanon, and Iran) do not allow travelers with Israeli stamps in their passports to enter their countries. If you're planning on visiting these countries, ask that your passport not be stamped.

PHOTOCOPIES. It is a good idea to photocopy the page of your passport that contains your photograph, passport number, and other identifying information, along with other important documents such as visas, travel insurance policies, airplane tickets, and traveler's check serial numbers, in case you lose anything. Carry one set of copies in a safe place apart from the originals and leave another set at home. Consulates also recommend that you carry an expired passport or an official copy of your birth certificate in a part of your baggage separate from other documents.

LOST PASSPORTS. If you lose your passport, immediately notify the local police and the nearest embassy or consulate of your home government. To expedite its replacement, you will need to know all information previously recorded and show identification and proof of citizenship. In some cases, a replacement may take weeks to process, and it may be valid only for a limited time. Any visas stamped in your old passport will be irretrievably lost. In an emergency, ask for immediate temporary traveling papers that permit you to re-enter your home country. Your passport is a public document belonging to your nation's government. You may have to surrender it to a foreign government official, but if you don't get it back in a reasonable amount of time, inform the nearest mission of your home country.

NEW PASSPORTS. All applications for new passports or renewals should be filed several weeks or months in advance of your planned departure date—remember that you are relying on government agencies to complete these transactions. Most passport offices do offer emergency passport services for an extra charge. Citizens residing abroad who need a passport or renewal should contact their nearest embassy or consulate.

VISAS AND WORK PERMITS

Visas are not required for citizens of most countries, including Australia, Canada, Ireland, New Zealand, South Africa, the UK, and the US. Visas issued at entry are valid for three months but are extendable: extensions are normally granted for six months to one year at offices of the **Ministry of the Interior,** 1 Reḥov Shlomtzion Ha-Malka, Jerusalem (☎(02) 629 02 22) or Shalom Tower, 9 Reḥov Ahad Ha-am, 14th fl., Tel Aviv (☎(03) 519 33 33). Cruise ship passengers visiting Israel are issued landing cards allowing them to remain in the country as long as the ship is in port.

Admission as a visitor does not include the right to work, which is authorized only by a **work permit.** For temporary work in Israel, have your employer in Israel contact the Office of the Interior and arrange a work visa before you leave. Entering Israel to study requires a **student visa** ($US25, free for US citizens). For more information, see **Alternatives to Tourism,** p. 68.

IDENTIFICATION

When you travel, always carry two or more forms of identification on your person, including at least one photo ID; a passport combined with a driver's license or birth certificate is usually adequate. Many establishments, especially banks, may require several IDs in order to cash traveler's checks. Never carry all your forms of ID together; split them up in case of theft or loss. It is useful to bring extra passport-size photos to affix to the various IDs or passes you may acquire along the way.

STUDENT AND TEACHER IDENTIFICATION. The **International Student Identity Card (ISIC),** the most widely accepted form of student ID, provides discounts on sights, accommodations, food, and transportation. The ISIC is preferable to an institution-specific card (such as a university ID) because it is more likely to be recognized (and honored) abroad. All cardholders have access to a 24-hour emergency helpline for medical, legal, and financial emergencies (in North America call (877) 370-ISIC, elsewhere call US collect +1 (715) 345-0505), and US cardholders are also eligible for insurance benefits (see **Insurance,** p. 49). Many student travel agencies issue ISICs, including STA Travel in Australia and New Zealand; Travel CUTS in Canada; USIT in the Republic of Ireland and Northern Ireland; SASTS in South Africa; Campus Travel and STA Travel in the UK; and Council Travel (www.counciltravel.com/idcards/default.asp) and STA Travel in the US (see p. 58). The card is valid from September of one year to December of the following year and costs AUS$15, CDN$15, or US$22. Applicants must be degree-seeking students of a secondary or post-secondary school and must be of at least 12 years of age. Because of the proliferation of fake ISICs, some services (particularly airlines) require additional proof of student identity, such as a school ID or a letter attesting to your student status, signed by your registrar and stamped with your school seal. The **International Teacher Identity Card (ITIC)** offers teachers the same insurance coverage as well as similar but limited discounts. The fee is AUS$13, UK£5, or US$22. For more info, contact the **International Student Travel Confederation (ISTC),** Herengracht 479, 1017 BS Amsterdam, Netherlands (☎ +31 (20) 421 28 00; fax 421 28 10; email istcinfo@istc.org; www.istc.org).

YOUTH IDENTIFICATION. The International Student Travel Confederation issues a discount card to travelers who are 25 years old or under but are not students. This one-year **International Youth Travel Card** (**IYTC;** formerly the **GO 25** Card) offers many of the same benefits as the ISIC. Most organizations that sell the ISIC also sell the IYTC for the same prices (see above).

CUSTOMS

Upon entering Israel, you must declare certain items and pay a duty on the value of those articles that exceed the allowance established by Israel's customs service. The following items are prohibited: gambling equipment, illegal drugs, pornographic materials, weapons, fresh meat, and plants. It is wise to make a list, including serial numbers, of any valuables that you carry with you from home; if you register this list with customs before your departure from home and have an official stamp it, you will avoid import duty charges and ensure an easy passage upon your return. Be especially careful to document items manufactured abroad. Israel also has a value-added tax that can be claimed upon departure (see **Taxes,** p. 41)

Upon returning home, you must declare all articles acquired abroad and pay a **duty** on the value of articles that exceed the allowance established by your country's customs service. Keeping receipts will help establish values when you return. Goods and gifts purchased at **duty-free** shops abroad are not exempt from duty or sales tax at your point of return; you must declare these items as well. "Duty-free" merely means that you need not pay a tax in the country of purchase.

MONEY

If you stay in hostels and prepare your own food, expect to spend anywhere from US$20-40 per person per day. **Accommodations** start at about US$8 per night for a bed in a hostel and US$15 per night for a single, while a basic sit-down meal costs US$8. Carrying cash with you, even in a money belt, is risky but necessary; personal checks from home are usually not accepted and even traveler's checks may not be accepted in some locations.

CURRENCY AND EXCHANGE

The primary unit of currency is the **New Israeli Shekel (NIS).** Notes come in denominations of NIS200, NIS100, NIS50, NIS20, and NIS10; coins come in NIS10, NIS5, NIS1, NIS0.50, 10 agorot, and 5 agorot. There are 100 agorot in a shekel. The currency chart below is based on published exchange rates from August 2000. Rates were relatively stable during 2000

CURRENCY

US$1 = NIS4.07 (NEW ISRAELI SHEKEL)	NIS1 = US$0.25
CDN$1 = NIS2.74	NIS1 = CDN$0.37
UK£1 = NIS6.13	NIS1 = UK£0.16
IR£1 = NIS4.66	NIS1 = IR£0.21
AUS$1 = NIS2.37	NIS1 = AUS$0.42
NZ$1 = NIS1.84	NIS1 = NZ$0.54
SAR1 = NIS0.58	NIS1 = SAR1.72
EUR€ = NIS3.67	NIS1 = EUR€0.27
E£1 = NIS1.17 (EGYPTIAN POUNDS)	NIS1 = E£0.86
JD1 = NIS5.73 (JORDANIAN DINARS)	NIS1 = JD0.17

As a general rule, it's cheaper to convert money in Israel than in your home country. However, it is advisable to bring enough foreign currency to last for the first 24-72 hours of a trip to avoid being penniless after banking hours or on a holiday, though ATMs in Israel are open 24 hours and accept most major American credit cards. Travelers living in the US can get foreign currency from the comfort of their home; **International Currency Express** (☎ (888) 278-6628) will deliver foreign currency for over 120 countries or traveler's checks overnight (US$15) or second-day (US$12) at competitive exchange rates.

Watch out for commission rates and check newspapers for the standard rate of exchange. In Israel, **post offices** usually have the best rates and charge no commission. Banks generally also have good rates. A good rule of thumb is to go to only banks that have at most a 5% margin between their buy and sell prices. Bank Ha-Poalim charges no commission for up to $100, while most other banks charge about 2%. Since you lose money with each transaction, **convert in large sums** (unless the currency is depreciating rapidly). Banks are generally open Su, Tu, and Th 8:30am-12:30pm and 4-5:30pm, M and W 8:30am-12:30pm, F and holidays 8:30am-noon. Using an ATM card or a credit card will often get you the best possible rates.

If you use traveler's checks or bills, carry some in small denominations (US$50 or less), especially for times when you are forced to exchange money at disadvantageous rates. However, it is good to carry a range of denominations since charges may be levied per check cashed.

Many services and shops accept Australian, Canadian, and US dollars and British pounds in addition to shekels. If you purchase more than $50 of goods at a shop approved by the Ministry of Tourism, you are entitled to a discount of at least 5% of the purchase price. For the most part, the prices are inflated far above what's necessary to compensate, so you should still bargain (see **Tipping and Bargaining,** p. 40). If you pay in foreign currency, you will receive change in shekels, and you will be exempt from the domestic **Value Added Tax (VAT)** on goods and services (see **Taxes,** p. 41).

TRAVELER'S CHECKS

Traveler's checks are one of the safest and least troublesome means of carrying funds, since they can be refunded if stolen. Several agencies and banks sell them, usually for face value plus a small percentage commission. (Members of the American Automobile Association and some banks can get American Express checks commission-free; see **Driving Permits and Insurance,** p. 63). **American Express** and **Visa** are the most widely recognized. If you're ordering checks, do so well in advance, especially if you are requesting large sums.

Each agency provides refunds if your checks are lost or stolen, and many provide additional services, such as toll-free refund hotlines in the countries you're visiting, emergency message services, and stolen credit card assistance.

In order to collect a **refund for lost or stolen checks,** keep your check receipts separate from your checks and store them in a safe place or with a traveling companion. Ask for a list of refund centers when you buy your checks, leave a list of check numbers with someone at home, and record check numbers when you cash them. Never countersign your checks until you are ready to cash them, and always bring your passport with you when you plan to use the checks.

American Express: in Australia call (800) 251 902; in New Zealand (0800) 441 068; in the UK (0800) 521 313; in the US and Canada (800) 221-7282. Elsewhere call US collect +1 (801) 964-6665; www.aexp.com. Traveler's checks are available in shekels at 1-4% commission at AmEx offices and banks, commission-free at AAA offices (see p. 63). *Cheques for Two* can be signed by either of 2 people traveling together.

Citicorp: In the US and Canada call (800) 645-6556; in Europe, the Middle East, or Africa call the UK +44 (020) 7508 7007; elsewhere call US collect +1 (813) 623-1709. Traveler's checks available in 7 currencies at 1-2% commission. Call 24hr.

Thomas Cook MasterCard: In the US and Canada call (800) 223-7373; in the UK call (0800) 62 21 01; elsewhere call UK collect +44 (1733) 31 89 50. Checks available in 13 currencies at 2% commission. Thomas Cook offices cash checks commission-free.

CREDIT CARDS

Credit cards are generally accepted in Israel, but only in relatively upscale places. Major credit cards—**MasterCard** and **Visa** are welcomed most often—can be used to extract cash advances in NIS from associated banks and ATMs throughout Israel. Credit card companies get the wholesale exchange rate, which is generally 5% better than the retail rate used by banks and other currency exchange establishments. All ATMs require a four digit **Personal Identification Number (PIN).** You must ask your credit card company for a PIN before you leave; without it, you cannot withdraw cash with your credit card outside your home country. If you already have a PIN, check with the company to make sure it will work in Israel.

Credit cards often offer an array of other services, from insurance to emergency assistance. **American Express** (US ☎ (800) 843-2273) has a travel service in addition to a 24-hour emergency hotline (☎ (800) 554-2639 in the US and Canada; from abroad call US collect (202) 554-2639). Benefits include baggage loss and flight insurance, sending mailgrams and international cables, and holding your mail at one of the more than 1700 AmEx offices around the world. For more information about AmEx services see p. 40 and p. 55.

CASH CARDS

Popularly called ATM (Automated Teller Machine) cards, cash cards are widespread in Israel. However, you'll probably get a blank stare if you ask for an ATM machine: call it a *kaspomat*. You should have no problem finding machines in the cities, though in rural areas and small towns they are far less available. Depending on the system that your home bank uses, you can probably access your own personal bank account whenever you need money. ATMs get the same wholesale exchange rate as credit cards, but there is often a limit on the amount of money you can withdraw per day (usually about US$500), and your bank might charge a hefty service fee per withdrawal. Memorize your PIN code in numeric form since machines elsewhere often don't have letters on their keys. Also, if your PIN is longer than four digits, ask your bank whether the first four digits will work, or whether you need a new number.

The two major international money networks are **Cirrus** (US ☎(800) 424-7787) and **PLUS** (US ☎(800) 843-7587 for the "Voice Response Unit Locator"). **Bank HaPoalim** ATMs take bank cards affiliated with Cirrus and often Plus networks for free, but your home bank may charge you. Inquire before you go.

GETTING MONEY FROM HOME

AMERICAN EXPRESS. Cardholders can withdraw cash from their checking accounts at any major AmEx office (listed in the Practical Information sections), up to US$1000 every 21 days (no service charge, no interest). AmEx also offers Express Cash at any of their ATMs in Israel; withdrawals are automatically debited from the cardmember's checking account or line of credit. Green card holders may withdraw up to US$1000 in a seven day period. There is a 2% transaction fee for each cash withdrawal, with a US$2.50 minimum/$20 maximum. To enroll in Express Cash, cardmembers may call (800) 227-4669 in the US; outside the US call collect +1 (336) 668-5041. The AmEx national number in Israel is (715) 343 79 77.

WESTERN UNION. Travelers from the US, Canada, and the UK can wire money abroad through Western Union's international money transfer services. In the US, call (800) 325-6000; in Canada (800) 235-0000; in the UK (0800) 833 833; in Israel (177) 213 141. The rates for sending cash are generally US$10-11 cheaper than with a credit card, and the money is usually available within an hour. For the nearest Western Union location, consult www.westernunion.com.

US STATE DEPARTMENT (US CITIZENS ONLY). In dire emergencies only, the US State Department will forward money within hours to the nearest consular office, which will then disburse it according to instructions for a US$15 fee. Contact the Overseas Citizens Service, American Citizens Services, Consular Affairs, Room 4811, US Department of State, Washington, D.C. 20520 (☎(202) 647-5225; nights, Sundays, and holidays 647-4000; http://travel.state.gov).

TIPPING AND BARGAINING

Tipping in Israel is increasingly moving toward American standards, but for the time being, a 10% tip will suffice in restaurants, bars, and hotels. Check whether a service charge is already included in the bill; in restaurants, gratuity is frequently included for parties of six or more.

Bargaining in Israel is the norm (for bargaining tips, see p. 120). There are very few places where you can't bargain; the "NOs" are limited for the most part to department stores, drug stores, supermarkets, and restaurants with fixed-price menus. Ask hostel owners if they offer any "discounts." Chances are they'll knock 5-10% of the price. A good strategy is to wait inconspicuously by the side until an Israeli makes a purchase. If your price seems higher, bargain. And if there are only tourists in the vicinity, definitely bargain, especially in markets.

TAXES

Israel offers a VAT (Value Added Tax) refund to tourists purchasing more than US$50 worth of goods at a shop approved by the Ministry of Tourism. To collect the 17% refund, you must be a foreign passport holder who is not an Israeli citizen, and you must pay for your purchase in foreign currency (cash or international credit cards). Approved stores will be marked; look for a the Ministry of Tourism insignia or a sign reading "V.A.T. Refund." For details, pick up a copy of the *Customs Guide for the Reimbursement of VAT to Tourists* or *Tourist Information: Customs and VAT* at the airport. In order to collect your refund, you will need to present a VAT invoice/receipt at the point of departure from Israel (if you are leaving from Ben-Gurion International Airport, go to the 24-hour Bank Leumi counter). Be sure to ask for the invoice and fill it out in the shop. Both your purchase and the invoice must be sealed in a bag at the shop and must remain sealed until your departure. Pack the sealed bag in your **hand luggage,** as you will need to present it for inspection. The official will stamp the invoice and refund the VAT in US dollars; if the bank cannot scrape together enough, the refund will be mailed to your home address. Eurocheques may be written in shekels and counted as foreign currency for discounts. The bank does charge a commission: US$2 on refunds of up to US$30; US$5 on refunds ranging from US$30 to US$100; and US$8 for refunds greater than US$100. If you leave Israel from a departure point other than Ben-Gurion Airport, the refund will be mailed to your foreign address, with no charge. Note that no VAT is charged on items purchased in Eilat, which is a free trade zone. For information on large purchases, consult the Ministry of Tourism.

SAFETY AND SECURITY

EMERGENCY NUMBERS. These emergency numbers can be dialed from anywhere in Israel. **Police:** 100. **Emergency:** 101. **Fire:** 102.

Safety in Israel is not guaranteed. The most effective ways to avoid terrorism are to follow current events before leaving and to read English newspapers while there. Several web pages have current information, including the pages of the US Embassy in Israel (www.usis-israel.org.il) and the US State Department (www.state.gov). In 2000, Israel experienced increased warnings of terrorism after its withdrawal from Lebanon.

BLENDING IN. Tourists are particularly vulnerable because they often carry large amounts of cash and are not as street savvy as locals. Luckily, Israel has a very large immigrant population and many foreign (predominantly English-speaking) students, so not speaking Hebrew doesn't automatically scream "tourist." To avoid unwanted attention, try to blend in as much as possible. Respecting local customs (in some cases dressing more conservatively) may placate would-be hecklers. This is particularly tricky in Israel because the dress code and attitudes vary so significantly by region. In brief, cities covered in this book fall into three major categories: modest and religious (Jerusalem, Tzfat, the West Bank, Gaza); immodest, secular, and down-right sexy (Tel Aviv, Eilat), where baggy jeans and a t-shirt might attract more attention than a mini-skirt and mesh tank top; and somewhere in between (Haifa, Be'er Sheva, and much of the rest of the country).

Familiarize yourself with your surroundings before setting out; if you must check a map on the street, duck into a cafe or shop. Also, carry yourself with confidence, as an obviously bewildered bodybuilder is more likely to be harassed than a stern and confident 98-pound weakling. If you are traveling alone, be sure that someone at home knows your itinerary and **never admit that you're traveling alone.**

EXPLORING. Extra vigilance is always wise, but there is no need for panic when exploring a new city or region. Find out about unsafe areas from tourist offices, from the manager of your hotel or hostel, or from a local whom you trust. You may want to carry a **whistle** to scare off attackers or attract attention. Whenever possible, *Let's Go* warns of unsafe neighborhoods and areas, but there are some good general tips to follow. When walking at night, stick to busy, well-lit streets. Do not attempt to cross through parks, parking lots, or other large, deserted areas. Buildings in disrepair, vacant lots, and unpopulated areas are all bad signs. The distribution of people can reveal a great deal about the relative safety of the area; look for children playing, women walking in the open, and other signs of an active community. Keep in mind that a district can change character drastically between blocks. If you feel uncomfortable, leave as quickly and directly as you can, but don't allow fear of the unknown to turn you into a hermit. Careful, persistent exploration will build confidence and make your stay in an area much more rewarding.

TERRORISM. Terrorism is a threat in Israel, as it is everywhere, from Oklahoma City to Manchester. Travelers need not feel like powerless bystanders, however. The chances of becoming a victim of terrorism are relatively low and can be lowered further by taking certain precautions. You should be aware of the possibility of danger without letting it paralyze you.

Avoid crowded areas and do not visit the West Bank or the Gaza Strip in the days following the announcement of a new building project or on the anniversary of previous attacks. Traveling in the **Palestinian territories** can be dangerous, especially in a car with the yellow license plates that identify the vehicle as Israeli. Jewish travelers should avoid identifying themselves as such. Simply placing a baseball cap over a *kippah* can prevent stares and hostility. Demonstrations by Palestinians and Israelis in the West Bank have led to confrontations and clashes with the police, and some turn deadly. Stone throwing and other forms of protest can occur without warning and escalate quickly. Be aware of potential unrest in the West Bank by staying up to date with the news and contacting the consular division of the United States Consulate General (see p. 36).

Public transportation has been the target of several terrorist bombings, particularly local buses in Jerusalem and Tel Aviv. Most bus bombings have occurred in the early morning rush hour; if your plans are flexible, avoid bus travel at this time.

Travelers in Israel are more likely, however, to be affected by anti-terrorist measures than by terrorism itself. The Israeli soldiers on every corner are there for your protection, but the prevalence of gun-toting 20-year-olds can be a little shocking. Do not leave bags unattended in public places. Termed "*Ḥefetz Ḥashood*," (suspicious package) these bags are dealt with in a serious manner. They will be destroyed within minutes since in the past bombs have been left in trash cans (which now have only small receptacles) or on street corners. Finally, expect stringent security measures, including bag searches or metal detectors, at museums, bus stations, shopping malls, and public events.

As of February 1998, the Israeli government has had the responsibility to supply the entire population with **gas masks** in times of emergency. The ministry of tourism has declared that there are enough masks for all tourists; those residing in hotels will receive them directly from these hotels, while others will receive them from designated department stores.

GETTING AROUND. More Israelis have been killed in car accidents than in all of the country's wars combined. Israel has a bad reputation when it comes to driving, and with good reason. Drunk driving is prevalent, and the windy, hilly roads don't help. If you are using a **car,** learn local driving signals and wear a seatbelt. Children under 18kg (40lbs) should ride only in a specially-designed carseat, available for a small fee from most car rental agencies. Study route maps before you hit the road; some roads, particularly in the Negev and in the Golan, have poor (or nonexistent) shoulders or few gas stations. In some regions, road conditions necessitate driving far more slowly and more cautiously than you would at home. In most cases you will be presented with two options for reaching your destination: the scenic route or the highway. Make sure you know what you're getting into if you choose the former—the roads are often barely wide enough for one car, yet buses will blast past you in the opposite direction.

If you plan on spending a lot of time on the road, you may want to bring spare parts. For long drives in desolate areas invest in a cellular phone and a roadside assistance program. Car phones are ubiquitous in Israel, and most rental cars have them built in. When you rent the car, you'll have to determine whether you want the more expensive with-phone plan. Cellular phones (or "pelephones," as Israelis call them) are responsible for many car-accidents. As a result, the laws regarding them are stringently enforced. Do not hold the phone while you are driving (all rental cars should come with phone stands anyway). If you do, you're likely to be hit with another car, a heavy fine, or both. Be sure to park your vehicle in a garage or well-traveled area, and use a steering wheel locking device in larger cities.

Sleeping in your car is one of the most dangerous (and often illegal) ways to get your rest. If your car breaks down, wait for the police to assist you.

Let's Go does not recommend **hitchhiking** under any circumstances, particularly for women. For more information see **Getting Around,** p. 62.

SELF-DEFENSE. There is no sure-fire set of precautions that will protect you from all the situations you might encounter when you travel. A good self-defense course will give you more concrete ways to react to different types of aggression. **Impact, Prepare,** and **Model Mugging** can refer you to local self-defense courses in the US (☎(800) 345-5425) and Vancouver, Canada (☎(604) 878-3838). Workshops (2-3hr.) start at US$50; full courses run US$350-500. Both women and men are welcome.

FURTHER INFORMATION The following government offices provide travel information and advisories by telephone, fax, or the web.

Australian Department of Foreign Affairs and Trade: ☎(2) 6261 1111; www.dfat.gov.au.

Canadian Department of Foreign Affairs and International Trade (DFAIT): In Canada call (800) 267-6788 in Canada, elsewhere call +1 (613) 944-6788; www.dfait-maeci.gc.ca. Call for their free booklet, *Bon Voyage...But.*

New Zealand Ministry of Foreign Affairs: ☎(04) 494 8500; fax 494 8511; www.mft.govt.nz/trav.html.

United Kingdom Foreign and Commonwealth Office: ☎(020) 7238 4503; fax 7238 4545; www.fco.gov.uk.

US Department of State: ☎(202) 647-5225, auto faxback (202) 647-3000; http://travel.state.gov. For *A Safe Trip Abroad,* call (202) 512-1800.

FINANCIAL SECURITY

PROTECTING YOUR VALUABLES. To prevent easy theft, don't keep all your valuables (money, important documents) in one place. **Photocopies** of important documents allow you to recover them in case they are lost or filched. Carry one copy separate from the documents and leave another at home. Fortunately, Israel is a very small country, so it's easy to leave your valuables in a safe deposit box in Jerusalem or Tel Aviv. You'll always be within a couple hours of your ticket home. Label every piece of luggage both inside and out. Carry as little money as possible, keep some aside to use in an emergency, and never count your money in public. **Don't put a wallet with money in your back pocket**. If you carry a purse, buy a sturdy one with a secure clasp, and carry it crosswise on the side, away from the street with the clasp against you. Secure packs with small combination **padlocks** which slip through the two zippers. A **money belt,** a nylon, zippered pouch with a belt that sits inside the waist of your pants or skirt, combines convenience and security; you can buy one at most camping supply stores. A **neck pouch** is equally safe, though far less accessible. Refrain from pulling out your neck pouch in public. Avoid keeping anything precious in a fanny-pack (even if it's worn on your stomach): your valuables will be highly visible and easy to steal. Many hostels and hotels in Israel have secure and reliable safes that are worth the nominal charge.

CON ARTISTS AND PICKPOCKETS. Among the more colorful aspects of large cities are **con artists.** Con artists and hustlers often work in groups, and children are among the most effective. They possess an innumerable range of ruses. Be aware of certain classics: sob stories that require money, rolls of bills "found" on the street, mustard spilled (or saliva spit) onto your shoulder distracting you for enough time to snatch your bag. Be especially suspicious in unexpected situations. Do not respond or make eye contact, walk away, and keep a solid grip on your belongings. Contact the police if a hustler is particularly insistent or aggressive.

In crowds and especially on public transportation, **pickpockets** are amazingly deft at their craft. Rush hour is no excuse for strangers to press up against you on the bus. If someone stands uncomfortably close, move away and hold your bags tightly. Pickpocketing is particularly common in the crowded markets, where you'll barely be able to tell where your own hands are. If you're headed for the markets, leave whatever you don't need somewhere safe. Also, be alert in public telephone booths. If you must say your calling card number, do so very quietly; if you punch it in, make sure no one can look over your shoulder.

ACCOMMODATIONS AND TRANSPORTATION. Never leave your belongings unattended; crime occurs in even the most demure-looking hostel or hotel. If you feel unsafe, look for places with either a curfew or a night attendant. *Let's Go* lists locker availability in hostels and train stations, but you'll need your own **padlock.** Lockers are useful if you plan on sleeping outdoors or don't want to lug everything with you, but don't store valuables in them. Most hotels also provide lock boxes free or for a minimal fee.

Don't trust anyone to "watch your bag for a second." If you travel by **car,** don't leave valuables—such as radios or luggage—in it while you are away. If your tape deck or radio is removable, hide it in the trunk or take it with you. If it isn't, at least conceal it under something else. Similarly, hide baggage in the trunk—although savvy thieves can tell if a car is heavily loaded by the way it sits on its tires.

DRUGS AND ALCOHOL

A meek "I didn't know it was illegal" will not suffice. Remember that you are subject to the laws of the country in which you travel, not to those of your home country; it is your responsibility to familiarize yourself with these laws before leaving. If you carry **prescription drugs** while you travel, it is vital to have a copy of the prescriptions themselves when you cross borders.

Israeli drug laws are not lenient. Cannabis is widely smoked, widely prosecuted, and disdained by most Israelis. Sentences range from heavy fines to imprisonment, though foreigners are most likely to experience deportation. Purchasing drugs in Israel is risky, since many dealers double as informers. Police periodically sweep the hostels, especially in Eilat and some areas of Tel Aviv. Quantities of more than 15g will land you in prison with a drug-dealing charge, and smuggling drugs across Israeli borders is bound to get you in trouble. The thorough security searches are meant to prevent terrorism, but there isn't much that slips through.

The drinking age in Israel is 18, and for the first time, bars and discotheques are beginning to enforce it. Eilat in particular has begun to card stringently; a foreign driver's license usually serves as adequate identification. Avoid public drunkenness; it can jeopardize your safety and earn the disdain of locals.

HEALTH

Common sense is the simplest prescription for good health while you travel. Travelers complain most often about their feet and their gut, so take precautionary measures: drink lots of fluids to prevent dehydration and constipation, wear sturdy, broken-in shoes and clean socks, and use talcum powder to keep your feet dry. To minimize the effects of jet lag, "reset" your body's clock by adopting the time of your destination as soon as you board the plane.

BEFORE YOU GO

Preparation can help minimize the likelihood of contracting a disease and maximize the chances of receiving effective health care in an emergency. For tips on packing a basic **first-aid kit** and other health essentials, see p. 50.

In your **passport,** write the names of any people you wish to be contacted in case of a medical emergency, and also list any allergies or medical conditions of which you would want doctors to be aware. Matching a prescription to a foreign equivalent is not always easy, safe, or possible. Carry up-to-date, legible prescriptions or a statement from your doctor stating the medication's trade name, manufacturer, chemical name, and dosage. While traveling, be sure to keep all medication with you in your carry-on luggage.

IMMUNIZATIONS

The CDC (see below) advises that there are no special requirements for travel in Israel. Nevertheless, extensive travel makes you more prone than usual to disease. Take a look at your immunization records before you go. Travelers over two years old should be sure that the following vaccines are up to date: MMR (for measles, mumps, and rubella); DTaP or Td (for diptheria, tetanus, and pertussis); OPV (for polio); HbCV (for haemophilus influenza B); and HBV (for hepatitis B). Hepatitis A vaccine and/or immune globulin (IG) is a good idea. Check with a doctor for guidance through this maze of injections.

USEFUL ORGANIZATIONS AND PUBLICATIONS

The US **Centers for Disease Control and Prevention** (**CDC;** ☎(877) FYI-TRIP; www.cdc.gov/travel), which is an excellent source of information for travelers, maintains an international fax information service. The CDC's comprehensive booklet *Health Information for International Travelers*, an annual rundown of disease, immunization, and general health advice, is free on the website or US$22 via the Government Printing Office (☎(202) 512-1800). The **US State Department** (http://travel.state.gov) compiles Consular Information Sheets on health, entry requirements, and other issues for various countries. For quick information on health and other travel warnings, call the **Overseas Citizens Services** (☎(202) 647-5225; after-hours 647-4000), contact a US passport agency or a US embassy or consulate abroad, or send a self-addressed, stamped envelope to the Overseas Citizens Services, Bureau of Consular Affairs, #4811, US Department of State, Washington, D.C. 20520. For information on medical evacuation services and travel insurance firms, see http://travel.state.gov/medical.html. The **British Foreign and Commonwealth Office** also gives health warnings for individual countries (www.fco.gov.uk).

For detailed information on travel health, including a country-by-country overview of diseases, try the **International Travel Health Guide,** Stuart Rose, MD (Travel Medicine, US$20; www.travmed.com). For general health information, contact the **American Red Cross** (☎(800) 564-1234, M-F 8:30am-4:30pm).

MEDICAL ASSISTANCE ON THE ROAD

Medical care in Israel is equivalent in quality to that in the West. For minor illnesses, go to a pharmacy. Israeli law requires that at least one pharmacy in a neighborhood be open or on call at all times. Pharmacists offer medical advice as well as medication; most speak English. In more serious situations, see a doctor.

Almost all Israeli doctors speak nearly fluent English. Because Israel's system of socialized medicine has only recently begun to be privatized, private practice is very expensive, and medical insurance is a must. Medical care in Israel is generally more available and of higher quality than in the Palestinian territories.

If you are concerned about access to medical support while traveling, there are support services you may employ. The *MedPass* from **Global Emergency Medical Services (GEMS),** 2001 Westside Dr., #120, Alpharetta, GA 30004 (☎(800) 860-1111; fax (770) 475-0058; www.globalems.com), provides 24-hour international medical assistance, support, and medical evacuation resources. The **International Association for Medical Assistance to Travelers** (**IAMAT;** in the US ☎(716) 754-4883, in Canada (416) 652-0137, in New Zealand (03) 352 2053; www.sentex.net/~iamat) has free membership, lists English-speaking doctors worldwide, and offers detailed info on immunization requirements and sanitation. If your regular **insurance** policy does not cover travel abroad, you may wish to purchase additional coverage (see p. 49).

Those with medical conditions (diabetes, allergies to antibiotics, epilepsy, heart conditions) may want to obtain a stainless-steel **Medic Alert** ID tag (first-year US$35, $15 annually thereafter), which identifies the condition and gives a 24-hour collect-call number. Contact the Medic Alert Foundation, 2323 Colorado Ave, Turlock, CA 95382 (☎(800) 825-3785; www.medicalert.org).

ENVIRONMENTAL HAZARDS

The geographic diversity in Israel is extraordinary, and the environmental risks are correspondingly broad. The most common health problems are related to the heat, particularly in the desert.

Heat exhaustion and dehydration: Heat exhaustion, characterized by dehydration and salt deficiency, can lead to fatigue, headaches, and wooziness. Drink plenty of fluids (when hiking drink a liter every hr.), eat salty foods (e.g. crackers), and avoid dehydrating beverages (e.g. alcohol, coffee, tea, and caffeinated soda). Wear a hat, sunglasses, and a lightweight longsleeve shirt in hot sun. Continuous heat stress can eventually lead to **heatstroke,** characterized by a rising temperature, severe headache, and cessation of sweating. Victims should be cooled off with wet towels and taken to a doctor.

Sunburn: Wear plenty of sunscreen, preferably SPF-15 or higher. If you're heading toward the Negev or Golan, particularly hiking, buy sunscreen in the city and bring it with you. Apply it liberally and often to avoid burns and to reduce the risk of skin cancer. If you are planning on spending time near water or in the desert, you are at risk of getting burned, even through clouds. Remember to slather the tops of your feet, which are exposed to the sun all-day. Protect your eyes with good sunglasses, since ultraviolet rays can damage the retina of the eye. If you get sunburned, drink more fluids than usual and apply Calamine or an aloe-based lotion.

PREVENTING DISEASE

INSECT-BORNE DISEASES

Many diseases are transmitted by insects—mainly mosquitoes, fleas, ticks, and lice. Be aware of insects in wet or forested areas, especially while hiking and camping. **Mosquitoes** are most active from dusk to dawn. Wear long pants and long sleeves, tuck your pants into your socks, and buy a mosquito net. Use insect repellents, such as DEET, and soak or spray your gear with permethrin (licensed in the US for use on clothing). Consider natural repellents that make you smelly to insects, like vitamin B-12 or garlic pills. To stop the itch after being bitten, try Calamine lotion or topical cortisones (like Cortaid), or take a bath with a half-cup of baking soda or oatmeal. **Ticks**—responsible for Lyme and other diseases—can be particularly dangerous in forested regions. Pause periodically to brush off ticks using a fine-toothed comb on your neck and scalp. Do not try to remove ticks by burning them or coating them with nail polish remover or petroleum jelly.

FOOD- AND WATER-BORNE DISEASES

Prevention is the best cure: be sure that everything you eat is cooked properly and that the water you drink is clean. Tap water is generally safe for drinking in Israel. If you need to drink water from nature, purify it first by bringing it to a rolling boil or treating it with **iodine tablets,** available at any camping goods store. Other edible dangers include raw shellfish, unpasteurized milk, and sauces containing raw eggs. Watch out for food from markets or street vendors that may have been fried in rancid cooking oil. Always wash your hands before eating, or bring a quick-drying purifying liquid hand cleaner like Purrell. Your bowels will thank you.

Traveler's diarrhea (*shilshul* in Hebrew): Results from drinking untreated water or eating uncooked foods; a temporary (and fairly common) reaction to the bacteria in new food ingredients. Symptoms include nausea, bloating, urgency, and malaise. Try quick-energy, non-sugary foods with protein and carbohydrates to keep your strength up. Over-the-counter anti-diarrheals (e.g. Immodium) may counteract the problems, but can complicate serious infections. The most dangerous side effect is dehydration; drink 8oz. of water with ½ tsp. of sugar or honey and a pinch of salt, try decaffeinated soft drinks, or munch on salted crackers. If you develop a fever or your symptoms don't go away after 4-5 days, consult a doctor. See a doctor for treatment of diarrhea in children.

Dysentery: Results from a serious intestinal infection caused by certain bacteria. The most common type is bacillary dysentery, also called shigellosis. Symptoms include bloody diarrhea (sometimes mixed with mucus), fever, and abdominal pain and tenderness. Bacillary dysentery generally only lasts a week, but it is highly contagious. Amoebic dysentery, which develops more slowly, is a more serious disease and may cause long-term damage if left untreated. A stool test can determine which kind you have; seek medical help immediately. Dysentery can be treated with the drugs norfloxacin or ciprofloxacin (commonly known as Cipro). If you are traveling in high-risk (especially rural) regions, consider obtaining a prescription before you leave home.

Hepatitis A: A viral infection of the liver acquired primarily through contaminated water. Symptoms include fatigue, fever, loss of appetite, nausea, dark urine, jaundice, vomiting, aches and pains, and light stools. The risk is highest in rural areas and the countryside, but it is also present in urban areas. Ask your doctor about the vaccine (Havrix or Vaqta) or an injection of immune globulin (IG; formerly called gamma globulin).

Parasites: Microbes, tapeworms, etc. that hide in unsafe water and food. **Giardiasis,** for example, is acquired by drinking untreated water from streams or lakes all over the world. Symptoms include swollen glands or lymph nodes, fever, rashes or itchiness, digestive problems, eye problems, and anemia. Boil water, wear shoes, avoid bugs, and eat only cooked food

Schistosomiasis: Also known as *bilharzia*; a parasitic disease caused when the larvae of flatworm penetrate unbroken skin. Symptoms include an itchy localized rash, followed in 4-6 weeks by fever, fatigue, painful urination, diarrhea, loss of appetite, night sweats, and a hive-like rash on the body. If exposed to untreated water, rub the area vigorously with a towel and apply rubbing alcohol. Schistosomiasis can be treated with prescription drugs. In general, swimming in fresh water should be avoided.

Typhoid fever: Caused by the salmonella bacteria; common in villages and rural areas in the Middle East. While mostly transmitted through contaminated food and water, it can be acquired by direct contact with people. Early symptoms include fever, headaches, fatigue, loss of appetite, constipation, and sometimes a rash on the abdomen or chest. Antibiotics can treat typhoid, but a vaccination (70-90% effective) is recommended.

OTHER INFECTIOUS DISEASES

Rabies: Transmitted through the saliva of infected animals; fatal if untreated. By the time symptoms appear (thirst and muscle spasms), the disease is in its terminal stage. If you are bitten, wash the wound thoroughly, seek immediate medical care, and try to have the animal located. A rabies vaccine, which consists of 3 shots given over a 21-day period, is available but is only semi-effective.

Hepatitis B: A viral infection of the liver transmitted via bodily fluids or needle-sharing. Symptoms may not surface until years after infection. Vaccinations are recommended for health-care workers, sexually-active travelers, and anyone planning to seek medical treatment abroad. The 3-shot vaccination series must begin 6 months before traveling.

Hepatitis C: Like Hep B, but the mode of transmission differs. IV drug users, those with occupational exposure to blood, hemodialysis patients, and recipients of blood transfusions are at the highest risk, but the disease can also be spread through sexual contact or sharing items like razors and toothbrushes that may have traces of blood on them.

AIDS, HIV, STDS

Acquired Immune Deficiency Syndrome (AIDS) is a growing problem around the world. The World Health Organization estimates that there are 30 million people infected with HIV virus, and women now represent 40% of all new HIV infections.

The easiest mode of HIV transmission is through direct blood-to-blood contact with an HIV-positive person; *never* share intravenous drug, tattooing, or other needles. The most common mode of transmission is sexual intercourse. Health professionals recommend the use of latex condoms. Since it may not always be easy to buy condoms when traveling, take a supply with you for your trip.

Israel has several organizations devoted to HIV/AIDS, including the **Jerusalem AIDS Project,** P.O. Box 7956, Jerusalem 91077 (☎(02) 679 76 77; www.aidsnew.org.il), which provides education and support. Their website lists several links to other HIV/AIDS organizations. **HIV support line:** ☎600 200 200.

For detailed information on **Acquired Immune Deficiency Syndrome (AIDS)** call the **US Centers for Disease Control's** 24-hour hotline at (800) 342-2437, or contact the **Joint United Nations Programme on HIV/AIDS (UNAIDS),** 20 av. Appia, CH-1211 Geneva 27, Switzerland (☎ +41 (22) 791 36 66; fax 791 41 87). Council's brochure, *Travel Safe: AIDS and International Travel,* is available at all Council Travel offices and on their website (www.ciee.org/Isp/safety/travelsafe.htm).

Sexually transmitted diseases (STDs) such as gonorrhea, chlamydia, genital warts, syphilis, and herpes are easier to catch than HIV and can be just as deadly. **Hepatitis B** and **C** are also serious STDs (see **Other Infectious Diseases,** above). Though condoms may protect you from some STDs, oral or even tactile contact can lead to transmission. Warning signs include swelling, sores, bumps, or blisters on sex organs, the rectum, or the mouth; burning and pain during urination and bowel movements; itching around sex organs; swelling or redness of the throat; and flu-like symptoms. If these symptoms develop, see a doctor immediately.

WOMEN'S HEALTH

HOTLINES. There are a number of women's support groups and 24-hour hotlines that can be dialed from anywhere in Israel.

Rape Crisis Center: ☎1202
Breast cancer: ☎(03) 566 75 55
Family planning: Tel Aviv ☎(03) 510 15 11; Jerusalem ☎(02) 624 84 12
Pregnancy loss: ☎(02) 563 83 40
Women in Distress: ☎(09) 950 57 20

Women traveling in unsanitary conditions are vulnerable to **urinary tract** and **bladder infections,** common and severely uncomfortable bacterial diseases that cause a burning sensation and painful and sometimes frequent urination. To avoid these infections, drink plenty of vitamin-C-rich juice and water and urinate frequently, especially right after intercourse. Untreated, these infections can lead to kidney infections, sterility, and even death. If symptoms persist, see a doctor. Most hospitals in Israel have a separate women's care facility.

Women are also susceptible to **vaginal yeast infections,** a treatable but uncomfortable illness likely to flare up in hot and humid climates. Wearing loosely fitting trousers or a skirt and cotton underwear will help. Yeast infections can be treated with an over-the-counter remedy like Monostat or Gynelotrimin. Bring supplies from home if you are prone to infection, as they may be difficult to find on the road. Some travelers opt for a natural alternative such as plain yogurt and lemon juice douche if other remedies are unavailable.

Tampons and **pads** are generally available in Israel, but your preferred brands may be hard to find; it may be advisable to take supplies along. **Reliable contraceptive devices** may also be difficult to find. Women on the pill should bring enough to allow for possible loss or extended stays. Bring a prescription, since forms of the pill vary a good deal. Women who use a diaphragm should bring enough contraceptive jelly. Though condoms are generally available, you might want to bring your favorite brand before you go, as availability and quality vary.

Women considering an **abortion** abroad should contact the **International Planned Parenthood Federation (IPPF),** Regent's College, Inner Circle, Regent's Park, London NW1 4NS (☎ (020) 7487 7900; fax 7487 7950; www.ippf.org), for more information. Abortions in Israel are only permitted on limited health grounds. For further information, consult the *Handbook for Women Travellers*, by Maggie and Gemma Moss (Piatkus Books, US$15).

INSURANCE

Travel insurance generally covers four basic areas: medical/health problems, property loss, trip cancellation/interruption, and emergency evacuation. Although your regular insurance policies may well extend to travel-related accidents, you may consider purchasing travel insurance if the cost of potential trip cancellation/interruption is greater than you can absorb.

Medical insurance (especially university policies) often covers costs incurred abroad; check with your provider. **Medicare does not cover foreign travel.** Canadians are protected by their home province's health insurance plan for up to 90 days after leaving the country; check with the provincial Ministry of Health or Health Plan Headquarters for details. **Homeowners' insurance** (or your family's coverage) often covers theft during travel and loss of travel documents (passport, plane ticket, railpass, etc.) up to US$500.

ISIC and **ITIC** provide basic insurance benefits, including US$100 per day of in-hospital sickness for a maximum of 60 days, US$3000 of accident-related medical reimbursement, and US$25,000 for emergency medical transport (see **Identification,** p. 37). Cardholders have access to a toll-free 24-hour helpline for medical, legal, and financial emergencies overseas (US and Canada ☎ (877) 370-4742, elsewhere call US collect +1 (713) 342-4104). **American Express** (☎ (800) 528-4800) grants most cardholders automatic car rental insurance (collision and theft, but not liability) and ground travel accident coverage of US$100,000 on flight purchases made with the card.

Prices for travel insurance purchased separately generally run about US$50 per week for full coverage, while trip cancellation/interruption may be purchased separately at a rate of about US$5.50 per US$100 of coverage.

INSURANCE PROVIDERS. Council and **STA** (see p. 58) offer a range of plans that can supplement your basic coverage. Other private insurance providers in the **US and Canada** include: **Access America** (☎ (800) 284-8300); **Berkely Group/Carefree Travel Insurance** (☎ (800) 323-3149; www.berkely.com); **Globalcare Travel Insurance** (☎ (800) 821-2488; www.globalcare-cocco.com); and **Travel Assistance International** (☎ (800) 821-2828; www.worldwide-assistance.com). Providers in the **UK** include **Campus Travel** (☎ (01865) 258 000) and **Columbus Travel Insurance** (☎ (020) 7375 0011). In **Australia,** try **CIC Insurance** (☎ 92 02 80 00).

PACKING

Pack light: lay out only what you absolutely need, then take half the clothes and twice the money. The less you have, the less you have to lose (or store, or carry on your back). Any extra space will be useful for souvenirs or items you might pick up along the way. If you plan to hike, also see **Camping and the Outdoors,** p. 53.

IMPORTANT DOCUMENTS. Don't forget your passport, traveler's checks, ATM and/or credit cards, and adequate ID (see **Identification,** p. 37).

LUGGAGE. If you plan to cover most of your itinerary by foot, a sturdy **frame backpack** is unbeatable. For the basics on buying a pack, see p. 53. Toting a **suitcase** or **trunk** is fine if you plan to stay in one or two cities and explore from there, but a very bad idea if you're going to be moving around a lot. In addition to your main piece of luggage, a **daypack** (a small backpack or courier bag) is a must.

CLOTHING. No matter when you're traveling, it's always a good idea to bring a **warm jacket** or wool sweater, a **rain jacket** (Gore-Tex® is both waterproof and breathable), sturdy shoes or **hiking boots,** and **thick socks. Flip-flops** or waterproof sandals are crucial for grubby hostel showers. Jeans are heavy and difficult to wash; take khakis or light cotton **trousers** instead. You may also want to add one dressier outfit and maybe a nicer pair of shoes if you have the room: many Israeli discotheques have dress codes. In some areas and especially holy sites, both men and women should cover their knees and upper arms to avoid offending local rules of modesty. Women should consider bringing one light but long skirt for holy sites.

FOOTWEAR. Appropriate shoes are vital: well-cushioned **sneakers** are good for walking. For hiking, a pair of **hiking boots** with good ventilation is a must (see p. 54). Don't be fooled at the entrance to a hike if you see a large group of Israelis in sandals: Israelis will wear sandals anywhere. A double pair of socks—light absorbent cotton inside and thick wool outside—will cushion feet, keep them dry, and help prevent blisters. Talcum powder in your shoes and on your feet can prevent sores. Break in your shoes before you leave home.

SLEEPSACKS. Some hostels require that you either provide your own linen or rent sheets from them. Save cash by making your own sleepsack: fold a full-size sheet in half the long way, then sew it closed along the long side and one of the short sides.

CONVERTERS AND ADAPTERS. In Israel, electricity is 220 volts AC, enough to fry any 110V North American appliance. 220V electrical appliances don't like 110V current, either. Visit a hardware store for an adapter (which changes the shape of the plug) and a converter (which changes the voltage). Don't make the mistake of using only an adapter (unless appliance instructions explicitly state otherwise).

TOILETRIES. Toothbrushes, towels, cold-water soap, talcum powder (to keep feet dry), deodorant, razors, tampons, and condoms are often available, but may be difficult to find, so bring extras along. **Contact lenses,** on the other hand, may be expensive and difficult to find, so bring enough extra pairs and solution for your entire trip. Also bring your glasses and a copy of your prescription in case you need emergency replacements. If you use heat-disinfection, either switch temporarily to a chemical disinfection system (check first to make sure it's safe with your brand of lenses), or buy a converter to 220V.

FIRST-AID KIT. For a basic first-aid kit, pack bandages, aspirin or other painkiller, antibiotic cream, a thermometer, a Swiss Army knife, tweezers, moleskin, decongestant, motion-sickness remedy, diarrhea or upset-stomach medication (Pepto Bismol or Immodium), an antihistamine, sunscreen, insect repellent, burn ointment, and a syringe for emergencies (get an explanatory letter from your doctor).

STRAIGHT FLUSH As a result of mass urbanization and agricultural efforts, Israel suffers from a chronic water shortage. Up to 60 percent of much-needed rainfall is lost in evaporation each year, eliciting a steadfast conservationist mentality among Israelis. Their ecological efforts manifest themselves in water-saving devices such as micro-drip sprinklers, machines that recycle household and industrial fluids, and—the two levered toilet. All johns are equipped with a double jointed flushing device specific for either, er. . . number one or number two. The inner part of the handle is darker and less flexible, and it packs a more powerful goosh that takes everything down with it. The outer part of the lever is pushed for lighter substances.

FILM. If you are not a serious photographer, you might want to bring a **disposable camera** or two rather than an expensive permanent one. Despite disclaimers, airport security X-rays *can* fog film, so buy a lead-lined pouch at a camera store or ask security to hand inspect your film. Always pack film in your carry-on luggage, since higher-intensity X-rays are used on checked luggage.

OTHER USEFUL ITEMS. For safety purposes, you should bring a **money belt** and small **padlock.** Basic **outdoors equipment** (plastic water bottle, compass, waterproof matches, pocketknife, sunglasses, sunscreen, hat) may also prove useful. Quick repairs of torn garments can be done on the road with a needle and thread; also consider bringing electrical tape for patching tears. Doing your **laundry** by hand (where it is allowed) is both cheaper and more convenient than doing it at a laundromat—bring detergent, a small rubber ball to stop up the sink, and string for a makeshift clothes line. **Other things** you're liable to forget: an umbrella; sealable **plastic bags** (for damp clothes, soap, food, shampoo, and other spillables); an **alarm clock;** safety pins; rubber bands; a flashlight; earplugs; and a small calculator.

ACCOMMODATIONS

HOSTELS

A HOSTELER'S BILL OF RIGHTS Unless stated otherwise, you can expect that every hostel has: no lockout, no curfew, free hot showers, secure luggage storage, and no key deposit.

Hostels are generally dorm-style accommodations, often in large rooms with bunk beds, although some hostels do offer private rooms for families and couples. Most hostels in Israel offer co-ed and women only accommodations. They sometimes have bike or moped rentals, storage areas, and laundry facilities. There can be drawbacks: some hostels close during certain daytime "lock-out" hours, have a curfew, don't accept reservations, or impose a maximum stay. In Israel, a bed in a hostel will average around US$10, though prices vary dramatically by region. Hostels do not have to pay taxes on US dollars, which means that at most places, American greenbacks will be more welcome than shekels.

For their various services and lower rates at member hostels, hostelling associations, especially **Hostelling International (HI),** can definitely be worth joining. HI hostels are several dollars more expensive and marginally cleaner. Any Israel branch of HI offers discounted coupons (4 nights NIS48; 7 nights NIS99; 10 nights NIS139) at one of their 20 locations. HI's web page lists the web addresses and phone numbers of all national associations and can be a great place to begin researching hostelling in a specific region (www.iyhf.org). Most student travel agencies (see p. 58) sell HI cards, as do the national hosteling organizations listed below. All prices below are valid for **one-year memberships** unless otherwise noted.

Australian Youth Hostels Association (AYHA), 422 Kent St., Sydney NSW 2000 (☎(02) 9261 1111; fax 9261 1969; www.yha.org.au). AUS$49, under 18 AUS$14.50.

Hostelling International-Canada (HI-C), 400-205 Catherine St., Ottawa, ON K2P 1C3 (☎(800) 663-5777 or (613) 237-7884; fax 237-7868; email info@hostellingintl.ca; www.hostellingintl.ca). CDN$25, under 18 CDN$12; life $175.

Israel Youth Hostels Association (ANA), 1 Shazar St., P.O. Box 6001, Jerusalem 91060 (☎(02) 655 84 00; fax 655 84 30). Youth Travel Bureau organizes tours to Israel, Egypt, and Jordan. Write for *Israel on the Youth Hostel Trail.*

An Óige (Irish Youth Hostel Association), 61 Mountjoy St., Dublin 7 (☎(1) 830 4555; fax 830 5808; email anoige@iol.ie; www.irelandyha.org). IR£10, under 18 IR£4.

Youth Hostels Association of New Zealand (YHANZ), P.O. Box 436, 193 Cashel St., Christchurch 1 (☎(03) 379 9970; fax 365 4476; email info@yha.org.nz; www.yha.org.nz). NZ$40, ages 15-17 NZ$12, under 15 free.

Hostels Association of South Africa, 73 St. George's St. Mall, 3rd fl., P.O. Box 4402, Cape Town 8000 (☎(021) 424 2511; fax 424 4119; email info@hisa.org.za; www.hisa.org.za). SAR50, under 18 SAR25; lifetime SAR250.

Scottish Youth Hostels Association (SYHA), 7 Glebe Crescent, Stirling FK8 2JA (☎(01786) 89 14 00; fax 89 13 33; www.syha.org.uk). UK£6, under 18 UK£2.50.

Youth Hostels Association (England and Wales) Ltd., Trevelyan House, 8 St. Stephen's Hill, St. Albans, Hertfordshire AL1 2DY, UK (☎(01727) 85 52 15; fax 84 41 26; www.yha.org.uk). UK£12, under 18 UK£6, families UK£24.

Hostelling International Northern Ireland (HINI), 22-32 Donegall Rd., Belfast BT12 5JN, Northern Ireland (☎(01232) 32 47 33; fax 43 96 99; email info@hini.org.uk; www.hini.org.uk). UK£7, under 18 UK£3.

Hostelling International-American Youth Hostels (HI-AYH), 733 15th St. NW, #840, Washington, D.C. 20005 (☎(202) 783-6161 ext. 136; fax 783-6171; email hiayhserv@hiayh.org; www.hiayh.org). US$25, under 18 free.

YMCA AND YWCAS

Not all **Young Men's Christian Association (YMCA)** locations offer lodging; those that do are often in urban downtowns, which can be convenient but a little gritty. YMCA rates are usually lower than a hotel's but higher than a hostel's and may include the use of TV, air-conditioning, pools, gyms, access to public transportation, tourist information, safe deposit boxes, luggage storage, daily housekeeping, multilingual staff, and 24-hour security. Many YMCAs accept women and families (group rates often available), and some will not lodge people under 18 without parental permission. There are several ways to make a reservation, which must be made at least two weeks in advance and paid for in advance with a traveler's check, US money order, certified check, Visa, or Mastercard in US dollars. **Y's Way International,** 224 E. 47th St., New York, NY 10017 (☎(212) 308-2899; fax 308-3161; email ysway@ymcanyc.org) will make reservations for YMCAs in East Jerusalem, Gaza, and Nazareth for a small fee (US and Canada US$3, elsewhere US$5).

HOME EXCHANGE AND RENTALS

Home exchange offers the traveler various types of homes (houses, apartments, condominiums, or villas), plus the opportunity to live like a native and to cut down on accommodation fees—usually only an administration fee is paid to the matching service. Most companies have pictures of member's homes and information about the owners. A great site listing many exchange companies can be found at www.aitec.edu.au/~bwechner/Documents/Travel/Lists/HomeExchangeClubs.html. In some cities it is possible to rent a room in a **private home.** The GTIO and some private travel agencies can arrange accommodations. Consider finding a place on your own; prices should be no more than what you would pay at a hostel. Exercise caution, as quality varies. While home rentals are more expensive than exchanges, they can be cheaper than comparably-serviced hotels. Both home

exchanges and rentals are ideal for families and for travelers with special dietary needs; you often get your own kitchen, maid service, TV, and telephones.

HomeExchange, P.O. Box 30085, Santa Barbara, CA 93130 (☎ (805) 898-9660; fax 898-9199; email admin@HomeExchange.com; www.homeexchange.com).

Intervac International Home Exchange, contact Dan Arbel, P.O. Box 2045 Herzliya, Israel 46120 (☎(09) 955 71 08 or 91 70; email scandi@inter.net.il; www.intervac.com).

The Invented City: International Home Exchange, 41 Sutter St., #1090, San Francisco, CA 94104 (☎(800) 788-2489 in the US or (415) 252-1141 elsewhere; fax 252-1171; email invented@aol.com; www.invented-city.com). For US$75, you get your offer listed and unlimited access to the database containing thousands of homes.

Hometours International, Inc., P.O. Box 11503, Knoxville, TN 37939 (☎(865) 690-8484; email hometours@aol.com; www.thor.he.net/~hometour) helps find short-term **apartment rentals** in Jerusalem, Tel Aviv, and Netanya from the US. They also have **bed-and-breakfast, kibbutz,** and **moshav** locations (US$50, half goes toward rent).

CHRISTIAN HOSPICES

If you plan to sleep in Nazareth, Jerusalem, Jaffa, Tiberias, or on Mount Tabor, consider staying in a **Christian hospice.** They are designed to provide reasonably-priced room and board for Christian pilgrims, but most listed in this book welcome other tourists as well. Though austere, the hospices are located in important religious centers and are usually quiet, comfortable, and impeccable. Usually, they have early curfews and most also serve cheap, filling meals. Bed and breakfast costs US$18-25 per person at most places.

CAMPING AND THE OUTDOORS

Israel's campsites usually provide electricity, sanitary facilities, public telephones, first aid, a restaurant or store, a night guard, and on-site or nearby swimming areas. In July and August most sites charge NIS10-20 per night.

USEFUL ORGANIZATIONS

Those interested in **environmental protection** can contact **Adam Teva V'din** (☎(03) 562 40 44). For information about camping, hiking, and biking, write or call the organizations listed below.

Israeli National Parks Authority, 35 Jabotinsky St., Ramat Gan 52511 (☎(03) 576 68 88; fax 751 18 58). Material on parks and historic sites.

Society for the Protection of Nature in Israel (SPNI; Ha-Ḥevra LeHaganat Ha-Teva), 4 Ha-Shfela St., **Tel Aviv** (☎(03) 638 86 74; fax 688 39 40); other offices in major cities. In the **US,** ASPNI, 28 Arrandale Ave., Great Neck, NY 11024 (☎(212) 398-6750; fax 398-1665; www.spni.org). Call (800) 323-0035 for reservations and nature trails brochure. Organizes hikes, sight-seeing tours in English, and camping trips. Dues US$36 per year (tax deductible; includes discounts on trips). Local SPNI organizations are listed in the Practical Information Section of each town.

The Mountaineers Books, 1001 SW Klickitat Way, #201, Seattle, WA 98134 (☎(800) 553-4453; email alans@mountaineers.org; www.mountaineersbooks.org). Over 400 titles on hiking, biking, mountaineering, natural history, and conservation.

CAMPING AND HIKING EQUIPMENT

WHAT TO BUY

Good camping equipment is both sturdy and light. Camping equipment is generally more expensive in Australia, New Zealand, and the UK than in North America.

Sleeping Bag: Most sleeping bags are rated by season ("summer" means 30-40°F at night; "four-season" or "winter" often means below 0°F). They are made either of **down** (warmer and lighter, but more expensive and miserable when wet) or of **synthetic**

material (heavier, more durable, and warmer when wet). Prices may range from US$80-210 for a summer synthetic to US$250-300 for a good down winter bag. **Sleeping bag pads** include foam pads (US$10-20), air mattresses (US$15-50), and Therm-A-Rest self-inflating pads (US$45-80). Bring a **stuff sack** to store your bag and keep it dry.

Tent: The best tents are free-standing, with their own frames and suspension systems; they set up quickly and only require staking in high winds. Low-profile dome tents are the best all-around. When pitched their internal space is almost entirely usable, which means little unnecessary bulk. Tent sizes can be somewhat misleading: two people *can* fit in a two-person tent, but will find life more pleasant in a four-person. If you're hiking, stick with a smaller tent that weighs no more than 5-6 lbs (2-3kg). Good two-person tents start at US$90, four-person tents at US$300. Seal the seams of your tent with waterproofer, and make sure it has a rain fly. Other tent accessories include a **battery-operated lantern,** a **plastic groundcloth,** and a **nylon tarp.** If you are camping in Israel in the summer, you are extraordinarily unlikely to need rain protection for your tent.

Backpack: Internal-frame packs mold better to your back, keep a lower center of gravity, and flex adequately to allow you to hike difficult trails. **External-frame packs** are more comfortable for long hikes over even terrain, as they keep weight higher and distribute it more evenly. Make sure your pack has a strong, padded hip-belt to transfer weight to your legs. Any serious backpacking requires a pack of at least 4000 in^3 (16,000cc), plus 500 in^3 for sleeping bags in internal-frame packs. Sturdy backpacks cost anywhere from US$125-420—this is one area in which it doesn't pay to economize. Fill up any pack with something heavy and walk around the store with it to get a sense of how it distributes weight before buying it. Either buy a **waterproof backpack cover,** or store all of your belongings in plastic bags inside your pack: many hikes in the Golan are along the water and may even require that you get wet.

Boots: Be sure to wear hiking boots with good **ankle support.** They should fit snugly and comfortably over 1-2 pairs of wool socks and thin liner socks. Break in boots over several weeks to spare yourself from painful and debilitating blisters.

Other Necessities: Synthetic layers, like those made of polypropylene, and a **pile jacket** will keep you warm even when wet. A **"space blanket"** will help you to retain your body heat and doubles as a groundcloth (US$5-15). Plastic **water bottles** are virtually shatter- and leak-proof. Bring **water-purification tablets** for when you can't boil water. Although most campgrounds provide campfire sites, you may want to bring a small **metal grate** or **grill** of your own. For those places that forbid fires or the gathering of firewood, you'll need a **camp stove** (the classic Coleman starts at US$40) and a propane-filled **fuel bottle** to operate it. Also don't forget a **first-aid kit, pocketknife, insect repellent, calamine lotion,** and **waterproof matches** or a **lighter.**

AND WHERE TO BUY IT

The mail-order/online companies listed below offer lower prices than many retail stores, but a visit to a local camping or outdoors store will give you a good sense of the look and weight of certain items.

Campmor, P.O. Box 700, Upper Saddle River, NJ 07458 (in the US ☎(888) 226-7667, elsewhere call US +1 (201) 825-8300; www.campmor.com).

Discount Camping, 880 Main North Rd., Pooraka, South Australia 5095, Australia (☎(08) 8262 3399; fax 8260 6240; www.discountcamping.com.au).

Eastern Mountain Sports (EMS), 327 Jaffrey Rd., Peterborough, NH 03458 (US ☎(888) 463-6367; www.emsonline.com) Call for the branch nearest you.

L.L. Bean, Freeport, ME 04033 (US and Canada ☎(800) 441-5713; UK (0800) 891 297; elsewhere, call US +1 (207) 552-3028; www.llbean.com). If your purchase doesn't meet your expectations, they'll replace or refund it.

Mountain Designs, 120 Wickham St., Fortitude Valley, Queensland 4006, Australia (☎(07) 3216 1866; fax 3216 1855; www.mountaindesign.com.au).

Recreational Equipment, Inc. (REI), Sumner, WA 98352 (☎(800) 426-4840 or (253) 891-2500; www.rei.com).

YHA Adventure Shop, 19 High St., Staines, Middlesex TW18 4QX, UK (☎(01784) 458 625; fax 464 573; email inflo@yhaadventure.co.uk; www.yhaadventure.co.uk).

WILDERNESS SAFETY

Stay warm, stay dry, and stay hydrated. The vast majority of life-threatening wilderness situations results from a breach of this simple dictum. On any hike, however brief, you should pack enough equipment to keep you alive should disaster befall. This includes a **first-aid kit** (see p. 50), a **reflector,** a **whistle, high energy food,** and extra **water.** In winter, dress in warm layers of **synthetic materials** (designed for the outdoors) or in **wool,** and bring **raingear,** a **hat,** and **mittens.** Pile fleece jackets and Gore-Tex raingear are excellent choices. Never rely on **cotton** for warmth. This "death cloth" will be absolutely useless should it get wet. Make sure to check all equipment for any defects before setting out.

Check **weather forecasts** and pay attention to the skies when hiking. Weather patterns can change suddenly. **Flash floods** are not uncommon (occurring most often in the winter and spring), and several hikers in Israel have been killed. Consult the local park officials on the same day of the hike to decide if it is safe. Whenever possible, let someone know when and where you are going hiking, either a friend, someone at your hostel, a park ranger, or a local hiking organization. Do not attempt a hike beyond your ability—you may be endangering your life.

Don't crash in areas not officially designated for camping. Certain stretches of beach are off-limits for security reasons, and others are full of thieves (Haifa, Tel Aviv, and Eilat). **Women should not camp alone.** Always heed **mine** warning signs. Wars have left an excess of mines, many of which are active and dangerous.

For **further information,** consult *How to Stay Alive in the Woods*, by Bradford Angier (Macmillan, US$8). See **Health,** p. 45 for information about outdoor ailments such as heatstroke, hypothermia, giardia, rabies, and insects.

KEEPING IN TOUCH

MAIL

SENDING MAIL TO AND RECEIVING MAIL IN ISRAEL

Letters sent to Israel should be marked "air mail" or "par avion." Airmail letters under 1oz. between North America and Israel take 4-7 days (US$1). From Australia, airmail takes 5-7 days (AUS$1.20 for small letters up to 20g, AUS$1.50 for larger letters up to 20g). There are four ways to arrange pick-up of letters sent to you while you are abroad.

General Delivery: Mail can be sent to Israel through **Poste Restante** (the international phrase for General Delivery) to almost any city or town with a post office. The service tends to be fairly reliable. Address *Poste Restante* letters to the post office, highlighting the last name. For example: Nicole JOSEPH-GOTEINER, Poste Restante, street address (where available), City, Israel. The mail will go to a special desk in the central post office, unless you specify a post office by street address. Postal codes are unnecessary in Israel. As a rule, it is best to use the largest post office in the area, since mail may be sent there regardless. When possible, it is usually safer and quicker to send mail express or registered. Bring a photo ID, preferably a passport, for pick-up. There is no surcharge. If the clerks insist that there is nothing for you, have them check under your first name as well. *Let's Go* lists post offices in the **Practical Information** section for each city and most towns.

American Express: AmEx's travel offices throughout the world offer a free **Client Letter Service** (mail held up to 30 days and forwarding upon request) for cardholders who contact them in advance. Address the letter in the same way shown above. Some offices will offer these services to non-cardholders (especially AmEx Travelers Cheque holders), but call ahead to make sure. *Let's Go* lists AmEx office locations for most large cities in **Practical Information** sections; for a complete, free list, call US (800) 528-4800.

Federal Express: (in the US and Canada ☎(800) 463-3339). If regular airmail is too slow, Fed Ex can get a letter from New York to Israel in three days; rates between two non US locations are prohibitively expensive. Do not send items by Fed Ex (or any other express delivery service) to a post office.

Post office Express Services: These can be purchased at your local post office, and they bridge the gap in prices and speed between FedEx and regular mail. Post offices will hold letters sent using these services if no signature is required. From the US Global Priority Mail can get a letter to Israel within 5 working days (often faster) for US$5.

SENDING MAIL FROM ISRAEL

Post offices are usually open Sunday through Tuesday and Thursday 8am-12:30pm and 3:30-6pm, Wednesday 8am-2pm, and Friday 8am-1pm. They are closed on Saturdays and holidays. In larger cities, some offices may keep longer hours. On the street, yellow mailboxes are for mail sent within the same city; red mailboxes are for all other mail. Most post offices offer international **Express Mail Service (EMS),** which supposedly takes three days (in reality, at least four).

Aerogrammes, sheets that fold into envelopes and travel via airmail, are available at post offices for NIS1.40. Mark them "par avion." Most post offices charge exorbitant fees or simply refuse to send aerogrammes with enclosures. Airmail from Israel averages 5-9 days, although times are unpredictable from small towns.

Surface mail is by far the cheapest and slowest way to send mail. It takes one to three months to cross the Atlantic and two to four to cross the Pacific—appropriate for sending large quantities of items you won't need to see for a while, such as souvenirs or other articles you've acquired along the way.

TELEPHONES

TELECARDS AND METERED PHONES

PLACING INTERNATIONAL CALLS. To call Israel from home or to place an international call from Israel, dial:

1. The **international dialing prefix.** To dial out of **Australia,** dial 0011; **Canada** or the **US,** 011; **Israel, Republic of Ireland, New Zealand,** or the **UK,** 00; **South Africa,** 09.
2. The **country code** of the country you want to call. To call **Australia,** dial 61; **Canada** or the **US,** 1; the **Republic of Ireland,** 353; **New Zealand,** 64; **South Africa,** 27; the **UK,** 44; **Israel,** 972.
3. The **city** or **area code.** *Let's Go* lists the phone codes for cities and towns in Israel opposite the city or town name, alongside the following icon: ☎. If the first digit is a zero (e.g., 03 for Tel Aviv), omit it when calling from abroad (e.g., dial 011 972 3 from Canada to reach Tel Aviv).
4. The **local number.**

Public telephones are everywhere. Look for pay phones in public areas, especially train stations, as private ones are often more expensive. Older telephones devour *asimonim* (tokens) even for local calls (NIS0.50) and should be avoided for international calls—making a connection may take hours and bucketfuls of *asimonim.* Far more common are the beige-colored phones (marked with yellow signs) that operate with **Telecards,** available at the post office (20 units NIS10.50, 50 units NIS23, 120 units NIS52). Telecards are the least expensive option for long distance and international calls (roughly NIS5.90 per min. to the US). International rates drop by up to 50% late at night and on Saturday and Sunday.

Bezek, Israel's phone company, has offices with metered phones for international calls in Tel Aviv and Jerusalem. It may be more economical to call overseas from there, because they charge only for the time you were on the phone; phone cards must be purchased with a fixed set of units, and you may be left with extra units at the end of the call. Nonetheless, there's nothing you can do at a telephone office that you can't do from a pay phone. English telephone directories are available at hotels and main post offices, or dial 144 for the **operator** or **information.**

Although incredibly convenient, in-room hotel calls invariably include an arbitrary and sky-high surcharge (as much as US$10).

CALLING CARDS

Calling card calls are billed either collect or to your account. Wherever possible, use a calling card for international phone calls, as the long-distance rates for national phone services are often more expensive. **To obtain a calling card** from your national telecommunications service before you leave home, contact the appropriate company below.

Australia: Telstra **Australia Direct** (☎13 22 00).

Canada: Bell Canada **Canada Direct** (☎(800) 565-4708).

Ireland: Telecom Éireann **Ireland Direct** (☎(0800) 25 02 50).

New Zealand: Telecom New Zealand (☎(0800) 00 00 00).

South Africa: Telkom South Africa (☎09 03).

UK: British Telecom **BT Direct** (☎(800) 34 51 44).

US: AT&T (☎(888) 288-4685); **Sprint** (☎(800) 877-4646); or **MCI** (☎(800) 444-4141).

CALLING CARD ACCESS NUMBERS. To call home with a calling card, contact the Israeli operator for your service provider by dialing:

AT&T: ☎800 94 94 949.
Sprint: ☎800 938 70 70.
MCI WorldPhone Direct: ☎800 940 27 27.
Canada Direct: ☎800 949 41 05.
BT Direct: ☎177 440 27 27.
Ireland Direct: ☎177 353 27 27.
Telecom New Zealand Direct: ☎177 640 27 27.
Telkom South Africa Direct: ☎177 270 27 27.

COLLECT CALLS

The expensive alternative to dialing direct or using a calling card is to place a collect call through an international operator; dial **188** for an overseas operator. An English-speaking operators from your home nation can be reached by dialing the appropriate service provider listed above, and they will typically place a collect call even if you don't possess one of their phone cards.

EMAIL AND INTERNET

Israel is a highly networked country, with computer technology as one of its major industries. Try cybercaptive.com or netcafeguide.com to help you find cyber-cafes in Israel. *Let's Go* lists cybercafes in most locations.

Free, **web-based email** providers include Hotmail (www.hotmail.com), RocketMail (www.rocketmail.com), and Yahoo! Mail (www.yahoo.com). Many free email providers are funded by advertising and some require subscribers to fill out a questionnaire. Almost every internet search engine has an affiliated free email service.

Travelers who have the luxury of a laptop with them can use a **modem** to call an internet service provider. Long-distance phone cards specifically intended for such calls can defray normally high phone charges. Check with your long-distance phone provider to see if they offer this option.

ESSENTIALS

GETTING THERE

BY PLANE

When it comes to airfare, a little effort can save you a bundle. If your plans are flexible enough to deal with the restrictions, courier fares are the cheapest. Tickets bought from consolidators and standby seating are also good deals, but last-minute specials, airfare wars, and charter flights often beat them. Shop around, be flexible, and persistently ask about discounts. Students, seniors, and those under 26 should never pay full price for a ticket. Special deals to Israel may be advertised in publications targeted at Jewish and Arab communities in your home country.

FLIGHT PLANNING ON THE INTERNET. The Web is a great place to look for travel bargains–it's fast, it's convenient, and you can spend as long as you like exploring options without driving your travel agent insane.

Many airline sites offer special last-minute deals on the Web. Other sites compile the deals for you–try www.bestfares.com, www.onetravel.com, www.lowestfare.com, and www.travelzoo.com.

STA (www.sta-travel.com) and **Council** (www.counciltravel.com) provide quotes on student tickets, while **Expedia** (msn.expedia.com) and **Travelocity** (www.travelocity.com) offer full travel services. **Priceline** (www.priceline.com) allows you to specify a price, and obligates you to buy any ticket that meets or beats it; be prepared for odd routes. **Skyauction** (www.skyauction.com) allows you to bid on both last-minute and advance-purchase tickets.

Just one last note–to protect yourself, make sure that the site uses a secure server before handing over any credit card details. Happy hunting!

DETAILS AND TIPS

Timing: Airfares to Israel peak between mid-June and mid-August, and holidays are also expensive periods. Midweek (M-Th morning) round-trip flights run US$40-50 cheaper than weekend flights, but they are generally more crowded and less likely to permit frequent-flier upgrades. Traveling with an "open return" ticket can be pricier than fixing a return date when buying the ticket.

Route: Round-trip flights are by far the cheapest; "open-jaw" (arriving in and departing from different cities) and round-the-world, or RTW, flights are pricier but reasonable alternatives. Patching one-way flights together is the least economical way to travel. Flights between capital cities or regional hubs will offer the most competitive fares.

Boarding: Whenever flying internationally, pick up tickets for international flights well in advance of the departure date, and confirm by phone within 72 hours of departure. Most airlines require that passengers arrive at the airport at least 2 hours before departure. One carry-on item and two pieces of checked baggage is the norm for non-courier flights. Consult the airline for weight allowances.

Fares: Flights to Israel land at Ben-Gurion airport (see p. 142). Sample round-trip fares from: **New York** US$700-1100; **London** US$310-400; and **Sydney** US$1250-1450.

BUDGET AND STUDENT TRAVEL AGENCIES

A knowledgeable agent specializing in flights to Israel can make your life easy and help you save, too, but agents may not spend the time to find you the lowest possible fare—they get paid on commission. Students and under-26ers holding **ISIC and IYTC cards** (see **Identification,** p. 37), respectively, qualify for big discounts from budget travel agencies. Most flights from budget agencies are on major airlines, but in peak season some may sell seats on less reliable chartered aircraft.

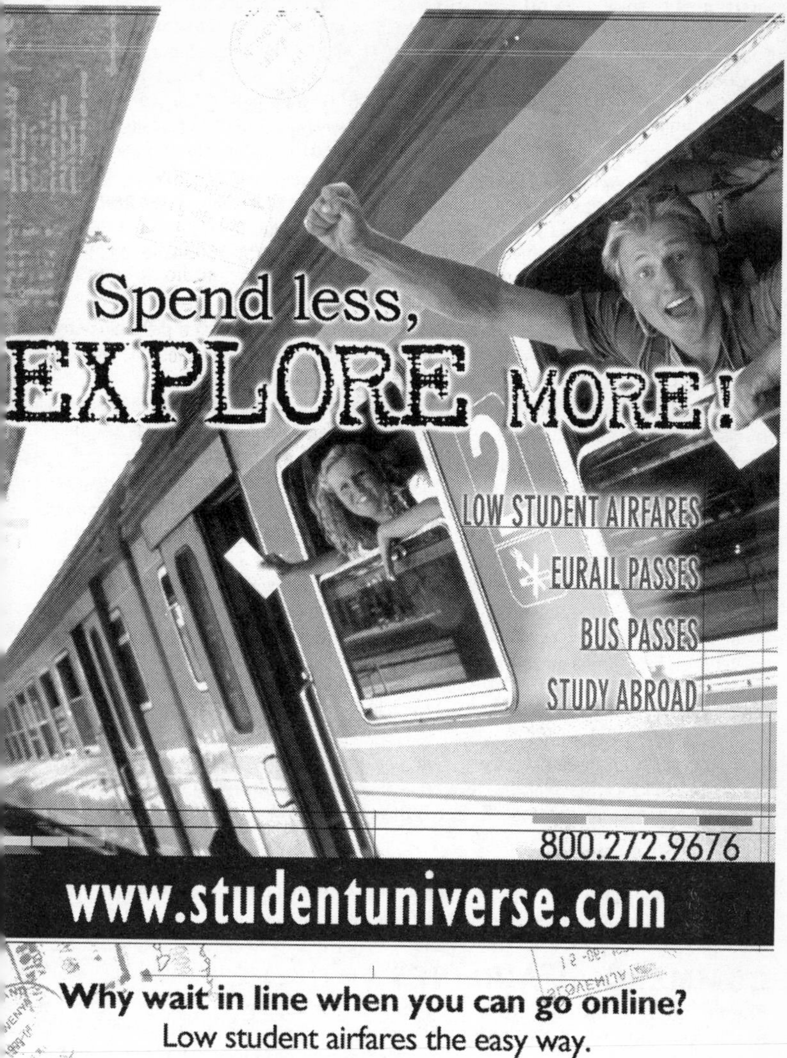
Spend less,
EXPLORE MORE!
LOW STUDENT AIRFARES
EURAIL PASSES
BUS PASSES
STUDY ABROAD
800.272.9676
www.studentuniverse.com
Why wait in line when you can go online?
Low student airfares the easy way.
Go ahead... put your feet up and
plan your trip.
student universe.com
IT'S YOUR WORLD. EXPLORE IT

usit world (www.usitworld.com). Over 50 **usit campus** branches in the UK (www.usitcampus.co.uk), including 52 Grosvenor Gardens, **London** SW1W 0AG (☎(0870) 240 1010); **Manchester** (☎(0161) 273 1721); and **Edinburgh** (☎(0131) 668 3303). Nearly 20 **usit now** offices in Ireland, including 19-21 Aston Quay, O'Connell Bridge, **Dublin** 2 (☎(01) 602 1600; www.usitnow.ie), and **Belfast** (☎(02890) 327 111; www.usitnow.com). Offices also in Athens, Auckland, Brussels, Frankfurt, Johannesburg, Lisbon, Luxembourg, Madrid, Paris, Sofia, and Warsaw.

Council Travel (www.counciltravel.com). US offices include: Emory Village, 1561 N. Decatur Rd., **Atlanta,** GA 30307 (☎(404) 377-9997); 273 Newbury St., **Boston,** MA 02116 (☎(617) 266-1926); 1160 N. State St., **Chicago,** IL 60610 (☎(312) 951-0585); 931 Westwood Blvd., Westwood, **Los Angeles,** CA 90024 (☎(310) 208-3551); 254 Greene St., **New York,** NY 10003 (☎(212) 254-2525); 530 Bush St., **San Francisco,** CA 94108 (☎(415) 566-6222); 424 Broadway Ave E., **Seattle,** WA 98102 (☎(206) 329-4567); 3301 M St. NW, **Washington, D.C.** 20007 (☎(202) 337-6464). **For US cities not listed,** call (800) 2-COUNCIL (226-8624). In the UK, 28A Poland St. (Oxford Circus), **London** W1V 3DB (☎(020) 7437 7767).

CTS Travel, 44 Goodge St., **London** W1 (☎(020) 7636 0031; fax 7637 5328; email ctsinfo@ctstravel.com.uk).

STA Travel, 6560 Scottsdale Rd., #F100, Scottsdale, AZ 85253 (☎(800) 777-0112; fax (602) 922-0793; www.sta-travel.com). A student and youth travel organization with over 150 offices worldwide. Ticket booking, travel insurance, railpasses, and more. US offices include: 297 Newbury St., **Boston,** MA 02115 (☎(617) 266-6014); 429 S. Dearborn St., **Chicago,** IL 60605 (☎(312) 786-9050); 7202 Melrose Ave., **Los Angeles,** CA 90046 (☎(323) 934-8722); 10 Downing St., **New York,** NY 10014 (☎(212) 627-3111); 51 Grant Ave., **San Francisco,** CA 94108 (☎(415) 391-8407); 4341 University Way NE, **Seattle,** WA 98105 (☎(206) 633-5000); 2401 Pennsylvania Ave., Ste. G, **Washington, D.C.** 20037 (☎(202) 887-0912). In the UK, 11 Goodge St., **London** WIP 1FE (☎(020) 7436 7779 for North American travel). In New Zealand, 10 High St., **Auckland** (☎(09) 309 0458). In Australia, 366 Lygon St., **Melbourne** Vic 3053 (☎(03) 9349 4344).

Travel CUTS (Canadian Universities Travel Services Limited), 187 College St., **Toronto,** ON M5T 1P7 (☎(416) 979-2406; fax 979-8167; www.travelcuts.com). 40 offices across Canada. Also in the UK, 295-A Regent St., **London** W1R 7YA (☎(020) 7255 1944).

Travel Avenue (☎(800) 333-3335) rebates commercial fares to or from the US and offers low fares for flights anywhere in the world. They also offer package deals, which include car rental and hotel reservations, to many destinations.

COMMERCIAL AIRLINES

The commercial airlines' lowest regular offer is the **APEX** (Advance Purchase Excursion) fare, which provides confirmed reservations and allows "open-jaw" tickets. Generally, reservations must be made seven to 21 days ahead of departure, with seven- to 14-day minimum-stay and up to 90-day maximum-stay restrictions. These fares carry hefty cancellation and change penalties (fees rise in summer). Book peak-season APEX fares early; by May you will have a hard time getting your desired departure date. Although APEX fares are probably not the cheapest possible fares, they will give you a sense of the average commercial price, from which to measure other bargains. Specials advertised in newspapers may be cheaper but have more restrictions and fewer available seats.

El Al is the only Israel based carrier, and it provides flights to many European and American destinations. More information can be found on the El Al website at www. elal.co.il. Most major airlines fly to Israel.

OTHER CHEAP ALTERNATIVES

AIR COURIER FLIGHTS

Couriers help transport cargo on international flights by guaranteeing delivery of the baggage claim slips from the company to a representative overseas. Generally, couriers must travel light (carry-ons only) and deal with complex restrictions on their flight. Most flights are round-trip only with short fixed-length stays (usually one week). Most also operate only out of the biggest cities, like New York. Generally, you must be over 21 (in some cases 18), have a valid passport, and procure your own visa, if necessary. Groups such as the **Air Courier Association** (☎(800) 282-1202; elsewhere call US +1 (303) 215-9000; www.aircourier.org) and the **International Association of Air Travel Couriers** (☎(561) 582-8320; fax 582-1581; www.courier.org) provide their members with lists of opportunities and courier brokers worldwide for an annual fee. For more information, consult *Air Courier Bargains* by Kelly Monaghan (The Intrepid Traveler, US$15) or the *Courier Air Travel Handbook* by Mark Field (Perpetual Press, US$10).

STANDBY FLIGHTS

Traveling standby requires considerable flexibility in arrival and departure dates and cities. Companies dealing in standby flights sell vouchers rather than tickets, along with the promise to get to your destination (or near your destination) within a certain window of time (typically 1-5 days). You call in before your specific window of time to hear your flight options and the probability that you will be able to board each flight. You can then decide which flights you want to try to make, show up at the appropriate airport at the appropriate time, present your voucher, and board if space is available. Vouchers can usually be bought for both one-way and round-trip travel. You may receive a monetary refund only if every available flight within your date range is full; if you opt not to take an available (but perhaps less convenient) flight, you can only get credit toward future travel. Carefully read agreements with any company offering standby flights as tricky fine print can leave you in a lurch. To check on a company's service record in the US, call the Better Business Bureau (☎(212) 533-6200). It is difficult to receive refunds, and clients' vouchers will not be honored when an airline fails to receive payment in time. One established standby company is **Airhitch,** 2641 Broadway, 3rd fl., New York, NY 10025 (☎(800) 326-2009; fax 864-5489; www.airhitch.org) and Los Angeles, CA (☎(888) 247-4482). Airhitch's head European office is in **Paris** (☎ +33 (01) 47 00 16 30); there's also one in **Amsterdam** (☎ +31 (20) 626 32 20).

CHARTER FLIGHTS

Charters are flights a tour operator contracts with an airline to fly extra loads of passengers during peak season. Charters can sometimes be cheaper than flights on scheduled airlines, some operate nonstop, and restrictions on minimum advance-purchase and minimum stay are more lenient. However, they fly less frequently than major airlines, make refunds difficult, and are almost always booked. Schedules and itineraries may also change or be cancelled at the last moment (as late as 48 hours before the trip, and without a full refund), and check-in, boarding, and baggage claim are often much slower. As always, pay with a credit card, and consider traveler's insurance against trip interruption (see **Insurance,** p. 49).

Discount clubs and **fare brokers** offer members savings on last-minute charter and tour deals. Study their contracts closely; you don't want to end up with an unwanted overnight layover.

TICKET CONSOLIDATORS

Ticket consolidators, or **"bucket shops,"** buy unsold tickets in bulk from commercial airlines and sell them at discounted rates. The best place to look is in the Sunday travel section of any major newspaper, where many bucket shops place tiny ads. Call quickly, as availability is typically limited. Not all bucket shops are reliable, so pay by credit card and insist on a receipt that gives full details of restrictions and refunds. For more info, check the website **Consolidators FAQ** (www.travel-library.com/air-travel/consolidators.html) or the book *Consolidators: Air Travel's Bargain Basement*, by Kelly Monaghan (Intrepid Traveler, US$8).

Travel Avenue (☎(800) 333-3335; www.travelavenue.com) will search for cheap flights from anywhere for a fee. Other consolidators worth trying are **Interworld** (☎(305) 443-4929); **Pennsylvania Travel** (☎(800) 331-0947); **Cheap Tickets** (☎(800) 377-1000; www.cheaptickets.com); and **Travac** (☎(800) 872-8800; www.travac.com). Yet more consolidators on the web include the **Internet Travel Network** (www.itn.com); **SurplusTravel.com** (www.surplustravel.com); **TravelHUB** (www.travelhub.com); and **The Travel Site** (www.thetravelsite.com). These are just suggestions to get you started; *Let's Go* does not endorse any of these agencies. As always, be cautious, and research companies before you hand over your credit card number.

BY BOAT AND BY LAND

Ferries depart from Israel for Greece and Cyprus and from Sharm al-Sheikh for Hurghada in Egypt. For more information see **Tel Aviv,** p. 142; **Haifa,** p. 176; and **Sharm al-Sheikh,** p. 366.

Tourists can cross into Egypt from Eilat at the Taba **border crossing.** For Sinai stays of 14 days or less, get a **Sinai-only visa** stamp on the Egyptian side of the border. This visa limits travel to the Gulf of Aqaba coast as far south as Sharm al-Sheikh (but not the area around Sharm al-Sheikh, including Ras Muhammad) and to St. Catherine's monastery and Mt. Sinai (but not sites in the vicinity of St. Catherine's). Unlike ordinary one-month Egyptian visas, the Sinai-only visa has no grace period; you'll pay a hefty fine if you overextend your stay. For more border crossing information into **Egypt,** see p. 351.

There are three border crossings from Israel into Jordan: one in Jericho at the King Hussein/Allenby Bridge in the West Bank, one in Beit She'an in the North of Israel, and one in Eilat. Travelers to Petra usually cross at Eilat, which is only a few hours away. For more information on crossing into **Jordan,** see p. 344.

GETTING AROUND

BY BUS

Buses are the most popular and convenient means of travel. Except for the **Dan Company** (☎(03) 639 44 44) in Tel Aviv and the **Arab buses** serving the West Bank, Galilee, and Gaza, the **Egged Bus Cooperative** (www.egged.co.il) has a monopoly on intercity and most intracity buses in Israel. The modern, air-conditioned buses are either direct *(yashir)*, express, or local *(me'asef)*. Students with ISICs receive a 10% discount on some fares; show your ID first to the ticket seller, then to the driver, then to the ticket inspector. Buses are sometimes crowded, especially on Saturday nights after Shabbat and during morning and afternoon rush hours. You can shove your way into and out of the bus as long as you preface each push with the word *sliḥa*, as Israelis do.

Most bus stations have printed schedules, often in English. Egged has intercity **information lines** in the major cities (in Tel Aviv ☎(03) 694 88 88; Haifa (04) 854 95 49; Jerusalem (02) 530 47 04). For information on local lines, call the area's central bus station. Signs in stations direct you to buy your ticket at the ticket window. This is only really necessary for highly-traveled, long-distance routes; otherwise, buy the ticket from the driver. Most local bus rides cost NIS5. A *kartisia* available from any bus driver, gives you 11 local rides for the price of 10 (NIS47); a one month pass that includes unlimited local rides in Haifa, Jerusalem, and Tel Aviv costs NIS188. Buses between cities usually leave from the central bus station *(taḥanah merkazit)*. Roundtrip tickets may be 10% cheaper.

BY TAXI AND SHERUT

Israeli companies offer both private and less expensive **sherut** (shared) taxis. Regular private taxi rides are called *special* (pronounced "spatial"). City taxis operating as *special* must use a meter *(moneh);* make the driver turn it on. Offers of special but unspecified "discount" rates (translation: no meter and an exorbitant fare) should be adamantly refused. If you can estimate a decent price, you'll get a better rate by setting the price before you enter the taxi. Taxi drivers do not expect tips but accept them.

Sherut taxis hold up to seven people. Certain companies operate *sherut* taxis seven days a week from offices in each city. Intercity *sherut* operate on loose schedules, departing when they fill up; on Saturdays, they often whiz along the streets in search of passengers. Intracity *sherut* never follow a schedule. Most routes have set fares comparable to bus prices; ask for quotes at tourist offices or from the nearest Israeli. Always settle on a price before you depart.

BY CAR

While widespread public transportation makes cars generally unnecessary; some places (especially the Golan and Negev) are most easily reached by a rented car. Roads are usually well-marked, and maps are available at all tourist offices. Israelis drive on the right side of the road. The legal driving age is 17, but most agencies rent only to credit-card holders 21 or older (a few will rent to 18-year-olds). Rentals usually cost about US$55-70 per day with a 250km daily limit. There is often a discount for rentals of three days or more. Prices in shekels are considerably higher in some cases, and deals arranged beforehand from overseas are often much cheaper. See **Practical Information** in each city for agency addresses.

INTERNATIONAL DRIVING PERMIT (IDP)

If you plan to drive while in Israel, you can use an International Driving Permit (IDP), though an American license valid for at least three months from time of entry works just as well. It may be a good idea to get an IDP anyway, in case you're in a situation (e.g. an accident or stranded in a small town) where the police do not know English. Information on the IDP is printed in 10 languages, including Arabic.

Your IDP, valid for one year, must be issued in your own country before you depart. An application for an IDP usually needs to include one or two photos, a current local license, an additional form of identification, and a fee.

Australia: Contact your local Royal Automobile Club (RAC) or the National Royal Motorist Association (NRMA) if in NSW or the ACT (☎(08) 9421 4444; www.rac.com.au/travel). Permits AUS$15.

Canada: Contact any Canadian Automobile Association (CAA) branch office or write to CAA, 1145 Hunt Club Rd., #200, K1V 0Y3. (☎(613) 247-0117; www.caa.ca/CAAInternet/travelservices/internationaldocumentation/idptravel.htm). Permits CDN$10.

Ireland: Contact the nearest Automobile Association (AA) office or write to the UK address below. Permits IR£4. The Irish Automobile Association, 23 Suffolk St., Rockhill, Blackrock, Co. Dublin (☎(01) 677 9481), honors most foreign automobile memberships (24hr. breakdown and road service ☎(800) 667 788; toll-free in Ireland).

New Zealand: Contact your local Automobile Association (AA) or their main office at Auckland Central, 99 Albert St. (☎(9) 377 4660; www.nzaa.co.nz). Permits NZ$8.

South Africa: Contact the Travel Services Department of the Automobile Association of South Africa at P.O. Box 596, 2000 Johannesburg (☎(11) 799 1400; fax 799 1410; http://aasa.co.za). Permits SAR28.50.

UK: To visit your local AA Shop, contact the **AA Headquarters** (☎(0990) 44 88 66), or write to: The Automobile Association, International Documents, Fanum House, Erskine, Renfrewshire PA8 6BW. To find the location nearest you that issues the IDP, call (0990) 50 06 00 or (0990) 44 88 66. For more info, see www.theaa.co.uk/motoringandtravel/idp/index.asp. Permits UK£4.

US: Visit any American Automobile Association (AAA) office or write to AAA Florida, Travel Related Services, 1000 AAA Drive (mail stop 100), Heathrow, FL 32746 (☎(407) 444-7000; fax 444-7380). You don't have to be a member to buy an IDP. Permits US$10. AAA Travel Related Services (☎(800) 222-4357) provides road maps, travel guides, emergency road services, travel services, and auto insurance.

CAR INSURANCE

Most credit cards cover standard insurance. If you rent, lease, or borrow a car, you will need a **green card,** or **International Insurance Certificate,** to certify that you have liability insurance and that it applies abroad. Green cards can be obtained at car rental agencies, car dealers (for those leasing cars), some travel agents, and some border crossings. Rental agencies may require you to purchase theft insurance in countries that they consider to have a high risk of auto theft.

BY TRAIN

Rail service is useful only for travel along the northern coast. Trains are slightly cheaper than buses, but they stop during Shabbat. Avoid traveling on Friday afternoons when the trains are most crowded. Students with an ISICs enjoy a 10% discount for tickets over NIS20.50. See www.isarail.com for more information.

BY THUMB

The incidence of sexual harassment and assault has increased dramatically in recent years. License plates carry meaning: yellow are Israeli, black with a צ are army, red are police, blue or gray are occupied territories, and white are diplomatic. Those who hitch in the Negev or Golan (where sometimes the only option is a military vehicle) run the risk of getting a ride that doesn't go all the way to their destination, in which case they are stranded. Hitchers flag cars by pointing to the far side of the road with the index finger. *Let's Go* does not recommend hitchhiking. *Tremping*, as it is called, is not what it used to be in Israel.

SPECIFIC CONCERNS

WOMEN TRAVELERS

Women exploring on their own inevitably face some additional safety concerns, but it's easy to be adventurous without taking undue risks. If you are concerned, you might consider staying in hostels which offer single rooms that lock from the inside or with religious organizations that offer rooms for women only; many co-ed hostels in Israel offer women-only rooms as well. Communal showers in some hostels are safer than others; check them before settling in. Stick to centrally located accommodations and avoid solitary late-night treks or metro rides.

When traveling, always carry extra money for a phone call, bus, or taxi. **Hitching** is never safe for lone women or even for two women traveling together. Look as if you know where you're going (even when you don't) and consider approaching older women or couples for directions if you're lost or feel uncomfortable.

Generally, the less you look like a tourist, the better off you'll be. Israeli women generally dress in Western style, making it fairly easy to blend in. In the Palestinian territories, and in both the Orthodox Jewish and Arab sections of Israel, however, it is advisable to dress modestly (nothing sleeveless or tight and skirts and pants well below the knees) and adhere to local standards of behavior as much as possible. This is particularly important when visiting religious sites. Wearing a conspicuous **wedding band** may help prevent unwanted overtures. Some travelers report that carrying pictures of a "husband" or "children" is extremely useful to help document marriage status. Even a mention of a husband waiting back at the hotel may be enough in to discount your potentially vulnerable, unattached appearance.

Your best answer to verbal harassment is no answer at all; feigned deafness, sitting motionless and staring straight ahead at nothing in particular will do a world of good that reactions usually don't achieve. The extremely persistent can sometimes be dissuaded by a firm, loud, and very public "Go away!" in Hebrew ("lech!") or even in English. Don't hesitate to seek out a police officer or a passerby if you are being harassed. *Let's Go: Israel* lists emergency numbers in the Practical Information listings of most cities. Memorize the national emergency numbers (see p. 41). Carry a **whistle** or an airhorn on your keychain, and don't hesitate to use it in an emergency. An **IMPACT Model Mugging** self-defense course will not only prepare you for a potential attack, but will also raise your level of awareness of your surroundings as well as your confidence (see **Self Defense,** p. 43). Women also face some specific health concerns when traveling (see **Women's Health,** p. 48).

FURTHER READING

A Journey of One's Own: Uncommon Advice for the Independent Woman Traveler, Thalia Zepatos. Eighth Mountain Press (US$17).
Adventures in Good Company: The Complete Guide to Women's Tours and Outdoor Trips, Thalia Zepatos. Eighth Mountain Press (US$7).
Active Women Vacation Guide, Evelyn Kaye. Blue Panda Publications (US$18).

TRAVELING ALONE

There are many benefits to traveling alone, including independence and greater opportunities to interact with the residents of the region you're visiting. On the other hand, any solo traveler is a more vulnerable target of harassment and street theft. Lone travelers need to be well-organized and look confident at all times. Try not to stand out as a tourist, and be especially careful in deserted or very crowded areas. If questioned, never admit that you are traveling alone. Maintain regular contact with someone at home who knows your itinerary.

Tel Aviv is something of a haven for lone Americans and Europeans looking for a few months work in the hopping beach-side city. The hostels and pubs are crammed with wise-but-friendly veterans of the solo scene. Jerusalem has large communities of expatriate Americans and Europeans who are generally very welcoming and can give good tips.

For more tips, pick up *Traveling Solo* by Eleanor Berman (Globe Pequot, US$17). A number of organizations supply information for solo travelers, and others find travel companions for those who don't want to go alone, including **Connecting: Solo Travel Network,** P.O. Box 29088, Delamont RPO, Vancouver, BC V6J 5C2 (☎/fax (604) 737-7791; www.cstn.org; membership US$25-35) and the **Travel Companion Exchange,** P.O. Box 833, Amityville, NY 11701 (☎(631) 454-0880 or (800) 392-1256; www.whytravelalone.com; US$48).

OLDER TRAVELERS

Senior citizens are eligible for a wide range of discounts on transportation, museums, movies, concerts, restaurants, and accommodations. If you don't see a senior citizen price listed, ask, and you may be delightfully surprised.

Agencies for senior group travel are growing in enrollment and popularity. These are only a few:

ElderTreks, 597 Markham St., Toronto, ON, Canada, M6G 2L7 (☎(800) 741-7956; fax (416) 588-9839; email eldertreks@eldertreks.com; www.eldertreks.com).

Elderhostel, 75 Federal St., Boston, MA 02110 (☎(800) 426-8056, outside the US +1 (978) 323-4141; email registration@elderhostel.org; www.elderhostel.org). Programs at colleges, universities, and other learning centers in Israel on varied subjects lasting 1-4 weeks. Must be 55 or over (spouse can be of any age).

The Mature Traveler, P.O. Box 50400, Reno, NV 89513 (☎(775) 786-7419, credit card orders (800) 460-6676). Has soft-adventure tours for seniors. Subscription$30.

Walking the World, P.O. Box 1186, Fort Collins, CO 80522 (☎(970) 498-0500; fax 498-9100; email walktworld@aol.com; www.walkingtheworld.com), organizes trips to Israel for the 50+ traveler.

FURTHER READING

No Problem! Worldwise Tips for Mature Adventurers, Janice Kenyon. Orca Book Publishers (US$16).

A Senior's Guide to Healthy Travel, Donald L. Sullivan. Career Press (US$15).

Unbelievably Good Deals and Great Adventures That You Absolutely Can't Get Unless You're Over 50, Joan Rattner Heilman. Contemporary Books (US$13).

BISEXUAL, GAY, AND LESBIAN TRAVELERS

Listed below are contact organizations, mail-order bookstores and publishers which offer materials addressing some specific concerns.

Society for the Protection of Personal Rights, P.O. Box 37604, Tel Aviv 61375 (☎(03) 629 36 81; fax 525 23 41), or P.O. Box 3592, Haifa (☎(04) 867 26 65), a main organization for gay and lesbian concerns in Israel. A community center, library, and coffee shop are in the basement of 28 Naḥmani St., Tel Aviv. The society's gay and lesbian hotlines are the **White Line** (Ha-Kav Ha-Lavan; ☎(03) 732 55 60; Su-Th 7:30-11:30pm) and the **Gay Hotline** (☎(03) 629 36 81; Su-Tu, Th 7:30-10:30pm).

Association of Gay Men, Lesbians, Bisexuals and Transgenders in Israel (GLBT), 28 Nachmani St., P.O Box 37684, Tel Aviv 61375. (☎(03) 620 43 27; fax 525 23 41; email info@nif.org; www.liquanet.co.il/vip/klaf) The only national gay and lesbian association in the Middle East.

Gay's the Word, 66 Marchmont St., London WC1N 1AB (☎(020) 7278 7654; email sales@gaystheword.co.uk; www.gaystheword.co.uk). The largest gay and lesbian bookshop in the UK, with both fiction and non-fiction titles. Mail-order service available.

KLAF (☎(03) 516 56 06). Israel's lesbian feminist community. Open M-W 11am-5pm.

Giovanni's Room, 345 S. 12th St., Philadelphia, PA 19107 (☎(215) 923-2960; fax 923 0813; www.queerbooks.com). An international feminist, lesbian, and gay bookstore with mail-order service which carries the publications listed here.

International Gay and Lesbian Travel Association, 4331 N. Federal Hwy., #304, Fort Lauderdale, FL 33308 (☎(954) 776-2626; fax 776-3303; email IGLTA@aol.com; www.iglta.com). An organization of over 1350 companies serving gay and lesbian travelers worldwide. Call for lists of travel agents, accommodations, and events.

International Lesbian and Gay Association (ILGA), 81 rue Marche-au-Charbon, B-1000 Brussels, Belgium (☎/fax +32 (2) 502 24 71; www.ilga.org). Not a travel service. Provides political information, such as homosexuality laws of individual countries.

TRAVELERS WITH DISABILITIES

Those with disabilities should inform airlines and hotels when making arrangements for travel; some time may be needed to prepare special accommodations. Call ahead at restaurants, hotels, parks, and other facilities to find out about the existence of ramps, the widths of doors, the dimensions of elevators, etc.

The following organizations provide information or services that might be of assistance:

Yad Sarah, 124 Herzl St., Jerusalem 96187 (☎(02) 644 44 44; fax 644 44 23; www.yadsarah.org.il). With 76 branches throughout Israel, it is the country's largest volunteer organization. Free loan of medical and rehabilitative equipment, oxygen service, and transport service for persons in wheelchairs. Call the English speaking P.R. director at least 2 weeks in advance to book airport pick-up and for help with special needs.

FURTHER READING

Spartacus International Gay Guide. Bruno Gmunder Verlag. (US$33).

Damron's Accommodations and *The Women's Traveller*. Damron Travel Guides (US$14-19). For more information, call US ☎(415) 255-0404 or (800) 462-6654 or check their website (www.damron.com)

Ferrari Guides' Gay Travel A to Z, *Ferrari Guides' Men's Travel in Your Pocket*, *Ferrari Guides' Women's Travel in Your Pocket*, and *Ferrari Guides' Inn Places*. Ferrari Guides (US$14-16). For more information, call (602) 863-2408 or (800) 962-2912 or check their website (www.q-net.com).

The Gay Vacation Guide: The Best Trips and How to Plan Them, Mark Chesnut. Citadel Press (US$15).

Gayellow Pages ($US 16). Call (212) 674-0120, email gayellow@banet.net, or check the website at http://gayellowpages.com.

Mobility International USA (MIUSA), P.O. Box 10767, Eugene, OR 97440 (☎(541) 343-1284 voice and TDD; fax 343-6812; email info@miusa.org; www.miusa.org). Sells *A World of Options: A Guide to International Educational Exchange, Community Service, and Travel for Persons with Disabilities* (US$35).

Moss Rehab Hospital Travel Information Service (☎(215) 456-9600; www.mossresourcenet.org). An information resource center on travel-related concerns for those with disabilities.

Society for the Advancement of Travel for the Handicapped (SATH), 347 Fifth Ave., #610, New York, NY 10016 (☎(212) 447-7284; www.sath.org). Advocacy group publishing a quarterly color travel magazine *OPEN WORLD* (free for members, US$13 for nonmembers). Also publishes a wide range of info sheets on disability travel facilitation and accessible destinations. Annual membership US$45, students and seniors US$30.

MINORITY TRAVELERS

Immigration from Ethiopia as well as an influx of foreign workers from Southeast Asia has recently made minority travelers stand out a little less. Still, Israelis are known for their abrupt and direct method of questioning, and some comments could be interpreted as offensive. Aside from a slew of questions, minority travelers are unlikely to encounter harassment in Israel, particularly in large cities that see many tourists, such as Jerusalem and Tel Aviv. Smaller towns and less-populated regions may bring some unwanted attention, but it probably won't amount to more than staring. Jews traveling in Arab areas such as East Jerusalem, the West Bank, and Gaza should make their tourist status pronounced and avoid external signs of their religious affiliation (i.e. wear a hat instead of a *kippah*).

TRAVELERS WITH CHILDREN

Family vacations often require that you slow your pace and always require that you plan ahead. When deciding where to stay, remember the special needs of young children; if you pick a small hotel, call ahead and make sure it's child-friendly. If you rent a car, make sure the rental company provides a car seat for younger children. Be sure that your child carries some sort of ID in case of an emergency or in case he or she gets lost.

Restaurants may have children's menus and discounts. Virtually all museums and tourist attractions also have a children's rate. Children under two generally fly for 10% of the adult airfare on international flights (this does not necessarily include a seat). International fares are usually discounted 25% for children from two to 11. Finding a private place for **breast feeding** is often a problem while traveling, so pack accordingly.

ESSENTIALS

FURTHER READING.

Backpacking with Babies and Small Children, Goldie Silverman. Wilderness Press (US$10).

How to take Great Trips with Your Kids, Sanford and Jane Portnoy. Harvard Common Press (US $10).

Have Kid, Will Travel: 101 Survival Strategies for Vacationing With Babies and Young Children, Claire and Lucille Tristram. Andrews and McMeel (US$9).

DIETARY CONCERNS

Vegetarians will have an easy time keeping themselves happily fed in Israel. Some of the most common and cheapest Middle Eastern food, such as the ubiquitous falafel, is vegetarian. In addition, many restaurants are vegetarian because of the kosher restriction on mixing milk and meat. The Hebrew Israelite Community has a chain of good vegan restaurants (see **Tel Aviv: Food,** p. 151).

For more information about vegetarian travel, contact the **North American Vegetarian Society,** P.O. Box 72, Dolgeville, NY 13329 (☎(518) 568-7970; email navs@telenet.com; www.cyberveg.org/navs/) or take a look at *The Vegetarian Traveler: Where to Stay if You're Vegetarian*, Jed Civic. Larson Pub. (US$16).

ALTERNATIVES TO TOURISM

STUDYING ABROAD

There are a number of options for study in Israel, ranging from intensive language classes to cultural programs. The requirements vary depending on the program; a tourist visa may be sufficient for a short summer language program, whereas a university class requires testing and a study visa. Study visas can be obtained from an Israeli embassy or consulate prior to departure or from an Office of the Interior once in Israel. Show the original letter of acceptance at an educational institution (US$25 plus US$5 mailing charge; fees not applicable for US citizens), a return ticket, application form, passport valid for one year from date of arrival, proof of sufficient funds, and two photos; those under 18 also need a notarized letter indicating the consent of both parents. More information and application forms are on the web at www.israelemb.org/consular/consular_frame.htm.

UNIVERSITIES

Most American undergraduates enroll in programs sponsored by US universities. However, if your Hebrew is already good, local universities can be much cheaper than an American university program, though it can be hard to receive academic credit. Schools that offer study abroad programs to foreigners are listed below.

Programs for foreign students range in length from one summer to four years. **Year-abroad** programs usually begin with a four- to nine-week *ulpan* to learn Hebrew before the semester begins in October. Classes are usually in English; those who know Hebrew have the option of taking regular university courses. University programs are usually preceded by a *mekhina* (see **Mekhinot,** below). Admission for undergraduates requires proficiency in Hebrew and often at least one year of college. For all programs contact: **Israel Student Authority,** 15 Hillel St., Jerusalem (☎(02) 624 11 21) or the New York consulate's **Office of Academic Affairs.** The Israeli Embassy in Washington, D.C. also maintains a web page which provides additional information at www.israelemb.org/highered/index.html.

During much of the *intifada*, all four West Bank universities—Birzeit, Bethlehem, Hebron, and An-Najah—were closed by the Israeli authorities as security threats. Today, some West Bank schools are still only open sporadically.

Bar Ilan University, Ramat Gan, 52900, Israel (☎(03) 531 81 21; fax 535 49 18; www.biuny.com)

Ben-Gurion University, Overseas Student Programs, 342 Madison Ave., #1224, New York, NY 10173 (☎(212) 687-7721; email bguosp@haven.ios.com; www.bgu.ac.il). In Israel, contact the Center for International Student Programs, P.O. Box 653, Be'er Sheva 84105 (☎(07) 646 11 11; email osp@bgumail.bgu.ac.il). Students must be enrolled at an accredited college or university.

Birzeit University, Student Affairs Office, Birzeit University, P.O. Box 14, Birzeit, West Bank, Palestine (☎(02) 298 20 00; fax 281 06 56; email par@birzeit.edu; www.birzeit.edu/pas). Runs a Palestine and Arab Studies Program, with courses in Modern Standard Arabic, Colloquial Arabic, and the social sciences and arts. Semesters are in spring, summer, and fall. May also have information on other organizations that administer programs in the West Bank or East Jerusalem.

Haifa University, 352 7th Ave., New York, NY 10001 (☎(888) 562-8813 or (212) 685-7880; email university-of-haifa@worldnet.att.net), or University of Haifa, Haifa 31905 (☎(04) 824 07 66; email rcbs702@uvm.haifa.ac.il; www.haifa.ac.il).

Hebrew University of Jerusalem, 11 E. 69th St., New York, NY 10021 (☎(212) 472-2288; fax 517-4548). United Kingdom Friends of the Hebrew University, 3 St. Johns Wood Rd., London NW8 8RB (☎(020) 7266 3214; fax 7289 5549). In Israel, Rothberg International School, Mt. Scopus, Jerusalem 91905 (☎(02) 588 26 07; fax 582 70 78; email admission@roth.huji.ac.il; www.huji.ca.il).

Technion-Israel Institute of Technology, contact the American Technion Society National Office, 810 7th Ave., 24th fl., New York, NY 10019 (☎(212) 262-6200; fax 262-6155) or the Institute directly at Technion City, Haifa (☎(04) 822 15 13; fax 823 51 95; email parddir@tx.technion.ac.il; www.technion.ac.il).

Tel Aviv University, Office of Academic Affairs, 360 Lexington Ave., New York, NY 10017 (☎(212) 557-5820; fax 687-4085), or P.O Box 39040, Tel Aviv 69978 (☎(03) 640 81 11; fax 640 95 98; email tauinfo@post.tau.ac.il; www.tau.ac.il).

Weizmann Institute of Science, P.O. Box 26, Reḥovot 76100 (☎(08) 934 21 11; fax 934 41 07; email webmaster@weizmann.ac.il; www.weizmann.ac.il).

MEKHINOT

Students who are not proficient in Hebrew but wish to enter a full undergraduate degree program usually first enroll in *mekhina* (preparation) programs, providing a year of intensive Hebrew and a chance to develop study plans. *Mekhinot* are offered by universities and other schools of post-secondary education. Note that *mekhina* participation does not guarantee acceptance to a university; students must still take entrance examinations.

ULPANIM

An *ulpan* is a program providing intensive Hebrew and Jewish culture instruction. Israel has about 100 *ulpanim*. **Kibbutz Ulpanim** offers instruction together with work. Contact the **Kibbutz Aliya Desk** (see **Kibbutzim,** p. 71).

For information about *ulpanim* in Jerusalem, contact City Hall (☎(02) 629 66 66 or 77 77). Two of the city's better known *ulpanim* are **Beit Ha-Noar Ha'lvri,** 105 Ha-Rav Herzog, Jerusalem 92622 (☎(02) 678 94 41; fax 678 86 42), and **Mo'adon Ha'Oleh,** 9 Alkalai St., Jerusalem (☎(02) 563 37 18; fax 563 49 10).

Ulpan Akiva Netanya offers a live-in program at its seaside campus for students from around the world—Jews, non-Jews, Israelis, and new immigrants. The daily program includes five hours of Hebrew study, social and cultural activities, tours, trips, and special Shabbat activities. Three-, eight-, 12-, and 20-week courses are accredited by several universities. Costs vary. Contact: **Ulpan Akiva Netanya,** P.O. Box 6086, Netanya 42160, Israel (☎(09) 835 23 12 or 13 or 14; fax 865 29 19; email ulpanakv@netvision.net.il; www.ulpan-akiva.org.il), or **JCC Ulpan Center,** 15 W. 65th St., 8th fl., New York, NY 10023 (☎(212) 580-0099; fax 799-0254).

OTHER LANGUAGE SCHOOLS

In addition to *ulpanim*, there are a number of language programs run by foreign universities, independent international or local organizations, and divisions of Israeli universities.

Berlitz Language Centers, 37 Sha'ul Ha-Melekh Ave., Tel Aviv 64298 (☎(03) 695 21 31; fax 695 21 34); 40 W. 51st St., New York, NY 10020 (☎(212) 765-1000); or at any of their locations world-wide. Administers programs of study in Hebrew and Arabic. Also offers cultural training. Check out interactive "Berlitz World" at www.berlitz.com.

Language Immersion Institute, 75 South Manheim Blvd., The College at New Paltz, New Paltz, NY 12561 (☎(914) 257-3500; fax 257-3569; email lii@newpaltz.edu; www.newpaltz.edu/lii). Language instruction at all levels in Hebrew and Arabic. Weekend courses at New Paltz and in New York City. US$750 per 2 weeks.

OTHER ACADEMIC PROGRAMS

Biblical Archaeology Society, 4710 41st St. NW, Washington, D.C. 20016 (☎(202) 364-3300; fax 364-2636; www.bib-arch.org). Organizes travel/study tours that center around archaeological sights. Also publishes the Biblical Archaeological Review.

College Semester Abroad, School for International Training, Admissions, Kipling Rd., P.O. Box 676, Brattleboro, VT 05302 (☎(802) 257-7751; fax 258-3248; email info@sit.edu; www.sit.edu). Runs semester-long program jointly held in Israel and Jordan. Financial aid available and US financial aid is transferable.

International Association for the Exchange of Students for Technical Experience (IAESTE), 10400 Little Patuxent Pkwy., #250, Columbia, MD 21044 (☎(410) 997-3068; fax 997-5186; email iaste@aipt.org; www.aipt.org). Operates 8- to 12-week programs in Israel for college students who have completed 2 years of study in a technical field. Non-refundable US$50 application fee; apply by Dec. 16 for summer placement.

FURTHER READING

Academic Year Abroad 2000/2001 (Institute of International Education Books, US$45).

Vacation Study Abroad 2000/2001 (Institute of International Education Books, US$43).

Peterson's Study Abroad 2001 (Peterson's, US$30).

WORKING ABROAD

If you plan to work in Israel, you must obtain a work visa; if you already have a job lined up, have your employer contact the Ministry of the Interior (see p. 37). For computer gurus, finding a job in Israel should be easy; for others, the job market is pretty stiff, especially since unemployment is high. Friends in Israel can help expedite work permits or arrange work-for-accommodations swaps. In some sectors (like agricultural work) permit-less workers are rarely bothered by authorities.

American or European companies with branches in Israel are a possible source of employment. Another option is volunteer work in exchange for room and board. Some people look for temporary jobs in Eilat upon arrival, where high tourism provides openings in hotels and restaurants. Be wary of scams that exploit foreigners' unfamiliarity with the laws in order to get free labor.

The **Jewish Agency** is a good clearinghouse for work and volunteer opportunities throughout the country. Their representatives will help you find a kibbutz, a place to study Hebrew, or a volunteer organization. The multilingual staff is trained to work with immigrants and long-term visitors. English speakers should ask for Tziki Aud. Write or call the Information and Service Center, P.O. Box 31677, Jerusalem 91030 (☎(02) 623 20 99 or 623 18 23; fax 623 53 28; www.jafi.org.il).

KIBBUTZIM

Israel's 250 kibbutzim (singular kibbutz), communal settlements whose members divide work and profits equally, are often eager for volunteers. Kibbutzim vary greatly in size, wealth, number of volunteers, and ideology. Volunteers generally work six eight-hour days per week, with a few days off per month, and they receive a small monthly allowance in addition to room and board and various other benefits; the work is generally physical, in agriculture, industry, or service. Prior knowledge of Hebrew is helpful, but certainly not necessary; non-speakers can even study Hebrew through combined work/study *ulpan* programs (see **Ulpanim,** p. 69). Accommodations are most often in dormitory settings. Kibbutz life can be seductive in its routine, and many volunteers find themselves staying longer than planned. A written promise of placement on a kibbutz before arriving in Israel helps with passport authorities.

To apply for any kibbutz program, contact your local Kibbutz Aliya Desk or the main office, 633 3rd Ave., 21st fl., New York, NY 10017 (☎(800) 247-7852; fax (212) 318-6134; email kibbutzdsk@aol.com). Applicants must be 18-35 and have no children; there is a two-month minimum commitment and no maximum stay length. After being interviewed and given the appropriate application and medical forms, you will be sent to the **Kibbutz Program Center, Volunteer Office,** 18 Frishman St., Center Ben-Yehuda, 3rd fl., Tel Aviv 61030, where you will be assigned to a kibbutz. (☎(03) 527 88 74 or 524 61 56; fax 523 99 66. Open Su-Th 8am-2pm.) **Project 67,** 94 Ben-Yehuda St., Tel Aviv 63345, also places volunteers on kibbutzim and *moshavim*. (☎(03) 523 01 40. Open Su-Th 9am-4pm.)

These agencies provide official volunteer appointments, but kibbutz volunteering can be arranged informally as well. Many find that visiting a kibbutz, seeking out the volunteer leader, and asking if they need help is a preferable method, one that allows the would-be volunteer to test the environment rather than having to cope with a blind assignment (it also avoids registration fees). On the other hand, working through the agencies provides the security of a prompt match.

MOSHAVIM

Moshavim, agricultural communities in which farms and homes are privately owned and operated, provide a somewhat different work experience from kibbutzim. You will receive free lodging with a family or with other workers. In return, you work a six-day week, at least eight hours per day. Workers are paid about US$300 per month and are expected to pay for their own food. Applicants must be ages 18-35 and physically fit. Contact **Volunteers Moshavim Movement,** 19 Leonardo da Vinci St., Tel Aviv (☎(03) 695 84 73).

ARCHAEOLOGICAL DIGS

Work on archaeological digs consists largely of digging pits, shoveling shards, and hauling baskets of dirt for up to 10 hours per day in searing heat, beginning at 5am; don't dream of discovering ancient treasures.

The "Dig for a Day" program by Archaeological Seminars is designed for the curious tourist. The three-hour program at the Beit Guvrin National Park includes a short seminar on the history of the area, excavation, a crawl through an unexcavated cave system, and a tour of the park (US$17). Individuals are taken on Fridays; the rest of the week is for groups. Reservations are a good idea. Write to P.O. Box 14002, Jaffa Gate, Jerusalem 91140 (☎(02) 627 35 15; email office@archesem.com).

Many archaeological excavations employ volunteers for extended periods of time, providing room and board in exchange for hard manual labor. Current digs and contact people are listed at www.israel.org/archdigs.html.

TEACHING ENGLISH

Several services employ English-speakers to teach English in Israel. Requirements vary by program.

International Schools Services, Educational Staffing Program, P.O. Box 5910, Princeton, NJ 08543 (☎(609) 452-0990; www.iss.edu). Recruits teachers and administrators for American and English schools in Israel. US$150 application fee.

Office of Overseas Schools, US Department of State, Room H328, SA-1, Washington, D.C. 20522 (☎(202) 261-8200; fax 261-8224; www.state.gov/www/about_state/schools/). Keeps a comprehensive list of schools abroad and agencies that arrange placement for Americans to teach abroad.

World Teach, Center for International Development, 79 John F. Kennedy St., Cambridge, MA 02138 (☎(800) 483-2240 or (617) 495-5527; www.worldteach.org). Volunteers teach English, math, science, and environmental education for 6-12 months in Israel.

VOLUNTEERING

Volunteer jobs are readily available almost everywhere. You may receive room and board in exchange for your labor. You can sometimes avoid the high application fees charged by the organizations that arrange placement by contacting the individual workcamps directly; check with the organizations.

Shatil, a project of the **New Israel Fund,** 1625 K St. NW, #500, Washington, D.C. 20006 (☎(202) 223-3333) or P.O Box 53395, Jerusalem 91534 (☎(02) 672 35 97; fax 673 51 49; email shatil@shatil.nif.org.il; www.nif.org.il), places volunteers with organizations working in areas such as civil and human rights, Jewish-Arab coexistence, the status of women, and religious tolerance.

The Volunteers for Israel, 330 W. 42nd St., #1618, New York, NY 10036 (☎(212) 643-4848; fax 643-4855; www.members.aol.com/vol4israel/), places participants in non-combat support jobs in the Israeli military. The 3-week program involves menial work such as washing dishes or mending equipment. You will wear army fatigues and boots and sleep in army barracks, but don't expect to carry an Uzi or keep the uniform afterwards. The program offers reduced airfare on El Al, provided you fulfill your commitment. Non-refundable application fee US$100, under 24 US$50.

Volunteers for Peace, 1034 Tiffany Rd., Belmont, VT 05730 (☎(802) 259-2759; www.vfp.org). Arranges placement in workcamps in Israel. Annual *International Workcamp Directory* US$20. Registration fee US$200. Free newsletter.

LIVING EXPERIENCES

Project Otzma is a 10-month volunteer leadership development program for 20-24 year-olds (college graduates preferred). Participants live and work in kibbutzim, youth *aliya* villages, immigrant absorption centers, and areas of urban renewal, as well as study, travel throughout the country, and live with host families. The program costs US$1850. Contact Council of Jewish Federations, 111 8th Ave., New York, NY 10011 (☎(877) GO-OTZMA; fax (212) 284-6838; email otzma@cjfny.org; www.cjfny.org/otzma/index.htm).

Livnot U'Lehibanot: To Build and To Be Built, 110 E. 59th St., 3rd fl., New York, NY 10022 (☎(212) 613-1413; fax 760-2783; email livnot@livnot.org.il; www.livnot.org.il), or 27 Ben-Zakkai, Katamon, Jerusalem 93585 (☎(02) 679 34 91; fax 679 34 92), offers three-week or three-month study and work experiences in Jerusalem and Tzfat for 21-30 year-olds. These experiences involve four hours per day of discussion-oriented classes exploring Jewish heritage and the land of Israel and four hours per day of building and community service projects, plus hikes throughout the country.

FURTHER READING

International Jobs: Where they Are, How to Get Them, Eric Koocher. (Perseus Books, US$17).

Work Abroad: The Complete Guide to Finding a Job Overseas, Clayton Hubbs. (Transitions Abroad, US$16).

International Directory of Voluntary Work, Victoria Pybus. (Vacation Work Publications, US$16).

Teaching English Abroad, Susan Griffin. (Vacation Work, US$17).

THE WORLD WIDE WEB

The internet is an invaluable resource in planning a trip to Israel. Most major organizations in Israel have complete webpages, as do many accommodations and services. Many hostels offer internet access, and there are cybercafes in all major cities. Some of the more generally helpful websites are listed here.

LEARNING THE ART OF BUDGET TRAVEL

How to See the World: www.artoftravel.com. A compendium of great travel tips, from cheap flights to self defense to interacting with local culture.

Rec. Travel Library: www.travel-library.com. A fantastic set of links for general information and personal travelogues.

Shoestring Travel: www.stratpub.com. An e-zine focusing on budget travel.

INFORMATION ON ISRAEL

InfoTour (www.infotour.co.il). The Israel Ministry of Tourism's official page; chock-full of detailed information sorted by region. At tourist offices, pick up the Tourist Yellow Pages, a slim volume with excellent major city maps and listings for everything from alternative medicine to zoos.

United States Embassy, Israel (www.usis-israel.org.il) includes frequently updated information on travel warnings, US policy toward Israel, and other information relevant to American travelers.

The CIA World Factbook (www.odci.gov/cia/publications/factbook/index.html) has tons of vital statistics on Israel. Check it out for an overview of Israel's economy and an explanation of its system of government.

Foreign Language for Travelers (www.travlang.com) can help you brush up on your Hebrew and Arabic.

MyTravelGuide: www.mytravelguide.com. Country overviews, with everything from history to transportation.

AND OUR PERSONAL FAVORITE...

Let's Go: www.letsgo.com. Our recently revamped website features photos and streaming video, info about our books, a travel forum buzzing with stories and tips, and links that will help you find everything you could ever want to know about Israel.

JERUSALEM

ירושלים القدس ☎02

There are men with hearts of stone,
and there are stones with hearts of men.
—Rav Kook

When the sun sets over the Judean hills, Jerusalem's white stone turns to gold and peace seems to be within the city's grasp. The domes, spires, and minarets of the worship of three faiths rise over the Old City walls in quiet harmony. But Jerusalem is not always as serene as its evening breeze and rooftop view. The white stone, from which all of Jerusalem's new buildings are constructed, is indelibly, if invisibly, stained with the blood of centuries.

In this city that has been the battleground and spoil of countless holy wars, the magnificent spirituality that defines Jerusalem bursts forth from every square inch of space; it cannot be escaped. As Israeli poet Yehuda Amiḥai commented, the "air over Jerusalem is saturated with prayers and dreams, like the air over industrial cities. It's hard to breathe."

Spiritual over-saturation doesn't hinder Jerusalem's magnetic attraction; it heightens it. Jews, from ultra-Orthodox to secular, Christians of all denominations, Muslims, missionaries, pilgrims and tourists from every continent, mystics, and raving lunatics all come to Jerusalem with their spiritual baggage in tow. The time warp is most evident on a city bus, where black robes, habits, and *kefyehs* mingle with halter tops and baseball caps. Jerusalem is the modern capital for ancient peoples and a headline grabber for age-old disputes. Every street here is a crucible, and, for better or for worse, every footstep has an element of prayer.

HIGHLIGHTS OF JERUSALEM

The **Via Dolorosa** (p. 116) winds through the crowded Old City *souq* to Jesus' tomb. Contemplate the miracle of the Resurrection over an apple-flavored tobacco smoke in an Arab coffeehouse in the **Muslim Quarter.**

Wonder anew at the glory of negative spaces in the works of Rodin and Picasso at the **Israel Museum's** sculpture garden (p. 132).

Spend a morning at the **Yad va-Shem** Holocaust memorial museum (p. 133) for a powerful reminder of the atrocities committed by Nazis in WWII Europe.

Wade by candlelight through **Hezekiah's Tunnel** (p. 124), dry off on the walk back to **Dung Gate,** (see **The Gates,** p. 109) and spend the afternoon exploring the intricate Islamic architecture of the mosques of the **Dome of the Rock** (p. 111).

HISTORY

BIBLICAL TIMES, THE GREEKS, AND THE ROMANS. During Jerusalem's 5000 years, 18 conquerors have presided over the city. Archaeological findings indicate that Jerusalem (Jebus, then) was a Canaanite settlement for 2000-3000 years before King David's conquest around 1000 BCE (II Samuel 5). David established Jerusalem as the capital of the Israelite kingdom; his son Solomon extended the city's boundaries northward to include the present-day Temple Mount (see **The Iron Age,** p. 7). Solomon built the First Temple on the Mount, where sacrificial observances were centralized and the Ark of the Covenant kept.

The Israelite kingdom split shortly after Solomon's death in 933 BCE. The tribes of the northern Kingdom of Israel created their own capital, while those of the south retained Jerusalem as the center of the Kingdom of Judah. Over three prosperous centuries, Judah's citizens developed Judaism and the Jewish identity, until a Babylonian army led by King Nebuchadnezzar besieged the city and forced its capitulation in 596 BCE. The Babylonians kidnapped the aristocracy and kept Jerusalem disarmed and powerless. When Zedekiah instigated a rebellion 10 years later, a wrathful King Nebuchadnezzar ordered the exile of the Jews to Babylon and the burning of Jerusalem's finest buildings, including the Temple. In 539 BCE, however, the Babylonians succumbed to Cyrus of Persia who permitted the Jews to return from exile (2 Chronicles 36). Reconstruction commenced soon thereafter, and in 515 BCE the Second Temple was rededicated (Ezra 6:15-18).

Jerusalem enjoyed more than a century of undisturbed revival under the Persians until Alexander the Great swept through the city in 332 BCE (see **Greeks and Nabateans,** p. 8). Hellenization was soon embraced by much of the educated population. After a century and a half of Hellenic rule and a brief spell of Egyptian Ptolemaic control, the Seleucid Empire took Jerusalem (198 BCE). King Antiochus IV forbade all Jewish practices, including Shabbat observance, circumcision, and the reading of the Torah. When he installed the cult of Zeus in the Temple, non-Hellenized Jews revolted. The rebels, led by Judas Maccabeus, were successful. In 164 BCE, the temple was resanctified and the priestly hierarchy assumed control of the city. The resulting Hasmonean dynasty zealously ruled the area's Jews for the next century.

The Roman general Pompey seized control of Jerusalem in 64 BCE, ushering in six and a half centuries of Roman rule (see **Romans,** p. 9). The Romans installed Herod the Great, the child of a Jewish father and Samaritan mother, to reign over what they called the Kingdom of Judea. While occupying the throne (37-4 BCE), Herod commanded the reconstruction of the temple and the creation of the well-known and partially extant Western Wall to better support the enlarged Temple Mount. In 6 CE the Romans bequeathed the governance of the province to a series of procurators, the most famous of whom was Pontius Pilate. Sixty years later, the Jews revolted against Rome. The Roman commander Titus crushed the revolt after four years, destroying the temple, razing the city, and casting many Jews into slavery or exile; life in the diaspora had begun. After the Bar Kokhba Revolt (a second Jewish revolt named for its leader) ended in 135 CE, the city was further destroyed by Emperor Hadrian and declared off-limits to the Jews.

That very year Hadrian built a new city over Jerusalem, Aelia Capitolina, to serve as a Roman colony. The pattern of the present-day Old City corresponds to that of Hadrian's city; it is divided into quarters by two major roads (the Cardo and Decumanus) and oriented north to south. You can see the remains of the Cardo in the Old City's Jewish Quarter. When Roman Emperor Constantine adopted and legalized Christianity in 331 CE, his mother Eleni visited the Holy Land in order to identify and consecrate Christian sites (see **The Byzantines,** p. 9). Subsequent Byzantine rulers devoted their energies to the construction of basilicas and churches for the glorification and celebration of the city's Christian heritage.

MUSLIM RULE AND THE CRUSADES. Following a brief period of Persian rule in the early 7th century, Muslim Caliph Omar conquered Aelia in 638 (see **Early Arabs,** p. 9). The Temple Mount was cleansed and hallowed anew as a center of Muslim worship. In 691 his successors completed the Dome of the Rock (see p. 111). Under the tolerant Muslim rule, Jews were allowed to return to the city.

In the 10th century, Jerusalem fell into Egyptian hands. The Fatimid despots destroyed all synagogues and churches and passed on their policy of persecuting non-Muslims to their successors, the Seljuk Turks. Their rumored closing of pilgrimage routes enraged Western Christians and added fuel to the fire of the Crusades, culminating in the Christian capture of Jerusalem in 1099 (see **Crusades,** p. 10). With cries of *"Deus vult"* (God wills it), the Crusaders mercilessly slaughtered Jerusalem's Muslim and Jewish inhabitants. The Crusader Kingdom of

Jerusalem Overview
JERUSALEM FOREST
MOTZA ILIT
Sderot Ben Gurion
SEE WEST JERUSALEM MAP
Kanfei Nesharim
HAR NOF
BEIT ZAYIT
Sderot Herzl
Wolffsohn
Bank of Israel
University Stadium
Givat Ram
Hebrew University (Givat Ram Campus)
JERUSALEM FOREST
Mt. Herzl
Yad Vashem
Herzl's Grave
Herzl Museum
Shmuel Beyth
Jerusalem Forest Recreation Centre
Ein Kerem
Hantke
Church of St. John
EIN KEREM
Bezalel Barak
Ha-Rav Uziel
Hantke
Church of the Visitation
Russian Convent
KIRYAT HA-YOVEL
TO HADASSAH MEDICAL CENTER
Golomb
Szold
KIRYAT MENAHEM
Golomb
ORA
N
0
1000 yards
0
1 kilometer
Kenyon Yerushalayim (Shopping Mall)
Teddy Stadium

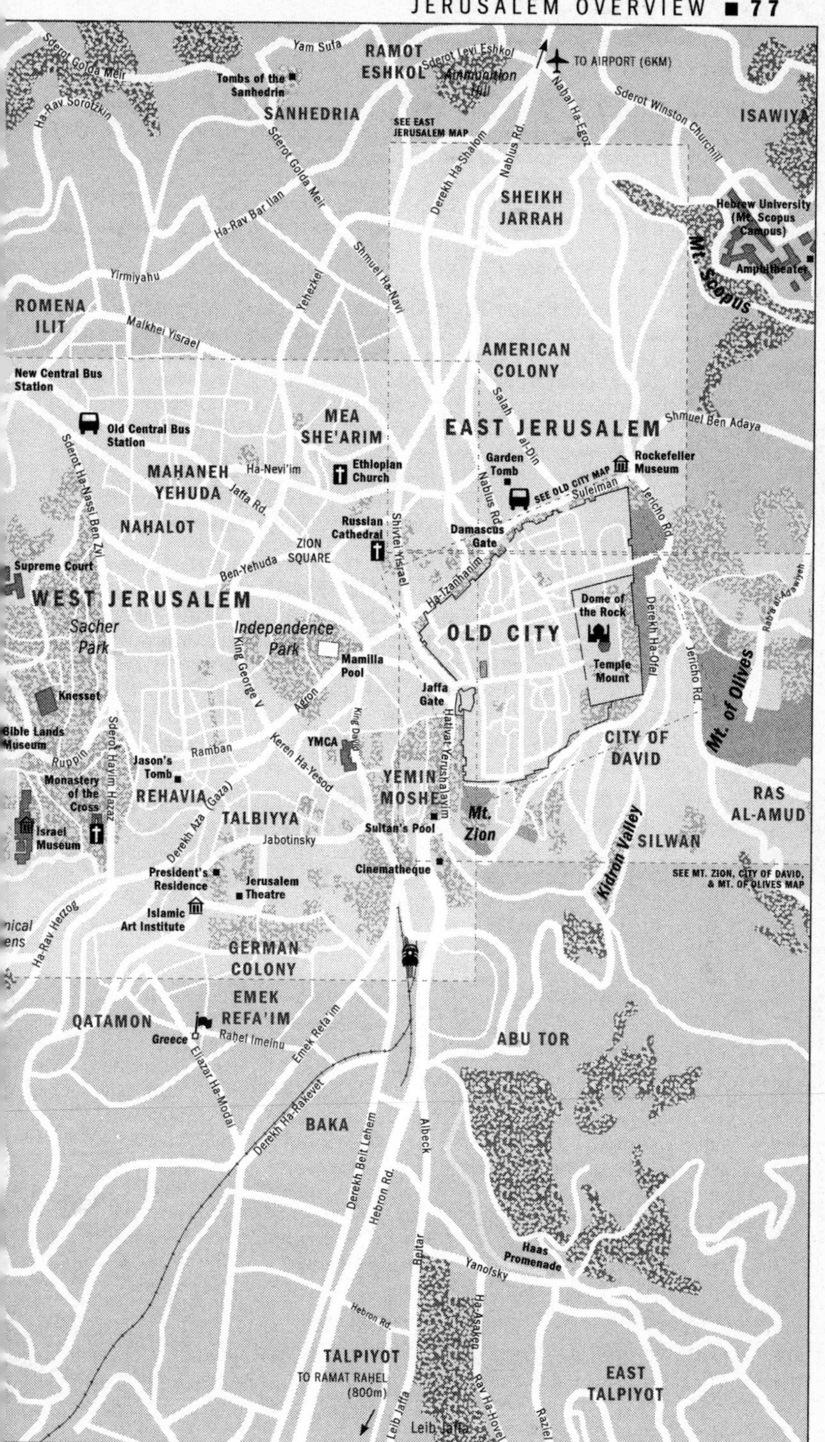
RAMOT ESHKOL
Ammunition Hill
TO AIRPORT (6KM)
Tombs of the Sanhedrin
SANHEDRIA
ISAWIYA
SEE EAST JERUSALEM MAP
SHEIKH JARRAH
Hebrew University (Mt. Scopus Campus)
Amphitheater
Mt. Scopus
ROMENA ILIT
AMERICAN COLONY
New Central Bus Station
Old Central Bus Station
MEA SHE'ARIM
EAST JERUSALEM
MAHANEH YEHUDA
Ethiopian Church
Garden Tomb
Rockefeller Museum
SEE OLD CITY MAP
NAHALOT
Russian Cathedral
Damascus Gate
ZION SQUARE
Supreme Court
WEST JERUSALEM
Dome of the Rock
Sacher Park
Independence Park
OLD CITY
Mamilla Pool
Temple Mount
Mt. of Olives
Knesset
Jaffa Gate
Bible Lands Museum
YMCA
CITY OF DAVID
Jason's Tomb
YEMIN MOSHE
Monastery of the Cross
REHAVIA
RAS AL-AMUD
TALBIYYA
Mt. Zion
Israel Museum
Sultan's Pool
Kidron Valley
SILWAN
President's Residence
Cinematheque
SEE MT. ZION, CITY OF DAVID, & MT. OF OLIVES MAP
Jerusalem Theatre
Islamic Art Institute
GERMAN COLONY
EMEK REFA'IM
QATAMON
Greece
ABU TOR
BAKA
Haas Promenade
TALPIYOT
TO RAMAT RAHEL (800m)
EAST TALPIYOT
Yam Sufa
Sderot Golda Meir
Ha-Rav Sorotzkin
Sderot Levi Eshkol
Nahal Ha-Egoz
Sderot Winston Churchill
Nablus Rd.
Derekh Ha-Shalom
Ha-Rav Bar Ilan
Shmuel Ha-Navi
Yehezkel
Yirmiyahu
Malkhei Yisrael
Salah al-Din
Shmuel Ben Adaya
Sderot Ha-Nassi Ben Zvi
Ha-Nevi'im
Jaffa Rd.
Suleiman
Jericho Rd.
Shivtei Yisrael
Ben-Yehuda
Ha-Tzanhanim
Rab'a al-Adawiyeh
Derekh Ha-Ofel
King George V
Agron
King David
Hativat Yerushalayim
Sderot Hayim Hazaz
Ramban
Keren Ha-Yesod
Ruppin
Derekh Aza (Gaza)
Jabotinsky
Ha-Rav Herzog
Rahel Imeinu
Emek Refa'im
Eliazar Ha-Modai
Derekh Ha-Rakevet
Derekh Beit Lehem
Hebron Rd.
Albeck
Beitar
Yanofsky
Ha-Asaken
Rav Ha-Hovel
Leib Jaffa
Raziel

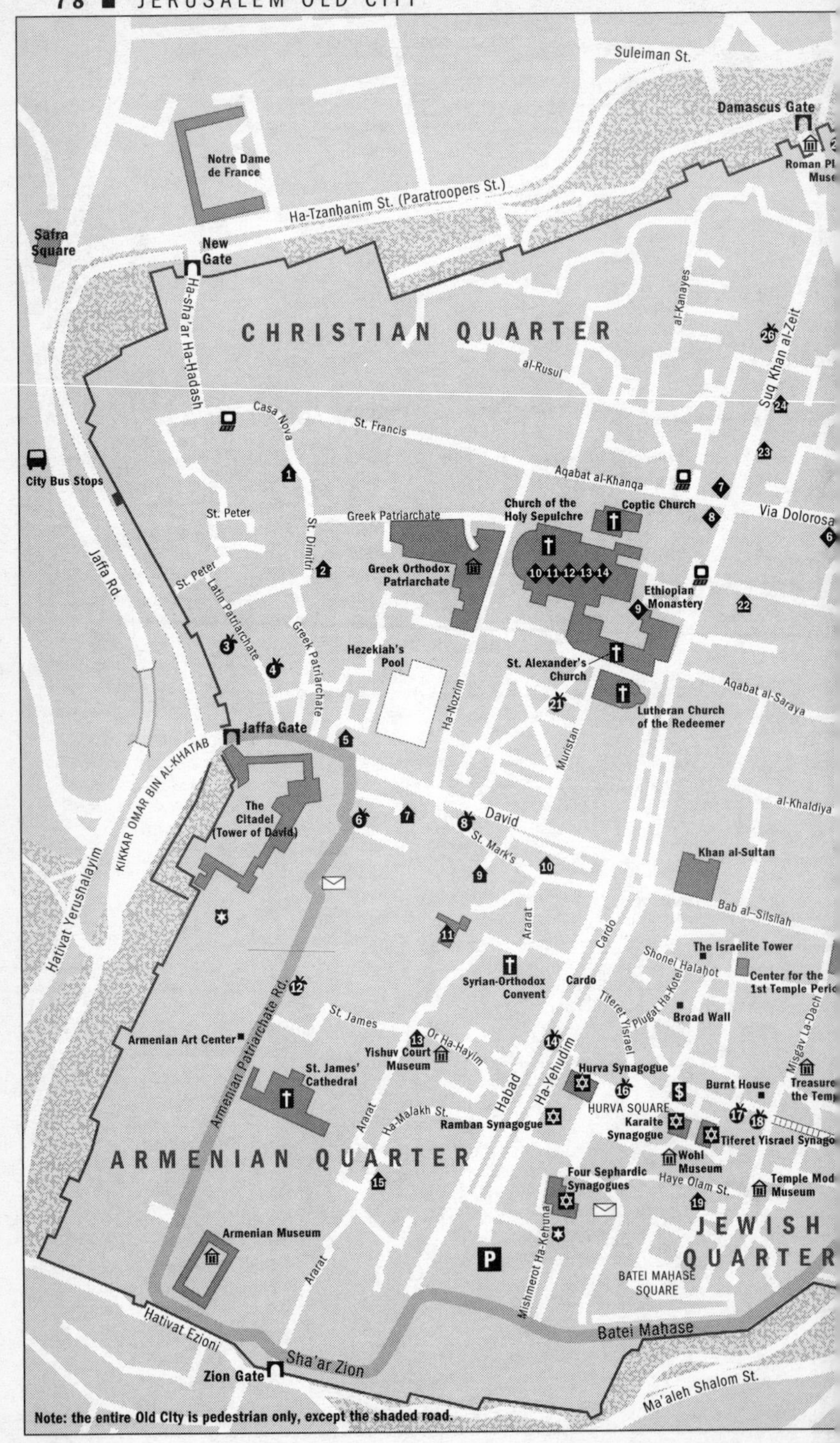

Suleiman St.
Damascus Gate
Notre Dame de France
Ha-Tzanhanim St. (Paratroopers St.)
Safra Square
New Gate
Ha-sha'ar Ha-Hadash
CHRISTIAN QUARTER
al-Kanayes
al-Rusul
Suq Khan al-Zeit
Casa Nova
St. Francis
City Bus Stops
Aqabat al-Khanqa
Church of the Holy Sepulchre
Coptic Church
Via Dolorosa
St. Peter
Greek Patriarchate
St. Dimitri
Greek Orthodox Patriarchate
Jaffa Rd.
Latin Patriarchate
Ethiopian Monastery
Hezekiah's Pool
St. Alexander's Church
Aqabat al-Saraya
Ha-Nozrim
Lutheran Church of the Redeemer
Muristan
Jaffa Gate
KIKKAR OMAR BIN AL-KHATAB
The Citadel (Tower of David)
David
St. Mark's
al-Khaldiya
Khan al-Sultan
Hativat Yerushalayim
Bab al-Silsilah
Ararat
Cardo
The Israelite Tower
Shonei Halahot
Center for the 1st Temple Period
Syrian-Orthodox Convent
Plugat Ha-Kotel
Tiferet Yisrael
Broad Wall
Misgav La-Dach
Armenian Patriarchate Rd.
St. James
Armenian Art Center
Or Ha-Hayim
Yishuv Court Museum
Ha-Yehudim
Hurva Synagogue
Habad
Burnt House
Treasures of the Temple
St. James' Cathedral
HURVA SQUARE
Ha-Malakh St.
Ramban Synagogue
Karaite Synagogue
Tiferet Yisrael Synagogue
ARMENIAN QUARTER
Wohl Museum
Four Sephardic Synagogues
Haye Olam St.
Temple Model Museum
JEWISH QUARTER
Armenian Museum
Mishmerot Ha-Kehuna
BATEI MAHASE SQUARE
Hativat Ezioni
Batei Mahase
Sha'ar Zion
Zion Gate
Ma'aleh Shalom St.
Note: the entire Old City is pedestrian only, except the shaded road.

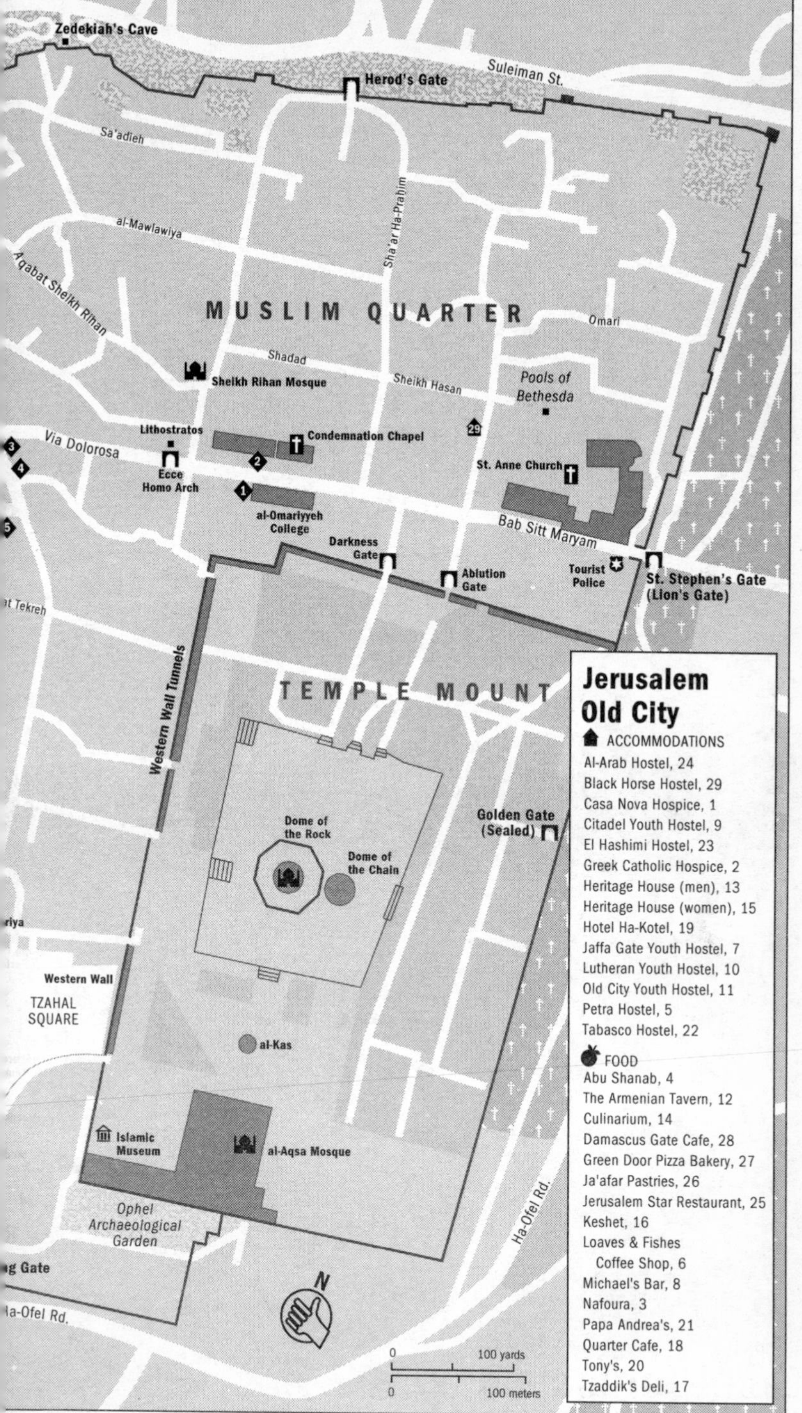

Jerusalem Old City

ACCOMMODATIONS

Al-Arab Hostel, 24
Black Horse Hostel, 29
Casa Nova Hospice, 1
Citadel Youth Hostel, 9
El Hashimi Hostel, 23
Greek Catholic Hospice, 2
Heritage House (men), 13
Heritage House (women), 15
Hotel Ha-Kotel, 19
Jaffa Gate Youth Hostel, 7
Lutheran Youth Hostel, 10
Old City Youth Hostel, 11
Petra Hostel, 5
Tabasco Hostel, 22

FOOD

Abu Shanab, 4
The Armenian Tavern, 12
Culinarium, 14
Damascus Gate Cafe, 28
Green Door Pizza Bakery, 27
Ja'afar Pastries, 26
Jerusalem Star Restaurant, 25
Keshet, 16
Loaves & Fishes Coffee Shop, 6
Michael's Bar, 8
Nafoura, 3
Papa Andrea's, 21
Quarter Cafe, 18
Tony's, 20
Tzaddik's Deli, 17

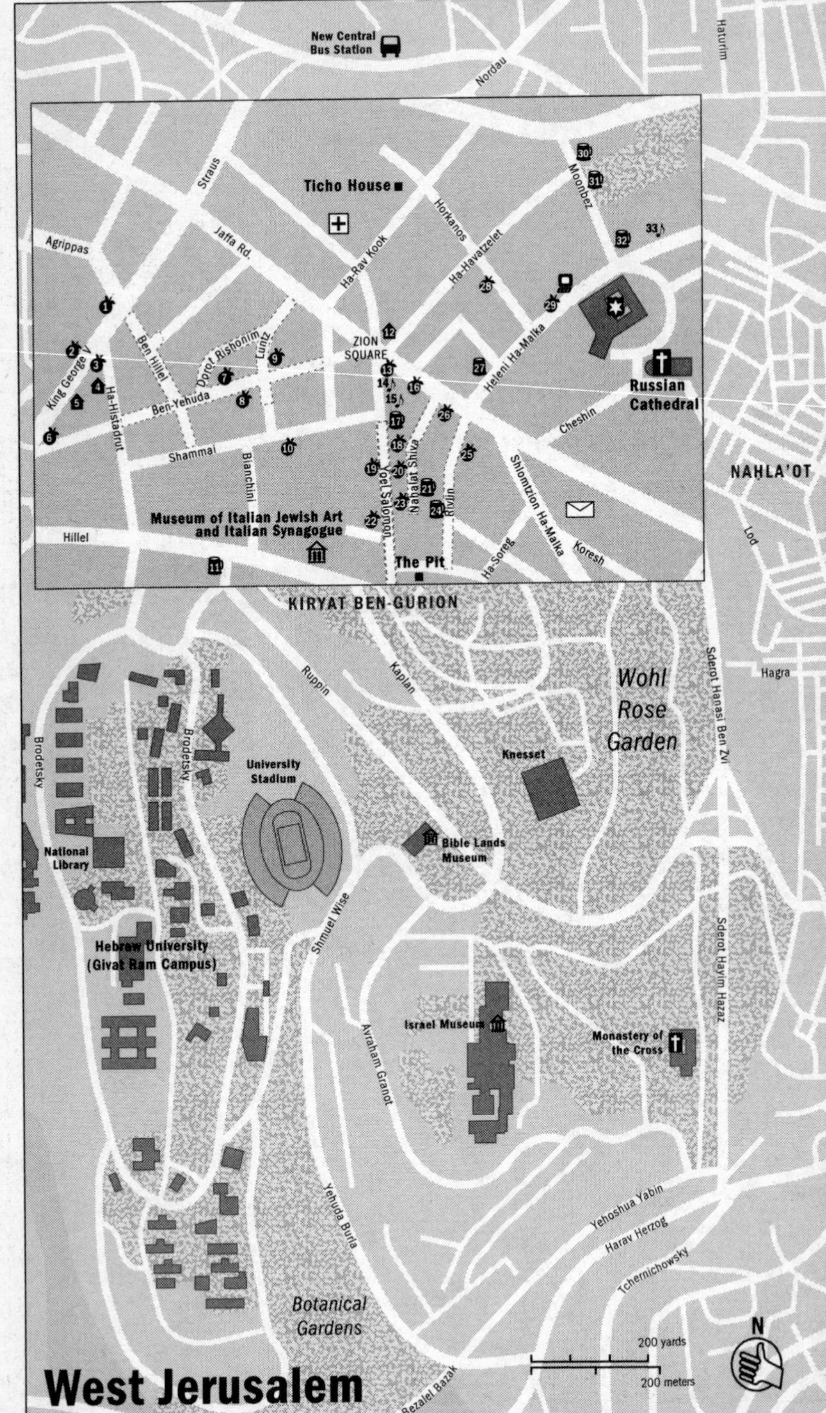

New Central Bus Station
Nordau
Haturim
Ticho House
Straus
Agrippas
Jaffa Rd.
Ha-Rav Kook
Horkanos
Ha-Havatzelet
Moonbez
King George V
Ben Hillel
Dorot Rishonim
Luntz
ZION SQUARE
Heleni Ha-Malka
Russian Cathedral
Ha-Histadrut
Ben-Yehuda
Shammai
Bianchini
Yoel Salomon
Nahalat Shiva
Rivlin
Cheshin
Shlomtzion Ha-Malka
NAHLA'OT
Museum of Italian Jewish Art and Italian Synagogue
Hillel
The Pit
Ha-Soreg
Koresh
Lod
KIRYAT BEN-GURION
Ruppin
Kaplan
Wohl Rose Garden
Sderot Hanasi Ben Zvi
Hagra
Brodetsky
Knesset
University Stadium
Bible Lands Museum
National Library
Shmuel Wise
Hebrew University (Givat Ram Campus)
Sderot Hayim Hazaz
Israel Museum
Monastery of the Cross
Avraham Granot
Yehuda Burla
Yehoshua Yabin
Harav Herzog
Tchernichowsky
Botanical Gardens
200 yards
200 meters
N
Bezalel Bazak
West Jerusalem

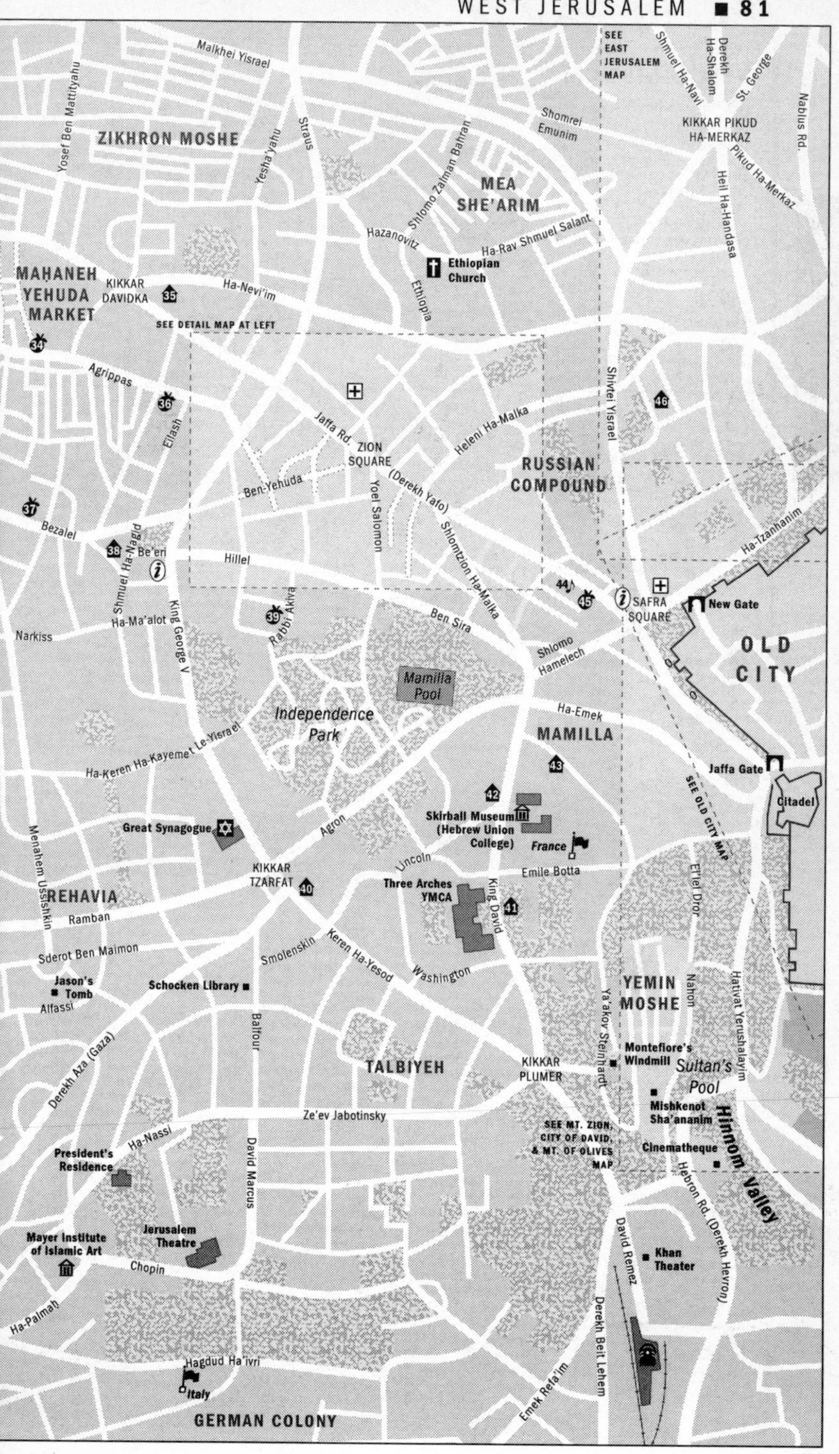

ZIKHRON MOSHE
MEA SHE'ARIM
MAHANEH YEHUDA MARKET
KIKKAR DAVIDKA
SEE DETAIL MAP AT LEFT
SEE EAST JERUSALEM MAP
KIKKAR PIKUD HA-MERKAZ
Ethiopian Church
ZION SQUARE
RUSSIAN COMPOUND
SAFRA SQUARE
New Gate
OLD CITY
Mamilla Pool
Independence Park
MAMILLA
Jaffa Gate
Citadel
SEE OLD CITY MAP
Skirball Museum (Hebrew Union College)
France
Great Synagogue
KIKKAR TZARFAT
Three Arches YMCA
REHAVIA
Jason's Tomb
Schocken Library
YEMIN MOSHE
Montefiore's Windmill
Sultan's Pool
KIKKAR PLUMER
TALBIYEH
Mishkenot Sha'ananim
Hinnom Valley
SEE MT. ZION, CITY OF DAVID, & MT. OF OLIVES MAP
Cinematheque
President's Residence
Mayer Institute of Islamic Art
Jerusalem Theatre
Khan Theater
Italy
GERMAN COLONY
Malkhei Yisrael
Yosef Ben Mattityahu
Yesha'yahu
Straus
Shlomo Zalman Bahran
Shomrei Emunim
Shmuel Ha-Navi
Derekh Ha-Shalom
St. George
Nablus Rd.
Pikud Ha-Merkaz
Heil Ha-Handasa
Hazanovitz
Ha-Rav Shmuel Salant
Ethiopia
Ha-Nevi'im
Agrippas
Eliash
Jaffa Rd.
(Derekh Yafo)
Heleni Ha-Malka
Shivtei Yisrael
Ben-Yehuda
Yoel Salomon
Shlomtzion Ha-Malka
Ha-Tzanhanim
Bezalel
Be'eri
Shmuel Ha-Nagid
Hillel
King George V
Ha-Ma'alot
Narkiss
Rabbi Akiva
Ben Sira
Shlomo Hamelech
Ha-Emek
Ha-Keren Ha-Kayemet Le-Yisrael
Agron
Menahem Ussishkin
Lincoln
Emile Botta
King David
Ramban
Sderot Ben Maimon
Smolenskin
Keren Ha-Yesod
Washington
Ettel Dror
Nahon
Hativat Yerushalayim
Alfassi
Balfour
Ya'akov Steinhardt
Derekh Aza (Gaza)
Ze'ev Jabotinsky
Ha-Nassi
David Marcus
Hebron Rd. (Derekh Hevron)
David Remez
Chopin
Ha-Palmah
Derekh Beit Lehem
Emek Refa'im
Hagdud Ha'ivri
34
35
36
37
38
39
40
41
42
43
44
45
46

West Jerusalem

ACCOMMODATIONS
Beit Bernstein Hostel (HI), 41
Beit Gesher, 42
Beit Shmuel Guest House (HI), 43
Davidka Hostel (HI), 37
Diana's House, 47
Hotel Noga, 39
Jerusalem Inn Guest House, 5
The King David Hotel, 44
My Home in Jerusalem Hotel, 6
Zion Square Hostel, 13

FOOD
Alumah, 1
Amigos, 21
Au Sahara, 46
Babette's Party, 11
Cafe Chagall, 9
Gizmongolia, 3
Katzefet, 30
Korea House, 10
Magic Fruit Juice, 24
Marzipan Bakery, 7
Melekh Ha-Falafel, 36
Misadonet, 23
Mr. Juice, 14
Nevatim, 8
Pampa Grill, 26
The Pie Shop, 19
Pinati, 4
Shalom Falafel, 38
Spaghettim, 40
Stanley's, 29
Taco Taco, 17
Village Green, 27
The Yemenite Step, 20

PUBS
Casso, 29
Egon, 22
Kanabis/Tarabin House, 32
Mike's Place, 28
Sergey, 34
Shanty, 18
Strudel, 31
Syndrome, 12
The Tavern Pub, 25

NIGHTLIFE
Glasnost, 35
Goa, 45
Q, 15
The Underground, 16

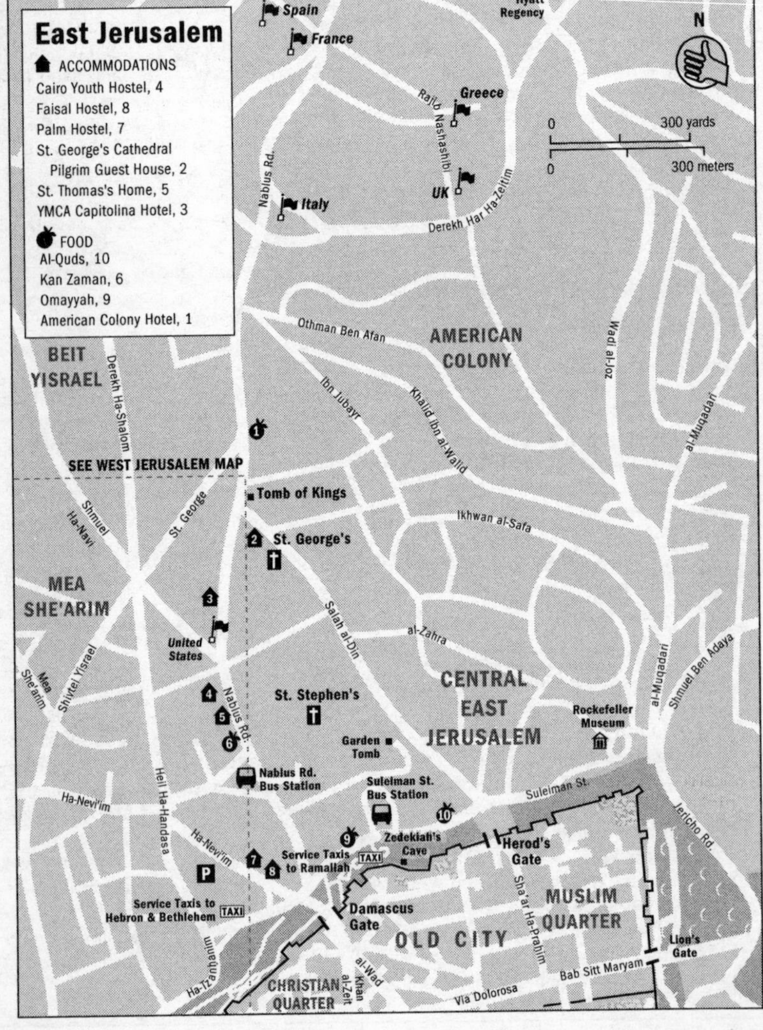

Jerusalem lasted almost 90 years. During this time, churches were built or rebuilt, hospices, hospitals, and monastic orders were founded, and non-Christian sites of worship were desecrated. In 1187 Salah al-Din expelled the Crusaders and both Muslims and Jews once again began to resettle the city. Jerusalem became a thriving center for Muslim scholarship from the 13th to the 15th century under the Mamluks.

OTTOMAN RULE AND EUROPEAN INFLUENCE. In 1516, Jerusalem capitulated to the Ottoman Turks, the city's rulers for the next 400 years (see **Mamluks and Ottomans,** p. 11). In 1537, Ottoman emperor Suleiman the Magnificent set out to rebuild the city walls, a task that took four years. The planners deviated from the older design, leaving Mount Zion and King David's tomb beyond the walls (see **The Walls,** p. 109). This negligence infuriated Suleiman, who had the architects' heads put outside the walls, too. In later centuries, many foreign countries began demanding extra-territorial rights for their citizens living under Ottoman rule. The world political climate forced the Ottoman sultan to issue the 1856 "Edict of Toleration" for all religions. The small, deeply religious Jewish and Christian communities in Jerusalem still needed charity from abroad to make ends meet, but the trickle of immigrants coming from Europe and Russia increased to a steady flow.

Sir Moses Montefiore, a British Jew, took several trips to Palestine between 1827 and 1874, sponsoring Jewish settlements outside the city walls. These areas expanded into bustling neighborhoods, the foundations of West Jerusalem (see **Zionism,** p. 11). Heavier Western influence and the influx of European immigrants led to the designation of Jerusalem as an independent *sanjak* (Ottoman province) in 1889, with its own *pasha* (governor) appointed directly from Istanbul.

Ottoman rule over Jerusalem ended in 1917, when the city fell without resistance to the British army. Both Jews and Arabs came to resent the increasing influence of the British in Jerusalem (see **British Mandate,** p. 12). During World War I, Britain made separate declarations to both Zionists and Arab nationalists, implying that each would eventually gain sovereignty over the city. In the end, though, the British kept Palestine as a League of Nations Mandate. Under British rule, tension between the Jewish and Arab communities heightened, bursting into violent confrontations in 1929 and 1933, and virtual civil war between 1936 and 1939.

The uneasy World War II truce between Arabs and Jews dissolved when the war ended, and violence ravaged Palestine for the next three years. The British announced that they were no longer capable of governing the country. They solcited a settlement from the newly formed United Nations, which divided Palestine into separate Jewish and Arab states, leaving Jerusalem an international city.

1948 TO THE PRESENT. In the war that followed the 1948 British evacuation (see **Partition and War,** p. 13), West Jerusalem and the Jewish Quarter were besieged by Arabs, who blocked the only road out of the city. West Jerusalem held out until the cease-fire, but the Jewish Quarter of the Old City capitulated to the Jordanian Arab Legion after exhaustive house-to-house fighting. Jordan destroyed much of the ancient quarter and dynamited synagogues. The Jordanian-ruled and Israeli sectors of the city were separated by a buffer zone for nearly two decades.

When the 1967 (Six-Day) War broke out, Israel requested that Jordan not get involved; King Hussein attacked West Jerusalem anyway. In the course of the war, Israel captured East Jerusalem, the Old City, and the West Bank from the Jordanians. On June 29 of that year, Israel declared the newly unified Jerusalem its "eternal capital." The walls separating the Israeli and Arab sectors were torn down, and life under Israeli rule began for Jerusalem's Arabs.

The 25 years following the 1967 War saw large scale construction outside the Old City. Land owned by Palestinians who had fled during the war was taken over by Israel (see **PLO and Jordan,** p. 14). Vast new Israeli housing developments were built north and south of the city, assuring a Jewish presence in areas previously under Jordanian rule. The old campus of the Hebrew University on Mount Scopus, maintained as a military post since 1948, was expanded. Intensive gardening projects blossomed throughout the city, including parks that encircle the Old City.

The 1987 outbreak of the *intifada* (uprising) of Palestinians protesting Israeli occupation had some effect on Jerusalem, though demonstrations were more common in West Bank towns (see **Intifada,** p. 16). The Palestinians made it clear that they regarded East Jerusalem as a part of the West Bank and the future capital of their desired state. Meanwhile, clashes between the Israeli army and stone-throwing Palestinians, as well as occasional stabbings of Jews in the Old City, turned East Jerusalem and the Old City into alien territory for Jewish Israelis and visitors. Matters were made worse in October 1990 when fighting broke out between Jews and Palestinians at the Western Wall. Israeli police killed 17 Palestinians and wounded almost 150 others during the ensuing crackdown. In February 1996, the militant Palestinian group Hamas brought bloodshed to West Jerusalem in two bus bombings that killed dozens; the following summer, a pair of suicide bombings only weeks apart caused the deaths of 20 bystanders.

The future of Jerusalem is perhaps the most sensitive issue of the current Israeli-Palestinian negotiations. Israel adamantly refuses to discuss withdrawing from its capital, while Palestinians fervently oppose abandoning claims to their most important city.

SAFETY WARNING. Tensions sometimes make East Jerusalem and parts of the Old City unfriendly to Israelis and Jewish foreigners. Jewish travelers should make their tourist status as pronounced as possible and speak English. Wearing a *kippah* is a bad idea in Arab parts of town (cover it with a baseball cap).

GETTING THERE AND AWAY

Flights: Ben-Gurion Airport (Info for all airlines ☎03 972 33 44. El Al English info ☎03 972 33 88. Automated flight reconfirmation ☎03 972 23 33) is only an hour from Jerusalem and easily accessible; you do not need to go to Tel Aviv first, no matter how early your flight, thanks to the 24hr. *sherut* service offered by Nesher (see **Taxis,** below). For a hassle-free airport experience, bags for El Al flights can be checked in and inspected in advance at 7 Kanfei Nesharim St., 1st fl. (☎651 57 05; fax 651 57 03), on the corner of Jaffa Rd. near the central bus station. Open Su-Th 2-10pm for next-day flights, 2-7pm for same-night flights.

Trains: As of summer 2000, the **Remez Square Station** (☎673 37 64), was closed "until further notice." The station is southwest of the Old City, just south of Liberty Bell Park; take buses #21 or 48 from downtown. Status posted on the web at www.israrail.org.il.

Buses: Egged Central Bus Station (☎530 47 04; www.egged.co.il), on Jaffa Rd. (see **Getting Around,** below). 10% ISIC discount on long-distance trips, generally only on tickets purchased at the ticket counter and not on the bus. Drivers often inspect ISIC cards upon boarding. Times, frequencies, and prices listed here are based on the summer 2000 schedule; call for current information (or go to the station, since they often ignore the phone). Info desk open Su-Th 6am-8:30pm, F 6am-3pm. To: **Arlozorov terminal** (#480; every 15-20min. Su-Th 6am-10:30pm, F 6am-4:30pm, Sa 8:20-

11pm); **Be'er Sheva** Direct (#470; 1½hr.; every 45min.-2hr. Su 6:20am-6:15pm, M-Th 6:45am-6:15pm, F 10:20am-sundown, Sa 8:20pm; NIS27) or via **Kiryat Gat** (#446; 1¾hr.; every 15min.-1hr. Su-Th 6am-9pm, F 6am-sundown, Sa sundown-10:35pm); **Ben-Gurion Airport** (#423, 428, 945, or 947; 1hr.; every 15-40min. Su-Th 6am-8:35pm, F 6am-sundown, Sa sundown-10pm; NIS21); **Eilat** (#444; 4½hr.; Su-Th 7, 10am, 2, and 5pm; F 7, 10am, and 2pm; less frequent in winter; NIS61); **Haifa** Direct (#940; 2hr.; every 15-45min. Su 6am-7:30pm, M-W 6:30am-7:30pm, Th 6:30am-8:30pm, F 6:45am-sundown, Sa sundown-10pm; NIS40) or via **Netanya** (#947; 2hr.; every 20-40min. Su-Th 6am-8:30pm, F 6am-sundown, Sa sundown-10pm); **Tiberias** (#961, 963, or 964; 3hr.; every hr. Su-Th 7am-7:30pm, F 7am-3pm, Sa 8:15-9:15pm); **Tel Aviv Central Station** (#405; 1hr.; every 10-25min. Su-Th 5:40am-midnight, F 6am-sundown, Sa sundown-midnight; NIS18). Egged buses don't go into any Palestinian towns in the West Bank; they stop only at Jewish settlements or sites. For example, bus #160 to Kiryat Arba stops outside Hebron. Two bus stations serve the West Bank. Suleiman Street Station, in East Jerusalem between Herod's and Damascus Gates, serves routes south while Nablus Road Station serves points north. See appropriate sections of West Bank and **West Bank: Getting There,** p. 308, for information on travel to the West Bank from Israel.

Taxis: Jerusalem is served by two main **intercity sherut taxi** companies. **Ha Bira** (☎625 45 45), at the corner of Ha-Rav Kook St. and Jaffa Rd. (near Zion Sq.), goes to **Tel Aviv** (every 20min. 6am-2am; NIS18, after 11:30pm NIS19, Shabbat NIS20). Office open Su-Th 5:30am-11pm and F 5:30am-5:30pm. **Nesher,** 21 King George St. (☎625 72 27 or 623 12 31), provides 24hr. door-to-door service to the airport from anywhere in Jerusalem (NIS40, reserve at least 4hr. ahead). *Sherut* taxis to other locations leave from the central bus station. Split among a group they can be as cheap as buses. To West Bank towns, *service* taxis (the Arab equivalent of the *sherut*) leave from outside of Damascus Gate (see **West Bank: Getting Around,** p. 309).

Car Rental: Many rental companies have offices on or near King David St., not far from the Hilton and King David Hotel. All prices include full insurance. Many companies increase their prices during July-Sept., sometimes by as much as US$15 per day. **Budget,** 23 King David St. (☎624 89 91; fax 625 89 86; www.budget.co.il), has cars starting at US$45 per day, US$40 per day for 3-day rentals, including unlimited mileage; 23+. **Eldan,** 24 King David St. (☎625 21 51; www.eldan.co.il), has one-day rentals beginning at US$38 (100km included), US$38 per day for one week or longer with unlimited mileage. **Superdrive,** 10 King David St. (☎625 08 43), rents to drivers 18 and older. US$50 per day, US$48 for 3 days. July-Aug. US$60 per day. Drivers ages 21-22 pay US$17 extra per day, age 18-20 US$35 extra. Credit cards accepted. Open Su-Th 8am-6pm, F 8am-1pm. Call ahead.

GETTING AROUND

Most distances in Jerusalem make for reasonable, pleasant walks, for those who don't mind the heat and the hills (see **Walking Tours of the Old City,** p. 102). All sections of the city are easily reachable by bus from the **central bus station** (info ☎530 47 04) on Jaffa Rd., west of city center just past the Maḥaneh Yehuda district (NIS5 per ride within Jerusalem; NIS47 *kartisia* buys 11 rides, 20 for those under 18). The current central bus station is temporary; the old one, farther west on Jaffa Rd., across from the Binyanei Ha-Umma Convention Center, is being rebuilt and will supposedly be finished sometime in 2001. A dazzling (and dizzying) **city bus map** is available at the information desk. Arab buses run irregularly every day; Egged service stops at about 4:30pm on Friday and resumes after sunset on Saturday. Taxis are widely available. Try **Reḥavia Taxi** (☎625 44 44 or 622 24 44) for 24-hour service.

COMMON BUS ROUTES:

#1: To Mea She'arim and Dung Gate/Western Wall.

#3: To Jaffa Gate, Shivtei Yisrael, Ha-Nevi'im, and Maḥaneh Yehuda.

#4 AND 4A: To Emek Refa'im, Keren Ha-Yesod, King George, Ramat Eshkol, and Mount Scopus.

#6, 8, 13, 18, AND 20: To Zion Sq.; get off at the intersection of Jaffa Rd. and King George St. Buses #6 and 20 continue to Jaffa Gate; #6 goes on to the Kenyon mall.

#9 AND 27: To the Knesset, the Israel Museum, the Hebrew University at Givat Ram, West Jerusalem center, and Mount Scopus.

#17: To Reḥavia, Mount Herzl, and Ein Kerem.

#21: To Talpiyot, Hebron Rd., King David St., and Mount Herzl.

#23: To Damascus Gate, Suleiman St. bus station, East Jerusalem, and Herod's Gate.

#99 (THE JERUSALINE): From Jaffa Gate or central bus station, passes 34 major tourist sights on a 2hr. loop. Su-Th at 10am, noon, 2, and 4pm; F 10am and noon. Runs less frequently in winter. One loop NIS28.

ORIENTATION

Known as **Yerushalayim** in Hebrew and **al-Quds** (the holy) in Arabic, Jerusalem is a sprawling city, most of which was only developed in the last 50 years of the capital's three-millennium history.

WEST JERUSALEM. This section includes Jewish parts of Jerusalem, from French Hill in the northeast and East Talpiyot in the southeast, to Kiryat Menaḥem in the southwest and Ramot in the northwest. The main street is **Jaffa Rd.** (Derekh Yafo), running west-to-east from the central bus station to the Old City's **Jaffa Gate.** Roughly midway between the two, **Zion Sq.** (Kikkar Tzion) sits at the corner of Jerusalem's triangular *midraḥov* bounded by Jaffa Rd., **Ben-Yehuda St.,** and **King George St.** Upscale eateries line **Yoel Salomon St.** and **Rivlin St.,** off Zion Sq.

North of the city center, the **Russian Compound's** hip bar scene hugs the old-world **Mea She'arim** like spandex on a *yenta*. Northwest on Jaffa Rd. are the teeming outdoor markets of **Maḥaneh Yehuda** and, further down, the central bus station. Southwest of the triangle are the Knesset building and the hilltop Israel Museum complex. The beautiful **Independence Park** lies south of the city center, ringed by luxury hotels; farther south are the cafes of **Emek Refa'im** and the discotheques of **Talpiyot.** The artists' district of **Yemin Moshe** huddles southeast of Zion Sq.

OLD CITY. Jerusalem's most important historical and religious sites are concentrated within the walls of the Old City, which is still divided into the four quadrants laid out by the Romans in 135 CE. **Jaffa Gate** and **Damascus Gate,** the two main entrances to the Old City, tend to be good reference points for locating sights and hostels. To reach Jaffa Gate from West Jerusalem, walk down **Jaffa Rd.** to the very end and continue straight across the intersection, or take buses #6, 20, 21, or 99. To reach Damascus Gate, walk to the end of Jaffa Rd. and take a left onto **Ha-Tzanḥanim St.** (Paratroopers St.); from further up Jaffa St. (e.g. near the **Maḥaneh Yehuda market**), walking straight down Ha-Nevi'im St. is more direct. Buses #1, 2, 37, and 44 go to Damascus Gate.

The two main roads in the Old City are the roof-covered **David St.,** beginning inside Jaffa Gate and turning into **Bab al-Silsilah St.** (Gate of the Chain) as it approaches the Temple Mount, and **Suq Khan al-Zeit,** beginning inside Damascus Gate and turning into the **Cardo** as it crosses David St.

Damascus Gate is Arab East Jerusalem's entryway into the Old City, leading right to the heart of the **Muslim Quarter's** *souq* (market). Just inside Damascus Gate, the road forks into al-Wad St. (on the left) and Suq Khan al-Zeit St. (on the right). This area is less safe after dark; those staying here should plan to return to hostels by nightfall. The Cardo leads into the **Jewish Quarter;** this quarter is also directly accessible through **Dung Gate.** The **Armenian Quarter** is to the right as you enter through Jaffa Gate and is directly accessible via **Zion Gate.** Inside Jaffa Gate to the left is the **Christian Quarter,** which can also be reached directly from the **New Gate.** Of the other three gates, **St. Stephen's Gate** (Lion's Gate) is closest to the both the **Mount of Olives** (outside the Old Cty) and the start of the **Via Dolorosa; Herod's Gate** enters into a less-touristed section of the Muslim Quarter, and the entrance at the **Golden Gate** is blocked.

EAST JERUSALEM. The old, invisible **Green Line** separating Jordan from pre-1967 Israel runs along **Derekh Ha-Shalom** (Peace Rd.) and is still a good general demarcation between Palestinian and Jewish areas of Jerusalem. **East Jerusalem** is the name normally given to the Palestinian parts of Jerusalem just outside the Old City to the north and east; it sometimes includes the Old City. **Suleiman St.,** in front of Damascus Gate, and **Salah al-Din St.,** which runs out from Herod's Gate, are the main roads in central East Jerusalem. **Ha-Nevi'im St.** (Musrada in Arabic), which runs in from Jaffa Rd. in West Jerusalem, converges with **Nablus Rd.** at Damascus Gate; the small but busy area has many falafel and *shawarma* stands, fruit vendors, dry goods stores, and hostels, all with cheaper prices than practically anywhere else in Jerusalem. Central East Jerusalem is the financial and cultural hub of the Arab community.

PRACTICAL INFORMATION

OLD CITY

TOURIST AND FINANCIAL SERVICES

Tourist Office: The tourist information office in Safra Sq. in West Jerusalem is superior to those in the Old City and worth the 10min. walk from Jaffa Gate (see p. 109). The **Tourist Information Center** (☎628 03 82), on the left just inside Jaffa Gate, sells books, postcards, phone cards, maps, and stamps. Books Egged bus tours. Also has money exchange and Internet (NIS0.50 per min.). Open Su-Th 8am-7pm, F 8am-4pm.

Special Interest Tourist Offices: Christian Information Center (☎627 26 92; fax 628 64 17; email cicts@netmedia.net.il; www.cits.org), inside Jaffa Gate, opposite the Tower of David. Offers information on Jerusalem's pilgrimage sights and Christian accommodations. Open M-Sa 8:30am-1pm. **Franciscan Pilgrims Office,** P.O. Box 186 (☎627 26 97), in the same building as the Christian Information Center. Talk to the priest here about going to Christmas midnight mass in Bethlehem. Open M-F 9am-noon and 3:30-5:30pm, Sa 9am-noon. **The Swedish Christian Study Center** (☎626 42 23; fax 628 58 77; email scsc@palnet.com), next door to the Christian Information Center (closer to David St.), features a sunny reading room and library and a 360-degree rooftop view. Primarily for Swedes, but the friendly staff will answer questions for anyone in a bind. Open M-Sa 9am-1pm. **The Jewish Student Information Center,** 5 Beit El St. (☎628 26 34; fax 628 83 38; e-mail jseidel@netmedia.net.il; www.geocities.com/athens/7613), in Ḥurva Sq. in the Jewish Quarter. Run by the friendly and enthusiastic 24hr.-a-day, one-man info factory Jeff Seidel, who also gives guided tours of the underground Kotel tunnels. He may want to discuss religion. Shabbat home hospitality available with Orthodox Jewish families. The center sells the comprehensive Jewish *Student's Travel Guide* (US$9) with religious information for most countries around the world.

Guided Tours: The highly recommended **Zion Walking Tours** (☎628 78 66; mobile 050 305 552; www.zionwt.co.il) offers 8 inexpensive guided routes on different days of the week in and around the Old City. Their most popular tour is of the four quarters of the Old City (3hr.; daily 9, 11am, and 2pm; US$10, students US$9, entry fees included). Their office is located right inside Jaffa Gate, opposite the Tower of David. **Israel Archaeological Seminars,** 34 Habad St. (☎627 35 15; fax 627 26 60; email office@archesem.com; www.archesem.com), in the Jewish Quarter, offers walking tours in addition to day-long archaeology excursions all over Israel. A guided tour of the politically sensitive **Western Wall tunnels** requires reserving a ticket **in advance** for an hour- long tour (NIS30-40). Individuals are not permitted to enter the tunnels or excavations without a guide (☎627 13 33; fax 626 48 28; www.hakotel.org). Probably the most popular tour offered from the Old City is not of the Old City—most hostels organize daily sunrise tours of the Dead Sea area (3am-3pm). Run by **Alternative Palestine Tours.** (NIS90 for transportation and guide; admission and food not included.)

Banks: Bank Mizrahi, 26 Tiferet Yisrael St. (☎627 31 31; fax 628 84 29), in the Jewish Quarter. Look for the blue sign in Ḥurva Sq. Hefty commission for foreign exchange. Open Su-Th 9am-2pm and 5-7pm; M, W, F 9am-noon. Has the only **ATM** and automated **currency exchange machine** in the entire Old City. There are money changers around the Old City that have lower rates but don't charge commission; make sure they don't give you old bills, which are not accepted at most establishments.

EMERGENCY AND COMMUNICATION

Police: (☎622 62 22). Inside Jaffa Gate to the right, next to the Tower of David. 24hr.

Pharmacies: Jaffa Gate Pharmacy (☎628 38 98), the first left from Jaffa Gate, immediately on the right. Open daily 9am-8pm. **Habash Pharmacy,** 104 al-Wad St. (☎627 24 27; fax 628 81 57), in the Muslim Quarter. Open daily 8:30am-8pm.

Medical assistance: Austrian-Arab Community Clinic, Qanatar Khadeir Rd. (☎627 32 46), off al-Wad St., in the Muslim Quarter, and across the street from the Austrian Hospice. Open Sa-W 8am-7pm, Th 8am-4pm. **Kupat Holim** (☎627 16 08), in the Jewish Quarter above the Cardo and across from Ḥurva Sq. Hours are erratic.

Internet Access: The cheapest connections are found mostly in the Muslim Quarter. **Mike's Center,** 172 Khan al-Zeit St. (☎628 24 86), at the turn-off for the 9th Station of the Cross, boasts "the fastest line in Israel." NIS12 per hr. **Freeline Internet Cafe** (☎627 19 59), on St. Francis St. around the corner from the 7th station, offers free tea and coffee while you work. NIS13 per hr. Open daily 9am-midnight.

Post Office: (☎629 06 86), inside Jaffa Gate, across from the Tower of David, marked by a red sign. Open Su-Th 7:30am-2:30pm, F 8am-noon. Smaller branch in the Jewish Quarter down Plugat Ha-Kotel St.

WEST JERUSALEM

TOURIST AND FINANCIAL SERVICES

Tourist Information: MTIO, 3 Safra Sq. (☎625 88 44), in the City Hall complex off Jaffa Rd. From behind the large water fountain in the municipal plaza, the entrance is on the right. Excellent computerized information. Offers pamphlets and maps, but doesn't have Carta's Map (NIS36), the best of the city, available at Steimatzky's (see **Bookstores,** p. 89). MTIO open Su-Th 8:30am-4pm, F 8:45am-1pm.

Religious Information: See **Old City Special Interest Tourist Offices,** p. 87.

Tours: The municipality sponsors a free Shabbat **walking tour** in English (☎625 88 44) from 32 Jaffa Rd. near Zion Sq. (2½hr., Sa 10am, rotates among several routes). *This Week in Jerusalem* lists guided tours throughout the city (also posted at the MTIO office). Sunrise tours to Masada and the Dead Sea (NIS90) and day tours to the Galilee (NIS120) are available through most hostels in the area, or by contacting **Alternative Tours** (☎/fax 628 32 82; email raed@jrshotel.com; www.jrshotel.com). **Society for the Protection of Nature in Israel (SPNI),** 13 Heleni Ha-Malka St. (☎625 23 57), runs expertly guided but relatively expensive tours throughout Israel and Sinai. Tours range from half-day explorations of Jerusalem to 15-day Israel odysseys. Office open Su-Th 9am-6:45pm, F 9am-12:30pm.

Budget Travel: Mazada Tours, 19 Jaffa Rd. (☎623 57 77; fax 625 54 54), the street behind the main post office at Jaffa Rd. Guided trips to Jordan (starting from 2 days, US$270) and Egypt (starting from 4 days, US$104) and transportation service to Cairo (daily 7:30am; Su, Tu, and Th also at 7:30pm; morning bus US$35, evening bus US$40; round-trip good for 40 days US$50 for morning bus, US$60 for evening bus). Prices 25% higher in Aug. and Dec. Reserve at least 2 days in advance; they can help with getting visas. Open Su-Th 9am-6pm, F 9am-3pm. **Better Travel Connections (B.T.C.),** 2 Ha-Soreg St. (☎623 39 90; fax 625 78 27; www.btctravel.com), off Shlomtzion Ha-Malka St., on the 5th floor. Offers numerous trips around Israel, ranging from a variety of half-day tours (US$26) to an 8-day "biblelands" tour (US$787), plus 2- to 3-day trips to Jordan (from US$145, not including visa and taxes) and 4-day jaunts to Egypt (from US$169). Open Su-Th 9am-6pm, F 9am-1pm. **Neot Ha-Kikar,** 5 Shlomtzion Ha-Malka St. (☎623 62 62; fax 623 61 61; www.neot-hakikar.com). Specializes in 1- to 6-day Sinai tours from Eilat (US$59-US$290). Open Su-Th 9am-5pm, F 9am-12:30pm. **ISSTA,** 31 Ha-Nevi'im St. (☎621 36 00). ISIC cards NIS40; bring photo and proof of student status. Student discounts on airfare, car rentals, and **Eurail** passes. Open Su-Tu and Th 9am-7pm, W and F 9am-1pm. Additional offices inside La-metayel camping store (☎624 31 78) and at Hebrew University campuses on Mount Scopus (☎582 61 16) and Givat Ram (☎651 87 80).

Consulates: UK, 19 Nashashibi St. (☎541 41 00), in East Jerusalem near Sheikh Jarrah. Open M-F 9am-noon. **US,** 27 Nablus Rd. (☎622 72 00, after-hours emergency ☎622 72 50; www.uscongen-jerusalem.org/consular), in East Jerusalem. Open for passport renewals and other services M-F 8:30-11:30am. Notary service Tu 1-3pm. Closed for Israeli and US holidays and last Friday of each month. Administrative offices at 18 Agron St. in West Jerusalem (☎622 72 30). Other foreign consulates in Tel Aviv (see p. 89).

Currency Exchange: City Change, 30 Jaffa Rd. (☎625 87 58). Open Su-Th 9am-6pm, F 9am-1pm. **Money Net,** 8 Ben Hillel St. (☎622 23 18; fax 623 27 88), on the *midraḥov*. Open Su-Th 9am-6pm, F 9am-1pm. Both give better rates than banks and charge no commission. The **post office** (see **Central Post Office,** p. 91) offers the same rates, also commission-free. **Bank Ha-Poalim** (emergency ☎03 567 49 99), in Zion Sq. Open Su, Tu-W 8:30am-1pm; M, Th 8:30am-1pm and 4-7pm; F 8:30am-12:30pm. **ATM** accepts Cirrus, Plus, and major credit cards. **Bank Leumi,** 21 Jaffa Rd. (emergency ☎03 514 94 00), next to the post office. Open Su-Th 8:30am-2:45pm, F 8:30am-noon.

American Express: 19 Hillel St. (☎624 69 33; fax 624 09 50), near McDonald's. Full service office with commission-free traveler's check cashing, purchasing, and replacement for cardholders. Holds mail, but not packages. For traveler's check emergencies, call 24hr. ☎800 943 86 94. Open Su-Th 9am-4:30pm, F 9am-noon.

LOCAL SERVICES

Bookstores: Sefer ve-Sefel, 2 Ya'abetz St. (☎624 82 37), on the *midraḥov,* off Jaffa St., just east of King George St. Jerusalem's best place for new and used books. Open Su-Th 8am-8pm, F 8am-2:30pm. **Steimatzky,** 39 Jaffa St. (☎625 01 55); other locations at 7 Ben-Yehuda St. and 9 King George St. Great for maps, magazines, and travel books. Open Su-Th 8:30am-7pm (Ben-Yehuda location until 8pm), F 8:30am-2pm. **Dani Books,** 57 Jaffa St. (☎623 12 03). Varied selection, numerous discount racks, and used book exchange. Open Su-Th 8:30am-7:30pm, F 8:30am-2pm. **SPNI Bookstore,** 13 Heleni Ha-Malka St. (☎625 23 57), often has the lowest prices on guidebooks and maps. **Judaica Book Center,** 5 Even Israel St. (☎622 32 15), off Agrippas St. near the city center, is the best English bookstore for new Judaica. Open Su-Th 10am-7:30pm, F 9am-2pm.

Cultural Centers: American Cultural Center, 19 Keren Ha-Yesod St. (☎625 57 55; fax 624 25 60; email acc-jer@usis-israel.org.il), near the Agron-King George intersection, right after King George St. turns into Keren Ha-Yesod St. The center's sizeable library covers any subject remotely related to the United States. Several computers and a large CD-ROM collection. Free and open to anyone; only Israeli or Palestinian residents may take out books. Open Su-Th 10am-4pm, F 9am-noon. Closed on all Israeli and US holidays. **Alliance Francaise,** 8 Agron St. (☎625 12 04), across the street from Supersol. French culture club for francophones of any nationality. Frequent activities such as movie nights, wine and cheese concerts, and art exhibits. Nominal charge for events. Pick up a tri-monthly schedule or call for event information.

Gay and Lesbian Services: Jerusalem Open House (JOH), 7 Ben-Yehuda St., 3rd floor (☎625 31 91; email gayj@hotmail.com; www.poboxes.com/gayj), on the *midraḥov*. A community center with a small library, lounge, and bulletin boards. Organizes and advertises activities, concerts, discussion and support groups, poetry readings, folk dancing, and occasional excursions. Call or visit for a schedule of events. Office open Su, Th 4-8pm; Tu 10am-3pm; F 10am-2pm. Open house every Su and Th 8-10pm. **KLAF** (☎625 12 71; www.aquanet.co.il/vip/klaf), is an organization for lesbian feminists, with activities all over the country. On the line every W 8-10pm. **The Other 10% (Ha-Asiron Ha-Aḥer;** ☎653 54 54; www.poboxes.com/asiron), is Hebrew University's organization for gay, lesbian, bisexual, and transgendered students. Hosts activities during the school year, Oct.-June.

Ticket Agencies: Bimot, 8 Shammai St. (☎625 09 05), and **Kla'im,** 12 Shammai St. (☎625 68 69). Discount tickets for students and tourists for concerts, shows, and sporting events around Jerusalem. Ask about English performances. Both open Su-Th 9am-7pm, F 9am-1pm.

Laundry: Laundry Place, 12 Shammai St. (☎625 77 14), convenient location near the *midraḥov*. Self-service NIS19 per load, includes dryer and detergent. Membership for long-term stays. Open Su-Th 8:30am-midnight, F 8:30am-sunset, Sa sunset-midnight.

Camping Supplies: La-metayel, 5 Yoel Salomon St. (☎623 33 38; fax 623 33 52; www.lametayel.com) has the most extensive (and expensive) stock of camping gear (and an impressive array of travel books). Open Su-Th 10am-9pm, F 10am-2:30pm. **Orcha Camping,** 12 Yoel Salomon (☎624 06 55), near Cafe Kapulsky, is affiliated with SPNI (members get discounts on merchandise). Open Su-Th 8am-7pm, F 8am-3pm.

EMERGENCY AND COMMUNICATIONS

Medical Emergency: ☎101. **Magen David Adom First Aid,** 7 Ha-Memgimel St. (☎652 31 33). Turn right at the end of Jaffa Rd. (past the bus station) and take the next left. Their **Terem Clinic** (☎652 17 48) is open 24hr. and will see anyone on a walk-in basis for both emergencies and non-emergencies; most insurance plans are accepted, as is direct payment by credit card. Newspapers list hospitals on duty for emergencies.

Police: Emergency ☎100. In the Russian Compound (☎539 11 11), off Jaffa Rd. in West Jerusalem. **Tourist desk** (☎675 48 11), on Cheshin St. just off Jaffa Rd., near the post office. An Old City branch (☎622 62 22), on the right, is inside Jaffa Gate.

Fire: ☎102.

Help Lines: M'Lev Center for Crisis Counseling (☎654 11 11 or 800 654 111) has a general help line and referrals for English speakers. The **Rape Crisis Center** (☎1202 from anywhere in Israel) is staffed 24hr. **Eran Emotional Health Hotline** (☎1201) assists tourists daily 8am-11pm. **Alcoholics Anonymous,** 24 Ha-Palmaḥ St. (☎563 05 24 or 583 00 92). **AIDS Hotline** (☎03 528 77 81), staffed M and Th 7:30-10pm. The weekly "In Jerusalem" insert in *The Jerusalem Post* lists many other support groups.

Services for the Disabled: Yad Sarah Organization, 124 Herzl Blvd. (☎644 44 25; fax 644 44 23; email info@yadsarah.org.il; www.yadsarah.org.il). Free loans of medical equipment. Offers wheelchair van for airport pick-ups (NIS150, order 2 weeks in advance) and rides anywhere within Jerusalem for fares comparable to those of taxis. Open Su-Th 9am-7pm, F 9am-12:30pm.

Pharmacy: Superpharm, 3 Ha-Histadrut (☎624 62 44 or 624 62 45; fax 624 75 75), between Ben-Yehuda and King George St. Open Su-Th 8:30am-11pm, F 8:30am-3pm, Sa sundown-11pm. **Alba Pharmacy,** 42 Jaffa St. (☎625 37 03). Open Su-Th 7am-7pm, F 7am-2pm. Another branch at 7 Ben-Yehuda St. (☎625 77 85). Open Su-Th 9am-7:30pm, F 9am-2pm. Two pharmacies are on rotating duty nightly and on Shabbat; check newspaper listings.

Hospital: see **Medical Emergency,** above.

Telephones: Solan Communications, 2 Luntz St. (☎625 89 08; fax 625 88 79), on the *midraḥov*, off Ben-Yehuda St. Telegram and international fax services (NIS13 first page, NIS8 each additional page), private booths for local and international calls (NIS3 per min. to most countries), and expensive cellular phone sales and rentals (US$2.89 per day, plus US$0.69 per min. for outgoing calls within Israel, US$0.39 per min. for incoming calls). Open Su-Th 8am-11pm, F 8am-5pm, Sa 5pm-midnight. An additional branch is inside Jaffa Gate. **Global GSM,** 22 King David St. (☎625 25 85 or 1 800 252 585), rents cellular phones at a more reasonable rate (US$1 per day, plus US$0.49 per min. for outgoing calls within Israel; incoming calls are free). Open Su-Th 9am-7pm, F 9am-1pm. **Bezeq 24hr. Information:** ☎144.

Internet Access: Cheaper in the Old City (see p. 88). The **Netcafe,** 9 Heleni Ha-Malka St. (☎624 63 27), uphill from Jaffa Rd. Private and friendly. NIS7 for 15min.; NIS25 per hr. Also offers sandwiches and light meals (kosher, dairy); "www.mmm.com" and "the gigabyte" NIS12-15. Open Su-Tu 11am-10pm, W-Th 11am-late, F 10am-3pm, and Sa 9pm-late. **Strudel Internet Cafe and Wine Bar,** 11 Moonbaz St. (☎623 21 01; fax 622 14 45), in the Russian Compound. Not too private. It doubles as a bar at night. NIS6 for 15min. Happy hour 7-9pm and midnight-12:30am (15min. computer time and a beer NIS13). Open M-F 10am-late, Sa 3pm-late.

Central Post Office: 23 Jaffa Rd. (☎629 06 47). **Poste Restante** for no fee. **Money exchange, Western Union, telegram,** and **fax** services available. Also sells phone cards. Open Su-Th 7am-7pm, F 7am-noon. For telegrams, dial 171 (24hr.). Branch post offices in most neighborhoods; look for a bright red awning.

ACCOMMODATIONS

OLD CITY

The Old City is what draws so many people to Jerusalem and often keeps them longer than they intended to stay; stop into any Old City hostel and you'll invariably find dozens of travelers who have canceled return flights or postponed further travel plans in order to spend more time within the enchanting walls.

Most of Jerusalem's cheapest hostels—from quiet sanctuaries to hang-from-the-rafters hangouts—are located in (or just outside) the Old City. Accommodations here are definitely more interesting and benefits include unbelievable rooftop views, proximity to major sights, and free wake-up calls from mosque *muezzins*.

Old City accommodations generally fall into two categories: quieter, cleaner establishments that sometimes have curfews, including Christian guest houses, and the sometimes less clean, more fun, and correspondingly less safe hostels, some of which feature bars or lax alcohol policies. Some of the latter operate without government permits—nevertheless, many patrons swear by them as the only way to meet cool fellow travelers and get to know the Old City. Use caution: even the most rambunctious of alleyways turns into a dark ghost town after nightfall.

Petty theft is a problem; use private lockers where available. Women traveling alone should be especially discriminating in choosing a hostel, as there have been reports of harassment in some hostels. Remember not to use the colorful shops as landmarks for finding your way back to your hostel because they all close by 8pm.

SAFETY WARNING. Be extremely **cautious** in the empty streets of the Old City after dark. Those staying in the Muslim quarter, **especially women,** should not walk alone and should make their tourist status pronounced. Only the busiest streets in the Old City are lit at night, so learn the way to your bed during the day. According to the Old City tourist office, the most commonly reported crime is **pickpocketing.** Many areas of the city, especially the Arab market, are very crowded, making pickpocketing easy. Carry your wallet in a front pocket or in the main compartment of your backpack, never in a back pocket of either pants or pack. When visiting mosques, you may be prohibited from carrying anything inside; avoid leaving valuables outside and hide them in your backpack if you have no other choice. (See **Safety and Security,** p. 41.)

MUSLIM QUARTER

El Hashimi Hostel and Hotel, 73 Suq Khan al-Zeit St. (☎628 44 10; fax 628 46 67; e-mailhashimi@alami.net;www.palestinehotels.com/cities/jerusalem/al-hashimi/index.html). Take the right fork from Damascus Gate. Squeaky clean bathrooms in each room. Single-sex dorms available. Fans in dorms; A/C in private rooms. Heat in winter. TV lounge. Internet access. Reception 6am-3am. Check-out 10:30am. Curfew 3am. Dorm beds NIS20; singles US$25-35; doubles US$30-45; triples US$50-70. 15% discount for stays longer than 2 nights (not applicable to dorm prices). Credit cards and traveler's checks accepted.

Al-Arab Hostel, Khan al-Zeit St. (☎628 35 37; email alarab@netvision.net.il). Take the right fork from Damascus Gate, before El Hashimi. A crowded party hostel with some of the cheapest beds in town and all the amenities: kitchen/cafe, *nargilah,* free tea and coffee, Internet service, laundry, satellite TV, and luggage storage. Reception 24hr. Roof bed NIS14; dorms NIS18; singles and doubles NIS60; triples NIS70.

Tabasco Hostel, 8 Akabat Tekreh St. (☎628 11 01; fax 628 34 61), just off Khan al-Zeit St.; take the right fork from Damascus Gate and look for the red Tabasco sign past El Hashimi. Huge, cheap hostel with rowdy international crowd. Bedouin-style "Tea" Room downstairs buzzes at all hours, especially happy hour (7-8 and 10-11pm; 2 beers NIS10). Hot showers 6am-10pm only. Lockers NIS2 per day; key deposit NIS20. Reception 24hr. Lock-out noon-2pm. Check-out 11am. Roof bed NIS15; dorms NIS20; private rooms NIS85, with bath NIS150.

Black Horse Hostel, 28 Aqabat Darwish St. (☎627 60 11; fax 628 60 39), near Lion's Gate, under a green awning. Laid back; not too loud but not lifeless. Amenities include a kitchen, bar, and Bedouin-tent-style sitting room. Check-out noon. Dorms NIS15; private rooms NIS80-100, mother-in-law owns the nicer rooms across the street.

ARMENIAN QUARTER

Lutheran Youth Hostel (☎628 21 20; fax 628 51 07), on St. Mark's Rd., the first alley off David St., on the right when coming from Jaffa Gate. Half hostel and half guest house. The large fountained garden and overhanging dining hall are reserved for private guests, but the hostel part has its own calm garden and enormous kitchen with free tea and coffee. Breakfast included for private rooms. Reception 6am-10:45pm. Check-in noon. Check-out 10am. Lockout for hostel guests 9am-noon. Curfew 10:30pm, flexible until midnight. Guests must be under 35 (also flexible, especially when business is slow). Large single-sex dorms NIS33; singles US$40-48; doubles US$72-80; prices fluctuate according to the value of the Deutschmark. No reservations for dorms. Credit cards accepted for guest house only.

Jaffa Gate Youth Hostel (☎627 64 02), in the Jaffa Gate area across from the Tower of David; a black and pink sign points down a short alley to the reception. TV lounge, patio, tiny common kitchen, and priceless rooftop view. Check-in until midnight. Check-out 10am. Curfew midnight. No smoking or alcohol. Small dorms NIS40; singles NIS60, with A/C and bath NIS80; doubles NIS100, with bath NIS160. Ask for a discount.

The Old City Youth Hostel (HI), 2 Ararat St. (☎628 86 11). Walk down David St. into the market and follow the signs: a right onto St. Mark's Rd. and a right again across from the Lutheran Hostel. Hauntingly spacious and nicer than most hostels, but also much more expensive. Breakfast included. Check-in 7-9am and 5-10pm. Check-out 9am. Lock-out 9am-5pm. Curfew midnight. Dorms NIS65; NIS5 discount for HI members. Private rooms (for 1-6 people) US$40 per room.

Citadel Youth Hostel, 20 St. Mark's Rd. (☎627 43 75; email citadelhostel@netscape.com), off David St., on the first alleyway to the right (when coming from Jaffa Gate), up the road from the Lutheran Hostel. Dark, somewhat musty private rooms with vaulted ceilings and a cavernous dorm room. Shared bathrooms. Several small lounge areas, satellite TV, and common kitchen. Check-out 10am. Flexible midnight curfew; just ask for the key and promise to come back quietly. Dorms NIS40, students NIS25; singles US$25-50; doubles US$35-60.

JEWISH QUARTER

Heritage House. Office: 90 Ḥabad St. (☎627 19 16). Men's hostel: 2 Or Ha-Ḥayim St. (☎627 22 24). Women's hostel: 7 Ha-Malakh St. (☎628 18 20). Free nightly classes (optional) at the men's hostel. Kosher dairy kitchen for guests. Lock-out 9am-5pm. Curfew midnight, 1am in the summer and on Shabbat. Dorm accommodations only; free except on Shabbat (NIS20).

Hotel Ha-Kotel, 18 Haye Olam Rd. (☎/fax 627 62 77; mobile 05 380 00 02; email hakotelh@zahav.net.il), near the Western Wall. A chain of beautifully furnished rooms (all with A/C, fridge, and microwave on request) organized in response to the shortage of accommodations in the Jewish Quarter. Ideal for families. Check in at Mama's Deli in Ḥurva Sq. Reservations required. Doubles weekdays US$80, Shabbat and holidays US$125; flexible, minimal rates for additional people.

CHRISTIAN QUARTER

Petra Hostel, 1 David St. (☎628 66 18), just inside Jaffa Gate, on the left before the entrance to the market. Built more than 175 years ago, this is the oldest accommodation in the Old City. Mark Twain and Herman Melville stayed here. Has fantastic rooftop views (some say the best in the city) and a vast, sunny lounge. Pool table, bar, Internet, laundry, and kitchen. Full breakfast NIS14. Luggage storage NIS1 per hr., or NIS5 per day. Check-out 10am. Roof mattresses NIS20, with sheets and blanket NIS25; rooftop tents (in winter only) NIS25; dorms NIS32, weekly rate (paid in advance) NIS28 per night; private rooms US$35-50. Reservations accepted only for morning arrivals.

Casa Nova Hospice (☎628 27 91 or 626 20 74; fax 626 43 70), on Casa Nova Rd. From Jaffa Gate, take the second left up Greek Patriarchate Rd.; from New Gate, turn left on Casa Nova and follow it as it curves to the right. Italian-speaking Christian pilgrim's heaven. Breakfast included. Half and full board available. Private baths. Reception 5am-11pm. US$22 per person; single supplement US$15. Reservations required.

Greek Catholic Hospice (☎627 19 68; fax 628 66 52). From Jaffa Gate take the second left onto Greek Patriarchate Rd. The elegant hospice is on the right, under a sign that reads "Patriarchat Grec-Catholique." The attached church had its moment of fame in March 2000 when visited by the pope; a plaque outside commemorates the occasion. Breakfast included. Half and full board available. Singles US$39; doubles US$58; triples US$72. Reservations recommended.

WEST JERUSALEM

Accommodations in West Jerusalem are generally roomier and safer than their Old City counterparts. They are correspondingly more expensive, and what they boast in amenities they lack in rustic charm. Hostels here are better for club-goers; most establishments have no curfew and some are located directly above the action. The 17% VAT can be avoided by paying in non-Israeli currency.

Privately-run small-scale bed-and-breakfasts are excellent alternatives to hostels. They are often more private and comfortable, and they provide some contact with an Israeli family. The **Home Accommodation Association** (☎645 21 98; www.bnb-jerusalem.co.il) is a group of independent apartment owners who offer rooms of all ranges. These all come with a telephone, TV, kitchenette bathroom, and usually air-conditioning. Prices range from US$25-70 per night, including breakfast (discounts for longer stays). No collective office can answer queries, so each B&B owner must be contacted individually. View the list of rooms (with pictures) on their website or request a list. A list is also available from the government tourist office in Safra Sq. (see **Tourist Information,** p. 132). **Good Morning Jerusalem** (☎623 34 59; email gmjer@netvision.net.il; www.accommodation.co.il) is an accommodations agency, which charges 20-30% commission to match room requests.

Zion Square Hostel, 42 Jaffa Rd. (☎624 41 14; fax 623 62 45; email jrpool@inter.net.il; www.zionsquarehostel.homestead.com/opening.html), in a fantastic location. A/C, laundry service, Internet (with a web camera), cable TV, 24hr. reception and security, lockers, and luggage storage. Some rooms have balconies overlooking Zion Sq. Breakfast included. Check-out 10am. Dorms NIS60; doubles NIS190.

Hotel Noga, 4 Bezalel St. (☎625 45 90, after 2pm ☎/fax 566 18 88; ask for Mr. or Mrs. Kristal). From the city center, walk down King George, turn right onto Be'eri, left onto Shmuel Ha-Nagid, and right onto Bezalel. Comfortable walk to Maḥane Yehuda or to the area of the Knesset and Israel Museum. Managers leave after 2pm and each floor has one full bath and kitchen. For longer stays, ask about the apartment down the block. Singles US$32; doubles US$40; triples US$50; small roof-top bungalow US$25 for one person, US$35 for two. 2-night min. stay. Reservations highly recommended.

Beit Gesher, 10 King David St. (☎624 10 15; fax 625 52 26), across from the Hilton Hotel. Clean and airy 39-room hostel in a beautiful, old building, frequented by youth groups in the summer but quieter the rest of the year. All rooms with private bath and A/C. No double beds. Breakfast US$7. Reception 24hr. Check-in after noon. Check-out 11am. Singles US$38; doubles US$54; add US$14 per person for 3rd and 4th people. Reservations highly recommended.

My Home in Jerusalem Hostel, 15 King George St. and 2 Ha-Histadrut St. (☎623 22 35; fax 623 22 36; email myhome@netvision.co.il; www.myhome.co.il), on the left, one block from Jaffa Rd.; a newer building with more rooms is around the corner. Take bus #8, 9, 31, or 32 from the central station. Decently clean rooms, cable TV lounge, and prime location. Shared bathrooms. The second building has more stairs, but nicer, carpeted rooms. Breakfast included. Reception and check-in 24hr. Check-out 10:30am. Dorms US$16 (more if you pay in NIS); doubles US$60. Prices vary by season.

Diana's House, 10 Hulda Ha-Neviah St. (☎628 31 31; fax 628 44 11; email dr-adiv@zahav.net.il). From Safra Sq., take Shivtei Yisrael past the municipality, turn right through the small park, continue down Natan Ha-Navi; Hulda is the next left. Israel's first gay B&B ("straight-friendly"). The architect proprietor named the house for his now-departed dog. Cable TV, VCR, jacuzzi with view of the Dome of the Rock, laundry and Internet available. Breakfast included. Singles US$45; doubles US$75. Studio apartments also available. Call ahead.

Beit Shmuel Guest House (HI), 6 Shamma St. (☎620 34 56; fax 620 34 67), off King David St. on the uphill (southern) side of the Hilton. Part of the Beit Shmuel Center for Progressive Judaism complex; accessible through Hebrew Union College. Take bus #18 and 21 from central bus station. Breezy central courtyard for sitting or eating. A/C; heat in winter. Limited number of wheelchair-accessible rooms. Breakfast included. Reception 7am-11pm. Check-in 3pm. Check-out 10am. Reservations required. 6-bed dorms (not always available) US$25, HI members US$20.50; singles US$65/$US42.50; doubles US$76/US$61. Low season prices drop US$8-10 for private rooms.

Beit Bernstein Hostel (HI), 1 Keren Ha-Yesod St. (☎625 82 86; fax 624 58 75). Small, somewhat dark and crowded hostel, across from the Supersol supermarket and within walking distance of both the Old City and the Israel Museum area. Frequented by groups in the summer. Breakfast included. Reception 7-9am and 3pm-midnight. Flexible midnight curfew. Reservations required. Doubles and triples NIS60 per person.

Davidka Hostel (HI), 67 Ha-Nevi'im St. (☎538 45 55; fax 538 87 90). Take bus #27, 35, 36, or 39 from central bus station. Mega-hostel with 250 beds in clean, though dull, A/C rooms. Watch out for the hordes of high schoolers. Breakfast included. Reception 24hr. Check-out 10am. Reservations recommended. Dorms US$22; singles US$43-50; doubles US$63. US$1.50 per person HI discount. MC, V.

Jerusalem Inn Guest House, 6 Ha-Histadrut St. (☎625 12 94; fax 625 12 97; email jerinn@netvision.net.il; www.jerusaleminn.co.il), off King George St., one block from Ben-Yehuda St. Take bus #14, 17, 31, or 32 from the central station to the first stop on King George. A technology-friendly 12-room hotel with keypad access and surveillance video. All rooms with fan, digital safe, cable TV, and heating in winter. Some rooms have private bath, A/C, and/or balconies. No visitors; front door locked at night. No smoking. Reception Su-Th 8am-midnight, F 8am-4pm, Sa 2-11pm. Check-out 11:30am; no check-out on Sa. Singles US$38; doubles US$56, with A/C and private bath US$84; triples with A/C and private bath US$112. Credit card required for reservation.

The King David Hotel, 23 King David St. (☎620 88 88; fax 620 88 82; email kingdavid@danhotels.com; www.danhotels.com). First opened in 1931, this majestic hotel has a long history and an impressive list of former guests. You cannot afford to stay here. You can, however, stroll around the gardens or order a drink while relaxing on the terrace overlooking the Old City. The rooms are impossibly comfortable and luxurious. If you *must* know, singles start at US$260; doubles US$280, before taxes.

LONGER STAYS

For a stay longer than two months, consider renting an apartment. During July and August, college students go on vacation and many rent out their flats. A single room in a shared apartment will cost at least US$250-400 per month. The best source of information is the classified section of the local weekly *Kol Ha-Ir*. *Kol Ha-Ir* also prints apartment request ads in Hebrew for free. The bulletin boards at Hebrew University and upstairs at the Israel Center on the corner of Strauss and Ha-Nevi'im St. may also be helpful (many postings are written in English). A more thorough but expensive option is the **She'al Service,** 19 King George St. (☎800 248 248; email malin@netvision.net.il; www.malin.co.il), which maintains voluminous English listings and will keep you posted by fax for a full month for NIS149 (one-time print-out of all listings NIS49). See their website for free listings access in Hebrew. (Open Su-Th 8am-7pm, F 8am-1pm.)

EAST JERUSALEM

East Jerusalem contains a beautiful and vibrant slice of Palestinian life and represents a stark contrast to the western parts of the city. However, it is also a hotbed of political tension. Feel out the situation before deciding to stay here. Remember that this area can be unsafe at night, though most travelers don't have problems. Visibly Jewish travelers (particularly men in *kippot*) should exercise caution.

Although not technically in the Old City, the hostels right outside Damascus Gate provide easy access to the Muslim Quarter and with equally easy access to the Russian Compound, they can be an excellent (and cheap) alternative to staying within the walls. Several hostels line the parking lot at the base of Ha-Nevi'im St., which intersects Suleiman St. across from Damascus Gate. Buses #1, 2, 23, 37, and 44 go to Damascus Gate from the city center.

Cairo Youth Hostel, 21 Nablus Rd. (☎627 72 16), on the left when coming from Damascus Gate; from the central bus station take bus #27. Perhaps not the most aesthetically pleasing hostel, but it wears its age well; the friendly, laid-back atmosphere will quickly overshadow the drabness of the walls. Comfortable TV sitting area, a view-lover's roof, and an immaculate kitchen. Heat in winter. Reception 24hr. Check-out 10am. Curfew 1am (flexible). Roof mattress NIS15; coed and single-sex dorm beds NIS20; private room for 1-4 people NIS90.

Faisal Hostel, 4 Ha-Nevi'im St. (☎628 75 02; email faisalsam@hotmail.com), in the parking lot opposite Damascus Gate, on the right. Crowded bunks, satellite TV lounge, cramped kitchen, and a computer with Internet access (NIS10 per hr.; a 5min. email check is free). Large but cozy bar on patio overlooking Ha-Nevi'im St, where *service* drivers can be heard yelling at almost all hours (don't expect a sound sleep if your room is on that side). Reception 24hr. Check-out 11am. Curfew 1am. Coed and single-sex dorm beds NIS20; private doubles and triples NIS80.

Palm Hostel, 6 Ha-Nevi'im St. (☎627 31 89), opposite Damascus Gate, just past the Faisal Hostel. Small but comfortable; has the same noise problem as Faisal. Upper common room for eating, smoking, and watching videos. Heat in winter. Reception 24hr. Check-out 10am. Curfew midnight. Dorms NIS25, students NIS20; private rooms NIS100-120, NIS80-100. Ask for discounts for longer stays.

St. George's Cathedral Pilgrim Guest House, 20 Nablus Rd. (☎628 33 02; fax 628 22 53; email sghostel@netvision.net.il), on the grounds of St. George's Cathedral on Nablus Rd., about 10min. past the Garden Tomb. Wonderful but expensive place to stay. Rooms have TV, bathroom, phone, fan, and sumptuous bedding. Guard 24hr. Cafe and sitting area in an airy and green courtyard. Breakfast included. Reception 8am-10pm. Check-out 10am. Reservations required. Singles US$62; doubles US$95; triples US$115. 10% service not included; discounts available in off-season.

YMCA Capitolina Hotel, 29 Nablus Rd. (☎628 68 88; fax 627 63 01), next door to the American consulate, in the magnificent YMCA building. Very comfortable rooms with full bath, many with balcony. Beautiful sitting rooms and restaurant on the top floor with epic views of the city. Breakfast included. Lunch and dinner US$10. Sports facilities downstairs, including an Olympic-sized pool, at a nominal charge. Reception 24hr. Reservations highly recommended. Singles US$60; doubles US$92, add a bed to make a triple at a small additional charge. 15% service not included.

St. Thomas's Home, 6 Chaldeen St. (☎628 26 57; fax 628 42 17), at the site of the Syrian Catholic Patriarchate. From Damascus Gate, walk up Nablus Rd. and take the alleyway to the left just before the Cairo Hostel. Clean but old rooms provide quiet comfort for globe-trotting pilgrims. All rooms with private bath. Heated in winter. Breakfast included. Reception 9am-9:30pm. Check-out 11am. Curfew 9:30pm. Reservations required. Singles US$31; doubles US$51; triples US$76.50.

FOOD

OLD CITY

While several tourist-priced places entice the mobs around Jaffa Gate, the cheaper Middle Eastern restaurants crowd in the narrow alleyways of the Old City. In the Muslim Quarter, the chicken restaurants on **Suq Khan al-Zeit,** inside Damascus Gate, are popular with locals (look for the huge rotisseries and follow the smell). Interchangeable sit-down restaurants line al-Wad Rd. and Bab al-Silsilah St. At Damascus Gate falafel is NIS5; at Jaffa Gate the same meal goes for NIS10. Crates of fresh fruit, veggies, and herbs abound both inside and outside Damascus Gate. Street vendors sell fresh, soft sesame *ka'ak* throughout the *souq;* ask for *za'tar* to go with it and dip away (NIS2-3). The market also drips with honey-drenched Arab pastries for NIS12-24 per kilo. **Ja'far Sweets,** 42 Suq Khan al-Zeit St. (☎628 35 82), offers the hottest, gookiest, most authentic pastries in the market, bar none. Take out or eat in with the locals. Open daily 8am-8pm. Small **supermarkets** can be found throughout the Old City, particularly in and near the Jewish Quarter.

MUSLIM QUARTER

The Green Door Pizza Bakery (☎627 62 71), off al-Wad St. Coming in Damascus Gate, make a sharp left when the road forks. Abu Ali has been serving his renowned Arabic-style pizza for over two decades. Filling, one-person pizzas (NIS6) are topped with cheese, egg, meat, and as many vegetables as he has. He'll also do individual orders, including vegetarian. Eat in and you get free tea and coffee. Open daily 6am-11pm.

Damascus Gate Cafe (☎627 42 82), on the immediate left, right inside Damascus Gate; look for the "The Gate Cafe" sign. The large shaded terrace grants welcome respite from the daily racket of the gate. Sit and "gate-watch" while eating *shawarma* (NIS15) or a full breakfast (NIS28). Open daily 7:30am-8pm or later.

Jerusalem Star Restaurant, 32 al-Wad Rd. (☎628 71 75). Cool interior with wood-painted walls and deep carpeting. One of the best deals in town. Traditional *musakhan* NIS30; hummus plate NIS5. Open daily 8am-10pm.

ARMENIAN QUARTER

Michael's Bar, 3 St. Mark's St. (☎052 949 560), off David St., uphill from the Lutheran Hostel. Possibly the best falafel in Jerusalem, but the real reason to come is for Michael, one of the Old City's most charming residents. This is not an eat-on-the-run type of place; prepare to kick back over a beer or glass of wine for an hour or more. Michael is also an excellent source for shopping and travel advice; consult with him to find out what a reasonable price is before you start haggling with shop owners. Falafel NIS8; shish kebab or *shawarma* NIS12. Open daily 10am-10pm.

The Loaves and Fishes Coffee Shop (☎626 40 90), inside Jaffa Gate, across from the Tower of David, hidden among more gaudy places. The awning simply says "The Coffee Shop." Ivy stenciling, Jerusalem-tiled tables, A/C, and a no-smoking rule make this one of the most pristine restaurants in the Old City. They modestly refer to their meat-and-cheese lasagna (NIS38) as the best in Israel. Sandwiches NIS15-16; unlimited salad bar NIS30. Many vegetarian options. Open Tu-Su 11am-6:30pm.

The Armenian Tavern, 79 Armenian Orthodox Patriarchate Rd. (☎627 38 54). Take a right inside Jaffa Gate and follow traffic on the too-narrow street. Tavern is on the left and down the steps. Blissfully cool and warmly appointed, with tile-studded walls and indoor fountain. Specialties include *khaghoghi derev* (minced meat in grape leaves; NIS35) and pepper salads (NIS7). Open Tu-Su 11am-11pm. Credit cards accepted.

JEWISH QUARTER

Keshet, 2 Tiferet Yisrael St. (☎628 75 15), in Ḥurva Sq. Delicious dairy food includes Jewish specialties like potato latkes with sour cream and applesauce, served with a fresh salad and house dressing (NIS40). When it's not oppressively hot, eat outside and watch the tour groups. Open Su-Th 9am-7pm, in winter until 6pm; F 9am-sundown.

Quarter Cafe (☎628 77 70), in the Jewish Quarter above the Burnt House; look for the sign on the way to the Western Wall. The hidden steps behind the cashier's desk lead to roof tables with an epic view of the Temple Mount. A little pricey for self-serve food, but some people will do anything for a good view. Dairy main dish with 2 side dishes NIS38-50, full breakfast NIS42. 10% *Let's Go* discount. Open Su-Th 9am-7pm, F 9am-3:30pm; in winter Su-Th 9am-6pm, F 9am to sundown.

The Culinarium (☎626 41 55; fax 628 42 38), in the Jewish Quarter Cardo. In a delightfully cartoonish (and cheesy) Roman manner, waiters in armor wrap patrons in togas, adorn them with plastic laurel wreaths, and bring out plate after plate of chicken, fish, salad, pita, and olive oil. Lunch US$17. Dinner US$29 (includes live music and juggling show). Lunch Su-F noon-4pm; dinner 6:30pm-midnight. By reservation only. Credit cards accepted.

Tony's (☎627 77 61). Facing away from the Western Wall plaza, take the archway to the right below the tall staircase; the stylish dairy restaurant is on your left. This one-time cave has been artfully transformed into an attractive and elegant cove. Sit downstairs to get the most of the coziness. Scrumptious Galilee Salad NIS44; soup du jour NIS20. Open Su-Th 8:30am-10pm, F 8:30am-1pm.

Tzaddik's Deli (☎627 21 48), on Tiferet Yisrael St., across from the Burnt House. One of the only real New York style delis in Israel, although portions are usually much more generous in the Bronx. Hot corned beef sandwich NIS29; daily specials NIS20-30. Open Su-Th 9:30am-9:30pm, F until 1hr. before Shabbat, Sa from 1hr. after Shabbat.

CHRISTIAN QUARTER

Abu Shanab Pizza and Bar, 35 Latin Patriarchate Rd. (☎626 07 52), the first left from Jaffa Gate. An old favorite of natives and tourists alike. Candlelight gleams off the stone walls and intimate tables. Mini individual pizzas NIS13-18; Oriental salads NIS7-10; assortment of cocktails NIS20. Happy hour every night 6-7pm, all drinks 2-for-1. Live jazz occasionally. Open M-Sa 10am-11pm.

Papa Andrea's, 64 Aftemeos St. (☎628 44 33), near the Church of the Holy Sepulchre. From Jaffa Gate, walk straight ahead into the market and take the 2nd left onto Aftemeos St. Third floor rooftop location is a good place to get away from the hubbub of the market. Pleasant, clean, and sunny. Delicious Jerusalem plate appetizer makes a filling vegetarian meal (NIS35); carnivores should try the lamb *shishlik* (NIS50). 10% *Let's Go* discount. Open daily 8am-midnight.

Nafoura, 18 Latin Patriarchate St. (☎626 00 34; fax 626 00 62), first left inside Jaffa Gate, 2 blocks in. Classical music, brand-new gleaming crystal chandeliers, and burbling tiled fountains in the back terrace make this the most elegant and simply beautiful restaurant in the Old City. One of the few places in Jerusalem to get a pork cutlet (NIS40). 10% *Let's Go* discount. Open daily 12:30-11pm.

WEST JERUSALEM

West Jerusalem's restaurant scene reflects the international makeup of its growing population. Dining here spans a full spectrum of price ranges, from fried falafel to fancy French. Restaurants with outdoor tables line the Salomon, Rivlin, and Ben-Yehuda St. *midraḥovot*, all within a couple square blocks in the city-center. Look for inexpensive "business lunch" specials at many city-center restaurants. Many establishments straddle the boundaries between restaurant, bar, and cafe, so check all listings to find the right place, or go to the Jerusalem specific website, www.go-out.com, which is jam-packed with most listings in town.

For the cheapest of the fresh and the freshest of the cheap, head for the raucous open-air **Maḥaneh Yehuda** market between Jaffa Rd. and Agrippas St., west of the city center. Elbow past bag-laden fellow shoppers to the fruit and vegetable stands, pita bakeries, and sumptuous displays of pastries that line the alleys. There's a small grocery store *(makolet)* with rock-bottom prices at almost every corner. Ten pitas go for NIS3 or less; 1kg grapefruit, tomatoes, or zucchini goes for the same price. The stands along Etz Ha-Ḥayim St. sell the best *ḥalva* (a dessert like sesame marzipan) at NIS14-16 per kg. The best hours to visit the *shuk* are at closing time (Su-Th 7-8pm, F 1-2hr. before sundown), when merchants lower their prices shekel by shekel to sell off the day's goods. Friday morning prices are the highest, but they plummet in the afternoon, when thousands scramble through the alleys in a frantic effort to stock up for Shabbat. The worst market day is Sunday, when things are still slow after the weekend.

Supermarkets include **Supersol,** on the corner of Agron and King George St. (☎625 06 57. Open Su-M 7am-midnight, Tu-Th 24hr., F until 3pm, Sa sundown-midnight), and **Co-Op** supermarket, in the basement of the Ha-Mashbir department store at the intersection of King George and Ben-Yehuda St. (☎625 78 30. Open Su-Th 8am-7:30pm and F 8am-2:30pm.) The small **Drugstore 2000,** 21 Shammai St. (☎624 74 40), at the corner of Luntz St. and the *midraḥov*, is not a drugstore, but Jerusalem's only 24hr. supermarket.

Spaghettim, 8 Rabbi Akiva St. (☎623 55 47; fax 625 70 11), off Hillel St. Bear left at the sign, through the gates of an Italian-style villa. Snappy and elegant restaurant serves spaghetti prepared in over 75 different methods, from "gorgonzola spinachi" (NIS38) to "vanilla and brandy" (NIS25). Beautifully lit interior and refreshing outdoor seating. Open daily noon-midnight.

The Yemenite Step, 10 Yoel Salomon St. (☎624 04 77). Grand stone building with high ceilings and outdoor seating. Try the heavenly *malaweh,* their specialty, which resembles a large, flat, flaky croissant (with honey NIS18; with meat or veggie fillings NIS38 and up). Open Su-Th noon-12:30am, F noon-4pm, Sa after sundown-1am.

Misadonet, 12 Yoel Salomon St. (☎624 83 96), when coming from Zion Sq., turn right into the marked alleyway and right again past Orcha Camping. Authentic Kurdish kitchen; serene atmosphere with traditional decor. Traditional specialties include *kubeh* (made from semolina and stuffed with minced meat or vegetables) and *mujadara* (rice and lentils doesn't begin to describe it). Many vegetarian options. Soups NIS18-22; entrees NIS24-58. Open Su-Th noon-11pm, F noon-sundown, Sa sundown-11:30pm.

Taco Taco, 35 Jaffa Rd. (☎625 50 70), marked by a bright green sign between Yoel Salomon St. and Naḥalat Shiva. Affordable Mexican bar with fast service and fresh ingredients made to order 'round the clock. Beef or chicken taco with cheese NIS12; quesadilla NIS18. Open Su-W 11:30am-2am, Th-Sa 24hr. Happy hour daily 7-8pm.

Au Sahara, 17 Jaffa Rd. (☎625 42 39), opposite the Municipality, a few steps away from the rowdy downtown restaurant scene. This is probably the closest to a home-cooked meal in Jerusalem's restaurants. The Moroccan kitchen has maintained North African decorations and couscous-based recipes. Eggplant with minced meat NIS20; veal with nuts and prunes NIS40. Open Su-Th 12:30-3pm and 6:30-11pm.

Amigos, 19 Yoel Salomon St. (☎623 41 77). Delicious Mexican place is a welcome change from the hordes of generic Italian joints around it. The brightly colored walls and music make for a lively atmosphere. Order any steaming fajita plate (steak and chicken NIS72) and get a homemade margarita free. Daily lunch special includes main dish and salad (NIS35). Open Su-Th noon-1am, F noon-sunset, Sa after sunset-1am.

Korea House, 7 Naḥalat Shiva St. (☎625 47 56), follow the signs into the alley off Yoel Salomon. Run by a friendly Korean family. One of the few places in Israel to get roast pork (NIS55). Daily lunch special: NIS30 for soup, side dish, main dish, and dessert. For the communally oriented, full 4-person share-a-meal NIS200. Numerous vegetarian options. Open daily noon-midnight.

Stanley's, 3 Horkanos St. (☎625 94 59; fax 623 52 59), just off Heleni Ha-Malka, between Jaffa Rd. and the Russian Compound. A hotspot for international dignitaries, Israeli celebs, and all-round bigwigs who enjoy the French-South African cuisine (dishes range from *medallions de foie gras* in port wine sauce to *boerwors* and ostrich fillet). Dinners are expensive, but the business lunch at noon is an unbelievable deal: the same food, with soup or salad, costs NIS24-35. Open daily noon-midnight. Reservations recommended for dinner.

Gizmongolia, 9 Heleni Ha-Malka St. (☎624 04 90), off Jaffa Rd., next door to the Netcafe right before the Russian Compound. Unique among Jerusalem restaurants: all you can eat NIS80. Open buffet features 12 kinds of raw beef, chicken, and fish, among various sauces and veggies. Step 1: fill your plate to overflowing. Step 2: hand it to the chef, who cooks it up as you like. Step 3: Repeat. There's also an à la carte menu with entrees around NIS50. Open Su-Th 12:30-11:30pm, Sa sunset-11:30pm.

VEGETARIAN/DAIRY

Alumah, 19 Agrippas St. (☎625 50 14), just between King George St. and Maḥaneh Yehuda. The one-time restaurant has turned into a factory, but still maintains a storefront and tables for the discriminating eater. The ultimate in health food: completely natural *pareve* (non-dairy) meals made using whole grains milled on location, homemade *tempeh*, purified water, rice milk, and olive oil. No margarine, sugar, yeast, aluminum, or microwaves used. Meals are served with rice, chunky veggies, and two slices of crusty, thick sourdough bread. Open Su-Th 7am-7pm, F 7am-2pm.

Nevatim, 10 Ben-Yehuda St. (☎625 20 07), under a large but subtle wooden sign. Unquestionably the crunchiest place on the *midraḥov;* also one of the most affordable. Impressive assortment of soups (from *miso* to *borscht;* small bowl NIS15), plus veggie burgers (NIS17), grilled tofu (NIS17), and delicious, unlimited homemade bread. Open Su-Th 10am-10pm, F 10am-before sundown.

JERUSALEM

Village Green, 33 Jaffa St. (☎625 30 65), between Rivlin St. and Naḥalat Shiva. Even carnivores will marvel over the salad bar here, which is priced according to weight (min. NIS13), while others satisfy their appetites with blintzes (NIS18), vegan burgers (NIS18), and other healthy a la carte options. Open Su-Th 9am-10pm, F 9am-3pm. More romantic location on 1 Bezalel St. (☎625 14 64), off King George in the city center, with similar menu and hours.

Cafe Chagall, 5 Ben-Yehuda St. (☎623 33 31), on the corner of Luntz St. A veritable fixture of the *midraḥov*. High quality, reasonably priced dairy restaurant, with decor inspired by the famed Jewish artist. The 12 types of fresh salad (NIS34-41), each more than a full meal, are the best deal here, but be sure to save some room—just reading the selection of desserts (NIS20 each) is enough to provoke drooling. Open Su-Th 7am-midnight, F 7am-sundown, Sa after sundown-2am.

The Pie Shop, 9 Yoel Salomon St. (☎054 832 933). Turn left into the alleyway when coming from Zion Sq. Specializes in all manner of crusty comestibles. Six kinds of "vegetable pie" (a.k.a quiche; with salad and a drink NIS30) and 9 kinds of deliciously sweet fruit pies (NIS18; a la mode NIS23). Strawberry, the hands-down favorite, is rarely available; ask about the seasonal fruit special. Open Su-Th 2pm-2am, F 10am-3pm, Sa sundown-2am; in winter Su-Th 10am-2am, F 10am-2pm, Sa sundown-2am.

CHEAP QUICKIES

There is nothing like the quest for cheap falafel to unite tourists and natives. Creating the ultimate falafel or *shawarma* is an art all its own, and dozens of dens throughout Jerusalem are busily engaged in the pursuit of greatness. *Me'orav*, a mix of inner parts grilled with onions and packed in pita pockets, is a specialty of the stands on Agrippas St., behind Maḥaneh Yehuda. International franchises like McDonald's and Kentucky Fried Chicken, found mostly in the Zion Sq. area, are often more expensive than the traditional Middle Eastern fast food

Melekh Ha-Falafel V'ha-Shawarma (King of Falafel and Shawarma, ☎636 53 72), on the corner of King George and Agrippas St. Acclaimed parlor dominates the midtown scene; the tiny store is always packed, no matter what hour. Savory falafel NIS8; *shawarma* NIS12. Open Su-Th 8:30am-11pm, F 8:30am-3pm.

Pinati, 13 King George St. (☎625 45 40), on the corner of Ha-Histadrut St. Specializes in old-school Middle Eastern food. Has an excellent reputation and strong following with the locals. During lunch it's full of middle-aged workers on their break; rarely a tourist in sight. Hummus and *fuul* platter (NIS14) is a long-time favorite, as are the rice and *fasulyeh* beans (NIS10). Open Su-Th 8am-8pm, F 8am-3pm.

Pampa Grill, 3 Rivlin St. (☎623 14 55). High quality South American grill that will delight any carnivore. The small take-out section offers the best deals; huge chicken or beef baguette and unlimited fried onions NIS17. Indoor and outdoor seating next door features a more extensive menu; lunch special daily noon-5pm, NIS30. Open Su-Th noon-midnight, F noon-sunset, Sa after sunset-midnight.

JERUSALEM, CITY OF GOLDEN ARCHES The opening of a large McDonalds just off the *midraḥov* on Hillel St. a few years ago was met with angry protest by religious Jews, who were infuriated by the burger tycoon's disregard of *kashrut*, religious laws that determine what observant Jews eat, which prohibits mixing meat and dairy products (see **Food and Drink,** p. 30). The menu items aren't the only controversial issue—while most other establishments have agreed to close for Shabbat, McDonalds remains open seven days a week, employing Jewish youth. Although the meat that they use is kosher, they continue to serve cheeseburgers, which does not make Orthodox Jews McPleased.

Shalom Falafel, 36 Bezalel St. (☎623 14 36), on the right a few blocks from the city center; look for the crowd huddled outside. Passing motorists often park on the street, risking tickets for this outstanding, non-greasy falafel. Falafel NIS8; *esh tanoor* (falafel in lafa bread) NIS9. Open Su-Th 9am-9pm.

Gagou de Paris Bakery, 14 King George St. (☎625 03 43), the best place in the city center for steaming morning goodies or lunchtime snacks, including a dozen kinds of bread. Small tuna sandwich NIS10. Open Su-Th 7am-8:30pm, F 7am-3pm.

SWEET QUICKIES

Babbette's Party, 16 Shammai St. (☎814 11 82), near the corner of Yoel Salomon. A happy addition to the sweet-tooth scene. Israelis flock just to get a whiff of Babbette's 14 amazing Belgian waffle varieties (butter and cream NIS14; Grand Marnier NIS17). Also hands-down the best hot chocolate in Israel, some would say in the world (NIS8). Open Su-Th 4pm-2:30am, F 11am-sunset, Sa after sundown-2:30am.

Magic Fruit Juice, at the corner of Ben-Yehuda and King George St. Fresh-squeezed juice stands are scattered on and near the *midraḥov,* but this one is generally regarded as the best of the lot. Choose among mango, fig, carrot, peach, watermelon, and the rest of the juice rainbow, or take a chance on the daily cocktail (small NIS4; large NIS10). Open Su-Th 8am-10pm, F 8am-sunset.

Marzipan Bakery, 44 Agrippas St. (☎623 26 18), at one end of the Maḥaneh Yehuda market, sells *ruggelaḥ* to die for—eat a kilogram (NIS20) and you just might. Open Su-Th 7am-7pm, F 7am-mid-afternoon.

Mr. Juice, 37 Jaffa Rd. (☎622 10 66), next to Taco Taco. Another strong contender in the blender wars, specializing in exotic and refreshing four-fruit combos whipped up on the spot (large NIS10; 1L NIS20). Open Su-Th 8am-midnight, F 8am-4pm.

Katzefet (☎625 37 22), on the *midraḥov* at the corner of Ben-Yehuda and Luntz St., under the large sign proclaiming "Special Ice Cream." Excellent ice cream (1 scoop NIS6), although the specialty is frozen yogurt, blended on the spot with your choice of fresh fruits, nuts, or chocolates (small with 3 flavors NIS8). Open Su-Th 9am-2am, F 9am-sunset, Sa after sunset-2am.

EAST JERUSALEM

East Jerusalem is crawling with vendors selling falafel, spicy kebab, *ka'ak,* and ears of corn, all for less than NIS5. Follow the smoke, smells, and solicitations to the corner of Suleiman and Nablus. Boxes along Suleiman St. and in the *souq* by Damascus Gate overflow with some of the cheapest produce in the city.

Kan Zaman (☎628 32 82; www.jrshotel.com), on the patio of the Jerusalem Hotel, just behind the bus station on Nablus Rd. Glass-enclosed garden restaurant with delicate tables shaded by vines. Sandwiches NIS30-35; meat and fish meals NIS40-60. Go Sa after 8pm for their highly regarded Lebanese buffet (NIS70) with live classical Arabic music. Open daily 11am-11pm.

Omayyah Restaurant, 21 Suleiman St. (☎628 61 02), across the street and to the right from Damascus Gate. Authentic Palestinian kitchen dishes up standard *shawarma* and shish kebab, but also some less commercial specialties like the "upside down" rice patty (a.k.a. *maqlubeh;* NIS22). Soft drinks NIS3. Open daily 9am-midnight.

American Colony Hotel Restaurant (☎627 97 77; www.theamericancolony.com), in the courtyard of the American Colony Hotel, a few blocks past the US Consulate on Nablus Rd. At night, a cab from the city center (NIS11) is a must; the hotel is several long blocks into East Jerusalem. The fountained courtyard of this historic and picturesque luxury hotel is the city's most romantic and idyllic refuge. Spectacular food, priced for special nights only, but worth it. Starter buffet US$12; entrees US$13-30. Open 6:30-10:30am, noon-3pm, and 7-9:45pm. Reservations recommended.

Al-Quds Restaurant, 23 Suleiman St. (☎627 39 63). Facing away from Damascus Gate, cross the street and turn right; keep walking to reach the unmistakable and popular eatery. Dozens of whole chickens roast on the storefront rotisserie. Take-away half a chicken for NIS25. Open daily 7am-midnight.

CAFES

Tmol Shilshom, 5 Yoel Salomon St. (☎623 27 58; www.tmol-shilshom.co.il). Enter from Naḥalat Shiva St. This bookstore-cafe, named after a Shai Agnon book, is frequented by writers and poets such as Yehuda Amiḥai; he and other local greats give occasional readings here (sometimes in English; call in advance or check the web page for dates), while aspiring writers scrawl over coffee and tea (NIS8-14). Renowned all-you-can-eat breakfast buffet every Friday morning (NIS39.50). Internet NIS7 for 15min. Gay-friendly. Open Su-Th 8am-2am, F 8am-before sunset, Sa after sundown-2am.

Noctorno, 7 Bezalel St. (☎625 85 10), off King George St. away from the *midraḥov*, at the corner of Ha-Gidem St. Small and cozy; a quiet but funky alternative to the crowded cafes just two blocks away. Espresso NIS5; salads NIS25; sandwiches NIS20. Open Su-Th 7am-midnight. F 7am-4pm, Sa after sundown-12:30am.

Second Cup, 4 Shammai St. (☎623 45 33), on the *midraḥov*, at the corner of Ben Hillel St. Hugely popular with non-Israelis and others who appreciate professionally roasted coffee (they've begun to sell it by the kg). Large cafe is great for quick morning croissant and coffee (NIS10) or a cup of hot apple cider (NIS8). Students often curl up in the comfy armchairs and library-like alcoves before exams. Open Su-Th 6am-1am, F 6am-sunset, Sa after sundown-1am.

Cafe Ta'amon, 27 King George St. (☎625 49 77), across the street from the old Knesset. A legendary hole-in-the-wall where older Israeli writers and intellectuals mingle with vodka lovers. Owner Mordekhai Kop's IOU book is a veritable *Who's Who in Israel*. Coffee, tea, soups (NIS15), and pastries (NIS7). Friday is *cholent* day, when regulars come for the traditional Jewish meat and potato stew (NIS20). Open Su-Th 6am-11pm, F 6am-4pm, Sa (in winter only) after sundown-1am.

Riff-Raff, 19 Ben Hillel St. (☎625 02 91), on the corner next to McDonald's. Sandwich and espresso bar draws a young, buzzing crowd at any hour; it's a good place to go if you're still awake when the clubs shut down. Gay-friendly. Espresso NIS6; huge selection of sandwiches NIS20-30; generous breakfast NIS28. Open 24hr.

Cafe Atara, 15 Ben-Yehuda St. (☎625 01 41). Atara was the first eatery on the street when it opened in 1938 (not in its current location). Its rich history has earned it a steady following. Selection of toasted sandwiches NIS28; salads NIS31-41; dessert pies NIS21. Open Su-Th 7:30am-midnight, F 7am-3pm, Sa after sundown-midnight.

SIGHTS

OLD CITY

There's something about this tiny plot of land that made it holy, not only for Jews, Christians, and Muslims, but to dozens of ancient religious groups as well. Excavations under the Old City have uncovered over 20 distinct layers of civilization. Before beginning a tour, it's helpful to get an idea of what the city looked like in ages past. The **Holyland Hotel** (☎643 77 77) in Bayit va-Gan in West Jerusalem has an excellent, knee-high model of Jerusalem circa 66 CE, toward the end of the Second Temple Period. (Bus #21 from downtown. Open daily 8am-10pm. NIS44, students with ISIC NIS25.) For a cheaper and more local introduction, start with the informative films at the Tower of David and at the Center for Jerusalem in the First Temple Period.

WALKING TOURS OF THE OLD CITY

The Old City is only about one square kilometer; a walking tour is a great way to get to know it. The following two suggested routes cover most of the Old City and nearby sites, with almost no overlap. If you only have a few days in Jerusalem, take Tour 1 on the first day, Tour 2 on the second, then spend some time looking at the individual sights in West Jerusalem. If you have more time, break up Tour 2 into two days, as suggested below. All **bolded** locations have separate listings later in the text; look under the section indicated at the beginning of the paragraph. Both routes are free, but many optional sights along the way require entrance fees; those are marked with a ($). See individual sight listings for the exact prices. For guided tours, see **Tours,** p. 87. For a **wheelchair-accessible** tour through the Old City, start in the parking lot in the Jewish Quarter (which can be reached through Zion Gate or Jaffa Gate) and follow the arrows with the wheelchair icon.

TOUR 1: HIGHLIGHTS

Starting and ending point: Jaffa Gate. Approximate walking time (without side trip to Mount Zion): 1½-2hr. Including all sights: 3-4hr. Best time to go: M-Th any time, but many of the sights along the way (including the Ramparts walk at the end) close at 4:30 or 5pm. Entrance fees (without side trip): NIS138, students NIS79. Modest dress recommended.

Inside Jaffa Gate, turn to the right and enter the **Tower of David** ($) for an introductory film about Jerusalem. Climb up to the Phasel Tower for an amazing view of the Old City. Leaving the Tower of David, continue to your right, following Armenian Patriarchate Rd. into the **Armenian Quarter** (see p. 92). Under the short tunnel, turn to your right and peek into the **Armenian Art Center** for shopping or browsing. To your left is the **St. James Cathedral.** Continue down the road away from Jaffa Gate, stopping next at the **Armenian Museum** ($) on your left. From there, the road curves to the left; **Zion Gate** will appear on your right.

Side trip: Mount Zion (see p. 121). *Approximate walking time: 15-20min. Including all sights: 1hr.* Exit through Zion Gate, and follow the path as it veers slightly to the right (rather than going down into the parking lot). Follow the signs for the **Dormition Abbey;** go into the basilica and down to the beautiful crypt. Leaving the abbey, backtrack a few steps, then turn right and come next to the **Cenacle** (site of the Last Supper) and **Tomb of David,** both entered through the door to the Diaspora Yeshiva, on your left. Exit through the back entrance of the *yeshiva,* which will put you almost right across the street from the small, but powerful, **Chamber of the Holocaust** ($). Next, head downhill and across the main road to the Christian Cemetery and **Schindler's Grave.** Head back up the main road and back through Zion Gate to continue with the tour. **End of side trip.**

Back inside the Old City walls, the road curves to the left and heads into the **Jewish Quarter** (see p. 93). Walk through the parking lot on your right to the far corner, where you will find the **Four Sephardic Synagogues** ($). Mishmerot Ha-Kehuna Rd. continues past the complex and leads into **Ḥurva Square.** The entrance to the **Herodian Quarter and Wohl Archaeological Museum** ($, get the combo ticket) is on your right; the exit is further down, so you'll have to walk back uphill to return to Ḥurva Sq. At the northeastern corner of the square, turn right on Tiferet Yisrael St. (at the Mizrahi Bank). The **Burnt House** ($) will be tucked away on your left just before the entrance to the **Quarter Café.** Continue past Bonker's Bagels and Tzaddik's Deli; at the next street (Misgav Ladach), a detour to the left will bring you to the **Treasures of the Temple Museum** ($), while a detour to the right leads to the **Temple Model Museum** ($). Returning from either detour, go down the steps and through the security point to enter Tzaḥal Sq., the plaza in front of the **Western Wall** (women who don't have their shoulders covered will be given a shawl). If you've been holding it until now, there are **public restrooms** by the men's side of the wall (to the left when facing the wall). Leave the plaza through the tunnel on the northwestern side (near the restrooms). Past the security point, you will be entering the busy **Muslim Quarter** (see p. 97) on al-Wad Rd. You can take al-Wad straight through to Damascus Gate, getting a taste of the busy *souq* along the way. Exit through Damascus Gate. A detour up the stairs to the right and along the outside of the wall leads to **Zedekiah's Cave** ($). If you decide to go here, buy the combo ticket; you'll use more of it in a few minutes and the rest of it if you go to **Hezekiah's Tunnel** and the **Ophel**

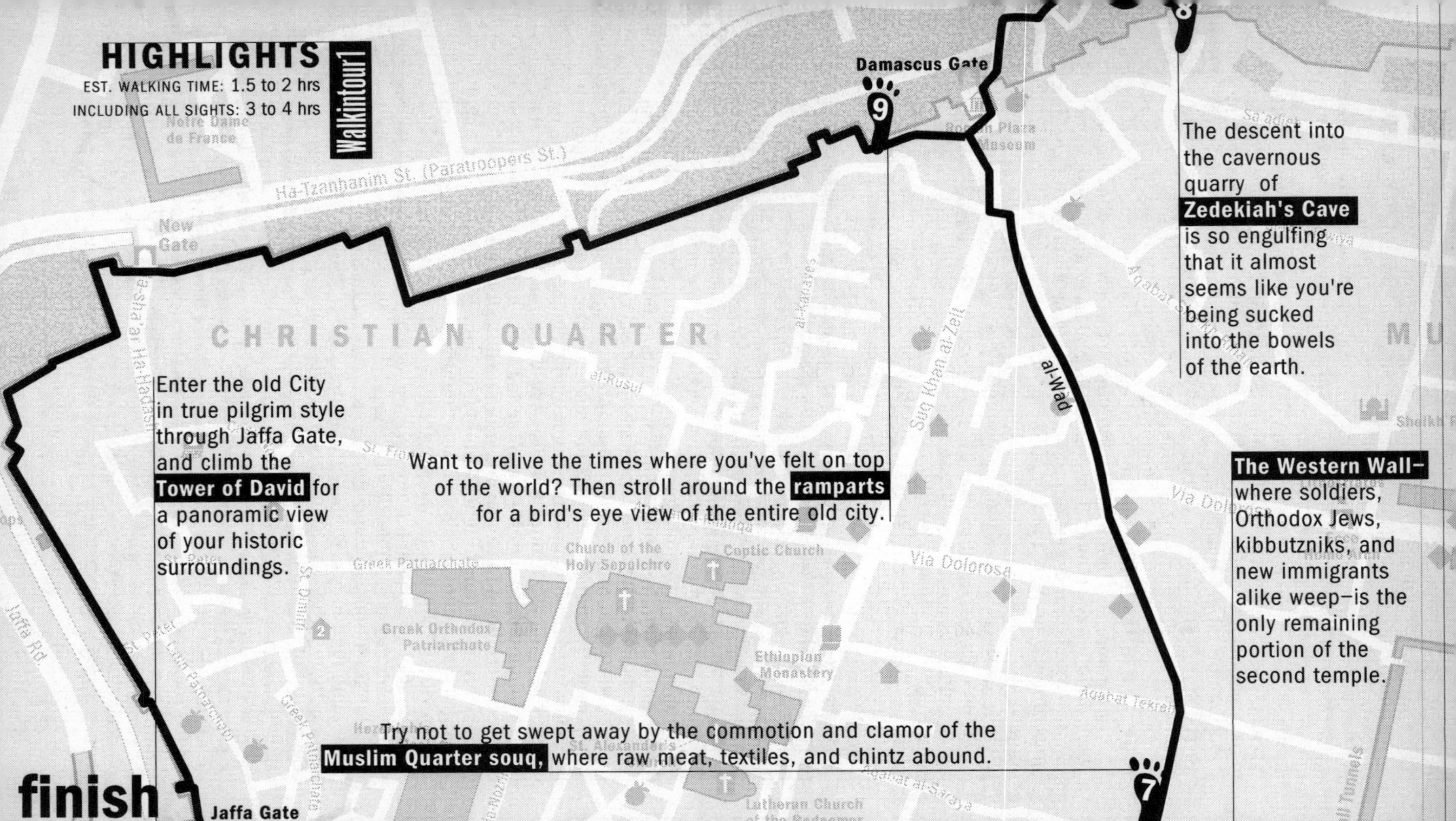
HIGHLIGHTS
EST. WALKING TIME: 1.5 to 2 hrs
INCLUDING ALL SIGHTS: 3 to 4 hrs
Walkintour1
Notre Dame de France
Ha-Tzanhanim St. (Paratroopers St.)
New Gate
Damascus Gate
9
Roman Plaza Museum
8
CHRISTIAN QUARTER
Enter the old City in true pilgrim style through Jaffa Gate, and climb the Tower of David for a panoramic view of your historic surroundings.
Want to relive the times where you've felt on top of the world? Then stroll around the ramparts for a bird's eye view of the entire old city.
The descent into the cavernous quarry of Zedekiah's Cave is so engulfing that it almost seems like you're being sucked into the bowels of the earth.
The Western Wall—where soldiers, Orthodox Jews, kibbutzniks, and new immigrants alike weep—is the only remaining portion of the second temple.
Try not to get swept away by the commotion and clamor of the Muslim Quarter souq, where raw meat, textiles, and chintz abound.
al-Khanqa
al-Rusul
Suq Khan al-Zeit
al-Wad
Via Dolorosa
Church of the Holy Sepulchre
Coptic Church
Greek Patriarchate
Greek Orthodox Patriarchate
Ethiopian Monastery
St. Alexander's
Lutheran Church of the Redeemer
Aqabat al-Saraya
Aqabat Tekreh
Jaffa Rd.
St. Peter
Latin Patriarchate
St. Dimitri
Jaffa Gate
7
finish

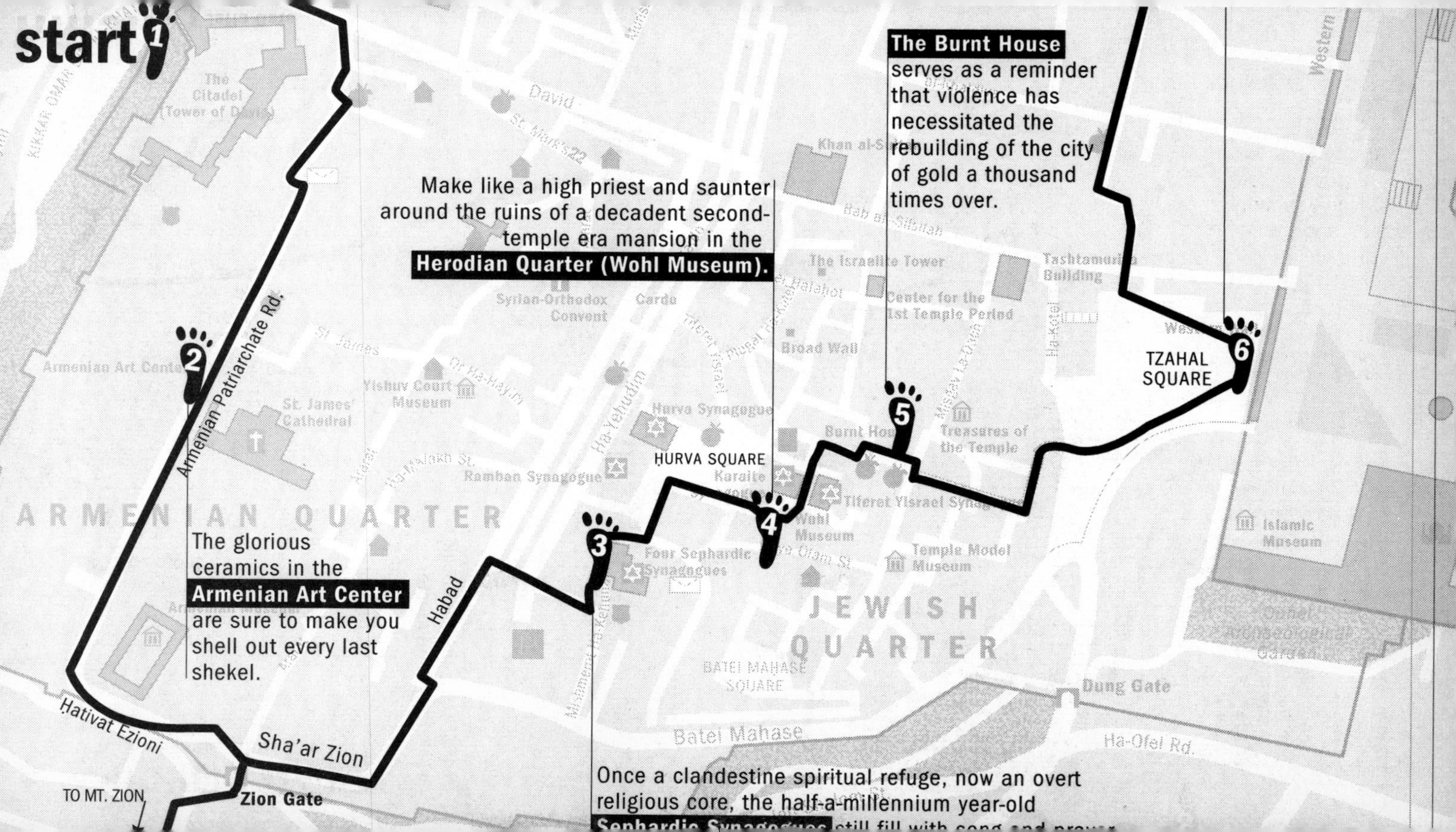
start 1
The Citadel (Tower of David)
David
St. Mark's
Armenian Patriarchate Rd.
Armenian Art Center
St. James
St. James' Cathedral
Yishuv Court Museum
Or Ha-Hayim
Syrian-Orthodox Convent
Cardo
Ha-Yehudim
Hurva Synagogue
HURVA SQUARE
Ramban Synagogue
Karaite
Tiferet Yisrael
Broad Wall
The Israelite Tower
Center for the 1st Temple Period
Khan al-S
Bab al-Silsilah
Burnt House
Treasures of the Temple
Misgav La-Dakh
Tiferet Yisrael Synagogue
Wohl Museum
Temple Model Museum
Four Sephardic Synagogues
Ha-Kotel
Tashtamuriya Building
TZAHAL SQUARE
Western
Islamic Museum
Ophel Archaeological Garden
ARMENIAN QUARTER
JEWISH QUARTER
BATEI MAHASE SQUARE
Batei Mahase
Dung Gate
Ha-Ofel Rd.
Habad
Sha'ar Zion
Hativat Ezioni
Zion Gate
TO MT. ZION
The glorious ceramics in the Armenian Art Center are sure to make you shell out every last shekel.
Make like a high priest and saunter around the ruins of a decadent second-temple era mansion in the Herodian Quarter (Wohl Museum).
The Burnt House serves as a reminder that violence has necessitated the rebuilding of the city of gold a thousand times over.
Once a clandestine spiritual refuge, now an overt religious core, the half-a-millennium year-old

Follow Jesus' last steps on the **Via Dolorosa.**
Wander about the enormous **Church of the Holy Sepulchre,** which marks Jesus' crucifixion site.
The Temple Mount is the birthplace of three religions: Judaism, Islam, and Christianity, and is now occupied by the devastatingly beautiful **Dome of the Rock,** precious to its Muslim worshipers.
Hidden behind the **Church of St. Anne** is the pool where Jesus is said to have cured the infirm.
If the ancient monuments and renovations of the **Cardo** don't raise your eyebrows, the hefty price tags in the surrounding stores will.
finish
MUSLIM QUARTER
Lions Gate
Bab Sitt Maryam
Via Dolorosa
al-Wad
Khan al-Zeit
TEMPLE MOUNT
Dome of the Rock
OLD CITY
Bab al-Silsilah St.
David St.
Western Wall
Habad
JEWISH QUARTER
ARMENIAN QUARTER
Dung Gate
Archaeological Garden
CITY OF DAVID
Warren's Shaft
Zion Gate
Chamber of the Holocaust
Ma'a lot Ir David
Hezekiah's Tunnel
Wadi Hilwa
Kidron Valley
Palombo Museum
Shiloah Pool
4
5
6
7
8
9
10

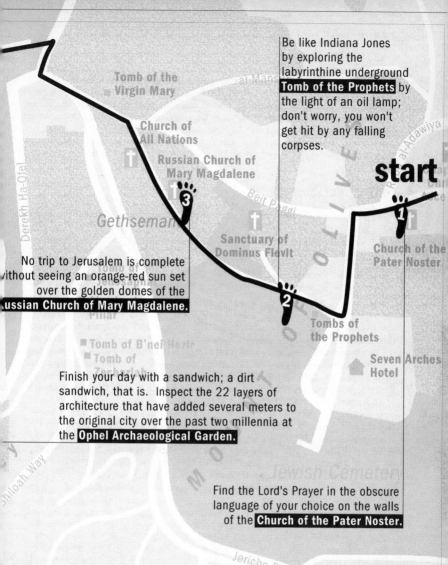

start

Be like Indiana Jones by exploring the labyrinthine underground **Tomb of the Prophets** by the light of an oil lamp; don't worry, you won't get hit by any falling corpses.

No trip to Jerusalem is complete without seeing an orange-red sun set over the golden domes of the **Russian Church of Mary Magdalene.**

Finish your day with a sandwich; a dirt sandwich, that is. Inspect the 22 layers of architecture that have added several meters to the original city over the past two millennia at the **Ophel Archaeological Garden.**

Find the Lord's Prayer in the obscure language of your choice on the walls of the **Church of the Pater Noster.**

Prepare to get soaked in the waist-deep waters of **Hezekiah's Tunnel,** designed by King Hezekiah to hide the city's water supply and deter invaders.

RELIGION

EST. WALKING TIME: 2 hrs

INCLUDING ALL SIGHTS: 5 to 6 hrs

Archaeological Garden another day (can be combined with Tour 2). Back at Damascus Gate, take the stairs on your left (when facing away from the gate) down to the entrance of the **Roman Plaza Museum** ($) and the **Ramparts Promenade** ($; see p. 109), both included in the combo ticket. The Roman Plaza Museum is only worth entering if you already have the combo ticket; otherwise, just get the ticket for the Ramparts. Take the ramparts back to Jaffa Gate, overlooking the **Christian Quarter.** *Free alternative:* return to Jaffa Gate along the outside of the walls, or go back into Damascus Gate, take the right fork (Khan al-Zeit Rd.) through the *souq*, and turn right when you reach David St.; continue uphill until you get back to Jaffa Gate.

TOUR 2: RELIGION

Starting point: Chapel of Christ's Ascension (Mount of Olives). Ending point: Dung Gate. Approximate walking time (not including Western Wall Tunnel tour or City of David side trip): 2hr. Including all sights: 5-6hr. Best time to go: early morning (not before 8:30am, when the Pater Noster opens), on a Tu or Th if possible. Do not go on F or Su. Entrance fees (not including Tunnel tour or side trip): NIS44, students NIS30. A taxi to the starting point should cost NIS15. Modest dress required. If you have more time, consider breaking this tour into two halves: the first day, do the Mount of Olives and Via Dolorosa; the second day, do the Temple Mount and City of David; arrange to take a tour of the Western Wall Tunnels either afternoon.

Take a taxi to the top of the **Mount of Olives** (see p. 125), disembarking at the unimpressive **Chapel of Christ's Ascension** ($). If you decide to skip the chapel, start instead at the much more memorable **Church of the Pater Noster,** just downhill from the chapel. Leaving the church, follow the road down and to the left. Walk past the top of the paved path to stop in front of the Seven Arches Hotel for a fabulous view of the Old City. Backtrack a few steps and head down the path, stopping along the way at each of the Mount of Olives sights: the **Tombs of the Prophets, Sanctuary of Dominus Flevit, Russian Church of Mary Magdalene, Church of All Nations,** and **Tomb of the Virgin Mary.** At the bottom of the path, turn right onto Jericho Rd. Take the second left up to **St. Stephen's Gate** (a.k.a. Lion's Gate). Not far from the gate, find the **Church of St. Anne** on the right. Continue up the road to the start of the **Via Dolorosa.** Follow Jesus' last steps according to the route detailed on p. 116, stopping at each of the **Stations of the Cross** and ending up in the **Church of the Holy Sepulchre.** Leaving the church, turn right onto the Muristan; climb the tower in the **Church of the Redeemer** ($), on your left, for a spectacular view of the Old City, including the path down the Mount of Olives you just climbed.

Now you're on your way to the **Temple Mount** ($; see p. 110); try to get there as close to 1:30pm as possible. To get to the entrance to the Temple Mount, continue to the end of the Muristan and turn left onto David St. On the way, stop in at the **Cardo,** a wide street, which is filled with ancient pillars, foreign tour groups and pricey Judaica shops. Backtrack to David St. which turns into Bab al-Silsilah St., which leads directly up to the Temple Mount. The sights in the complex include the **Dome of the Rock, al-Aqsa Mosque,** and the small **Islamic Museum.** Exit down the ramp that leads toward Dung Gate and go through the security point to enter Tzaḥal Sq., the plaza in front of the **Western Wall.** Take a guided tour of the **Western Wall Tunnels** ($, must be arranged in advance) or head up the steps into the Jewish Quarter to see more of the synagogues or sights not covered in Tour 1.

Side trip: City of David (see p. 123). If you're not totally exhausted yet or don't have extra days to explore Jerusalem, skip the rest of the Jewish Quarter sights and head over to the **City of David** instead: exit Dung Gate, turn left on Ha-Ofel Rd., right on Ma'alot Ir David St., and enter the **Visitors Center** on your left. Walk downhill to the entrance for the **Gihon Spring** and wade through **Hezekiah's Tunnel** ($). On the way back, use the last piece of your combo ticket to enter the **Ophel Archaeological Garden** ($; see p. 113), to the right inside Dung Gate.

ON THE PERIMETER

THE WALLS

The present walls of the Old City, with a total circumference of 4km, were built by Suleiman the Magnificent in 1542. The city had gone without walls since 1219, when al-Muazzan tore them down to prevent the Crusaders from seizing a fortified city. There are eight gates to the Old City, some of which have names in three languages: Hebrew (Jewish), Latin (Christian), and Arabic (Muslim). The most commonly used names are listed below.

Topping the Old City walls, the **Ramparts Promenade** provides an amazing overview of the Old City. The most popular place to start is Jaffa Gate; climb the hidden steps immediately on the left, just before the jewelry store. The 20-minute stretch from here to Damascus Gate curves around the Christian Quarter, affording views of Old City rooftops on one side and both West and East Jerusalem on the other. At Damascus Gate, it is possible to either descend into the market or continue on toward St. Stephen's Gate, the beginning of the Via Dolorosa. Ascent to the ramparts is possible only at Jaffa and Damascus Gates. To ascend the ramparts from **Damascus Gate,** face the gate from the plaza outside and go down the steps on the right, passing under the bridge and entering through the ancient carriageway to the left of the Roman Plaza. *(Promenade open daily 9am-5pm. NIS14, students NIS7; combined ticket to ramparts, Temple Mount excavations (Ophel), Roman Plaza, Zedekiah's Cave, and Hezekiah's tunnel NIS35. Tickets good for five days.)*

THE GATES

Jaffa Gate is the traditional entrance for pilgrims. It is the sole entrance in the western Old City wall and thus the most convenient from West Jerusalem. There has been a gate on this site since 135 CE; the fortified right-angle tower has since been breached by an adjacent cobbled road.

New Gate was opened in 1889 to facilitate access to the Christian Quarter. The gate sits just a few steps from Jaffa Gate, along the northern wall.

Damascus Gate was built over the Roman entrance to the Cardo. It faces East Jerusalem and provides direct access to the busy Muslim Quarter. Many of the Old City's cheaper hostels are in the vicinity.

Herod's Gate stands to the east of Damascus Gate and reaches the deeper sections of the Muslim Quarter.

St. Stephen's Gate, also known as **Lion's Gate,** is along the eastern wall. It faces the Mount of Olives and marks the beginning of the Via Dolorosa.

Golden Gate, blocked by Muslim graves, has been sealed since the 1600s. It is thought to lie over the Closed Gate of the First Temple, the entrance through which the Messiah will purportedly pass (Ezekiel 44:1-3).

Dung Gate, on the southern wall, opens onto the Western Wall plaza. First mentioned in 445 BCE by Nehemiah, it was given its name in medieval times because dumping dung here was considered an especially worthy act.

Zion Gate, on the opposite end of the ancient thoroughfare from Damascus Gate, connects the Armenian Quarter with Mount Zion.

TOUR OF DUTY One of the most competitive professions in Israel is the tour guide. Each year, over 500 (and some years as many as 1000) applicants hope to get into one of three tour guide schools, but each admissions committee takes only a lucky 45. After two years of intense training in religion, archaeology, geology, botany, zoology, folklore, and history, about two-thirds of the admitted class receives the coveted license. To even be considered, applicants must speak at least two foreign languages fluently, but many candidates speak three or four. Once licensed, guides must complete annual recertification courses, where they are kept up to date on new sights and archaeological discoveries (see **Guided Tours,** p. 87 and **Tours,** p. 132).

THE TOWER OF DAVID (CITADEL)

To the right inside Jaffa Gate. 24hr. info ☎626 53 33. Museum open Apr.-Oct. Sa-Th 9am-5pm, F 9am-2pm; Nov.-Mar. Sa-Th 10am-4pm, F 10am-2pm. NIS35, students and seniors NIS25, children 5-12 NIS15; includes tour in English Su-F at 11am only. Nighttime programs several nights per week. Occasional international jazz shows Oct.-June; call for dates.

The Citadel complex gives an outstanding historical introduction to the Old City. The Citadel, also called the Tower of David (*Migdal David* in Hebrew), resembles a Lego caricature of overlapping Hasmonean, Herodian, Roman, Byzantine, Muslim, Mamluk, and Ottoman ruins, but nothing from David's era (during his reign, this area was outside the city and unsettled). The tower provides a superb vantage point for surveying the Holy City. Winding through the rooms of the fortress, the high-tech, information-packed museum tells the story of the city in Hebrew, Arabic, and English. Begin with the excellent 14-minute introductory movie.

THE TEMPLE MOUNT

The entrance to the Mount is up the ramp, just right of the Western Wall. It is also accessible from the end of Bab al-Silsilah St. Visitors may enter the Temple Mount area Sa-Th 7:30-11am and 1:30-2:30pm; hours are subject to change during Ramadan and other Islamic holidays, usually open 7:30-10:30am. Tickets are sold until 3pm at a booth between al-Aqsa Mosque and the museum (to the right when entering from the ramp). NIS38, students NIS25. The Mount is sometimes closed to visitors without notice.

SECURITY. Remember that the area is highly sensitive—incidents in the past have resulted in violence. Any conspicuous action, no matter how innocent, may result in ejection. **Modest dress** is required and wrap-around gowns are provided for those who need them. Be aware that many sections considered **off-limits** by the police are not marked as such, including the walls around al-Aqsa, the area through the door to the south between al-Aqsa and the museum, the garden walkway along the eastern wall, and the Muslim cemetery. Bags and packs are not permitted inside al-Aqsa or the Dome of the Rock and must be left outside along with your shoes; theft is not usually a problem, but you should refrain from bringing valuables when you visit. **Photography** is permitted on the Temple Mount, but not inside al-Aqsa or the Dome of the Rock.

The **Temple Mount** (al-Haram al-Sharif in Arabic, Har Ha-Bayit in Hebrew), a 35-acre area in the southeastern corner of the Old City, is one of the most venerated religious sites in the world. A spiritual magnet, the hill is central to Judaism and Islam, and it served as a holy site for at least 10 ancient religions. The Temple Mount is traditionally identified with the biblical Mount Moriah, where God asked Abraham to sacrifice his son Isaac (Genesis 22:2). King Solomon built the First Temple here in the middle of the 10th century BCE (2 Chronicles 3:1), and Nebuchadnezzar destroyed it in 587 BCE, when the Jews were led into captivity (I Kings 5-8; II Kings 24-25). The Second Temple was built in 516 BCE, after the Jews' return from exile (Ezra 3-7). In 20 BCE, King Herod rebuilt the temple and enlarged the Mount, reinforcing it with four retaining walls. Parts of the southern, eastern, and western retaining walls still stand. Religious scholars believe that the Holy of Holies, the most sacred and important spot on the Temple, where only the High Priest was allowed to enter once a year, was closest to what is now the **Western Wall,** making this wall the holiest approachable site in Judaism. Some Jews won't ascend the Mount because of the chance that they will walk on the Holy of Holies, which is off-limits until the Messiah arrives.

Christians remember the Second Temple as the backdrop to the Passion of Christ. Like the First Temple, the Second Temple lasted only a few hundred years. In the fourth year of the Jewish Revolt (70 CE), Roman legions sacked Jerusalem and razed the Second Temple. Hadrian built a temple to Jupiter over the site, but the Byzantines destroyed it and used the platform as a municipal sewage facility. After Caliph Omar conquered Jerusalem in 638 CE (just six years after Muhammad's death) he ascended the Mount and began the clean-up himself, personally removing an armful of brown gook.

DOME OF THE ROCK AND AL-AQSA MOSQUE. The Umayyad caliphs built the two Arab shrines that still dominate the Temple Mount: the silver-domed **al-Aqsa Mosque** (built in 715 and rebuilt several times after earthquakes) and the magnificent **Dome of the Rock** (built in 691). A stunning display of mosaics and metallic domes, the complex is the third-holiest Muslim site after the Ka'ba in Mecca and the Mosque of the Prophet in Medina. According to Muslim tradition, this is the point to which God took Muhammad on his mystical Night Journey *(miraj)* from the Holy Mosque at Mecca to the outer Mosque (*al-aqsa* means "the farthest") and then on to heaven. The Dome of the Rock surrounds what Muslims believe to have been Abraham's makeshift altar where he almost sacrificed Ishmael, his son by Sarah's maid Hagar (not Isaac, as Christians and Jews believe).

The dome, once of solid gold, was eventually melted down to pay the caliphs' debts. The domes of the mosques and shrines were plated with lusterless lead until the structures received aluminum caps during the restoration work done from 1958 to 1964. The golden hue of the Dome of the Rock was previously achieved with an aluminum-bronze alloy, but in 1993 the dome was re-coated with new metal plates faced with a thin coating of 24-karat gold, leaving it more brilliant than ever. Many of the tiles covering the walls of the Dome of the Rock were affixed during the reign of Suleiman the Magnificent, who had the city walls built in the 16th century. Ceramic tiles were added in the 1950s and 60s through the private funds of the late Jordanian King Hussein.

ISLAMIC MUSEUM. Some of this museum's most interesting relics include elaborately decorated Qur'ans and a collection of crescent-topped spires that once crowned older domes. The museum is next to the al-Aqsa Mosque, to the right when entering from the ramp entrance beside the Western Wall.

OTHER SIGHTS. Between the al-Aqsa Mosque and the Dome of the Rock is **al-Kas,** a fountain, where Muslims perform ablutions (washing hands and feet) before prayer. Built in 709 CE, the fountain is connected to underground cisterns capable of holding 10 million gallons. The **arches** on the Temple Mount, according to Muslim legend, will be used to hang scales to weigh people's good and bad deeds. Next to the Dome of the Rock is the much smaller **Dome of the Chain,** the exact center of al-Haram al-Sharif, where Muslims believe a chain once hung from heaven that could be grasped only by the righteous.

JEWISH QUARTER

Known as "Ha-Rovah" by Israelis, the picturesque Jewish Quarter is in the southeast quadrant of the Old City, the site of the posh Upper City during the Second Temple era. The quarter extends from Ha-Shalshelet St. (Bab al-Silsilah) in the north to the city's southern wall, and from Ararat St. in the west to the Western Wall in the east. From Jaffa Gate, either head down David St. and turn right at the first large intersection just before it becomes Bab al-Silsilah, or turn right (past the Tower of David) onto Armenian Orthodox Patriarchate Rd. (in the direction of traffic) and make the first left onto St. James Rd. The high arch over the Ḥurva Synagogue, visible from most parts of the Jewish Quarter, marks Ḥurva Sq., a convenient reference point for Jewish Quarter sights.

After being exiled when the Second Temple was destroyed, Jews settled here again when they returned to Jerusalem in the 15th century. The Jewish community grew from 2000 in 1800 to 11,000 in 1865, when settlement began outside the walls. Today, about 650 families live in the Jewish Quarter.

Much of the Jewish Quarter was damaged in the 1948 War, and after two decades of Jordanian rule the Quarter lay in ruins. After the Israelis annexed the Old City in 1967, they immediately began extensive restoration of the neighborhood. City planners made archaeological discoveries with every lift of the shovel and have managed to gracefully integrate the ancient remains into the new neighborhood. Today the Jewish Quarter is an upper-middle-class neighborhood, with an almost exclusively Orthodox Jewish (and largely American) population.

THE WESTERN WALL. The 67m long, 18m tall wall (Ha-Kotel Ha-Ma'aravi in Hebrew, or just "The Kotel") is only a small part of the 488m long retaining wall of the Temple Mount; the rest is now part of Arab houses in the Muslim Quarter. Built around 20 BCE, the Wall was the largest section of the Temple area that remained standing after its destruction in 70 CE. The Wailing Wall, a dated moniker, refers to Jewish worshipers who visited in centuries past to mourn the destruction of the Temple. Today's visitors, Jewish or otherwise, often see the Wall as a direct connection with God, and tuck written prayers into its cracks. Don't expect your scribbles to wait there for the Messiah; all notes are periodically removed from the overburdened wall and buried, in accordance with Jewish Law. An innovative service from Bezeq (the telephone company) lets you fax in urgent messages to be deposited in the crevices (fax 561 22 22). About 3m off the ground, a gray line indicates the surface level before 1967. Nearly 20m of Herodian wall still lies underground. The Herodian stones are identifiable by their carved frames; Byzantines, Arabs, and Turks added the smaller stones above.

Pre-1948 photos show Orthodox Jews praying at the wall in a crowded alley; after the 1967 War, the present plaza was built. Israeli paratroopers are now sworn in here to recall the Wall's capture. The Ministry of Religion has decreed that all rules applying to Orthodox synagogues also apply to the Wall. Men must cover their heads (paper *kippot* are in a box by the entrance) and women must cover their legs (wraps can be borrowed from the Holy Sites Authority). The prayer areas for men and women are separated by a screen, with the Torah scrolls kept on the men's side. Because Orthodox men are not allowed to hear women's voices singing, observers will notice that the men's side is much louder and more active than the women's side. Since 1989, a group called the Women of the Wall has been pushing for equal rights; in April 2000, the Israeli Supreme Court finally granted women the right to wear a *tallis* (prayer shawl), read from the Torah, and hold group services. As of July 2000, controversial time tables were in developmental stages, so that each group could have a time to pray at the Wall without offending others. By next year, the solution will presumably have taken effect; ask around for current information but keep in mind that this is a very sensitive issue.

Named for the English archaeologist who discovered it, **Wilson's Arch** is located inside an arched room to the left of the Wall, accessible from the men's side. It was once part of a bridge that spanned Cheesemakers' Valley, allowing Jewish priests to cross from their Upper City homes to the Temple. A peek down the two illuminated shafts in the floor of this room gives a sense of the Wall's original height (women may not enter). The Wall continues from here through closed tunnels for over 500m. A number of rooms branch off from the tunnels, including what is thought to have been a chamber of the Sanhedrin, the supreme court of ancient Israel. Women and groups can enter the passageways through an archway to the south, near the telephones. Underneath the Western Wall is an underground passage where Jewish radicals hid explosives in the early 1980s in a plot to destroy the Dome of the Rock. For tours of the passage, contact the Archaeological Seminars or the Jewish Student Information Center (see **Tours,** p. 87).

Friday evenings are the best time to visit the Wall, when Jews come from all over the city (and world) to usher in Shabbat. The festivities start before sundown and go until late. Many visitors on these evenings are invited to traditional Shabbat meals following the prayers; if you would like to be guaranteed a place, contact the Jewish Student Information Center in advance (see p. 87). Half a dozen bar mitzvahs occur at the Wall on Monday and Thursday mornings. These ceremonies mark the coming of age of Jewish boys. Photography is appropriate at these occasions, but not on Shabbat or holidays. On other nights, the Wall is brightly lit, the air cool, and the atmosphere reflective and quiet. *(The Wall can be reached by foot from Dung Gate, the Jewish Quarter, Bab al-Silsilah St., or al-Wad Rd.)*

OPHEL ARCHAEOLOGICAL GARDEN. The excavations at the southern wall of the Temple Mount are known as "Ophel," though the name technically refers to the hill just outside the southern wall, where the City of David is located. Scholars have uncovered 22 layers from 12 periods of the city's history. A tunnel leads out to the steps of the Temple Mount. *(From the Western Wall, head out past the security point toward Dung Gate; the entrance to the ruins is on the left just before the gate. ☎625 44 03. Open daily 7am-5pm. NIS14, students NIS7. Combo tickets for Ophel, Burnt House, Herodian Quarter, and Last Ditch Battle Museum NIS26, students NIS24.)*

CARDO. Down Or Ḥayim St., between Ḥabad St. and Ha-Yehudim St., the staircase descends to the remains of Jerusalem's main thoroughfare during Roman and Byzantine times. The enormous remaining pillars suggest its original monumental proportions. The uncovered section is built over a Byzantine extension of Emperor Hadrian's Cardo Maximus, which ran from Damascus Gate to about as far south as David St. Archaeologists suspect that Justinian constructed the addition so that the Cardo would extend as far as the Nea Church (beneath Yeshivat Ha-Kotel). Sheltered by the Cardo's vaulted roof are the best Judaica shops in Jerusalem; most are fairly expensive, but the quality warrants the hefty price tags. Near the entrance to the Cardo, there is a climb down to an excavated section of the Hasmonean city walls and remains of buildings from the First Temple period. Farther along the Cardo is an enlarged mosaic reproduction of the Madaba map, the 6th-century plan of Jerusalem discovered in Jordan. *(Make a left at the bottom of the stairs on Ha-Yehudim St. Cardo open and illuminated Su-Th until 11pm.)*

HERODIAN QUARTER AND WOHL ARCHAEOLOGICAL MUSEUM. This museum consists of the huge excavation of three mansions, thought to belong to the family of a High Priest during the Second Temple period. Nine colorful mosaic floors were discovered in the ruins, five of which were probably in ancient bathrooms. After the Western Wall tunnels, this is perhaps the most interesting Old City excavation. *(Entrance is on Ha-Kara'im St., off Ḥurva Square, near Tony's Market. ☎628 34 48. Open Su-Th 9am-4:30pm, F 9am-12:30pm. NIS15, students NIS13. Combined ticket to Burnt House and Herodian Quarter NIS19, students NIS16.)*

BURNT HOUSE. The Burnt House is the remains of a priest's dwelling from the Second Temple era. In 70 CE, the fourth year of the Jewish Revolt, the Romans destroyed the Second Temple and broke into Jerusalem's Upper City, burning its buildings and killing its inhabitants. The excavation of the Burnt House provided direct evidence of the destruction of the Upper City. Near a stairwell, the bones of a severed arm were found, but a few years ago the remains were taken and buried according to Jewish law. Sound and light shows are set inside the Burnt House, re-creating the events of its destruction—with virtual fire, of course. *(On Tiferet Yisrael St. From Ḥurva Sq., turn right at the Mizrahi Bank. ☎628 72 11. Open Su-Th 9am-4:30pm, F 9am-12:30pm. NIS9, students NIS7. English presentations every hour on the half hour.)*

LAST DITCH BATTLE MUSEUM. Previously named the One Last Day Museum, the building displays the photojournal of the British journalist John Phillips, who lived in the Old City during the Jordanian siege of 1947-1948. Dubbed the modern-day Josephus Flavius, Phillips recounts life during the siege. The museum contains a surprisingly fascinating photography exhibit and five-minute silent documentary film. *(Newly relocated, in the first storefront on the left when entering the commercial center on the Cardo. Open Su-Th 9am-5pm, F 9am-1pm. NIS6, students NIS5.)*

FOUR SEPHARDIC SYNAGOGUES. The Synagogue of Rabbi Yoḥanan Ben-Zakkai, the Prophet Elijah Synagogue, the Middle Synagogue, and the Istanbuli Synagogue were built by Mediterranean Jews starting in the 16th century. At the time, there were laws against building synagogues, so they were called study centers. The Middle Synagogue is the most recent; it was a courtyard until a roof was put over it in 1835. The four synagogues (with religious services held twice a day) remain the spiritual center of Jerusalem's Sephardic community. A Portuguese *minyan* (a religious service with at least 10 participants) gathers in the Istanbuli room on Shabbat. An exhibition features photographs of the synagogues before their destruction in the 1948 and 1967 wars. *(Down Mishmerot Ha-Kehuna St., near the Jewish Quarter parking lot. ☎ 628 05 92. Open Su-Th 9am-4pm, F 9am-noon. NIS7, students NIS4.)*

TREASURES OF THE TEMPLE MUSEUM. The folks at the Temple Institute are hoping to rebuild the Jewish High Temple and to recapture its original look and feel. Their plan requires relocation of the Dome of the Rock. Muslim worshipers are not amused. The small museum is filled with gorgeous paintings and sacrificial instruments built to the specifications written in the Talmud and suitable for use in the anticipated Third Temple. A film (either 10 or 26 min.) gives history on the second temple and is a good introduction for people planning to go on a tour of the Western Wall tunnels. *(19 Misgav Ladakh St., off Tiferet Yisrael Rd.; turn left when coming from Ḥurva Sq. ☎ 626 45 45. Open Su-Th 9am-5pm, F 9am-noon. NIS20, students NIS15.)*

TEMPLE MODEL MUSEUM. The museum showcases reconstructions of the furniture of the Temple and clothing worn by its priests. Featured is a model of the proposed Third Temple. *(On Misgav Ladakh St., off Tiferet Yisrael Rd., to the right when coming from Ḥurva Sq., under the archway. ☎ 626 44 66. Open Su-Th 10am-5pm. NIS10, students NIS8.)*

ḤURVA SYNAGOGUE. A single stone arch soars above the ruins of the synagogue in the square named for it, forming the center of the Jewish Quarter. Built in 1700 by followers of Rabbi Yehuda the Ḥasid, the synagogue was destroyed by Muslims, thereby earning its ominous title (*ḥurva* means "ruin"). In 1856 the building was restored as the National Ashkenazic Synagogue, only to be destroyed again during the 1948 War. In 1967, renovators opted to rebuild only the single arch as a reminder of the destruction. *(On Ha-Yehudim Rd., around the corner from Ḥurva Sq.)*

YISHUV COURT MUSEUM. This small museum exhibits 19th-century life in the Jewish Quarter. The rooms in this one-time home each depict a different element of life, from childbirth to haberdashery. One especially interesting attraction is the synagogue, built in the room where the famed mystic rabbi the Arizal was born. Rooms are furnished with period artifacts donated by the quarter's citizens, including a collection of ancient wooden Torah cases. *(6 Or Ḥayim St., on the right when coming from St. James Rd. and Jaffa Gate. Open Su-Th 9am-3pm, F 10am-1pm. NIS14, students NIS11, children NIS8.)*

HOLOCAUST MEMORIAL HALL. The sculpture and room inside were designed by Agam, designer of the Dizengoff fountain in Tel Aviv. The brass tree contains 1200 brilliant leaves, and the ceiling and floor tiles can be grouped into Stars of David. *(Opposite the plaza from the Wall, on the right, halfway up the stairs to Bab al-Silsilah St. Open Su-Th 11am-6pm.)*

KARAITE SYNAGOGUE. Established by the divergent Karaite sect of Judaism, this synagogue is now the center of the Karaite community in Jerusalem (see **the Karaites,** p. 25). Visitors aren't allowed to enter, but there's a tiny, one-room museum with a window onto the synagogue. *(From Ḥurva Sq., go down Ha-Karaim St. (parallel to Tiferet Yisrael St.) and take your first left. No regular hours, but the caretakers live upstairs. Ring the bell any day but Saturday.)*

TIFERET YISRAEL SYNAGOGUE. Built by Ḥasidic Jews during the 19th century, this synagogue was destroyed by Jordan in 1948. The ruins aren't terribly interesting, housing only a few old photographs that depict the house of worship's heyday. *(Across from the Karaite Synagogue, also accessible from the upstairs door of the Quarter Cafe.)*

RAMBAN SYNAGOGUE. This synagogue was named for Rabbi Moshe Ben-Naḥman, also known as Naḥmanides ("Ramban" is an acronym for his name). Inside is a letter written by the rabbi describing Jerusalem's Jewish community in 1267, the year he arrived from Spain. During a period of nearly four centuries (1599-1967), Jews were forbidden to worship here and the building had stints as a store, butter factory, and mosque. Today it is open for morning and evening prayers. *(On Ha-Yehudim Rd., next door to the more prominent Ḥurva synagogue.)*

BROAD WALL. This Israelite wall, which once encircled the City of David, the Temple Mount, and the Upper City, was built by King Hezekiah in the 7th century BCE and, along with his famous tunnel, formed part of the city's defenses (see **Citadel**, p. 111). The chunk of wall is 7m thick—much broader than the current Ottoman fortifications. *(On Plugat Ha-Kotel Rd., off Ha-Yehudim Rd.)*

ISRAELITE TOWER. The tower is part of the same defense system as the Broad Wall. Beneath it lie the remains of two older towers that were important bastions for the first wall built in the north. Maps indicate how the city walls have changed over the centuries, but the exhibit is fairly dull. *(Continue left on Plugat Ha-Kotel and turn right onto Shonei Ha-Lakhot St. Open Su-Th 9am-5pm, F 9am-1pm. NIS4, students NIS3.)*

CENTER FOR JERUSALEM IN THE FIRST TEMPLE PERIOD. This academic center has a small but fascinating museum and screens a 35-minute, partially 3D film presentation about Jerusalem in the First Temple period. The film and exhibit provide an excellent alternative for those who don't wish to tackle the City of David's many steps and Hezekiah's Tunnel's knee-deep waters. *(Across the street from the Israelite Tower. ☎628 62 88; fax 628 85 93. Open Su-Th 9am-4pm, F 9am-1pm; July-Aug. Su-Th 9am-6pm, F 9am-1pm. NIS12, students NIS10. Call for a schedule of English shows.)*

ARMENIAN QUARTER

Cloistered in the southwestern corner of the Old City, Jerusalem's small Armenian Christian population lives in the shadow of tragedy. The Turkish massacre of one and a half million Armenians in 1915 remains one of the century's little-noticed genocides and persecution of those fleeing to Palestine has caused their numbers to dwindle even further. The 1000 Armenians remaining in the Quarter are haunted by this devastating past: posters mapping out the genocide line the streets. Although the **Armenian Compound,** their residential area, is not open to the public, the few available glimpses of Armenian culture are fascinating.

ST. JAMES CATHEDRAL. The spiritual center of the Quarter, the cathedral was originally constructed during the 5th century CE, Armenia's golden age, to honor two St. Jameses. The first martyr, St. James the Greater, was beheaded in 44 CE by Herod Agrippas. His head, supposedly delivered to Mary on the wings of angels, rests under the altar. St. James the Lesser, entombed in a northern chapel, was the first bishop of Jerusalem, but he was run out of town by Jews who disliked his version of Judaism. Persians destroyed the cathedral in the 7th century, Armenians rebuilt it in the 11th, and Crusaders enlarged it in the 12th. *(The massive cathedral is on Armenian Orthodox Patriarchate Rd., the main paved road leading right from Jaffa Gate. The entrance is on the left past the tunnel, under an arch reading "Couvent Arménien St. Jacques." ☎628 23 31; www.armenian-patriarchate.org. Open daily 6-7:30am during the morning service and 3-3:30pm during the Vespers service. Modest dress required.)*

ARMENIAN MUSEUM. Chronicling the history of Armenia from pre-Christian times to the 1915 genocide, the small museum displays weapons and religious artifacts. *(On Armenian Orthodox Patriarchate Rd., on the left from Jaffa Gate. ☎628 23 31; fax 626 48 62. Open Sa-Th 9am-4:30pm. NIS5, students NIS3.)*

ARMENIAN ART CENTER. The center is one of the few Armenian ceramic shops still painting tile and pottery by hand. Items are more expensive than the machine-made items sold in the *souq*, but the heavy, handmade dyes lend a richness to the colors. The traditional and intricate designs are unmatched elsewhere. The best pieces are kept hidden from spying competitors; ask to see some of the work kept in the back of the store. *(On Armenian Orthodox Patriarchate Rd., across from St. James Cathedral. ☎628 35 67 or 628 43 05. Open M-Sa 9am-7pm. Tiles, doorhangings, plates, and other objects from NIS20 and up—way, way up. Pieces available by advance order.)*

SYRIAN ORTHODOX CONVENT. Also known as St. Mark's Church. Aramaic, the ancient language of the Levant, is spoken here during services and in casual conversation. The Syrian Church believes the room in the basement to be the site of St. Mark's house and the Last Supper (most other Christians recognize the Cenacle on Mount Zion as that hallowed place). Decorated with beautiful gilded woodwork, the chapel contains a 150-year-old Bible in Old Aramaic and a painting of the Virgin Mary supposedly painted by St. Mark himself. *(Turn left from Armenian Orthodox Patriarchate Rd. onto St. James Rd. and left onto Ararat St. The convent, marked by a vivid mosaic, is on the right after a sharp turn in the road. Open daily 8am-4pm. Ring the bell if the door is closed.)*

CHRISTIAN QUARTER AND VIA DOLOROSA

In the northwest corner of the Old City, the Christian Quarter surrounds the Church of the Holy Sepulchre, the site traditionally believed to be the place of Jesus' crucifixion, burial, and resurrection. The alleyways of the Quarter pass small churches and chapels of various denominations, and the streets bustle with pilgrims, nuns, monks, and merchants peddling rosaries and holy water.

The **Via Dolorosa** (Path of Sorrow) is the route that the cross-bearing Jesus followed from the site of his condemnation (the Praetorium) to the site of his crucifixion and grave. Each event on his walk has a chapel commemorating it; together these chapels comprise the 14 Stations of the Cross. The present route was mapped out during the Crusader period and passes through the Muslim and Christian Quarters. Modern New Testament scholars have suggested alternate routes based on recent archaeological and historical reconstructions.

To begin the walk taken by Jesus and millions of tourists and pilgrims, start at St. Stephen's Gate. When coming from Damascus or Jaffa Gates, it is necessary to walk along part of the Via Dolorosa to get to the starting point. While this may cause temptation to see the stations out of order, following the traditional sequence will provide a more rewarding experience. On Fridays at 3pm (summer 4pm), a group of pilgrims led by Franciscan monks walk the Via Dolorosa starting at al-Omariyyeh College (the first station) and welcome additional guests.

THE STATIONS OF THE CROSS

I. One bone of contention between sects involves the starting point of Jesus' final walk as a mortal. It is generally agreed that Jesus was brought before Pontius Pilate, the Roman procurator, for judgment. Normally, Roman governors fulfilled their duties in the palace of Herod the Great, south of Jaffa Gate and the Citadel area. But on feast days such as Passover, the day of Jesus' condemnation, the governor and his soldiers presumably based themselves at the Antonia Fortress (also built by Herod) to be closer to the Temple Mount. Reflecting this holiday relocation, the **Tower of Antonia,** in the courtyard of **al-Omariyyeh College,** is considered to be the **First Station,** where Jesus was condemned. The station is not marked. For one of the best views of the Dome of the Rock plaza, walk into the courtyard of the school, turn left, and ascend the steps on the right. (*Just past an archway, 200m from St. Stephen's Gate, a ramp with a blue railing on the left returns to the courtyard.)*

II. Across the Via Dolorosa from the ramp is a Franciscan monastery; inside on the left is the **Condemnation Chapel,** complete with a three-dimensional relief above the altar. This is the **Second Station,** where Jesus was sentenced to crucifixion. On the right is the **Chapel of the Flagellation,** where he was first flogged by Roman soldiers. Inside the Chapel of the Flagellation, on the right, a crown of thorns adorns the dome. *(Open daily Apr.-Sept. 8-11:45am and 4-6pm; Oct.-Mar. 8-11:45am and 1-5pm.)*

Continuing along the Via Dolorosa, pass beneath the **Ecce Homo Arch,** built on the site of Pontius Pilate's mansion, where Pilate looked down upon Jesus and cried, "Behold the Man." The arch (identifiable by its two windows) is actually part of the triumphal arch that commemorated Emperor Hadrian's suppression of the Bar Kokhba Revolt in the 2nd century. Half of the arch is inside the **Convent of the Sisters of Zion,** beneath which the **Lithostratos** excavations have cleared a large chamber thought by some to be a judgment hall, making it an alternative First Station. Within the excavations is evidence of a pagan game called the Game of King, which Roman soldiers played to torment prisoners. *(Open M-Sa 8:30am-5pm. NIS6, students NIS4.)*

III. Although the following stations—the destinations of countless pilgrims—are all marked, they are nonetheless difficult to spot. Immediately after the Via Dolorosa turns left onto al-Wad Rd., look left for the door to the Armenian Catholic Patriarchy. To the left of the door is the **Third Station,** where Jesus fell to his knees for the first time. A small Polish chapel inside a blue gate marks the spot; a relief above the entrance, marked "III Statio," depicts Jesus kneeling beneath the cross.

IV. At the **Fourth Station,** a few meters farther on the left, just beyond the Armenian Orthodox Patriarchate, a small chapel commemorates the spot where Jesus saw his mother. Look for a metal plaque that simply says "IV" and a relief of Jesus and Mary above light blue iron doors, to the left of an arched alleyway.

V. Turn right on the Via Dolorosa to reach the **Fifth Station,** where Simon the Cyrene volunteered to carry Jesus' cross. Look for the brown door on the left, with the inscription "V St."

VI. Fifty meters farther, the remains of a small column designate the **Sixth Station** (marked with a "VI"), where Veronica wiped Jesus' face with her handkerchief. The mark of his face was left on the cloth, now on display at the Greek Orthodox Patriarchate on the street of the same name. Look for a pair of doors on the left, one green and one dark brown; the column is set into the wall between the doors.

VII. The **Seventh Station,** straight ahead at the intersection with Khan al-Zeit, marks Jesus' second fall, precipitated by the sudden steepness of the road. In the first century, a gate to the countryside opened here, and tradition holds that the notices of Jesus' condemnation were posted on it.

VIII. Crossing Khan al-Zeit, ascend Aqabat al-Khanqa and look left past the Greek Orthodox Convent for the stone Latin cross that marks the **Eighth Station.** Here Jesus turned to the women who mourned for him, saying, "Daughters of Jerusalem, do not weep for me, weep rather for yourselves and for your children" (Luke 23:28). The small stone is part of the wall and difficult to spot; a large red-and-white sign sticking out of the wall makes the task much easier.

IX. Backtrack to Khan al-Zeit, take a right, walk for about 50m through the market, ascend the wide stone stairway on the right (at Mike's Center), and continue through a winding passageway to the **Coptic Church.** The remains of a column to the left of the door mark the **Ninth Station,** where Jesus fell a third time. The Coptic complex there also contains three small churches, all of which are still in use.

X-XIV. The fastest way to the rest of the stations is to go through the Ethiopian Monastery, to the left when facing the Ninth Station. The Ethiopians possess no part of the Holy Sepulchre itself, so they have become squatters on the roof. The modest compound houses a small but spiritual church; enter through the roof and descend, exiting next to the Church of the Holy Sepulchre, where the Via Dolorosa ends. The placement of the last five stations inside the Church of the Holy Sepulchre contradicts an alternative hypothesis that the Crucifixion took place at the skull-shaped Garden Tomb (see p. 139), on Nablus Rd. in East Jerusalem.

The **Church of the Holy Sepulchre** marks Golgotha, also called Calvary, the site of the Crucifixion. The location was first determined by Eleni, mother of the Emperor Constantine, during her pilgrimage in 326 CE. Eleni thought that Hadrian had erected a pagan temple to Venus and Jupiter on the site in order to divert Christians from their faith. She sponsored excavations and uncovered the tomb of Joseph of Arimathea and three crosses, which she surmised had been hastily left there after the Crucifixion as the Sabbath approached. Constantine built a church over the site in 335, which was later destroyed by the Persians in 614, rebuilt, and destroyed again (this time by the Turks) in 1009. Part of the church's foundations buttress the present Crusader structure, built in 1149. When the present building was erected, its architects decided to unite all the oratories, chapels, and other sanctuaries that had cropped up around the site under one monumental cross. By 1852, tremendous religious conflicts had developed within the Holy Sepulchre. The uninterested Ottoman rulers divided the church among the Franciscan, Greek Orthodox, Armenian Orthodox, Coptic, Syrian, and Ethiopian churches. The first three are the major shareholders, entitled to hold masses and processions and to burn incense in their shrines and chapels.

One of the most revered buildings on earth, the church is also somewhat decrepit. Bickering among the various denominations has kept it in a state of perpetual construction. Damage caused by major fires in 1808 and 1949 and an earthquake in 1927 demanded a level of cooperation and a pooling of resources that could not be mustered. Restoration work in any part of the basilica implies ownership, making each sect hesitant to assist and eager to hinder the others. The result is that little, if anything, is ever accomplished. In 1935 the church was in such a precarious state that the colonialists desperately propped it up with girders and wooden reinforcement. Since 1960, partial cooperation has allowed the supportive scaffolding to be gradually removed. To this day, however, the question of who gets to change a light bulb can rage into a month-long controversy.

The church's entrance faces the slab on which Jesus was supposedly anointed before he was buried. To continue along the stations, go up the stairs to the right just inside the entrance. The chapel at the top is divided into two naves: the right one belongs to the Franciscans, the left to the Greek Orthodox. At the entrance to the Franciscan Chapel is the **Tenth Station,** where Jesus was stripped of his clothes, and at the far end is the **Eleventh Station,** where he was nailed to the cross. The **Twelfth Station,** to the left inside the Greek chapel, is the unmistakable site of the Crucifixion: a life-size Jesus, clad in a metal loincloth, hangs among oil lamps, flowers, and enormous candles. Between the eleventh and twelfth stations is the **Thirteenth Station,** where Mary received Jesus' body. The station is marked by an odd statue of Mary adorned with jewels, a silver dagger stuck into her breast.

Jesus' tomb on the ground floor is the **Fourteenth** (and final) **Station.** The Holy Sepulchre, in the center of the rotunda, is a large marble structure flanked by huge candles. The first chamber in the tomb, the **Chapel of the Angel,** is dedicated to the angel who announced Jesus' resurrection to Mary Magdalene. A tiny entrance leads from the chapel into the sepulchre itself, an equally tiny chamber lit by scores of candles and guarded by priests. The raised marble slab in the sepulchre covers the rock on which Jesus' body was laid. Nudging the back of the Holy Sepulchre is the even smaller **Coptic Chapel.** To the right of the Sepulchre, the **Chapel of Mary Magdalene** marks where Jesus appeared to her after his resurrection.

The rest of the church is a dark labyrinth of small chapels through which priests, pilgrims, and chatty tourists wander. Because the various denominations can't agree on an interior decorator, the building houses only religious paintings and oil lamps. Near the eastern end, steps lead down to two chapels commemorating the discovery of the true cross. In a small chapel on the ground floor just below Calvary, a fissure runs through the rock, supposedly caused by the earthquake following Jesus' death. According to legend, Adam (of Adam and Eve) was buried beneath Calvary, allowing Jesus' blood to drip through this cleft and anoint him. *(Church open daily 5am-8pm, in winter 4am-7pm. Men and women must cover their knees.)*

OTHER RELIGIOUS SIGHTS

CHURCH OF ST. ANNE. Commemorating the birthplace of Jesus' mother Mary, the church is one of the best-preserved pieces of Crusader architecture in Israel. It survived the Islamic period intact because Salah al-Din used it as a Muslim theological school (hence the Arabic inscription on the tympanum above the doors). Extensive excavations behind the church clearly show the layers of history; the ruins of a 5th-century basilica cover those of a 2nd- or 3rd-century chapel. The church itself has fantastic acoustics. *Let's Go* used to suggest that visitors try singing quietly in the front rows, but there's now a sign informing people that "This is a holy place for prayer and religious hymns only"—oops. The cool, beautiful crypt has a beaten-copper cross and inlaid stone floors.

Within the grounds of the church is the **Pool of Bethesda,** straight ahead and down the stairs. Crowds of the infirm used to wait beside the pool for an angel to disturb the waters since the first person in after the angel would supposedly be cured. Jesus also healed a sick man here (John 5:2-9). *(Near St. Stephen's Gate, through the large wooden doors on the right. Church and grounds open M-Sa 8am-12:45pm and 2-6pm; in winter M-Sa 8am-12:45pm and 2-5pm. NIS6, students NIS4.)*

ST. ALEXANDER'S CHURCH. Built over the Judgment Gate, the church marks the end of the Roman Cardo, through which Jesus exited the city on his way to Calvary. First-century stones line the floor and two pillars from the original Cardo are visible. Next to the gate is a small hole in the ancient wall—this is the famed Eye of the Needle, through which latecomers would sneak into the city when the gates were closed at night. The Russian Orthodox Palestine Society owns the church. *(Located on the right just after turning off al-Wad St. toward the Holy Sepulchre. ☎627 49 52. Open M-Sa 9am-1pm and 3-5pm. Ring bell. Prayers for Czar Alexander III Th 7am. NIS5.)*

LUTHERAN CHURCH OF THE REDEEMER. The church is off al-Wad St., across the street from St. Alexander's. Enter around the corner on Muristan St. and climb a seemingly endless spiral staircase (actually 178 steps) to the bell tower for an amazing view. *(☎627 61 11. Open M-Sa 9am-1pm and 1:30-5pm. English service Sunday 9am; in German at the Crusader chapel next door. NIS3, students NIS2.)*

MUSEUM OF THE GREEK ORTHODOX PATRIARCHATE. The museum is a more recent addition to the Christian Quarter. Under the Patriarch Benedictos Papadopoulos, the scattered liturgical riches, gifts of pilgrims, and early printings of the Patriarchate's 19th-century press were arranged in a reconstructed Crusader building. *(On the street of the same name. ☎627 11 96. Open Tu-F 9am-1pm and 3-5pm, Sa 9am-1pm. NIS3.)*

MUSLIM QUARTER (EXCLUDING VIA DOLOROSA)

The Muslim Quarter can be the most exciting of the four quarters; it is also the most conservative. Women should **dress modestly.** During the day, the main streets are crowded with tourists and merchants. At night, the quarter becomes dark, isolated, and possibly dangerous. This is the largest and most heavily populated quarter in the Old City. The architecture dates mostly from the Ayyubid and Mamluk periods. Old City walking tours will pass through here; inquire with individual tour groups for more detailed excursions (see p. 87). Self-appointed tour guides of varying quality linger around Jaffa Gate; agree on a price before setting out. Don't pay more than NIS15 for a trip around the Quarter.

Damascus Gate, the main entrance to the Quarter, is one of the finest examples of Islamic architecture around. The main thoroughfare and western border of the quarter is **Khan al-Zeit Rd.,** leading from Damascus Gate to David St., with an infinite array of booths selling spices, candy, clothing, sandals, and souvenirs. **Al-Wad Rd.** connects the Western Wall area to Damascus Gate. A right off al-Wad Rd. onto the **Via Dolorosa** leads to an array of small ceramics shops.

SOUQ. The bustling *souq* is crammed at all hours; watch out for heavily laden wagons and tiny tractors, which charge gleefully at the crowds of shoppers. Palestinian crafts such as Hebron-style wine glasses, mother-of-pearl inlaid boxes, ceramic tiles, and spherical Jerusalem candles are beautiful; other items (cheap t-shirts and plastic Domes of the Rock) aren't. For those who cannot throw out enough t-shirts to fit an *argeileh* (waterpipe) into their packs, a short but powerful smoke (NIS1-2) at an *ahwa* (coffeeshop) provides adequate consolation. The apple tobacco is especially delicious. Several local haunts inside Damascus Gate rent *argeilehs* for NIS5 and they'll keep refilling the coals until your lungs say stop. Women should make sure the *ahwa* is not exclusively male.

Do not buy from the first air-conditioned wonderland you enter. Often, the same wares are sold from closet-like alcoves for a lot less. There's a lot of supply in this market—remember the rules of economics and use them to your advantage. There's no backing off—you must be prepared to pay any price you offer.

GETTING THE BEST DEAL: THE FINE ART OF HAGGLING In any of Israel's numerous flea markets and *shuks*, all budget travelers must participate in one fundamental struggle: defending the honor of English-speaking people everywhere by not getting ripped off (too much). Many describe bargaining as a dance, and to avoid stepping on anyone's toes or revealing that you have two left feet, keep the following tips in mind:

- Learn the numbers one through ten and basic phrases ("lo!", "kama zeh?", for more see inside back cover). If you can get through the experience without having to resort to English, more power (and shekels) to you.
- Be prepared to walk away empty-handed and don't show too much interest in an item. Keep in mind that every vendor from Akko to Jerusalem probably has 30 of them. If they discover you've become attached to an item, the battle is already lost.
- A counter-offer of one-half the offered price is generally appropriate, but use lower fractions for prices that seem unduly high.
- At some point in the bargaining process, you are expected to start walking away and the salesmen generally reserve the biggest price drop for that point in the "dance."
- Finally, if you really want something but he just won't go down another shekel, keep in mind how much one shekel is actually worth and just surrender and buy the chintzy little thing.

Much decorative masonry in the *souq* is characteristic of Mamluk architecture. Paintings of the Dome of the Rock and the Ka'ba shrine of Mecca adorn doorways; a painting of the latter signifies that a member of the family has been on the *hajj*, the Islamic pilgrimage to Mecca and Medina. The red and green painted dots on some whitewashed doors and walls are not graffiti; they too indicate the *hajj*.

BAB AL-SILSILAH ST. The stretch of Bab al-Silsilah St. (Gate of the Chain) extending from the end of David St. to the Temple Mount is partly founded on the ancient Mamluk causeway that crossed the Tyropoeon Valley, linking the upper city to the temple platform. There are sites to see here, but none to enter. At the end of the first alley to the left stands the **Khan al-Sultan** (or al-Wakala), a remarkably preserved Crusader-period *caravanserai*, an inn which provided lodging for merchants and their donkeys. Just past Misgav Ladakh St. (further down the street on the right) is the **Tashtamuriya Building,** housing the tomb of its namesake (d. 1384). The multitude of Mamluk institutions can be attributed to a system of succession that prevented them from passing wealth on to their children; constructing public institutions was the best way to preserve their legacy.

Continuing down Bab al-Silsilah St. to its intersection with Western Wall St. (HaKotel) leads to the **Kilaniya Mausoleum,** with its characteristic Mamluk stalactite half-dome. The **Turba Turkan Khatun** (Tomb of Lady Turkan) is at #149. At the end of Bab al-Silsilah St. , on the right and often surrounded by tour guides in training, is the **Tankiziya Building,** built by a Mamluk slave who worked his way up to become governor of Damascus in 1312, and then back down to imprisonment and execution in Alexandria 30 years later. This venerated structure, on the site of the original seat of the *Sanhedrin*, is currently controlled by the Israelis due to its proximity to the Western Wall and Temple Mount.

ROMAN SQUARE MUSEUM. The Roman Square museum, one of the Muslim Quarter's oft-visited sights, is not actually within the Old City walls, but just outside and underneath them. The museum, at the Damascus Gate entrance to the Ramparts, is set among the excavations from Aoelia Capitolina (the name given to Jerusalem by Emperor Adrianus in 135 CE). Although the archaeology is fascinating, the museum itself is fairly dull. Its centerpiece is a copy of the 6th-century **Madaba map** from Jordan, the earliest known blueprint of Jerusalem's layout. *(Exiting Damascus Gate, go down the stairs to your left. Open Sa-Th 9am-5pm, F 9am-2pm. NIS8, students NIS4. Combo ticket to the museum, Ramparts Promenade, Zedekiah's Cave, Hezekiah's Tunnel, and the Ophel Archaeological Garden NIS35.)*

ZEDEKIAH'S CAVE. Also known as King Solomon's Quarries, the cave extends far beneath the Muslim Quarter. According to tradition, stones from the quarry were used in the construction of the First Temple, but archaeological and geological evidence suggest that the cave was used no earlier than the Second Temple period. *(Entrance is about halfway between Damascus Gate and Herod Gate; exiting Damascus Gate, follow the wall to the right. Open Sa-Th 9am-4pm, F 9am-2pm. NIS10, students NIS8.)*

NEAR THE OLD CITY

MOUNT ZION AND ENVIRONS

MOUNT ZION. Rising outside the city walls opposite Zion Gate and the Armenian Quarter, Mount Zion *(Har Tzion)* has long been considered the site of the Tomb of David, the Last Supper, and the descent of the Holy Spirit at Pentecost. The name Zion, which is also applied to Israel as a whole, was first seized by King David when he conquered the eastern territory. During the siege of the Jewish Quarter in 1948, the area around **Zion Gate** was the scene of some of the fiercest fighting in Jerusalem; bombshell pockmarks remain. *(To reach the mount, exit the Old City through Zion Gate, near the Jewish Quarter parking lot, and take the short path opposite the gate, bearing right at the Franciscan convent. At the next fork, a left leads to the Cenacle and David's Tomb; a right leads to the Dormition Abbey.)*

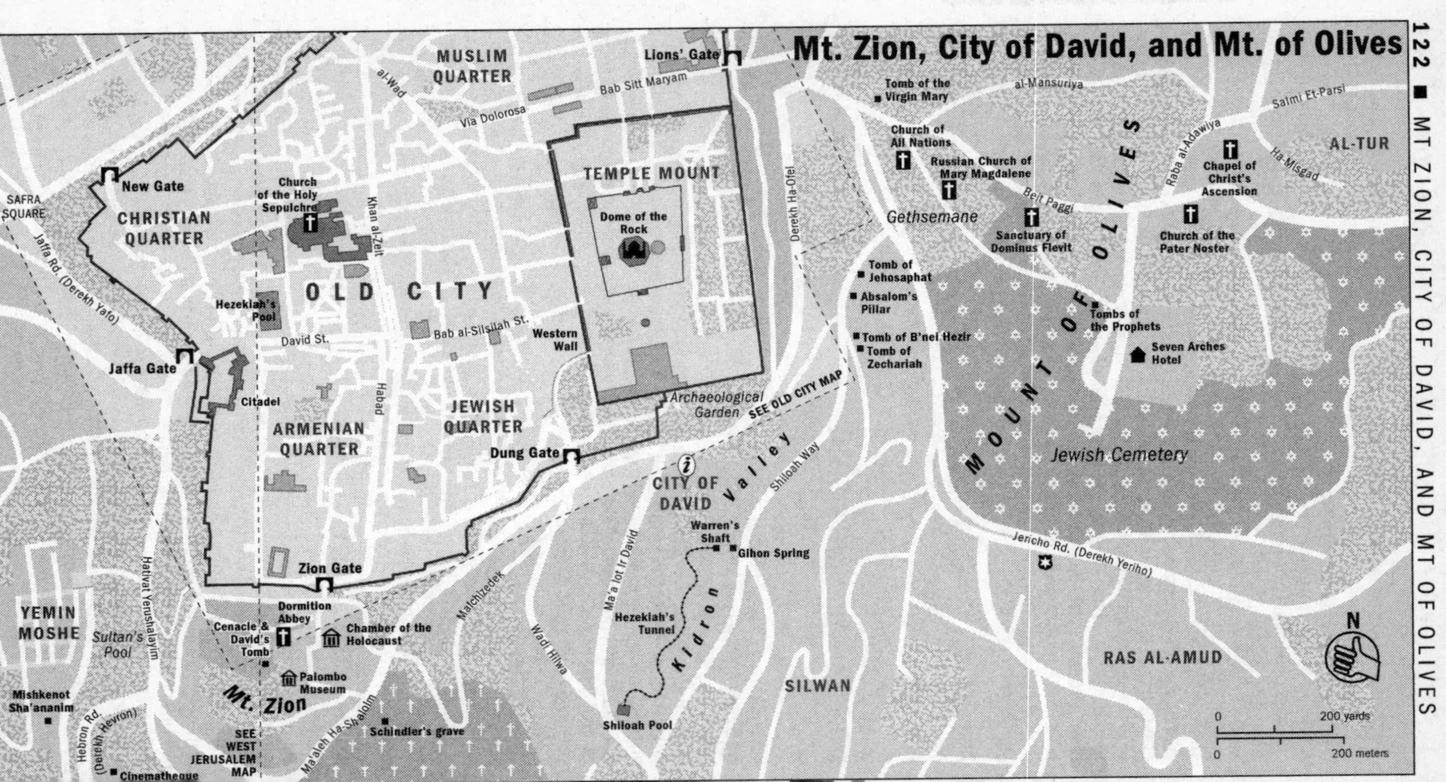
Mt. Zion, City of David, and Mt. of Olives
MUSLIM QUARTER
Lions' Gate
Bab Sitt Maryam
al-Wad
Via Dolorosa
Tomb of the Virgin Mary
al-Mansuriya
Salmi Et-Parsi
Church of All Nations
Russian Church of Mary Magdalene
Raba al-Adawiya
Chapel of Christ's Ascension
Ha-Misgad
AL-TUR
New Gate
SAFRA SQUARE
CHRISTIAN QUARTER
Church of the Holy Sepulchre
Khan al-Zeit
TEMPLE MOUNT
Dome of the Rock
Derekh Ha-Ofel
Gethsemane
Beit Paggi
Sanctuary of Dominus Flevit
Church of the Pater Noster
MOUNT OF OLIVES
Jaffa Rd. (Derekh Yafo)
OLD CITY
Hezekiah's Pool
Tomb of Jehosaphat
Absalom's Pillar
Tombs of the Prophets
David St.
Bab al-Silsilah St.
Western Wall
Tomb of B'nei Hezir
Tomb of Zechariah
Seven Arches Hotel
Jaffa Gate
Citadel
Habad
JEWISH QUARTER
Archaeological Garden
SEE OLD CITY MAP
ARMENIAN QUARTER
Dung Gate
Kidron Valley
Shiloah Way
Jewish Cemetery
CITY OF DAVID
Warren's Shaft
Gihon Spring
Ma'a lot Ir David
Jericho Rd. (Derekh Yeriho)
Hativat Yerushalayim
Zion Gate
Malchizedek
YEMIN MOSHE
Sultan's Pool
Dormition Abbey
Cenacle & David's Tomb
Chamber of the Holocaust
Wadi Hilwa
Hezekiah's Tunnel
N
RAS AL-AMUD
Palombo Museum
Mishkenot Sha'ananim
Mt. Zion
SILWAN
Hebron Rd. (Derekh Hevron)
SEE WEST JERUSALEM MAP
Ma'aleh Ha-Shalom
Schindler's grave
Shiloah Pool
0
200 yards
0
200 meters
Cinematheque

COENACULUM (CENACLE). The no-frills appearance of this church, identified by most as the site of the Last Supper, is due in part to an attempt by the British Mandate to avoid sectarian disputes by forbidding any change to the building. The Cenacle was converted from a mosque into a church almost four centuries ago, but the mosque's *mihrab* (prayer niche) is still visible in the southern wall. A group in Ein Kerem, on the outskirts of Jerusalem, runs Last Supper reenactment dinners in a variety of languages. *(Take the left fork after the Franciscan convent and ascend a stairway through the Diaspora Yeshiva door on the left. Open Sa-Th 8am-8pm, F 8am-2pm.)*

DAVID'S TOMB. Archaeologists are skeptical about the authenticity of this site; it is written that kings and only kings were buried within the city, and Mount Zion was never encompassed by David's walls. The historical check, however, does little to reduce the fervor of worshipers at the tomb, many of whom whisper David's own psalms in the small, dim chamber. *(To enter, go through the Cenacle, descend the stairs, and turn right around the corner. Open Sa-Th 8am-6pm, F 8am-2pm; in winter Su-Th 8am-5pm, F 8am-1pm. Free, although members of the yeshiva next door happily accept donations. Modest dress required; men should cover their heads with the available cardboard kippot.)*

BASILICA OF THE DORMITION ABBEY. This huge, fortress-like edifice was completed in 1910 and commemorates the death of the Virgin Mary. Parts of the precariously situated basilica were damaged during battles in 1948 and 1967 and were never repaired. A gold mosaic rises above the apse, the floor is inlaid with symbols of the zodiac and the apostles, and the crypt holds a figure of the Virgin, with Jesus surrounded by all the women of the Bible above her. Head down to the bathrooms; by the entrance are the excavated ruins of a Byzantine church. *(Off the right fork of the road leading to the Cenacle. ☎565 53 30. Open M-Th, Sa 9am-noon and 12:30-6pm; F, Su 10am-noon and 12:30-6pm. Free. Call for info on occasional classical music concerts.)*

CHAMBER OF THE HOLOCAUST. Nowhere near the scale of the Yad Va-Shem museum in West Jerusalem, this small, simple memorial museum was the first of its kind in Israel and is at least as moving as the newer, more modern ones. The museum's few rooms contain haunting photographs, memorabilia, and newspaper clippings from the Holocaust, as well as memorial plaques covering the walls. *(Across the street from the back entrance of David's Tomb; can also be reached by bearing left at the Franciscan convent. Open Su-Th 8am-5pm, F 8am-2pm. NIS10, students NIS5, seniors NIS6.)*

SCHINDLER'S GRAVE. Visitors pay homage to Oskar Schindler, the man credited with saving more than 1300 Jews from Nazi persecution, by placing stones on his grave. *(In the Christian Cemetery across the main road, downhill from the other Mount Zion sights. The gate is open at erratic hours. Once inside, go down two flights of stairs.)*

THE CITY OF DAVID

As far as the archaeologists working to uncover this massive site are concerned, any exploration of Old Jerusalem must begin outside its walls, right here in the most ancient part of the city. The City of David housed the throne of the biblical Kings of Israel and was included within the walls during the First Temple period, while today's walled city dates from the mostly Hellenic period of the Second Temple. The earliest origins of biblical Jerusalem are still shrouded in mystery, but archaeologists have confirmed that the Ophel ridge, just south of the Old City walls, is the site of Jebus, the original Canaanite city King David captured and made his capital.

Excavations of the site indicate that the Jebusites were confined to an area of about eight acres. The city's location above the Kidron Valley was selected for its proximity to the Giḥon Spring and its defensibility on the ridge. In times of peace, townspeople passed through a "water gate" to bring water into the city. For continued supply during times of siege, an underground tunnel provided access to a large reservoir. David's strategy for taking Jebus relied on finding the water source; his soldier Joab succeeded when he found a natural shaft that led up to the tunnel and therefore into the city. In 1867, Warren confirmed this biblical account when he discovered the long, sleek shaft that now bears his name. For many years, archaeologists believed that water was drawn up through this shaft, but recent excavations found the continuation of the tunnel that led to the reservoir; the current theory is that the natural shaft was covered or ignored by the Jebusites and never used for drawing water. In the 1960s, Kathleen Kenyon located the Jebusite city walls, which date from 1800 BCE and lie just above the Giḥon Spring.

Later, King Hezekiah devised a system to prevent David's strategy from being turned against the Israelites; he built a 500m long tunnel to bring the Giḥon waters into the city walls and hid the entrance of the spring, preventing invaders from finding water when they camped outside the wall. In 1880, a few years after the tunnel was excavated, a local boy discovered an inscription carved by Hezekiah's engineers describing the jubilant moment when the north and south construction crews met underground. The original inscription is in Istanbul, but a copy is on display at the Israel Museum (see p. 132).

Recent years have seen tension in this much-disputed area. Claiming the legacy of the ancient Jewish capital, Israeli nationalists have established a Jewish presence in the midst of the almost entirely Arab Silwan; Arab homes were quietly purchased for very large sums and Jewish families brought in. The Jewish bastion is perched precariously and conspicuously in the Arab neighborhood. Unaware tourists may find themselves walking into a potentially dangerous situation. As always in politically sensitive areas, make your tourist status pronounced, read newspapers, and consult tourist offices before exploring.

The excavations in the northern part of the Ophel, **Section G,** were halted in 1981 when a group of Orthodox Jews protested that the area might be the Jewish cemetery mentioned in the diaries of several medieval pilgrims. After considerable and sometimes violent political dispute, the Supreme Court of Israel ruled that the site should be closed. As a compromise, the Israeli government promised that digging would continue only under rabbinic supervision. No bones have been found, and the excavations ceased in the late-90s due to a lack of funding.

Sloshing with a flashlight or candle through **Hezekiah's Tunnel** is one of Jerusalem's most enjoyable adventures, but it's best not to do it alone. The water is never deeper than thigh-high, and wading through it takes about 45 minutes. Start at the Giḥon Spring source on Shiloah Way and emerge at the Pool of Shiloah (Silwan in Arabic, Silo'am in Hebrew). Check in at the Visitors Center for a map and detailed instructions. *(Open Su-Th 9am-5pm, F 9am-2pm. NIS12, students NIS6.)*

Beside the Visitors Center is an ancient, subterranean **cistern,** 15m in diameter and about 5m high, suspected by some to be the biblical pit into which the prophet Jeremiah was thrown (Jeremiah 38). The cistern can only be entered as part of the guided tour offered through the Visitors Center. Past the Visitors Center, descend the stairs to the hillside ruins known as **Area G.** The foundations of a house here date from the First Temple period. Archaeologists found 51 clay seals in the house, representing 46 different names, leading some to speculate that this was possibly a post office or official archive building.

About 100m past the entrance to the City of David, away from Area G, is a small museum with photos of the most recent excavations. A spiral staircase leads down to **Warren's Shaft.** (Open Su-Th 9am-4pm, F 9am-1pm. NIS8, students NIS6.) With a flashlight, the entire length of the wall that Joab scaled is visible. Nearby is the recently excavated **Spring House** (Beit Ha-Ma'ayan), which accessed the ancient pool. There are plans to host a sound and light show inside the structure that currently covers the (now dry) pools.

Sights in the City of David are poorly marked and difficult to appreciate without guidance. The **City of David Visitors Center** provides an excellent three-hour tour of the excavations. Tours in English Su, Tu, and Th at 10:30am, with additional days and times during the summer. NIS39, students NIS35, children NIS26; admission to all sights included. Book by phone at least one day in advance. The tour involves many **stairs and wading** through Hezekiah's Tunnel (wear shorts and shoes that can get wet, and bring a flashlight if you can). To get to the Visitors Center from town, take bus #1 to Dung Gate. Facing away from the gate, make a left downhill, then the first right, downhill onto the unmarked Ma'alot Ir David St.; the center is immediately on the left. (☎800 252 423 or 626 23 41. Open Su-Th 9am-5pm, F 9am-2pm.)

THE KIDRON VALLEY AND THE MOUNT OF OLIVES

The best way to visit the churches, tombs, gardens, and observation point is to start at the top and walk down the winding road that passes through the hill's sights. In the morning, this route yields sparkling views of the Old City. Most churches are closed on Sundays and from about noon to 3pm. A taxi from Damascus Gate to the top should cost NIS15-20.

Christians revere the historic **Kidron Valley,** which runs between the Old City and the Mount of Olives, as the path of the last walk of Jesus. To get there, turn left from Dung Gate and walk up the narrow Ha-Ophel Rd. A new paved sidewalk leads to an observation point for the valley, the Mount of Olives in front of it, and the four tombs directly below; a map on the floor explains the vista. Running north-to-south are the **Tomb of Jehosaphat** and **Absalom's Pillar,** allegedly the tomb of David's favored but feisty son (II Samuel 15-18). A dirt path on the left leads to the impressive rock-hewn **Tomb of B'nei Hezir** and the **Tomb of Zechariah.** The tombs are accessible from the base of the Mount of Olives or via a new staircase near the observation point just past Ma'alot Ir David St. on Ha-Ophel Rd. **Women travelers should not visit the Mount of Olives alone.**

The bone-dry slopes of the **Mount of Olives** (Har Ha-Zeitim in Hebrew, Jabal al-Zeitoun in Arabic) to the east of the Old City are dotted with churches marking the sites of Jesus' triumphant entry into Jerusalem, his teaching, his agony and betrayal in Gethsemane, and his ascension to heaven. Jews believe that the Messiah will arrive in Jerusalem from the Mount of Olives. Tradition holds that the thousands of people buried here will be the first to be resurrected upon his arrival.

For a monumental view of the Old City, check out the observation promenade outside the **Seven Arches Hotel.** From here look to the north: the bell tower of the **Augusta Victoria Hospital** on Mount Scopus marks the highest point in Jerusalem (903m above sea level). Feel free to explore the luxurious interior of the hotel and other magnificent vistas from behind its many windows.

CHAPEL OF CHRIST'S ASCENSION. Built in 392, this was the first church erected to commemorate Christ's ascension. It is the geographical apex of noteworthy sites in the area, if not the aesthetic peak. Toward the end of the 11th century, the Crusaders adorned the tiny chapel with columns and arches, and in the late 12th century Salah al-Din fortified it and added a domed roof. The interior contains a candle-lighting stand and a sacred footprint, unidentifiable after generations of non-sacred treadings of relic-happy pilgrims. The chapel is not particularly interesting except on and near Ascension Day, when Christians from several denominations set up camp in the small courtyard during the celebration. *(Open daily 8am-5pm; ask a guard in the mosque courtyard if closed. NIS3.)*

CHURCH OF THE PATER NOSTER. When St. Eleni founded this church in the 4th century, she named it the Church of the Disciples; it is also referred to as the **Church of the Eleona** (Greek for "olive grove"). This was the site of the grotto where Jesus revealed the "inscrutable mysteries" to his disciples—foretelling the destruction of Jerusalem and his Second Coming. The church commemorates the first recitation of the Lord's Prayer *(pater noster)*. Polyglots can read the prayer in over 80 languages (including Quechua, Sotho, and Old Frisian) on the tiled walls. In the midst of the translations is the tomb of the Princesse de la Tour d'Auvergne, who worked here for 17 years (1857-74) and financed the excavations and renovations. The Lord's Prayer was her favorite prayer, and she was determined to uncover the long-lost grotto where it was originally taught. The urn above the tomb holds the heart of her father, the Italian politician and poet Baron de Bossi. *(Below the Chapel of Christ's Ascension, under an orange sign reading "Carmelite Convent." Open M-Sa 8:30-11:45am and 3-4:45pm.)*

TOMBS OF THE PROPHETS. This site is the supposed resting-place of the prophets Malachi and Ḥaggai. Archaeological evidence, however, suggests that the graves are far too recent—probably dating from the 4th century CE. The glass-enclosed home on the premises is the residence of the caretaker, who will show visitors around downstairs with a kerosene lamp if asked. *(With your back to the Seven Arches, turn right and go down the gray cement path to the left. Several meters down, a large green gate on the left leads to two cavernous tunnels. Open Su-F 8am-3pm.)*

To the left of the tombs is an easy-to-miss orange sign with rubbed-off black lettering marking "This Common Grave" of those who died defending the Jewish Quarter in 1948. Next to the Common Grave lies the **National Cemetery,** and farther down the path sprawls the immense **Jewish Graveyard,** the largest Jewish cemetery in the world. Take the stone staircase on the left for another small observation point and access to the Jewish graves.

SANCTUARY OF DOMINUS FLEVIT. The sanctuary was erected in 1955 to mark the spot where Jesus wept for Jerusalem (Luke 19:41); hence the Latin name meaning "The Lord wept." The chapel incorporates a Byzantine mosaic and altar; the apse end is one large window, with a dazzling view of the Dome of the Rock. The glass shards of broken liquor bottles cemented to the top of the walls serve to protect the property from trespassers. *(Downhill from the Tombs of the Prophets, on the right. Open Mar.-May 8am-5pm, June-Oct. 8am-6pm.)*

RUSSIAN CHURCH OF MARY MAGDALENE. Czar Alexander III built the church in 1885 in the lavish 17th-century Muscovite style and dedicated it to his mother, the Empress Maria Alexandrovna. It is adorned with seven golden onion domes. The crypt houses the body of a Russian grand duchess, smuggled to Jerusalem via Beijing after her death in the Russian Revolution. Now a convent, the church claims a part of the Garden of Gethsemane. *(Past the Sanctuary of Dominus Flevit. ☎ 628 43 71. Ordinarily open Tu and Th 10am-noon.)*

CHURCH OF ALL NATIONS AND THE GARDEN OF GETHSEMANE. Built with contributions from many European countries, the Church of All Nations faces west toward the Old City. Among its highlights is a magnificent gold and red facade portraying Jesus bringing peace to all nations. Inside, mosaics and sculptures depict Jesus' last days, including the proverbial kiss of death, but the real highlight is the **Rock of the Agony,** where Jesus was so impassioned that he sweat blood (Luke 22:44). Although the site has been venerated since the 4th century, the present building, designed by Barluzzi, was built after World War I. The garden outside is where Jesus spent his last night in prayer and was betrayed by Judas (Mark 14:32-43). *(The church is on the left near the bottom of the main path; the entrance is on the side. Open daily Apr.-Oct. 8am-noon and 2:30-6pm; Nov.-Mar. 8am-noon and 2:30-5pm.)*

TOMB OF THE VIRGIN MARY AND GROTTO OF GETHSEMANE. The steep stairs down to Mary's tomb were built to prevent pagans from riding horses into the sacred space. To the right, the natural grotto is another candidate for the site of Jesus' betrayal and arrest. *(At the bottom of the main path, on the right. Open daily 8am-noon and 2:30-5:30pm. At the exit onto the main road are telephone booths and taxis. Damascus and St. Stephen's Gates are within walking distance. A taxi to the city center should cost NIS15.)*

WEST JERUSALEM

West Jerusalem is best known for the eateries, dance clubs, and sandal stores of the pedestrian *midraḥov*. The ever-popular city center *(merkaz ha-ir)* provides welcome entertainment for tourists, but explorations of West Jerusalem's subtler side—its elegant neighborhoods, well-kept parks, and impressive museums—are often more rewarding.

Jerusalem has been dubbed "a city of neighborhoods" for good reason. Each of its twenty-something neighborhoods has a distinct flavor. A sampling of the subtleties: in the artist-haven Baqa'a, it is hardly possible to walk through the streets without hearing piano practice; the Ultra-Orthodox Mea She'arim area is one of the last strongholds of the Yiddish language; in Qatamon, 7th-generation Jerusalemites mingle with English-speaking university students; the German Colony, sometimes jokingly referred to as the "Sixth Borough," is replete with New Yorkers who have made *aliya*, or immigrated to Israel.

Since 1860, when a few Jews moved outside the walls of the Old City, West Jerusalem has flourished. By municipal law, all new buildings must be cased with off-white Jerusalem stone, creating a harmony between the uninspired developments of the 50s, ritzy displays of the 90s, and the ancient buildings of the Old City.

ZION SQUARE AND ENVIRONS

Zion Square (Kikkar Tzion) is the center of West Jerusalem and one of the few places in the city that is lively at all hours. Less than 1km from the Old City along **Jaffa Rd.,** it is the epicenter of the pedestrian malls of Ben-Yehuda, Yoel Salomon, Naḥalat Shiva, and Rivlin St. and a good reference point.

Intersecting Jaffa Rd. just northwest of Zion Sq. and forming another boundary of the *midraḥov* is **King George St.,** a bustling extension of the city center. At the corner of King George and Ben-Yehuda St., uphill from Jaffa Rd., is the area's largest **mall,** Ha-Mashbir. Three blocks further away from Jaffa Rd., the enormous and ornate **Great Synagogue of Jerusalem,** 58 King George St., is an inspiring architectural compromise between modernity and religion. (☎624 71 12. Open Su-Th 9am-1pm, F 9am-noon.) Services here on holidays and Jewish new months feature an excellent men's choir meant to recall the Levites' choir in the ancient Temple.

Across from Zion Sq. on the other side of Jaffa Rd., Ha-Rav Kook St. eventually crosses Ha-Nevi'im St. and turns into the quiet, stone-wall-lined Ethiopia St. At the end of Ethiopia St. on the right is the handsome **Ethiopian Church,** built between 1874 and 1901. Inscriptions in Ge'ez, the ancient language of Ethiopia, adorn the gate and doors; black-robed monks and nuns live in the surrounding compound and care for the distinctive, blue-domed church, which feels oddly like a cross between a church, mosque, and synagogue. (☎628 28 40. Open daily 9am-1pm and 2-6pm. Remove your shoes before entering.) Directly across from the entrance to the church, at #11, is the one-time home of the founder of the modern Hebrew language, **Eliezer Ben-Yehuda.**

MEA SHE'ARIM

Mea She'arim ("Hundredfold," an invocation of plenty), lies just north of Ethiopia St., on the other side of Ha-Nevi'im St. To get there from Zion Sq., take Jaffa Rd. and turn right onto Nathan Strauss St. (the continuation of King George St.); continue until it intersects with Ha-Nevi'im St. (Bank Ha-Poalim is on the corner). This intersection is known as Kikkar Shabbat (walk through on a Friday night around 11pm to find out why), the unofficial beginning of Mea She'arim.

WARNING! Signs in the area caution, "Do not enter our neighborhood unless your dress and conduct conform to the standards described below," and then proceed to request that women wear at least knee-length skirts (not pants), elbow-length sleeves, and nothing tight-fitting. Men should wear below-the-knee pants. Visitors are also advised not to enter in groups; other signs remind outsiders that this is a residential area, not a "touristic site." Be warned that extremists have been known to stone tourists whom they deem improperly dressed. Whether you're Jewish or not, take these warnings seriously to avoid offending local Ḥasidim and being asked to leave the area.

The neighborhood, one of Jerusalem's oldest, is among the few remaining Jewish *shtetl* communities like those that used to flourish in pre-Holocaust Eastern Europe. Several thousand Ultra-Orthodox Jews live here and in the neighboring **Geula** (Hebrew for "redemption"), preserving traditional habits, dress, customs, and beliefs with painstaking diligence. If your newfound grasp of Hebrew lets you down, it may be because you're hearing Yiddish, spoken by residents who consider Hebrew too holy for daily use. The neighborhood, just like the Orthodox suburbs to the north and northwest of the city, is largely conservative, but Mea She'arim's relatively few extremists receive a good deal of publicity for opinions and actions that do not necessarily reflect those of the entire community. The Neturei Karta ("City Keepers"), the most extreme sect of the Satmar Ḥasidim, oppose the Israeli state, argue that Jewish law prohibits the legitimate existence of a Jewish country until the coming of the Messiah. While other Ultra-Orthodox Jews hold similar views, the Neturei Karta once went so far as to ask Yasser Arafat to accept them as a minority in the future Palestinian state.

Mea She'arim is probably the cheapest place in the world for Jewish books and religious items. Although the quality is not as high as in the Jewish Quarter of the Old City, the stores along Mea She'arim St. have vast, affordable selections (see **Judaica,** p. 138). The neighborhood also has some of the city's best **bakeries,** most of which are open all night on Thursdays, baking *ḥallah* and cake for Shabbat.

GIVAT RAM

ISRAELI SUPREME COURT. This impressive neighborhood is the seat of the Israeli Supreme Court, completed in late 1992. The designers combined Modernist flair with themes from ancient Jerusalem's architectural traditions. See if you can find the spot from which the cover photo on your *Let's Go* book was taken. This architectural masterpiece is worth visiting for the aesthetic experience as well as an understanding of the complex, constantly changing Israeli justice system (keep in mind that Israel has no constitution). Anyone may sit in on a trial—it's like Court TV, only live and in Hebrew. The best time to catch a court session is in the morning, just after the work day begins. *(☎675 96 12; fax 652 71 18; email marcia@supreme.court.gov.il. Open Su-Th 8:30am-2:30pm. English tour Su-Th noon; call for summer schedule. With advance notice, can accommodate most special needs, including touch tours for the blind.)*

WOHL ROSE GARDEN. The Wohl Rose Garden, which forms a walking path between the Supreme Court and the Knesset, is a sublime picnic spot with beautifully manicured lawns and flowers. Take the path on the right when exiting the Supreme Court building, or climb up to it from anywhere on the main street; leaving the Knesset compound, the path is also on your right. Near the back of the Supreme Court, part of the garden has been converted into a Garden of All Nations; a path winds past several dozen small plots growing native shrubs from countries around the world.

KNESSET. Once at the **Knesset,** discover why Israeli schoolteachers compare excessively rowdy pupils to Parliament members. Free tours include an explanation of the structure of the Israeli government, a look at the magnificent Marc Chagall mosaics and tapestries (yes, those are woven not painted) that adorn the building, and a peek into the room in which some of the most important decisions have been made—the cafeteria. *(On Eliezer Kaplan St. directly across from the Israel Museum. From the central bus station or Jaffa Rd. take bus #9 or 24 and ask the driver where to get off. Passports are required for entrance as part of a detailed search. ☎675 33 33. Tours last 30min.; Su and Th; call to find out when the English tours begin and arrive at least 15min. early. Open sessions M and Tu 4pm, W 11am; call to make sure that the Knesset is in session.)*

ARDON WINDOW. The Ardon Window in the **Jewish National and University Library** is another Givat Ram sight worth looking into—or, better still, out of. One of the largest stained-glass windows in the world, it depicts Jewish mystical symbols in rich, dark colors. The library, which boasts the world's largest collection of Judaica and Hebraica materials, also features temporary exhibits displaying different aspects of their collection. *(Take bus #9, 24, or 28 from the city-center. ☎658 50 27. Open Su-Th 9am-7pm, F 9am-1pm. Free.)*

REḤAVIA

South of Independence Park lie some of Jerusalem's most elegant and affluent residential areas. Reḥavia, the area trisected by Azza Rd. and Ramban St., was founded in the 1920s and became the refuge for the many German Jews fleeing Nazi persecution in the 1930s. For years, it was famous as a German high-culture enclave, where dark wood library shelves were lined with Goethe and Schiller while Mozart grooved on the gramophone. Today, the legacy lives on in the many International Style houses, designed in the best German Modernism tradition. Flowery hedges fill the spaces between the well-kept stone buildings, making a walk around the neighborhood's lush streets a verdant pleasure.

In the middle of Reḥavia on Alfassi St. is **Jason's Tomb** (near 12 Alfassi St., the sign says "Rock Cut Tomb"), built around 100 BCE as the burial site of a wealthy Hasmonean-era Jewish family. Pottery found at the site indicates that three generations were buried there, while charcoal drawings on the plastered porch wall depict ships, suggesting that one of the deceased was involved in naval excursions. The pyramid topping the tomb is a reconstruction. Farther east past Azza Rd. is the **Prime Minister's official residence,** in the heavily guarded house at the corner of Balfour St. and Smolenskin St. Next door on Balfour St. is the **Schocken Library,** designed by renowned architect Erich Mendelssohn, who resided in Jerusalem in the late 1930s (he lived in the windmill on Ramban St. near Kikkar Tzarfat, now a ritzy shopping complex).

TALBIYYA AND QATAMON

Farther south are the neighborhoods of **Talbiyya** (Komemiyut) and **Qatamon** (Gonen), still known by their pre-1948 Arabic names. The ornate villas, one of which was the home of renowned cultural theorist Edward Said, have become favorites of Hebrew University faculty and, more recently, well-to-do professionals. The official residence of the **Israeli President** is on Ha-Nassi (President) St., and the plush **Jerusalem Theater** is on the other side of the block, on the corner of Chopin St. and Marcus Rd.

On the other end of Jabotinsky St. from the President's House is **King David St.,** running northward to the base of Shlomtzion Ha-Malka St. and Shlomo Ha-Melekh St., which runs uphill to Safra Sq. and the Old City. Just south of the intersection with Jabotinsky St. is the sprawling, green **Liberty Bell Park** (Gan Ha-Pa'amon). An amphitheater, basketball courts, climbable sculptures, and a Liberty Bell replica grace the lawns. On Saturday nights, the park hops with folk-dancing festivities (take bus #14, 18, or 21 from the center). Three hundred meters up King David St. toward the city center, the **Three Arches YMCA,** built in 1933, has an imposing bell tower with impressive views of the whole city. (☎569 26 92. NIS5.)

YEMIN MOSHE AND MISHKENOT SHA'ANANIM

In the valley between King David St. and the Old City lies the restored neighborhood of **Yemin Moshe.** It was here that Sir Moses Montefiore, a British Jew, first managed to convince a handful of residents from the Old City's overcrowded Jewish Quarter to spend occasional nights outside the city walls, thus founding West Jerusalem. To strengthen the settlers' confidence, Montefiore built Mishkenot Sha'ananim (Tranquil Habitations), a small, picturesque compound with crenelated walls resembling those of the Old City. The original buildings, located at the bottom of the hill, now house an exclusive municipal guest house and a pricey French restaurant. Montefiore also erected his famous **stone windmill,** which now contains a tiny free museum. (Open Su-Th 9am-4pm, F 9am-1pm.) Yemin Moshe is crammed with artists' studios and galleries; a plaza with a fountain beneath the exclusive King David Apartments makes this a lovely spot to wander. The stepped street of Ḥutzot Ha-Yotzer leads up to Ḥativat Yerushalayim St.; at #16 is the studio of Motke Blum, whose subtle cityscapes brilliantly evoke Jerusalem in oil. The now-dry **Sultan's Pool** (see p. 137) sits in the valley below. Named after Suleiman the Magnificent, who renovated this Second Temple reservoir in the 16th century, the pool figures prominently in Palestinian novelist Jabra Ibrahim Jabra's *The Ship*. Today, the Sultan's Pool is most famous for its open-air concerts and annual art fair in July or early August.

GERMAN COLONY AND HAAS PROMENADE

The **German Colony,** a neighborhood of somber European houses and spacious Arab villas, surrounds Emek Refa'im St., a beautiful upscale avenue with a lively cafe scene. Buses #4, 14, and 18 run here from the city-center. To the southeast, the **Haas Promenade** is a hillside park that commands unbelievable views of the Old City and the Dead Sea. The dusk experience alone is worth the trip. On foot, walk south on Hebron Rd., bear left onto Albeck St., and turn left onto Yanofsky St. Bus #8 runs from King George St. to the corner of Albeck St. and Yanofsky St.

NORTHERN OUTSKIRTS

TOMBS OF THE SANHEDRIN. A park carpeted with pebbles and pine needles houses the Tombs of the Sanhedrin. Composed of 70 esteemed male sages and leaders, the Sanhedrin was the ancient high court of the Jews; it ruled on legal matters and even reviewed Jesus' case. Separate burial areas were designated for the members. *(Take bus #2 from the city center to Ha-Sanhedrin St., off Yam Suf St. Open Su-F 9am-sunset. Free.)*

AMMUNITION HILL. Before the Six-Day War, Ammunition Hill (Givat Ha-Taḥmoshet) was Jordan's most fortified position in the city, and it commanded much of northern Jerusalem. Taken by Israeli troops in a bloody battle, the hill now serves as a memorial to the Israeli soldiers who died in the Six-Day War. The somber, architecturally striking museum is housed in a reconstructed bunker with a detailed account of the 1967 battle. *(Buses #4, 9, 25, and 26 stop at the foot of the hill, in Ramat Eshkol, north of the Old City. ☎582 84 42. Open Su-Th 8am-6pm, F 8am-2pm; closes 1 hr. earlier in winter. NIS10, students NIS8.)*

HEBREW UNIVERSITY OF JERUSALEM. After 1948, the Hebrew University of Jerusalem had to relocate from **Mount Scopus** (Har Ha-Tzofim), where it was founded in 1925, to the new campus in Givat Ram. From 1948 to 1967, Mount Scopus was a garrisoned Israeli enclave in Jordanian territory. Every week for 19 years, UN supplies were flown in to relieve the community; every week, seven Israeli soldiers were let in and seven were let out. After 1967, all but the natural and physical sciences departments moved back to the original campus. Massive reconstruction was funded largely by international donors, whose names emblazon the libraries, promenades, and pebbles that comprise modern Mount Scopus. Free guided tours depart from the Bronfman Reception Center in the Sherman Administration Building. Pick up a map from the Reception Center for an unguided stroll around Israel's top university and browse through the bookstore, library, computer labs, and botanical gardens. For a fabulous view of Jerusalem, head to the lookout point, outside the university gates along the south side of the campus. The **Hecht Synagogue** in the Humanities building overlooks the Old City and is reputed to have the most magnificent view of Jerusalem in the entire city. Enter the synagogue via the Sherman Building. The university's gorgeous **amphitheater** faces the Palestinian Territories. *(Take bus #4a or 9 from the city-center. Tours Su-Th 11am.)*

WESTERN OUTSKIRTS

MOUNT HERZL PARK. Heading out of the city center along Herzl Blvd. eventually leads to Mount Herzl Park, named for Theodor Herzl, a newspaper correspondent who made the most prominent modern articulations of Zionism and lobbied for the creation of a Jewish state (see **Zionism,** p. 11). Herzl was buried here in 1904; since then, the site has become the final resting place for many other of the nation's great leaders, including Ze'ev Jabotinsky, Levi Eshkol, Golda Meir, and Yitzḥak Rabin. A small museum encapsulating the energy of Theodor Herzl is near the entrance, but it has been closed for over a year with no projected re-opening date. Nearby is the **Israeli Military Cemetery,** the resting place of fallen soldiers. *(Take bus #13, 16-18, 20-21, 23-24, 26-27, or 39. Open Su-Th 8am-6:45pm, F 8am-2pm, Sa 9am-6:45pm.)*

JERUSALEM FOREST AND EIN KEREM. The scenic Jerusalem Forest and the pastoral village of Ein Kerem, just west of Mount Herzl, are perfect for picnics and short hikes. Formerly an Arab village, tiny Ein Kerem (Fountain of Vines) is the traditionally recognized birthplace of **John the Baptist.** The tranquil streets of this thriving artists' colony are now lined with charming studios and craftshops. *(To get to the village, take city bus #17, west from the central bus station or Zion Sq. Every 20-30min.)*

The **Church of St. John,** with its soaring clocktower, marks the spot where John was born. The church displays several paintings, including the *Decapitation of Saint John.* In the church's **Grotto of the Nativity** there is a lovely Byzantine mosaic of pheasants—the symbol of the Eucharist. Ask the guardian for a key. *(☎641 36 39. Open Apr.-Sept. Su-F 8am-6pm; Oct.-Mar. Su-F 8am-5pm. Free.)*

Across the valley, down Ma'ayan St. from St. John's gate, the **Church of the Visitation** recalls Mary's visit to Elizabeth and contains a rock behind which the infant St. John hid when the Romans came to kill babies. *(☎641 72 91. Open May-Sept. Su-F 8am-6pm; Oct.-Apr. Su-F 8am-5pm. Free.)* The newer Upper Chapel depicts the glorification of Mary. The pink tower belongs to the **Russian Monastery.** *(☎625 25 65 or 641 28 87; only Russian spoken. Visit by appointment only.)*

HADASSAH MEDICAL CENTER. The synagogue at the Hadassah Medical Center, near Ein Kerem (not to be confused with Hadassah Hospital on Mount Scopus), houses the magnificent Chagall Windows, Marc Chagall's fantastical stained-glass depictions of scenes from Genesis 49 and Deuteronomy 33. Chagall donated the windows to the hospital in 1962. When four of the windows were damaged in the 1967 War, Chagall was sent an urgent cable. He replied, "You worry about the war, I'll worry about my windows." Two years later he installed replacements. Three of the windows still contain bullet holes. *(From Jaffa Rd., take bus #27 or 19 to the end, about 45min. ☎677 62 71. Synagogue open Su-Th 8am-1:15pm and 2-3:45pm, F 8am-1pm. NIS10, students and seniors with ID NIS5. Free tours in English Su-Th every hr. 8:30am-12:30pm and 2:30pm, F every hr. 9:30-11:30am.)*

JEWISH NATIONAL FUND TREE-PLANTING CENTER. About 4km behind the hospital is a Jewish National Fund tree-planting center. Follow the orange "Planting Center" signs (or take a taxi). You can plant your own tree and participate in the program that has reforested vast tracts of land in northern Israel. *(☎670 74 11 or 1 800 223 484; email plantatree@kkl.org.il. Trees US$10 each. Open Su-Th 8:30am-3pm, F 8:30am-noon.)*

EAST JERUSALEM

GARDEN TOMB. The skull-shaped rock formations here, first noticed in 1860 by Otto Thenius, have led some to believe that this quarry hillside is Golgotha (the "place of the skull"), the site of Christ's crucifixion. A nearby rock-cut tomb is that of Joseph of Arimathea, who placed Jesus' body in his own tomb after the Crucifixion. A group of Christians not affiliated with any one church now maintains the lovely garden that surrounds Skull Hill and the empty tomb. *(A short distance up Nablus Rd., on the right when coming from Damascus Gate; follow the signs. ☎627 27 45; www.gardentomb.com. Open M-Sa 8:30am-noon and 2-5:30pm. All are invited to attend the English service Su 9am. Free, but donations encouraged.)*

BASILICA OF ST. STEPHEN. The stately but seldom-visited basilica was consecrated in 439 CE. Impressive paintings of the 14 stations of the cross line the interior. The church runs an elementary school, within the high protective walls. *(6 Nablus Rd., just past the Garden Tomb. ☎582 81 49. No regular visiting hours, just ring the bell.)*

ST. GEORGE'S CATHEDRAL. This cathedral, which features a gothic-style nave and one of Jerusalem's most impressive organs, is the cathedral church of the Anglican Episcopal Dicocese of Jerusalem and the Middle East. The 100-year-old cathedral is now home to both Arabic and English speaking congregations, both of which welcome visitors at their services. *(On the right, past the intersection and the gas stations along Nablus Rd. ☎628 32 61. Open daily 6:30am-6:30pm. Free. Also runs a beautiful guest house, see p. 96.)*

TOMBEAU DES ROIS (TOMB OF THE KINGS). Judean kings were once thought to be buried here, but evidence shows that the tomb was in fact built in 45 CE by the Mesopotamian Queen Helena for her family. The deep tombs are dimly lit and practically require crawling to enter. *(On Salah al-Din St. at the intersection with Nablus Rd. Open M-Sa 8am-1pm and 3-5pm. NIS3.)*

ROCKEFELLER ARCHAEOLOGICAL MUSEUM. This museum records the region's history, beginning with the 250,000-350,000 year old remains of the "Galilee Man" (the oldest remains from the Levant), and it chronicles the cultural impact of imperialism. Check out the impressive, intricately carved wood panels from the 9th-century al-Aqsa Mosque. The museum was designed in the 1920s by British architect Austen S. B. Harrison in his inimitable Orientalist-Gothic style. *(In East Jerusalem on Suleiman St. at the northeastern corner of the Old City walls. Take Egged bus #1 toward the Old City from the city center. ☎628 22 51. Open Su-Th 10am-5pm, F-Sa 10am-2pm. NIS26, students NIS16.)*

MUSEUMS

ISRAEL MUSEUM

Take bus #9 or 17 from King George St. On foot, walk up King George, turn onto Ramban, cross Hazaz, and walk up Ruppin St. ☎670 88 11; fax 563 18 33; www.imj.org.il. Open Su-M and W-Th 10am-5pm, Tu 4-10pm, F 10am-2pm, Sa 10am-4pm. The Shrine of the Book is open the same hours except on Tu, open 10am-10pm. English Museum Highlights tours Su-M and W-F 11am, Tu 4:30pm. English guided tours of the Shrine Su-M and W-Th 1:30pm, Tu 3pm, and F 12:45pm. Admission to museum and Shrine NIS37, students NIS30, children (3-17) NIS20, family NIS108. Fee includes EZ-listening audio guide and admission to Rockefeller Museum; go to the Rockefeller first and the reciprocal deal saves NIS5. Repeat visit within one month half-price. NIS125 annual student membership allows unlimited entrance to the Israel and Rockefeller Museums.

The Israel Museum is the largest and most comprehensive museum in Israel. With extensive collections of antiquities, sculptures, ancient and modern art, books, the legendary Dead Sea Scrolls, and even a childrens' section with hands-on exhibits, the museum has nearly as many facets as the country itself.

Rock and rust enthusiasts should go straight to the **archaeology** section (pick up a map upon entering), where an extensive collection of tools and weapons records 30,000 years of human habitation in the Fertile Crescent. Guided English "Archaeological Treasures" tours are given on Monday and Thursday at 3pm. Straight ahead from the bottom of the steps is the **ethnography** exhibit, tracing the important events of the Jewish life cycle. Guided English "Jewish Heritage" tours of the Judaica and ethnography galleries are given Sunday and Wednesday at 3pm.

The museum boasts a fabulous collection of **art,** including the largest display of Israeli art in the world. There is a fairly large Impressionist and Post-Impressionist collection and even a few period rooms (including a spectacular French Rococo *salon* donated by the Rothschilds). The **Weisbord Pavilion,** directly across from the ticket building, houses a few Rodin sculptures, early modern paintings, and temporary exhibitions. The **Billy Rose Sculpture Garden** displays some incredible masterpieces by Henry Moore, Auguste Rodin, and Pablo Picasso. Pick up a schedule of evening outdoor concerts at the museum, and try to visit on a Tuesday night when the garden is illuminated.

The museum's biggest attraction is the **Shrine of the Book,** which displays the Dead Sea Scrolls. Hidden for 2000 years in the Caves of **Qumran** (see **Qumran,** p. 267) near the Dead Sea, the scrolls date from the 2nd century BCE to 70 CE and were written by an apocalyptic, monastic Jewish sect called the Essenes. The scrolls contain fragments of every biblical text except the Book of Esther. These texts are nearly identical to their modern versions, supporting claims for the historical dating of the Hebrew Bible. The building's white dome and black walls symbolize the struggle between the Sons of Light and Dark, an important theme to the Qumran sect, and was designed to resemble the covers of the pots in which the scrolls lay hidden (though when the fountains are on it looks more like a Hershey Kiss taking a shower).

YAD VA-SHEM

Don't plan to do too much right after a visit; the museum's several buildings deserve some time and take an emotional toll. To get to Yad Va-Shem, take bus #13, 16-18, 20-21, 23-24, 26-27, or 39 and get off at the huge, red arch just past Mount Herzl. Turn around and take a left on Ein Kerem St., then follow the signs down Ha-Zikaron St. for about 10min. Info ☎ 644 35 65 or 644 35 62; www.yad-vashem.org.il. Open Su-Th 9am-5pm, F 9am-2pm. Free. Free guided tours in English available by appointment.

Meaning "a memorial and a name," Yad Va-Shem is the largest of Israel's Holocaust museums. Memorializing an event as broad-sweeping and traumatic as the Holocaust cannot be accomplished with any single medium; the juxtaposition of Nazi records, the testimony of victims, and documentation of resistance creates a powerful and disturbing experience. It's best to start at the **Historical Museum,** which traces the origins of the Holocaust through photographs, documents, and relics. The exhibit ends with a simple, powerful memorial: symbolic tombs showing the number of Jews who were killed in each country and a tiny shoe that belonged to one of the Holocaust's 1.5 million younger victims. **The Hall of Names** (closes 15min. before museum) contains an achingly long row of archive shelves with lists of all known Holocaust victims. Visitors may fill out a Page of Testimony, recording the name and circumstances of death of family members killed by the Nazis. **The Hall Of Remembrance** houses a *ner tamid* (eternal fire) to memorialize the Holocaust's victims, with the names of many concentration camps engraved into the floor. The nearby **art museum** displays drawings and paintings composed by Jews in the ghettos and concentration camps, while below it in the small **Children's Hall** is a display of toys and dolls which outlived their young owners. In the same room are visitors' books in which to share your impressions; reading through the thoughts and reflections left by others is at least as powerful as the formal exhibits. By far the most haunting part of Yad Va-Shem is the stirring **Children's Memorial,** where mirrors are positioned to create the illusion of an infinite sea of candles, while a recorded voice recites the names and ages of young victims. The **Avenue of Righteous Gentiles** honors non-Jewish Europeans who risked their own safety to aid Jews fleeing Europe. The **Valley of the Communities** is an enormous labyrinthine memorial dedicated to the destroyed villages of Europe. Carved in stone are the names of *shtetls* that are no more; surviving family members wander around in search of their former towns.

OTHER MUSEUMS

BIBLE LANDS MUSEUM. This museum records the ancient history of every geographic locale mentioned in the Bible. Ancient pottery, jewelry, seals, and figurines comprise the private collection of Dr. Elie Borowski, a Canadian antiquities collector. For an educational interlude, check out the interactive computer program on cylindrical stamps and seals. *(Across the street from the Israel Museum. Take bus #9 or 17 from King George St. ☎ 561 10 66; www.blmj.org. Open Su-Tu and Th 9:30am-5:30pm, W 9:30am-9:30pm (Nov.-Apr. 1:30-9:30pm), F 9:30am-2pm, Sa 11am-3pm. English tour Su-F 10:15am, W 10:15am and 5:30pm, and Sa 11am. NIS28, students and children NIS15.)*

TICHO HOUSE. On display are watercolors and drawings by artist Anna Ticho, who lived here with her prominent oculist husband, Dr. Avraham Albert Ticho, who opened Jerusalem's first eye clinic in 1912. His collection of *menorahs* is also on display. The elegant building and well-groomed gardens are a relaxing city respite; the attached restaurant serves a classy all-you-can-eat wine, cheese and salad buffet on Tu nights for NIS65. *(9 Ha-Rav Kook St. About 2 blocks up the hill from Zion Sq. ☎ 624 50 68 or 624 41 86. A small library shows a videotape of Anna Ticho's life and work upon request. Open Su-Th 10am-5pm, Tu 10am-10pm, F 10am-2pm. Free.)*

WOLFSON MUSEUM. This museum houses a wonderful collection of Jewish religious and ceremonial objects. Note the texts painted on eggshells and the Samaritan Torah. The museum also has a room of detailed dioramas depicting scenes from Jewish history. *(On King George St. next door to the Great Synagogue, on the 3rd floor of the Heḥal Shlomo building. ☎ 624 79 08. Open Su-Th 9am-1pm. NIS13, students NIS10.)*

SKIRBALL MUSEUM. Part of **Hebrew Union College,** the American Reform Movement's outpost in Israel, this small archaeological museum has an excellent exhibit of artifacts from Tel Dan, Gezer, and Aroer, three ancient cities. The plaza was designed by noted Israeli architect Moshe Safdie. *(13 King David St. ☎ 620 33 33. Open Su-Th 10am-4pm, Sa 10am-2pm. Free.)*

MAYER INSTITUTE FOR ISLAMIC ART. The institute displays a significant collection of miniatures, paintings, and carpets from the Islamic world. Visitors may also take advantage of the comprehensive research library covering subjects in Islamic art and archaeology. *(2 Ha-Palmaḥ St. Around the corner from Ha-Nassi St. Take bus #15 from the center of town. ☎ 566 12 91. Open Su-M and W-Th 10am-3pm, Tu 10am-6pm, F-Sa 10am-2pm. Library open Su and W 9am-3pm. NIS14, students NIS9, under 18 NIS7; free on Sa.)*

MUSEUM OF ITALIAN JEWISH ART AND ITALIAN SYNAGOGUE. The small but impressive collection includes silverwork, tapestries, and gilded Torah arks, including 18th-century pieces from the Conegliano Veneto Synagogue. Services in the restored, old-world synagogue are open to the public Friday nights and Saturday mornings. *(27 Hillel St., in city center near the midraḥov. ☎ 624 16 10. Open Su, Tu-W 9am-5pm; M 9am-2pm; Th-F 9am-1pm. NIS15; students, seniors, and children NIS10.)*

THE UNDERGROUND PRISONERS MUSEUM. This museum commemorates the work of Israel's underground movement in pre-1948 struggles against British rule. Originally erected by Russian pilgrims, the hall was converted during the British Mandate into Jerusalem's main prison and is now a small but powerful exhibit. *(Behind the municipal tourist office in Safra Sq., off Shivtei Yisrael St. ☎ 623 31 66. Open Su-Th 8am-4pm. NIS8, students and seniors with ID NIS4.)*

BLOOMFIELD SCIENCE MUSEUM. Kids will leap at the chance to interact with scientific phenomena in fun, hands-on exhibits covering topics such as gravity, waves, electricity (be prepared for a few shocks), and lasers. *(Take bus #9, 24, or 28 to Hebrew University, Givat Ram campus; the museum is opposite the stadium. ☎ 561 81 28. Open M and W-Th 10am-6pm, Tu 10am-8pm, F 10am-1pm, Sa 10am-3pm. NIS27, students and seniors NIS15.)*

NIGHTLIFE

Tel-Avivians hate to admit it, but Jerusalem's nightlife is no longer joke-worthy. Once the city's conservative majority is safely tucked into bed, the bar and club scene comes to life, peaking Thursday to Saturday nights. Friday night in Jerusalem is like a dam bursting; the flood of energy into the cityscape would make a rabbi's hair curl. Cultural events, from lunchtime chamber music to the early summer **Israel Festival,** add to Jerusalem's arts scene. Buy Friday's *Jerusalem Post* for the "In Jerusalem" insert, the best weekly info in English; *Kol Ha-Ir* provides the best info in Hebrew. The municipal tourist office in Safra Sq. (see **Tourist Information,** p. 88) also gives out detailed monthly calendars in English. The JOH can help you find gay nightlife (see p. 90). In June, look out for **Student Day** at Hebrew University, with trips during the day and fireworks at night.

BARS

In the **Russian Compound** (Migrash Ha-Russim), two blocks down Heleni Ha-Malka St. east of Zion Sq. (toward the Old City), neon beer signs glow through the crisp night air in the shadow of the stately Russian Orthodox church, luring alcohol lovers like moths. After midnight, stylish bars in old stone buildings fill to capacity (and overflow into the street) with a young, hip crowd. It's not hard to choose a haunt to suit any mood; they're all concentrated around two blocks and many offer extra entertainment like jazz or karaoke on certain nights. The **midraḥov** area offers some less rowdy and more plain escapes from this crazy scene; it's only five minutes away, so you can easily hop back and forth.

RUSSIAN COMPOUND

Mike's Place, 7 Heleni Ha-Malka (☎052 670 965), on the corner of Horkanos. Tightly packed (but in a cozy way) English-speaking crowd puts away Guinness, smokes *nargilah* (NIS15), and digs excellent live music every night starting around 10:30pm. Happy hour daily 5-8pm (all drinks half price) and midnight-12:30am (cocktails and shots half price). Also serves light pub food (pizza NIS10; cheesy fries NIS20). No cover. Open daily 5pm-3am.

Kanabis, 11 Moonbaz St. (☎623 29 29), upstairs from Tarabin. Large bar-restaurant-dance floor with outdoor terrace overlooking the Moonbaz scene. Karaoke M-Tu nights beginning at 10pm. Beautiful circular bar with 3-page cocktail menu. Individual pizzas and salads NIS30-35. Cover Th-Sa NIS30; M-Tu NIS25 works as a food and drink voucher; W free. Open M-Sa 8:30pm-4am.

Sergey, 15 Heleni Ha-Malka St. (☎625 85 11), at the corner of Moonbaz St. No-frills bar packed with an intellectual twenty-something crowd of Bezalel Art Institute students so hip they don't even wear black. Decent selection of food. Pizza NIS30; crepes NIS28; salads NIS30-36. Beer NIS16-25; mixed drinks NIS30 and up. Min. charge on weekends NIS20. Open daily from 7pm.

Tarabin House, 9 Moonbaz St. (☎623 29 29). Mellow oasis among the rowdy pubs and dance clubs, with candles, pastoral Bedouin murals on the walls, and jungle-prints. *Nargilah* lover's paradise; all-you-can-smoke NIS25. Moderately priced small meals and many, many cocktails (NIS30). 21+ (flexible). Open daily 8pm-morning.

Strudel Internet Cafe and Bar, 11 Moonbaz St. (☎623 21 01), anchoring the western end of the block. Popular with Anglophone expats, Strudel retains a cool atmosphere despite the packs of American Hebrew University students gathering forces on their way to the Underground. Don't expect privacy while surfing. Happy hour 7-9pm and midnight-12:30am (half-price drinks). Open M-F 10am-late, Sa 3pm-late.

ON OR NEAR THE MIDRAḤOV

Shanty, 4 Naḥalat Shiva St. (☎624 34 34), in the alleyway between Yoel Salomon and Rivlin St., tucked in the corner. An Israeli enclave in a tourist domain; ensures an absence of teens by carding hard. Candle-lit room and outdoor tables always filled to capacity. Huge drink list with prices slightly lower than other nearby bars; buy an alcoholic drink and get a soft drink for NIS4. Excellent salads (NIS38) and house specialties (NIS21-36). Open Su-Th 7pm-late, F and Sa 8pm-even later. Kitchen closes at 11pm.

Syndrome, 18 Hillel St. (☎054 805 210), on the corner of Rabbi Akiva, underneath Cafe Aroma, at the end of the row of stores. Friendly and casual atmosphere. No food, no coffee, just alcohol, chips, *nargilah* (NIS15), and music. Happy hour nightly 8-9pm (half-price draft beer). Live music performances (mostly blues and rock) on small stage almost every night 10pm-1am. Cover NIS10-30 (depending on who's playing), including a beer. Open daily 8pm-2am or later.

The Tavern Pub, 16 Rivlin St. (☎624 45 41). Supposedly Jerusalem's oldest pub—putting it at the ripe old age of 30. A magnet for all types, from European tourists and American college students to Israeli locals hoping to meet tourists and students. Eight kinds of draft beer (1 pint NIS16-20) and innumerable international beers. Cocktails NIS22 and up. Live music every other Th in winter. Open daily 3pm-5am.

Egon, 9 Naḥalat Shiva St. (☎622 24 58), accessible from the arch at 14 Rivlin St. Crowded outdoor cafe-bar-restaurant with a very lively, casual atmosphere and large outdoor screen showing sports or music videos. Full bar serves over 50 kinds of international beer (NIS14-35), 40 kinds of ice cream (NIS17), and light meals. Smoke unlimited sweet *nargilah* for NIS14. Free backgammon. Open 24hr.

CLUBS

While many clubs cluster in the city center, larger clubs are on or near Ha-Oman St. in **Talpiyot,** Jerusalem's southern industrial neighborhood, down Hebron Rd. Take bus #21 from the city center until midnight; a taxi back should cost NIS15-20. Talpiyot clubs are more expensive than those in the city center and most close in the summer. They also open, close, and move more frequently than the city center clubs; go to Ha-Oman 17 first and ask where to find other local hot spots.

Ha-Oman 17, 17 Ha-Oman St. (☎678 16 58; www.haoman.com), in Talpiyot. The city's largest and best dance club. Still relatively unknown among tourists (which is either good or bad, depending on who you ask). Huge after-parties on major holidays. Two huge indoor dance floors with large bar, populated mostly by scantily-clad Israeli university students. Mostly techno and pop. Th 23+, F 19+. Cover NIS70. Open Th-F midnight-dawn (or later). Closed July-Aug.

The Underground, 1 Yoel Salomon St. (☎625 19 18), is the dance club everyone hates but goes to anyway, with a bar and batcave-like disco below. Sweaty, grinding dancers shed layers of clothing as the hours go by. Drinks NIS15 and up; buy one get one free during happy hour (daily 8-9pm). 18+. Cover Su-W after 10:30pm NIS20, Th-Sa NIS30; includes one drink. Open nightly 7:30pm-4am.

Glasnost, 15 Heleni Ha-Malka St. (☎625 69 54), past Moonbaz when coming from Jaffa Rd. In the heart of the bar scene in the Russian Compound. Large outer courtyard overflows with toe-stepping Israelis. Live salsa every M 9pm-3am (NIS25), crash course 8-9pm (NIS35 includes both). Tu Reggae, Th house party, F-Su pub only with tables and chairs crowding out the dance floor (no cover). 21+.

Q, 1 Yoel Salomon St. (☎622 25 16), next to and above the Underground. In past years, this was Jerusalem's most decidedly gay club; nowadays, it's simply a smaller, more upscale competitor to the Underground (although still gay-friendly). Crowded on Th nights. 22+. Cover NIS40-70, depending on the DJ. Open Th-Sa 11pm-morning.

Goa, 19 Jaffa Rd., across from the Municipality. "Psychadelic" doesn't even begin to describe this place; the loud trance music and blacklight-illuminated paintings and wall hangings of 'shrooms and Shiva surrounding the small dance floor are trippy enough. When the room starts spinning too much, head upstairs to the even trippier lounge area, complete with fluorescent bean-bags. Cover Th-F NIS20. Open M-Sa 9pm-4am.

THEATER AND FILM

Gil Movie Theater (☎678 84 48), in the Kenyon shopping mall (bus #6), shows the latest Hollywood flicks on 8 screens. Most films are in English with Hebrew subtitles. Call or check newspaper listings for times. NIS27.50.

Jerusalem Cinematheque (☎672 41 31; www.jer-cin.org.il), on Hebron Rd. in the Hinnom Valley, southwest of the Old City walls; walk downhill past Jaffa Gate, or take bus #7, 8, 21, 30, 44, or 48. Two screens show different films every evening. Tickets NIS28; unlimited movies for a year NIS450. Ask about a student discount. Call about Friday night "movie marathons." The annual **Jerusalem Film Festival** takes over the entire theater for the early weeks of July, bringing international films to the city and introducing local creations. Pick up a free book of listings (also in English) at the Cinematheque or municipal tourist office, or check the website (http://go.walla.co.il/jff) or the Friday supplement of the *Post.* Some films require advance ticket purchase.

J.E.S.T. Theater (Jerusalem English-Speaking Theater; ☎642 09 08; www.tande.com/jest). Amateur group performs 3 or 4 English plays per year. Community theater attracts a large expat crowd.

Khan Theater (☎671 82 81), across from the railway station in Remez Sq. Egged buses #7, 8, 21, 30, and 48 pass by the railway station. Built by Ottoman Turks in the 1880s as a caravan stop. Contains an intimate theater, restaurant, art gallery, and cafe featuring Hebrew stand-up comedy and classical music concerts. Rarely frequented by tourists, but the concerts and plays, mostly in Hebrew, are critically acclaimed.

Palestinian National Theater (al-Nuzha al-Hakawati Theater; ☎628 09 57), off Nablus St., near the American Colony Hotel. Walk up Nablus St. and take the first right after the intersection with Salah al-Din St. 15m down on the right a metal gate guards a parking lot; the theater entrance is inside the lot. Take a taxi at night. Has survived through years of Israeli occupation and IDF raids. Stages plays and musicals, many of which are political; English synopses are sometimes provided. From the end of June to mid-July, the theater hosts the **Jerusalem International Theater Festival,** a gathering of international troupes with several English-language plays; The **International Puppet Festival** is in October. Most tickets NIS20. Ticket office open Tu-Su 9am-5pm.

DANCE

International Cultural Center for Youth, 12 Emek Refa'im St. (☎566 41 44), in the German Colony. Take bus #4, 14, or 18. Coed, teacher-led folk dancing every Tu. Beginner 7-8pm, advanced 8-11:30pm. NIS20.

Hebrew Union College, 13 King David St. (☎620 33 33). Outdoor Israeli Folk Dancing every Su 8-9pm for beginners, 9-11:45pm for advanced. Teacher-led. NIS18.

House for Hebrew Youth (Beit Ha-No'ar), 105 Ha-Rav Herzog St. (☎678 94 41). Take bus #6, 17, 19, 31, or 32. Holds folk-dancing classes. Coed W and Sa 8:30pm-12:30am, Th 8pm-midnight (NIS18); women-only Tu 6:30-8pm (NIS15).

Ulpan Machol, 105 Ha-Rav Herzog St. (☎679 56 26), in the same building as the youth center. Ballet, modern, and jazz dance classes daily Sept.-July. Great range of classes beginner to advanced; one-time only participation also welcome. NIS45 per class. Intensive 8hr. classes during two weeks in July (entire course NIS650; one-week NIS400). Call for details.

MUSIC

Yellow Submarine, 13 Ha-Rekavim St. (☎656 66 11). This theater-cafe features a different kind of performance 3-4 nights a week. Frequent musical guests from unknown locals to Israeli superstars. Party for those 30+ after 11pm every other Th; for students every F (during the school year). Stand-up comedy marathon in Hebrew every other Sa. Full bar and light Mexican food. Call for a schedule of events. NIS30-60.

Pargod Theater, 94 Bezalel St. (☎623 17 65), on the corner of Nissim Bekhar St. in Naḥalot. Hip, young crowd comes for jazz and special performances. Billboard in front announces special events.

Jerusalem Symphony Orchestra (☎561 14 98; www.jso.co.il). Performs frequently at the Jerusalem Theater on David Marcus St. and the Henry Crown Symphony Hall, 5 Chopin St. A schedule of events is available on the website. NIS90-165; 30% student discount on night of show. Season runs Sept.-June.

Ein Kerem Music Center (☎641 42 50), on Ha-Ma'ayan St., opposite Mary's Well in Ein Kerem. Take bus #17 from the central bus station or Zion Sq. Features weekly classical music and operatic performances, usually on F or Sa night. Tickets cost NIS45 at the door; 25% student discount. Call for a schedule of events.

Diaspora Yeshiva Band (☎671 68 41; email diaspora@netvision.net.il), in Asaf's Cave, in the Mount Zion Cultural Center near David's Tomb. Bids Shabbat goodbye Sa at 9pm (in winter 8:30pm) with Ḥasidic dancing and English, Hebrew, and Yiddish music–a uniquely Jerusalem experience. NIS10. Call to make sure there is a performance.

Sultan's Pool (*Brekhat Ha-Sultan;* ☎629 80 66), in Yemin Moshe, downhill from Jaffa Gate. Seize any opportunity to attend a performance. Open in summer only. Tickets for American or British rock stars start at NIS80.

SHOPPING

Budget shopping in Jerusalem can be fun for those who keep their wits about them. Often the deal of the century is found after relentless comparison shopping or by bargaining until blue in the face (for bargaining tips, see **The Fine Art of Haggling,** p. 120). It's best to pay in foreign currency to avoid the 17% VAT. Otherwise, be sure to get a receipt and refund form to be redeemed at the airport or border crossing stations. If you're feeling homesick for large shopping malls, take bus #6 to the **Kenyon Yerushalayim,** a 3-story monstrosity with everything from a supermarket and post office to Tower Records and countless trendy clothing stores.

JEWELRY

Jewelry can be bought in many places in Jerusalem—in Arab *souqs*, on the Ben-Yehuda *midraḥov*, or from the fine shops on King David St. **Eilat stone,** a green or turquoise semi-precious stone from the hills around Eilat, is a common element in rings, necklaces, earrings, and pendants. Booths of cheap rings and trinkets abound at **The Pit,** also known as "The Cat Market" *(shuk ha-ḥatulim)*, an open-air market near the base of Rivlin and Yoel Salomon St. that features odd trinkets, jewelry and clothing. Merchants set up shop every afternoon and evening. On Friday, they start at 10am and end before Shabbat. On Saturday, they hawk from nightfall until past midnight.

CRAFTS

Israel is home to many accomplished artisans. Pieces are often made from olivewood, Jerusalem stone, and other native materials. Most of the best deals are found in the Old City; in West Jerusalem, art stores with higher quality (and higher priced) items line the *midraḥov*. At **Kakadu,** 1 Rivlin St., Reut Shaher hand-designs beautiful pinewood trays, notebook covers, and other gift items with elegant, whimsical animal motifs. (☎625 64 12. Open Su-Th 9am-9pm, F 9am-4pm. Credit cards accepted.) **Lifeline for the Old,** 14 Shivtei Yisrael St., behind the Municipality, is a small workshop and market selling high-quality crafts produced by the elderly and disabled. Proceeds are used to fund the project and to provide support services for Lifeline's workers. (☎628 78 29; email lifeline@netmedia.net.il; www.lifeline.org.il. Open Su-Th 9am-6pm and F 9am-12:30pm, in winter Su-Th 9am-4pm and F 9am-12:30pm.)

JUDAICA

If you're looking for *menorot, mezuzot, kippot,* or other ritual items, this is the right city. The *Talmud* says it is not enough to fulfill the commandments; one must beautify the ritual with pieces of art. As a result, making ceremonial objects has been a practical outlet for talented Jewish artists. Rows of inexpensive Judaica shops crowd the streets of Mea She'arim. **Chen Eilat,** 11 Mea She'arim, has a huge selection of cheap *ḥallah* covers, *tallit* bags, and other things Jewish. (☎537 01 28. Open Su-Th 9am-8pm, F 9am-2pm. Credit cards accepted.) Slightly higher quality goods can be found in the Ben-Yehuda *midraḥov*. Most shops will personalize items like knitted *kippot* within two days. For truly high-quality merchandise, head to the Jewish Quarter Cardo, where the craftsmanship, individuality, and price of Judaica skyrockets. Here, too, however, great deals can be found: *mezuzot* carved out of Jerusalem stone are as low as US$3.

MUSIC

The cheapest place to buy CDs and tapes in Jerusalem is in the *souq* of the Old City's Muslim Quarter. Unfortunately, most merchandise is pirated; there have been reports of tourists being fined for such purchases, although this is rare. **Picadelly Music,** 4 Shatz St., right off Ben-Yehuda St. on the *midraḥov*, has a good selection of Israeli and international CDs, often at discount prices. (☎624 79 83. Open Su-Th 8:30am-8pm, F-8:30am-3pm, Sa sundown-10pm.) For a larger selection, try **Tower Records,** 19 Hillel St. (Open Su-Th 10am-10pm, F 9:30am-4pm.) There is another branch at the Kenyon Yerushalayim shopping mall.

NEAR JERUSALEM

ABU GHOSH אבו גוש أبو غوش

Overlooking the Judean hills west of Jerusalem, the Arab village of Abu Ghosh is revered by Christians and Jews alike as an early site of the Ark of the Covenant, which King David later moved to Jerusalem (I Chronicles 13:5-8). In caravan days, the town was the last stop on the way to Jerusalem; its 18th-century namesake, Sheikh Abu Ghosh, required pilgrims to pay a toll here as they traveled to the Holy City. Historically, the Arabs of the village have always had good relations with neighboring Jewish settlements and the State of Israel, even during the 1948 War.

GETTING THERE. To get to Abu Ghosh, take Egged bus #185 or 186 (45min.; every 30min. Su-Th 6:10am-10:15pm, F 6:10am-4:45pm, NIS8.30) from the central bus station and get out at the crest of the road, just past the restaurants. *Sherut* traveling between Jerusalem and Tel Aviv will stop at the turnoff, 2km downhill from Abu Ghosh, for roughly the same price.

FOOD. There are several restaurants to curb midday hunger on the road between the village's two main sights. The verdant **Caravan Inn Restaurant** (☎534 27 44) has slightly pricey main dishes; *shishlik* (NIS35-40), *schnitzel (*NIS32), and Turkish salad appetizer (NIS10) served on a breezy terrace, overlooking Abu Ghosh and the hills of Jerusalem. Open daily 11am-11pm. At a lower altitude, **Mifgash Ha-Kfar,** around the corner from the crusader church, feeds today's hungry crusaders hummus and falafel plates (NIS12) and *tabule (*NIS10) at indoor or shaded outdoor tables. (☎570 06 88. Open daily 9am-9pm.)

SIGHTS. Two churches grace the hills of Abu Ghosh. **Notre Dame de l'Arche d'Alliance** (Our Lady of the Ark of the Covenant), at the top of the hill (turn right across from the old police station), was built on the site of the Ark's ancient holding place. The current church was built in the 1920s on the ruins of a demolished Byzantine church; beautiful fragments of the original mosaics are integrated into the marble floor. (☎534 28 18. Open daily 8:30-11:30am and 2:30-6pm.)

In the beautiful garden below the sacred hill stands the magnificently preserved **Crusader Church of the Resurrection,** built in 1142 and acquired by the French government in 1873. Excavations beneath the church have uncovered remains dating back to Neolithic times; the crypt contains evidence of a Roman fortification. Today, ten monks and twelve sisters reside in the monastery and make their living from the **ceramics** hand-crafted in their small pottery studio. To reach the church, walk down the main road past the restaurants, turn right at Mahmoud Rashid Abu Ghosh St., and head for the minaret of the mosque next door. Buzz for entrance at the blue door to the right. Ask for Father Olivier, a popular monk who is known to give good advice and who has been featured in Israeli newspapers. (☎534 27 98 or 533 56 70. Open M-W, F-Sa 8:30-11am and 2:30-5:30pm. Free, but donations welcome. Regular morning mass M-Sa 11:30am, vespers 6pm; Gregorian chant Su 10am, vespers 5pm. Modest dress required.)

FESTIVALS. Abu Ghosh is usually a pretty quiet little village, but the excellent acoustics at both churches have attracted choirs and musicians from around the country. Twice a year, during the Jewish holidays of Sukkot (Oct. 2-9, 2001) and Shavuot (May 28, 2001), the **Abu Ghosh Vocal Music Festival** fills the town with melodious sounds and multitudes of people. During the winter months, the Notre Dame church hosts classical music concerts on the last Saturday of each month. Tickets aren't cheap, ranging from NIS67-110 for each event at the festival, but the artists are among the best in Israel. *(Tickets and information. ☎(03) 604 47 25 or (02) 624 08 96; during the festival (02) 534 00 66; email agfestiv@inter.net.il.*

SOREQ CAVE (ME'ARAT HA-NETIFIM)

The cave is 19km southwest of Jerusalem. Take bus #415 or 420 to Beit Shemesh, 10km west of the cave (45min., every 25min.-1hr. 6-9:30am, NIS14). From Beit Shemesh call Moniyot Ha-Mercaz (☎991 48 33; open 6:30am-midnight) and take a NIS45 taxi to the site. ☎991 11 17. Open Sa-Th 8:30am-4pm, F 8:30am-1pm. NIS18, students NIS15; includes a short audio-visual program at the entrance and a guided tour every day but Friday. Photography and solo wanderings are permitted on Friday only.

The stalagmite and stalactite cave in the **Avshalom Reserve** (a.k.a. Me'arat Ha-Netifim or Soreq Cave) contains spectacular speleological splendors. Discovered less than 30 years ago when a routine blast at a nearby quarry exposed a view into the cave, this site has been transformed into a major tourist attraction. The artificial lighting and paved pathways may disappoint adventurous spelunkers but can't detract from the natural majesty.

LATRUN לטרון

Bus #404, 409, 433, or 435, from either Jerusalem (30min., every 30min., NIS16.90) or Ramla (15min., NIS14.90). Ask the driver in advance to stop in Latrun and remind him.

A stern hilltop sentinel on the highway between Tel Aviv and Jerusalem, Latrun blends monasticism with an ancient tradition of militarism. The Bible says Joshua fought the Canaanites here, and Latrun later served as base camp for the Romans, Richard the Lionhearted, and Salah ad-Din. In 1917, the British took Latrun from the Turks and built a giant police fortress. Israeli forces tried unsuccessfully to capture Latrun in 1948 in order to get supplies to the besieged city of Jerusalem. Only by carving out a new road (dubbed the **Burma Road**) almost overnight to circumvent Latrun were Israeli forces able to defend Jerusalem. In 1967, the Israelis recaptured Latrun from the Jordanians and were able to build a more direct highway between Tel Aviv and Jerusalem.

The **Armored Corps Museum,** above the Alon filling station, contains 120 armored battle vehicles from Israel and surrounding countries. Highlights include an exhibit of stamps featuring armed forces from all over the world and a model of the tank planned by Leonardo da Vinci over 500 years ago. There is also a memorial to the 4864 armored corps soldiers killed in battle. (☎08 925 52 68. Call ahead to arrange a tour with an English guide at no extra charge. NIS20, students NIS15, children NIS10. Open Su-Th 8:30am-4:30pm, F 8:30am-12:30pm, Sa 9am-4pm.)

Famous for its **wine,** the hillside **Latrun Monastery** offers beautiful views of the surrounding area's nearby biblical sites, including Emmaus, Agalon, and Bethoron. A church and peaceful gardens sit beside the monastery. On Saturdays, a short film describing the life of a monk is screened. The French Trappist Order, part of the great monastic family of St. Benedict, founded the monastery as a center for silent contemplation and reflection. The shop near the main gate offers a wide selection of wines and spirits. To reach the monastery, whose orange rooftops are visible across the Tel Aviv-Jerusalem highway, go right and downhill from the gas station. Pass the front of the monastery; the entrance road will be on your left. (☎925 51 80; fax 925 50 84. Church and gardens open M-Sa 8am-noon and 3:30-5pm; shop open M-Sa 9am-1pm and 2:30-6:30pm.)

After his resurrection, Jesus was said to have appeared to two of his disciples on the site of the **Emmaus (Nicopolis) Church** (Mark 16:12-13, Luke 24:13-31), now the French Prehistorical Research Center. To reach the church, turn left out of the gas station and walk along the Tel-Aviv-Jerusalem highway for about 15 minutes. Another 100m along the road is the entrance to the **Canada Park,** a beautifully forested area with water holes and the remains of an amphitheater.

TEL AVIV-JAFFA

תל אביב-יפו

☎03

Proudly secular and downright sexy, Tel Aviv pulses with cutting-edge energy. Ever since the 1940s and 1950s, when authors and poets crowded the intimate cafes of Dizengoff Street, Tel Aviv has dedicated itself to taking Israeli culture in new directions. Still a bastion of the literati, Tel Aviv has expanded into other fields as well; most Israeli bands rocket to stardom from local clubs, and dozens of theater groups debut everything from Broadway exports to avant-garde Israeli plays. Today, the city's exuberant youth spends its time shopping for combat boots and navel rings in trendy Sheinkin Street boutiques, bronzing at the beach on Shabbat, and clubbing 'til sunrise.

Not surprisingly, given its never-ending quest to stay current, Tel Aviv is a very political city. Despite the effort to make Jerusalem the recognized capital, most countries keep their foreign embassies here. For a brief period during the Gulf Crisis in the winter of 1991, Tel Aviv became a target for Saddam Hussein's SCUD missiles. As modern and international as the city is, CNN videos of gas masks being distributed to children demonstrated the unique tension that exists here. It was also here in November 1995 that Yigal Amir, a Jewish student, fired the bullet that killed Prime Minister Yitzḥak Rabin (see **Assassination of Rabin,** p. 17). The assassination cast a shadow over all of Israel, but no place felt it more acutely than Tel Aviv. The Middle East peace process has taken its toll since then; in the last few years, Hamas bombings have claimed a number of lives in the city. However, political developments in the peace process leave residents hopeful that the recent calm will remain the norm.

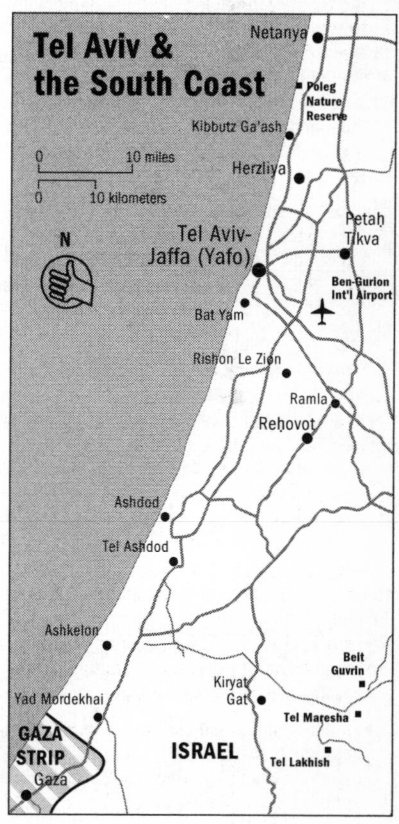

Tel Aviv sprouted from Jaffa (*Yafo*, or "beautiful," in Hebrew; *Yafa* in Arabic), its neighboring city, at the end of the 19th century. Jewish settlers, unhappy with the crowded and dilapidated condition of Jaffa and its high Arab population, founded the first two exclusively Jewish neighborhoods just to the north in 1887 and 1891. In 1909, the Jewish population of Jaffa parcelled out another northern area, naming it Atuzat Bayit (Housing Property). One year later, the suburb was renamed Tel Aviv (Spring Hill) after the town Theodore Herzl had envisioned in his turn-of-the-century utopian novel, **Altneuland** (Old-New-Land; see **Zionism,** p. 11). Appealing to bourgeois Jewish immigrants from Eastern Europe, the new town quickly developed in the 1920s and 1930s and soon became the largest Jewish town in Palestine.

Far from forgotten, Jaffa is still an integral part of Tel Aviv and one of the oldest functioning harbors in the world. Though once the busiest port in the region, Jaffa has primarily harbored small fishing boats since the rise of modern shipping centers in Haifa and Ashdod. Restaurants and galleries cater mostly to tourists, but next to Tel Aviv's sky-scraping hotels and glossy storefronts, the winding cobble-stone alleys and stunning sea vistas of Old Jaffa provide a breath of salty Mediterranean air.

HIGHLIGHTS OF TEL AVIV-JAFFA

Chat with the architect-inhabitant of the Surrealist **Hermit's House** (p. 166) before strolling down to Herzliya's beautiful shoreline for a quiet afternoon of sun.

Haggle your head off at the **Shuk Ha-Pishpeshim** (p. 164) in old Jaffa.

Get up close and personal with Tel Aviv chic on **Sheinken St.,** (p. 152) then disco 'til dawn in the myriad of clubs and pubs.

GETTING THERE AND AWAY

Flights: Ben-Gurion Airport (English recorded info ☎972 33 44), 22km southeast of Tel Aviv in Lod. Egged bus #475 to the airport leaves from the 6th floor of the New Central Bus Station (every 30min. Su-Th 5:20am-11:40pm, F 5:20am-4:50pm, Sa 8:30-11:30pm; NIS10). Shuttle bus #222 makes a round-trip between the airport and Tel Aviv, passing most of the major hostels (every hr. Su-Th 4am-midnight, F 4am-7pm, Sa noon-midnight; NIS16; last shuttle departs from airport Su-Th, Sa 11pm). Taxis from the airport to Tel Aviv run at a fixed tariff (about NIS70 during the day, NIS88 at night or on Shabbat, each piece of luggage NIS2).

Trains: Central Train Station (☎577 40 00), on Arlozorov St., across from Namir Rd. Take bus #10 or 18 from the city center or bus #27 from the New Central Bus Station. Open Su-F 6am-11pm. A/C trains leave every 30min. to: **Acre** (NS29); **Ashdod** (every 2hr., NIS13) via **Be'ersheva** (NIS23.50); **Hadera** (NIS16); **Haifa** (NIS21); and **Nahariya** (NIS39.50) via **Netanya** (NIS11). 10% discount with ISIC card on fares NIS20.50 and above. Lockers NIS5-10.

Intercity Buses: Operated by **Egged** (☎694 88 88). 10% discount with ISIC card on fares NIS20.50 and above.

New Central Bus Station has departures on the 6th floor to: **Be'er Sheva** (#370; every 20min. Su-Th 6am-11pm, F 6am-4:40pm, Sa 8:30-11pm; NIS20.50); **Hadera** (#852 or 872; 1hr.; every 30min. Su-Th 7am-11:30pm, F 8am-4:30pm, Sa 8:30pm-midnight; NIS17); **Haifa** #900 direct (1¼hr.; every 25min. Su-Th 7:30am-8:40pm, F 7:30am-4:35pm, Sa 8:30-10pm; NIS20.50) or late-night #901 express (1¼hr.; every 20min. Su-Th 9:15-11pm; NIS20.50); **Jerusalem** (#405; 1 hr.; every 15min. Su-Th 5:40am-midnight, F 6am-5:30pm, Sa 8:30pm-midnight; NIS18); **Netanya** (#605; 45 min.; every 25min. Su-Th 8am-9:15pm, F 8am-4:30pm, Sa 8:30am-10pm; NIS13); and **Zikhron Ya'akov** (#872; 2hr.; every 30min. Su-Th 7am-11:30pm, F 8am-4:30pm, Sa 8:30pm-midnight; NIS22.50).

Arlozorov terminal, on Arlozorov St., across from Namir Rd. To: **Be'er Sheva** (#380; 1¾ hr.; every 15min. Su-Th 6am-8:30pm, F 6am-4:30pm, Sa 8:30-10:30pm; NIS20.50); **Haifa** (#910; 1¼hr.; every 15min. Su-Th 7:45am-8:45pm, F 7:45am-4:30pm, Sa 8:30-10pm; NIS20.50); and **Jerusalem** (#480; 50min.; every 15min. Su-Th 6am-10pm, F 6am-4:30pm, Sa 8:30pm-midnight; NIS18).

Ferries: Caspi, 1 Ben-Yehuda St. (☎517 57 49), in the Migdalor Bldg. 20% discount for passengers under 24 and students under 30. Port tax NIS100/US$22. Fares drop for round-trip tickets. To: **Piraeus** (3 nights; Su and Th 8pm, NIS424/US$106; in winter Th 7pm, NIS384/US$96) via **Cyprus** (1 night; NIS232/US$58; in winter NIS192/US$48) and **Rhodes** (2 nights; NIS404/US$101; in winter NIS364/US$91).

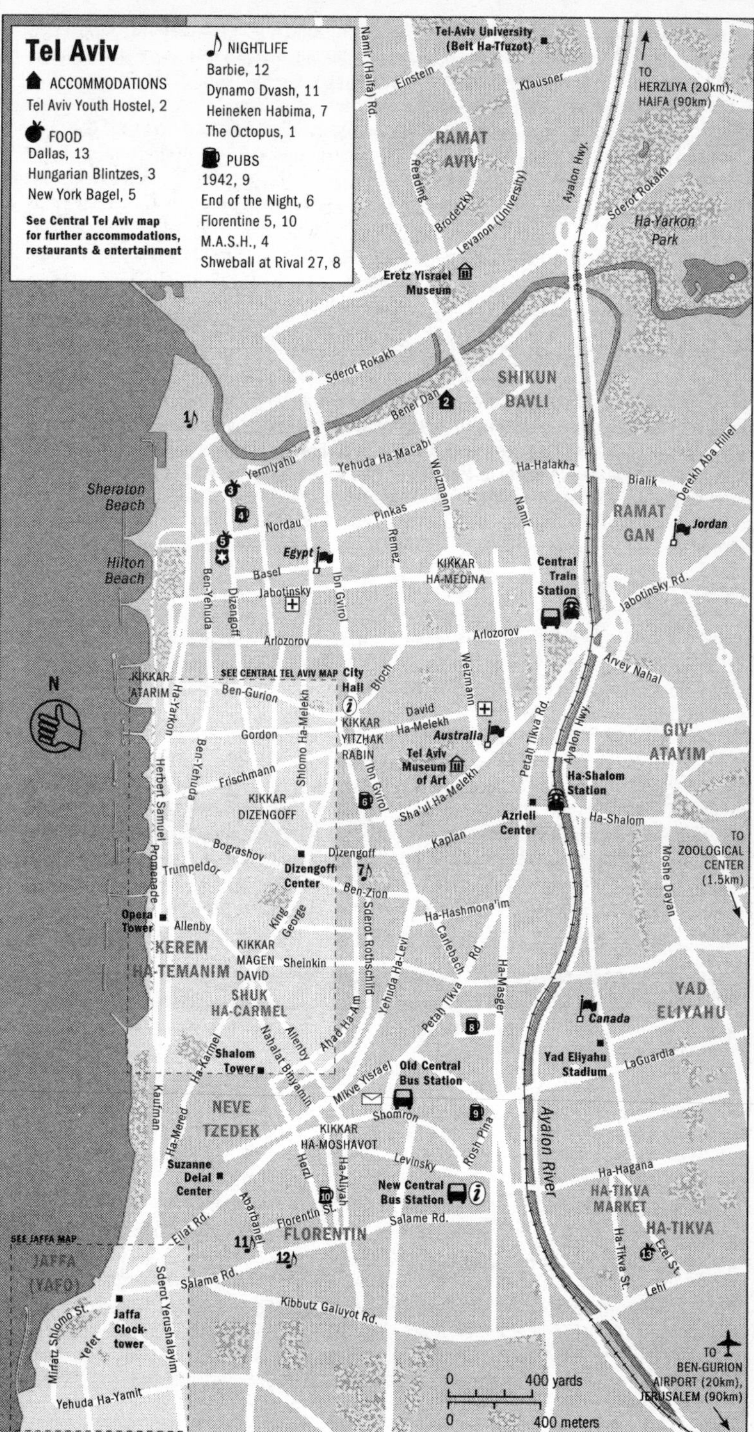

Tel Aviv
ACCOMMODATIONS
Tel Aviv Youth Hostel, 2
FOOD
Dallas, 13
Hungarian Blintzes, 3
New York Bagel, 5
See Central Tel Aviv map for further accommodations, restaurants & entertainment
NIGHTLIFE
Barbie, 12
Dynamo Dvash, 11
Heineken Habima, 7
The Octopus, 1
PUBS
1942, 9
End of the Night, 6
Florentine 5, 10
M.A.S.H., 4
Shweball at Rival 27, 8
Tel-Aviv University (Beit Ha-Tfuzot)
TO HERZLIYA (20km), HAIFA (90km)
RAMAT AVIV
Ha-Yarkon Park
Eretz Yisrael Museum
SHIKUN BAVLI
Sheraton Beach
Hilton Beach
RAMAT GAN
KIKKAR HA-MEDINA
Central Train Station
SEE CENTRAL TEL AVIV MAP
City Hall
KIKKAR YITZHAK RABIN
Tel Aviv Museum of Art
GIV' ATAYIM
Ha-Shalom Station
Azrieli Center
KIKKAR DIZENGOFF
Dizengoff Center
TO ZOOLOGICAL CENTER (1.5km)
Opera Tower
KEREM HA-TEMANIM
KIKKAR MAGEN DAVID
SHUK HA-CARMEL
YAD ELIYAHU
Yad Eliyahu Stadium
Shalom Tower
Old Central Bus Station
NEVE TZEDEK
KIKKAR HA-MOSHAVOT
Suzanne Delal Center
New Central Bus Station
HA-TIKVA MARKET
HA-TIKVA
FLORENTIN
SEE JAFFA MAP
JAFFA (YAFO)
Jaffa Clock-tower
Ayalon River
TO BEN-GURION AIRPORT (20km), JERUSALEM (90km)
0 400 yards
0 400 meters

Intercity sheruts: Across the street from the New Central bus station exit (platform 410), to your left (with your back to the bus station). *Sheruts* leave whenever most of the 10 seats fill up. To: **Haifa** (1hr., NIS22); **Jerusalem** (45min., NIS18); **Nazareth** (1hr., NIS25); and **Netanya** (20min., NIS10).

Car Rental: Gindy Ltd. Rent-a-Car, 132 Ha-Yarkon St. (☎527 83 44). Manual NIS200/US$50 per day, automatic NIS240/$60 per day. 200km per day limit but weekly rental discounts with unlimited mileage available. 21+; drivers under 24 have $1000 deductible in case of accident. **Avis,** 113 Ha-Yarkon St., (☎527 17 52). Manual NIS184/US$46 per day, automatic starts at NIS200/US$50 per day. 23+, 26+ for larger automatics. 250km per day limit. **Rent-a-Reliable-Car,** 155 Ha-Yarkon St. (☎524 97 94). Manual NIS280/US$70 per day, 20+; automatic starts at NIS300/US$75, 24+. All companies require driver to have had a license for at least two years.

GETTING AROUND

Tel Aviv is mostly manageable by foot. On a hot August afternoon, though, a NIS4.70 bus ride may seem like the deal of the century. Buses in Tel Aviv are frequent, air-conditioned, and comfortable; definitely take them to sights north of the Yarkon, in the Ha-Tikva area, in the Tel Aviv University area, or in Jaffa, which are all beyond easy walking distance from the city center.

The **New Central Bus Station,** 108 Levinsky St. (☎638 40 40) can be scary and painful the first time you experience it, but the basics are easy enough. Most local buses (Dan) and local and intercity sheruts leave from the 4th floor; exit at platform 416 for local buses and platform 410 for sheruts. A few local buses with destinations outside Tel Aviv (Ramat Gan, Ramat Aviv) leave from the 1st floor. Intercity buses (Egged) leave from the 6th floor; the 4th and 6th floors have information kiosks. **Baggage check** rooms are on the 6th floor, down a small flight of stairs near the information kiosk. (NIS10 per item per day. Open Su-Th 7am-7pm, F and holiday eves 7am-3pm.)

Buses within Tel Aviv are operated by **Dan,** 39 Sha'ul Ha-Melekh (☎639 33 33 or 639 44 44). They generally run Sunday to Thursday 5:30am-midnight, Friday 5am-5pm, Saturday 8:15pm-12:30am, but some stop running earlier. Buses cost NIS4.70 and do not run on Shabbat. For extended stays, consider buying Dan's **monthly bus pass** (NIS176). Unlike intercity buses, local buses travel both ways, so you must be conscious of the direction. Fortunately, bus stops have clear English signs with a green marker pointing to the current stop. Decide whether you need to follow the blue or red directional path and stand on the side of the street where the appropriately colored arrow matches the flow of traffic. The most frequent and important seven routes are:

IMPORTANT BUS ROUTES

#4: From the New Central Bus Station (4th floor), runs parallel to the coastline up Allenby and Ben-Yehuda St. and back. Every 5min.

#5: From the New Central Bus Station (4th floor), runs up Rothschild Blvd. and Dizengoff St. to Dizengoff Ctr., then turns right to run down the lengths of Nordau and Yehuda Ha-Maccabee before turning around. Every 5min.

#10: Runs from train station along Arlozorov St., turns left to go down the coast along Ben-Yehuda St., Herbert Samuel St., and Kaufman St. to Jaffa. Weaves back up through the Florentin area along Herzl St. to Rothschild Blvd. before turning back. Every 15min.

#18: Runs from the train station along Sha'ul Ha-Melekh through Dizengoff Square to Ben-Yehuda and then Allenby before heading down to Florentin along Ha-Aliya and Salame Rds. and turns around after reaching Bat Gam. Every 5-10min.

#25: Runs from Tel Aviv University down Namir Rd. then Yehuda Ha-Maccabee to Ibn Gvirol. After turning right and going for a few blocks on Arlozorov, turns left to follow Shlomo Ha-Melekh and King George down to Shuk Ha-Carmel. Until 9:30pm, continues to Bat Yam along the coast, but otherwise turns around at the *shuk*. Every 15 min.

#27: From the New Central Bus Station (1st floor), runs along Petaḥ Tikva Rd. and to Haifa Rd., Central Train Station, then along Levanon St. to Tel Aviv University, the *kenyon* (shopping mall) in Ramat Gan, and back. Every 10-15min.

#46: From the New Central Bus Station (1st floor) to Jaffa and back along Yefet St. Every 8-10min., every 15min. at night.

Sherut taxis run along the routes of buses #4 and 5, and are numbered accordingly. At NIS4.50, they're cheaper than the bus and will stop anywhere along the route. Call a taxi anytime (☎524 90 90 or 527 19 99). **Rent-A-Scooter**, 136 Ha-Yarkon St. (☎681 57 78), provides an alternative to public transportation (NIS100/US$25 per day, 10% discounts for a week, 20% for two weeks; min. age 18).

ORIENTATION

Located in the center of Israel's Mediterranean coastline, Tel Aviv is 63km northwest of Jerusalem and 95km south of Haifa. The two main points of entry into Tel Aviv are **Ben-Gurion Airport** and the **New Central Bus Station.** Frequent bus and *sherut* (minibus) service from the airport is supplemented by the vans that warring hostels send to lure potential customers.

Tel Aviv is rather easy to navigate once you learn the few main roads that run parallel to the coastline and a few big intersections. The **tayelet** (promenade) extends from Jaffa up to Gordon beach (about two-thirds of the way to the port). Parallel and one block inland is **Ha-Yarkon St. Ben-Yehuda St.** is another block inland. All three streets are lined with hotels, cafes, and restaurants—prices generally go down as you go further from the shore. **Dizengoff St.,** home to some of Tel Aviv's trendy cafes and bars, runs parallel to Ben-Yehuda before swerving away from the coast toward **Kikkar Dizengoff,** an elevated plaza surrounded by shops and a cineplex. Dizengoff St. then continues to intersect the next big coastal-parallel, **Ibn Gvirol St.,** with its arcades and cafes. On Ibn Gvirol, a few blocks above this intersection is **Kikkar Yitzḥak Rabin,** in front of City Hall.

The third square to know is **Kikkar Bath November,** where Ben-Yehuda intersects **Allenby St.** Almost all of the hostels in Tel Aviv are either on or near Ben-Yehuda or Allenby. Further down, Allenby intersects **King George St.** and **Sheinkin St.** at **Kikkar Magen David**. This intersection is also the starting point of **Shuk Ha-Carmel** and the **midraḥov** (pedestrian mall) of **Naḥalat Binyamin.** Between the *shuk* and the shore are the winding alleyways of **Kerem Ha-Temanim** (the Yemenite Quarter) and below the *shuk* lies the neighborhood of **Neve Tzedek,** which has profited from a recent infusion of yuppies. Allenby continues most of the way to the bus station. Below the bus station, framed by **Herzl St., Ha-Aliya St., and Salame St.,** is the bohemian **Florentin** neighborhood.

Still another parallel, much farther from the coast, is **Namir Rd.,** a major thoroughfare that leads to Tel Aviv's northern exit; the **train station,** which has service to all major cities, is at the intersection of Namir Rd. and **Arlozorov St. Jaffa** and its waterfront lie farther south, outside the downtown area. The entrance to **Old Jaffa,** marked by a famous **clocktower,** lies at the intersection of **Eilat St.** and **Goldman St.**

PRACTICAL INFORMATION

TOURIST AND FINANCIAL SERVICES

Tourist Information Office: (☎639 56 60; fax 639 56 59), in the New Central Bus Station, 6th floor, near platform 630. From the city center, take bus #4 or 5. Provides hotel and tour reservations, maps of Tel Aviv and other Israeli cities, and information on food, shopping, and cultural events. Open Su-Th 9am-5pm, F 9am-1pm. A kiosk in the City Hall Lobby (☎521 85 00) gives out maps and information about Tel Aviv only. Open Su-Th 9am-2pm.

Tours: SPNI, 19 Ha-Sharon St. (☎638 86 74), near the intersection with Petaḥ Tikva Rd. Their English-speaking guides lead the best 1-12 day tours, year-round. Day tours NIS200/US$50-NIS300/US$75. Open Su-Th 8am-4:30pm, F 8-11am. **Egged Tours,** 59 Ben-Yehuda St. (☎527 12 12). Not as spectacular as SPNI. Guided tours around Israel. Half-day tour of Tel Aviv NIS120/US$30; full-day tour of Jerusalem NIS232/US$58. **United Tours,** 113 Ha-Yarkon St. (☎522 20 08), offers tours around the country in English, Hebrew, French, and German. Day tours NIS232-296/US$58-74; 10% student discount with ISIC if booked directly from their office.

Budget Travel: ISSTA, 128 Ben-Yehuda St. (☎521 05 55), at Ben-Gurion St. For ISICs, bring a photo, current student ID, and NIS40; Youth Hostel cards NIS35. Open Su-Th 9am-noon and 3-7pm, F 9am-noon. **Mona Tours,** 25 Bogorochov St. (☎621 14 33), specializes in student and charter rates. Must be under 28 to book flights; proof of age required. Open Su-Th 9am-6pm, F 9am-1pm. Both take credit cards.

Embassies and Consulates: Australia, 37 Sha'ul Ha-Melekh Blvd., Europe House, 4th fl. (☎695 04 51). Open M-Th 8am-noon. **Canada,** 3 Nirim St. (☎636 33 00), next to basketball stadium in Yad Eliyahu. Open for visas M-Th 8am-4:30pm, F 8-1:30pm. **South Africa,** Top Tower, Dizengoff Ctr., 16th fl. (☎525 25 66). Enter through gate #3. Open M-F 9-11am, W 9-11am and 2-3pm. **UK** (also serves travelers from **New Zealand**), 1 Ben-Yehuda St., Migdalor Bldg., 6th fl. (☎510 01 66 for passports and visas). Open M-Th 1:30-3:30pm and F noon-1pm. **US,** 71 Ha-Yarkon St. (☎519 75 75), just a few blocks north of Allenby St., on the left side. Open for passports M, W 8:30-11am and 2-3:30pm; Tu, Th 8:30-11am; F 8:30am-12:30pm; for visas M-F 7:30am-2:30pm. **Egypt,** 54 Basel St. (☎546 51 51 or 546 51 52), just off Ibn Gvirol. For a visa, bring a passport, photo, and NIS75 (U.S. citizens NIS50)—be sure to specify planned visits beyond the Sinai, or they'll automatically issue a "Sinai Only" visa. Open Sa-Th 9-11am. **Jordan,** 14 Aba Hillel (☎751 77 22), in Ramat Gan. Pre-arranged visas (NIS30) are required for crossing to Jordan via Allenby Bridge (see p. 344). Open Su-Th 9:30am-12:30pm.

Currency Exchange: Any post office will change money without commission. **Change Point,** 106 Ha-Yarkon St. (☎524 55 05; open Su-Th 9am-6pm, F 8:30am-1pm), and **Change Spot,** 140 Dizengoff St. (☎524 33 93; open Su-Th 9am-7pm, F 9am-2pm), also offer no-commission exchange. Banks usually exchange currency M-Th 8:30am-2pm, F 8:30am-noon for US$6 or 5% commission.

Banks: Most banks are open Su, Tu, Th 8:30am-12:30pm and 4-5:30pm; M, W, F, and holiday eves 8:30am-noon. Main bank offices: **Bank Ha-Poalim,** 104 Ha-Yarkon St. (☎520 06 12); **Israel Discount,** 16 Mapu St. (☎520 32 12); and **Bank Leumi,** 130 Ben-Yehuda St. (☎520 37 37). Branches throughout the city and suburbs.

American Express: 57 Rothschild Blvd. (☎966 20 50). Mail held for cardholders, but no packages. For lost AmEx traveler's checks, call the toll-free 24hr. line (☎177 440 86 94). Changes traveler's checks at bank rates without commission. Cardholders can buy traveler's checks with a passport and personal checks (1% service charge) or cash (3% service charge). Open Su-Th 9am-5pm, F 9-11am.

LOCAL SERVICES

Shopping Hours: In general, 8:30am-7pm, but many stores stay open until 10pm, especially in malls. Most are open late on Th night, and almost all close F by 2pm.

English Bookstores: The Book Boutique, 190 Dizengoff St. (☎527 45 27). The best place for used English-language books in Tel Aviv. A vast selection of texts, plus free lemonade for thirsty bibliophiles. The friendly owner buys and exchanges books, too. Open Su-Th 10am-7pm, F 10am-3pm. **Katzman Gallery Books,** 152 Dizengoff St. (☎523 52 43). A wide selection of magazines, comics, and cheap used books, which they'll buy back afterwards for half-price. Usually open Su-Th 10:30am-8pm, F 8am-3pm. **Steimatzky** has many locations, including 107 Allenby Rd., 109 Dizengoff St., the Opera Tower at 1 Allenby Rd., and Kikkar Ha-Medina. Open Su-Th 8:30am-11pm, F 8:40am-2pm, Sa after sunset-11pm.

Library: British Council Library, 140 Ha-Yarkon St. (☎522 21 94). A peaceful, A/C haven with English-language books, newspapers, videocassettes, and magazines. Open to the public M-Th 10am-1pm and 4-7pm, F 10am-1pm.

Camping Supplies: LaMetayel (☎528 68 94), Dizengoff Center, on the 3rd floor, near the Lev Cinema. The largest camping store in the area, with a full range of equipment and information. The place to meet young Israelis gearing up for their post-military grand tour. Open Su-Th 10am-8:30pm, F 10am-2pm. **Steve's Packs** (☎525 99 20), next door, has a narrower selection, but may be more affordable. Open Su-Th 9:30am-8:45pm, F 9:30am-3pm, Sa 7-10:45pm. **Maslool Travelers' Equipment and Information Center,** 47 Bogroshov St. (☎620 35 08). Buys used equipment. Offers advice and maps (some free, some NIS20-40) for hiking all over Israel. 10% *Let's Go* discount. Open Su-Th 9am-10pm, F 9am-4pm, Sa 7:30-10:30pm.

Film Developing: Fotofilm, 84 Allenby St. (☎517 12 41). 1hr. developing (NIS13), lenses, film, and video supplies. Open Su-Th 9am-6pm, F 9am-2:30pm.

Ticket Agencies: Rococo, 93 Dizengoff St. (☎527 66 77). Open Su-Th 9am-7pm, F 9am-2pm. **Hadran,** 90 Ibn Gvirol St. (☎527 97 97), north of Kikkar Yitzḥak Rabin. **Castel,** 153 Ibn Gvirol St. (☎604 76 78). **Le'an,** 101 Dizengoff St. (☎524 73 73). All sell tickets for concerts, plays, sporting events, and other performances. Discount student tickets sometimes available. MC, V; no checks.

Laundry: Self-service laundromats abound, and hostels and hotels often have their own laundry services. Most hostels allow non-guests to use machines. **Kikkar Dizengoff Laundry,** right near the fountain, on your right when coming from the city center, has coin-operated machines. Washers NIS10; dryers NIS1 for 3min. Open 24hr.

EMERGENCY AND COMMUNICATIONS

Emergency: Police: ☎100. **Ambulance:** ☎101. **Fire:** ☎102.

24hr. Crisis Lines: Rape Crisis (☎517 61 76 for women, 517 91 79 for men). **Alcoholics Anonymous** (☎578 66 63). **Drug Counseling** (☎688 64 64). All speak English.

Pharmacy: Superpharm (☎620 37 98 or 620 09 75), on the bottom floor of Dizengoff Center. Open Su-Th 9:30am-10pm, F 9am-3:30pm, Sa 6:30-11pm. Another location, in the London Minister building, at the intersection of Ibn Gvirol and Sha'ul Ha-Melekh St. Open 24hr. **Nayanpharm,** 75 Ben-Yehuda St. (☎522 91 21) next to the Supersol. Open Su-Th 9am-11pm, F 9am-3pm, Sa 7:30-10:30pm.

Hospitals: Ichilov Hospital, 6 Weizmann St. (☎697 44 44). **Assuta,** 58-60 Jabotinsky St. (☎520 15 15).

Telephones: Solan Communications, 13 Frischmann St. (☎522 94 24; fax 522 94 49). Private booths for international calls (NIS7 per min). Telecards, international calling cards, fax services. Open Su-Th 10am-9pm, F 8am-3pm. **RSM Communications,** 80 Ha-Yarkon St. (☎516 83 66; fax 516 81 26; email fones@rentafone.co.il). Cellular phone rentals with voice mail NIS4/US$1 per day; local calls NIS2 per min.; international calls NIS5 per min.; incoming calls free. Open Su-Th 9am-5:30pm, F 9am-2pm.

Internet Access: Private Link, 78 Ben-Yehuda St. (☎529 98 89). Time purchased can be used over the course of one month: NIS18 per hr., NIS85 for 5hr. Open 24hr. **Maslool Travelers' Equipment and Information Center,** 47 Bogroshov St. (☎620 35 08). NIS8 for 30min. Open Su-Th 9am-10pm, F 9am-4pm, Sa 7:30pm-10:30pm. **Webstop,** 28 Bograshov St. (☎620 26 82). NIS33 per hr.; NIS24 from 9am-noon, 10:30pm-1am. Open daily 9am-1am. Most hostels with Internet access also allow non-guests.

Post Office: 7 Mikveh Yisrael St. (☎564 36 51), 2 blocks east of the south end of Allenby St. **Poste Restante, fax, telegram, and telex.** Open Su-Th 8am-6pm, F 8am-noon. Other branches throughout the city.

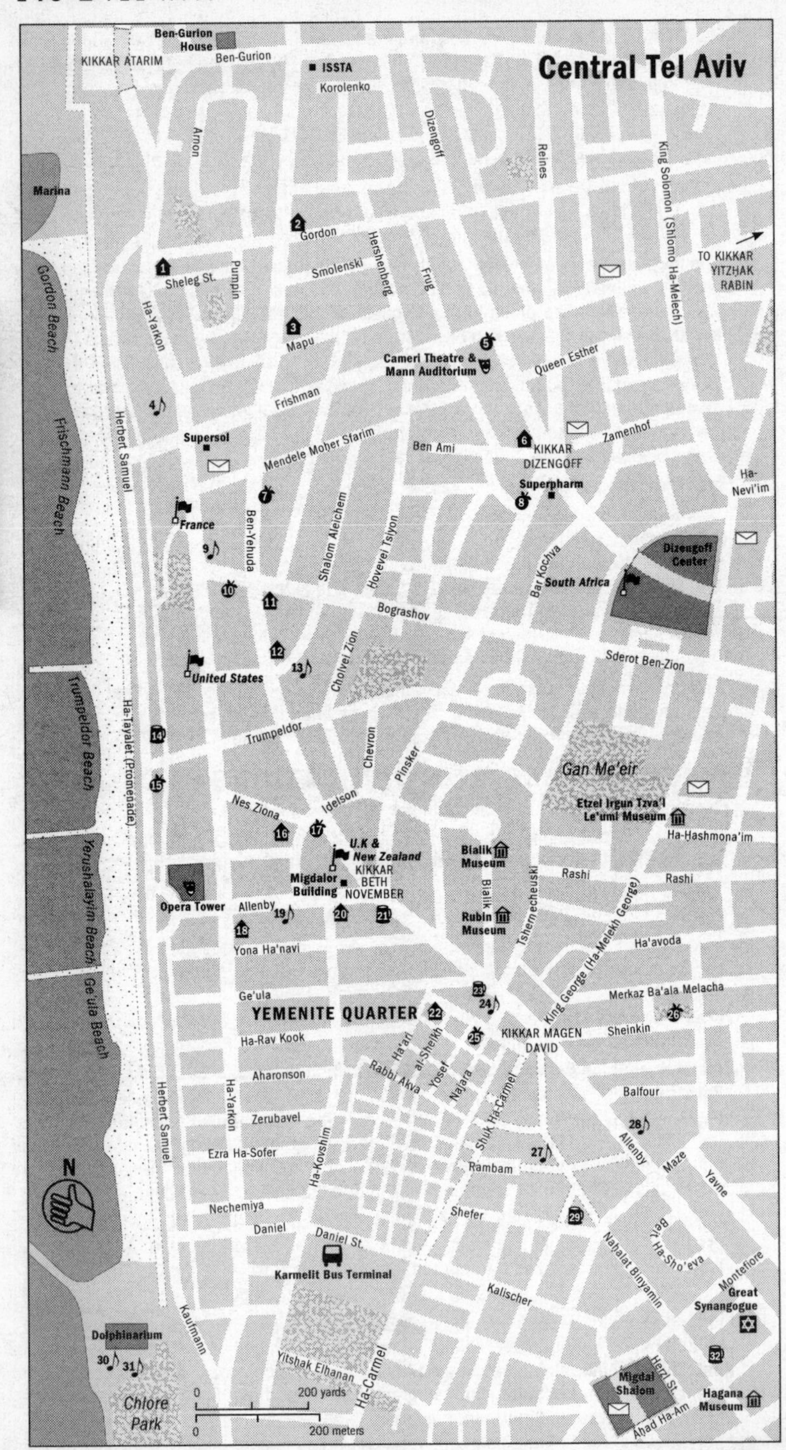
Central Tel Aviv
Ben-Gurion House
KIKKAR ATARIM
Ben-Gurion
ISSTA
Korolenko
Arnon
Dizengoff
Reines
King Solomon (Shlomo Ha-Melech)
Marina
Gordon
Hershenberg
TO KIKKAR YITZHAK RABIN
Sheleg St.
Pumpin
Smolenski
Frug
Gordon Beach
Ha-Yarkon
Mapu
Cameri Theatre & Mann Auditorium
Queen Esther
Frishman
Frischmann Beach
Herbert Samuel
Supersol
Mendele Mohher Sfarim
Ben Ami
KIKKAR DIZENGOFF
Zamenhof
Ha-Nevi'im
Superpharm
France
Ben-Yehuda
Shalom Aleichem
Hovevei Tsiyon
Bar Kochva
Dizengoff Center
South Africa
Bograshov
Sderot Ben-Zion
United States
Cholvei Zion
Trumpeldor Beach
Ha-Tayalet (Promenade)
Trumpeldor
Chevron
Pinsker
Gan Me'eir
Etzel Irgun Tzva'I Le'umi Museum
Nes Ziona
Idelson
Ha-Hashmona'im
U.K & New Zealand
KIKKAR BETH NOVEMBER
Bialik Museum
Yerushalayim Beach
Migdalor Building
Rashi
Opera Tower
Allenby
Bialik
Tshernecheuski
King George (Ha-Melekh George)
Rubin Museum
Yona Ha'navi
Ha'avoda
Ge'ula
Ge'ula Beach
Merkaz Ba'ala Melacha
YEMENITE QUARTER
KIKKAR MAGEN DAVID
Sheinkin
Ha-Rav Kook
Ha'ari
al-Sheikh
Rabbi Akva
Yosef
Najara
Aharonson
Balfour
Shuk Ha-Carmel
Zerubavel
Ezra Ha-Sofer
Ha-Kovshim
Maze
Yavne
Rambam
N
Nechemiya
Shefer
Daniel
Daniel St.
Beit Ha-Sho'eva
Nahalat Binyamin
Montefiore
Karmelit Bus Terminal
Kalischer
Great Synangogue
Dolphinarium
Kaufmann
Yitshak Elhanan
Ha-Carmel
Migdal Shalom
Herzl St.
Ahad Ha-Am
Hagana Museum
Chlore Park
0
200 yards
200 meters
1 2 3 4 5 6 7 8 9 10 11 12 13 14 15 16 17 18 19 20 21 22 23 24 25 26 27 28 29 30 31 32

Central Tel Aviv

ACCOMMODATIONS
Dizengoff Square Hotel, 6
Gordon Hostel, 1
Gordon Inn Guest House, 2
Ha-Yarkon 48 Hostel, 18
Home Hostel, 22
Hotel Nes Ziona, 16
The Mograby Hostel, 20
Momo's Hostel, 12
No. 1 Hostel, 3
Noa Hostel, 11

FOOD
Big Mama, 25
El Gaucho's, 8
Falafel 101, 5
Itzik Ve'Ruthie, 26
Off Side, 17
A Taste of Life, 7
Thai House Restaurant, 10
Yotvata Ba'Ir, 15

PUBS
The Buzz Stop, 14
He-She, 29
Joey's Bar, 21
Lola, 23
The Out, 32

NIGHTLIFE
Azimut, 19
Camelot, 13
Daniel's Punchnight, 31
Fetish, 27
The International Dance Bar, 4
Pacha, 30
The Scene, 24
The Second Floor, 28
Soweto, 9

ACCOMMODATIONS

The Tel Aviv hostel scene really has its act together. There's a bed for every budget, and most places come with all the fixings travelers crave. Even better, the vast majority of hostels practically qualify as beachfront property. Most cluster on Ben-Yehuda and Ha-Yarkon St., with some just off Allenby Rd. or Dizengoff St. Bus #222 makes a round-trip between the airport and Tel Aviv and passes most hostels. When choosing, keep in mind that drunken revelry and honking horns downtown may continue through the wee hours. Also, consider the hostels in Jaffa (see p. 162). Hostels fill up quickly in the summer, especially the private rooms, so make reservations if possible. Almost all have 24hr. reception, kitchen, safe and storage, and Internet access. A huge influx of long-term travelers and day-laborers gives a lived-in feel to some places; daily work can often be found through the hostel managers. Sleeping on the beach is illegal and dangerous; theft and sexual assault are not uncommon, and the zamboni-like machines that sweep the beaches every night for bombs could crush a traveler or at least give a rude awakening.

Ha-Yarkon 48 Hostel, 48 Ha-Yarkon St. (☎516 89 89; fax 510 31 13; email info@hayarkon48.com; www.hayarkon48.com). Take bus #4 or 16 from the central bus station. The bright rooms and showers win popularity contests, but everyone spends their time in the TV lounge playing pool for free, drinking beer in reception, or on the rooftop bar. Small breakfast included. Laundry NIS8. Key deposit NIS20. Check-out 10:30am. 6-bed dorms NIS42/US$10.50, NIS120/US$30 for 3 nights, NIS142/US$38 for 4 nights, NIS252/US$63 for 7 nights. Private rooms NIS176/US$44, with fan and bath NIS208/US$52, with A/C and bath NIS228/US$57. Rooftop mattress NIS35/US$8.75 in summer if all beds are taken.

Gordon Hostel, 2 Gordon St. (☎522 98 70; fax 523 74 19; email sleepin@inter.net.il), on the corner of Ha-Yarkon St. Take bus #4 or 5 from the central bus station, and get off at Gordon St. Though the hostel is as close to the beach as you can get without getting sand in your sheets, most of the clientele sunsoaks on the rooftop lounge. Wash and dry NIS14. Check-out 10:30am. Lockout 11am-2pm. Dorms (coed or female-only) NIS36/US$9, NIS224/US$57 per week. Rooftop mattress NIS27/US$6.75. Students and repeat visitors receive 10% discount.

Gordon Inn Guest House, 17 Gordon St. (☎523 82 39; fax 523 74 19; email sleepin@inter.net.il, www.psl.co.il/gordon-inn), just off Ben-Yehuda St. From the central bus station take bus #4 to Ben-Yehuda and Gordon St. More polished and proper than most in the price range, the Guest House resides conveniently between Dizengoff Center and the beach. Posh bar/cafe open until 3am. Breakfast included. Wash and dry NIS25. Max stay 2 weeks, negotiable. Check-in 2pm. Check-out 11am. All rooms have A/C, some have balconies. Rooms in back are quieter. 7-8 bed dorms (coed) NIS64/US$16; singles NIS184/US$46, with bath NIS228/US$57; doubles NIS236/US$59, NIS284/US$71; triples NIS288/US$72, NIS340/US$85; quads NIS340/US$85, NIS396/US$99. Prices 10-15% lower Nov.-June, except holidays.

Dizengoff Square Hostel, 13 Ben-Ami St. (☎522 51 84; fax 522 51 81; email dizengof@trendline.co.il; www.dizengoff-hostel.co.il), off Dizengoff Sq., across from the Chen cinema. Take bus #5 from the central bus station to Dizengoff Sq. Colorful paint, plaster sculptures in the TV/pool table room, and a breezy rooftop terrace keep the oldest hostel in Tel Aviv fresh and funky. Small breakfast included. Laundry NIS6. Check-out 10:30am. Lockout 10:30am-2:30pm. 4-8 bed dorms (coed and single sex) NIS38/US$9.50, NIS232/US$58 per week, with A/C NIS46/US$11.50. Private rooms NIS188/US$47; with A/C, bath, TV, and fridge NIS216/US$54.

Tel Aviv Youth Hostel/Guest House (HI), 36 B'nei Dan St. (☎544 17 48; fax 544 10 30, email telaviv@iyha.org.il), near Ibn Gvirol St. Take bus #5, 24, or 25 to the Weizmann St. and Yehuda Ha-Macabbe intersection and walk up one block to B'nei Dan. This spotless and shiny hostel is more of a Park Place (huge nearby playground and playing courts) than a Boardwalk (long schlep from the beach). Large breakfast included. Check-out 10am. All rooms have A/C and private rooms have bath. 4-bed dorm NIS70/US$17.50, with bath NIS88/US$22; singles NIS148/US$38; doubles NIS224/US$56; triples NIS288/US$72. NIS6 surcharge for nonmembers. Discounts for longer stays.

No. 1 Hostel, 84 Ben-Yehuda St., 4th floor (☎523 78 07, email sleepin@internet.net.il). One block to your left as you face the sea from Gordon Inn; follow the same directions. There's a time to party and a time to relax, or so claims this middle sibling in the Gordon family. The highly social atmosphere is tempered by a midnight quiet rule. Sunny reception lounge has cable TV, pool table, and an arcade game. Breakfast included. Laundry NIS14. Check-in 2pm. Check-out 10:30am. Rooms have showers and fans. Dorms NIS39/US$10, NIS238/US$60 per week; singles NIS140/US$35; doubles NIS160/US$40; quads NIS160/US$140. Rooftop mattress in summer NIS31/US$8.

Home Hostel, 20 al-Sheikh St. (☎517 67 36). Take bus #4 from the central bus station along Allenby St. until Bialik St.; go behind Allenby 56 and turn right. As cheap as it gets, and, in terms of rooms and facilities, you get what you pay for; but, the family-like atmosphere, meals on Saturday, and a bed on your birthday are all free. Saintly owner can get discounts at local bars and clubs and find jobs for clientele. Breakfast included. Kitchen available. Dorms (coed and female-only) NIS30/US$8, students NIS27/US$7.

Hotel Nes Ziona, 10 Nes Ziona St. (☎510 60 84), just off Ben-Yehuda. Take bus #4 from the central bus station to the Opera Tower or bus#222 from the airport to the first stop on Ben-Yehuda. Simple, airy rooms provide a pleasant escape from the grunge of the backpacking world. All rooms have TV and A/C. Some have balconies. Check-in and check-out noon. Singles NIS140/US$35, with bath NIS196/US$49; doubles with bath NIS200-240/US$50-60 depending on size; triples with bath NIS240-300/US$60-75.

Noa Hostel, 34 Ben-Yehuda St. (☎620 00 44 or 528 14 45 to reach guests; fax 528 33 03). Bus #4 from the central bus station passes the hostel. Laid-back clientele play pool and watch TV in the lounge or BBQ on the roof. Check-out 11am. All rooms have A/C, some have balconies. 6-bed dorms NIS35/US$9; 5-bed dorms NIS40/US$10; 4-bed dorms NIS38/US$9.50. Private rooms NIS140/US$35, with bath NIS160/US$40. Discounts for longer stays.

The Mograby Hostel, 30 Allenby St. (☎510 24 40; email mugrabyhostel@hotmail.com; www.inisrael.com/mograby). Take bus #4 from the central bus station to the first stop on Ben-Yehuda. Long-term crowd of day-laborers chills in the rooftop tents (NIS32/US$8) or the lively social room of this centrally located hostel. Laundry NIS12. Check-out 11am. Some rooms have A/C or balcony for no extra charge. 6-bed dorms (coed or female only) NIS35/US$8.50, NIS210/US$52 per week; singles NIS120/US$30, with shower NIS130/US$32, with bath NIS150/US$37; doubles NIS140/US$35, NIS150/US$37, NIS160/US$40.

Momo's Hostel, 28 Ben-Yehuda St. (☎528 74 71; fax 528 07 97; email momos28@hotmail.com). Take bus #4 from the central bus station to the huge El Al building. Momo's has beds, a bar, and a snooker table, all wrapped in a no-frills package. Sometimes provides free airport pickup (☎180 055 33 44). Wash and dry NIS15. Check-out 11am. 4-8 bed dorms (single-sex and coed) with fans NIS35/US$140; private rooms NIS100/US$25, with bath NIS130/US$32.50, with A/C and TV NIS160/US$40. 10% discount for week long stays.

FOOD

Come mealtime, Tel Aviv rises above and beyond the call of duty. Restaurants range from Tex-Mex to Southeast Asian, from falafel and hummus to French *haute-cuisine.* After a brain-melting day at the beach, however, fast food and frozen yogurt may sound just as good. Luckily, there's plenty of time to decide—most restaurants stay open until midnight or later, all week long.

For quick, cheap belly-fillers, head to the self-service eateries on **Ben-Yehuda** or **Allenby** where stuff-your-own falafel goes for under NIS10. The trick for serious penny-pinchers is to find a place selling falafel by the pita and keep refilling it until your stomach hits the ground. The only better deal is the free food given out by the Hare Krishnas in Gan Me'ir Park, just off King George St. The eateries, just a block past the extortionist beachfront refreshment stands, are the best option for beachbums. For the late-night crowd, many of the bakeries along Allenby between Shuk Ha-Carmel and Ha-Yarkon St. sell bagel toasts. (NIS5-8. Open 24hr.) Bakeries, falafel stands, and fast-food joints line the **Dizengoff Sq.** area. **Domino's** delivers medium-sized pizzas for NIS50, plus NIS5 per topping. (☎527 23 30 for northern locations, 562 77 70 for southern locations or after midnight.)

For a more civilized experience than that of the deep-fried and dripping tahini sort, there are several options. In **Little Tel Aviv,** bistros offering Eastern European, Middle Eastern, and Far Eastern fare at fairly reasonable prices line Yermiyahu St., which runs between Dizengoff and Ben-Yehuda, just before they intersect. Much more expensive fish restaurants are nearby in the **port.** Some of the most authentic and cheap food can be found in **Kerem Ha-Temanim** (the Yemenite Quarter), along Ge'ula St. and Ha-Rav Kook St. Small red-roofed houses on narrow streets offer salads and pita (NIS10), spicy meats (NIS20-35), and fried dough snacks (NIS15-25).

Israelis flock from nearby cities to the **Shechunat Ha-Tikva** area for the outdoor cafes and restaurants selling cheap beer and their renowned chicken, lamb, and beef kebab. Take bus #15, 16, or 41 to Ha-Tikva—it's too far and unsafe to walk. The Ha-Tikva Market, between Ezel St. and Ha-Tikva St., just below Ha-Hagana St., is a carnivore's carnival or a vegetarian's hell. The market also sells some of the freshest produce available in the city. Closer to the center of town, reluctant spenders should shop at the large, outdoor **Shuk Ha-Carmel.** When coming from Allenby, the produce carts are toward the back. To catch prices at their lowest (and crowds at their rowdiest), shop an hour or two before the beginning of Shabbat. Dizengoff Center hosts a **food fair** where people sell their homemade goodies—everything from Greek baklava (NIS1-3) to Chinese dumplings (NIS12 for 6. Open Th 6-10pm, F 10am-4pm.) **Supermarkets** can be found throughout town. **Supersol,** 79 Ben-Yehuda St., near Gordon St., may be the most convenient. (Open Su-M 7am-midnight, Tu-Th 24hr., Sa after sundown.) **Co-op** has supermarket branches right in Dizengoff Sq., in the basement of the Ha-Mashbir department store in Dizengoff Center. (Open daily 7am-8pm.)

The restaurants listed take credit cards unless otherwise noted.

Itzik Ve'Ruthie, 53 Sheinkin St. (☎685 27 53), serves the most scrumptious sandwiches (NIS5-15) in the city. The homemade soda (NIS2) alone is worth squeezing past all the locals crammed into this tiny shop. Open Su-Th 5am-4pm, F 5am-2pm.

Falafel 101, 99 Dizengoff St., near the corner of Frischmann St., should be the model for all other falafel stands. For NIS10, get piping-hot falafel, a large selection of salads, and a drink. Open Su-Th 8am-midnight, F 8am-4pm. No credit cards.

Big Mama, 13 Najara St. (☎517 50 65). Look for the blue and red neon sign on the back right corner of the walkway behind Allenby 58. Gobble down the best pizza this side of Italy (NIS25-34), or try one of the indulgently creamy pasta dishes (NIS28-34). Open Su noon-2am, M-W and F noon-3am, Th noon-4am.

TEL AVIV-JAFFA

A Taste of Life, 60 Ben-Yehuda St. (☎620 31 51). A vegan paradise run by members of the Black Hebrew community, a group whose dietary laws prohibit both milk and meat (see **Dimona,** p. 285). Entrees like wheatfurters, veggie *shawarma,* and soy barbecue twists served *à la carte* (NIS15) or with two sides and a salad (NIS42). Cleanse your palate on the excellent soymilk ice cream (NIS6.50) and other non-dairy, no-egg desserts. Open Su-Th 9am-11pm, F 9am-3pm, Sa after sundown-midnight.

Hungarian Blintzes, 35 Yermiyahu St. (☎544 16 97 or 605 06 74), near the port. Turn right off Dizengoff St. and continue for a block. Locals jonesing for hungarian goulash blintzes (NIS32) flock to this intimate bistro. Sweeter options like jam (NIS25) and poppy seed cream (NIS30) also available. Open Su-Th 1pm-1am, Sa sundown-1am.

Yotvata Ba'Ir, 78 Herbert Samuel St. (☎510 79 84). There's a green and orange neon sign off the *tayelet*. Kibbutz Yotvata, renowned producers of dairy goods, ventures into the city with this well-lit oasis of fresh veggies, cheeses, and fruits. Menu highlights include salads large enough to feed a small army (NIS45-47) and pancakes masquerading as sundaes (NIS27-39). Open daily 7am-3am.

Dallas Restaurant, 68 Ezel St. (☎687 43 49), in the Ha-Tikva neighborhood, a few blocks past the *shuk*. Bus #15 and 16 go past the restaurant. Outstanding Yemenite restaurant serves up every cow part, including heart (NIS13), testicles (NIS10), and udder (NIS10). Open Su-Th noon-2am, F 11am-1hr. before sundown, Sa 8:30pm-2am.

New York Bagel, 215 Ben-Yehuda St. (☎605 35 72), above Jabotinsky St. Something from the diaspora makes a welcome return to Israel, namely bagels (NIS3), with cream cheese (NIS13) and nova lox (NIS22). Open Su-Th 7:30am-11pm, F 7am-3pm.

El Gaucho's, 57 Pinsker St. (☎528 37 88), just off Dizengoff Square. The beef is almost as tender as the loving care extended by the waitstaff of this Argentinian steakhouse. Business lunch includes steak, fries, salad, and a drink (NIS49; served M-F noon-6pm). Open Su-Th noon-11:30pm, Sa after sundown-midnight.

Off Side (☎516 49 05), at the intersection of Ben-Yehuda and Idelson St. Look for the neon chicken. The half-chicken and two veggie sides are as close as you can get to mom's homemade dishes in under 5 minutes (NIS30, less for take-out). Open Su-Th 10am-11pm, F 10am-2:30pm.

Thai House Restaurant, 8 Bograshov St. (☎517 85 68), just off Ben-Yehuda St. This restaurant brings a delicately spiced taste of the Far East to the Middle East. Their specialties are coconut milk casseroles (NIS38-58), but *Pad Thai* (NIS28) can be found as well. Top it all off with a fried banana in mango sauce (NIS12). Open daily noon-11pm.

CAFES

Crowd-gazing is an art in Tel Aviv; chairs on the sidewalk and cafe-au-lait can be found just about anywhere in the city. **Sheinken St.,** one of the hippest promenades in town, has a long tradition of artsy liberalism. Along **Ben-Yehuda, Dizengoff,** and **Ibn Gvirol,** three parallel streets, a number of cafes serve local neighborhood folk and weary shoppers alike. **Basel St.** (near its intersection with Ibn Gvirol St., a block above Jabotinsky St.) recently sprouted its own crop of chichi cafes for hipper-than-thou Sheinken expats.

Tamar Cafe, 57 Sheinken St. (☎685 23 76), provides a quintessential Sheinken experience. Immortalized in a song by the Israeli pop trio Mango ("Living on Sheinken/drinking coffee at the Tamar Cafe/my dream is to make a short film"), the Tamar is crammed with locals arguing about who's more liberal. Open Su-Th 7am-8pm, F 7am-5pm.

Babblefish, 13 Rabbi Akiva (☎516 45 85), near the corner of Najara St., to the right of the *shuk* from Allenby. This adorable, cherry-pink hole-in-the-wall cafe serves a mean sangria (NIS12) and cheap salads (NIS15-20). Live percussion and funk DJ on Friday nights. Open Su-F noon-2am.

Ilan's Coffee Shop, 90 Ibn Gvirol St. (☎523 53 34). Tables are a prized commodity in Tel Aviv's first espresso bar. Renowned for their fantastic home brew "Angela Mia" (NIS6-16), they also recently crossed the fence into the whole-leaf tea business (NIS6-14). Another location at 20 Carlebach St. Open Su-Th 6:30am-10pm, F 6:30am-3pm.

Kassit, 117 Dizengoff St. (☎522 38 55). The elderly clientele screaming at each other were the Bohemians and poets who made Kassit the classic Dizengoff political cafe. Serves good toasts (NIS22-27) and Eastern European food. Open daily 9am-10pm.

Cafe Nordau, 145 Ben-Yehuda St. (☎524 01 34), on the corner of Arlozorov. Good food in generous portions served to a largely, but not exclusively, gay clientele; distributes Hazman Havarod (Tel Aviv's gay newspaper) and provides current info on gay life and hot spots. Full meals NIS36-44. Open M-W 8am-1am, Th-Su 24hr.

My Coffee Shop and Bar, 39 Allenby St. (☎528 40 71), on the corner of Bialik St., is the place to go after a night of clubbing. Coffee NIS9. For a few more shekels get caramel cream, coconut, and mocha concoctions. Open 24hr.

Orna Ve' Ella, 33 Sheinkin St. (☎620 47 53). Sheinkin sophisticates line up for a table at this elegant cafe. Delectable food served in somewhat stingy portions, but homemade sorbets (NIS18) and innovative chilled soups (NIS20) make a nice snack. Open Su-Th 10am-midnight, F 10am-5pm, Sa 11am-12:30am.

SIGHTS

ROOFTOP OBSERVATORY. When haggling, shoving, and sunning take their toll, rise above it all. Look down on the chaos of the market and the city from the observatory in **Migdal Shalom.** The tower rises 34 stories skyward and the penthouse affords a breathtaking view, although the gating does give it a somewhat caged-in feel. The mosaic walls were made by artists Naḥum Gutan and David Sharir. *(1 Herzl St. and Aḥad Ha-Am St. Enter through the Eastern Wing beneath the underpass. ☎517 73 04. Open Su-Th 10am-6:30pm, F 10am-2pm. NIS15, students and seniors NIS10.)*

KIKKAR YITZḤAK RABIN. Formerly Kikkar Malkhei Yisrael (Kings of Israel Sq.), the square was renamed in 1995 in memory of Prime Minister Yitzḥak Rabin. On November 4, 1995, Rabin was assassinated by Yigal Amir, a Jewish student, during a crowded peace rally. The square has since drawn mourners who have painted large portraits of Rabin and left candles, flowers, and poetry. The official memorial, surrounded by five years' worth of candlewax, is next to the City Hall. *(Just off Ibn Gvirol St., between Arlozorov St. and Ben-Gurion St.)*

DIZENGOFF SQUARE. The capital of the maze that is Dizengoff St. hosts an ever-changing scene, from retirees feeding pigeons in the midday sun to late-night punks cluttering the overpass stairs. The revolving, multicolored, fire-spitting, **fountain,** designed by illustrious Israeli artist Agam, crowns the square in an unsurpassed celebration of municipal kitsch. The tunes come from the fountain itself, which orchestrates its own hourly multimedia show to music ranging from Ravel's Bolero to Israeli folk songs. *(At the intersection of Dizengoff St., Ben-Ami St., and Pinsker St.)*

GREAT SYNAGOGUE. Completed in 1926 and renovated in 1970, this huge domed building showcases arches and stained-glass windows that are replicas of those from European synagogues destroyed during the Holocaust. *(110 Allenby St., near the corner with Rothschild Blvd. ☎560 49 05 or 560 40 66. Open Su-F 10am-5pm, Sa 7:30-11:30am. Sa prayer open to the public; head coverings and modest dress required.)*

Near the synagogue is **Independence Hall,** where the founding of the State of Israel was proclaimed in 1948. *(16 Rothschild Blvd. ☎517 39 42. Open Su-Th 9am-2pm.)*

ZOOLOGICAL CENTER. This combination drive-through safari park, circus, and zoo features 250 acres of African game in a natural habitat. Stare over a *wadi* at impossibly cute gorillas and Syrian bears, or let an ostrich poke its head into your car for a bite of candy. People without picnics can have lunch at the moderately priced restaurant, and those without a car can ride the park's own vehicles through the habitat. Pedestrian tours are offered as well. *(In Ramat Gan. Take bus #30, 35, or 43 from Tel Aviv or bus #67 within Ramat Gan. From the bus stop, go 0.5km down Ha-Tzvi Blvd. with the park on your right; the zoo entrance is on the right. ☎631 21 81 or 674 49 81. Open Su-Th July-Aug. 9am-5pm, Mar.-June and Sept.-Oct. 9am-4pm, and Nov.-Feb. 9am-2:30pm; open year round F 9am-1pm, Sa 9am-3pm. Visitors may remain on the grounds 2hr. after entrance gate closes. NIS42, students and children NIS32; with circus NIS49, students and children NIS42; extra NIS5 charge to ride on park's bus.)*

The beast-watching madness continues outside the Zoological Center in the massive **Ramat Gan National Park,** which rents boats. *(Open 24hr. Free.)*

TEL AVIV UNIVERSITY. Home to the superb **Beit Ha-Tfutzot** (see **Museums,** p. 155), the university remains Ramat Aviv's star attraction. The vast central lawn is flanked by palm trees, well-kept memorial gardens, and Modernist sculpture. When facing the fountains, the first building on the right is the **Sourasky Central Library.** *(☎640 84 23. Open Su-Th 9am-9pm, F 9am-12:30pm. Non-students NIS22.)* From here, the gently sloping path leads directly to the glitzy new main gate complex on Levanon St. The **Genia Schreiber University Art Gallery,** in the pink pavilion right next to the gate, keeps its modern art collection on the cutting edge by changing it every two months. *(☎640 88 60. Open Su-Th 11am-7pm. Free.)* Students give free tours focusing on the campus' unique Bauhaus and neo-postmodern architecture every Monday at 11am. Meet at the bookstore next to the Art Gallery. Grab a snack at the Gilman or Law cafeterias for a peek at the student scene. *(Both buildings are on the left side of the fountain; the law school is closer to the main gate. Croissants NIS4, yogurt NIS3.50, sodas NIS4. Bus #27 from the central bus station or bus #24 or 25 from Allenby near the shuk go to gate #2, which leads into the central lawn.)*

WALKS AND PARKS

While Tel Aviv may not boast a laundry list of ancient synagogues and castles, its historic neighborhoods supplement the short list of highlights. These turn-of-the-century neighborhoods make perfect strolling grounds for those who wish to escape some of the chaos of the city.

Neve Tzedek, just west of the intersection of Herzl St. and Aḥad Ha-Am St., is Tel Aviv's oldest Jewish neighborhood outside of Jaffa and one of the few with a 100-year-old history. The area is being gradually renovated to accommodate local yuppies attracted to the Mediterranean-village charm of its narrow streets and stone architecture. Happily unrenovated is **Kerem Ha-Temanim** (the Yemenite Quarter), northwest of Allenby St. and King George St., near Shuk Ha-Carmel. This area firmly maintains its village feel despite relentless sky-scraping all around it.

Those who wish to soak in the newness of Tel Aviv's culture congregate at the waterfront **promenade,** where preteens neck, vendors hawk, and folk dancers strut their stuff all night long. The wide sidewalks of **Dizengoff St.** are still among the more crowded catwalks in town, though they are no longer at the peak of their glory due to the mutant-growth of shopping arenas in the area. The young and the restless generally roam here and on **Sheinken St.,** while the bold and the beautiful head uptown to the northern parts of **Dizengoff St., Ibn Gvirol St., and Basel St.**

Tel Aviv has a number of options for the athletically-inclined as well. East of Namir (Haifa) Rd. (bus #25) is the **Sportek** (☎699 03 07), a collection of sports fields, a jogging track, and a miniature-golf course. (Open 4-10pm. Free.) Tel Avivians crowd **Ha-Yarkon Park,** just across the river from Sportek, home to a little train, water park, and bird safari. Nearby is **Gan Ha-Yehoshua;** barbecue some kebab and play some *matkot* (paddleball), and you'll fit right in. To go to Gan Ha-Yehoshua from the city center, take bus #47 or 48 from King George, bus #21 from Dizengoff St., or bus #28 from the first floor of the central bus station.

MUSEUMS

THE ERETZ YISRAEL MUSEUM. A veritable eight-ring circus, the Eretz Yisrael museum consists of eight pavilions covering vastly different topics spread over an archaeological site that is still being excavated. The most famous attraction in the complex is the **Glass Pavilion,** with one of the finest collections of glassware in the world. The **Nehushtan Pavilion,** with its cave-like entry way, holds the discoveries of the excavations at the ancient copper mines of Timna, better known as King Solomon's Mines, located just north of Eilat. Across the patio, the **Kadman Numismatic Museum** traces the history of the region through ancient coins. The **Ceramics Pavilion** contains ancient Canaanite pottery, exhibits explaining its production, and artist Moshe Shek's ceramic sculptures. Across the entrance area, past the grassy amphitheater, is the **Man and His Work Center,** an exhibition of Middle Eastern folk crafts and techniques. Follow the road to the right and go up the stairs to reach the **Tel Qasile Excavations,** which have revealed a 12th-century BCE Philistine port city and ruins dating from around 1000 BCE. The area at the top of the hill contains the remains of three separate Philistine temples built on top of each other. Down the hill to the south are scattered remnants of the residential and industrial quarter of the city. Past the Philistine town is the **Folklore Pavilion,** with Jewish religious art, ceremonial objects, and ethnic clothing. The Eretz Yisrael complex also houses a library of over 30,000 books and periodicals (some in English) and the **Lasky Planetarium.** *(2 Levanon St., in Ramat Aviv (the northernmost part of the city). Buses #7, 24, 25, or 74 from the New Central Bus Station stop at the museum. ☎641 52 44. Open Su-Tu and Th 9am-3pm, W 9am-5pm, F-Sa 10am-2pm. NIS28, students NIS22, children NIS20; includes access to all 8 pavilions and the Eretz Yisrael Library. Planetarium NIS20, in Hebrew.)*

BEIT HA-TFUTZOT (THE DIASPORA MUSEUM). Also in Ramat Aviv, this outstanding museum chronicles the history of Jewish life outside the land of Israel, from the Babylonian exile (596 BCE) to the present day. A display of synagogue models shows how Jews incorporated local architectural ideas in building their houses of worship; they resemble Italian villas, American ranches, and Chinese pagodas. There's even a model of a synagogue designed by architect **Frank Lloyd Wright.** Short films and multimedia displays throughout the museum highlight everything from the culture of the Yemenite Jewish community to the evolution of Yiddish theater. The museum also has a **Genealogy Department** that can trace the family trees of Jews whose relatives have registered. The **Chronosphere,** offering English multimedia presentations at 12:30 and 2:30pm, is a good introduction to the museum. *(On the Tel Aviv University Campus in Ramat Aviv. Buses #24 and 25 stop at the closest gate to the museum (Gate #2), but #27 stops near the rear gate not far away. ☎646 20 20; email bhmuseum@tau.ac.il; www.bh.org.il. Open Su-Tu and Th 10am-5pm, W 10am-7pm, F 9am-2pm. NIS22; students, children, and seniors NIS16.)*

TEL AVIV MUSEUM OF ART. The museum holds a sizeable collection of Israeli and international art. The handsome lobby boasts a Lichtenstein, and the museum itself runs the gamut from Impressionism (Renoir, Monet, Corot, and Pissaro) to Surrealism (including de Chirico and Magritte) to cutting-edge multimedia installations by more recent artists. Rotating thematic exhibits are exceptionally well-curated and range from "Music in Art" to "Stage Design." An English program listing special exhibits and events is available in the ticket booth or the This Week in Tel Aviv insert in Friday's Jerusalem Post. *(27 Sha'ul Ha-Melekh Blvd. Buses #7 and 18. ☎696 12 97 or 695 73 61; www.tamuseum.co.il. Open M and W 10am-4pm, Tu and Th 10am-10pm, F 10am-2pm, Sa 10am-4pm.Gallery tours in English W 11:30am. NIS30, students NIS24, seniors and children NIS15.)*

HA-GANAH MUSEUM. This museum relates the history of the Israeli Defense Force (IDF). Two movies (in Hebrew and English) tell the stories of the Exodus, the first ship to make *aliya*, and the Palmaḥ. *(23 Rothschild Blvd., between Allenby St. and Naḥalat Binyamin. ☎560 86 24. Open Su-Th 9am-4pm. NIS8; students, seniors and children NIS4.)*

RUBIN MUSEUM. Located in the former residence of Reuven Rubin, this collection of his oil paintings represents the formative years of Israeli art. *(14 Bialik St. ☎525 59 61. Open Su-M and W-Th 10am-2pm, Tu 10am-1pm and 4-8pm, Sa 11am-2pm. NIS15, students NIS7.50.)*

ETZEL IRGUN TZVA'I LE'UMI MUSEUM. The displays trace the pre-1948 history of late Israeli prime minister Menaḥem Begin's military movement that struggled against British Mandatory rule. *(38 King George St., in the Likud party headquarters. ☎528 40 01 or 525 33 07. Open Su-Th 8am-4pm. NIS8, students and seniors NIS4.)*

BEIT BIALIK MUSEUM. The former home of Ḥayim Naḥman Bialik, one of Israel's greatest poets, now houses his manuscripts, photographs, articles, letters, and 94 books (with translations in 28 languages). The building is maintained almost exactly as it was when he died. An English brochure is available, but there are no English translations on the displays. *(22 Bialik St., a block up Allenby, across from the shuk. ☎525 45 30. Open Su-Th 9am-5pm, Sa 11am-2pm, closed on Sa in August. Free.)*

DAVID BEN-GURION HOUSE. Peruse books, pictures, and mementos (including letters from Ben-Gurion to John F. Kennedy, Winston Churchill, and Charles de Gaulle) of Israel's first prime minister. In the Hillel Cohen Lecture Hall next door, invade Ben-Gurion's privacy even further as you examine his passports and one of his salary slips. *(17 Ben-Gurion Ave. ☎522 10 10. House and lecture hall open Su-Th 8am-3pm, F 8am-1pm. Open erratically on Sa 11am-2pm. Free.)*

BEACHES

Tel Aviv may party night after night, but somehow it manages to fit a busy day of sun and surf in between. Beaches have lifeguards on duty. (May-June and Sept.-Oct. 7am-5pm, July-Aug. 7am-7pm, and Nov.-Apr. 7am-2:30pm.) Since all of Tel Aviv's beaches are rife with theft, use the free safes at most hostels.

From north to south, the beaches are Sheraton, Hilton (behind those hotels), Gordon, Frischmann, Trumpeldor (at the ends of those streets), and the **Jerusalem beach** at the end of Allenby Rd. (originally set up to give people from Jerusalem a place to play); the last four are almost one continuous beach. The southern coastline, with fewer amenities and no luxury hotels, tends to be quieter during the day, though this is gradually changing now that the *tayelet* (promenade) has been extended all the way to Jaffa. The **Sheraton beach** is also quite peaceful. **Gordon Beach** overflows with foreign tourists and people trying to pick them up, while the **Hilton beach** swarms with native surfers and people trying to pick them up. Avoid that whole scene altogether at **Nordau Beach**, a religious beach. (Men: M, W, and Sa; women: Su, Tu, and Th.)

The **Octopus Diving and Sport Center**, at the marina, provides scuba diving courses and equipment. (☎527 35 54. 5-day course NIS1100 but expect to pay at least NIS410 more for a certificate, mask, and log book.) **Surfboards** (☎524 21 39) can be rented near the marina at Kikkar Atarim for NIS80 per hour.

ENTERTAINMENT

PERFORMING ARTS

For the most detailed information on performance schedules and other activities in the Tel Aviv area, see *Tel Aviv Today*, *Events in Tel Aviv*, and *This Week in Tel Aviv*, all free at the tourist information office and major hotels.

The **Suzanne Delal Center**, 5 Yeḥiely St. (☎510 56 56), in Neve Tzedek, has indoor and outdoor dance, theater, and musical performances. Take bus #8, 10, 25, or 61 from downtown or #40 or 46 from the central bus station. The center is best known as the home of the Inbal and Bat Sheva dance companies, both of which perform contemporary ethnic dances. (Box office open daily 9am-5pm. Inbal: ☎517 37 11, call 8am-8pm; NIS60. Bat Sheva: ☎517 14 71; NIS45-60, 20% discount with foreign passport.) **Beit Lessin**, 34 Weizmann St. (☎694 11 11), has live jazz acts (NIS30-70). The **Tel Aviv Cameri Theater**, 101 Dizengoff St., at the corner of

Frischmann St., offers simultaneous translation earphones during 8:30pm performances on Tuesday. (☎523 33 35. Tickets NIS100-125.) **Habima Theater,** 2 Tarsat Blvd., the national theater of Israel, also offers simultaneous translation at some performances. (☎629 55 55 or 620 77 77. Tickets NIS85-150, 20% student discount.) In the same complex, the **Mann Auditorium** (☎528 91 63) is home to the **Israeli Philharmonic Orchestra** (box office ☎525 15 02) which plays modern Israeli works as well as more internationally known pieces. Be prepared for a cough-fest like no other when the orchestra pauses—the crowd of season ticket holders is older than the auditorium.

There are also more than 40 **movie theaters** showing American and Israeli flicks. Check the *Jerusalem Post* for English listings for the artsy **Tel Aviv Cinemathèque,** 2 Sprinzak St. (☎691 71 81), at the intersection with Carlebach St., or the more mainstream **Chen Cinema** (☎528 22 88) in Dizengoff Sq.

VISUAL ARTS

Art galleries line **Gordon St.,** between Dizengoff St. and Ben-Yehuda St., and are scattered elsewhere throughout the city. **The Stern Gallery,** 30 Gordon St. (☎524 63 03), showcases artwork by a father and son team. **M. Pollack,** 42 King George St. (☎528 13 36), near the Etzel Irgun Tzva'i Le'umi Museum, displays an extensive collection of antique maps of the world.

SHOPPING

If there's one thing Israelis love more than 80s music, it's huge shopping malls. **Azrieli Center,** 132 Petaḥ Tikvah Rd. (☎608 11 98), is the tallest mall in Israel—at least for now—and has a huge movie theater with the latest American fare. (Open Su-Th 10am-10pm, F 9:30am-3pm, Sa 8-11pm.) Closer to the center of town, **Dizengoff Center** overflows with stores, fast-food, video arcades, and two cineplexes. (Open Su-Th 9am-midnight, F 9am-3pm and 8pm-noon.)

Plan your dream wedding or the debutante ball you never had in the ritzy shops around **Dizengoff St.** and **Sderot Nordau.** Trendy clothing and jewelry boutiques line **Sheinken St.** While many Tel Avivians fill their clubbing closets here, the price tags can be rather steep. Remember, all it takes is one good accessory: **Schwartz's Fancy Feathers,** on the corner of Rambam and Naḥalat Binyamin, has wall-to-wall feather boas. Two meters of their pure tactile pleasure go for NIS20-40. (☎272 36 52. Open Su-Th 9am-6pm, F 9am-2pm.)

For a more down-and-dirty shopping experience, head to the famed **Shuk Ha-Carmel,** at the intersection of Allenby Rd. and King George St. While waving polyester undergarments and red plastic sandals, vendors extol their products' virtues to strollers. Farther down from Allenby Rd., fresh fruit and vegetables go for the lowest prices in the city. Huge mounds of plucked chickens make for a fowl sight. Near the *shuk*, Naḥalat Binyamin, parallel to Allenby one block closer to the sea, becomes a street fair on Tuesdays and Fridays. From 10am to 4pm (weather permitting) local artists and craftspeople sell artsy jewelry, pottery, original paintings, Judaica, kids' toys, and bizarre candelabras. Musicians and mimes fill the cobblestone street to entertain those weary of shopping. Other bargains can be found at Jaffa's **flea market** (see p. 164).

NIGHTLIFE

LIVE MUSIC

Young Israeli rock bands have appointed Tel Aviv their headquarters and play the clubs nightly. In addition, two amphitheaters at Ha-Yarkon Park hold concerts. *Ha-Ir (The City)*, a weekly Hebrew magazine, has a section called "Akhbar Ha-Ir," with comprehensive listings. For listings in English, check the brochure *This Week in Tel Aviv*, produced by *The Jerusalem Post.*

Barbie, 40 Salame Rd. (☎681 67 57), halfway between Herzl St. and Marzuk Veezar. Only accessible by taxi. Look for a gray striped awning or a big crowd. Garage-like place is frequented by some of the best rock bands in Israel. Cover NIS10-50 depending on the band's fame. Shows Su-F 10pm and midnight.

Heineken Habima (☎528 21 74), on the left side of Kikkar Habima, at the top of Rothschild Blvd. Locals groove to local bands by the neon and candlelight. Beer NIS15-20. Cover NIS25, weekends NIS30. Open M-Sa at 10:30pm.

Camelot, 16 Shalom Aleichem St. (☎528 52 33). The basement echoes with live blues and R&B, while the upstairs pub stays mellow, with DJs on W, F, and Sa. Cover NIS35-80 for downstairs. Open daily 9pm-4am. Reserve at least a day before for good bands.

Daniel's Punchnight (☎510 88 92), in the Dolphinarium next to Pacha. The waitstaff are also the performers at this packed dance-bar and grill. 21+. Cover NIS30. Open Tu-Sa 10pm-4am.

DISCOS

Tel Aviv's dance scene is always on the move; the *only* club one year may be empty the next and a hardware store after that. To really enjoy Tel Aviv's nightlife, you may have to reset your internal clock. The music sometimes starts early, but no one arrives before midnight and places tend to peak around 3am. Friday is the hottest. Those who really want to earn their nocturnal merit badges should keep an eye out for after-party signs; different clubs take turns hosting these 6:30am (Saturday morning) bashes that tunnel on until noon.

Pacha (☎510 20 60). This sprawling club in the Dolphinarium overlooks the ocean. The hedonistic playground has two dance floors (Th house and 80s, F-Sa all house), a lounge for *nargilah* (NIS15), masseuses, and more glittered and pierced navels than you can count. Th 23+, F-Sa 18+. Cover NIS60-100. Open Th at 1am, F-Sa at midnight.

The Octopus (☎620 01 31), at the port. Turn right at the end of Yermiyahu St., near the Superpharm, and continue 300m to the cluster of clubs. After Thursdays and Fridays of hard-core trance, the crowd chills out at the Saturday sundown party (5:30pm) then grooves up for 70s night fever (midnight). Cover Th NIS80, F-Sa NIS60.

The Scene, 56 Allenby Rd. (☎510 85 23). A catwalk of a club, the Scene serves as the prime stomping grounds for Tel Aviv's starlets in sequins. Club goes loco for salsa on Thursday. Monday is gay night. 23+. Cover NIS50. Open M-Sa 10pm-4am.

The Second Floor, 67 Allenby Rd. Head under the blue wooden sign around back and up the stairs. Wild crowd spills out onto the balcony of this 70s-style apartment or retreats to the many chill-out rooms to enjoy pool, *nargilah*, or rooftop jazz. 20+. Cover NIS30. Open Th-F at 10pm, occasional jazz soirées on Friday afternoons.

Dynamo Dvash, 59 Abarbanel St. (☎683 51 59), a small street off Salame St., on your left when coming from Herzl St. DJs from all over the world craft "brain dance" electronica high above the warehouse floor. 21+. Cover NIS40-70. Open Th, F at midnight.

Fetish (☎510 88 07), on Rambam St., off Naḥalat Binyamin. Despite the name, this trendy dance club is pretty vanilla. The international crowd gets shaken up on James Bond Saturdays and kicks it up for salsa Thursdays.

Azimut, 26 Allenby St. (☎517 74 97), right near the Opera Tower. Though Azmut draws a tourist crowd, it indulges the Israeli obsession with the new wave decade. Go thirsty; the cover (NIS60) includes drinks. 20+. Open Th, F.

The International Dance-Bar, 109 Ha-Yarkon St. (☎527 59 57). A new theme every night–Salsa Sundays, hip-hop Tuesdays, 80s Wednesdays, and house on weekends–but the great seaview from the back patio stays constant. Beer NIS12-20. 21+. Open daily 8pm. Only a disco in summer.

Soweto, 61 Ha-Yarkon St. (☎516 02 22), at the corner of Trumpeldor St. Very rowdy crowd rolls to rap and reggae early into the morning. Occasional dance contests. Cover: women NIS30, men NIS40. Open F-Sa.

DON'T ASK, DON'T TEL AVIV Today, Tel Aviv is home to Israel's most thriving gay community. From the soaring attendance at the annual gay pride day party (now held in Ha-Yarkon Park) to the large number of gay clubs, pubs, and establishments with "gay nights," the community is present, active, and powerful. The best ways to find out what's going on are by catching leaflets on Sheinkin St. and reading *Ha-Zman Ha-Varod*.

BARS

After an exhausting day of suntanning at the beach, many travelers just want an evening of good company and icy Carlsbergs. And why bother with pricey club covers when you can join the rest of the crowd dancing in the aisles and on the tables? Rowdy but generic bars abound around hostel-heavy **Ha-Yarkon St.** and **Allenby Rd.** Israelis—often charged cover when tourists are not because of their tendency toward smaller bar bills—head inland to bars with a little more character. Several great options are hidden away on the Ibn Gvirol sidestreets and in Florentin. As with clubs, the general closing time is "when the last customer leaves," which can be as early as midnight or 1am on weekdays, but as late as 6am on weekends.

1942, 27 Rosh Pina St. (☎688 96 92 or 052 448 516), a few blocks from the central bus station. For all your nightlife needs, this gorgeous place has a mod checkerboard dance floor, a pub with the city's cheapest (and best decorated) cocktails (NIS20-28), and an Arabian-style loft for *nargilah* (NIS20). Cover: NIS40 includes one drink; NIS60 for all you can eat and drink. Prove it's your birthday and everything is free. Open daily at 9pm, but only a dance bar Th-Sa. Also hosts an after-party at 6:30am on Sa.

Shweball at Rival 27, 27 Rival St. (☎687 43 64), off Ha-Massger St. Look for the graffiti mural reading "Rival 27." Relive your childhood, this time with alcohol. Join the friendly, young Israeli crowd for beer (NIS14-20), cocktails (NIS28, 35 for flaming versions), and games like pick-up sticks, Connect Four, and *taki*, the Israeli version of Uno. Open M-Th and Sa at 9pm, F at 10pm. Fills up at about 11pm.

End of the Night, 16 Ibn Gvirol St. (☎695 00 91), just above Dizengoff. Look for a big orange sign that reads 'Mongol'. Twentysomething locals pile on top of each other to jam to the well-chosen hip-hop and funk. 21+. Open Th-Sa at 11:30pm.

Florentine 5, at that address (☎682 66 34), just off Herzl St. If the candlelight, Israeli classics, and sophisticated crowd don't mellow you out, the *nargilah* (NIS15) just might do the trick. Open daily at 9pm.

He-She, 8 Ha-Shomeret St. (☎510 09 14), off Shefer St. Tel Aviv's most popular gay bar, thanks to a devoted crowd of locals and tourists. Beer NIS20. Open M-Sa at 8pm.

The Out, 45 Naḥalat Binyamin (☎560 2391), a few blocks after the pedestrian mall, on the corner of Montefiore. Two-floor cozy gay bar with red lights and wood floors that lend a mellow ambiance, especially on romantic-themed Tuesdays. Israeli rock on Mondays, but the house goes house on weekends. Beer NIS12-18, happy hour prices until 11pm. Open Sa-W at 9, Th-F at 10.

Joey's Bar, 42 Allenby St. (☎517 92 77). Shake the bartender's hand when you enter and pound the beers until you're numb enough to get a tattoo next door. *Let's Go* does not recommend getting tattoos while intoxicated. Beer NIS14. 25+, 18 for tourists. Open daily noon-8am.

M.A.S.H. (More Alcohol Served Here), 275 Dizengoff St. (☎605 10 07), at the intersection with Ben-Yehuda. Near the port; take bus #4. The testosterone runs high and the Brit accents are thick. The legendary burgers and the big-screen TV make for particularly wild sports nights. Beer NIS14-23, pitchers NIS30-64. Open daily 11am-5am.

Lola, 54 Allenby St. (☎516 78 03), the blue building next to the Scene. Music and passion are always in fashion at this bar. Israeli students prefer this welcome haven of dusky blue on the Allenby strip of neon. Beer NIS20-35. 20+. Open daily at 9pm.

The Buzz Stop, 86 Herbert Samuel (☎510 08 69), across from the *tayelet*. A boisterous crowd of tourists on a mission: inebriation. Beer NIS12-16. Live band Sa at 9pm. Open 24hr. Kitchen serves its cheap, greasy fare 9am-3am.

DAYTRIPS FROM TEL AVIV

REḤOVOT רחובות ☎08

The Weizmann Institute is a 30min. walk back along Herzl St. from the central bus station. The bus from Tel Aviv (45min.) makes a stop directly across the street from the Institute, so watch for its large gates on the left and get off early to avoid backtracking. Return buses and sherut to Tel Aviv stop at the bus stop to the right when exiting the Institute.

Reḥovot, renowned as a center of technological and agricultural research, is home to three research institutions: the prestigious Weizmann Institute of Science, the research facilities of the Faculty of Agriculture of Hebrew University, and the Development Study Center, specializing in rural development. Due to the large number of recent immigrants from the former Soviet Union, Yemen, and Ethiopia, the crowded city is an interesting cultural and socioeconomic mixture; the streets are filled with falafel vendors and wealthy scientists.

The world-famous **Weizmann Institute of Science** is named for Israel's first president, Dr. Ḥaim Weizmann, the chemist who discovered an innovative way to produce acetone. This smelly fluid proved essential to England's World War I military effort, as well as to manicurists everywhere as nail polish remover. Weizmann's discovery gave him the political clout necessary to persuade Lord Balfour to issue the 1917 Balfour Declaration, a statement of British support favoring the establishment of a Jewish national homeland. In 1934, Weizmann founded a chemistry research center in Reḥovot to carry out his mandate that Jews in Palestine stay on the cutting-edge of scientific research and development. Over the years this research facility has expanded to encompass all major fields of science and it is responsible for Israel's first computer and particle accelerator.

Tourists can visit the **Weizmann House** where Weizmann lived while President of Israel. Walk to the back of the house to see Weizmann's grave. A nearby building holds the Weizmann Archives, a collection of the scientist-statesman's papers. At the northern end of the campus, next to the solar tower, is the **Garden of Science,** which houses a collection of interactive science exhibits. Tickets, maps, and an introductory film are at the **Visitors Center.** (☎934 45 00. Film. Self-guided tour and visit to Weizmann House NIS25, students NIS15. Open Su-Th 9am-4pm. Combined ticket to also see Garden of Science NIS40. Call in advance to schedule tour of Weizmann House and view the film in English. NIS25, students NIS15. Garden of Science open Su-Th 10am-5pm.)

Located about a mile from the Weizmann Institute is the **Ayalon Institute,** a kibbutz where 1930s and 40s Jewish freedom fighters in Palestine secretly manufactured over two million bullets between 1945 and 1948. Call to schedule an English tour of the underground factory and a screening of a historical video. (☎930 05 85. Open Su-Th 8:30am-4pm, F 8:30am-1pm, Sa 9am-4pm. NIS15, children NIS11, students NIS10. From the Weizmann Institute gate turn right and walk about 20 minutes to Ha-Damah St. or take a bus toward Tel Aviv and ask the driver to stop at Kiryat Hadamah. Walk down Hadamah (there will be a sign for the Ayalon Institute), and turn left on Ḥaim Holtzman; the museum is up the hill to the right.)

The cheapest falafel stands (NIS6) are on Herzl St. south of the turnoff to the main bus station. Another alternative is to stop by the lively *shuk* on Levkovitz St. between the bus station and Herzl St.

ASHDOD אשדוד ☎08

Express bus #320 goes directly to Ashdod from Tel Aviv (45min., every 20min., NIS13.80). From the bus station walk one block toward the beach and enter the building with flags in front to get a free map of Ashdod from the information booth on the left.

Eight kilometers of sandy beach and wide, palm-tree-lined boulevards give Ashdod the feel of a Florida beach resort. The Philistines made Ashdod the capital of their great trade empire 2000 years ago. Today, Ashdod's port retains its role as an important commercial center, but the city is also in the midst of a building boom in hopes of attracting more tourists. Ashdod's central bus station adjoins the glistening **Merkaz Ha-Ir** mall, where Domino's and McDonald's compete for the attention of the largely Russian-speaking population. Ashdod is spread far out and up, with clusters of white high-rise apartment buildings interspersed with palm trees. A stroll down Shavei Tzion St. leads to a beach complete with boardwalk and marina. All day Wednesday, there is a market on the beach; otherwise it is remarkably clean and deserted on weekdays. To get to the main drag of pricey shops, cafes, and restaurants on Rogozin St., take bus #8 (NIS4) from the bus station.

Ashdod's history lives on at the small but well-kept **Corine Maman Ashdod Museum,** 16 Ha-Shayatim St. With its multimedia exhibit on the world of Philistines. Get off the Tel Aviv bus or local bus #8 at the old central bus station (a few stops before the new one). In apparent deference to past philistinism, the current residents have erected large signs at major intersections that point the wrong way; ignore these. Take a right on Keren Ha-Yesod, another right on Ha-Shayatim St., and then follow the signs from there. *(☎854 30 92. NIS16, students NIS10. Open Su-Th 9am-4pm, Sa 10:30am-1:30pm. Call ahead to see the video in English.)*

At this time there is only one hotel in Ashdod, though plans for more are in the works. The **Hotel Orly,** 22 Nordau St., (☎856 53 80; fax 856 53 82.) Two blocks from Miami Beach and accessible from bus #8; it is a bit pricey but its rooms are very comfortable with air-conditioning, cable TV, and refrigerator; many have a view of the ocean. (Singles US$65; doubles US$80; suites US$100. Breakfast included.)

Miami Beach and Lido Beach are where the hippest crowds gather on Friday and Saturday nights. The **Thai-Town Beach Bar Restaurant** by the prominent white tower is open 24 hours, 7 days a week, and on weekend nights you can hang out at the bar at the top of the tower. (Beer NIS15.)

JAFFA (YAFO) יפו يافا

According to the Bible, the recalcitrant prophet Jonah shirked his divine calling and fled to Jaffa to catch that fated boat to Tarshish (Jonah 1:3). Jaffa makes an appearance in the New Testament as well; it was here that Peter had a vision telling him that the Gospel extended outside the confines of Judaism and that the dietary laws no longer applied. The standard repertoire of conquerors stomped through Jaffa. In 1468 BCE, the Egyptians captured Jaffa by hiding soldiers in human-sized clay jars brought into the city market. King David conquered the city around 1000 BCE, and under Solomon it became the main port of Judea until King Herod's Caesarea usurped that title. In the 12th century CE, the First Crusaders, Salah al-Din, Richard the Lionheart, the Muslims, and Louis IX all had a go at the city. Finally, in 1267 the Mamluks overpowered the city, and, apart from a brief stay by Napoleon around 1800, Jaffa remained an Arab stronghold.

The first Jewish settlers, who were mostly merchants and artisans from North Africa, arrived in 1820 and built the "Jewish House," a temporary hostel. The increased settlement of the area encountered protest, and in 1929, 1936, and 1939, Jaffa was the scene of anti-Zionist riots. When Jewish fighters captured the Arab section of Jaffa in 1948, most of Jaffa's Arab population fled the city. Jaffa was officially incorporated into the Tel Aviv municipality in 1950.

After the 1948 War, Jaffa was left in ruins, and the areas around it filled with prostitution, drugs, and crime. In the late 1960s, the Tel Aviv Municipality decided to turn Jaffa into an artists' colony to clean it up. Under the auspices of the Old Jaffa Development Company, whose name is still on many signs today, each artist bought a section of the ruins, eventually transforming them into today's galleries. An Israeli folk song describes Jaffa as possessing a "mysterious and unknown" element that allows its atmosphere "to seep like wine into the blood." Indeed, Jaffa's stone houses, cobblestone alleys, and charming galleries do intoxicate.

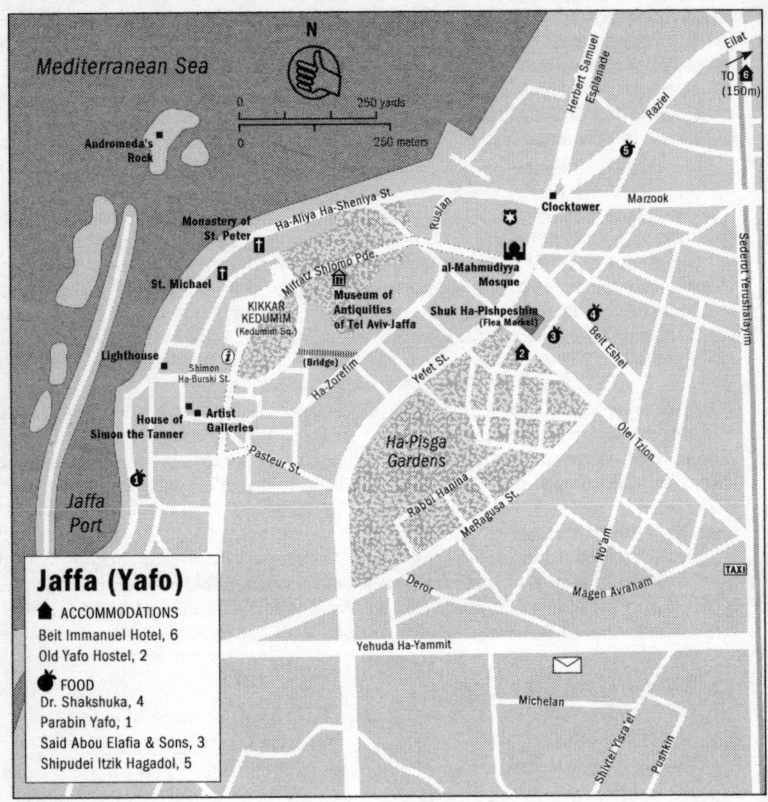

ORIENTATION

The **Jaffa Clocktower,** completed in 1906, stands by the entrance to Jaffa from Tel Aviv and is a useful landmark. A free 2-hour **tour** of Old Jaffa by the Tourism Association begins here Wednesday at 9:30am, though many people line up at 9am. Bus #46 from the New Central Bus Station lets off in front of the clocktower, and bus #10 from Ben-Yehuda St. or Allenby St., near the Opera Tower, stops just a couple minutes before it. A couple blocks past the clocktower, head right and the road becomes the **Mifratz Shlomo Promenade,** which leads to the **Old City** and provides stunning views of Tel Aviv's action-packed coast and skyline. Alternatively, a left turn onto **Beit Eshel St.** will you bring you to the *shuk.*

ACCOMMODATIONS

If all the beds in Tel Aviv are full, or if you just want something that feels a little less like a college dorm, the two hostels in Jaffa provide fabulous alternatives.

Old Yafo Hostel, 8 Olei Tzion St. (☎682 23 70; fax 682 23 16; email ojhostel@shani.net). Walk one block past the clocktower on Yefet St. and turn left onto Olei Tzion St. It's rare that a hostel feels enchantingly antique without an accompanying layer of grime, but the Old Yafo manages superbly. Fully stocked bookshelves and a large rooftop garden make for delightful finishing touches. Kitchen available. Storage for non-guests NIS1. Laundry NIS10. Internet NIS10 for 15min. Reception 8am-11pm. Check-out noon. No curfew, but lights off at 11pm. Payment in any major foreign currency avoids 17% VAT. 6-bed dorms (coed or female-only) NIS40/US$8.50. Singles NIS147/US$30; with TV, bath, A/C, and kitchen NIS226/US$46. Doubles NIS168/US$34; with TV, bath, A/C, and kitchen NIS246/US$50. Curfew 11pm.

Beit Immanuel Hostel, 8 Auerbach St. (☎682 14 59; fax 682 98 17; email beitimm@netvision.net.il; www.inisrael.com/beitimmanuel). From the clocktower, head toward Tel Aviv on Raziel St. for 5min. until it turns into Eilat St. Turn right after 12 Eilat St. onto Auerbach St. On bus #46, get off on Eilat St. near the gas stations. This family-oriented Christian hospice has a garden and playground. Breakfast included. Dinner NIS40. Shabbat NIS60. Laundry NIS10. Reception 7am-11pm. Check-in 3pm. Check-out 1pm. Lockout 10am-noon. Curfew 11pm. All rooms have A/C. Dorms NIS48/US$12; singles with bath NIS180/US$45; doubles with bath NIS280/US$70.

FOOD

The maze of narrow streets surrounding the Jaffa Clocktower is peppered with cheap falafel stands (NIS7-10), *al-ha'esh* (barbecue) meat establishments, and sweets vendors, some of which are open 24-hours. The cafes and restaurants in the Old City tend to be generic, but the surrounding gardens and views of the Mediterranean make them some of the loveliest tourist traps imaginable. For a touch of romance and a big hit to the wallet, head to Jaffa Port, off Pasteur St. on the far side of the artists' colony, where picturesque waterfront restaurants offer seafood so fresh the gills are almost moving (daily catch entrees NIS42 and up). Jaffa is also one of the best places to get a great meal on Shabbat.

Said Abou Elafia and Sons, 7 Yefet St. (☎681 23 40), one block behind the Jaffa clocktower. Popularly known as "Aboulafia," this bakery is so famous that its name is used by Israelis to denote all stuffed-pita foods. Try the zatar-spiced toasts, flaky Iraqi pita with cheese, or honey-drenched baklava, all for NIS3-8. Take-out only. Open 24hr. Cash only.

Parabin Yafo, 20 Ogan St. (☎518 09 62), in the port, about 400m past the fancy fish restaurants. Feel like a sheikh, or at least incredibly chic, while lounging on pillows and puffing *nargilah* (NIS17) in this cavernous, lantern-lit hideaway. A late-night staple among the locals, there's a line from 10pm on of large groups jonesing for their huge salads (NIS25-27), creamy hummus plates (NIS12-18), and an orgasmic chocolate cake (NIS24). Open Sa-Th 8:15pm-3am, F 10:45pm-6am. Credit cards accepted.

Shipudei Itzik Hagadol/Big Itzik's Skewers, 3 Raziel St. (☎518 18 02), a couple blocks before the clocktower. Sign in Hebrew only; look for green neon. Hungry locals meet, greet, and eat skewered meat at this clean, friendly establishment. Herbivores and carnivores can achieve peaceful coexistence over a sampler platter of 18 salads (NIS14 per person), sizzling kebabs (NIS15 each), and huge, warm pita. Open Sa-Th 11am-1am.

Dr. Shakshuka, 3 Beit Eshel (☎682 28 42), corner of Yefet St. Libyan food in the heart of Old Jaffa. Eponymous dish is the *shakshuka*—a mouth watering tomato and egg concoction (NIS18). Open Su-Th 9am-1am, F 9am-sundown, Sa sundown-midnight.

Ilana Goor Museum Cafe, 4 Mazal Dagim St. (☎683 76 76). Situated in the heart of the artists' colony, this rooftop cafe overlooking the port is the trendiest place to grab a bite in the Old City. Take in the artsy ambiance that makes the NIS10 cup of coffee seem worth it. Don't miss the great museum downstairs (see **Ilana Goor Museum,** below). Open Su-Th, Sa 10am-6pm; F 10am-4pm.

SIGHTS

CLOCKTOWER AND ENVIRONS. Built in 1906 to celebrate the 25th anniversary of Sultan Abdul Hamid II's ascension to power, the clocktower marks the entrance to Jaffa from Tel Aviv. Originally, the clocktower's four faces were split between Israeli and European time for the convenience of European sailors. On the right of the clocktower is the **al-Mahmudiyya Mosque,** an enormous structure erected in 1812 that only Muslims may enter. Head to the right and up the hill along the Mifratz Shlomo Promenade to the **Museum of Antiquities of Tel Aviv-Jaffa,** which contains artifacts from Neolithic to Roman times and a collection of coins found in the area. *(☎682 53 75. Open Su-Th 9am-1pm. NIS10, students and seniors NIS5.)*

KIKKAR KEDUMIM. The old city's tourist center is Kikkar Kedumim. Following signs to the Visitors Center, head down to the underground plaza to the excavations from 2300-year-old Tel Yafo, get a short history lesson, and pick up free maps. *(Continue along Mifratz Shlomo past the Napoleonic Cannons, pass the* ***Church of St. Peter*** *and go up a large staircase. Open Su-Th 9am-10pm, F 9am-2pm, Sa 10am-10pm. Free. Church open daily 8-11:45am and 3-5pm; public masses in English Sa 8pm and Su 9am.)*

To the right of the Kikkar, just before the cafes and shops, a small alleyway leads to the colorful **Greek Orthodox Church of St. Michael,** worth a brief tour. *(Open daily 8-11:45am and 3-5pm.)*

HA-PIGSA GARDENS. The wooden footbridge from Kikkar Kedumim leading to the gardens is used by both Arab and Jewish couples to take wedding pictures (Tu and Th evenings are especially busy). The gardens contain a small, modern amphitheater for summer concerts, an excavation of an 18th-century BCE Hyksos town and a later Egyptian city, as well as look-out point. The point offers Jaffa's best view of the coast, Tel Aviv, and **Andromeda's Rock.**

GALLERIES. Past the tourist center, a large ramp leads to the museums, restaurants, and galleries that make up Jaffa's artists' colony. You can also get there by winding through the gardens, away from the sea. The 20th century hits Old Jaffa in the playful form of the **Ilana Goor Museum,** which houses both Goor's artwork and her personal collection. Fun and funky jewelry, sculptures, and furniture (including a psychedelic painted piano) are spread throughout the artist's home; the bookshelf in Goor's sitting room is also worth a browse. *(4 Mazal Dagim St. ☎683 76 76. Open Su-Th and Sa 10am-8pm, F 10am-4pm. NIS24, students and seniors NIS20.)*

A little further down the same road, **Studio Hundleman,** sells silk-screen originals depicting scenes of Israel and Ḥasidic Jewish life. The friendly owners are happy to answer questions and explain their techniques. Miniatures are affordable at US$10-30. *(14 Mazal Dagim St. ☎683 45 93. Open Su-Th 10:30am-10:30pm, F 10:30am-sundown, Sa sundown-10:30pm. Ring the bell.)*

Another spot worth a browse is the **Frank Meisler Gallery,** home of kitschy, interactive, extremely expensive sculptures made of gold, silver, bronze, and pewter. Check out the human figurines whose stomachs open up to expose what "they're really made of"—usually sexy women and lascivious goodies. *(25 Mazal Arie St. ☎681 35 02. Open Su-Th 9am-11pm, F 9am-4pm, Sa 6pm-11pm.)*

JAFFA PORT. The port, past the bottom of the artists' colony to the right along Pasteur St. was the perfect depth for King Solomon when he imported rafts of cedars from Lebanon to build his temple. It was too shallow, however, for larger ships. The infamous port caused Dutch sailors to term the impossible as "entering Jaffa." Today, the port is more accessible and is an active fisherman's wharf.

SHUK HA-PISHPESHIM. Back in town, Jaffa's large Shuk Ha-Pishpeshim (Flea Market) is one of the livelier markets in Israel, with roofed rows of overflowing stalls offering dust-covered Middle Eastern knick-knacks, hand-dyed clothing,

Persian carpets, leather goods, and brassware. A vast selection of enormous *nargilah* (waterpipes) is also available. The *shuk* is squeezed between Olei Tzion and Beit Eshel St. It's busiest on Fridays when special permits are not required and is closed on Saturdays. For tips on bargaining, see **The Fine Art of Haggling,** p. 120. *(To reach the flea market, go one block past the clocktower along Yefet St., and turn left.)*

TAYELET. Heading in the opposite direction from the clocktower brings you to the southern end of the *tayelet* which, since it was extended to Jaffa in 1999, has made the beach there more accessible but also more crowded.

NEAR TEL AVIV

HERZLIYA הרצליה ☎03

Named after Theodore Herzl by the seven Zionist pioneers who settled the area (see **Zionism,** p. 11), Herzliya is more colloquially known as "the Bank of Israel" because of the affluent tourists and Israeli vacationers who flock to its beautiful shores. In the never-ending battle for the "best beach in Israel" title, Herzliya is a prime contender. Only 15km outside of Tel Aviv, Herzliya makes a great daytrip from the city; it's a good thing too, because there are no budget accommodations.

ORIENTATION AND PRACTICAL INFORMATION. Herzliya's **bus station** is at the corner of **Ben-Gurion St.** and **Ha-Atzma'ut Rd.** Buses #501 (35min., every 20min. 5:30am-11:30pm, NIS7) and 502 (30min., every 15min. 9am-7pm, NIS7) run between Herzliya and Tel Aviv. They stop running at around 5:30pm on Friday and start again at 8:20pm on Saturday. The town's cultural hub, the **Yad Labanim Memorial Center,** is at the corner of Ben-Gurion St. and **Ha-Banim St.;** from the bus station, head two blocks left along Ben-Gurion St. The main shopping area in Herzliya can be found by turning right from the central bus station, and making a left onto **Sokolov St.** after a few blocks. City bus #29 goes to the beaches in Herzliya's suburb, Herzliya Pituah. (10-30min. depending on traffic, NIS5).

FOOD. It's a good idea to eat in town before hitting the beach. There are refreshment stands right off the ocean, but they have high prices and little variety. Ben-Gurion has a number of cheap eats, including the falafel stand at 10 Ben-Gurion St., diagonally across from the central bus station. Tuvya, an Egyptian expat who charms his patrons in English, French, Arabic, and Hebrew, serves deliciously fresh falafel (NIS7) and a variety of salads. There is also a **supermarket** in the shopping center on the left side of Ben-Gurion St., one block before Sokolov St. (Open Su-Th 9am-7pm, F 9am-1pm.)

BEACHES. The beaches in Herzliya Pituah range from the large, soft-sanded variety to the small and rocky type. The **Dabesh Beach** and **Arcadia Beach,** near the marina at the end of the bus line, belong to the former category and accordingly, charge admission (NIS12, children NIS8). While the size and sand of the **Sidna Ali** beach pales in comparison, admission is free, and it is the only beach without wall-to-wall umbrella lounge-chairs. People walking the 1km from Sidna Ali to the pay-beaches (to your left as you face the sea) or those claiming to stay at one of the hotels (for example, Hotel Arcadia or Hotel Ha-Sharon) are often not required to pay. From the bus stop in Sidna Ali, the beach is up the hill and through the gate.

The Sidna Ali beach has other reasons to visit as well. The **Sidna Ali Mosque** allows modestly dressed visitors to visit when it is not prayer time. Women must cover their heads and shorts are forbidden. After the Mamluks destroyed the area during the Third Crusade, the mosque was named after one of Salah al-Din's soldiers who died in a battle on the hill on which the mosque stands.

HERMIT'S HOUSE. Herzliya's most worthwhile attraction is an inhabited sand castle known as the Hermit's House. This fantastical residence built into the side of a cliff by "hermit" **Nissim Kakhalon** is a must-see for anyone to whom "arts and crafts" is not incompatible with Surrealism. Kakhalon claims, "I make it from my love. I make it good." In other words, he spent 29 years turning other people's garbage (tires, toys, tiles, etc.) into this hallucinogenic maze of winding tunnels, flower-strewn antechambers, and plush gardens. Even more impressive, everything in the artful interior is absolutely functional, from the bathroom ceiling made entirely of Maccabee Beer bottles to the loveseat with a mirrored mosaic on one side and a huge sculpted stone face on the other. Nothing goes to waste here: Kakhalon even uses the manure from his family of goats to grow fragrant basil. Kakhalon's tours depend on the extent to which his guests are appreciative. This hermit is quite friendly, after all, and more showman than recluse. During the week, Kakhalon runs a cafe serving hummus (NIS15) and smoked fish (NIS50). (9am-sundown; hours erratic; closed for Shabbat.)

BEIT RISHONIM. Zionist history buffs may enjoy the Beit Rishonim (Founders' Museum), 8-10 Ha-Nadiv St.(☎950 42 70). From Sokolov St. turn right on Ha-Nadiv St. and continue two blocks. The museum narrates the history of Herzliya, beginning with its days as a colony in 1924, using computerized presentations as well as items from the early settlement period. (Open M 8:30am-12:30pm and 4-6:30pm, Tu-Th 8:30am-12:30pm. NIS8, students and children NIS4, seniors free.)

OTHER SITES. The **Yad Labanim Memorial Center** houses the diminutive and avant-garde **Herzliya Museum of Art** (☎09 955 10 11 or 950 23 01; www.adgo.co.il/herzliya_museum). The contemporary exhibits are well worth the short trip from the bus station. (Open Su, Tu, and Th 4-8pm; M, W, F, and Sa 10am-2pm. Free.) An outdoor amphitheater is attached to the building and overlooks the museum's modern **Sculpture Garden.** It is the setting of concerts by the **Herzliya Chamber Orchestra** (☎09 950 0761) once every couple of months, as well as an annual theatrical festival in May.

RISHON LE ZION ראשון לציון ☎03

Rishon Le Zion ("First to Zion"), founded in 1882 by 17 Russian immigrant families with the financial help of Baron de Rothschild, was the first modern Jewish settlement in Palestine. Since its founding, Rishon has been the site of several important firsts for Israel. In Rishon, the Jewish National Fund was created, the Israeli flag was first flown, and the world's first national Hebrew school opened its doors. Once a covert hotbed of Zionist resistance, Rishon has become another sprawling suburb in the ever-expanding Tel Aviv.

GETTING THERE AND AROUND. Buses #201, 174, and 301 from Tel Aviv stop at Rishon's old bus station in the historical district (30min., every 20min., NIS7.20) on their way to the new bus station in a mall on the other side of town. Buses back to Tel Aviv can be caught on the main highway—keep walking on Barshovsky St. past Nafis until you reach the highway and bus stop. The last bus back to Tel Aviv leaves around 11:30pm. Rishon today is divided by Highway 4 into east and west sections. Most of the sights of interest to tourists lie in the eastern section of town along Herzl St. To reach the base of the *midraḥov*—an uphill pedestrian walkway leading to many of the town's sights—continue to the right past the bus stop on Herzl St. for two blocks and make a left toward the fountain.

FOOD AND ENTERTAINMENT. The *midraḥov* in the historic district is lined with falafel stands. In the **old industrial section** of Rishon, outside the town's historic area, hip restaurants and clubs attract an eclectic clientele. To get to the old industrial section, take bus #85 from the bus station or catch a pink, orange, and white *sherut* #85 at the stand on Herzl St. across from the bus station and ask to be let off at Barshovsky St. or Nafis (NIS4.50). Both will stop at an intersection; from there, walk down Barshovsky St. where the establishments' signs are visible.

The place for twenty-somethings to be seen on Friday and Saturday nights is the Yemenite restaurant **Nafis,** 12 Moshe Beker St., which serves everything from hummus plates (NIS10) to hamburger meals (NIS38), and specializes in Yemenite pastries. (☎966 76 77 open 24hr. English menu available.) Down the block from Nafis is **Formagio,** 2 Barshevsky St., a popular vegetarian Italian restaurant. Order the lunch special (NIS36) from 9am-6pm, for a heaping portion of pasta, salad, a pitcher of fresh juice, and coffee. (Open daily 9am-2:30am.) For a more lively evening head to **Peach Time,** 13 Moshe Beker St., where waiters serve hamburgers (NIS45) sing Hebrew and American pop songs, and the clientele is apt to get up on their chairs to dance along. (☎967 53 62. Open daily 9pm-4am.)

SIGHTS. A yellow line painted along Rishon's pavement marks **Pioneer's Way,** which leads to 18 of the town's historic sites, each marked with a descriptive plaque in both Hebrew and English. The path starts and ends at the museum's gate. A guide is available at the museum (NIS5). Most of Rishon's sights lie along the *midrahov.* The **Village Well** and other sights are along the first section, and the museum is a bit further up on the right, beyond where the *midrahov* changes into a regular street with traffic and a sidewalk.

RISHON LE ZION MUSEUM. Traces the history of the town from its pioneer days to the present. A tour of the museum includes a look at the first iron plow in Israel and a replica of the first Hebrew school room. Following the museum tour is a 10-minute sound and light show in the old **Village Well,** detailing the town's initial struggle to find a water source of its own. *(2-4 Ahad Ha-am St. On the right just above the midrahov and across from the Great Synagogue. ☎964 16 21 or 968 24 35. Open Su, Tu-Th 9am-2pm; M 9am-1pm and 4-7pm. Admission to museum and well NIS13, students NIS10. Free tours and admission 10am-2pm on the 1st Saturday of every month. For all tours, call ahead to request an English-speaking guide.)*

WINERY. The **Rishon Le Zion Winery,** was built by Baron Edmond de Rothschild in 1887 and used as a secret firing range by Zionist resistance fighters in the early 20th century. It currently produces Carmel Mizraḥi wine. One-hour tours of the winery feature an audio-visual presentation, an explanation of a remarkable life-size mural by German painter Gershom Schwarze, a tasting, and a souvenir bottle. *(25 Ha-Carmel St., on the left side. ☎965 36 62. Tours Su-Th 9 and 11am, 1, and 3pm. NIS13, students NIS11. To book a tour with an English-speaking guide and guarantee a taste of the wine, call in advance Su-Th 8am-4pm.)*

Across the street from the winery, **Rishon Wine** sells Carmel brand wine (NIS12.80-NIS80 per bottle) and liquor (vodka NIS15) at slightly discounted prices, and occasionally offers free tastings in the afternoon. *(98 Herzl St. ☎969 93 51. Open Su, Tu-Th 9am-1pm and 4:30pm-7:30pm; M 9am-1pm; F 9am-3:30pm.)*

Across the street from the museum is **Rishon's Great Synagogue.** Built in 1885, it fronted as a warehouse under Ottoman rule. It is possible to arrange a tour of the synagogue by calling the Rishon Le Zion Museum ahead of time. Other sights include the oldest Hebrew school still in use and a military base from the beginning of the century.

RAMLA רמלה ☎08

Founded in 716 by the formidable Umayyad Caliph Suleiman ibn Abd al-Malik, Ramla is the only town in Israel established and developed by Arabs. Until the arrival of the Crusaders in the 11th century, Ramla was the capital of Palestine and was known for its magnificent palaces and mosques. After the 1948 War, the Arab majority was forced to flee. Today the community is predominantly composed of Jewish immigrants and a Christian Arab minority. The diversity of Ramla's history and present population, as well as its vibrant *shuk* (town market), make the town worth a visit.

PRACTICAL INFORMATION

From **Tel Aviv,** take bus #245, 455, 450, or 451 (30min., every 20min., NIS9.50). From **Jerusalem,** take bus #401, 403, 411 (45min., every 30min., NIS14.90). Services include: **Police,** 80 Herzl St; **post office,** 4 Danny Mass St. (☎922 81 00); and **Bank Leumi,** 8 Herzl St. (☎927 70 77. Open Su, Tu, W 8:30am-1pm; M, Th 8:30am-1pm, 4:30-6pm. F 8:30am-noon. Changes money with commission.) The **shuk,** on Ze'ev Zabutinsky, is open every day until dark and is especially lively on Thursdays. The street is closed to traffic until the shops close at around 7pm.

FOOD

There are several affordable and tasty restaurant options in Ramla, involving mostly chickpeas and pita. One of the more popular falafel joints is **Baget Hazav Gershel,** 87 Herzl St., one block to the right from the bus station; look for the blue awning and NIS10 falafel. (Open Su-Th 7am-midnight, F 7am-5pm, Sa 8:30pm-midnight.) **Khalil Restaurant,** 6 Kehlat Detroit St., off of Herzl St. (look for a yellow sign with a dolphin), is a popular and more spacious place to enjoy a wide range of Middle Eastern specialties. The menu is in Hebrew, but ask for a hummus (NIS11) or meat plate (NIS20-40) and you'll receive a full meal. (Open daily 7am-7pm.) **Kshatot,** 10 Kehlat Detroit, a Chinese restaurant located on the grounds of an old church. Drink coffee in the outdoor courtyard or eat kosher Chinese food in a vaulted dining room for around NIS30 per dish. (Open Su-Th 10am-8pm.) A great alternative is to stop at the *shuk*, through a short alley and on a street to the left just before the park. The *shuk* offers a range of fresh fruits, veggies, sweets, and an assortment of random plastic gadgets, as well as plenty of falafel (NIS10).

SIGHTS

Ramla's sights are primarily religious and historical, and while they're not maintained tourist sights, their authenticity compensates for the disarray. Most of the mosques and churches that comprise Ramla's multi-religion pilgrimage are located in the center of the town, all within easy walking distance.

GREAT MOSQUE. The Crusader Cathedral of St. John became the Great Mosque when Ramla's Muslims recaptured the town from the Crusaders. Although the mosque consequently retains little of Muslim architecture, the well-preserved minaret is breathtaking, and the medieval vaulted arches are impressive. *(From the bus station walk right on Herzl St., turn left at the first intersection, and continue through the parking lot toward the towering minaret. The entrance is through a small green door on the side facing the parking lot. Open Su-Th 8am-4pm.)*

CHURCH OF ST. NICODEMUS AND ST. JOSEPH ARIMATHEA. Ramla is supposed to be the biblical Arimathea, where one of Jesus' earliest disciples, Joseph, is said to have lived. Together with St. Nicodemus, St. Joseph Arimathea made the preparations for Jesus' burial. The large stone Catholic complex was built in his honor in 1296, with money donated by European Catholics. Renovated in 1902, it now serves as a school as well. The monks at the 18th-century monastery next door claim that Napoleon Bonaparte stayed in the upstairs chambers during his unsuccessful campaign against the Turks. *(The complex is past the mosque at the corner of the main Herzl St. and Bialik St. The main gate into the church is on Bialik St.)*

TOWER OF FORTY MARTYRS. To reach the Tower, follow Herzl to Danny Mass St. Take a left on Danny Mass St., and the rectangular tower will be visible. Known as the **White Tower,** this minaret was a 14th-century addition to an 8th-century mosque, which is said to be the burial site of Muhammad's companions. A few stone arches and this tower are all that remain of the mosque. Napoleon is purported to have coordinated his attack on Jaffa from the top of the tower. Climb the steps to the top of the tower for a birds-eye view of Ramla and the surrounding area. The noises inside are not the screams of the martyrs but the sounds of the many birds who now use the tower as a nesting spot. Next to the mosque is a Muslim cemetery in a state of disrepair. *(Open Su-Th 8am-3pm, F 8am-1pm, Sa 8am-4pm.)*

DIANE AND ARTHUR BELFER LIBRARY. The sparkling glass and stone library is a remarkable, modern contrast to Ramla's other sites. The library opened in 1992 and signifies cooperative efforts between the New York Jewish community and Ramla's residents to improve the quality of life in Ramla. The books (including an English section) are upstairs and free for in-library use by all visitors. The free public bathrooms are the cleanest in town; there are also storage lockers upstairs for NIS1. *(Past Bialik St., at the corner of Herzl St. and Weizmann St. ☎922 12 87. Open Su-Th 10am-7pm, F 9am-noon. NIS5 adults, students and children NIS4.)*

SOUTH OF TEL AVIV

ASHKELON אשקלון ☎07

Ashkelon was first settled in the 3rd millennium BCE. Strategically located on Mediterranean naval and land transport routes, it was a spoil of war for nearly every empire of the ancient era, including the Philistines, Assyrians, Phoenicians, Greeks, Romans, Muslims, and Crusaders. First rising to prominence as one of the Philistines' five great cities, Ashkelon reached its zenith as an independent city-state during the Roman period.

Today, Ashkelon's main attractions are its sandy beaches, seaside national park, and well-known archaeological sites. With intensive development of the seaside resort area, upbeat marketing efforts, and ongoing construction of a municipal marina, Ashkelon is none-too-subtly aiming to recover its past greatness, this time as an upscale resort community.

GETTING THERE AND GETTING AROUND

Buses: Central Bus Station (☎677 82 22) on Ben-Gurion Blvd., about a 30min. walk from the beach. Information booth and bulletin board in Hebrew and English. To: **Be'er Sheva** (#363 and 364, 1½hr., every 45min.-1hr. 5:45am-8:05pm, NIS23.50); **Jerusalem** (#437, 1½hr., every 45min.-1hr. 5:50am-7:15pm, NIS22.50); **Tel Aviv** (#300, 301, and 311; 1¼hr.; every 15-30min. 5:20am-9pm; NIS18.20-21.50).

Local Transportation: Local bus #5 goes to Zephania Sq. in the heart of the Afridar neighborhood and to the *midrahov* in the Migdal area, stopping in between at the central bus station. Catch it on the Ben-Gurion (front) side of the station for Migdal, or on the right side of the station for Afridar (every 12-20min., NIS4). Bus #6 (also bus #13 July-Aug.) goes to the National Park and shoreline (NIS4).

Taxis: Moniot Ha-Merkaz (☎673 30 77), across Ben-Gurion Blvd. from the central bus station. *Sherut* to **Tel Aviv** (NIS16) and **Be'er Sheva** (NIS20).

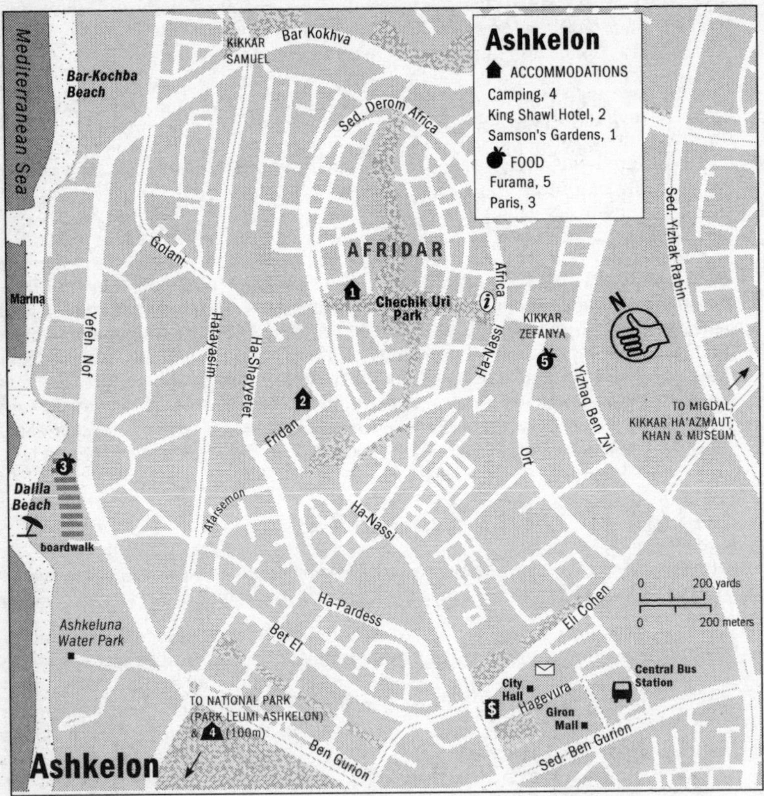

ORIENTATION AND PRACTICAL INFORMATION

Tourist Office: (☎673 24 12). In the City Hall, behind the bus station. Walk down the alley between the bus station and the Giron Mall to Ha-Gvurah St., turn a left, and continue halfway down the shopping center on the right. A Hebrew sign and flags fly in front, but the entrance is on the right. Assistance with travel to Israel's most touristed destinations and free brochures and maps for Ashkelon. Ask about tours to local sights and activities. Open Su-Th 8am-1pm and 4-6pm.

Currency Exchange: Bank Ha-Poalim (☎567 33 33), one block past the City Hall. **ATMs** accept NYCE, Cirrus, and major credit cards. Open Su, Tu, and W 8:30am-1:15pm, M and Th 8:30am-1pm and 4-6:30pm, F and holiday eves 8:15am-12:30pm. The **post office** in Migdal on the *midraḥov* has good rates with no commission.

Emergency: First Aid: (☎672 33 33.) **Police:** (☎677 14 44), at the corner of Ha-Nassi and Eli Cohen St. From the tourist office continue on Ha-Gvurah, and bear right.

Pharmacy: Super-Pharm (☎671 14 31). In the *kenyon* Giron, the shopping mall by the bus station. Open Su-F 8:30am-11pm, Sa 10am-midnight.

Post Office: (☎672 36 06). Behind the building with the town hall, near the *kenyon* Giron. Su-Th 8am-2:30pm, F 8am-noon.

ACCOMMODATIONS AND CAMPING

Cheap accommodations are lacking in Ashkelon; Tel Aviv is a 1¼-hour bus ride, making this an easy daytrip. **Camping** is normally available at the **Park Leumi Ashkelon** (Ashkelon National Park; ☎673 64 44). Those with tents can settle on one of the grassy areas for free. There are bathrooms, but no showers. As of late, most campsites are being used by foreign workers. Call before your visit to see if any are available to tourists. Entrance to the park is free by foot, NIS15 by car. The snack bar and beach-side restaurants in the park are convenient and relatively inexpensive (steak, *shishlik*, or hamburger in a pita NIS15-25). Camping on the beach adjacent to the city is dangerous and not recommended. Tent-campers within the park are also advised that there is no guard on duty from 8pm until 7am. Though not quite in the budget range, **Samson's Gardens** has spacious, clean, and incredibly comfortable rooms. Located in Afridar, the hotel can be reached from the bus station on local bus #4, which stops on the right side of the main bus station. Ask to be let off at "Ganeh Shamshon" and look for the blue and red Hebrew sign on the main street. From where the bus lets off on Derom Africa, walk up Zonabend St. to Hatamar St. The cozy villas are tucked away in the colorful gardens. All rooms include full bathroom, A/C, satellite TV, and complete Israeli breakfast. (Reception open until 10pm. Sept.-May; singles NIS255/US$50-55; doubles NIS315/US$65-70. June-Aug.: singles NIS300/US$63; doubles NIS355/US$75. Jewish holidays: Singles US$88; Doubles US$100. Cash only.) Also in the Afridar neighborhood is the slightly cheaper but less luxurious **King Shaul Hotel,** 28 Ha-Rakefet St. (☎734 12 45, fax 734 12 49), single NIS180/US$43; doubles NIS200/US$50. Rooms have A/C, refrigerator. Major credit cards accepted.

FOOD

The Herzl St. *midraḥov* in Migdal has the highest concentration of affordable eateries (falafel stands abound). Near the *midraḥov* is a lively *shuk* that sells fruits, vegetables, and nuts. From the *midraḥov,* take Ha-Kerem St. toward David Remez St.; the *shuk* is on the right (open M,W, Th 7am-7pm). There are a number of outdoor, locally frequented, inexpensive restaurants on the corner of Ha-Nasi and Zephania St. at the Afridar Center, with schnitzel, hamburger, steak, and pizza for about NIS20. **Delilah Beach boardwalk,** a stone plaza up toward the street from the beach, showcases the city's collection of fish restaurants (meals NIS35-80).

Chinese Restaurant Furama, 24 Ort St. (☎673 84 97). From the station, take bus #5 toward Afridar, get off at Zephania Sq., and backtrack a street to the highly visible front of the restaurant. Sweet and sour pork (NIS40), Kung Pao chicken (NIS40), wonton soup (NIS10), and egg rolls (NIS10) in an airy dining room. Open daily noon-3pm, and 7pm-midnight. Credit cards accepted.

Titanic, in the middle of the *midraḥov*. One of the more popular falafel joints. Get a falafel (NIS10) or satisfy your iceberg-sized hunger with a *shawarma* sandwich on delicious *lafah* bread (NIS18). Open daily 8am-9pm.

Nitsaḥon (☎675 12 00), the Romanian steak house at the end of the *midraḥov*. The town's best selection of steaks (NIS40-60), *me'orav* (mixed meat grill; NIS40), and kebab (NIS24). Open Sa-Th 9am-11pm. Reservations recommended F and Sa nights.

Paris (☎671 18 47) is the hippest of the bunch, with sharp decor, and an ocean view. Fish dishes with salad (NIS55-75), salads (NIS12-15), personal pizzas (NIS24-35), and cocktails (NIS25-45). Open daily 11am-2am. Credit cards accepted.

Hyperneto Supermarket (☎671 14 22) in the *kenyon* Giron (Giron Mall) next to the bus station, is your best bet for make-your-own romantic beachside meals. Open Su-Tu 7:30am-11pm, W-Th 7:30am-midnight, F 7am-3pm, Sa after sunset-11pm.

SIGHTS

ASHKELON NATIONAL PARK. The Ashkelon National Park was built on the site of 4000-year-old Canaanite remains, buried beneath ruins of Philistine, Greek, Roman, Byzantine, Crusader, and Muslim cities. Traces of the once-thriving Philistine city surround the picnic tables and snack bars of this well-used park. The infrequent bus #6 stops at a path leading to the park's entrance. The walk from the central bus station takes about 30min. and offers enticing views of the sea. From the station, turn right onto Ben-Gurion Blvd. and follow it to the T junction at the coast, before the soldiers' recreation facility (note the striking sculpture of Samson along the way). Turn left onto the road to the park; a small orange sign points the way.

The **Bouleuterion,** a series of Hellenistic and Roman columns and capitals, graces the park's center. It served as the Council House Square when Ashkelon was an autonomous city-state under Severius in the 3rd century CE. The courtyard-like area next to the Bouleuterion is actually the inside of a Herodian assembly hall; it contains two statues of Nike, the winged goddess of victory, and an Italian marble statue of the goddess Isis with her god-child Horus, sculpted between 200 BCE and 100 CE. Behind the Bouleuterion lies a preserved **amphitheater.**

Along the southern edge of the park are segments of a wall from the 12th-century **Crusader city.** A short hike past the amphitheater affords a close-up view of the walls and a glimpse of Ashkelon's Rothenberg Power Station. Most peculiar is the assembly of Roman columns jutting out of the ancient Byzantine sea wall on the beach. These massive marble columns were used to support the walls, which were destroyed in 1191 by Salah al-Din. Richard Lionheart partly restored them in 1192, as did Cornwall in 1240, only to have them demolished by the Sultan Baybars in 1270. *(☎673 64 44. Open daily 7am-7pm except rainy Saturdays in winter. Admission free, NIS15 with car. Free maps available at the main entrance.)*

ASHKELON KHAN AND ASHKELON MUSEUM. Ashkelon Khan, a 7th-century tower and courtyard, houses the Ashkelon Museum, which traces the history of Ashkelon from Roman times to the present and has a small collection of modern paintings and sculpture. The khan is past the *midrahov* at the very end of Herzl St.; look for the tower on the left, enter through the courtyard, and the museum door is on the left. *(☎672 70 02. Open Su-Th 8am-1pm, 4-8pm, F 9am-1pm, Sa 11am-1pm.)*

KIKKAR HA-ATZMA'UT (INDEPENDENCE SQUARE). A few blocks past the *midrahov* on Herzl St., this dilapidated intersection was the site of the first reading of Israel's Declaration of Independence in 1948.

BEACHES AND ENTERTAINMENT

Ashkelon's coast has four beaches where swimming is permitted; **Delilah Beach** is the most popular. Note the flag system: white flags signal safe bathing and black flags signal dangerously rough water. At Delilah Beach, breakwaters lessen the chance of black-flagging, and shady canopies and snack bars provide relief to sun-scorched bathers. Once the nighttime revelry begins, the crowd of sun bathers starts discoing to blaring Israeli pop music.

For sand-free water fun, try the **Ashkeluna water park** (☎673 99 70). Crowds of Israeli teenagers and youngsters from Be'er Sheva to Yavneh flock to Ashkeluna's extensive complex of water slides and games, set to the tune of Israeli pop. The water park is near Delilah Beach and the T-junction that branches off toward the national park. (Open daily May-Oct. 9am-4pm. Full day NIS50, after 1pm NIS30.)

DAYTRIPS FROM ASHKELON

BEIT GUVRIN NATIONAL PARK בית גוברין

To reach Beit Guvrin, first travel to Kiryat Gat, which is easily accessible by bus from ***Tel Aviv*** *(#369, 1hr. 15min., every 30min., NIS18);* ***Jerusalem*** *(#446, 1¼hr., every hr., NIS23.50) and* ***Ashkelon*** *(#025, 35min., every 30min, NIS11.50.) Bus #011 from Kiryat Gat goes directly to Kibbutz Beit Guvrin (25min.; Su-Th 8:05am and 5:10pm, F 8:05am and 2pm; return Su-Th 8:30am and 5:30pm, F 8:30am and 2:30pm; NIS8.50). If you miss the bus from Kiryat Gat,* ***Kiryat Gat Taxis*** *(☎393 60 09), in the back of the gas station to the left will take you to Beit Guvrin. (NIS60, but try haggling.) Call for a taxi from Beit Guvrin back to Kiryat Gat. The park is just off Rte. 35, near Kibbutz Beit Guvrin, across from the gas station. Bring plenty of portable shade (a hat or white scarf, sunglasses, and sunscreen) and at least 1½L of water.*

Beit Guvrin National Park, encompassing the ruins of Maresha and Beit Guvrin, is one of Israel's buried treasures. The complex caves and magnificent views make this site unforgettable. The biblical city of **Maresha** was one of the cities of Judah fortified by Rehoboam (Joshua 16:44). The area was later settled by Edomites, Sidonians, and eventually Greeks, who converted it into a bustling economic center. Before the turn of the first century BCE, the Hasmonean king John Hyrcanus I conquered the city and forced Judaism upon its inhabitants. The city was destroyed by the Parthian army in the year 40 BCE. Beit Guvrin became a flourishing Jewish settlement in the years between the destruction of the Second Temple and the Bar Kokhba Revolt (132-135 CE). During the Byzantine period, Beit Guvrin was mostly inhabited by Christians, and more recently, it was the site of an Arab village until Israel's War of Independence in 1948.

Upon entering through the main gate past the ticket office, turn left and follow the road to the Bell Caves. There is an information office behind the bathrooms on the left. Follow the signs to the large-domed **bell-shaped caves** carved by Greeks, Byzantines, and others as they quarried for limestone. Once dug, the caves were used for storage, penning animals, and water collection, and later became sanctuaries for hermits and monks. Saint John and others came here seeking solitude, and they often carved crosses and altars into the walls. More recently, Sylvester Stallone made his own mark in the caves with the filming of *Rambo III.*

The rest of the park is accessible by car, but there is also a 1.9km hiking trail from the Bell Caves that leads toward the **Sidonian Burial Caves** and the ancient city of **Maresha.** The trail is marked with white stone markers, and if you are lucky you may see mountain goats along the way. The trail passes the ruins of the church of St. Anne, originally built during the Byzantine era. Be careful not to wander from the trail as there are many hidden caves in the area.

Sidonians living in Maresha during the 2nd and 3rd centuries BCE buried their dead in decorated caves. Inside the caves you will see many burial niches and paintings of animals and mythological creatures. From the Sidonian caves continue up the hill to see the other caves of Maresha. Especially impressive are the dwelling houses and underground cisterns that connect to form a vast underground network of storage, work, and living rooms. Some of the caves were used for making olive oil, and the olive crushing and squeezing apparatus is on display in the **olive oil plant cave.** The **Columbarium** cave is an enormous room full of niches in which Mareshans raised pigeons for food, manure, and sacrificial purposes.

Even those who yawn at the sight of ruins will appreciate the unbelievable 360° view from atop Tel Maresha. On a clear day, Tel Aviv may be visible in the west, and the Hebron mountains in the east. The entire park site is well-tended with marked trails, bathrooms, and a snack area. On your way out be sure to check out the Roman amphitheater and bathhouse on the other side of the highway. Behind the nearby gas station is the **Beit Guvrin Restaurant,** a self-service cafeteria. *(Open daily 8am-9pm. ☎681 10 20 for the ticket office, ☎681 29 57 for the information office. Sites open Su-Th 8am-5pm, F 8am-4pm. Sept.-Apr 8am-4pm, F 8am-3pm. NIS18, students NIS15, children NIS9. The English brochure has a small map of the park.)*

YAD MORDEKHAI יד מרדכי

Buses #373, 374, and 379 stop at Mordekhai junction, but do not go directly to the kibbutz (every few hours, NIS9.50). If you get stuck in the late afternoon, go back to the bus stop on the highway and try flagging a passing bus from Rafah. ☎07 672 05 29. Museum and battlefield open daily 10am-4pm. Admission to museum and battlefield NIS16, children NIS14.

From May 19th to 24th, 1948, the 165 members of Kibbutz Yad Mordekhai withstood an attack by an Egyptian battalion of 2500. A model of the battle comes with soldiers, tanks, weapons, and a recorded explanation. The famous museum also illustrates the story of the Warsaw ghetto resistance movement.

MEDITERRANEAN COAST

The stretch of coastline north of Tel Aviv is home to much of Israel's population and most of its agricultural output. Zionists and refugees poured onto the beaches for the first half of the 20th century and drained the swamps of the coastal plain, clearing the path for a modern, industrial state. Still, safely removed from the country's two largest cities, the region maintains an old-world character. Life here moves at a more luxurious pace; the ways of the west haven't completely taken over yet and many old villages remain remarkably well preserved.

Picturesque beach towns, friendly kibbutzim, and significant archaeological ruins dot the shore between Tel Aviv and the Lebanese border. Indeed, the coast and its attractions are incredibly idiosyncratic and travelers sun-worshiping one day may find themselves in a Druze village the next, and in a Crusader fortress the day after that. Almost every day, however, is bound to be followed by a glorious Mediterranean sunset and a night of relaxed strolling along a promenade.

HIGHLIGHTS OF THE MEDITERRANEAN COAST

If you don't find the inner peace you seek in the stunning gardens of Haifa's **Baha'i Shrine** (see p. 184), try the nearby surrealist artist commune of **Ein Hod** (see p. 190).

Watch the waves toss foam against the white chalk cliffs and wander through the grottoes of **Rosh Ha-Nikra** (p. 212), the northernmost point of Israel's coastline.

HAIFA חיפה حيفا ☎04

Since the prophet Elijah fled the wrath of King Ahab to the caves of Mt. Carmel (I Kings 18-19), Haifa has harbored religious minorities. Crusaders built the first of several monasteries above **Elijah's Cave,** which eventually gave shelter to the wandering Carmelite Order of Monks. **German Templars** established Haifa's German colony, and the **Baha'i** built their world headquarters here. In the 1930s, waves of European Jews seeking refuge from Nazism poured onto Haifa's beaches.

As a result, Haifa developed the philosophy, "live and let live." When the British decided to construct a port in the city, Arabs and Jews flocked to the economic opportunities and worked side-by-side in factories. Though they went home to separate neighborhoods, the municipality as a whole employed and was supported by members of both communities. Of course, the War of 1948 affected Haifa like all other areas, with thousands of Arabs abandoning the city; but today, Haifa's population of a quarter million includes a sizeable Arab minority and a small Orthodox Jewish community, who live together with little tension. Haifa University has the largest Arab population of any university in Israel and a joint community center promotes relations at the local level, especially among children. Not surprisingly, supporters of the Israeli-Palestinian peace accords often cite Haifa as the paradigm for peaceful Jewish-Arab co-existence.

The construction of the port had long-lasting effects on the city. Factories and industrial districts came first to the shores of Haifa, and residential districts climbed their way up Mt. Carmel. For most of the 20th century, Haifa remained essentially a workers' city. Other businesses have since begun to grow, and the coast looks more like the Riviera every day. Still, Haifa still remains something of

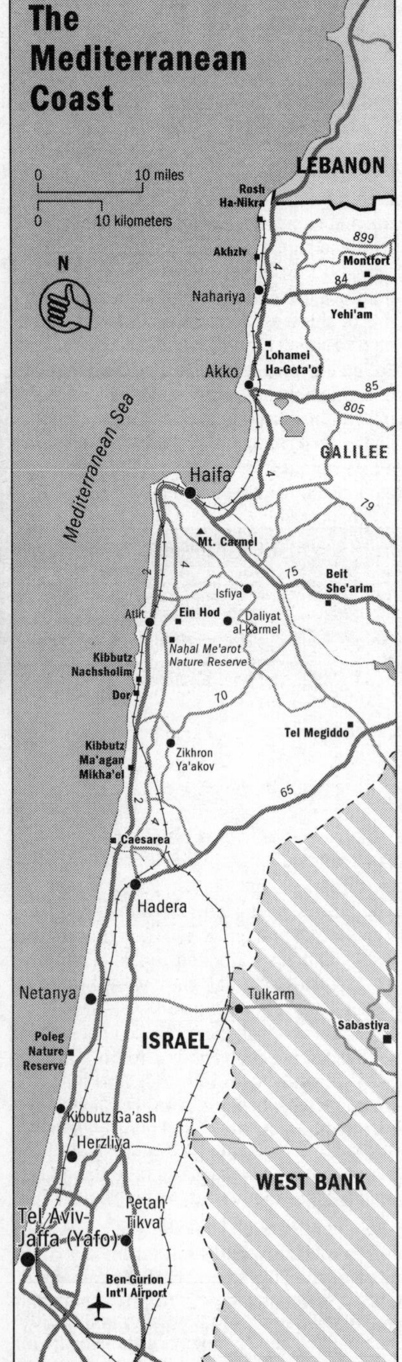

an underachiever. City residents are painfully aware of this fact and when asked about good places to eat or have fun, most will answer, "Well, I know a place that's pretty good for Haifa, but it's nothing like they have in Tel Aviv." For better or worse depending on your perspective, the unique topography, luxuriously wooded neighborhoods, and striking vistas remain Haifa's most memorable attraction.

GETTING THERE

Trains: Central station in Bat Galim (☎856 44 44), is connected by tunnels to the central bus station. Trains to: **Akko** (30 min., NIS11); **Hadera** (50 min., NIS16); **Nahariya** (40 min., NIS13); **Netanya** (NIS19.50) via **Binyamina** (45 min., NIS16); and **Tel Aviv** (1 hr., NIS21). The trip to Jerusalem requires a station change and will take longer than the bus. Trains are generally the best choice when traveling north. 10% discount with student ID. The tourist office has schedules. Credit cards accepted.

Buses: The **central bus station** (intercity info ☎851 22 08), is at Jaffa Rd. and Rothschild Blvd. Intercity buses generally run Su-Th from 5:15am-11:30pm, F 5:15am-5pm and Sa 5pm-midnight. Buses to: **Ben-Gurion Airport** (#945 and 947, 2hr., every 30min., NIS28); **Jerusalem** (#940 (direct) 2hr., #945 and 947 (via Ben-Gurion) 3hr; NIS40); **Nahariya** (#251, 271, and 272; 1¼hr.; every 15-20min.; NIS13.80) via **Akko** (50min., NIS11.50); **Nazareth** (#331 and 431, 1½hr., every 40 min., NIS18.20); **Tel Aviv** (#900 (direct) and 901 (express); 1½hr.; every 20min.; NIS20.50); and **Tiberias** (#430 (direct) and 431, 1½hr., every hr. 5:30am-8pm, NIS23.50).

Ferries: Terminal (☎851 82 45) next to Merkaz train station, off Ha-Atzma'ut St. Ferries to Cyprus and mainland Greece (Th 8pm, F 7pm, and sometimes Su 8pm. Security checks are often several hours prior to departure. Check ahead. South Africans need visas to enter both countries. Tickets at **Caspi Travel,** 76 Ha-Atzma'ut St. (☎867 44 44.

Open Su-Th 9am-5pm, F 9am-1pm.) For cruises, try **Mano,** 2 Sha'ar Palmer St. (☎866 77 22. open Su-Th 8:30am-5pm, F 8:30am-2pm). Ferry tickets also available through ISSTA.

Taxis: Most taxis leave from Eliyahu St. in Paris Sq., near the Carmelit stop or from Ha-Ḥalutz St. and Herzl St., near bus stops in Hadar. For *special*, home pick-up, taxis call **Kavei Ha-Galil** (☎866 44 44 or 22). To **Akko** (NIS80), **Nahariya** (NIS120), or **Lod** (NIS280). **Amal's Sherut Service** (☎866 23 24) will take you from 6 Ha-Ḥalutz St. in Hadar to **Tel Aviv** (NIS22) and **Ben-Gurion Airport** (NIS45). Other taxi services include **Carmel Ahuza** (☎838 27 27) and **Merkaz Mitzpeh** (☎866 25 25 or 866 83 83). For 24hr. direct service to Ben-Gurion Airport, try Kavei Ha-Galil or Amal.

Car Rental: Avis, 7 Ben-Gurion Blvd. (☎851 30 50); **Budget,** 46 Ha-Histadrut Blvd. (☎842 40 04); **Hertz,** Ha-Histadrut Blvd. (☎840 21 27); **Reliable,** 140 Yafo Rd. (☎850 79 07); **Eldan,** 95 Ha-Nassi Blvd. (☎837 53 03). All open Su-Th 8am-6pm, F 8am-2pm. Most require minimum age of 24; Eldan will rent to 21-year-olds with double insurance payments.

GETTING AROUND

BUSES. The **central bus station** (city line info ☎854 91 31), like the city itself, has three tiers. Intercity buses leave from the first floor, city buses depart from the second, and all buses arrive on the third. Intercity buses stop at the bus station and in Hadar along Herzl after 8pm. All urban rides cost NIS5; a 15-ride pass is NIS47.

On weekdays, buses run from about 5:30am to 11pm. On Fridays, they stop at around 4:30pm, depending on when Shabbat starts. **Saturday buses** usually begin running at 9:30am, run less frequently than on weekends and do *not* run from the central bus station, but from the Hadar area (many from Daniel St.) until about 6pm, when they switch back. **Sheruts** taper off a couple hours later than buses; many go to Hadar only (NIS4.50), while others follow specific bus routes.

Haifa's bus routes are extremely circuitous and a 20-minute walk (though uphill) may be a half-hour bus ride. To get **Downtown (Ha-Ir)** from the central bus station, take bus #17 or 41; from other parts of town, take any bus in the 70s. Almost every bus numbered 1-40 eventually stops in Hadar, but from the central bus station, #15 and 18 run most frequently. Those in the 20s go to **Carmel** and **Ahuza,** and #24 and 37 continue on to the **University of Haifa.**

SUBWAY. The best way to travel within Haifa is the Carmelit subway system (☎837 68 61), a train slanted just enough to make the ascent or descent seem flat. Though this subway has only one line, its six stops conquer steep hills and put most neighborhoods within walking distance. Starting from the bottom, the subway stops at Kikkar Paris, Solel Boneh, Ha-Nevi'im, Masada, Golomb, and Gan Ha-Eim. Yellow pavilions indicate entrances. Trains run every six to seven minutes. (Su-Th 6am-10pm, F 6am-3pm, 8pm-midnight, Sa in winter 7pm-midnight. NIS4.70 per ride for adults and children, NIS3 for seniors; 10-ride pass NIS42, NIS32.50 for seniors and those under 18. Credit cards accepted.)

CABLE CARS. A more scenic, but also more expensive alternative for getting from bottom to top and back again is to take the **Rakbal cable cars** (☎833 59 70). Colloquially known as "the Carmel's Eggs" for their ellipsoidal shape, the cable cars run down the Carmel's northwestern slope, shuttling between the orange-and-turquoise **Yotvata B'Ir** dairy restaurant on the Bat Galim Promenade and the **Stella Maris monastery** area at the mountain's peak. To Bat Galim, take bus #41 or 42; to Stella Maris take #25 or 26. (Open daily 9am-midnight in summer, 9am-7pm in winter; NIS16, round-trip NIS22.)

ORIENTATION

Situated on a small peninsula, Haifa rises from the Mediterranean coast up the steep, northern slopes of Mt. Carmel. It calls itself the "gateway of the North" for good reason; the cliffs of Rosh Ha-Nikra (and the Lebanon border) are less than 50km to the north. The Sea of Galilee is 70km to the east, and the ruins of Caesarea

40km to the south. The city itself is divided into three terraces and in this vertically oriented town, social stratification is more than just a metaphor; the rich really do live on the top, the poor at the bottom.

The **Ir Ha-Taḥtit area** (downtown) fans outwards from the port and **Ha-Atzma'ut Rd.** The Old City is one block back around **Yafo Rd.,** and it extends to the right (if facing the port) towards **Kikkar Paris,** the lowest stop of the Carmelit subway. Slightly higher up and to the left, the traditional Middle Eastern neighborhood **Wadi Nisnas** lies on and around **Khuri St.** Farther to left, **Ben-Gurion St.** runs uphill and intersects Yafo Rd. at the bottom, **Ha-Meginim Ave.** near the German Colony, **Allenby Rd.** near the **tourist office,** and **Ha-Geffen St.** at the first of the Baha'i gardens. Much further left on the lower terrace, the **central bus station** adjoins the **train station** at the intersection of Yafo Rd. and **Rothschild Boulevard,** in the **Bat Galim** neighborhood. Yafo then becomes **Ha-Hagana Ave.,** which curves around the peninsula to the beaches.

The middle terrace, the **Hadar** district, teeters precariously on the trendy-trashy border and is home to many clothing stores, cheap hotels, bakeries, and bazaar stands. The two main streets are **Herzl St.** and **Ha-Ḥalutz St.** Ha-Ḥalutz runs parallel to Herzl but one block down. Buses from Herzl go up the mountain, while buses from Ha-Ḥalutz go to the central bus station. The street parallel to and above Herzl is the quiet **Nordau Midraḥov** (pedestrian zone). **Balfour St.,** perpendicular to these three and bordering Nordau on the left as you face the port, leads up to **Masada St. and Hillel St.** Hadar's Carmelit stop is at the intersection of Herzl St. and **Ha-Nevi'im St.,** a few blocks past Balfour.

The highest area, known as **Carmel Center,** glitters with posh homes, five-star hotels, restaurants, and bars. This district is traversed by **Ha-Nassi Boulevard** and **Yefeh Nof St.** Both pass the Dan Panorama Hotel, next to the **Louis Promenade,** which offers a view of the lower city and the port area. One block up Ha-Nassi is **Gan Ha-Eim,** a peaceful park, near the last Carmelit stop. **Hayam Road** branches to the right off Ha-Nassi and **Wedgewood Ave.** to the left as you walk from the Carmelit stop. The **Cultural Center** and several cafes and bars are further up Ha-Nassi as it curves right. From Carmel Center, it's a long walk on Moriya St. or a quick ride on bus #24 or 37 to Ahuza—a yuppie district with cafes, restaurants, and Merkaz Ḥorev, a large shopping center.

PRACTICAL INFORMATION

TOURIST AND FINANCIAL SERVICES

Tourist Information Office: 48 Ben-Gurion St. (☎853 56 06; fax 853 56 10; email haifa5@netvision.net.il). Take bus #22 to the corner of Ben-Gurion and Ha-Gefen St. or walk several blocks to the left of Kikkar Paris Carmelit along Ha-Meginim Ave. and turn left on Ben-Gurion. Distributes free maps (more detailed ones NIS3), and the bimonthly Events in Haifa booklet. Free short film on Haifa's highlights. Open Su-Th 8:30am-6pm, F 8:30am-2pm.

Tours: Society for the Protection of Nature in Israel (SPNI), 18 Hillel St. (☎866 41 35), on the 4th floor. Has information and maps (NIS62, in Hebrew) on hiking trips into the Carmel Mountains. Tours must be arranged with the Tel Aviv office. Open Su-Th 9am-2pm, F 8am-1pm.

Budget Travel: ISSTA, 20 Herzl St. (☎868 22 22). ISIC NIS40 HI membership NIS30. Student rates on plane and ferry tickets. Open Su-Tu and Th 9am-7pm., in winter 9am-6pm; Also at the **Technion** (☎832 67 39; fax 832 67 41), in the Student Building. Open Su-Th 9am-5pm; in summer F 9-11:30am and Haifa University (☎825 39 51; fax 834 53 06), next to the #37 bus stop.

US Consulate: 26 Ben-Gurion St. (☎853 14 70; fax 853 14 76; email consage@netvision.net.il), in Hadar. Call Su-Th 9am-1pm (call first). In an emergency, call (03) 519 73 70.

Currency Exchange: Any post office will exchange money without charging a commmission. Also, no-commission services cluster around Palmer Sq., by the port, and by the Gan Ha-Eim Carmelit stop. Banks generally charge a commission: minUS$6, max15% **Bank Ha-Poalim,** 1 Ha-Palyam Blvd. (☎868 14 11). Currency exchange open M-Th 8:30am-2:30pm. F 8:30am-11:30am. **Bank Leumi,** 21 Yafo St. (☎854 71 11), in the new Ha-Meginim Tower (other branches throughout the city). Currency exchange open M-Th 8:30am-2:30pm and F 8:30am-noon.

American Express: Meditrad Ltd., 6 Ha-Yam St. (☎836 26 96). **Client Letter Service** available. Open Su-Th 8:30am-5pm, F 8:30am-12:30pm.

LOCAL SERVICES

Shopping Hours: Most shops open Su-Th 8:30am-1:30pm and 4-7pm, F 8:30am-1pm, and some open on Sa 8-11pm. Larger stores and malls usually open 8:30am-7pm.

English Bookstores: Steimatzky, 16 Herzl St. (☎866 50 42), has a large collection of paperbacks, magazines, and travel books. (Open Su-Th 8:30am-7pm, F 8:30am-2pm). **Books,** 5 Sirkin St. (☎862 69 10), one block below the Yehiel St. and Ha-Ḥalutz St. intersection. Buys and sells used books in a variety of languages, English included.

Film Developing: Photo-center, 1 Herzl St. (☎862 83 24). 45min. developing available for NIS45 plus NIS1 per picture. Open Sa-Th 8:30am-7:30pm, F 8:30am-2:30pm.

Camping Supplies: Ha Metayel, 2 Balfour St. (☎864 42 44), next to ISSTA. Open Su-M and Th 9am-7pm, Tu 9am-6pm, W 9am-2pm, F 9am-1pm. Also located on the 2nd floor of the central bus station.

Ticket Offices: Haifa Municipal Theatre, (☎860 05 00) puts on everything from classic Neil Simon to edgy new Israeli playwrights. There are also general ticket offices for an array of plays, musicals, and concerts. **Haifa,** 11 Baerwald St. (☎866 22 44). Open Su-W 9am-1pm and 4-7pm, Th-F 9am-1pm. **Garber,** 129 Ha-Nassi Blvd. (☎838 47 77). Open Su-Th 9am-1pm and 4-7pm, F 9am-2pm. **Nova,** 15 Nordau St. (☎866 52 72). Open Su-M and W-Th 10am-1pm and 4-6:30pm, Tu 10am-1pm, F 10am-1:30pm.

Laundry: Wash and Dry, 5 Ha-Yam Rd. (☎810 78 50), in Carmel Center. NIS12 for up to 7kg; NIS1 per minute to dry. Open Su-M 8:30am-5:30pm, Tu 8:30am-3pm, W-Th 8:30am-5:30 pm, F 8:30am-2pm.

Swimming Pools: Maccabee Pool, 19 Bikurim St. (☎838 83 41), in Central Carmel. Heated and covered in winter. Open Su, Tu, and Th 6am-2pm and 4-10pm, M and W 6am-2pm and 6:30-10pm, F 6am-2pm and 4-6pm. NIS40. The **Dan Panorama Hotel,** 107 Ha-Nassi Blvd. (☎835 22 22), has a pool open to the public Su-F 7am-5pm, Sa 7am-2pm and 4-5pm. NIS40. **Technion Pool** (☎829 33 00) has a 50m pool and a sauna, in addition to a few smaller pools. NIS45; 12-visit pass NIS450. Open Su and Th 6am-11pm, M and W 6am-8pm, Tu 6am-10pm, F and Sa 6am-6pm.

EMERGENCY AND COMMUNICATIONS

Emergency: First Aid: 6 Yitzḥak Sadeh St. **Police:** 28 Jaffa St. **Emotional First Aid** (☎867 22 22), open 24hr. English spoken.

Pharmacies: Ha-Ḥalutz, 12 Ha-Ḥalutz St. (☎862 06 29), in Hadar. Open Su-Th 8:30am-1pm and 4-7pm, F 8:30am-1pm. **Merkaz,** 130 Ha-Nassi Blvd. (☎838 19 79), in Carmel Center. Open Su-Th 8am-7pm, F 8am-2pm.

Hospitals: Rambam (☎854 31 11), in Bat Galim; **Benei Zion (Rothschild),** 47 Golomb St. (☎835 93 59); **Carmel,** 7 Michal St. (☎825 02 11); **Herzliya Medical Center** (HMC), 15 Ḥorev St. (☎830 52 22).

Post Office: Main branch at 19 Ha-Palyam Blvd. (☎830 41 82), offers **Poste Restante**. Other branches at Shabtai Levi and Ha-Nevi'im St. (☎864 09 17); 152 Jaffa Rd., on the corner of Sha'ar Palmer; 63 Herzl St. in Hadar; and 7 Wedgewood Blvd. next to #37 bus stop at Haifa University. Most open Su-Th 8am-5pm, F 8am-noon, except for the Shabtai Levi St. branch which is open until 6pm on Su-Th.

Internet: Nor-Em Internet Cafe. See accommodations below.

ACCOMMODATIONS

Options are slim, but growing in Haifa. The two picks listed here have made enormously welcome contributions to the budget scene. Also, the Haifa Tourist Board (☎853 56 06) now arranges **B&B stays in private homes** (NIS25-60). Religious hostels offer immaculate premises, but strict curfews thwart nightlife revelry. Beyond these options, buyer beware and take a good look around before committing.

Nor-Em Internet Cafe Bed & Breakfast, 27-29 Nordau St. (☎866 56 56; email info@norem.israel.net; www.norem.israel.net), off Ḥaim St., between Herzl St. and the Nordau *midraḥov*. Brand spanking new, this B&B offers spacious rooms, all with A/C and immaculate bathrooms. Laid-back, backpacker-friendly staff serves up drinks, sandwiches, and advice on the city 24 hours a day in the posh cafe. Check-out noon. 6-bed dorms (coed) NIS80/US$20; singles NIS160/US$40; doubles NIS220/US$55. 10% discount for stays longer than 3 days; 20% discount for stays longer than a week.

Port Inn, 34 Yafo St. (☎852 44 01; fax 852 10 03; email port_inn@yahoo.com), downtown. From the central bus station, take bus #3 or 5 to the intersection of Ha-Atzma'ut St. and Ben-Gurion. The Port Inn yearns to be your home away from home with a den-like social room, free use of the kitchen and coffee supplies, and a warm and advice-laden manager, who will even do your laundry (for NIS30). Internet NIS0.50 per min. A/C in all rooms. Reception 7:30am-midnight; ring the bell anytime. Check-out 11am. 6-bed dorms (single-sex and coed) NIS45/US$11.25, with breakfast NIS55/US$13.75; Singles and doubles NIS170/US$42.50, NIS200/US$50 with bath.

MEDITERRANEAN COAST

Carmel Youth Hostel (HI) (☎853 19 44; fax 853 25 16), 4km south of the city at Ḥof Ha-Carmel (Carmel beach). Bus #43 from the central bus station and 44 *alef* from Hadar go directly past the hostel. Though extremely far from the center of town and a schlep from the beach, this simple hostel offers large rooms, cool breezes, and shaded woods. All rooms with A/C and bath. Breakfast included. Lockers NIS6. Check-in 2pm-8pm. Check-out 10am. 6-bed dorms (single-sex) NIS80/US$20; singles NIS128/US$38; doubles NIS224/US$56; triples NIS288/US$72; quads NIS352/US$88; quints NIS416/US$416. HI-card carriers get NIS5 discount.

Bethel Hostel, 40 Ha-Geffen St. (☎852 11 10). Take bus #22 from central bus station to Ben-Gurion St., walk up to Ha-Geffen, and turn right. The hostel is on the right after a couple blocks. A buzz-killer during party time, but located in a quiet neighborhood close to the center of town. Christian volunteers keep the rooms sparklingly clean. All rooms have fans. Shared bath in hall. Free dinner on Shabbat and sometimes M and Th. No smoking. Under 18 must be with an adult. Check-in Sa-Th 5-10pm, F 4-9pm. New arrivals may leave bags in locked storage and return after 5pm to register. Lock-out 9am-5pm; strict 11pm curfew; wake-up 7am. 8- to 12-bed single-sex rooms NIS56/US$14.

FOOD

Downtown overflows with *shawarma* and falafel shops, the best option for meals on Shabbat. There's more falafel (there's always more falafel) to be found in Hadar along Herzl and Ha-Ḥalutz St., and slightly more expensive cafes dot the **Nordau Midraḥov** (pedestrian section). The lower, even-numbered end of Herzl St.—where the heady fragrance of fresh burekas and croissants wafts from a strip of bakeries—indulges a sweet tooth, but only until early evening. The area around the Gan Ha-Eim Carmelit stop serves a late night crowd with a mix of chain restaurants, ice cream stands, and several popular cafes and bars along Natanson St.

There is an inexpensive **fruit and vegetable market** just west of the Kikkar Paris station. Another **shuk** lies one block down from Ha-Ḥalutz St., around Yehiel St., where Haifans purchase cheap clothes, groceries, and wine. Finally, Khuri St. in Wadi Nisnas can satisfy any *shuk*-cravings on Shabbat. Be stubborn and bargain hard (see **The Fine Art of Haggling,** p. 120).

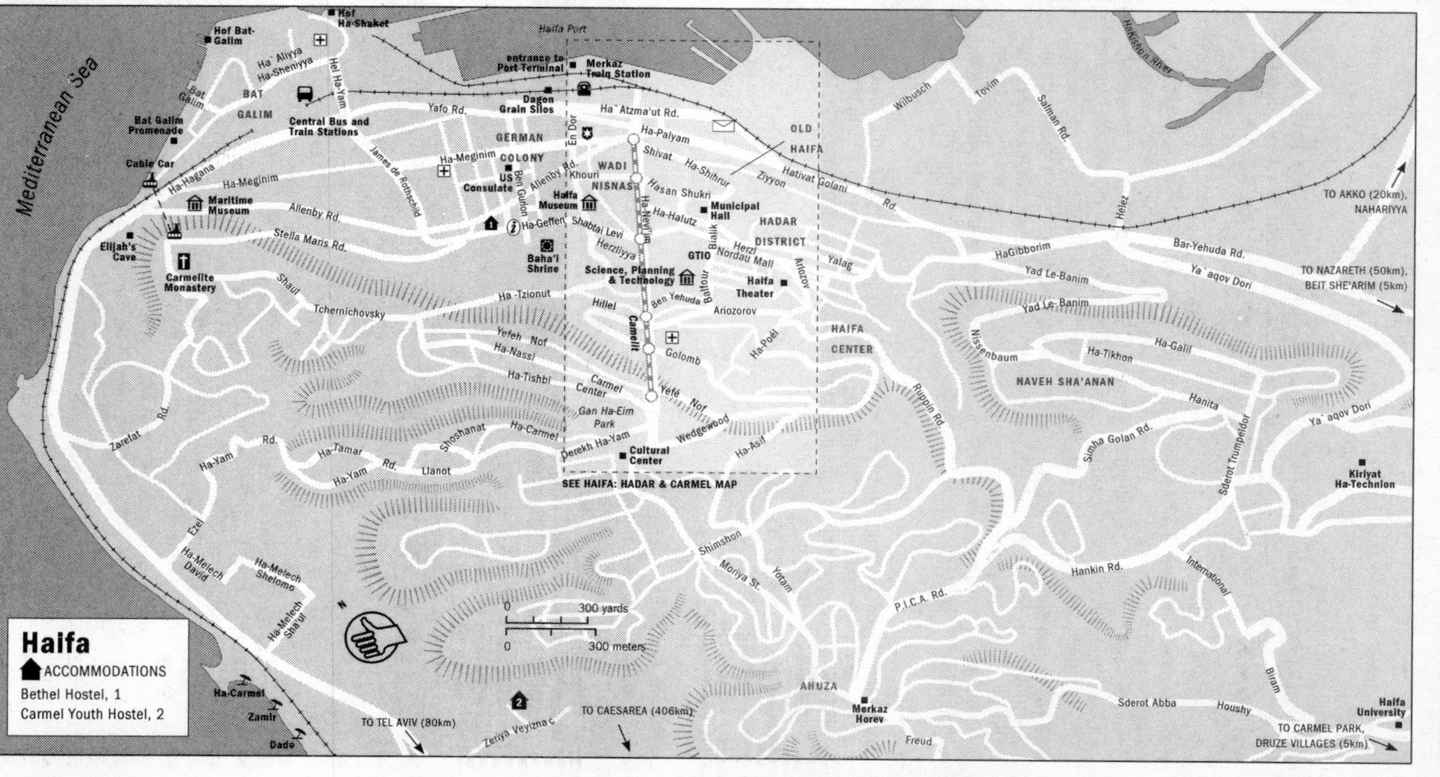

Haifa
ACCOMMODATIONS
Bethel Hostel, 1
Carmel Youth Hostel, 2
Mediterranean Sea
SEE HAIFA: HADAR & CARMEL MAP
TO AKKO (20km), NAHARIYYA
TO NAZARETH (50km), BEIT SHE'ARIM (5km)
TO CARMEL PARK, DRUZE VILLAGES (5km)
TO CAESAREA (406km)
TO TEL AVIV (80km)
Haifa University
Kiryat Ha-Technion
Merkaz Horev
Haifa Port
Merkaz Train Station
entrance to Port Terminal
Dagon Grain Silos
Central Bus and Train Stations
Hof Ha-Shaket
Hof Bat-Galim
Bat Galim Promenade
Cable Car
Elijah's Cave
Carmelite Monastery
Maritime Museum
US Consulate
Baha'i Shrine
Haifa Museum
Municipal Hall
Haifa Theater
Science, Planning & Technology
Cultural Center
Carmelit
GTIO
OLD HAIFA
HADAR DISTRICT
HAIFA CENTER
NAVEH SHA'ANAN
AHUZA
GERMAN COLONY
BAT GALIM
WADI NISNAS
Ha-Kishon River
Ha-Carmel
Zamir
Dado
0 300 yards
0 300 meters

DOWNTOWN

Iraqi Shishkebab, 59 Ben-Gurion St. (☎852 75 76). The owner will put anything in a pita to make the mother of all meals. Divine kebab skewers (NIS3 for 2) set a new standard for the culinary arts. Open Su-Th 12:30-10:30pm.

Ma'ayan Ha-Bira, 4 Natanson St. (☎862 31 93), in the midst of the shuk, look for Carlsburg signs on your left if coming from the Kikkar Paris Carmelit. This diner's claim to fame is its home-smoked meats (NIS20-38). Eastern European delicacies like *ikra* (fish salad, NIS15) and *kisonim* (meat dumplings, NIS15) also served. Open Su-F 8am-6pm. Credit cards accepted.

Jacko Seafood Restaurant, 12 Kehilat Saloniki St. (☎866 88 13), near the Kikkar Paris Carmelit station and parallel to, but one block past, the *shuk*. Owner is a former fisherman who still gets fresh seafood daily (entrees NIS30-60). Enjoy this unique hole-in-the-wall more cheaply with their Turkish desserts like *malaby* or semolina with coconut (NIS10). Open Su-F noon-11pm, Sa noon-6pm. Credit cards accepted.

Abu Yousef and Brothers (☎866 37 23), in Kikkar Paris across the street (away from the port) from the Carmelit. This spacious restaurant in the heart of downtown serves up Middle Eastern delights including kebab, *shishlik,* and *sinaya* with pine nuts (NIS30-40). All dishes come with fries, coffee, and pita on the side. A shot of licorice-flavored *'araq* (NIS7) makes a good *digestif.* Open Sa-Th 8am-midnight, F 8am-6pm.

HADAR

Tzimzhonit Ḥayim, 30 Herzl St. (☎867 46 67), has nourished vegetarians since the 1930s with Eastern European stewed veggies (NIS14) and sweet or savory blintzes (NIS15-17). However, there is something fishy about the vegetarian menu (fish delicacies NIS12-20). Open Su-Th 9am-8pm, F 9am-2pm.

Beneinu, 49 Hillel St. (☎852 41 55). Just "between us," it's the place to see and be seen by Hadar locals, Baha'is, and the international crowd. Chatty cafe by day, chic bar by night. Daily special quiche NIS27; Beer NIS14-22. Open Su-Th 9:30am-1am, F 9:30am-5pm and 8pm-2am, Sa 4pm-2am. Credit cards accepted.

CARMEL CENTER

Casa Italiana, 119 Ha-Nassi Blvd. (☎838 13 36), next to McDonald's. Perfect for wooing that special someone, or even just remembering what pizza (NIS26-39) is supposed to taste like, this precious gem has been run by the same family for 30 years. Pop makes the canneloni (NIS31.90, with mushrooms or meat) while mom cooks dessert (NIS15-27). Open Sa-Th 5pm-11pm. Credit cards accepted.

Sandwich Bar Carmel, 128 Ha-Nassi Blvd. (☎838 04 44). Tender love notes posted on the walls keep patrons occupied while they wait for their generously sized sandwiches (NIS16-19). Open 24 hr.

WALKS AND PARKS

A rule to live by in Haifa: always walk down, never walk up. Haifa's steep topography makes it a difficult place to negotiate on foot. Taking a bus or the Carmelit to the top of Carmel and working down through the city is a feasible (albeit circuitous) way of seeing each district's varied attractions. For more in-depth explorations of the heart of Haifa, the tourist offices provide a map criss-crossed with four **walking tours** (NIS3 each), each of which is supposedly 1000 steps. On Saturdays, the **Haifa Municipal Tourist Office** gives free, guided versions of the tours in English and Hebrew (2hr.; meet at 10am at the corner of Yefeh Nof and Sha'ar Ha-Levanon St. and dress modestly for stops at Baha'i holy places).

A stroll through the quiet, shrub-lined walkways of **Gan Ha-Eim** (Mother's Park), across from the Carmel Center Carmelit stop, offers a nice escape from the urban doldrums. The **Municipal Zoo** (☎837 23 90 or 837 28 86) houses a moderate number of beasts including the biggest snake in the Middle East. (Open Su-Th 8am-4pm, in summer until 6pm; F 8am-1pm; Sa 9am-4pm, in summer until 5pm. NIS20, students NIS18.) An **SPNI nature trail** begins in Gan Ha-Eim to the right of the shell-shaped stage. The blue signs mark a 2km foray around the zoo, through tangled greenery

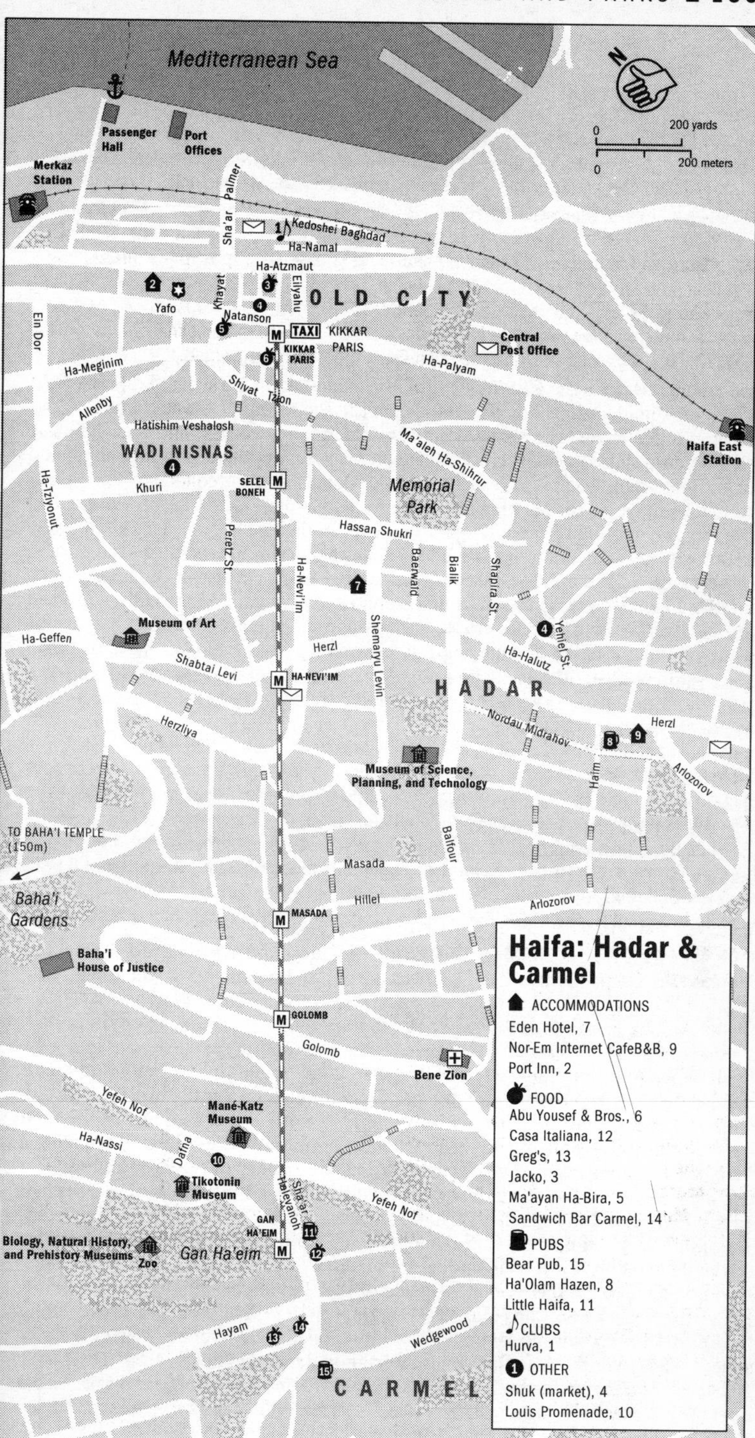
Mediterranean Sea
Passenger Hall
Port Offices
Merkaz Station
200 yards
200 meters
Kedoshei Baghdad
Ha-Namal
Sha'ar Palmer
Ha-Atzmaut
Yafo
Khayat
Natanson
Eilyahu
OLD CITY
TAXI
KIKKAR PARIS
Central Post Office
Ha-Palyam
Ein Dor
Ha-Meginim
Shivat Tzion
Allenby
Hatishim Veshalosh
WADI NISNAS
Ma'aleh Ha-Shihrur
Haifa East Station
Khuri
SELEL BONEH
Memorial Park
Ha-Tziyonut
Hassan Shukri
Peretz St.
Ha-Nevi'im
Baerwald
Bialik
Shapira St.
Museum of Art
Ha-Geffen
Shemaryu Levin
Yehiel St.
Herzl
Ha-Halutz
Shabtai Levi
HA-NEVI'IM
HADAR
Herzliya
Nordau Midrahov
Herzl
Museum of Science, Planning, and Technology
Haim
Arlozorov
TO BAHA'I TEMPLE (150m)
Balfour
Masada
Baha'i Gardens
Hillel
Arlozorov
MASADA
Baha'i House of Justice
GOLOMB
Golomb
Bene Zion
Yefeh Nof
Mané-Katz Museum
Ha-Nassi
Dafna
Tikotonin Museum
Sha'ar Halevanoh
Yefeh Nof
GAN HA'EIM
Biology, Natural History, and Prehistory Museums
Zoo
Gan Ha'eim
Hayam
Wedgewood
CARMEL
Haifa: Hadar & Carmel
ACCOMMODATIONS
Eden Hotel, 7
Nor-Em Internet CafeB&B, 9
Port Inn, 2
FOOD
Abu Yousef & Bros., 6
Casa Italiana, 12
Greg's, 13
Jacko, 3
Ma'ayan Ha-Bira, 5
Sandwich Bar Carmel, 14
PUBS
Bear Pub, 15
Ha'Olam Hazen, 8
Little Haifa, 11
CLUBS
Hurva, 1
OTHER
Shuk (market), 4
Louis Promenade, 10

into Wadi Lotam in lower Carmel (buses #3 or 5 will get you back uptown). For further information, contact the SPNI office. Wildlife without fencing or bars can be found at **Mount Carmel National Park,** the biggest park in Israel (15min. by bus #24, 37, or 192 from Gan Ha-eim). There are several marked trails in the park. The SPNI office has more information.

Back in the city, two smaller parks are well worth a visit. A collection of bronze sculptures by Ursula Malbin is in the **Sculpture Garden,** off Ha-Tzionut Ave., near the Baha'i Shrine. **Memorial Park,** off Hassan Shukri St. behind City Hall in lower Hadar, has a memorial for soldiers from Haifa who died in Israeli wars. The combination of shade and panoramic vistas makes it a perfect spot for picnics.

SIGHTS

BAHA'I SHRINE. The golden-domed Baha'i Shrine that dominates the Haifa skyline commemorates the Persian Sayyid Ali Muhammad (the Bab), the first Baha'i prophet. In 1890, Baha'ullah, the founder of the Baha'i faith (see **The Baha'i,** p. 24), selected this spot on Mt. Carmel, near where he pitched his tent following his exile from Persia to Akko, and instructed his son Abdu'l-Baha to bury the Bab here and build a great temple in his honor. Though the Bab was executed in 1850 for his religious teachings, devotees transferred his remains numerous times for almost 60 years to prevent them from falling into enemy hands. Finally, in 1909, the Bab was laid to rest as Baha'ullah had wished, inside the shrine, beneath the red carpet. Abdu'l-Baha built the preliminary structure and Shoghi Effendi, Guardian of the Baha'i religion from 1921 to 1957, embellished and expanded the structure. Modest dress is required and visitors must remove their shoes before entering the shrine. For a stunning view of the entire grounds, look up from Ben-Gurion St. or down from Yefeh Nof St., just past the Louis Promenade. *(Landscaping renovations and a project to create a pilgrim's walkway leading straight from the port all the way up to the shrine have closed the two main entrances until May 2001. Take bus #22 from the central bus station or downtown or bus #23, 25, 26, or 32 from Ha-Nevi'im and Herzl St. to Ha-Tzionut Ave., just above the shrine. Once the project is completed, visitors can ascend the stairs from Ben-Gurion at the bottom, or weave down through magnificent gardens from Yefeh Nof St. ☎835 83 58. Open daily 9am-noon; gardens open 9am-5pm. Free.)*

Other Baha'i buildings are scattered around the grounds, but are not open to the public. To the right of the shrine (as you face the port), the **International Baha'i Archives Building** houses Baha'i relics and historical materials. Further right, the marble **Universal House of Justice** is the center of international Baha'i operations.

MONASTERY OF THE CARMELITE ORDER. A Latin monk named Berthold founded the Carmelite order in 1156, but the Sultan Baybars destroyed the monastery in 1291. Originally built because the monks were not allowed to live in Elijah's Cave, the beautiful monastery, which stands on a promontory over Haifa bay, seems a more than reasonable replacement. The monks currently live in a relatively new church and monastery complex called Stella Maris (Star of the Sea), built in 1836 on the ruins of an ancient Byzantine chapel and a medieval Greek church. The inside of the chapel is crafted from marble, and its dome is crowned by paintings of Elijah flying heavenward in a chariot of fire, King David plucking a harp, the prophets Isaiah, Ezekiel, and Daniel, and scenes of the Holy Family. The exquisite statue of the Virgin Mary cradling the baby Jesus stands above a small cave where tradition says that Elijah's midsummer prayer for rain was answered. The monastery's small museum contains finds from the Byzantine and Crusader settlements on Mt. Carmel, including toes from a large statue of Jupiter that once stood on an altar on the mount. Because of the Carmelites' affinity for Elijah (St. Elias), the Feast of St. Elias (July 20) is a great time to visit. In the days preceding the Feast, Christian Arabs set up booths with food and games, and a carnival atmosphere takes over the complex. Knees and shoulders must be covered. *(Buses #25, 26, 30 and 31 climb Mt. Carmel to the monastery; get off at to the Seminar Gordon stop. A more expensive and scenic way to get to the monastery is via the Rakbal cable car from Bat Galim; see p. 177. ☎833 77 58. Open daily 6am-1:30pm and 3-6pm.)*

MEDITERRANEAN COAST

ELIJAH'S CAVE. Judaism, Christianity, and Islam all revere these grounds as sacred and even magical. According to the Bible, the caves at the base of Mt. Carmel sheltered Elijah from the wrath of the evil King Ahab and Queen Jezebel. They were more than a bit peeved at the prophet's drastic attempt to win the hearts of northern Israelites from Ba'al in the 9th century BCE when he brought down a heavenly fire to consume his sacrifices and then slaughtered the 450 priests of Ba'al (I Kings 18). Muslims revere Elijah as al-Khadar, the "green prophet" of the same-colored mountains, Jews believe he will return as the harbinger of the Messiah, and Christians hold that the caves safeguarded the Holy Family upon their return from Egypt. Adherents of each religion now pray quietly in the dim light. Modest dress is required, and there is no eating or drinking inside the cave. The religious (and not so religious) worshipers offering their blessings for you expect pocket change in return. *(230 Allenby St. The stairs leading to the cave's entrance are just across the street from the National Maritime museum, but construction may force you to go around to the left as you face the cave. Just across from the monastery entrance, an inconspicuous trail leads 1km down the Stella Maris ridge to the shrine at Elijah's Cave; do not attempt in sandals. ☎852 74 30. Cave open Su-Th 8am-5pm, F 8:30am-12:45pm. Free.)*

TECHNION. Real nerds can check out the Technion, Israel's internationally acclaimed institute of technology. The Coler Visitors Center has English-language newsletters and computerized displays describing the institution's history and achievements from its inception in 1913 to the present. *(Take bus #17 or 19 from downtown, Hadar, or central bus stations or 31 from Carmel Center to Kiryat Ha-Technion. ☎832 06 68 or 832 06 64. Open Su-Th 8am-2pm. Free.)*

OTHER SIGHTS. Various lookouts throughout the city provide breathtaking, panoramic views. Most accessible is the breezy **Louis Promenade,** next to the Dan Panorama Hotel on Yefeh Nof St. in Carmel Center. It commands stunning views of the port as well as the Upper Galilee, Lebanon, and even snowy Mt. Ḥermon on clear days. The observatory on the 30th floor of Haifa University's **Eshkol Tower** stretches farther up into the clouds, and, accordingly, offers broader but hazier views. *(Open Su-Th 8am-3pm. Free.)* The tower itself crowns the vast, flat main building that serves as the center of student activities. After hours, go all the way to the edge of the huge slab at the foot of the tower (above the bus stops) for less expansive views of the city below. The rest of the concrete campus is hardly remarkable, but it boasts a larger percentage of Arab students than any of Israel's other universities. *(Buses #24, 36, and 31 run to the university, a 30-minute trip from Carmel Center. Free student-guided tours Su-Th 10am-noon, starting from the main building.)*

MUSEUMS

HAIFA MUSEUM

The museum consists of 3 separately located buildings, each on a different level of the city. All are open M, W, and Th 10am-5pm, Tu 10am-2pm and 5-8pm, F 10am-1pm, and Sa 10am-2pm. A ticket admits the bearer to all three museums for three days in a row. Adult NIS22, children under 18 and students NIS16, seniors NIS11.

MUSEUM OF ART. This avant-garde collection ranges from simplistic blank canvases to downright wacky shoebox architecture. The museum has a small permanent collection but prides itself on its ever-changing, multi-national exhibits. *(26 Shabtai Levi St. in the Hadar district. Take bus #10, 12, 21, or 28. ☎852 32 55.)*

TIKOTIN OF JAPANESE ART. The Japanese tradition of displaying beautiful objects in harmony with the season has been embraced by this branch of the Haifa Museum. *Shoji*, sliding partitions made of wood and paper, soften the sunlight and make for delightful browsing. *(89 Ha-Nassi Blvd, in Carmel Center, between the Nof Hotel and the Dan Carmel Hotel. Take bus #3, 5, 21-23, 28, or Gan Ha-Eim Carmelit; ☎838 35 54.)*

NATIONAL MARITIME MUSEUM. The lowest branch of the Haifa Museum (in altitude, not quality). Chronicles 5000 years of maritime history. The intricately detailed ship models, the marine mythology collection, and the Department of Marine Ethnology have the most appeal for the average landlubber. *(198 Allenby Rd., opposite Elijah's Cave; bus #3, 5, 44, 45. ☎853 66 22.)*

OTHER MUSEUMS

REUBEN AND EDITH HECHT MUSEUM. This museum houses a permanent exhibit called *The People of Israel in the Land of Israel*, a magnificent collection of archaeological finds from university excavations across the country, as well as changing exhibits in its new wings. The small art wing contains Hecht's personal collection of Impressionist paintings and a few others from the Jewish School of Paris. *(On the 1st floor in the main building of Haifa University. ☎825 77 73 or 824 05 77. Open Su-M and W-Th 10am-4pm, Tu 10am-7pm, F 10am-1pm, Sa 10am-2pm. Call for tour info. Free.)*

MA'AGAN MIKHEAL SHIP PROJECT. The main exhibit for the next several years is the reconstruction of an amazingly preserved Phoenician ship from 500BCE. It was found off the coast of Caesarea, which didn't even have a port in 500BCE. *(Within the Hecht museum, but affiliated with Haifa University. Hours and information number the same as the Hecht museum.)*

CLANDESTINE IMMIGRATION AND NAVAL MUSEUM. Devoted to *Ha-Apala*, the story of European Jewish immigrants smuggled into Palestine during the British mandate (see p. 12). The museum showcases impressive displays on Jewish underground movements and a recreation of a Cyprus deportation camp. Perched atop the museum is the *Af-Al-Pi-Khen* (In Spite Of Everything), a ship that once ran the British blockade in the 1940s. *(204 Allenby Rd., next to the National Maritime Museum and opposite the lower cable car station; bus #3, 5, 43 or 44. ☎853 62 49. Open Su-Th 9am-4pm. NIS10, children and students NIS5, free for soldiers from any country.)*

MANÉ KATZ ART MUSEUM. While the museum usually displays sculptures and canvases by Mané Katz, a member of the Paris group of Jewish Expressionists that included Modigliani, Chagall, and Cremegne, it packs everything up in storage a few times a year for special exhibits of contemporary Israeli artists. *(89 Yefe Nof St., just behind Panorama Center. ☎838 34 82. Bus #21, 22, 23, or 28, or Gan Ha-Eim Carmelit. Open Su-M and W-Th 10am-4pm, Tu 2-6pm, F 10am-1pm, Sa 10am-2pm. Free, except during special exhibits when the price ranges between NIS10-25.)*

NATIONAL MUSEUM OF SCIENCE, PLANNING, AND TECHNOLOGY. Housed in the old Technion building, this museum boasts over 200 hands-on stations demonstrating technologies from telecommunications to architecture. Reclaim your childhood in the funhouse-like Mirrors & Optics Hall and repent for slacking off in high school in the Chemistry Exhibition lab. *(One block up from Herzl St., accessible from either Balfour St. or Shmaryahu Levin St. Bus #12, 21, 28, or 37 or Ha-Nevi'im Carmelit and walk right one block along Herzl St. to Shmaryahu Levin St. ☎862 81 11. Open Su-M and W-Th 9am-6pm, Tu 9am-7pm, F 10am-3pm, Sa 10am-5pm. NIS25, students NIS15, seniors NIS12.)*

MUSEUMS AT THE ZOO. These mediocre museums are worth a quick look only if you're already at the zoo (see p. 182). *(Prehistory open Su-Th 9am-3:45pm, F 8:30am-1pm, Sa 10am-2pm. Others open the same hours as the zoo. Zoo includes all museums: NIS20, students NIS18.)*

BEACHES AND ENTERTAINMENT

The beaches surrounding Haifa may not be as large as Tel Aviv's or as beautiful as Netanya's, but they're still a great place to sun-worship or take a see-and-be-seen stroll. Although free beaches sprawl all along the northern coast, the best lie just outside of the city in **Dor** (see p. 189) and **Atlit,** both accessible by bus #921. Within Haifa, **Ḥof Ha-Carmel** and **Ḥof Dado** are most pleasant (bus #43, 44 or 45; 15 min.). Hordes of Israelis pour down to these beaches on Friday and Saturday afternoons to play *matkot* (paddleball) and people-watch on the promenade; in summer, the bikini-clad and the men who love them hang out long after sunset. Near the central bus station **Ḥof Bat Galim** (bus #41, 42) has a more sedate promenade. On Tuesday evenings in summer, folk dancers kick it up at both promenades. **Ḥof Ha-Shaket** (Quiet Beach), is a true-to-name, separate-sex beach. (Women: Su, Tu, Th; men M, W, F; co-ed Sa.) Lifeguards work from 8am-6pm at each of the beaches.

During Pesach, the Municipal Theater puts on a number of Children's Plays at the Cultural Center in Carmel (information and tickets ☎860 05 00). In December, weekend nights bring concerts and small carnivals to Wadi Nisnas for the Feast of the Feasts. Free concerts (usually classical, but occasionally modern pop or religious) at the amphitheater in Gan Ha-Eim park (in summer W 6pm, Sa 9pm).

In the beginning of July, the nearby town of Carmiel fills with people coming to see the **Israeli Music and Dance Festival.** Carmiel is normally accessible from Haifa by buses #261 262, 361 and 501 (every 20-45min., NIS18), and Egged provides extra transportation during the festival. The artsy **Cinematheque,** 142 Ha-Nassi Blvd. (☎835 35 30), is next to the Cultural Center, a few blocks up from the Carmelit station, just after Ha-Nassi curves right. This theater shows cult classics, new Israeli films, *film noir,* and the latest American fare. (Su-Th shows at 7, 9:30pm and occasionally 5pm; F shows at 2 and 10pm; Sa shows at 5, 7 and 9:30pm. NIS27).

NIGHTLIFE

When asked about the sparse entertainment, Haifa's first mayor pointed to the factories and said, "There is our nightlife." Although today's Haifa is not exactly a bastion of Bacchanalia, times have changed since that sobering statement. Each terrace of the city specializes in one form of evening revelry. Downtown hosts the most popular dance floors around Ha-Atzma'ut St. These discotheques heat up on Thursday and Friday and shut down on Saturdays. Dress codes run from casual to nonexistent. While the Nordau *midraḥov* in Hadar may once have been the place for long evenings of *café au lait,* the current cafe gold mine resides on Masada and Hillel St., near the Masada Carmelit stop. As middle ground, Hadar is home to a couple good bars and the city's oldest dance club. Carmel Center has enough diversity of pubs to please both sophisticates and brewsky-swilling sailors.

PUBS

The Bear, 135 Ha-Nassi Blvd. (☎838 17 03), on the corner of Ha-Nassi and Wedgewood Ave., a few blocks up from the Carmel Center Carmelit stop. Everything seems sexier (even before the 4th beer) in this mellow, candlelit bar. Pleases the upper twenty-something crowd with indoor and outdoor seating and a monstrously large alcohol menu (beer NIS15-22; cocktails NIS27). Open daily 6pm-3am.

Little Haifa, 4 Sha'ar Ha-Levanon St. (☎838 16 58), between Ha-Nassi and Yefe Nof St., a block down from Gan Ha-Eim park. The oldest pub in the area, with a raucous decibel level matching its age. Drunk American sailors sing about home. Beer NIS10-12. Open M-Sa from 8:30pm until the ship leaves port.

Ha-Olam Hazeh (☎864 20 75), hidden away in a tiny nook on Ḥaim St. between Herzl St. and the Nordau *midraḥov*, right next to the Nor-Em Internet Cafe and B&B. This itsy-bitsy bar in Hadar teems with locals and hostel-dwellers alike on weekends and chills out with cocktails (NIS18-24) and tasty toasts (NIS22) on laid-back weeknights. Open daily 9pm-3:30am.

Camel Café, down the coast at Ḥof Ha-Carmel. Almost every customer has a delicious fruit shake (NIS18, with alcohol NIS27) and a navel ring. Skinny dipping is rumored to occur. Beer NIS15-21. Open daily 8am-sunrise.

CLUBS

Ḥurva (☎862 12 65), on Qedoshe Baghdad St. off Ha-Atzma'ut St. Probably best to take a cab. A veritable carnival of a club, Hurva offers one dance floor with alternative and Euro-techno downstairs and another one on the roof with MTV standards. Henna tattoos (NIS18). Beer NIS10-13, cocktails NIS18. Th 21+, F 18+. No dress code. Cover NIS30, students with ID NIS25. Open Th-F from 12:15am.

City Hall (☎862 88 02), on Shabtai Levi St., which Herzl turns into after crossing Ha Nevi'im St. Recently relocated from downtown to Hadar, this Ḥaifan institution opened its doors in the 80s, and its DJ has yet to leave the decade. Beer NIS12-15, free on Th. F men 23+, women 21+. No dress code. Beer NIS12-15. Open Th-Sa until the dancers collapse. Cover Th-F NIS40, Sa NIS35.

CAFES

Greg's, 3 Hayam St. (☎837 16 20), off Ha-Nassi Blvd. Ex-New Yorker Greg serves pricey but delicious coffee and steaming variations thereof (NIS8.50-22). A great place to stumble into after a long night. Open 24hr.

Martef 10, 142 Ha-Nassi Blvd. (☎824 07 62), enter around the back of the Rothschild Cultural Center which is next to the Cinemathèque. Prime stomping grounds for university students and intelligentsia-bent tourists. Local musicians wail late into the night on Fridays; poetry readings, debates, and lectures (in Hebrew) other nights from Nov.-June. Coffee NIS5, beer NIS12. Cover for music NIS35-40, other nights NIS25. Opens 8pm.

DAYTRIP FROM HAIFA

KIBBUTZ MA'AGAN MIKHA'EL AND TEL MEVORAḤ

To get to the aqueducts, take bus #921 from Ḥadera (20min., every 30min., NIS10) and ask the driver to let you off at the Moshav Beit Ḥananya. To get to the kibbutz, get off at the Ma'agan Mikha'el intersection. Walk 1½km down the road, cross a small bridge to the entrance of the kibbutz. The main office and nature reserve are 1km past the entrance.

North of Moshav Beit Ḥananya, excavations are in progress at **Tel Mevoraḥ**, where several important Roman artifacts have been unearthed. Two of the marble sarcophagi discovered in the ruins of a Roman mausoleum are on display in the Rockefeller Museum in Jerusalem (see p. 132).

Kibbutz Ma'agan Mikha'el (☎(06) 639 41 11), one of Israel's largest, most successful kibbutzim, is home to the National Preservation Society's **Nature Reserve,** renowned for the diversity of birds that flock to its frogponds. Reservations must be made in advance and are mostly for groups (☎(06) 639 41 66). Anyone, however, can stroll around the kibbutz's **Crocodile River and Roman Bridge,** a light, fun hike.

NEAR HAIFA

ZIKHRON YA'AKOV זיכרון יעקב ☎06

In 1882, 100 Romanians settled in Zikhron Ya'akov in response to the call of "the House of Jacob" (a.k.a. the Rothschilds) to rise up, settle Eretz Yisrael, and make it flourish as in Biblical days. Today, Zikhron sprawls happily among forested hills on swamplands drained with the generous financial assistance of Baron Edmond de Rothschild. A recent restoration of the cobblestone roads, red-roof villas and antique building facades has made Zikhron the latest suburban hotspot; third-generation descendants of the first Aliyah (meaning a permanent return to Israel) now live side-by-side with yuppies from the high-tech industries of nearby cities. Zikhron Ya'akov is best visited as a day trip from Haifa, since all the accommodations are overwhelmingly pricey.

ORIENTATION AND PRACTICAL INFORMATION

The **tourist office,** the white building behind the station, offers maps, brochures, and information about city events. (☎639 88 92; fax 639 24 22. Open Su-Th 9am-1pm, F 9am-1pm). To the right of the central bus station, two blocks past the concrete arches, is the newly renovated, cobblestone section of **Ha-Meyasdim Street** (also called Wine Road). Most of the sights are along this strip, as are a number of restaurants and art galleries. Budget travelers migrate to the falafel stands (NIS9) and the **supermarket** (open Su-Th 6:30am-8pm, F 6:30am-3pm) at the bottom of the hill, where the cobblestones end. On Fridays, the last bus out of town may be as early as 3:30pm. Bus #872 from Tel Aviv (2hr., every 30min., NIS22.50) and bus #202 from Haifa (40min., every hr., NIS17.30) stop at the small **central bus station.**

SIGHTS AND ENTERTAINMENT

CARMEL WINERY. Zikhron Ya'akov is best known for the Carmel Mizraḥi Winery, founded 118 years ago by the Baron himself. The winery now produces a significant share of Israel's domestic wine as well as a large stock for export. The one-hour tour includes a look at the old wine cellars, an audio-visual presentation, wine tasting, and a souvenir bottle. It's best to visit from August to November, the harvest season. *(☎629 09 77. Turn right from the central bus station onto Ha-Meyasdim St., continue downhill for a few blocks, and turn right onto Ha-Nadiv St. where the cobblestone ends. The winery is at the bottom of the hill, past the post office. Open Su-Th 8:30am-3:30pm, F 9am-1pm. NIS13, students NIS11, children NIS10. Call ahead for tours in English.)*

BEIT AHARANSON MUSEUM. The Beit Aharonson House Museum shows off the former digs of a town resident who set up a spy network to assist the British against the Turks during World War I. The intriguing tour (available in English) tells the story of Sarah Aharonson, who committed suicide in the house (see the nook where she had hidden the gun and the bed where she lay afterwards) rather than being taken by the Turks for torture and death. *(40 Ha-Meyasdim St., ☎639 01 20. Open Su-M 8:30am-3pm, Tu 8:30am-4pm, W-Th 8:30am-3pm, F 8:30am-1pm. Admission and tour NIS12, students NIS10, seniors NIS6.)*

FIRST ALIYAH MUSEUM. The First Aliyah Museum presents an exciting, if melodramatic, film reenactment of the first wave of Zionism, during which Zikhron Ya'akov was founded. *(☎629 47 47. Turn left on Ha-Nadiv St. from Ha-Meyasdim St. when the cobblestone ends; the museum is directly after the synagogue.Open Su-M 9am-4pm, Tu 9am-7pm, W-Th 9am-4pm, F 9am-1pm, Sa 10am-2pm. NIS15, seniors NIS12.)*

OTHER SIGHTS. Other sites of interest include the beautiful **Ohel Ya'akov Synagogue,** erected in 1886 (at the junction of Ha-Meyasdim and Ha-Nadiv St.). Just outside the city limits lies **Ramat Ha-Nadiv,** the Rothschild Family tomb and gardens. In his will, Baron Edmond de Rothschild asked that he "be buried in the rock of the land of Israel," and in 1950, his remains and those of his wife were placed here. *Sherut* taxis from the bus station on their way to Binyamina will stop on the far side of the park at the side road leading to the estate (NIS5). Resplendent views of the valley below enliven the remaining 15- to 20-minute walk. The cafe outside the gardens provides trail maps of the surrounding area, including a map to a natural spring. (Open Su-Th 8:30am-4pm, F 8:30am-2pm; crypt closed on Sa and holidays. Free.) The **Baron's Winery** (☎638 04 34), in Ramat Ha-Nadiv, is down the hill from the entrance to the tomb. The small winery gives tours and free wine-tasting for groups, but call ahead to tag along (NIS15; open Su-F 8am-4pm).

DOR דור ☎04

TEL DOR. The pristine **beach** at Dor is protected by four small, rocky islands. Each has a bird sanctuary, and all can be explored at low tide. The Tel Dor archaeological site is on the hill to the right as you face the sea, just past the Kibbutz Nachsolim beach; footwear is recommended. The site includes temples dedicated to Zeus and Astarte, as well as the ruins of a Byzantine church. Facing the sea, you can see Atlit on the right, Caesarea (or at least its power-generating towers) to the left, and Zikhron Ya'akov and the Arab village of Faradis on the hills behind you. *(☎639 09 22. Take bus #921 from either Haifa (30min., every 30min., NIS12) or Tel Aviv (2hr., every 30min., NIS22.50) or bus #202 from Zikhron Ya'akov (20min., every 1½ hrs., NIS8.50). After getting off at the Kibbutz Dor intersection, it's a 4km walk on a well-trafficked road past banana fields to the beach. Many people hitch rides from kibbutzniks going down this road. Open Sa-Th 7am-5pm, F 7am-4pm. NIS15, children NIS10.)*

HAMIZGAGA MUSEUM. Next to the beach, within the boundaries of **Kibbutz Naḥsholim,** the **Center of Nautical and Regional Archaeology,** also known as Hamizgaga Museum, displays objects found at Tel Dor and underwater archaeological treasures retrieved by the center's diving team. Exhibits include 4000-year-old anchors and sea-shell encrusted muskets thrown overboard by Napoleon's troops as they retreated from Acre. *(CONRAD; ☎639 09 50. Open Su-F, Sa, and holidays 10:30am-3pm. Admission and English film NIS10, students and seniors NIS7.)*

NATURE RESERVE. A few kilometers north, next to **Kibbutz Ein Karmel,** is the Naḥal Me'arot Nature Reserve, with prehistoric caves inhabited some 200,000 years ago. These caves are the only evidence in the world of Neanderthals and Cro-Magnons living simultaneously. Experienced guides explain the significance of the caves and can recommend or lead longer hikes in the surrounding area. English tours and film available. *(☎984 17 50 or 52. Bus #921 goes to the site from Haifa (20min., every 30min., NIS10) and from Tel Aviv (2hr., every 30min., NIS23.20). Get off at Ein Carmel Junction and walk a few minutes south along the road until you see a sign indicating the Nature Reserve. A few hundred meters east of the main road is the entrance to the caves. Open Su-Th 8:30am-4pm, F 8:30am-3pm. NIS18, under 18 NIS9.)*

BEIT SHE'ARIM בית שערים ☎04

Nineteen centuries ago, Beit She'arim functioned as the center of Jewish life, as evidenced by the subterranean graveyard that houses the rich and famous of ancient Israel. Following the Romans' destruction of Jerusalem in 70 CE, Judaism's hub shifted to the Galilee, and Beit She'arim became a prominent Jewish city. It once served as the gathering place for the Sanhedrin, which the Roman Empire recognized in the 2nd century CE as the Supreme Rabbinical Council and judicial authority over all of the world's Jews. Two hundred years later, when Jews were barred from Jerusalem's Mount of Olives cemetery, Beit She'arim became the site of a sacred Jewish burial ground. The flourishing city was burned down in 351 CE by the emperor Galus as part of his attempt to quash a Jewish rebellion. Since 1936, archaeologists have unearthed a labyrinth of some 20 caves, the walls of which are lined with dozens of intricately adorned sarcophagi. According to inscriptions found on the sarcophagi, many of the buried were brought from as far away as Sidon, Tyre, Babylon, or Southern Arabia. Rabbi Yehuda Ha-Nassi, patriarch of the Sanhedrin, compiled the *Mishnah* in Beit She'arim (see **Literature,** p. 31) and is among those buried in the catacombs. *(☎983 16 43. Open daily Apr.-Sept. 8am-5pm, Oct.-Mar. 8am-4pm. NIS14, children NIS6.)*

GETTING THERE. Transportation to the site goes only to the access road. Many buses from Haifa go near Beit She'arim, but buses #301 and 338 (20min., every 20min., NIS11.50) are the most convenient. Ask the driver to stop at the Beit She'arim archaeological site, not the *moshav*. From the bus stop, go to the far side of the grass circle and continue down Izrael St. After a 20min. walk, turn right at the T-intersection and then right again at the fork. Continue past the unimpressive ruins of an ancient synagogue and olive press as well as the steep road uphill on the left (which leads to a statue of the first modern Jewish settler of the region, the foundations of an ancient basilica, and a breathtaking view). Continue down the road as it hooks right to reach the entrance to the catacombs.

EIN HOD עין הוד ☎04

Though perched on the western slopes of Mt. Carmel, 14 kilometers south of Haifa, Ein Hod ("Spring of Grandeur") seems to reside in its own surrealist universe. Tin soldiers stand guard along winding, nameless streets, funky mobiles swing between trees, and bronze nudes recline lazily against fences in this small artists' colony. Established in 1953 by Marcel Janco (one of the founders of Dadaism), Ein Hod functions as a co-operative with about 90 members whose talents range from glass-blowing to needlework.

DADA BING, DADA BOOM Dadaism was an artistic movement founded in the 1920s that sought to undermine established society through satire, parody, and non-sequiturs. According to Hans Arp, cofounder of the Dada movement of Zurich, Dadaists "were seeking an art that would heal mankind from the madness of the ages." What they found was a style of cabaret performance that included simultaneous poetry reading, feeding a stuffed teddy bear fluffy meringues, and actors shouting, "We demand the right to piss on you in a variety of colors."

GETTING THERE. To get to Ein Hod, take bus #921 from Haifa, which heads south along the old Haifa-Ḥadera road (20min., every 30min., NIS10). From the junction where the bus stops, the town is a 2km walk uphill, but the magnificent view compensates. To get to the center of town, turn right at the colorful sign and then right again at the fork.

SIGHTS. The **Main Artists' Gallery** (☎984 25 48), one of the largest galleries in Israel, displays the work of resident artists. The fantastic exhibits change every four or five months. (Open Sa-Th 9:30am-5pm, F 9:30am-4pm. Free.) The **Janco-Dada Museum** (☎984 23 50) features paintings and *objets d'art* by contemporary Israeli Dadaist artists, a permanent display of Janco's work, a constantly changing exhibit introducing a new artist in the village, and a hilarious and informative film entitled "Excuse Me, What is Dada?" that outlines the origins of the Dada movement. (Open Sa-Th 9:30am-5pm, F 9:30am-2pm; NIS10, students NIS5.) In addition to the main gallery and the museum, residents have their own studios and shops throughout the village which are fun to browse around for window-shopping or chatting with the artist.

On Fridays during the summer, local musicians give evening concerts and comedians occasionally do stand-up in the small **amphitheater** in the center of town (info ☎984 20 29 or check local newspapers for listings, NIS20-60). No transportation is available after the shows, but locals insist that hitchhiking from Ein Hod to the main road is relatively safe. Turn left after the museums and branch off left again to ascend the blue-railed steps to the amphitheater. The small **Middle Eastern food stand** in the amphitheater offers cheap food, including the best salads (NIS13-20) and hummus around (M-Sa 10am-4pm, sometimes open in the evenings when there are shows). The house of Gertrude Kraus, a dance-artist who has strongly influenced most of Israel's dancers, now contains archives of Ein Hod's history, a collection of Kraus's work, and dance workshops. On one Saturday night a month, usually the first, **Beit Gertrude** holds chamber music concerts (NIS25). It's opposite from the Main Gallery, up the stairs on the left of the ritzy restaurant.

Workshops in glass-blowing, pottery, and other crafts are offered on Saturdays at which time no buses run and only residents can park their cars in the village (visitors park in the lot up the hill). The numerous "Pottery" signs lead to **Naomi and Zeev's Pottery Studio** (☎984 11 07), which offers 45-minute workshops in wheel-throwing for adults and hand-building for children. (Workshops offered Sa 10am until dark; NIS30, children NIS15; 50% off for *Let's Go* readers.). They also sell a wide variety of ceramics, including a large selection of clay whistles (NIS15-150). (Open 24hr. Just ring the bell outside for service anytime.) **Alex Arbell** gives glass-blowing demonstrations and holds a lottery for the resulting glass creatures (☎984 11 05. Tickets NIS6; must arrange in advance). He also rents out a beautiful unit with A/C, bath, and equipped kitchen (single NIS240/US$60, double NIS280/US$70, child NIS100/US$25). Discounts for longer stays and increased rates on weekends and holidays (varying NIS20-NIS70). Many of the other artists in the village offer demonstrations; ask any of the gracious inhabitants of Ein Hod.

ISFIYA AND DALIYAT AL-KARMEL ☎04

Isfiya and Daliyat al-Karmel are all that remain of 14 Druze villages that once prospered on the Carmel. In 1830, the Egyptian *pasha* crushed a rebellion and then destroyed the area's villages. Thirty years later, the Turks welcomed Druze back to Isfiya and Daliyat, hoping that the towns would serve as buffers against Bedouin marauders and Christian missionaries. Today, some 17,000 Druze make their homes here. Religious Druze elders sport thick mustaches, baggy pants, and flowing white headdresses. Observant Druze women wear dark robes and long white shawls (for more information see **The Druze,** p. 24). A large portion of the population, however, is secular. Unlike those residing in the Golan Heights, the Druze of the Carmel acknowledge their Israeli citizenship, and young men enlist in the army. Although Daliyat is by far the more touristed and interesting of the Druze villages, a visit to Isfiya provides more authenticity regarding Druze daily life and accommodations.

GETTING THERE

The Druze villages can be visited as a day trip from Haifa. Bus #22 (40min., departs infrequently 1-4:35pm, NIS5) leaves from the central bus station, stops in Isfiya, and then continues along the main road to Daliyat. The best option is to take a *sherut;* they leave from Kikkar Paris off Ha-Atzma'ut St. (to Isfiya NIS11, to Daliyat NIS12) and return from the Egged bus stops in Isfiya (across the street from the Stella Hospice) and Daliyat (at the top of the shuk). It is also possible to catch a bus or *sherut* to or from the University of Haifa. The last bus leaves Daliyat at 2:10pm, but *sherut* taxis run until 5pm, when stores close.

MEDITERRANEAN COAST

ACCOMMODATIONS

Isfiya's only accommodation is the heavenly **Stella Carmel Hospice,** 18 Abu Kish St. (☎04 839 16 92; fax 839 02 33; email stcarmel@netvision.net.il). A small, tree-shaded sign marks the hostel, which perches atop the hill on the side of the road opposite the PAZ gas station. Though run by the Anglican Church, it's open to all. A converted Arab villa, the hospice has a small, quiet library and a lounge covered in antique Persian rugs. The pleasant volunteer staff complements the serenely quiet atmosphere and provides free trail maps to the surrounding Carmel forest reserve. Hearty breakfast included. Doors locked at 10:30pm but keys are available for later return. Check-out 11am. Reservations one month in advance are recommended, but rooms sometimes available on shorter notice. (3-4 bed single-sex dorm NIS60/US$15; doubles with bath NIS275/US$65.)

SIGHTS

The scenic mountain road to the Druze villages inspires even the most agoraphobic of travelers to explore the outdoors. The inviting ridges and forests of the **Carmel Mountains** spread dramatically into the Yizre'el valley to the southeast and the Mediterranean to the west. SPNI has detailed trail maps, but ideal picnic spots are often just a few steps from the main road (see **Haifa, Practical Information,** p. 178). Down the road from the hospice, **Wadi Chiq** has well-marked forest trails.

SHUK. Tourists come to **Daliyat al-Karmel** to shop in the small *shuk* on the main road. The bazaar is busiest on Saturdays, but weekdays make for low prices and better conversation with locals. The recent surge of tourism has raised the kitsch factor; souvenir shops have taken over most of the bazaar. With rare exception, each store sells the same selection of enamel pottery, water pipes, wooden camels, jewelry, and wall hangings—much of the merchandise is actually imported from India or made in Gaza. Wheat stalk baskets are one of the few items still made locally. In a back room of the bazaar's **Mifqash Ha-Akhim Restaurant** is the **Druze Heritage House** (☎839 31 69), full of artifacts, photographs, and explanations of all things Druze. Ask the restaurant owner, Sheikh Fadel Nasser ad-Din, to let you take a peek, and feel free to ask questions. The house also hosts groups of 30 or more for lectures about the Druze people followed by tea and baklava (NIS12). Call ahead to ask about joining in.

BEIT OLIPHANT. The Zionist and Christian mystic **Sir Lawrence Oliphant** was one of few outsiders close to the Druze sect. In the late 19th century, he and his wife lived in Daliyat for five years, helping the Druze build their homes. Beit Oliphant now serves as a memorial to the scores of Druze soldiers killed in Israel's wars. A simple but eloquent memorial on the second floor displays the photographs of all the Druze slain in Israeli wars. Sir Lawrence sheltered Arab and Jewish insurgents against the British in a cave between the sculpture garden in the rear and the main house. Oliphant's secretary, the Hebrew poet **Naftali Hertz Imber,** wrote the words to "Ha-Tikva" (The Hope), Israel's national anthem, on the premises. At the far side of the football field, **Kir Ha-shalom** (Hebrew for "the wall of peace"), commemorates the Oslo Peace Accords. (*Turn right at the same end of the bazaar street as Mifqash Ha-Akhim restaurant and continue for 10min. Beit Oliphant is the stone building across from the domed marble sculpture, shortly after the road veers to the right).*

MUHRAQA. Four kilometers from Daliyat al-Karmel is the site where Elijah massacred 450 priests of Ba'al (I Kings 18:40), a weather-god who had enjoyed new popularity because of a harsh drought. **Muhraqa,** the site's Arabic name, refers to the burnt sacrifice that the prophet offered to God on an altar here. Pleased with the Israelites' renewed faith, God sent life-giving rain clouds, which the Carmelites later interpreted as symbols of the Virgin Mary, to whom their order is devoted. In 1886 they built a small **monastery** here. A short flight of stairs leads to magnificent rooftop views; on clear days Mt. Hermon is visible on the horizon. *(There is no bus service to the monastery, so a car or a taxi ride is necessary (NIS20-25 each way). If walking from Daliyat (not advisable), bear left at the only fork along the way. Monastery open M-Sa 8am-1:30pm and 2:30-5pm, Su 8am-1:30pm. Admission to the rooftop viewing area NIS1.)*

MEDITERRANEAN COAST

SOUTH OF HAIFA

NETANYA נתניה ☎09

Netanya celebrates laziness in all its glorious forms—baking on the beach, strolling aimlessly along the Promenade, and sipping coffee and people watching in Ha-Atzma'ut Square. In the 1920s, the town was established itself with a citrus-farm and a few diamond factories in the 1920s, but the tantalizing call of idyllic beaches and the prime location between Tel Aviv and Haifa soon made Netanya one of the most popular hotspots in Israel. In both location and ethos, Netanya leans closer to Tel Aviv; there are even rumors among the locals of mafia infiltration, but crime is far from a glaring problem in this resort town. A significant minority of the tourists hail from landlocked parts of Israel, but there is a decidedly European, especially French, presence in Netanya. Because of the large Russian immigrant population, signs and menus are more often in French and Russian than in English. While the crowd is mostly affluent retirees and families (increasingly more of the latter), students and lone travelers are heartily welcomed into the chilled-out subculture of the young locals.

ORIENTATION AND PRACTICAL INFORMATION

To get to the center of town from the **central bus station** (☎860 62 02), cross the intersection to **Sha'ar Ha-Gai St.** and follow the falafel stands one block to **Herzl St.,** the town's central artery and main shopping area. Turn left and after a few blocks, just past **Dizengoff St.,** Herzl St. empties into the **midraḥov** (pedestrian zone), lined with expensive outdoor cafes and *shawarma* stands. At the end of the *midraḥov* is **Ha-Atzma'ut Sq.** (Independence Sq.), marked by a central fountain, benches and palm trees. Most Netanyans spend their days and nights milling around this area. Stairs to the beach are at the back of the square. Also at the back of the square, on your right as you face the sea, is the entrance to the **Promenade,** a walkway along the cliffs overlooking the sea with an **outdoor amphitheater** and a few playgrounds.

TOURIST AND FINANCIAL SERVICES

Buses: Central bus station, 3 Binyamin Blvd. (☎860 62 02 or 860 62 22), on the corner of Binyamin Blvd. and Ha-Halutzim St. To: **Tel Aviv** (#601 and #605, 1hr., every 15min. 5:40am-10:30pm, NIS13); **Haifa** (#947, 45min., every 30min., NIS21.50); and **Jerusalem** (#947, 1½hr., every 30min., NIS38).

Sheruts: Across the street from the station on Binyamin Blvd. To Tel Aviv NIS11.

Taxis: The main services include **Ha-Shahar** (☎861 44 44), **Ha-Sharon** (☎882 23 23), **Hen** (☎833 33 33), and **Netanya** (☎834 44 43).

Car Rental: Hertz (☎882 88 90), **Avis** (☎833 16 19), and **Eldan** (☎861 69 82) have offices at Ha-Atzma'ut Sq.

Tourist Office: ☎882 72 86. Located at the very back corner of Ha-Atzma'ut Sq., next to the Diamond Center in a tiny brick building with an oddly angled roof. City maps, bus schedules, and event schedules. Many languages spoken. Don't be fooled by the large Foreign Resident and Tourist Center at 15 Herzl St.; it's an investment center. Open Su-Th 8am-6pm (until 4pm in winter), F 9am-noon.

Currency Exchange: Global Change (☎872 47 56; fax 872 47 59), on the left of Ha-Atzma'ut Sq., changes money with no commission. Open Su-Th 8am-7pm, F 8am-1pm. **Bank Ha-Poalim,** on the right as the *midrahov* empties into Ha-Atzma'ut Sq., is open Su-Tu and Th 8:30am-3pm, W 8:30am-1:30pm, and F 8:30am-12:30pm. **Bank Leumi** (☎860 73 33; fax 860 73 29), on the corner of Herzl and Weizmann St., is open Su and Tu-W 8:30am-1pm, M and Th 8:30am-1pm and 4:30-7pm, F 8:30am-noon. No exchange on Sundays. Commission NIS25.

LOCAL SERVICES

Bookstore: Steimatzky Booksellers, 4 Herzl St. (☎861 71 54), on the left of the *midrahov*. Sells books and magazines in Hebrew, English, and a variety of other languages. Open Su-Th 8am-8pm, F 8am-2pm.

Emergency: Magen David Adom First Aid: ☎862 33 33, or 862 33 35. **Police:** ☎860 44 44. **Fire:** ☎862 22 22.

Hospital: Laniado Hospital (☎860 46 66) is the main hospital. From the central bus station, head on Binyamin Blvd. several blocks past Herzl (street will become Sderot Weizmann). Turn left on Rabbi Akiva and right on Divrei Ha-Yamim. The hospital will be on your right.

Telephones: Solan, 8 Ha-Atzma'ut Sq. (☎862 21 31). Private booths for international calls. Fax, telegrams, and cellular phone rental. Open daily 8am-11pm.

Internet Access: Solan, (☎862 21 31) has private AC booths with dial-up connections. 15min. for NIS12/US$3, 30min. for NIS20, 1hr for NIS28. Open daily 8am-11pm. **Pinati Internet Cafe,** 15 Remez St. on the corner of Remez and Smilansky (☎862 46 04). In a small cafe selling ice cream (NIS6) and light meals (NIS19-35). 15min. for NIS8, 30min. for NIS15, 5hr. for NIS100. Open Su-Th 9am-9pm, F 9am-1pm.

Post Office: The central branch, 57 Herzl St. (☎862 15 77), offers **Poste Restante.** Another branch is located at 2 Herzl St. (☎862 77 97). Open Su-Tu and Th 8am-12:30pm and 3:30-6pm, W 8am-1:30pm, F 8am-noon.

ACCOMMODATIONS

A cheap-sleep can be hard to find in Netanya. The hotels, most of which line the beach along Gad Machnes St. and David Ha-Melekh St., are fairly expensive (single NIS240/US$60; doubles NIS300/US$75; add NIS110 for each additional adult). American cash can be used as a bargaining tool, hence prices in dollars don't often jive with standard conversion rates. Reservations are necessary to secure one of the few pleasant and affordable options; call at least two weeks ahead in the summer and a month in August. The most popular areas for **beach-sleeping** are near the cafes and on benches that line the promenade. Since camping on the beach is unsafe, especially for solo women, *Let's Go* does not recommend it.

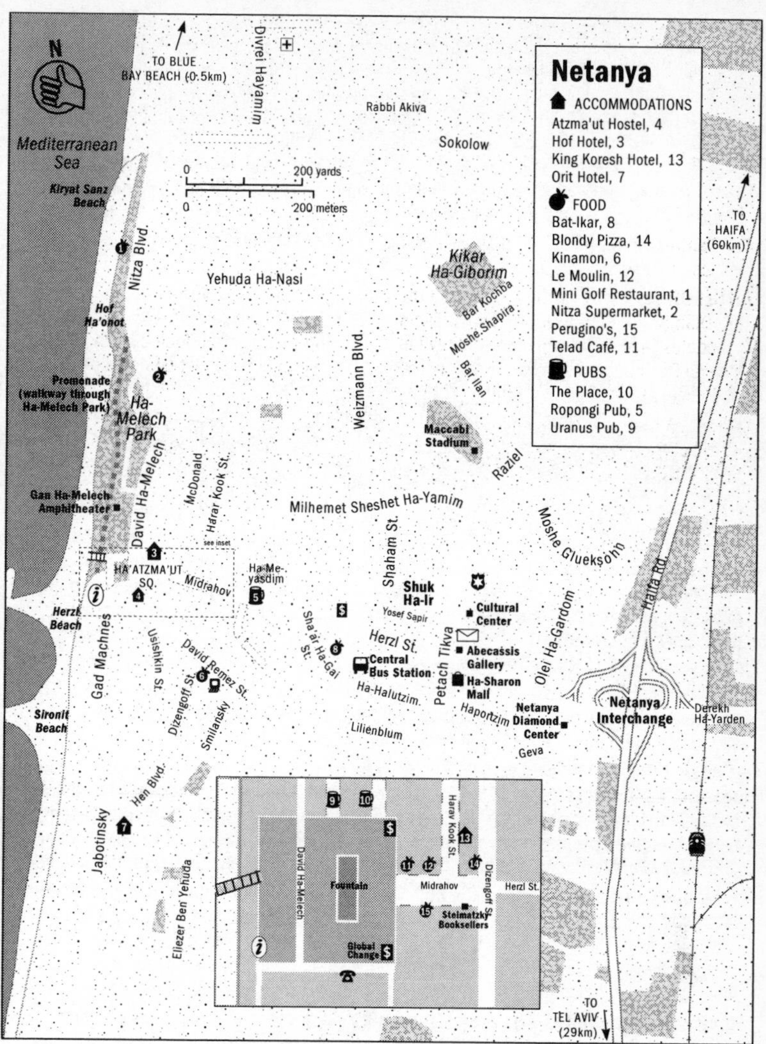

Orit Hotel, 21 Hen Blvd. (☎/fax 861 68 18; email orith@bezenqint.net), off Dizengoff several blocks to the left of Ha-Atzma'ut Sq. This hotel provides a peaceful atmosphere and many perks, including beach towels and a library of Scandinavian and English books. The amiable Swedish management will even pick up guests from the airport (NIS140/US$35). Scrupulously clean rooms, private baths, fans, and balconies. No smoking. Breakfast included. Reception 7am-11pm, but guests can borrow keys to return after it closes. Check-out 10am. Singles NIS170/US$35; doubles NIS240/US$50; each additional bed NIS95/US$20.

Atzma'ut Hostel, 2 Usishkin St (☎862 13 15; fax 882 25 62), at the corner of Ha-Atzma'ut Sq. and Usishkin St., on the left as you walk through the square from the *midrahov*. Within stumbling distance of both the square and the beach. The warm and accommodating owners allow early check-ins if a room is ready and luggage storage if it is not (NIS10). To avoid late night noise, ask for a room that does not overlook the square, preferably one with a view of the sea. A/C, fridges, and private baths in all rooms. Reception 24hrs. Check-out 11am. 6 and 10-bed (coed) dorms NIS50/US$10; singles NIS100/US$20; doubles NIS150/US$30.

MEDITERRANEAN COAST

King Koresh Hotel, 6 Harav Kook St. (☎861 35 55; fax 861 34 34). Turn right on Harav Kook St. just before Ha-Atzma'ut Sq. The princely sum is about as low as hotels in the area get. $5-15 student discount. All rooms have A/C, spic-and-span bathrooms, cable TV. Daily maid service provides fresh towels and linens. Complimentary safe and luggage storage available. Reception 24hr. Check-in and check-out noon. Singles NIS200/US$50; doubles NIS280/US$70; triples NIS350/US$90.

Ḥof Hotel, 9 Ha-Atzma'ut Sq. (☎862 44 22). One of the cheapest of the central hotels. Ḥof is as close to the action (and the noise) as one can get without sleeping on a bench in the square. TV and A/C in all rooms. Singles NIS180/US$45; doubles NIS200/US$50, triples NIS250/$62.50. Discounts for longer stays.

FOOD

Cheap food *is* available in Netanya. During the day, the **Shuk Ha-Ir** (the City Market) one block north of Herzl St. overflows with cheap produce and fresh pastries; Pita and hummus for NIS15 on the beach but prices go down and quality goes up closer to the central bus station. **Sha'ar Ha-Gai St.** is lined with self-service falafel stands where one can stuff just about anything into a pita. Just about any place in the square offers a Sabra breakfast–with two eggs, salad, roll and jam, coffee and juice - for NIS20. The blue-and-white **Telad Cafe,** on the right side of the square, serves particularly magnanimous portions. Stock up at the **Nitza Supermarket,** 8 Nitza Blvd. (☎862 82 16), off David Ha-Melech St.

MEDITERRANEAN COAST

Mini Golf Restaurant and Pub, 21 Nitza Blvd. (☎861 77 35), perches on the edge of a cliff overlooking the sea. Ideal for a lazy lunch or snack, the restaurant serves up inner peace, a great view, and scrumptious stuffed vegetables (NIS18, with pita), but no putt-putt. Closed on Shabbat.

Bat Ikar, 14 Sha'ar Ha-Gai St., across from the bus station, fills the tummies of weary travelers and locals alike, 24-hours a day, except on Shabbat. The house specialty, *sambusa* (delicate bread folded around your choice of stuffings, such as cheese and sauce or potatoes), is substantial enough for a light meal (NIS9-10). Pastries go for NIS1-4, any one of their 102 types of bread NIS1-3.

Kinamon, 13 Remez St. (☎832 25 44), on the corner of Dizengoff St. This candlelit, mellow restaurant serves far more than schnitzel and shishlik. The munchies platter, a heaping basket of stuffed pastries and vegetables, serves 2-3 (NIS33, add pesto for NIS2). Open Su-Th 8:30am-12:30am, F 8:30am-4:30pm and 7:30pm-12:30am, Sa 6:00pm-12:30am.

Le Moulin, 13 Ha-Atzma'ut Sq. (☎862 77 13), on the right side at the end of the *midraḥov*. This creperie adds a little French flair to the standard fare of the square. People-watch from the outside or chill inside with the A/C while noshing on entree crepes of egg, cheese or meat (NIS17-28) or dessert crepes oozing at the seams with chocolate, fruit, or ice-cream (NIS12-25). Open daily 8am-1am, closed for Shabbat.

Perugino's Crem Caffe, 4 Herzl St., on the left side of the *midraḥov*, offers gargantuan cinnamon buns and fritters (NIS6, 8 to sit), dense cream cakes (NIS13,16), and dozens of different cookies (NIS35 for about 40), but the strudel (NIS15 for a slice, NIS30 for the whole loaf) is the thing to get. Open daily in summer 8am-2am; off-season 8am-midnight. Closed on Shabbat.

SIGHTS AND ENTERTAINMENT

BEACHES. Netanya's **beaches** are certainly its *raison d'être.* The stunning Mediterranean coast in Netanya is clean, free, and stretches on for 11km. **Herzl Beach,** the most crowded one, just below Ha-Atzma'ut Sq., has waterslides, playing courts, and surfboards for rent. **Sironit Beach,** just to the left of Herzl as you face the sea, is the only one open year-round; the others are open from May to October. **Kiryat Sanz Beach,** farther north, caters to the religious sunsoakers with separate bathing hours for men and women (men: Su, Tu, Th mornings and M, W, F afternoons; women: M, W, F mornings and Su, Tu, Th afternoons).

FREE ENTERTAINMENT. The Netanya municipality organizes various forms of free entertainment almost every night during the summer and often during the winter. Stop by the tourist office for a complete listing of concerts, movies, and other activities. During the summer, you can watch the sun set over the Mediterranean while listening to classical music in the **Amphitheater** on the Promenade (check the tourist office for times). On Saturdays in summer, folk dance performers in Ha-Atzma'ut Square passionately incite the crowd to come join their revelry. Every Monday at noon, talented Russian musicians give classical concerts at 11 Ha-Atzama'ut Sq. *(☎884 05 34. NIS18, includes food at pre-concert reception.)*

ABECASSIS STUDIO. The art scene in Netanya is limited, but the small Abecassis Studio displays the work of Raphael Abecassis, an internationally acclaimed artist who works in the studio, using brilliant colors and modern design to portray ancient Sephardic themes. (*4 Razi'el St. next to the post office; from the midraḥov, walk 1km along Herzl St. and turn left on Razi'el St. ☎862 35 28. Open Su-Th 10am-1pm and 4-8pm, F 10am-1pm).*

THE RANCH. The ranch offers horseback riding all day and by moonlight and is perfect for families with children. The rides last about an hour and cost NIS80. Call ahead. (*For a small group, a NIS20 taxi to the ranch is both faster and cheaper than taking bus #29. Get off at Blue Bay Hotel if you do take the bus. Open 8am-7pm. Closing time varies depending on business).*

BARS AND PUBS

Uranus Pub, 13 Ha-Atzma'ut Sq. (☎882 99 19), is on the right as you enter Ha-Atzma'ut Sq. from the *midraḥov.* Fashioned after traditional English pubs, Uranus skips the frou-frou and gets back to basics with a wide selection of beer (NIS13-17), straight-up liquor (starting at NIS26), and a laid-back 20-something crowd. Open daily 8pm-5am.

Ropongi Pub, 9 Herzl St. (☎882 92 99), about halfway between the *midraḥov* and Binyamin Blvd., is packed with locals and an international crowd tossing back whatever beer and eating whatever sandwich Ropongi happens to be selling extra cheap that night (both NIS14-19).

The Place (☎844 32 11), down a flight of stairs from 11 Ha-Atzma'ut Sq. attempts to stem the exodus to Tel Aviv dance clubs with a barrage of bouncers, a strictly enforced dress code (no jeans, but spandex and cleavage almost mandatory), and plenty of neon and blacklight. Russian locals groove to international pop music. Those who opt against the steep cover (NIS50) can still hang out in the adjacent bar. Beer NIS14-20, cocktails NIS33-38. Open Th-Sa 10:30pm-6am.

CAESAREA קיסריה ☎06

At the end of the first century BCE, Herod the Great, vassal king of Judaea, established Caesarea Marit-ima (Caesarea of the Sea; Kay-SAHR-ya in Hebrew). In only twelve years, he constructed a resplendent city of innovative architecture, huge entertainment complexes, and a harbor designed to bring his kingdom to the top of the pecking order of eastern Mediterranean ports. The multi-layered ruins—astonishingly resilient despite riots and rebellions, pillage and plunder, and a partial sinking of the coastline—now constitute one of Israel's finest archaeological sites and most popular tourist attractions. Though Caesarea can feel rather like a tour-bus unloading zone, the extent of the excavations and the diversity of previous inhabitants and cultures is remarkable enough to intrigue even the most devout of off-the-beaten-path types.

Right next to the ruins, but miles away from the Kodak-mentality, is Kibbutz Sdot Yam. They haven't ignored the opportunity to profit off their prime location with tourist activities and accommodation offerings. However, a peaceful stroll along shaded and landscaped paths followed by a peek in the small museums and a chat with the delightful curators provides a nice yang to Caesarea's ying.

HISTORY OF CAESAREA

After conquering a small Phoenician harbor called Strato's Tower in the first century BCE, Augustus Caesar granted the land to his vassal king, Herod. Herod returned the favor and named the area Caesarea and its port Sebastos, the Greek version of Augustus. Herod transformed Caesarea and the port dramatically. Innovative architecture and infrastructure and large entertainment facilities for the Great Caesarea games attracted region-wide interest in the city; the harbor, the largest in the eastern Mediterranean and a quick ten-day jaunt from Rome, soon became a major port. After Herod died, the Roman senate put Archelaus, Herod's incompetent son, in charge of the port and its revenues. Within a decade, the Romans disposed of both Archelaus and the vassal-king position; Caesarea became a Roman province and remained the seat of Roman power in Judea until the fall of the Empire. In about 33 CE, Pontius Pilate, the Roman procurator of Caesarea from 26 to 36 CE, ordered the crucifixion of Jesus of Nazareth in Jerusalem. The first evidence of Pilate's existence outside the accounts of the Gospels and the historian Josephus, an inscription on a stone found in the Roman theater, was uncovered here in 1961.

Over the next four centuries, Caesarea, with a population of over 50,000, became the commercial and cultural center of the region. For the first two centuries, this population consisted of mostly pagans, Samaritans, and Jews. Ethnic conflicts expanded with the population. Josephus reports that a dispute over property rights between pagans and Jews led to a riot that left 20,000 Jews dead in 66 CE and ignited the six-year **Jewish Rebellion** (see **The Romans,** p. 9), which resulted in the destruction of Jerusalem's Second Temple in 70 CE. The Romans celebrated Jerusalem's fall by slaughtering thousands of Jews in Caesarea's amphitheater and crowning the commanding general Vespasian as Caesar.

By the third century CE, Caesarea had become a major center for Christianity. The school and library founded by Origen in the late third century drew Christian scholars from around the world. Eusebius, a great Christian sage who was born in Caesarea, declared Christianity the official religion of the empire when he served as Bishop of Caesarea. As Christianity established a stronghold over Caesarea, its intolerance grew. The Samaritans revolted several times in response to oppression and, in 555 CE, burned and destroyed much of the city. In response, the Byzantine Emperor Justinian brutally suppressed the rebels, killing thousands of Samaritans.

The Arab conquest of Palestine in 634 CE came late to Caesarea; the Byzantine navy maintained control of the sea and was able to supply the city for four years. When the Muslims finally conquered Caesarea, it became a major strategic defense against Byzantine naval invasion.

The Crusades brought both glory and destruction to Caesarea—over the course of two centuries, possession of the city changed four times. King Baldwin I took the city in 1101. During the raid of a mosque, his troops discovered a goblet, which was subsequently declared to be the Holy Grail and taken to Genoa. In 1187, however, Caesarea fell to Saladin, who destroyed the church and massacred the city's Christians. When Louis IX of France came to Caesarea in 1251, he ordered the restoration of the city's walls but that wasn't enough to prevent the invasion of Mameluke Sultan Beybars only 14 years later. His successor consigned Caesarea to six centuries of oblivion when he ordered its destruction.

GETTING THERE AND GETTING AROUND

Getting to Caesarea can be difficult. The only practical way is via **Ḥadera,** the nearest town. Buses to Ḥadera are plentiful: From **Tel Aviv** (#852 or 872, 1 hr., NIS17.20; **Netanya** (#706, 35min., every 30min., NIS8.30 or the #921, 1hr., every 40min., NIS17.2); **Haifa** (#945 40min., every 1½hr., NIS17); and **Jerusalem** (#945, 2hr., a few times per day, NIS33). From Ḥadera, however, only bus #76 goes to the ruins (30min., NIS8.30) and travels only a handful of times per day. The bus stops at the

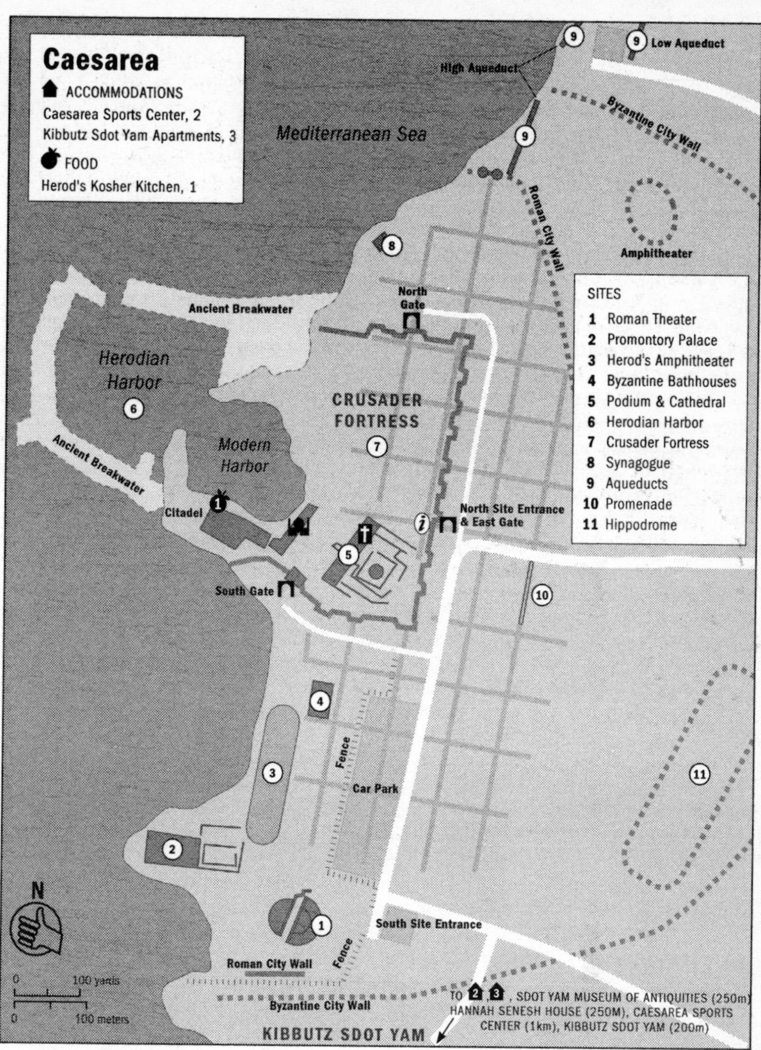

three entrances to the archaeological park: next to the Roman theater, near the eastern gate of the Crusader wall, and just south of the Crusader city wall (this stops upon request only). While it is possible to get a taxi from the station in Ḥadera (NIS30), finding one for the ride back from the ruins requires advance arrangements and costs about NIS10 more.

ACCOMMODATIONS

There are two options for budget accommodations around Caesarea. Friendly, quiet **Kibbutz Sdot Yam** (☎636 44 70 or 44; fax 636 22 11; email kef-yam@sdot-yam.org.il; www.kef-yam.co.il) feels like a ritzy summer camp, in a good way. To get to the reception office, get off bus #76 at the Roman theater. The kibbutz's main gate is on the left of the theatre, right next to the snack bar. Walk about 100 yards behind the tile factory, turn right at the fork in the road just after the tile factory, and follow the signposts to the "Kef Yam" office building at the end of the road. Fifteen private apartments (all with A/C, private bath, refrigerators, TV, and telephones) are ideal for families or for three- to four-person groups, while 6-bed dorms come with bath, TV, linens, and A/C. Reception open daily 7am-5pm but manager can be paged; in winter 7am-4pm. Check-out 10am. Safe available in office. Call at least one week in advance. (6-bed dorms Apr, May, and June, are NIS120/US$30 for one person, NIS80/US$20 for an additional adult and NIS72/US$18 for a child. Prices go up NIS10-20 from July-Oct. and down NIS10-20 from Nov.-Mar. Extra 15% charged on weekends and holidays.)

You never quite know who you'll meet at the **Caesarea Sports Center** (☎636 43 94; fax 636 46 11); the place is often full of volunteer archaeologists from around the world, as well as traveling sports teams. Facing the sea, the center is to the left of Kibbutz Sdot Yam. Walk parallel to the coastline, past the Hannah Senesh House; after passing through the parking lot, the Center is just behind the big brown building. *Let's Go* readers can negotiate with owner Shimshon for use of the sports facilities (yachting, basketball, volleyball, and training center) and for possible discounted bus fares. Rooms with A/C, TV, and private baths: single NIS180/US$45; double NIS320/US$80; quad NIS640/US$160. Hostel-style rooms with no A/C and shared bath are NIS92/US$46. Prices drop up to 50% in winter. Many visitors to Caesarea unroll their sleeping bags on the beach, but **camping** in some places, such as Ḥof Shonit Beach, is forbidden. Since sleeping on the beach is unsafe, *Let's Go* does not recommend it.

FOOD

Restaurant prices in Caesarea are as high as the Crusader walls. Establishments within the ruins (right at the harbor), such as **Herod's Kosher Restaurant** (☎636 11 03) and **Charley's Restaurant** (☎636 30 50), offer great views but mostly standard fare at outrageous prices (schnitzel, shislik, kebab go for NIS40-55). The **Sdot Yam Cafeteria** (☎636 45 14) in the kibbutz offers a taste of kibbutz life and kibbutz food like *ktsitsot*, salads, and mashed potatoes. All-you-can-eat breakfast buffet (NIS23, 7-10am), lunch (NIS38, noon-3pm), and dinner (NIS23, 6:30-8:30pm). Stock up on picnic supplies like fresh produce and other staples at Sdot Yam's mini-market **Markol** in the lower level of the dining hall building. *(☎636 43 58) Open Su, Tu, and Th 11am-1pm and 4-6pm, M and W 11am-1pm. Non-kibbutzniks pay 20% more, cash only.*

SIGHTS

THE ANCIENT CITY

Caesarea's main sights are the Roman city, ancient port, and large Crusader fortress. A map (NIS10) sold at the three entrances to the **Caesarea National Park** provides a good history of Caesarea, and a well-illustrated booklet (NIS17, includes map) explains each well-labeled site. *(Park open Su-Th 8am-5pm, F 8am-4pm; in winter Su-Th 8am-4pm, F 8am-3pm. NIS18, students NIS15. Hold onto your ticket stub!)*

The numbers below that follow the sight names correspond to the numbers on the Caesarea map. As they are ordered, the sights forms a large, rough loop around the park that should take roughly three hours. Visitors seeking the abridged version might want to skip the aqueducts, promenade and Hippodrome.

ROMAN THEATER (1). Constructed by Herod, the theater was designed to bring Hellenistic culture to the city. Though reconstructed numerous times in the first few centuries, remains from Herod's period are still evident, such as the drainage system, the spectators' seats *(cavea)*, and the multi-storied wall behind the stage *(scaena frons)*. The marble floor, on the other hand, covers the original plaster floor designed to look like marble. In the third and fourth centuries, Caesarea's elite flooded the orchestra with water using an intricate series of canals and aqueducts for mock battles and games; but by the sixth century, the tomfoolery got out of hand and the town's religious rulers turned the theatre into a fortress. Restored and reopened in 1961, this 4000-seat structure has hosted Eric Clapton, the Bolshoi Ballet, Joan Baez, and Julio Iglesias (concert schedule ☎636 13 58). The New Israeli Opera performs regularly throughout the summer (opera ticket office ☎03 692 77 77. *The theater is at the southernmost edge of the park, 500m to the left as you face the parking lot from the road from the entrance to the Roman city).*

PROMONTORY PALACE (2). The verdict is still not out on this mysterious structure carved into rock and jutting out into the sea. Although it was not originally believed to be an ornamental fish pond, excavations of four more rooms once decorated with mosaic floors and Herodian-era pottery indicate it may have been the palace of Herod, where he and the town's governors' lived. If this theory and the writings of Josephus Flavius are true, then the Jews of Jerusalem lay here for five days and nights begging Pontius Pilate to remove the images of Caesar he had placed on the Temple Mount.

HEROD'S AMPHITHEATER (3). Adjacent to the Promontory Palace lie the remains of Herod's Amphitheater. Herod originally built this 15,000 sq. meter, 15,000-seat complex as a hippodrome for chariot races and sporting events. According to Josephus, this is where Pontius Pilate announced that images of Caesar be placed on the Temple Mount, despite protest of the Jews lying on his front lawn (i.e. **Promontory Palace**) in protest. He ordered his soldiers to slaughter any Jews who refused his command. When the Jews submitted to impending execution instead of rioting in defiance, Pilate, overcome by their self-sacrifice, sanctioned the removal of the images.

BYZANTINE BATHHOUSES (4). Fed by the city's main aqueduct, Caesarea's bathhouses offered a freshwater change from the salty sea. The baths included a *frigidarium* (cold-water pool) and a *calidarium* (hot-water pool), which was heated by outdoor furnaces.

PODIUM (5). The site of Caesarea's first temple served as a place of worship over the full course of the city's history. Herod built the large podium as a platform for his Temple of Augustus. In the fifth century, Christians converted the temple into a martyrium, which may have been a destination for Christian pilgrimages. Under Arab rule, the podium provided the base of a mosque. In 1101, the Crusaders reconverted the podium into a church.

SEBASTOS—HERODIAN HARBOR (6). Now partially submerged, Herod's port extended along the ancient city to welcome distinguished visitors and merchantmen. Herod originally had high hopes of grand international renown for this port, but remains found on the breakwaters indicate that it was already in decline by the tsunami waves and earthquake of 115 CE. A constant stream of international archaeologists and volunteers continue to excavate not only Caesarea's dry ground, but its buried-in-water treasures.

CRUSADER FORTRESS (7). The walls of this fortress were built by Louis IX during his brief reign. The moat never held any water but its height and slanted bottom *(glacis)* provided defenders a double advantage. Remnants of Christian churches, Arab granaries, and residences are scattered about the area. Don't be surprised to find pieces of marble column used as street pavement—medieval contractors frequently re-used Roman remains when erecting cities.

SYNAGOGUE (8). The synagogue was in use from the Herodian period until the 8th century CE, providing the first evidence of the Jewish community in Caeserea during the Talmudic era. Several important archaeological finds were uncovered in the 1920s, including a Corinthian capital and synagogue oil lamps, both decorated with menorahs, mosaic floors, and a hidden cache of 3700 copper coins.

AQUEDUCTS (9). So far, three of the aqueducts that provided Ceasarea's water have been uncovered; two channeled water into the city from the north (the "high" aqueducts) and one from the south (the "low" aqueduct). The first high aqueduct was fed by the Shuni Springs of Mt. Carmel, northeast of present-day Binyamina and separated from Caesarea by a 400m sandstone ridge. The second aqueduct was built under Emperor Hadrian, and drew on springs east of Shuni. *(The aqueducts are a 1km walk north along the water. Alternatively, the road that runs along the Crusader walls also leads to the Roman aqueducts (and Caesarea's beach), but unless you've got great hiking shoes, not much on your back, and a love of pain, take the road instead of the rocky beach path).*

PROMENADE (10). Although most of the Roman ruins stand within the Crusader walls, several interesting relics lie outside the site proper. Across from the entrance to the Crusader city is an excavated **Byzantine street** and Caesarea's most famous find: colossal **Roman statues** from the second century CE. Kibbutzniks ploughing fields accidentally discovered the two headless figures, one of red porphyry, the other of white marble.

HIPPODROME (11). About 1km along the main road east of the theater stands an archway leading to the ruins of the **Roman Hippodrome** ("Circus"), now overgrown with banana and orange groves cultivated by nearby Kibbutz Sdot Yam. Constructed in the mid-second century CE, the hippodrome replaced Herod's Amphitheatre, which could no longer accommodate the huge population. In its heyday, the 450m by 90m racetrack could hold 30,000 spectators.

MEDITERRANEAN COAST

OTHER SIGHTS

A stroll through the peaceful **Kibbutz Sdot Yam** (see p. 173) provides a good antidote to the feel of the ruins. Shaded paths wind lazily through the well-manicured landscape, past kibbutzniks' cottages and a **playground** constructed from an airplane donated by the Air Force in gratitude for seven kibbutzniks who served about 25 years ago. The two museums in the kibbutz (follow the signs) are small but staffed by knowledgeable and amiable curators.

Most of the relics unearthed at Caesarea are on display at the **Sdot Yam Museum of Caesarea Antiquities** (☎636 43 67). The new archaeological garden and the museum's three rooms contain Jewish, Christian, Samaritan, and Muslim artifacts, Canaanite pottery, 3500-year-old Egyptian urns, and Roman coins and statues. Shield the eyes of any small children from the erotic oil lamps. Next to the museum is the **Hannah Senesh Memorial Centre** (☎636 43 66), built in honor of a Sdot Yam parachutist who died while trying to save Jews from the Nazis during World War II. Admission includes a short film about Senesh's life offered in six different languages. (*Both open Su-Th and Sa 10am-4pm, F and holiday eves 10am-2pm. Each museum NIS10, students and seniors NIS9).*

YOU'D LOSE YOUR HEAD TOO IF IT WEREN'T SCREWED ON Only one statue from the Caesarea ruins has survived the ages with its head intact. The minor sculpture of a court woman is currently in the Archaelogical Garden at Kibbutz Sdot Yam. While it's not surprising that statues would break at vulnerable points like necks and limbs over time, more of the blame resides with a sculpting technique common in the regicide-heavy times of the Roman empire. Sculptors would make one big, muscular body with the traditional leather skirt, mantle, and sash, and leave a groove in the headless neck. Heads, separately carved, could easily be switched when a new ruler came to power.

BEACHES AND ENTERTAINMENT

While the intensely blue water is cool and inviting, **swimming** within the walls of the city is not very economical. (NIS25, NIS19 children). Tickets can be bought at Charley's Restaurant (see p. 174) or at the office inside the crusader fortress walls. Unless you wish to snorkel in the ancient harbor, the free public beach behind the aqueduct is a better place to swim. Diving in the harbor is an expensive but rewarding experience. The **Caesarea Diving Center** (☎/fax 626 58 98) provides full scuba equipment (NIS170 per day), beginner lessons (half-day NIS190/US$50; fullday includes trip to sunken port NIS380/$US100, less for larger groups), and snorkeling gear for NIS58 per day. Those who plan to dive without a guide must bring their license, insurance, and log (open daily 9am-4pm). The **Kef Yam Office** (☎636 44 44) in the kibbutz offers glass-bottomed boat tours of the harbor (NIS32), wild tornado-boat rides off the beach (NIS45), and jeep tours to the Carmel Mountains (NIS520/US$130 for a 2hr. trip with up to 4 people). Reservations are required.

NORTH OF HAIFA

AKKO (ACRE) עכו عكا ☎04

Dominated by the emerald-domed, 18th-century **Mosque of al-Jazzar,** the Old City of Akko (*Akka* in Arabic, historically written "Acre" in English) is surrounded on three sides by the Mediterranean Sea. It gazes across the bay at Haifa's crowded skyline, but the city's stone fortresses and underground Crusader City lend it a character far removed from that of its modern coastal neighbor. Visitors can stroll through the colorful maze of the *souq* or escape to the city's South Promenade and toss back a Tuborg while the waves crash against the city's white walls.

The Canaanite city-state of Akko is first mentioned in the *Book of Curses,* which records the curses of pharaohs on their enemies in the 19th century BCE. After this happy entry onto the international stage, Akko was conquered by the usual suspects: Egyptians, Persians, Greeks, Hasmoneans, Romans, and Umayyads. Crusaders came to the city in 1104 on their campaign to recapture the Holy Land for Christianity. In 1187, with the battle of the Horns of Hattim, Salah al-Din defeated the Crusader forces in Akko; three years later, Richard the Lionheart arrived from England and recaptured the city. During the next century, Crusader kings transformed Akko into the greatest port of their empire and a world-class showpiece of culture and architecture. The Mamluks ended Crusader rule in 1291, and Akko remained impoverished until the Druze prince Fakhr al-Din rebuilt it almost 500 years later. The Muslims built their city directly over the Crusader network of tunnels and basements and left the subterranean labyrinth for wide-eyed tourists. After his unsuccessful siege of the city in 1799, Napoleon claimed that had Akko fallen, "the world would have been mine." After a stint under the Egyptian Ibrahim Pasha, Akko returned to Ottoman control. When the British captured the port in 1918, it held a predominantly Arab population of about 8000.

Akkan locals are eager to share thoughts on their home and their lives while offering much-needed guidance around the dizzying network of Old City streets. However, women traveling alone are strongly advised to be cautious with many of these would-be guides, and all solo travelers are advised to avoid the alleys of Old Akko after dark; stick to the well-lit promenade by the port for a safer stroll.

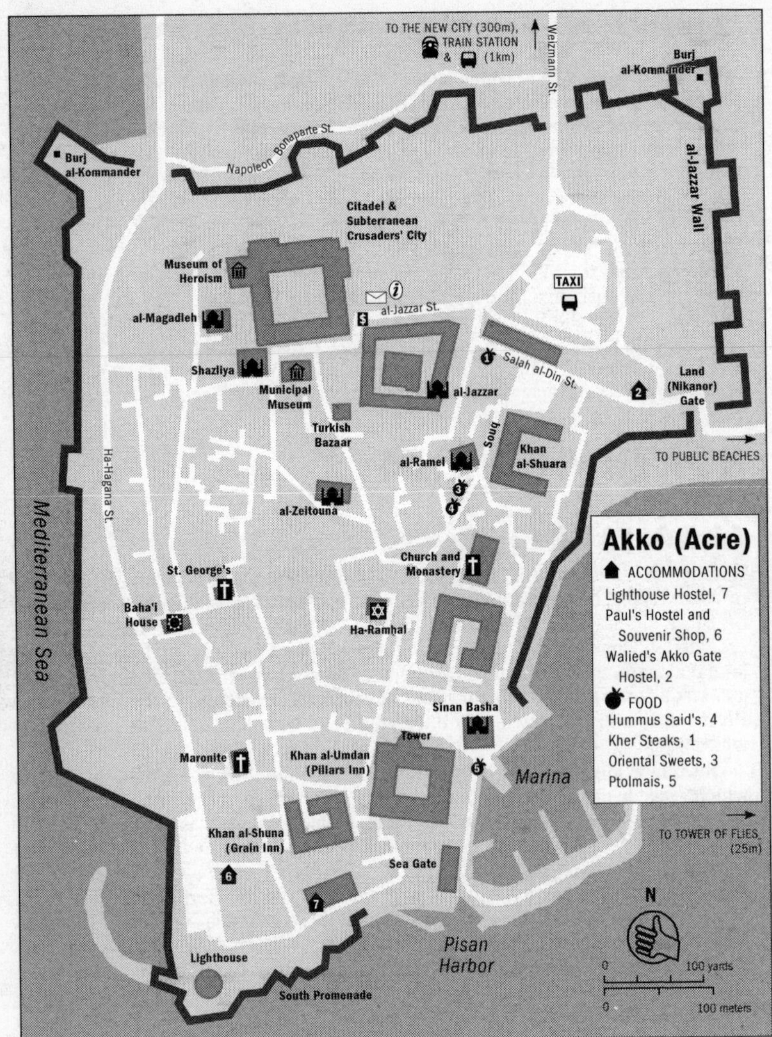

GETTING THERE AND GETTING AROUND

Trains: The **train station** (☎856 44 44) is on David Remez St., one street behind the central bus station. Trains are often the best way to get to and from Haifa, especially during rush hour. To: **Haifa** (40min., NIS11); **Nahariya** (10min., NIS6.50); and **Tel Aviv** (1¾hr., NIS29). Trains run every hr. Su-Th 5:30am-8:30pm, F 5:30am-3:30pm.

Buses: The **central bus station** (☎854 95 55) is on Ha-Arba'a St. in the new city. Buses go to **Haifa** (#271, 272, and 361; 45min.; every 20min.; NIS11.50; #271 makes local stops) and **Nahariya** (#271 and 272; 15min.; every 20min.; NIS7.20). Buses from platform #16 go to the **old city** until 6:30pm (NIS4).

Taxis: Sherut: off Ha-Arba'a St., across from the bus station. To: **Haifa** (NIS9); **Nahariya** (NIS7); and **Tel Aviv** (NIS25). **Special Taxis: Akko Ba'am** (☎981 66 66).

ORIENTATION AND PRACTICAL INFORMATION

In **New Akko,** the central bus station is on **Ha-Arba'a St.,** and the train station is one block behind it on **Remez St.** To get to the old city, turn left on Ha-Arba'a St. (with your back to the bus station), and after one block make a right on **Ben-Ami St.** Continue for a few blocks (past the bustling *midrahov*) and turn left on **Weizmann St. Ha-Atzma'ut St.,** the new city's major thoroughfare and home to the main post office and city hall, and Herzl St. also run between Ha-Arba'a St. and Weizmann St. Once in **Old Akko,** visitors will likely be dismayed by the lack of street signs—locals and monuments are the best (and only) navigational tools. **Al-Jazzar St.** and **Salah al-Din St.** extend in opposite directions from slightly different points near the main entrance on Weizmann St. Most museums are on al-Jazzar St., and the **souq** begins from a plaza off the right side of Salah al-Din St. when coming from Weizmann St. **Ha-Hagana St.** runs from the far side of the peninsula to the coast of the **Pisan Harbor,** which is lined with touristy restaurants, a pleasant promenade, and sitting areas with great bay views.

Tourist Office: Municipal Tourist Information Office Booth: (☎/fax 991 17 64), on al-Jazzar St. and across from the mosque, inside the same building as the post office. Open Su-Th 8:30am-6pm, F 8:30am-2:45pm, Sa 9am-5:45pm; in winter Su-Th 8:30am-5pm, F 8:30am-2:30pm, Sa 9am-5pm.

Currency Exchange: Mercantile Discount Bank (☎955 46 67), corner of al-Jazzar St. and Weizmann St. Open Su, Tu, W 8:30am-1pm; M, Th 8:30am-noon and 4:30-7pm; F 8:30am-1pm. **Bank Leumi** (☎995 63 33), on Ben-Ami St. near Weizmann St. Open Su, Tu, W 8:30am-1pm; M, Th 8:30am-1pm and 4:30-7pm; F 8:30am-noon. Both banks have **ATMs. Change Spot** (☎991 68 99), at the end of al-Jazzar St., across from the post office, changes currency with no commission. Open Su-F 8am-5pm.

Library: Canada-Akko Library, 13 Weizmann St. (☎991 08 60), near the old city. Delightful A/C reading room with multilingual collection, including many English books. Open Su-Th 9am-noon and 3-7pm; in winter 3-6pm.

Emergency: Magen David Adom (☎991 23 33).

Police: 16 Ha-Hagana St. (☎987 68 68).

Pharmacy: Merkaz (☎991 47 02), at the corner of Ben-Ami and Weizmann St. Open Su-Th 8am-1pm and 4-9pm, F 8am-1pm. Pharmacies rotate 24hr. duty; schedules are posted in the windows.

Hospital: Mizra Hospital (☎955 95 95), north of new Akko.

Internet Access: At the Canada-Akko Library. See above. NIS15 for 30min.

Post Office: Central branch at 11 Ha-Atzma'ut St. (☎306 66 66) offers **Poste Restante.** Open M, Tu, Th 8am-12:30pm and 3:30-6pm, W 8am-1:30pm, F 8am-12pm. Other branches at 53 Ben-Ami St. and on al-Jazzar St.

ACCOMMODATIONS

Dorm rooms are some of the cheapest in the area, yet remain rather empty. Quality varies greatly for even small price changes, so consider carefully before committing. All of the following will pick you up from the bus or train station; just call when you arrive. There are unofficial and unregulated rooms for rent in the old city; signs tend to cluster near the bus station, on the *midrahov* in the new city, or around the entrance to the old city. Get an opinion from the tourist office before making a decision. **Beach camping** is forbidden and dangerous.

Lighthouse Hostel, 175 Ha-Hagana St. (☎991 19 82, fax 981 55 3), at the end of Ha-Hagana St., a few minutes before the lighthouse. This gorgeous Turkish mansion is the place to stay in Akko. The huge dorms may be plain, but they are clean. The large, airy lounge with marble pillars can make even the grimiest backpacker feel like a sultan. Bike rental NIS35 per day. Kitchen available. Breakfast NIS15. Reception 24hr. Check-out 10am. Dorms (single-sex and coed) NIS25/US$6.25; singles NIS105/US$26.25; doubles NIS120/US$30. Cash only.

Walied's Akko Gate Hostel (☎991 04 10; fax 981 55 30); near the eastern Nikanor Gate on Salah al-Din St., a mere stumble from the beach. Sports a rooftop bar and a pool table (NIS25 per hr.). Kitchen available. Breakfast NIS25. Check-out 10am. Dorms (single-sex and coed) NIS25/US$6.25; rooms NIS120/US$30, with A/C and bath NIS200/US$50. Credit cards accepted.

Paul's Hostel and Souvenir Shop (☎991 28 57 or 981 76 86). Souvenir shop doubling as reception is just across from the lighthouse at the southern end of Ha-Hagana St. under a large yellow awning. For a down-and-dirty backpacker experience, this hostel has one large room stuffed with bunkbeds and a single bathroom. Climate control, summer and winter, consists of a few ceiling fans. Reception 24hr. Check-out 12pm. 20-bed dorms (coed) NIS20/US$5; private room with bath NIS100/US$25.

FOOD

The *souq*, a tumultuous avenue of butchers, bakers, candlestick-makers, and copper, brass, and leather vendors, bustles from 6am-5pm, though supplies start to run out after noon on busier days. Food stands along the *souq* offer kebab, falafel, and sandwiches (NIS5-10) as well as cheap, fresh produce and exotic spices. There are also food stands and supermarkets on Ben-Ami St. and Yehoshafat St. in the new city. More expensive options can be found in the Pisan harbor, where standard Middle Eastern meat and fish entrees go for NIS35-65.

Hummus Said's (☎991 39 45), in the midst of the *souq*, on your right when coming from the plaza off Salah al-Din St. Kick, shove, bribe: do whatever it takes to get through the hordes of locals. NIS12 buys 3 piping hot pitas, a plate of vegetables, and a deep dish of creamy hummus. If there are no tables open (and there won't be), try the takeout version, a pita stuffed with hummus, hot chickpeas, and vegetables (NIS3.50). Open M-Sa 6am until the food runs out, usually around 2pm.

Oriental Sweets, right next to Said's. Every possible combination of filo dough, nuts, and honey goes for NIS1-3, even cheaper if bought in large quantities. Open 8am-5pm.

Ptolmais Restaurant (☎991 61 12), on the left side of the marina, when facing the sea. One of the cheaper options on the marina, Ptolmais serves up lamb *shishlik* (NIS45) and various kebabs (NIS33), but herbivores just there for the great view might opt for hummus or tahini and pita (NIS13). Open daily 11am-midnight.

Kher Steaks, 1 Salah al-Din St. (☎596 85 25), on your immediate right when Weizmann turns to Salah al-Din. Mouth-watering grilled and skewered meats come with salad and chips in a plate (NIS35-40) or a pita (NIS17). Open daily 10am-midnight.

SIGHTS

The moats and dungeons of **Old Akko** speak clearly of the city's war-filled history. Guides—a.k.a. juice bar workers, waiters, and shopkeepers in their spare time—offer tours of varying quality and for varying prices. Ballpark figures are NIS15 for a sight and NIS120 for all of Akko, but make sure to verify beforehand. Women, especially, should ascertain what is expected in return for these tours.

CRUSADER CITY. Archaeologists first thought that the rooms in the Crusader City were built underground; they have since determined that al-Jazzar simply built his city on top of once above-land buildings. Much of the Crusader city still remains buried, but excavations expose more treasures each year. Most visible structures are part of the "Hospitaller's Quarter." Images of flowers or human forms on the columns are Crusader work, while abstract embellishments and

Arabic calligraphy come from Ottoman artisans. The 12th-century halls were probably part of a medical complex where the Hospitaller Order treated pilgrims. From the courtyard beyond the entrance hall, fortifications built by Fakhr al-Din and Tahir al-Omar are visible. Halfway down the stairs on the left and along the wooden path are the giant rooms of the Hospitaller Castle, called the **Knights' Halls,** built on top of 3rd-century BCE Hellenistic foundations. *(Across from the mosque on al-Jazzar St., in the same building as the tourist office. ☎991 17 64. Open Su-Th 8:30am-7pm, F 8:30am-3pm; in winter Su-Th 8:30am-4:45pm, F 8:30am-2pm. NIS25, children and students NIS22. Groups over 20: NIS21, children and students NIS18. Ticket includes access to all sights in the Crusader City and the Okashi Museum and comes with a hand-held audio tour in English, Hebrew, or German. Combination ticket available with Rosh Ha-Nikra.)*

CRYPT OF ST. JOHN. This large room was once a dining room where the Hospitallers held large feasts. Until excavations uncovered the *fleur-de-lis* in honor of Louis VII, archaeologists had mistakenly assumed the hall to be a large crypt; the Gothic architecture of the building resembles many European cathedrals. Next to the third column in the "crypt" is a staircase connected to a long underground passageway, which in turn leads to six adjacent rooms and a central courtyard. The passageway was originally dug by Romans as an elaborate 250m-long drainage tunnel, and the Crusaders used it as an escape tunnel during the Mamluk siege. It was restored by al-Jazzar to serve as a means of escape if Napoleon penetrated the city walls. The complex of arched rooms at the other end of the tunnel was used as a hospital for wounded knights. The Ottomans later turned the rooms into a post office, and the rooms now house a flock of pigeons whose eerie cooing echoes over visitors' heads. *(Down the path from the Knights' Halls.)*

MUNICIPAL MUSEUM. Built in 1775 by al-Jazzar, this building served as a **Turkish bath** until 1947, when it was damaged by the breakout next door (see **Museum of Heroism,** p. 208). Its rooms are appropriately named "hot," "cold," and "lukewarm." *(Accessible through the metal door opposite the crypt entrance or the main entrance around the corner from the plaza containing the post office. NIS8 for those without tickets to the Crusader City, students NIS4.)*

OKASHI MUSEUM. Named after late Akko resident Avshalom Okashi, a painter known for richly textured abstract paintings, landscapes, and architectural drawings of Akko and for "relying mainly on the secrets of the color black," this museum houses many of the artist's great works. *(Just past the Crusader City on al-Jazzar St. ☎951 66 97. Open Su-Th 8:30am-4pm, F 8:30am-2pm, Sa 9am-4:30pm. NIS10 for those without tickets to the Crusader City.)*

MOSQUE OF AL-JAZZAR. The third-largest mosque in Israel, it dominates the city with its green dome and towering minaret. Ahmed al-Jazzar ordered its construction in 1781 on what is believed to have been the site of San Croce, the original Christian cathedral of Akko. Inside is an attractive courtyard with Roman columns taken from Caesarea. Legend has it that al-Jazzar buried a large treasure underneath the mosque to ensure that there would be plenty of money to rebuild the place if it were ever destroyed. The tower was destroyed by an earthquake in 1927, but was promptly restored; the rest of the complex is in magnificent condition. Inside, in the green cage on the right side of the balcony, is a shrine containing a hair from the beard of the prophet Muhammad. Prayers are conducted five times a day, and visitors who arrive during a prayer session may be asked to wait. *(The entrance is a short walk on al-Jazzar St., across from the post office. Open daily 8am-7pm; in winter 8am-5pm. Closed periodically for 20min. during prayer time. NIS5, NIS3 after 4pm. Modest dress required; scarves available for those not already covered.)*

To the right of the mosque is a small building containing the **sarcophagi** of al-Jazzar and son; peek through the barred windows at the marble boxes, now covered with soil and green plants. Al-Jazzar turned the buried Crusader cathedral into an underground water reservoir that receiv.ed rainwater from the nearby Pasha gardens. The reservoir is accessible through a door and underground stairway at the left end of the mosque. Look for the small green sign and red arrows.

CITADEL. This stronghold, used by the British as their central prison, now houses the **Museum of Heroism,** a monument to Zionist fighters imprisoned by the British during the Mandate. The citadel, built in the late 1700s on 13th-century Crusader foundations, was used as an **Ottoman prison.** The most famous inmate during the Ottoman rule was Baha'ullah, founder of the Baha'i faith, who was imprisoned on the second floor in 1868. During the British Mandate, the prison housed about 560 inmates under the guard of about half as many British soldiers. Members of the Etzel, Ha-Gana, and Leḥi, including Ze'ev Jabotinsky, were incarcerated here for violent anti-British activities. Nine members of the resistance were sentenced to death by hanging between 1938 and 1947. The **Gallows Room** displays the noose along with photographs of the nine fighters. On May 4, 1947, Etzel members staged a prison break that freed 41 of their peers and enabled the escape of 214 Arab prisoners (later depicted in the movie *Exodus*, shot on location). Across the street from the museum looms **Burj al-Kuraim** (Fortress of the Vineyards), often referred to as the British Fortress despite its Crusader and Ottoman construction. *(The Citadel adjoins the Crusader City on Ha-Hagana St., opposite the sea wall. To reach the museum from the Old City, exit on Weizmann St. and take an immediate left on the path. At the entrance, follow the stone stairs down to the lower garden, then the metal stairs up and around the side of the prison. ☎991 82 64. Open Sa-Th 9am-6pm, F 9am-1pm. NIS8, students NIS4.)*

KHAN AL-UMDAN (INN OF PILLARS). The Khan al-Umdan is perhaps the most impressive of the many ancient inns or *caravanserai* near the market. Using 32 granite pillars taken from Caesarea, al-Jazzar built this *khan* for Ottoman merchants at the end of the 18th century. The lower stories of the courts served as rented storerooms for merchants, while the upper galleries served as boarding rooms. The *khan*'s slender clocktower, erected in 1906 for the jubilee of the Ottoman Sultan Abdulhamit, sports a Turkish half-moon and star. *(Entrance just past the Isnan Pasha Mosque and the fishing port, near the lighthouse.)*

THE CITY WALLS. A stroll along the Old City's cannon-spotted perimeter yields an interesting look at Akko's seaside defenses. Akko's security in recent centuries has relied upon the **al-Jazzar Wall,** running along the northern and eastern sides of the city and surrounded by a seawater moat. The best place from which to view the wall, which originally ran the length of the harbor, is **Burj al-Kommander** (Commander's Fortress), an enormous Crusader bastion at the northeastern corner. To enter the watchtower, climb the steps beginning where Weizmann St. meets the wall. Follow the green signs, which describe Napoleon's siege in reference to the walls, despite the fact that they were built after Napoleon's retreat; the deception works because the new walls are in form, if not appearance and dimensions, the same as the old. England blew up the original walls in the siege of 1840 (almost half a century after Napoleon), when the Egyptians were using them as an ammunition dump. The **Tower of the Flies,** the site of the original lighthouse, solemnly broods in the middle of the bay. Its fortifications were toppled by a devastating earthquake in 1837. At the eastern corner near the shoreline is **Land Gate** (also known as Nikanor Gate), once the only entrance to the city. Next to the marina, locals like to leap into the water from windows in the walls.

ENTERTAINMENT

Twice a year, Akko plays host to major performing arts events. Excellent acoustics in the Crusader City's halls make them the perfect location for the **Haifa Symphony Orchestra** in July and the acclaimed **Israel Fringe Theater Festival** each fall. The four-day dramatic extravaganza occurs during the Jewish festival of *Sukkot* (Oct. 2-9, 2001) and attracts small theater troupes from all over the country. Only a few of the performances are in English (check with the tourist office). During *Sukkot*, there are also prolific street performers.

Decent **beaches** for swimming are located just east of Akko's Old City; exit through the eastern Nikanor gate at the end of Salah al-Din St. by the Akko Gate hostel. Either settle for the **Wall Beach** directly outside the gate or follow the road for 15 minutes around the naval academy to **Purple Beach,** equipped with umbrellas, showers, and changing rooms. The latter charges a few shekels on Saturdays.

The **Morris Sabib Boat Company** (☎(05) 269 35 07 or (05) 095 56 63) gives 30-minute boat rides from the marina to the sea walls (NIS20, students NIS15), but will not depart until filled. A relaxed *nargilah* puff by the sea is the local choice for nightlife. **The Little Sultan,** a 24-hour kiosk across from the lighthouse and next to Paul's Souvenirs, serves *nargilahs* for NIS9, coffee for NIS5, and breakfast toasts for NIS12. Summer visitors can make a splash at the **Pisan Marina.**

DAYTRIP FROM AKKO

LOḤAMEI HA-GETA'OT

Loḥamei Ha-Geta'ot lies between Akko and Nahariya. To reach the kibbutz, take bus #271 from Akko or Nahariya (10min., every 20min., NIS7) or a sherut (NIS6.50).

Loḥamei Ha-Geta'ot ("Fighters of the Ghettos") is a kibbutz founded in 1949 by survivors of concentration camps and the Warsaw Ghetto uprising. It now houses an entire building dedicated to the stories of children and is one of Israel's most powerful Holocaust museums.

The **Ghetto Fighter's House** examines Jewish life in Eastern Europe during the years leading up to World War II and during the Holocaust. The exhibits on Jewish Youth resistance movements during the war and ghetto uprisings are particularly intriguing. While an entire floor chronicles the Nazi invasion of Europe, more specific exhibits relate the stories of Jews in Holland and Greece. (☎995 80 80; fax 995 80 07; email mgans@gfh.org.il. Free, but donation requested. Open Su-Th 9am-4pm; May-Sept., Su-Th 9am-6pm, F 9am-1pm.) The recently constructed **Yad La-Yeled** in a nearby building is a memorial to the 1.5 million children who perished in the Holocaust. The exhibition winds down an inscripted 4-story tower as it recounts the stories of children who experienced the Holocaust through audio-visual displays and recordings of stories collected from diaries, letters, and testimonies. The exhibits have English subtitles and translations. The museum complex also features a quiet, air-conditioned library where any visitor can research Jewish history; many Holocaust reference books are in English. (☎995 80 35. NIS10, students and children NIS9. Open Su-Th 10am-6pm, F 10am-1pm, Sa 10am-5pm; in winter Su-Th 10am-5pm, F 9am-1pm, Sa 10am-5pm. Library only open Su-Th.) The **Baha'i Gardens,** planted from 1952 to 1956, hold the villa and **shrine of Baha'ullah,** the prophet and founder of the Baha'i faith (see **The Baha'i,** p. 24). (The gardens are 2km south of the kibbutz, on the main Akko-Nahariya road. Take bus #271 (10min., every 20min., NIS7) or walk from the kibbutz towards Akko. ☎981 15 69. Free. Shrine open F-M 9am-noon; gardens open daily 9am-4pm. Modest dress requested.) The **Roman aqueduct** just outside the museum and to the south is well preserved, largely because it's not Roman. Al-Jazzar had it built in 1780 to carry water 15km from the Kabri springs to Akko. Over 15,000 people attend the national Holocaust Remembrance Day Ceremony in the nearby **amphitheater.**

NAHARIYA נהריה ☎04

Nahariya is literally a one-horse town—hang around Jabotinsky St. long enough, and you'll see the tired beast hauling tourists around in a white buggy. In 1935, Nahariya's first settlers tried their hands at farming, but because of stiff market competition, the relatively pleasant weather, and the beautiful coastline, they soon realized that the tourism industry was their best and only hope for survival. Most families and older people come to Nahariya to relish the slow-motion lifestyle; for travelers, it's a convenient, if expensive, base for its surrounding sites.

GETTING THERE AND GETTING AROUND

Trains: Station at 1 Ha-Ga'aton Blvd. (☎856 44 46). Trains to: **Akko** (10-15min., NIS6.50); **Haifa** (40min., NIS13); and **Tel Aviv** (1¾hr.; NIS35.50, students NIS29.50). Trains depart approximately every hr. Su-Th 5:20am-8:20pm, F 6:10am-2:10pm, Sa 9:15pm-noon; in winter 7:20pm-noon.

Buses: 3 Ha-Ga'aton Blvd. (☎992 34 34). Buses #270 (express), 271, and 272 go to **Haifa** (1hr., every 20min., NIS14) and #271 and 272 go to **Akko** (20min., every 20min., NIS7).

Sherut: Or Nahariya (☎992 78 88), on the right of the central bus station when facing the street, runs to **Akko** (NIS7). Sherut to **Haifa** (NIS12) in front of the bus station.

Car Rental: Avis, 31 Ha-Ga'aton Blvd. (☎951 18 80), beside the Penguin Cafe. Rents automatics NIS184/US$46 per day; manual NIS168/US$42 per day. Must be 23 and have had license for 2 years.

ORIENTATION AND PRACTICAL INFORMATION

Most sights and tourist resources are on **Ha-Ga'aton Blvd.** With your back to either the bus or train station on Ha-Ga'aton Blvd., **Jabotinsky Blvd.,** several blocks to the right, has many hotels and rooms to let. The beach is another block further along Ha-Ga'aton Blvd.; stop when you get wet.

Tourist Office: Municipal Tourist Information Office, 19 Ha-Ga'aton Blvd. (☎987 98 00), on the plaza of the Municipality Building before Herzl St. Open Su-W 8am-1pm and 4-7pm, Th-F 8am-1pm.

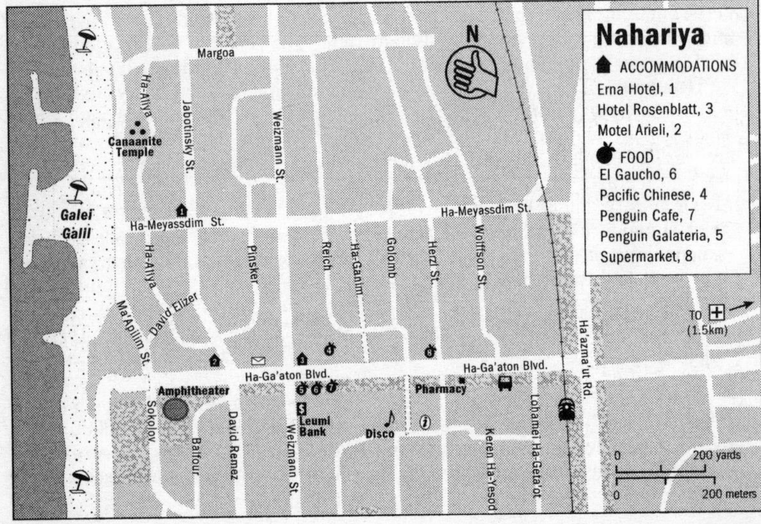

Currency Exchange: The **Post Office** gives bank rates for no commission, as does **Change Spot,** 36 Ha-Ga'aton Blvd. (☎951 27 60). Open Su-Th 9am-7pm, F 9am-2pm.

Bookstore: Doron Books, 32 Ha-Ga'aton Blvd. (☎992 10 79), has English newspapers, magazines, and paperbacks. Open Su-Th 7:30am-1:30pm and 4-7:30pm, F 8am-2pm.

Emergency: First aid: (☎991 23 33). **Fire:** (☎982 22 22).

Police: 5 Ben-Tzvi St. (☎992 03 44).

Pharmacy: Szabo Pharmacy, 3 Ha-Ga'aton Blvd. (☎992 04 54 or 992 11 97), in front of the bus station. Open Su-Th 8am-1:30pm and 4-7:30pm, F 8am-2:30pm.

Hospital: (☎985 05 05), Ben-Zvi St.

Post Office: 40 Ha-Ga'aton Blvd. (☎992 01 80), has **Poste Restante** and sells the cheapest international calling cards. Open Su-Tu, Th 8am-12:30pm and 3:30-6pm; W 8am-1:30pm; F 8am-noon.

ACCOMMODATIONS

Accommodations in Nahariya are quite expensive, especially in summer. Reservations are generally a good idea. In summer, rooms are sometimes available in private homes. "Rooms to Rent" signs are common on Jabotinsky St. (NIS75 or more; polite bargaining may help). The tourist office keeps a list of officially recognized bed and breakfasts, but not prices or descriptions; the quality range is large, so check them out first. For cheaper beds, head south to **Akko** (see p. 203).

Motel Arieli, 1 Jabotinsky St. (☎992 10 76), on the corner of Ha-Ga'aton Blvd., and a block from the beach. Leafy paths off the patio lead to clean, if somewhat cramped, bungalows. Reception 24hr. Check-out 10am. Singles NIS100/US$25, with bath and A/C NIS150/US$37.50; doubles with bath and A/C NIS200/US$50. Cash only.

Hotel Rosenblatt, 59 Weizman St. (☎992 00 69; fax 992 00 69), off Ha-Ga'aton Blvd. In furnishings and aura, this hotel vaguely resembles a 1970s country club—swimming pool included (in summer). All rooms have A/C, bath, and cable TV. Breakfast included. Reception 24hr. Check-out 11am. Singles NIS160/US$40; doubles NIS240/US$60. In winter NIS20/US$5 discount. Discounts available for longer stays; consult manager.

Erna Hotel, 29 Jabotinsky St. (☎992 98 52), a few blocks off Ha-Ga'aton Blvd. This quiet hotel rests close to the beach. Rooms have A/C, TV, and bath. Breakfast included. Singles NIS180/US$45; doubles NIS240/US$60; extra person NIS80/US$20.

FOOD

Nahariya suffers from a remarkable dearth of falafel stands (NIS10) and a glut of overpriced touristy cafes (bagel toast NIS35). The beaches and gardens make lush picnic grounds; shop at the **Co-op Tzafon supermarket** (☎992 72 10), on the corner of Ha-Ga'aton Blvd. and Herzl St. (open Su-Tu 7:30am-8pm, W 7:30am-8:30pm, Th 7:30am-9pm, F 7:30am-2:30pm), or at the fruit and vegetable stores on Herzl St. between Ha-Ga'aton Blvd. and Ha-Meyasdim St. Plan ahead for Shabbat.

Penguin Cafe, 31 Ha-Ga'aton Blvd. (☎992 00 27). Families and young couples crowd into this old standard, established when Nahariya was a six-year-old farm town. Cakes NIS19. Open Su-Th 8:30am-midnight, F-Sa 8:30am-2am.

Penguin Gelateria, 33 Ha-Ga'aton Blvd. (☎992 42 41), neighbor of Penguin Cafe and a bit cheaper. Dozens of sundae varieties (NIS21-29) and a huge Israeli breakfast (NIS25). Open daily 7am-3am.

El Gaucho, 33 Ha-Ga'aton Blvd. (☎992 86 35), serves Argentinian fish and meat entrees (NIS45-55) in a rustic setting. Open Sa-Th noon-midnight, F noon-1am.

Pacific Chinese Restaurant, 28 Ha-Ga'aton Blvd. (☎951 08 77), is the cheapest of the area's numerous Chinese restaurants. The business lunch served from noon-3pm is the best value (NIS35, with soup NIS40, takeaway NIS30). Vegetarian options NIS32-36.

SIGHTS AND ENTERTAINMENT

Nahariya slowly roasts visitors along its sandy strip. **Galei Galil,** a right turn from the end of Ha-Ga'aton Blvd., has a breakwater, a lifeguard, lots of sand, and a pool. (Open end of May-Oct. 8am-6pm. NIS20.) A **free beach,** past the end of the promenade, has neither a lifeguard nor a breakwater, but locals surf here anyway.

The dull but archaeologically important remains of a 4000-year-old **Canaanite Temple** dedicated to Asherah, the goddess of fertility, were discovered in 1947 on a hill next to the shore (30 Ha-Ma'apilim St., a 20min. walk to the right of the beach as you face the sea). The **Nahariya Municipal Museum,** in the Municipality Building just west of Herzl St., has exhibits on art, archaeology, malacology (the study of seashells), and the history of Nahariya. (☎987 98 63. Open Su, W 10am-noon and 4-6pm; Tu, Th 10am-noon. Free.) An ornate mosaic floor is all that remains of a 4th-century **Byzantine church** on Bielefeld St., near the Katzenelson School. (☎987 98 63; call ahead for a free visit.)

The tourist office isn't lying when they say, "Nahariya is hot, but not at night." Strolling along the Promenade is the most popular activity of all ages. Next to the beach are a couple of pubs with stupendous sunset views over the Mediterranean. Pub **Mul Ha-Yam,** a left turn after Ha-Ga'aton Blvd., meets the sand and steadfastly vends booze. (NIS14-20. ☎992 00 69. Open daily 5pm until the tide comes in.) All ages participate in fun **folk dancing** at the amphitheater, near the end of Ha-Ga'aton Blvd. (Late May to early Oct. W and Sa 7:30-9:30pm.) Those determined to kick it with the 30-60 something crowd can head to the **Carlton Hotel disco,** in the middle of town on Ha-Ga'aton Blvd. (Cover NIS50. Open F 10pm.) The **Hekhal Ha-Tarbout** (☎982 99 33), on Ha-Atzma'ut Rd., screens three movies in English.

DAYTRIPS FROM NAHARIYA

Loḥamei Ha-Geta'ot (see p. 209) can also be visited as a daytrip from Nahariya.

ROSH HA-NIKRA ראש הנקרה

Bus #20 and 32 depart from Nahariya to the site, but only a couple times per day (NIS8). Alternatively, sheruts to Shlomi will stop at the Misrafot Junction (NIS6); the site is a 3km uphill walk on the main road from there. ☎985 71 09. Cable car down to grottoes runs Apr.-June and Sept. Sa-Th 8:30am-6pm, F 8:30am-4pm; July-Aug. Sa-Th 8:30am-11pm, F 8:30am-4pm; Oct.-Mar. daily 8:30am-4pm. NIS34, students and seniors NIS29, children NIS27; discount ticket includes Akko sites.

The spectacular white chalk cliffs and grottoes of Rosh Ha-Nikra occupy the northernmost point on Israel's coastline. Rosh Ha-Nikra's caves, sculpted by millennia of lashing waves, nearly make one forget the mountain of barbed wire and the Uzi-toting soldiers who guard the tense Lebanese border only a few steps from the parking lot. The British enlarged the natural chalk grottoes when they bore a tunnel through the cliffs during World War II in order to complete a railway line linking Turkey with Egypt. The nearby kibbutz, smelling the chance for a new tourist trap, blasted additional tunnels through the rock to improve access to the sea caves, topped the cliffs with an observation point and cafeteria, and connected the highway to the caves with a cable car. Don't expect arduous spelunking here, a pleasant walk through the slippery grottoes is a half-hour affair.

The worse the weather, the better the show at Rosh Ha-Nikra—waves pound the gaping caverns, forming powerful whirlpools and echoing thunderously through the tunnels. Keep an ear open for the moaning cries of "The Bride" mixed in with the crashing waves; legend says she jumped out of a boat right near the cliffs to avoid an arranged marriage. Brown turtles visit to lay their eggs in the natural grottoes, and white doves nesting in cliffside cracks bring to life the Biblical verse, "My dove is hidden in the clefts of rock" (Song of Songs 2:14). Arrive early or be caught in the afternoon throngs of youth and tour groups.

MONTFORT AND NAḤAL KEZIV

*Frequent **buses** leave Nahariya from platform #6 for the Christian Arab village of **Mi'ilya** (#40, 41, 43, 44, and 45; 20min.; every 30min.; NIS10). From the stop, turn left and climb up the steep road toward Mi'ilya for about 30min. At the wooden sign for Montfort, the road veers right to Hilla. Continue straight and follow the red-and-white markers down the rocky path to the castle (another 30min.). The set of stone steps on the right is an alternate path to the ruins. The original trail turns to the right shortly, then travels across a small bridge and up the rocks to the castle. The site is currently under renovation and officially **closed,** but visitors have been known to prowl around.*

The Crusader **castle** of Montfort splendidly rewards a challenging hike; the windswept ruins overlook the western Galilee's steep Keziv Valley. The Knights Templar built the main structure early in the 12th century; Salah al-Din partially destroyed it in 1187. The Hospitaller Knights enlarged the fortress in 1230 and called it Starkenburg or Montfort ("strong mountain" in German or French). The complex's impressive 18m tower and 20m main hall stand among its remains.

Those who enjoy more strenuous pleasures should consider visiting by way of a longer hike, saving the castle for last. The four-hour hiking loop has spectacular views and begins at the lookout point on the road to Hilla (coming from Mi'ilya, turn right at the wooden sign). It descends into the Naḥal Keziv Valley and then circles back up to Montfort. Follow black- or blue-and-white markers down into the valley, green-and-white while along the river, and red-and-white up to the castle and back to Mi'ilya.

Several other trails branch off the loop. Following the river away from Montfort, green-and-white markers lead to the **Ein Tamir** and **Ein Ziv** springs. Ascending the slope opposite Montfort leads to **Goren Park** (follow red-and-white markers), a perfect vantage point for the castle (amazing at sunset). Bus #25 (8:15pm only) goes from the park to Shlomi, where there are *sherut* to Nahariya (NIS7).

Just north of Montfort is the **Naḥal Betzet Nature Reserve,** another fabulous stomping ground for hikers. Take bus #24 from Nahariya (30min.; departs 8:25am, 1, 3:30pm; NIS12), and ask the driver to stop at the path to Me'arat Keshet, or **Bow Cave.** Ascend the red-and-white marked trail for 20 minutes to reach the enormous cave, a natural arch affording dramatic views of the forested Galilean hills and cliffside caves. Descending into the cave requires ropes, and spelunkers should consult beforehand with SPNI. Walk across the arch to continue on the red-and-white marked path, which leads to a barbed wire fence after 30 minutes. The next two hours is a gentle descent into the **Betzet Wadi,** which flourishes with pink flowers and towering trees. Take a right on the blue path at the bottom of the *wadi*. At the large pipeline, follow the fence on the left, indicated by the red arrow, for five minutes until you see a gas station. Behind the station is a steep road that leads up to **Kibbutz Eilon** (700m), where a refreshment stand and some more small caves await. A 1km walk through the kibbutz reaches a stop for bus #28 back to Nahariya (8:10am, noon, 3:15, 5:15, 7:45pm; NIS10).

The Keziv River extends from deep in the Galilee to the Akhziv coastline (near the SPNI Field School). Serious hikers use the trail as the first or last leg of a three-day **Yam Le-Yam** trek from the Mediterranean to Galilee (for more information, see **From Sea to Shining Sea,** p. 214). SPNI has a field school in Akhziv and is an invaluable resource for planning any hike.

YEḤI'AM (JUDIN) FORTRESS מבצר יחיעם

Buses #39 and 42 from Nahariya stop at the kibbutz (20min., infrequently, NIS8). ☎ 04 985 60 04. Open Su-Th 8am-5pm, F and holidays 8am-4pm; closes an hour early during winter. NIS10, students NIS7, though kibbutzniks have hopped the fence during off hours.

In 1208, the Teutonic Knights inherited the **Judin Fortress,** built by the Templars in the 12th century. The Mamluk Sultan Baybars destroyed the fortress in 1265, and what can be seen today results from Bedouin governor Dahr al-Omar's restoration efforts in the 18th century.

In 1946, Jewish settlers moved back into the deserted castle and founded **Kibbutz Yeḥi'am.** Two years later, during the War of Independence, they became the most recent group to use it for protection. Though only half of the relief convoy reached the site, the kibbutz held out until Israeli forces took control of Western Galilee in May of 1948. The fortress still stands within the kibbutz grounds, the source of its new Hebrew name. Its nooks and crannies make for great exploration. Dancers, musicians, and artisans (in full period garb) crowd the fortress during *Sukkot* (Oct. 2-9 in 2001) for the **Days of Renaissance Festival** every year.

PEKI'IN (BKE'AH) פקיעין بقيعة

Bus #44 (50min., 7 per day, NIS14) makes the round-trip to Peki'in from Nahariya and will stop just above the cave upon request. Be sure to get off at Peki'in Ha-Atika (Old Peki'in), not Peki'in Ha-Ḥadasha (New Peki'in). At the blue-and-white sign, turn right and descend the stairs. At the large bush with houses behind it, turn right and walk between the two large rocks. The cave is a tiny hole about 3m away. A donation is requested.

Rabbi Shimon Bar-Yoḥai and his son Eliezer fled to Peki'in (Bke'ah in Arabic) when a Roman decree during the Bar Kokhba revolt banned the study of Torah (see **The Romans,** p. 9). For 12 years, this erudite duo hid in a small hillside cave and, sustained by a nearby spring and generous carob tree, delved into their illicit book of learning. It is during this period that Bar-Yoḥai is said to have composed the *Zohar*, the central text of Kabbalah (Jewish mysticism), though most evidence suggests it was composed about a millennium later. According to popular legend, Bar-Yoḥai's gaze started **angry fires** in the fields of those less worthy. When God saw this, he sent Bar-Yoḥai back into the cave to chill out for another year. In its present state, the cave does not live up to the legend surrounding it.

Peki'in is the only city in Israel claiming continuous Jewish occupation since the Second Temple period. Though now predominantly Druze, it has a Jewish presence, which endures in one remaining Jewish family and an 18th-century synagogue with Temple-era stones built into the wall. To visit the synagogue, continue down the staircase near the cave to Kikkar Ha-Ma'ayan with its oddly shaped pool. Follow the street at the far right of the square, turn left at the first intersection, and take the curving road down to the synagogue's white gate on the right. If the gate is closed, knock on the door with a blue star, around the corner and upstairs.

The sparkling **Peki'in Youth Hostel (HI)** (☎04 957 41 11; fax 957 41 16) has air-conditioned rooms with private bath. Take bus #44 from Nahariya to the first stop in Kfar Peki'in, and follow the signs for 2km. (Breakfast included. Reception 24hr. Check-out for members 11am; dorms NIS78/US$19.50, July-Aug. NIS89/US$22. Members get NIS5 discount. Credit cards accepted.)

FROM SEA TO SHINING SEA. One of Israel's most popular and challenging hikes is the three-to-four-day Yam L'Yam trek from the Mediterranean to the Sea of Galilee (or vice versa). The best place to start is at the Keziv Bridge in Akhziv, about 1km south of the SPNI Field School (☎982 37 62; also rents rooms). Contact SPNI for information and maps before attempting this hike. Cross the bridge and follow the green markers upstream along Naḥal Keziv for the first day. On the second day, the green path leads to the Druze village of Ḥurfish, a good place to restock on food. From Ḥurfish, follow the green or red markers up to the Hurbat parking lot, the next sleeping station. Black markers line the way from Hurbat to the peak of Har Meron (1½hr.). It's all downhill from here: follow the black marker down Naḥal Meron, which leads to Naḥal Amud, named for the large pillar carved out by the river. Israelis who haven't been to the Grand Canyon call it the eighth wonder of the world. The black markers on upper and lower Naḥal Amud lead to Kibbutz Hokkuk, next to the Sea of Galilee. From the kibbutz, buses #459 and 963 go to Tiberias. Plan ahead, bring a compass, and do as much walking as possible in the early morning. With proper planning, this trek can be the experience of a lifetime.

AKHZIV אכזיב

*All buses from platform #5 in **Nahariya** (buses #22-25 and 28) stop at the **Akhziv National Park** (10min., every hr., NIS7). Sherut (NIS6).*

The first historical records of Akhziv are 15th-century BCE Egyptian letters found in Tel Amarna, which describe it as a fortified Canaanite port city. The city switched hands during every major conquest, and eventually the Crusaders built the large **L'Ambert Castle** to defend the coastal road. Akhziv's war days are over now, and its current claim to fame is its sunny shoreline.

Built on the site of an 8th-century BCE Phoenician port town, the sprawling lawns and sheltered beach of **Akhziv National Park** are perfect for a relaxing day. Facilities include showers, changing rooms, and a playground. (☎04 982 32 63. NIS20, students NIS10. Open daily Apr.-Oct. 8am-5pm; July-Aug. 8am-7pm.) Two roads lead to the **Akhziv Beach:** one along the coast, currently closed off by the military, and a noncoastal road where buses stop. Every July a **Reggae Festival** stirs it up on the beach; call for details. (Begins 4km north of Nahariya and to the left of Akhziv National Park as you face the sea. ☎04 982 82 01. NIS18, children NIS9. Open Apr.-June and Sept.-Oct. 8am-5pm, July-Aug. 8am-7pm.)

The state of **Akhzibland** was founded in 1952 by the eccentric **Eli Avivi.** As the story goes, Eli was walking along the beach and saw the remnants of a village that the Israeli government had destroyed. Hopelessly in love, he claimed the land. The unamused Israeli government knocked down Eli's first house and arrested him on charges of "establishing a country without permission." Convinced that the land is worth fighting for, Eli has battled in the courts for 49 years. In winter 2000, he'll challenge the government's petition to bulldoze his Parliament.

An eye-catching figure in flowing robes, Avivi is unforgettable—especially when kvetchy customs officials try to figure out the "Akhzibland" stamp on your passport or when your Akhzibland marriage certificate proves less than adequate. The country is well guarded by eight lazy dogs (and two new puppies); the laws of the land are promulgated from the dilapidated parliament building.

Eli's Museum, housed in a deteriorated but striking Arab mansion, exhibits the benevolent dictator's extensive collection of mostly Phoenician implements and statue fragments found by Eli himself over the past 47 years. *(☎04 982 32 50. Open 24hr.)* Beds in one of Eli's breezy **guest rooms** above the museum or cabins next door cost NIS100, and sleeping in the rugged **camping area** costs NIS80 per person; the beach costs NIS20 for non-guests. These prices are entirely negotiable and may be waived for those who get on Eli's good side or help him with menial chores (such as landscaping, cleaning, or passing legislation) for 3 hours; 4 hours for lodging and food. The accommodations may not be the cleanest, but they're the best in the country. If you decide to stay at Akhzibland, be prepared for storytime in the evening; Eli's got a lot to say, since he's 187 years old.

The **Yad Leyad** monument across the road from Akhzibland commemorates the Palmaḥ soldiers who died during the "Night of the Bridges," when Jewish forces blew up numerous road and rail bridges to try to limit enemy mobility.

GALILEE הגליל الجليل

When the ancient Israelites described their country as flowing with milk and honey, they must have been talking about the Galilee. This lush and fertile region, bordering the West Bank to the south, the Golan to the east, Lebanon to the north, and the Mediterranean coast to the west, is laced by cool, refreshing rivers and carpeted with rolling, green hills. The Galilee was originally a province of the ancient Israelite kingdom, called Ha-Galil (the district) in Hebrew, whose inhabitants prospered by fishing and farming. As communities in the Galilee grew, religious leaders flocked to the area. Jesus grew up in Nazareth, performed many of his first miracles near the Sea of Galilee, and gave his famous sermon atop the Mount of Beatitudes. His apostles lived and taught in nearby Capernaum. Fifty years later, when Romans destroyed the second Temple in Jerusalem, the Sanhedrin relocated to the Galilee and resided there for the next 250 years. Dozens of armies swept through the region during the following millennium.

Despite a history of almost continuous war, today Galilee is one of the most peaceful areas in Israel. Since Israel captured the strategic Golan Heights in 1967 (see p. 14), putting the Galilee out of range of Syrian rockets, the region has blossomed into a tourist mecca. Busloads of pilgrims descend a massive metal staircase into the Jordan River at the site where John is believed to have baptized Jesus, banana boats and booze cruises skim over the Sea's blue waters to deposit passengers upon the bustling Tiberias promenade, and hikers crowd the trails of the Upper Galilee where Crusader fortresses keep watch over forested valleys. Meanwhile, the ancient synagogues of Tzfat and the churches of Nazareth continue to attract the faithful.

HIGHLIGHTS OF THE GALILEE

There's no better way to beat the heat in Tiberias than to take an evening swim in the lake known to Israelis as the **Kinneret** (p. 231).

You know the Sermon, now see the Mount. The **Mount of Beatitudes** (p. 233) provided the stage for the premiere of Jesus's famous oration.

Walk the winding streets of **Tzfat** (p. 234), the birthplace of Kabbalah and home to a thriving artists colony. Its mystical serenity makes for a peaceful escape.

SOUTHERN GALILEE

NAZARETH נצרת الناصرة ☎06

A vibrant center of Arab life in the Galilee, Nazareth (al-Nassra in Arabic, Natzrat in Hebrew) is a far cry from Christmas-card pictures of pastoral churches, quiet convents, and grazing sheep. Nazareth is indeed dear to Christian pilgrims as the setting of Jesus's younger years and the traditional home of Mary and Joseph, but it is also a gritty town. While devotees throng to a handful of neo-Gothic churches, drivers charge through dusty construction sites on the main road and crowds drift through the winding alleys of the hillside market.

Nazareth's population is roughly one third-Christian and two-thirds Muslim, with a small Jewish population. Unlike nationalist Palestinians in the West Bank, Nazarean Arabs are content as Israeli citizens. Life here, however, is worlds away from the beaches of Haifa and Tel Aviv. Visitors—especially women—should dress modestly to avoid harassment on the streets and difficulty entering churches. Parts of the city may be unsafe after dark.

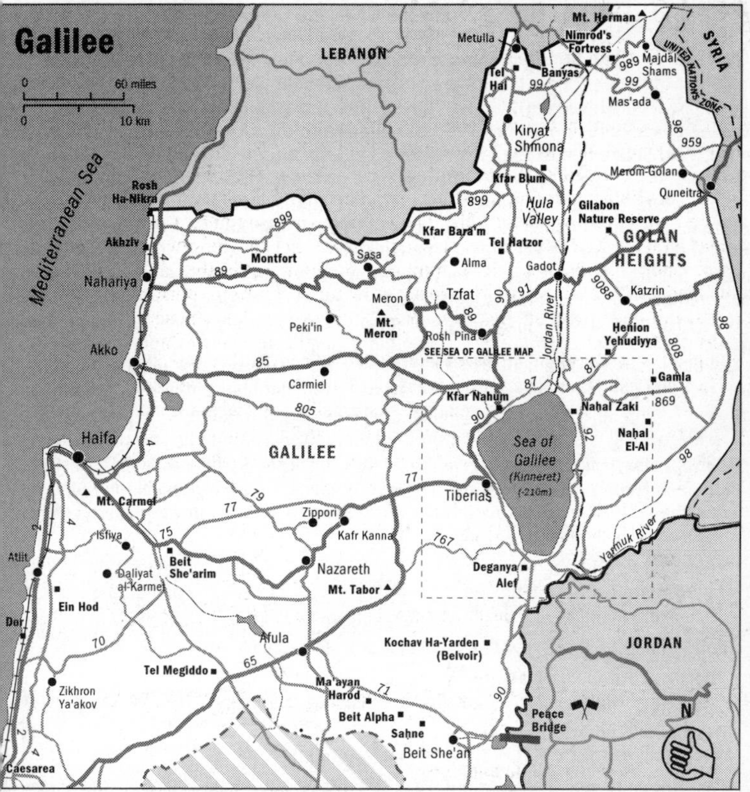

GETTING THERE AND GETTING AROUND

Buses: The **"bus station"** consists of several stops on Paul VI St., near Casa Nova St. When taking a bus to Nazareth, make sure it goes to Natzeret Ha-Atika, not Natzrat Illit. The upper city is a 20min. local bus ride from the old city. Buses leaving town head west on Paul VI St. The **Egged** info booth is on Paul VI St., just east of the intersection with Casa Nova. Open Su-F 7am-3pm. To: **Afula** (#355, 356, 357, 823, 824, and 953; 20min.; every 40min.-1½hr. Su-Th 5:25am-7:55pm, F 6am-3:30pm, Sa 4:15-9pm; NIS8); **Akko** (#343; 1½hr.; every 1-2hr. Su-Th 6:45am-5pm, F 6:45am-4:15pm; NIS21.50, students NIS19.50); **Haifa** (#331 and 431; 1hr.; every 1-2hr. Su-Th 5:40am-8:10pm, F 5:40am-5:10pm; NIS18); **Jerusalem** (#953, 3½hr., 6:30am, NIS40); **Tel Aviv** (#823 and 824 go from Natzrat Illit by way of Nazareth; 2½hr.; every 30min.-1hr. Su-Th 5:10am-7:40pm, F 5:45am-3:15pm, Sa 4-8:45pm; NIS32) via **Tel Megiddo** (45min., NIS13); and **Tiberias** (#431; 1hr.; every 1-2hr. Su-Th 6:50am-9:30pm, F 7am-5:30pm, Sa 7-10pm; NIS18).

Taxis: Ma'ayan (☎655 51 05), **Abu al-Assal** (☎655 47 45), **Galil** (☎655 55 36), and **Saiegh** (☎646 35 11). Taxis can be found all along Paul VI St.

Service: *Service* taxis gather on a small side street just off of Paul VI St. and across from the central bus stop. To: **Haifa** (NIS15); **Jenin** (NIS12); **Tel Aviv** (NIS25); and **Tiberias** (NIS18). *Service* run every day.

Car Rental: Europcar (☎655 41 29), at casa Nova St., next to the tourist office. 24+. Cars start at US$40 per day, automatics US$60 per day; min. 3-day rental. Open M-F 8:30am-6pm, Sa 8:30am-2pm. Credit card required.

GALILEE

ORIENTATION AND PRACTICAL INFORMATION

Nazareth is 40km southeast of Haifa and 30km southwest of Tiberias, on a hill north of the Jezreel Valley. All the Christian sights are located in the Arab **Old Nazareth** (Natzeret Ha-Atika). Upper Nazareth (Natzrat Illit), the newer, Jewish section of town, is residential and of little interest to tourists. The Arab town's main road, **Paul VI St.,** lies to the east of the sights. Its intersection with **Casa Nova St.,** just below the Basilica, is the busiest part of town. Uphill from Casa Nova St., among churches, is the market area. Higher quality accommodations and panoramic views are farther up the hill toward **Salesian St.** and Mary's Well. Obtain a **map** of the city from the GTIO (see **Tourist Office,** below), as few of the streets have signs. Nazareth's Christian community shuts down on Sundays, but most establishments are open on Shabbat. Although Arabic is the major language, everybody speaks Hebrew and the proprietors of most tourist sites also speak English.

Tourist Office: Government Tourist Information Office (GTIO) (☎657 30 03; fax 657 30 78), on Casa Nova St., near the intersection with Paul VI St., next door to Israel Discount Bank. Staff distributes brochures and colorful new maps. Computerized information available. Open M-F 8:30am-5pm, Sa 8:30am-2pm.

Currency Exchange: Money Net (☎655 25 40), on the south side of Paul VI St., just west of Casa Nova St. Exchanges cash and traveler's checks with no commission. Open M-Tu, Th-F 8:30am-7pm; W, Sa 8:30am-3pm. The **post office** also exchanges cash and traveler's checks with no commission.

Banks: Israel Discount Bank (☎602 73 33), on Casa Nova St. by the tourist office, has an **ATM.** Open Su, W, F 8:30am-1pm; M-Tu, Th 8:30am-12:30pm and 3:30-6pm. Bank Leumi and Arab Israeli Bank have **ATMs,** and are on Paul VI St. opposite the station.

Police (☎602 84 44), next to the post office by Mary's Well.

Pharmacy: Farah Pharmacy (☎655 40 18), next to Egged info, on Paul VI St. across from Bank Ha-Poalim. Open M, F 9am-7pm; Tu, Th 9am-1:30pm and 4-7pm; W, Sa 9am-2pm.

Hospitals: Nazareth Hospital (☎657 15 01 or 657 15 02), **Holy Family Hospital** (☎650 89 00), and **French Hospital** (☎650 90 00).

Post Office: Central branch (☎655 51 88), 2 blocks uphill from Paul VI St. from Mary's Well. Exchanges cash and travelers' checks and offers **Western Union** and **Poste Restante.** Open M-Tu, Th-F 8am-12:30pm and 3:30-6pm; W 8am-1:30pm; Sa 8am-noon.

ACCOMMODATIONS

During Christian holidays, it takes divine intervention to find a room here. At other times, hospices are crowded with tour groups but often have a bed to spare. There are very few budget accommodations in Nazareth, so call ahead if possible.

Sisters of Nazareth, P.O. Box 274 (☎655 43 04; fax 646 07 41). From Paul VI St., walk uphill on Casa Nova St. and turn left at the Basilica's entrance. This 150 year-old Catholic convent still looks brand-new. The courtyard was built over ruins from the first century, which the sisters claim contain the grave of St. Joseph. They offer tours of the excavations M-Sa 8:30am. Breakfast NIS16; lunch and dinner NIS36 each. Reception 6am-9pm. Check-in 4pm. Check-out 10am (flexible). Strict 9pm curfew. Private rooms have bathrooms and great views. Single-sex dorms NIS32/US$8; singles NIS100/US$24; doubles NIS160/US$38; triples NIS240/US$57. Reservations recommended.

Galilee Hotel (☎657 13 11; fax 655 66 27), on Paul VI St., 2 blocks west of Casa Nova St. This modern hotel offers clean, spacious rooms with A/C, telephones, and bathrooms with tubs. Reception 24hr. Check-in 2pm. Check-out noon. Singles NIS210/US$50; doubles NIS330/US$80; triples NIS420/US$100. Credit cards accepted.

Casa Nova Hospice (☎645 66 60; fax 657 96 30), on Casa Nova St. opposite the Basilica of the Annunciation. Comfortable and clean rooms with A/C, private bath, and phones, usually full of tour groups. Breakfast included. Lunch and dinner US$8 each.

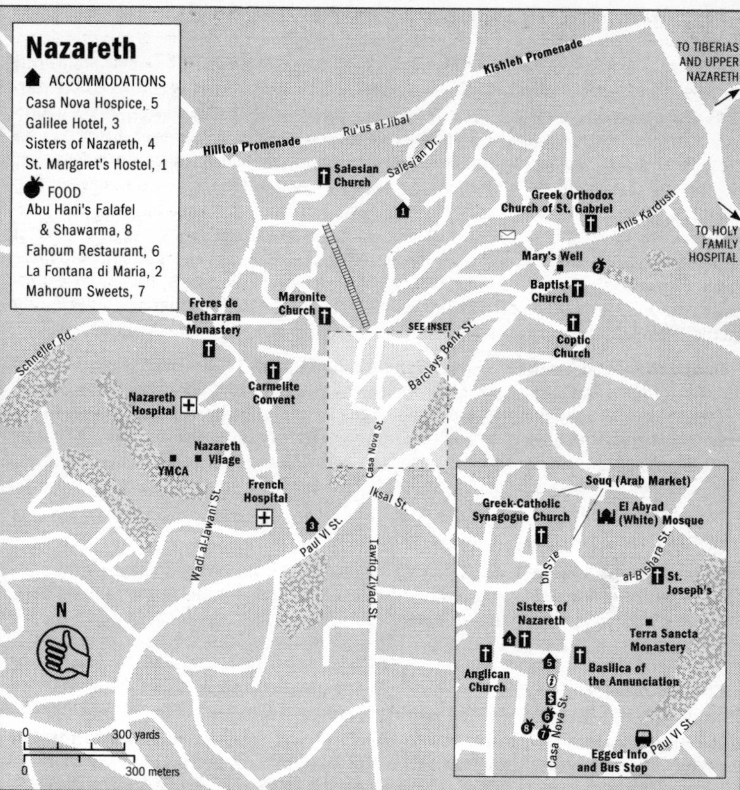

Check-out 8:30am. 11pm curfew. Singles NIS160/US$40; doubles NIS200/US$48; triples NIS290/US$72. 5% service charge. Traveler's checks accepted.

St. Margaret's Hostel (☎657 35 07; fax 656 71 66), off Salesian St. Climb the stairs from the *souq* to Salesian St. and turn right. At the wooden guard booth, turn right onto the downhill access road. By bus, take #9 or 13 west on Paul VI St. and get off on Salesian St. at the high school access road. Rooms arranged around a central courtyard have private baths and phones. Some have great views of Old Nazareth and some are a bit dank and musty. Breakfast included; lunch and dinner US$10 each. Reception 8am-midnight. Check-in and check-out noon. Flexible midnight curfew. Singles NIS225/US$50; doubles NIS310/US$70. Reservations recommended.

FOOD

Nazareth's cuisine is not known for diversity. Dozens of falafel stands and identical "Oriental" restaurants line the downtown streets. Restaurant hours are generally 7am-9pm, and many places are closed on Sunday. Several **food kiosks** can be found along the streets, but the biggest one is directly opposite the bakery. Besides that, the only options for late-night snacks are the *shawarma* stands along Paul VI St. near Casa Nova St. These usually stay open until midnight.

La Fontana di Maria (☎646 04 35), on Paul VI St., to the right of Mary's Well. Located inside a Turkish khan with high vaulted ceilings, this is Nazareth's only classy sit-down restaurant. House specialties include steak (NIS50), kebab (NIS40), and cornish hen (NIS50). Soups (NIS15) and salads (NIS10-25) are a bit cheaper. Open daily 11am-11pm. Credit cards accepted.

GALILEE

Abu Hani's Falafel and Shawarma, on Paul VI St., just west of the intersection with Casa Nova St. Look for the large sign in front advertising falafel and *shawarma* deals. This tiny place has some of the best and cheapest falafel (NIS7) and *shawarma* (NIS10) in town. Add NIS2 for a soda. Open M-Sa 9am-9pm.

Fahoum Restaurant (☎655 33 32), on Casa Nova St., on the left, just up from Paul VI St. This modern-looking restaurant actually dates back to before the creation of the state of Israel. Delicious chicken *shishlik* NIS35; St. Peter's Fish NIS50; kebab with chips NIS40; hummus plate NIS15. Open daily 8am-9pm. Credit cards accepted.

Mahroum Sweets (☎656 02 14), on Paul VI St., at the intersection with Casa Nova St. Gooey, sweet pastries in a shiny, mirrored interior. *Baklavah* NIS30 per kg; cookies NIS20 per kg; Coffee and tea NIS5. Open daily 8:30am-11pm.

SIGHTS

Nazareth received a much-needed 60 million dollar face-lift for the millennium that included repaving many of the old city streets, constructing new promenades with scenic vistas, and putting up prominent signs to help pilgrims find their way to the numerous religious sights in town. The majority of sights are clustered around Paul VI St. and the *souq*, but the new Nazareth Village hopes to draw tourists up the hill to experience life as it was in ancient times. Nazareth's churches are all free to visitors, but they happily accept donations.

BASILICA OF THE ANNUNCIATION. Nazareth is synonymous with churches and none is more prominent than the huge basilica that dominates downtown with its faceted lantern dome. Completed in 1969, the basilica is built on the site believed to be Mary's home, where the archangel Gabriel heralded the birth of Jesus. Inside the huge, bronze doors depicting the life of Jesus is the **Grotto of the Annunciation,** the site of Mary's home. A gallery overlooking the grotto is lined with a series of artistic interpretations of the Annunciation. Outside, Madonna and Child mosaics from nearly every country in the world grace the courtyard walls. Churches have marked this spot since 356 CE; excavations of churches and ancient Nazareth lie in a garden underneath the plaza, accessible from the upper floor of the basilica. *(Walk up Casa Nova St. from Paul VI St.; the entrance is on the right. ☎657 25 01. Open M-Sa 8am-5:30pm; Oct.-Mar. M-Sa 8am-4:30pm. Shorts not allowed.)*

ST. JOSEPH'S CHURCH. This church was built in 1914, on top of the cave thought to have been Joseph's house. The present structure incorporates remnants of a Byzantine church. Inside, stairs descend to caves that once stored grain and oil, as well as an early baptismal bath. Although this is usually referred to as Joseph's workshop, evidence suggests that these caves have been used since the late Stone Age. *(Next to the Basilica of the Annunciation, in the same plaza on Casa Nova St.)*

GREEK-CATHOLIC SYNAGOGUE CHURCH. Recently restored by a group of Italian archeology students, the church is built on the site of the synagogue where young Jesus is believed to have preached. Next door is the beautiful 18th-century Greek-Catholic Church of the Annunciation. Two hundred meters up from the church on street 6126, on the left in a small chapel, is the **Mensa Christi** stone where Jesus supposedly ate with his disciples after his resurrection. *(In the center of the Arab market. Enter the* souq *from Casa Nova St., turn left after the music shop, and follow the street to the right. Open M-Sa 8am-6pm. If closed ring the bell on the door to the left.)*

NAZARETH VILLAGE. This recent addition to the Nazareth tourist market is a re-creation of the town of Nazareth as it was during the life of Jesus 2000 years ago. The stone houses, synagogue, furniture, and tools were built using the same materials and techniques of the time period. Costumed villagers engage in activities such as weaving, carpentry, and wine-making. *(Up the hill towards Nazareth Hospital on al-Wadi al-Jawani St., on the left next to the YMCA. ☎645 60 42. NIS32, children NIS20. Open M-Sa 9am-5pm. Call ahead.)*

SOUQ. Nazareth's outdoor market is the best place in the city to buy olive wood camels and Bart Simpson underwear. It has been gutted and repaved in the last two years; today its white stones sparkle. Although perfectly safe in daylight, the market area is best avoided at night, when dope fiends lurk in its dark alleyways. *(Best reached via Casa Nova St. Open M-Sa 9am-5pm.)*

MARY'S WELL. Many believe that the well's water miraculously heals; recently it has begun to heal its once-ugly surroundings. Over the past few years, a new plaza, a few restaurants, and souvenir shops have sprouted nearby. The recently-built scenic promenades begin near here. From the well continue right along Paul VI St. to the Namsawi Promenade and then up the hill to the promenades and the Salesian Church. *(The well is northeast of the bus station on Paul VI St.)*

GREEK ORTHODOX CHURCH OF ST. GABRIEL. The Church of St. Gabriel stands over the town's ancient water source. The original church was erected in 356 CE over the spring where Mary drew water and where the Greek Orthodox believe Gabriel appeared. The present structure, built in 1750, has elaborate Byzantine-style paintings and an ornate gold chandelier in the center. *(Left and uphill from Mary's Well, just off Paul VI St. Open M-Sa 7am-9pm, Su 7am-1pm and 2-9pm.)*

SALESIAN CHURCH OF JESUS THE ADOLESCENT. This magnificent 80-year old Gothic church is perched on a hilltop overlooking the old city of Nazareth. Climb the winding 250-plus stairs past the Maronite Church through Nazareth's stone alleyways, or take bus #6 or 13 from the city center away from Mary's Well. The church is housed within a school; enter through the main entrance to the school. *(Open by appointment only. Call ☎646 89 54 to arrange a visit.)*

DAYTRIPS FROM NAZARETH

MOUNT TABOR הר תבור

From Afula, take bus #830, 835, or 841 to the base of the mountain (NIS8; tell the driver to stop at Har Tavor). From there, walk 2km through a Bedouin town to the spot where taxis shuttle pilgrims up to the top (round-trip NIS20). It is worth the money to avoid the climb up the road. Church open Su-F 8am-noon, 2-5pm. Modest dress required; no visitors during services.

Mount Tabor (Har Tavor in Hebrew), the traditional site of Christ's Transfiguration, has become a standard stop on pilgrimage tours. The 588 meter-high hilltop is shared by Franciscan and Greek Orthodox monks. The Catholic **Basilica of the Transfiguration,** built in 1924, sits atop a 6th-century CE Byzantine church, which marks the spot where Jesus spoke with Elias and Moses and was transfigured in the presence of apostles Peter, James, and John (Luke 9:28-36). A dirt path on the left just before the stone archway that leads to the Basilica goes to the **Church of Elijah,** built atop the **Cave of Melkhizedek.** The limestone fortification, once an Arab fortress called **al-Adil,** dates from 1211. Mt. Tabor is also the site where the prophetess Deborah led the Israelites to victory over Sisera's army (Judges 4-5). At the foot of the mountain is the Bedouin village of Shibli. Just down the hill from the taxi stop is the **Tent of Tavor** restaurant in an authentic Bedouin tent with a view of the Galilee countryside. Sit on mattresses and eat traditional Bedouin rice and meat for NIS45. (☎676 03 12. Open daily 9am-11pm.)

ZIPPORI צפורי

Bus #343 to Akko will stop at the junction, about 3km south of the site (every hr. 6:45am-2:25pm, NIS7). ☎(06) 656 82 72. Open Sa-Th 8am-4pm, F 8am-3pm; in winter Sa-Th 8am-3pm, F 8am-2pm. NIS18, students NIS15, children NIS9.

About 6.5km northwest of Nazareth, excavations at Zippori (Sepphoris) are uncovering a rich legacy from the Judeo-Christian, Roman, and Byzantine periods. The town was the seat of the Sanhedrin in the 3rd century CE, as well as one of the places where Rabbi Yehuda Ha-Nassi gathered the most learned rabbinic scholars to compile the *Mishnah*. Extensive finds include the remains of a 4000-seat Roman amphitheater, exquisite mosaics, a crusader fortress, and a synagogue. Archaeologists have found over 40 ancient mosaics here; the most famous is the enigmatic, gently smiling woman, now dubbed the "Mona Lisa of the Galilee." Within the crusader citadel are a variety of multimedia programs on the history of the city and an exhibit of archaeological finds. One kilometer east of the main excavations is an ancient reservoir carved into the bedrock; it was once part of the area's intricate, system of 13.5 kilometers of aqueducts. Christians believe Zippori was the town where Mary's parents Anne and Joachim lived. A Crusader Church stands over the site of their house.

TEL MEGIDDO (ARMAGEDDON) תל מגידו

Buses #823 and 824 run from Nazareth to Tel Aviv, stopping at Megiddo (45min.; every 30min.-1hr. Su-Th 5:10am-7:40pm, F 5:45am-3:15pm; NIS13). When the bus leaves Afula, remind the driver to stop at Megiddo Junction. From the junction, walk 1km north toward Yoqneam and Haifa, then turn left at the brown sign. ☎ *(06) 652 21 67. Open Sa-Th 8am-5pm, F 8am-4pm; in winter Sa-Th 8am-4pm, F 8am-3pm. NIS18, students NIS15.*

Bible fans and heavy metal gurus have heard of Armageddon, but few realize that the demonic battleground for the End of Days (Revelations 16:16) is actually "Ḥar Megiddo" (Mt. Megiddo), an ancient *tel* located just southeast of Haifa. Excavations of the site have uncovered twenty layers of ruins, ranging in time from the Neolithic Period (7000 BCE) to the end of the Persian Period (332 BCE).

The vision of Megiddo as an apocalyptic gathering place is derived from the city's central location. Commanding the crossroads between several ancient trading routes that linked Egypt to Syria and Mesopotamia, the fortress town was the site of many fierce battles. Megiddo was razed and rebuilt by numerous civilizations, including Canaanites, Hyksos, Egyptians, Assyrians, and Israelites. The most impressive remains include a Canaanite temple dedicated to Astarte (20th century BCE), chariot stables and a palace from Solomon's time (10th century BCE), a public grain silo built during the reign of the Israelite king Jeroboam II (8th century BCE), and a man-made tunnel engineered by King Ahab (9th century BCE) to allow access to water during a siege. Only a few of the ruins have been reconstructed, and excavations are still underway.

Before negotiating the *tel*, check out the **museum** at the site's entrance. It explains some of Megiddo's layers, displays a model of Solomon's chariot city, and shows a video in Hebrew and English. Three gift shops have each set up camp in strategic locations around the site; they wage their own capitalistic pitched battle daily. There is also an overpriced cafeteria next to the museum that has hot meals for NIS30 and salads for NIS18. (Open daily noon-5pm.)

From the observation point atop the *tel*, you can look out over the **Jezreel Valley** *(Emek Yizre'el)*, mostly swamp until 1920, when it was drained by Jewish immigrants. The lone mountain in the distance is Mt. Tabor; also visible are the Gilboa range and the hills of Nazareth. The water tunnel terminates outside the ruins, so make sure it's your last stop at the site. When you exit, turn right and walk 500 meters back to the museum entrance and main road.

TIBERIAS טבריה طبرية ☎06

To accommodate its diverse group of visitors—vacationing Israeli families, party-seeking youths, weary backpackers, and Christian pilgrims from Hong Kong, Alabama, and everywhere in between—Tiberias has become a bizarre mix of flash and trash. Stores hawking Virgin Mary night lights and baby Jesus key-chains shut down just when the disco ball starts to twirl in the bar next door, and cafe waiters, hostels owners, and shopkeepers stand ready to pounce on any passerby. Despite proposals to clean up the city, Tiberias remains a whiff of Israel at its rawest.

Herod Antipas, puppet king of Judea, built the city in 18 CE and named it for the Roman Emperor Tiberius. Despite the Romans' attempt to bring in settlers, most Jews, including Jesus, refused to enter the town because it was built on the site of older Jewish graves. Later, in the 2nd century CE, Rabbi Shimon Bar-Yoḥai declared the town pure, and it soon became the religious center of the Jews. Later conquests by Persians (614 CE), Arabs (636 CE), and Mamluks (1247 CE) emptied the Jews from the city. In the 16th century, during Ottoman rule, Sultan Suleiman the Magnificent handed the town over to a Jewish refugee from Spain, who re-established a Jewish state. The city's 1940 population of 12,000 was evenly divided between Jews and Arabs but, since the 1948 War, the population has remained almost entirely Jewish.

Though its central location and cheap beds make it an ideal touring base for the Galilee and the Golan, its position 200m below sea level guarantees a hot, humid, and mosquito-ridden July and August. Of course, the action in Tiberias is also hottest during those months, with increased transportation, the best parties, street fairs, and everybody's favorite, price gouging.

GETTING THERE AND GETTING AROUND

Buses: Bus Station (☎672 92 22), at the corner of Ha-Yarden St. and Ha-Shiloah St. To: **Haifa** (#430 (express) and 431; 1¾hr.; every hr. Su-Th 6am-6:30pm, F 6am-4:30pm, Sa 4:45-7pm; NIS23.50, students NIS21); **Jerusalem** (#961, 963, and 964; 3hr.; every 30-60min. Su-Th 5:50am-7pm, F 7:30am-3pm, Sa 4:30-9:45pm; NIS42, students NIS38); and **Tel Aviv** (#830, 835, 836, 840, and 841 (local); 2½-3hr.; every 30min. Su-Th 5:30am-9pm, F 6am-5pm, Sa 4-10pm; NIS35.50, students NIS32).

Taxis: *Sherut* and private cabs wait in the parking lot below the bus station and on Bibas St. To **Haifa** (NIS20) and **Tel Aviv** (NIS32). **Taxi Ha-Emek** (☎672 01 31) is at the corner of Ha-Shiloah St. and Ha-Yarden St.

Car Rental: Avis (☎672 27 66), in the parking lot below the bus station. All of the following are on Ha-Banim St. **Arad** (☎672 49 99). 21+, under 23 NIS90 extra. **Eldan** (☎679 18 22). 24+, 10% student discount. **Hertz** (☎672 39 39). 21+, under 23 NIS60 extra. **Budget** (☎672 08 64 or 672 34 96). 23+. All open Su-Th 8am-5pm, F 8am-2pm. 2 years driving experience required.

Bicycles: Hostel Aviv and **Maman Hostel** (see **Accommodations,** p. 224) are well stocked. 18-speed mountain bike for NIS40 per day with insurance and roadside assistance. Return on night of rental. Check with the tourist office regarding accident insurance before renting elsewhere.

ORIENTATION AND PRACTICAL INFORMATION

Tiberias has three tiers: the **old city** by the water, **Kiryat Shmuel,** the new city up the hill, and **T'verya Illit** (Upper Tiberias) at the top of the hill (bus #7-10, every 10min., NIS4.10). The upper sections are residential; all boozing, boating, and beaching takes place in the old city. **Ha-Galil St.** and **Ha-Banim St.** run parallel to the water; **Ha-Yarden St.** runs perpendicular to them to the north. **Ha-Yarkon St.** and **Ha-Kishon St.** intersect Ha-Galil St. and Ha-Banim St. to the south. The central **midraḥov** (pedestrian mall) runs from Ha-Banim St. to the waterfront **promenade.**

Tourist Office: Government Tourist Information Office (☎672 56 66), on Ha-Banim St., in the archaeological park next to the Jordan River Hotel. Free city maps and brochures. Open Su-Th 8am-1pm and 2-5pm (until 7pm in August), F 8am-noon.

Tours: Matan Tours (☎06 672 45 74 or 054 616148), offers a one-day tour from Tiberias of both Tzfat and Nazareth for NIS150.

Currency Exchange: Discount packages paid in US dollars are the way of business here. The post office on Ha-Yarden St. gives top rates with no commission. **Money Net** (☎672 40 48), next to Bank Leumi on the corner of Ha-Banim St. and Ha-Yarden St., also charges no commission. Open Su-M, W-Th 8:30am-1pm and 4-7pm; Tu 8am-1:30pm; F 8:30am-1pm. **Bank Ha-Poalim** (☎679 84 11), on Ha-Banim St. between Ha-Yarden St. and Ha-Yarkon St., has a 24hr. **ATM.**

Bookstore: Steimatzky (☎679 12 88), on Ha-Galil St. between Ha-Yarden St. and Ha-Yarkon St. A decent selection of English newspapers and magazines. Open Su-M, W-Th 8am-1pm and 4:30-7:30pm, Tu 8am-1pm, F 8am-2pm.

Laundromat: Panorama, 50 Ha-Galil St. (☎672 43 24), south of Ha-Kishon St. and across from the city wall remnants. Wash, dry, and fold 7kg for NIS40. Open Su-M, W-Th 8am-6pm; Tu, F 8am-2pm.

Camping Supplies: Terminal La-Metayel, 38 Ha-Yarden St. (☎672 39 72), between the bus station and Ha-Galil St. Open Su-F 9am-1:30pm and Su-M, W-Th 4-7:30pm.

Emergency: First Aid (☎679 01 11), corner of Ha-Banim St. and Ha-Kishon St. Open 24hr. **Police** (☎679 24 44). **Fire** (☎679 12 22).

Pharmacy: Superpharm, 42 Ha-Yarden St. (☎667 66 63), near the bus station. Open Su-F 8:30am-10pm, Sa 10am-11pm.

Internet Access: Big Ben, at the end of the *midraḥov* on the left. NIS20 for 30min. Open daily 8:30am-late. **Immanuel Internet Cafe** (☎672 36 20), in the Galilee Experience gift shop. NIS10 for 15min. Open Su-Th 8am-10pm, F 8am-5pm, Sa 5-10pm.

Post Office: Central office, 1 Kikkar Rabin (☎672 22 66), in the parking lot off Ha-Yarden St., between Ha-Atzma'ut St. and al-Hadef St. **Poste Restante, EMS,** and **Western Union.** Open Su-Tu, Th 8am-12:30pm and 3:30-6pm; W 8am-1:30pm; F 8am-noon.

ACCOMMODATIONS

Competition is fierce in Tiberias; at peak times, hostel "runners" swoop on visitors as they get off the bus. The scene is lively, but cheap beds are often deservedly so: look before paying and only pay for one night in advance. That being said, atmosphere goes a long way and varies widely between hostels. Don't be afraid to ask to switch to a different room if there's something wrong with the first one; Tiberias is not the place to value politeness over sanity. Speaking of sanity, all rooms (dorms included) have air-conditioning.

Prices rise between July and September and reservations for private rooms are recommended. The Jewish holidays of Pesaḥ, Rosh Ha-Shana, and Sukkot are mob scenes. There are many "Room For Rent" signs throughout the city. Be aware that private homes are unlicensed and therefore not subject to inspection. Lone travelers should avoid sleeping in private houses.

Maman Hostel (☎679 29 86), on Atzmon St. From the central bus station, walk right on Ha-Shiloaḥ St. Bubbly international crowd keeps cool in the pool or on a stool at the tropical bar. If the great atmosphere doesn't compensate for the thin dorm mattresses, the private rooms are pretty tasteful. Kitchen available. Free safe and storage. Check-out 10am. Dorms NIS25/US$6, July-Aug. NIS30/US$7.50. Singles with bath NIS100/US$25, NIS120/US$30; doubles NIS100/US$25, NIS150/US$37.50.

Hostel Aviv, 66 Ha-Galil St. (☎672 00 07 or 672 35 10), one block past the intersection with Ha-Banim St. Stomping grounds for the rough-and-rugged but oh-so-friendly backpacker crowd, Aviv has some of the cheapest (and smallest) rooms in the city. Management offers copious discounts and freebies. Kitchen available; free coffee supplies. Free safe; lockers NIS10. Internet NIS20 for 30min. Reception 24hr. Check-out 10am. Dorms (single-sex and coed) with bath NIS25/US$6, July-Aug. NIS30/US$7.50. Singles with bath, TV, and fridge NIS60-80/US$15-20; doubles with bath, TV, and fridge NIS100-120/US$25-30. Credit cards accepted.

Meyouḥas Hostel (HI) (☎672 17 75 or 679 03 50; fax 672 03 72), at the corner of Donna Gratzia St. and Ha-Yarden St., in a building made of local black basalt rock. Breakfast included. Free safe; lockers NIS6. Reception 24hr. Check-in 2pm. Check-out 10am. Dorms (coed) NIS52/US$13, July-Aug. NIS78/US$19.50. Singles with bath NIS128/US$38, NIS172/US$43; doubles with bath NIS224/US$56, NIS252/US$63. NIS8 student discount; NIS7 member discount. Credit cards accepted.

Naḥum Hostel (☎672 15 05; fax 671 74 37). Head right (as you face the sea) on either Ha-Shiloaḥ or Ha-Galil and turn onto Tavor St. Backpackers relax with a Goldstar in the rooftop bar before heading back to their huge dorms with kitchenettes, bathrooms, and thin foam mattresses. Dorms (coed and single-sex) NIS25/US$7. Private rooms with bath NIS100/US$25. Prices rise 20% in high season. 10% discount for stays longer than 3 days. Credit cards accepted.

Nof Ha-Galil Hotel (☎671 28 80; fax 671 28 90), in Kikkar Rabin Sq., across from the post office. The cheapest escape from the grime of the backpacking world, Nof Ha-Galil is quiet and polished. Reception 24hr. Check-out 11am. Singles NIS100/US$25; doubles NIS150/US$37.50. July-Aug. and holidays 2-day min. stay. 20% off Nov.-Mar.

Hotel Aviv (☎671 22 72), on Ahva St., a block up from Hostel Aviv. Spoil yourself (and your budget) with a weekend at Hostel Aviv's rich aunt. Holiday flats come with A/C, cable TV, kitchenette, full bath (with bathtub!), and balconies with great views. Singles NIS160/US$40; doubles NIS200/US$50; 8 person suites NIS400/US$100. Prices rise 40% in July-Aug.

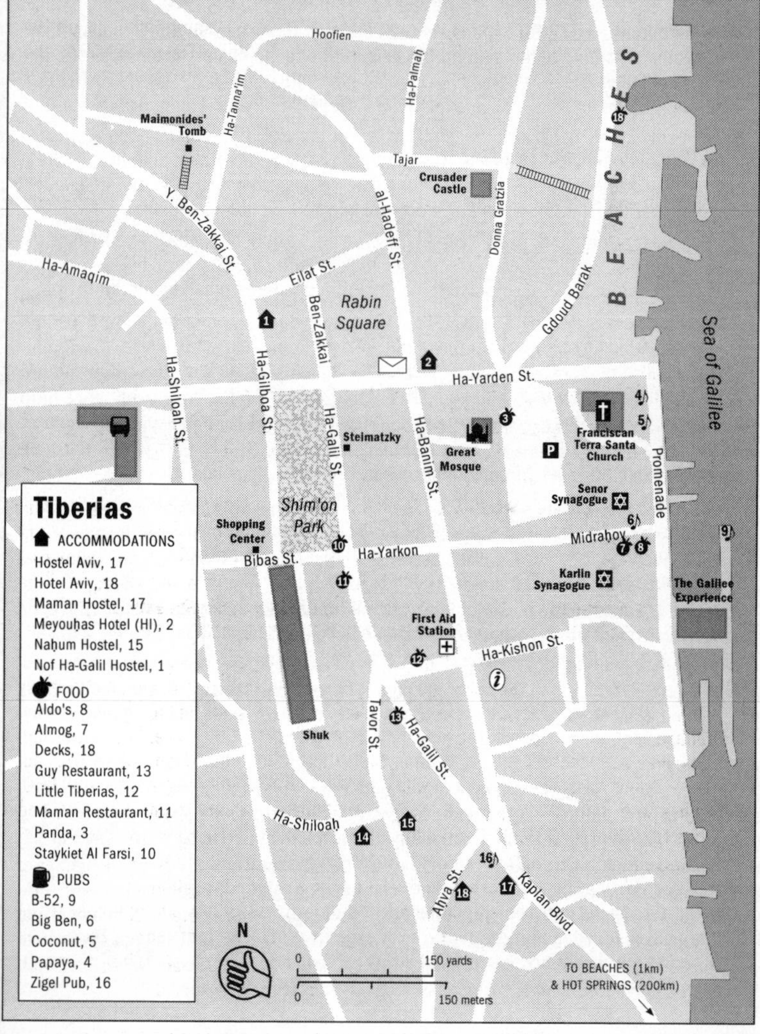

GALILEE

FOOD

Tiberias can easily meet all your beach and hiking picnic needs. The *shuk*, in a square block starting at Ha-Yarkon St. across from Shimron Park, sells cheap produce and baked goods every day except Shabbat. There is a **Supersol** supermarket on Ha-Banim St. (open Su-Th 8am-8:30pm, F 8am-4pm, Sa after sundown-10pm) and a **Hafer** supermarket on the corner of Ha-Banim and Ha-Yarden St. (open Su-Th 8am-9pm, F 8am-3pm, Sa 9-11pm).

The restaurant scene, plagued by too many tourists, is not nearly so ideal. Grilleries on Ha-Banim St. near the *midraḥov* serve *shishlik* with salad and pita for about NIS20. Waterfront seafood restaurants offer idyllic settings complete with jet skiers and plastic bottle flotillas. A dinner of **St. Peter's fish,** a Sea of Galilee specialty, costs about NIS35-50. Ha-Galil St., Ha-Banim St., and the squares in between burgeon with culinary possibilities, from Thai to Italian, but beware of menus that don't list prices.

Guy Restaurant (☎672 30 36), on Ha-Galil St., past Ha-Kishon St. when coming from the center of town. No frills and no big bills will be found at this fabulous Moroccan place. Stuffed veggies with rice NIS7-15, with meat NIS12-15; spicy meatballs NIS15; and some of the meanest coffee around NIS4. Open Su-Th noon-11pm, F noon-5pm.

Decks (☎672 15 38), at Lido Beach. Turn left at the end of the promenade and continue 200m down Gdoud Barak St. Cleanse your palate on the lemon and mint slushes (NIS20) and finish off with the heavenly apple crepes, drenched in sorbet and wine-soaked cherries (NIS25). Open Su-Th 6pm-midnight, Sa sundown-midnight.

Maman Restaurant (☎672 11 26), 21 Ha-Galil St. Locally beloved, Maman fills with Israeli regulars. Excellent hummus with pita and olives NIS12. St. Peter's fish at the lowest price around (NIS30). Open Su-Th 11am-11pm, F 11am-4pm, Sa sundown-11pm.

Little Tiberias (☎679 21 48 or 679 28 06), on the Ha-Kishon St. *midraḥov.* Families flock to this homey retreat from *midraḥov* mayhem. Huge salads (Greek and Caesar) NIS28; grilled meat NIS40-60; and indulgently creamy vegetarian dishes NIS34. Open daily noon-midnight. AmEx, MC, V.

Almog (☎672 12 72), on the *midraḥov* opposite Big Ben. By morning and late-night, a coffee bar; by day, another generic *midraḥov* restaurant. Desserts NIS12-23. *Shishlik* and kebab NIS30-50. 15% *Let's Go* discount. Open daily 9am-late. MC, V.

Panda, 32 Ha-Misgad Sq. (☎679 09 70), in the parking lot between Ha-Yarden St. and the *midraḥov.* Their business lunch (NIS42) will fill you and your weekly quota of greasy Chinese food. Combo dinners also make a good deal for groups (NIS72 for 2; NIS84 for 4). Open daily noon-midnight; lunch until 3:30pm.

Staykiet Al Farsi, on the corner of Bilas St. and Ha-Galil St., right next to Shimron Park. This glorified kiosk doesn't bother with the superfluous, just good grilled meat and salads (NIS27-37). Open Su-Th 10am-9pm, F 10am-2:30pm.

Aldo's (☎672 01 76), on the *midraḥov* on the far end from the promenade. Aldo's generous pizza slices (NIS7-8) are a great, cheap way to fill up. Open daily 11am-midnight.

SIGHTS

As the seat of Talmudic study in the 2nd and 3rd centuries CE, Tiberias hosted a number of influential scholars. Buried in the hills around Tiberias are several of the giants in Jewish thought, history, and Torah commentary. Modest dress is required for visiting the tombs; head coverings are provided for men. All that's left of the **Old City,** shaken by earthquakes and conquerors, is a few black basalt wall fragments scattered throughout the modern town. A **free tour** leaves from the Sheraton Moriah-Plaza hotel every Saturday at 10am.

MAIMONIDES' TOMB. The best-known of the scholars laid to rest in Tiberias is Moses Maimonides, the hugely influential 12th-century physician and philosopher whose works synthesized neo-Aristotelian-Arab philosophy with Judaism. According to legend, an unguided camel carried his coffin to Tiberias. The white half-cylinder is the actual tomb; the Hebrew inscription is a Jewish saying: "From Moses [the original] until Moses [Maimonides] there was no one like Moses [Maimonides]." Ask for the tomb of "Rambam," the Hebrew acronym for his full name (Rabbi Moshe Ben-Maimon). *(Walk out Ben-Zakkai St. from Ha-Yarden St.; the tomb is 2 blocks up on the right, up a wide stairway. Look for the red metal sculpture above the tomb.)*

BEN-ZAKKAI'S TOMB. Rabbi Yoḥanan Ben-Zakkai snuck out of besieged Jerusalem in a coffin, popped out of the casket in front of the Roman General Vespasian, and prophetically addressed him as "Caesar." When news of the old Caesar's death arrived, Vespasian graciously granted Rabbi Yoḥanan one wish. The rabbi chose to found a house of study with his students. *(Next to Maimonides' tomb, on Ben-Zakkai St.)*

RABBI AKIVA'S TOMB. Rabbi Akiva, a woodcutter who began to study only after age 40, is one of the more frequently quoted rabbis in the Talmud and was one of the students who helped carry Rabbi Yoḥanan out of Jerusalem. Believers gather to have their illnesses cured at the hillside tomb of Akiva's student, **Rabbi Meir Ba'al Ha-Nes,** above the hot springs. *(On the hillside directly above the city. See the GTIO city map for walking directions, or take bus #4, 4-aleph, 6, or 6-aleph and ask for directions.)*

FRANCISCAN TERRA SANCTA CHURCH. Also known as St. Peter's, the Terra Sancta Church was built in the 12th century to commemorate St. Peter's role in the growth of Christianity. The church is set back next to the Papaya Bar; look for the five crosses on the brown door (the symbol and color of the Franciscan church). The apse behind the altar is arched like the bow of a boat in honor of Jesus' fishing career. In the courtyard is a statue of the Virgin Mary created by Polish troops who lived in the church from 1942 to 1945. *(On the promenade in front of the Caesar Hotel. ☎672 05 16. Open daily 8:30am-6pm. Modest dress required.)*

CRUSADER CASTLE. The crumbling remains of a 12th-century **Crusader castle** overlook the Sea of Galilee. Admission includes coffee, a short historical tour, a sentinel's view of the water, and entrance to the art galleries now housed in the castle. *(A block past the Meaḥuz Youth Hostel on Donna Gratzia St. ☎672 13 75. Gallery open Su-Th 9am-1pm and 3-6pm, F 9am-1pm. NIS10.)*

GALILEE EXPERIENCE. The T-shaped wharf along the promenade is home to the 38-minute must-see film on the past 4000 years in the Galilee, emphasizing the life of Jesus and the formation of Israel. Composed of 2000 slides and 27 slide projectors, this is an informative way to escape the midday heat. *(Turn right at the end of the* midraḥov *onto the promenade. ☎672 36 20. Every hr. 8am-10pm except during Shabbat. NIS32, students NIS24. Screened in 12 languages.)*

LEHMANN MUSEUM. This small museum displays Tiberias's hot spring history. Walk out the museum's back door to reach the ruins of the Ḥammat Synagogues, six ancient buildings constructed on top of one another. The four upper synagogues were used from the 6th to the 8th centuries CE. Below these ruins are the remains of Roman spas, which still release scalding water. The jewel of the exhibit is a mosaic floor that was once part of three separate synagogues. *(Next to the spas. ☎672 52 87. Open daily 8am-4pm. NIS9, students NIS8, children NIS4.)*

KARNEI ḤITTIM. Salah al-Din defeated the Crusaders in 1187 at the Horns of Ḥittim. From the peak of this extinct volcano it is possible to see Jordan to the east, the Mediterranean to the west, and Tzfat to the north. The walk to the top of the hill takes about 50 minutes, but the view is more breathtaking than the climb. *(Bus #42, NIS7).*

BEACHES

For many **beaches** on the Galilee, you'll have to bring your own sand—otherwise, bring sandals for walking over the sizzling rocks. Beaches in the city and the immediate vicinity are owned by hotels that charge hefty fees in exchange for changing rooms, showers, boat rentals, and food. The beaches just north of town are located along Gdoud Barak Rd., off Ha-Yarden St.; those to the south lie off the main coastal road (Rte. 90, with which Ha-Galil merges).

Lido Kinneret, just off Ha-Yarden St., charges NIS20 for 45-minute boat rides on the lake, but they are often only available for groups. Waterskiing is NIS200/US$50 for 15 minutes. (☎672 15 38. Open daily 8am-5:30pm.) Just north of Lido, **Quiet Beach** (Ḥof Ha-Sheket), with a pool, an energetic DJ, and hordes of school kids, is anything but quiet. (☎670 08 00. Open daily 9am-6pm. NIS25, children NIS20.) Next in line to the north, **Blue Beach** boasts the largest swimming area and best view on the lake. (☎672 01 05. Open daily 9am-5pm. NIS25, children NIS20; NIS5 more on Shabbat.) A 15-minute walk from the city center or a short ride on bus #5-aleph south of Tiberias leads to **Ganim Beach.** (☎672 07 09. Open daily 9am-6pm. NIS20.) Next to it is **Holiday Inn Beach.** Look for the bridge connecting hotel and lakefront. Banana boats cost NIS30 for 15min. (☎672 85 36. Open 9am-6pm. NIS25, students NIS20.) There are three **religious beaches** on Gdoud Barak Rd.: **Ḥof Nifrad,** opposite the Scottish Guest House, welcomes visitors daily 9am to 5pm. (☎679 15 09. Open to women Su, Tu, Th; to men M, W, F. Free.) **Ḥof Mehadrin,** between Lido Kinneret and Quiet Beach, has the only unfenced beach on Barak Rd. and allows camping. The catch: it's men-only. (☎671 61 09. NIS10.) Next door, **Be'er Miriam** is for women only (NIS10). To avoid the hefty admission prices of most beaches, circle the old city walls at the southern end of the promenade and walk 200m along the dirt path through a field to a small **free beach.**

Those seeking a hotter and slimier time are in luck: Tiberias is home to the world's earliest-known hot mineral spring, **Ḥamei T'verya.** One legend maintains that the springs were formed in the Great Flood when the earth's insides boiled. Another holds that demons heat the water under standing orders from King Solomon. Cleanse body and wallet (NIS53, Sa NIS58; 20% student discount). The older building, **Tiberias Hot Springs,** has single-sex baths. (☎672 85 00. Open Su-F 7am-4pm.) The newer, coed building, **Tiberias Hot Springs Spa,** contains a fitness room and jacuzzis. A massage is NIS133 and a private mineral bath NIS99. (☎672 85 00. New spa open Su-M, W, F-Sa 8am-8pm; Tu, Th until 11pm.) The springs are 2km south of town on the coastal road; bus #5-aleph runs from the central bus station and Ha-Galil St. every 30 minutes.

A tangle of **waterslides** swishes 1km south of Tiberias at **Gal Beach.** (☎670 07 00. Open daily 9am-5pm. NIS50, students NIS40.) Walk or take bus #5-aleph from the central bus station or Ha-Galil St. The mother of all water parks is **Luna Gal,** operated by Moshav Ramot on the eastern shore. This aquatic extravaganza has bumper boats, slides, pools, waterfalls, an inner tube ride, and an excellent beach. (☎673 17 50. Open Su, Tu-W, F-Sa 9:30am-6pm; M, Th 9:30am-11pm. NIS65.)

ENTERTAINMENT

Nightlife in Tiberias centers on the *midraḥov* and promenade area. In summer, street musicians, popcorn vendors, and occasional palm-readers set up shop. Get out the white polyester duds and thigh-highs for Lido Kinneret Beach and Kinneret Sailing's **disco cruises,** one of Tiberias' trademarks. (Nightly 8-11pm. NIS15-25.) The **Sea of Galilee Festival** brings international folk troupes to Tiberias during the second week of July. Check the GTIO for info on this and other area festivals, including Ein Gev's **Passover Music Festival** and Tzemaḥ's **Tu b'Av Love Fest** (mid-Aug.), where happy young Israelis gather for some love, sweat, and rock 'n' roll.

Kibbutz Kinneret Discotheque (☎05 195 30 36 or 06 675 96 89), at the Kibbutz. Volunteers from neighboring *kibbutzim* and Tiberias expats guzzle cheap beer (NIS10) or groove inside at what is widely considered the best discotheque in the area. Cover NIS25, not always applicable for tourists. Open W at 9:30pm, F at midnight.

Coconut (☎05 328 85 25). Turn left at the end of the *midraḥov* and walk to the end of the promenade. This Gilligan's Island-esque hut has a nice view of the lake and a flashy little dance floor. Dancing is hottest on Friday, music is worst on Saturday (karaoke), and the place gets quiet and candlelit on Sunday. Beer NIS16-20; special tequila mixers NIS25. Open daily 8pm-morning.

Zigel Pub (☎05 285 35 82), where Ha-Galil St. and Ha-Banim St. merge. Israeli youth headquarters. If the disco trance and strobe light in the downstairs dance bar give you a headache, head upstairs to the comfy couches and cheap *nargilah* (NIS10). F-Sa dance bar, Tu, Th karaoke. Beer NIS16; cocktails NIS28. Open 10pm-morning.

Big Ben, on the left near the end of the *midraḥov*. This tourist bar gets rowdy late at night with young, drunken Brits (and a healthy dose of Americans and Israelis) giving each other the time of day. Beers NIS14-17; tropical cocktails like a 'Big Ben Kiss' NIS29. Fried snacks NIS19. Open 8:30am-late.

Papaya (☎05 124 12 00). Turn left onto the promenade from the *midraḥov;* it's just before Coconut. It's always summer in this beach hut, which serves spiked ice tea (NIS20) and alcoholic milkshakes (NIS25) to an older crowd. Long, slick bar and a tiny dance floor for salsa on Tuesdays. Requisite karaoke night on Thursday. Beer NIS15.

B-52, next to the Galilee Experience wharf. Dangling over the marina, this bar tends to be packed with Israeli youth drinking the advertised beer (look for the huge neon Tuborg sign). Place gets caliente for salsa Saturdays. Open daily 2pm-late.

GALILEE

DAYTRIPS FROM TIBERIAS

BEIT SHE'AN AND BORDER CROSSING בית שאן

From Tiberias, take bus #928, 961, 963, or 964 (50min., NIS19) to the Beit She'an bus stop. Walk to the main road through the mall, turn left, and make a right at the Bank Leumi, following signs to the site. ☎*658 71 89. Open Sa-Th 8am-5pm, F 8am-4pm; in winter Sa-Th 8am-4pm, F 8am-3pm. NIS18, students NIS15, children NIS9.*

THE TEL. One of the finest archaeological sites in the country, Beit She'an is a Sephardi (Jews of Middle Eastern descent) development town containing a vast complex of mostly Roman and Byzantine ruins. Excavations on and around **Tel al-Husn,** the oldest archaeological mound, have revealed 20 layers of settlements dating back as far as the 5th millennium BCE (Neolithic period). Of particular interest is the **Roman theater,** one of the largest extant Roman constructions in Israel. Built in 200 CE by Emperor Septimius Severus, the theater accommodated 7,000 riotous spectators in its three tiers of semi-circular seating. Newly renovated, it is now occasionally used for plays and dance performances. The remains of other grand structures branching off from the theater include a Byzantine bathhouse, and a Roman temple to Dionysus, god of wine and the principal god of the city. Long before it became a Philistine, Jewish, Greek, Roman, and eventually Turkish city, the region was occupied by the Egyptians; the 14th-century BCE ruins of the **Ashtaroth Temple,** built on the *tel* by Ramses III for his Canaanite allies, is a remainder of that period. North of the *tel* is the **Monastery of the Noble Lady Maria,** founded in 567 CE and abandoned after the Persian invasion of 614. The best time to visit the site is in the early morning, before the sun makes climbing the *tel* unbearable.

PEACE BRIDGE BORDER CROSSING. This is one of Israel's busiest border crossing into Jordan; allow at least an hour to cross, especially Th-S. From Beit She'an, take bus #16 (NIS8) or a taxi (☎658 84 55 or 658 64 80; NIS35) to the border. Once there, you'll pay a NIS64 exit fee, go through passport and customs control (where you can reclaim your VAT), and take a shuttle bus (NIS4) from in front of the Duty Free shop to the Jordanian side. A visa to enter Jordan (US$44) can be purchased on the spot. From the Jordanian border, a taxi to Amman is JD25. Coming from the Jordanian side, the exit fee is JD4; there is no entrance fee for Israel, but travelers who need a visa (see p. 37) must purchase one at the Israeli embassy in Amman; they are not available at the border. (☎ 06 658 64 44, 658 64 22, or 658 64 48; Jordanian terminal 00962 2 655 0523. Open Su-Th 6:30am-10pm, F, Sa 8am-8pm. For more info on crossing into Jordan, see p. 344.)

BELVOIR (KOKHAV HA-YARDEN) כוכב הירדן

About 25min. north of Beit She'an. Buses traveling between Beit She'an and Tiberias will stop at the bottom of the road to let you off, but the site is still 6km uphill—a long, tiring hike or easy hitchhike. Let's Go doesn't recommend hitchhiking; it is best reached by car. ☎ 658 17 66. Open Sa-Th 8am-5pm, F 8am-4pm; in winter Sa-Th 8am-4pm, F 8am-3pm. NIS14, students NIS12, children NIS6. Includes entrance to park.

In the middle of the 12th century, a Tiberias family established a farm atop a small mountain overlooking the Jordan River valley, on the site of the ancient Jewish city of Kokhav ("star"). Only 20 years later, they sold the land to the Knights of the Hospitaller Order, who were interested in the hilltop location for tactical rather than aesthetic reasons, turning the peaceful farm into a fortress. But even the knights couldn't ignore the scenery, naming their compound Belvoir (beautiful view). The strong fortress withstood multiple attacks by Muslin forces in 1182-1184, but finally fell to the Crusaders in 1187 and then to Salah al-Din's forces in 1189. The soldiers ravaged the fortress, which was later demolished even further by Salah al-Din's nephew to prevent the Crusaders from returning. The ruins remained unoccupied until the early 19th century, when local Bedouin families established a small village there, which they called Kaukab al-Hawa ("star of the winds"). The site was abandoned as its population fled during the 1948 war; preservation and reconstruction work was carried out from 1966-1968. The ruins are not as ancient or extensive as those at nearby Beit She'an, but here you have the leisure to wander around the old rooms.

Next to the fortress is a small **sculpture park** featuring the works of Israeli sculptor **Igael Tumarkin,** who now resides in Jaffa. A critic of Zionism and pioneer in environmental sculpture, Tumarkin (born in Germany, 1933) uses stone and metal to "paraphrase" history and mourn the death of ideals.

THE ROAD TO AFULA

Buses traveling between Beit She'an and Afula will stop at any of the sites upon request. Buses #411, 412, 415, 417, 829 and 953 make the 45min. trip every 30min. from 6am to 8pm, breaking for Shabbat.

Along the beautiful valley road from Beit She'an to Afula are several sights of natural and historical interest. **Gan Ha-Shlosha** (☎ 06 658 62 19; fax 658 78 22), also known as **Saḥne,** is about 8km west of Beit She'an.worth an afternoon excursion. Its waterfalls and crystal-clear swimming holes are refreshing in both summer and winter (at a constant 28°C). The springs have been popular since Roman times; the covered pool and waterslides haven't (open in summer Sa-Th 8am-5pm, F 8am-4pm; winter Sa-Th 8am-4pm, F 8am-3pm; NIS27, children NIS16). Watch out for theft on overcrowded weekends. A 10min. walk along the road behind the park leads to the **Museum of Regional and Mediterranean Archaeology** (☎ 658 63 52), a collection of Hellenistic and Islamic art and pottery gathered from a local Canaanite temple, an Israelite community, and a Roman colony (open Su-Th 9am-2pm, Sa and holidays 10am-2pm; park admission required to see the museum).

Within **Kibbutz Hefziba**, another 3km down the road toward Afula, is the beautiful 6th-century CE **Beit Alpha Synagogue** (☎ 06 653 20 04), whose highlight is a magnificently preserved mosaic of a zodiac wheel surrounding the sun god Helios, identified with the prophet Elijah. (Open Sa-Th 8am-5pm, F 8am-4pm; closes 1hr. earlier in winter. Admission NIS9, students NIS8, children NIS4.) Buses from Afula and Beit She'an stop at the entrance to the kibbutz. Don't be misled by the sign for Kibbutz Beit Alpha (1km closer to Beit She'an).

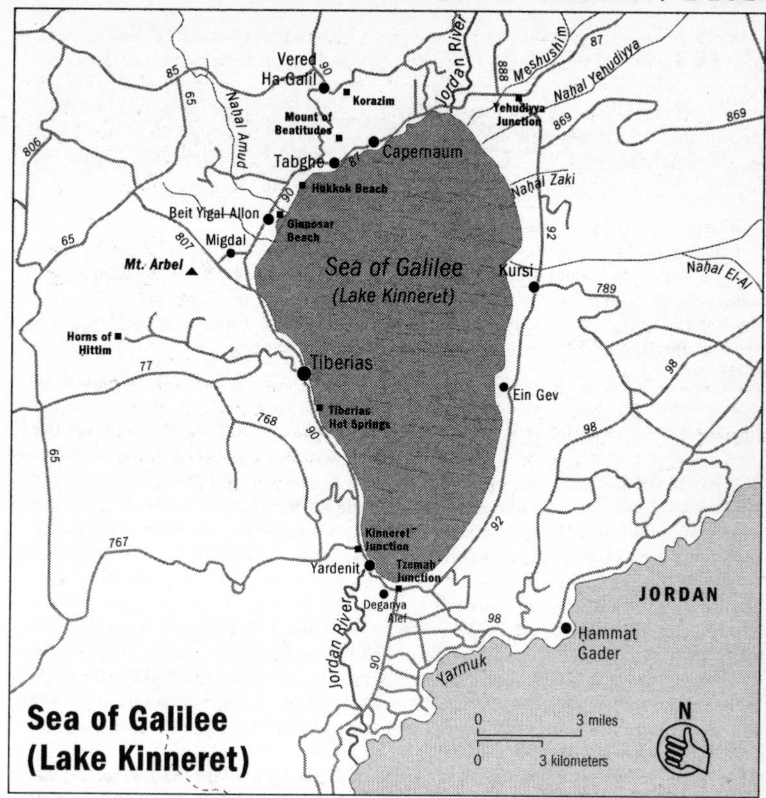

Sea of Galilee (Lake Kinneret)

GALILEE

SEA OF GALILEE (LAKE KINNERET) ☎06

Pleasant beaches, scenic trails, and historically and religiously significant sites grace the area that surrounds the Sea of Galilee. Campgrounds are available at several of the beaches around the Kinneret (contact the GTIO), or take advantage of cheap accommodations in Tiberias.

GETTING AROUND

All the sights on the Sea of Galilee are in some way accessible by bus from Tiberias, but renting a mountain bike is the more convenient and scenic way to go (see **Tiberias: Practical Information,** p. 223). A complete circuit of the lake (55km) takes four to five hours. Watch out for two tricky creatures: the furry little hyrax (a close relative of the elephant) and the screeching, careening Israeli driver (a close relative of the lemming). Leave as early as possible and bike clockwise around the lake to get the hilly part between Tiberias and Capernaum finished while your energy is high and the sun is low. Spring is the best time for biking; in July and August, the hills reach unbearable temperatures, but the ferries run more frequently and it's easier to catch one half-way around the lake. **Bring a lot of water.**

The **Lido Kinneret Sailing Co.** operates a ferry from Lido Beach to Capernaum, Ginosar Beach, Mt. of Beatitudes, and Tiberias. (☎672 15 38. 30-45min., NIS30. 8am-6pm.) Individuals with bicycles are welcome, but schedules are at the mercy of tour groups. The **Kinneret Sailing Company** runs cruises from Tiberias to Ein Gev on the east coast of the Sea of Galilee. During the second half of July and all of August, boats leave Tiberias daily at 10:30am, 12:30, and 3pm, and return from Ein Gev at 11:30am, 2:15, and 5:45pm. (☎665 80 08 or 665 80 09; fax 665 80 07. NIS20, children NIS15, with bicycle NIS30; round-trip NIS30, children NIS20).

ACCOMMODATIONS

The best accommodation option in the area is **Karei Deshei,** with beautiful gardens, a serene, private beach, and wonderful views of the Sea of Galilee. The clean, cool rooms make a great getaway from Tiberias. (Breakfast included. Reception 7am-10pm. Check-in 3pm. Check-out 10am; noon on Shabbat. Reservations recommended. A/C 4-6 bed dorms with bath NIS90; NIS112 on Fridays, holidays, and in July and Aug. Credit cards accepted.)

Camping is a good way to escape the city heat. Check out the MTIO/SPNI information office at Tzemaḥ on the southern tip of the lake, in the shopping strip across from Jordan Valley College; take bus #26 or 28. (☎675 20 56. Open daily 8am-4pm.) Their map (NIS22) shows the 25 lakeside campgrounds interspersed among the private beaches (NIS60 per car; free for car-less campers). Be wary of **theft.** Women should never camp alone.

SIGHTS ON THE SHORE

YIGAL ALLON CENTER. The low water level of the Galilee in 1985-86 had one serendipitous effect—the discovery of an **ancient boat** under a segment of a newly exposed lake bed off the beach of Kibbutz Ginnosar. Authorities encased its wooden frame in a fiberglass brace and hauled it to shore. The boat, dating from between 100 BCE and 100 CE, has been restored to near-pristine condition. Noting its age, some Christians have dubbed it "the Jesus boat." While it is a fishing boat, even of the sort the apostles might have used, archaeologists suspect it sunk in a great sea battle between the Romans and Jews in 66 CE, that was described by Josephus. It rests in a new wing of the Yigal Allon Center in an airtight glass tank, where it underwent several years of repair. Tickets also include admission to a museum with exhibits on the history of the Galilee, a Yigal Allon remembrance room, an observation tower, and "The Crossroads of War", a multimedia choose-your-own-adventure style look at different wars. *(Take bus #840, 841, 963, or 964. NIS6.60. ☎672 14 95. Open Su-Th 8am-5pm, F-Sa 8m-4pm. NIS16, children and students NIS14.)*

Shady, green Ginnosar Beach sits next door. *(☎670 03 00. Open 8:30am-6pm. NIS25, children NIS20. Paddle boats NIS50 per hr;, kayaks NIS40 per hr.)*

ḤAMMAT GADER. These hot baths, known as al-Himmeh in Arabic, lie in former Syrian territory. In Roman times, the town, combined with its other (Jordanian) half on the western side of the Yarmouk River, formed part of the Decapolis. While the more interesting remains lie in Jordan, the Roman ruins here, including a small pool once reserved for lepers, have been partially reconstructed. At the southwest corner of the complex sits the hottest spring in the area—so hot (51°C) that the Jews call it *Ma'ayan Ha-Gehinom* (Hell's Pool) and the Arabs call it *'Ain Maqla* (Frying Pool). The hot pool gets crowded with families; the leper pool does not. In one area, bathers slather on black mud that purportedly cures skin ailments. Ḥammat Gader also boasts an **alligator park,** where hundreds of large, sleepy gators sun themselves and slog through murky water. The first gators emigrated from Florida with a little help from park authorities, but the reserve now raises its young in a hothouse at the entrance to the ponds. *(30min. southeast of Tiberias. Bus #24 leaves from Tiberias: 9 and 10:30am, return at 1 and 3pm; F 8:45 and 10:30am, return noon and 1:15pm; NIS7.20. ☎665 99 99. Open M-Sa 7am-noon, Su 7am-4pm. Weekdays NIS50, after 5pm NIS43; F-Sa NIS55.)*

DEGANYA ALEF. Founded by Russian immigrants in 1909, Deganya Alef is Israel's first kibbutz and the birthplace of General Moshe Dayan. Today, the kibbutz manufactures diamond tools. A 1948 Syrian tank marks the entrance. *(Near the spot where the Jordan River flows out of the Sea of Galilee, about 8km south of Tiberias and west of Ḥammat Gader. From Tiberias take bus #22, NIS7.)*

MT. ARBEL. Among the best hikes in the area, the Mt. Arbel trail is to the northwest of the Sea of Galilee. The red trail leads from Moshav Arbel to the Arab village of Wadi Hamam. To start the hike, turn right and walk 1km. After another right turn on the next main road, walk 1km to Migdal Junction and take bus #459, 841, or 963 (NIS7) back to Tiberias. The entire hike should only take three to four hours. *(To get to Mt. Arbel, take bus #42 to Moshav Arbel; 7am, NIS7. Ask at the moshav for directions to Matzok Arbel.)*

NAḤAL AMUD. The Naḥal Amud stream flows from Mt. Meron all the way to Hukkok Beach on the lake. Along the banks are beautiful flowers and a natural pillar of rock. Serious backpackers use the trail as either the first or last leg of a multi-day **Yam Le-Yam hike** (see **From Sea to Shining Sea**, p. 214).

NEW TESTAMENT SIGHTS

According to the New Testament Jesus walked on the waters of the Sea of Galilee, and four of the most significant stories in Christian history are set in the steep hills of its northern coast. Modest dress is required for entrance to New Testament sights—no shorts above the knees or bare shoulders.

TABGHE

Take bus #459, 841, or 963 (20min., every hr., NIS11.50) to the Capernaum Junction (Tzomet Kfar Naḥum). Walk toward the sea, following the brown signs to Tabghe and Capernaum. Tabghe (Arabic), Heptapegon (Greek), or Seven Springs (English) houses two sites and lies about 1km down the road.

THE CHURCH OF THE BREAD AND FISH. This is the site where Jesus is said to have fed 5000 pilgrims with five loaves and two small fish (Matthew 14:13-21). The church is built around the rock upon which Jesus placed the bread, and a section of the mosaic has been removed to reveal part of the rock and the original 4th-century foundations. *(Open M-Sa 8am-6pm, Su 10am-5pm. Free.)*

Around the right side of the church, past the "private" sign and down the stairs, is a small hospice for Christian pilgrims; inquire at the office inside the church for information. *(☎672 10 61. Singles with A/C and bath NIS140/US$35; doubles with A/C US$30/NIS120.)*

CHURCH OF THE PRIMACY OF ST. PETER. This church commemorates the miracle of the loaves and fishes and the spot where Jesus made Peter "Shepherd of his People." According to the Book of John, Peter led the apostles on a fishing expedition 100m offshore from Tabghe. A man on shore called to them to throw their nets over the starboard side and assured them a catch. When the nets hit the water, a swarm of fish swam in. Peter jumped off the boat and swam to shore, where he found the man, whom he recognized as Jesus, preparing a meal for the Twelve Apostles. The Church of the Primacy is built around a rock said to be the table of this feast. A Persian invasion in 614 CE destroyed the 4th-century church at this spot. Franciscans rebuilt it with black basalt in 1933. On the seaward side of the church are the steps where Jesus called out his instructions; on the shoreline are the "thrones of the Apostles," a series of six double column bases. *(50m past the parking lot of the Church of the Bread and Fishes. ☎672 47 67. Open daily 8am-4:30pm. Free.)*

MOUNT OF BEATITUDES. Jesus is supposed to have delivered his Sermon on the Mount (Matthew 5) and chosen his disciples at this site. A church funded by Benito Mussolini stands on the Mount; its octagonal shape recalls the eight beatitudes. Symbols surrounding the altar inside the church represent the seven virtues (justice, charity, prudence, faith, fortitude, hope, and remembrance). The gardens around the site offer a spectacular view of the Sea of Galilee, Tiberias, and the Golan Heights. *(The small path to the Mount is next to the stop for bus #16, across the street from the entrance to St. Peter's Church. It's a 20min. walk uphill to the church. From the Mount, follow the road back 1km to catch bus #459, 841 or 963 back to Tiberias: NIS11.50. ☎672 67 12. Open daily 8am-noon and 2:30-5pm.)*

OUTSIDE OF TABGHE

CAPERNAUM. It was in Capernaum (Kfar Naḥum in Hebrew, Tel Num in Arabic), Peter's birthplace, that Jesus healed Simon's mother-in-law and the Roman Centurion's servant (Luke 4:31-37 and 7:1-10). A modern church arches over the ruins of a 5th-century octagonal church, marking the site believed to have held Peter's house. The ruins of a nearby **synagogue,** perched in the middle of the old town, contain Corinthian columns and friezes dating from the 4th century CE. The synagogue, discernible by the black, basalt foundation, is built on top of an older, first-century CE synagogue in which Jesus may have preached. A milestone recovered from the Via Maris, a 2nd-century CE Roman road built by the Emperor Hadrian, sits to the left of the synagogue. Since Capernaum did not participate in the first and second century Jewish revolts against the Romans, it survived unscathed. *(Buses #459, 841, and 963 from Tiberias pass the Capernaum junction about once an hour on the way north to Kiryat Shmona and Tzfat. Get off near the Capernaum ferry port and walk 1km to your left. From Tabghe, Capernaum is 2km further east on the coastal road, marked by a sign. Synagogue open daily 8:30am-4pm. NIS2.)*

MIGDAL. Also called "Magdala," the birthplace of Mary Magdalene lies north of Tiberias. An agricultural community founded in 1910 now accompanies the tiny, white-domed shrine and largely unexcavated ruins. *(Buses #50, 51, and 52 go to Migdal from Tiberias: 10min., infrequent. Buses #459, 841, and 963 run to the Migdal Junction, "Tzomet Migdal," a short walk away. When biking from Tiberias, wait until the second Migdal sign to turn off the road.)*

KURSI. The ruins of this Christian settlement, also known as Gergessa or Gerasa, date from early Byzantine times (5th-6th centuries CE). According to the New Testament, it was at Kursi that Jesus exorcised several demons from a man's body and caused the demons to possess a grazing herd of pigs; the pigs raced into the sea and drowned. Jesus' feat came to be known as the "Miracle of the Swine" (Luke 8:26-31, Matthew 8:23-34). The sight, popular with Christian pilgrims, harbors impressive remains of a large, Byzantine **monastery** and a small chapel—both reconstructed and with mosaic floors. *(On the eastern side of the lake, 7km north of Ein Gev. The ruins are 50m from the bus stop. Buses #15, 17, 18, 19, 20 and 22 run from Tiberias to Tzomet Kursi: 30min., every 30min. noon-7pm, NIS14. ☎673 19 83. Open Sa-Th 8am-5pm, F 8am-4pm; in winter Sa-Th 8am-4pm, F 8am-3pm. NIS9, students NIS8.)*

GALILEE

KORAZIM. These ruins are on the site of the unrepentant towns chastised by Jesus (Matthew 11:21). The **synagogue** here dates from the Talmudic period (3rd-4th centuries CE). The remains suggest a characteristic village of the time: housing quarters centered around a courtyard and a synagogue with ornamental pediments and a reconstructed interior cornice. *(Take bus #459, 841, or 963 and get off at Tzomet Korazim Junction: NIS11.50. Walk east 2km on the main road, past Vered Ha-Galil and Moshav Korazim to a parking lot on the right. Signs there lead to the town. ☎693 49 82. Open Sa-Th 8am-5pm, F 8am-4pm; in winter Sa-Th 8am-4pm, F 8am-3pm. NIS14, students NIS10.50.)*

YARDENIT. The Gospels say that John baptized Jesus in the Jordan River. Today, dozens of pilgrims and tourists come to the Yardenit Baptismal Area on the banks of the Jordan. *(Right off the coastal road; take bus #17, 19, 21, 22, 23 or 26 to Kibbutz Kinneret. ☎675 94 86. Open Su-Th 9am-6pm, F-Sa 8am-5pm.)*

NORTH OF THE SEA

TZFAT (SAFED) צפת صفد ☎06

Situated on Mt. Kenaan, the third highest peak in Israel, Tzfat is a city of mesmerizing tranquility. Streets wind through this city on a hill, raising aimless wandering to an artform. Stone buildings, brightly spotted with turquoise-colored doorways, fall over each other. Tzfat's beauty reflects not only its physical setting, overlooking the cool, lush greenery of the Galilean hills, but also a mystical way of life. In 1777, a rabbi who had trekked to Tzfat all the way from Europe ultimately packed up and left for Tiberias, complaining that the angels had kept him up at night.

The Talmud translates the town's name as "vantage point" because of the city's panoramic view, but others claim the name derives from the root for "anticipation." Jewish traditions are taken seriously in Tzfat; many people here await the arrival of the Messiah, who they believe will pass through on the way from Mt. Meron to Jerusalem. The modern-day mystics of the city may dress in uniformly black garb, but they come from diverse backgrounds; some are descendants of old *shtetl* rabbis, others are *baalei t'shuva* ("masters of return"), who turned to Ḥasidic Judaism after living much of their lives as agnostic real-estate agents or Buddhist backpackers. If Jerusalem is the city of gold, Tzfat is the city of turquoise, deeply steeped in the glory of its Kabbalistic masters.

Tzfat hasn't always been a bastion of spirituality. Its Crusader-built castle was captured by Salah al-Din in 1188, reconquered by the Knights Templar in 1240, and then lost again in 1266 to the Mamluk Sultan Baybars. It wasn't until the Middle Ages that many Jews arrived in Tzfat, seeking refuge in the relatively tolerant

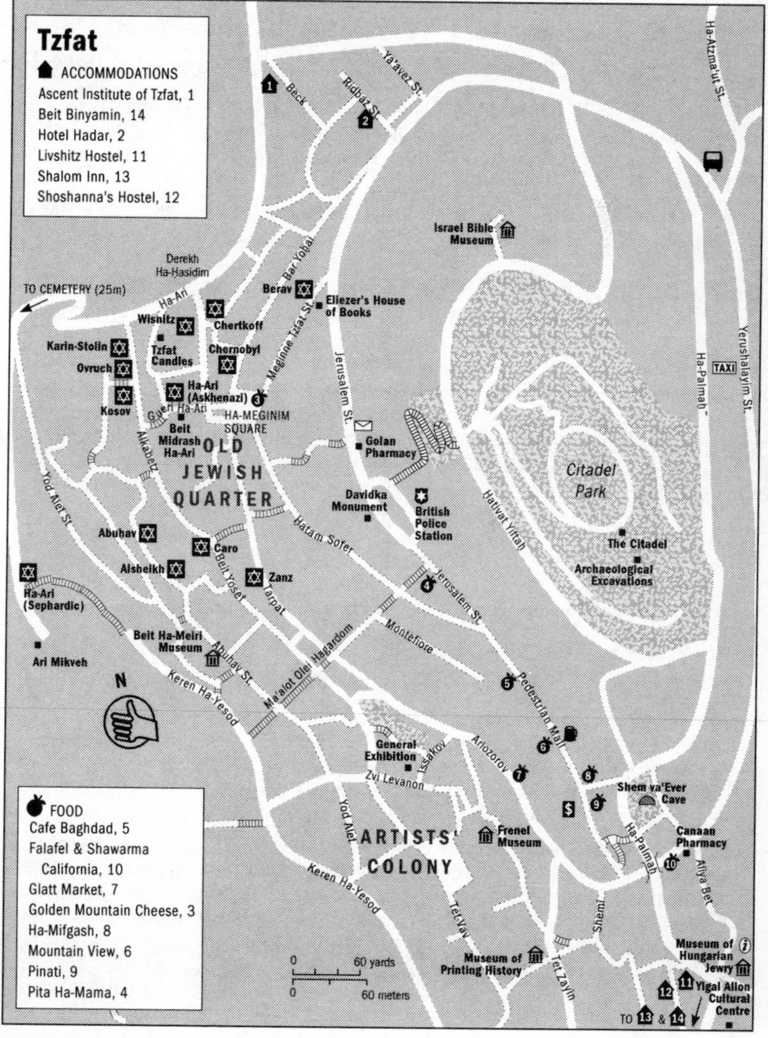

Ottoman Empire. After the Expulsion from Spain in 1492, Jewish exiles flocked to Tzfat, bringing with them the seeds of a mystical tradition. The subsequent century has become known as the Tzfat Renaissance. So many prominent leaders resided in Tzfat that an attempt was made to reestablish the Sanhedrin, the supreme rabbinical council, 1000 years after it had ceased to function. Rabbi Isaac Luria, often called Ha-Ari, arrived in Tzfat from Egypt in 1572 and established it as the center of Kabbalistic mysticism. His inspirational works, combined with poor conditions in Eastern Europe, drew an influx of Ḥasidic Jews from Poland in 1778. New settlements began in the second half of the 19th century and triggered violent Arab protest. By 1948, 12,000 Arabs lived in uneasy coexistence with 1700 Jews. In May 1948, Israeli Palmaḥ troops defeated the Iraqi and Syrian forces entrenched in the fortress at the top of Mt. Kenaan, and the Arab population fled with their armies.

GETTING THERE AND GETTING AROUND

Buses: Central bus station (☎692 11 22). Bus information booth open Su-Th 6:30-8:30am, 9am-1:30pm, 2-3pm; F 6:30-8:30am, 9am-1:30pm. To: **Haifa** via **Akko** (#361 and 362; every 30min. Su-Th 6:15am-7pm, F 6:10am-3:15pm, Sa after sundown; 2hr.; NIS30); **Jerusalem** (#964, daily 7:15am, NIS47); **Kiryat Shmona** (#501 and 511; every hr. Su-Th 5:50am-7:30pm, F 5:50am-4pm; 1hr.; NIS18); **Tel Aviv** (#846, 5:35 and 8:15am, 3hr., NIS44); and **Tiberias** (#459, every hr. 6:50am-7pm, 1hr., NIS17).

Taxis: Kenaan Taxis (☎697 07 07), next to the bus station. *Sherut* to **Tiberias** and **Rosh Pina.** Look for white minivans.

ORIENTATION AND PRACTICAL INFORMATION

The city can be divided into three districts: the **park area,** at the top of the mountain (ringed by Jerusalem St.), the **artists' quarter,** southwest and down the hill, and the **synagogue quarter** (Old City), immediately to the north of the artists' quarter on the other side of Ma'alot Olei Ha-Gardom St. Tzfat is arranged in curved terraces descending on the west from the castle ruins atop **Gan Ha-Metzuda** (Citadel Park). **Jerusalem (Yerushalayim) St.,** behind the central bus station, follows the lines of what was once the castle's moat and makes a complete circle around Citadel Park. Heading left from the major intersection beside the bus station, on the western side of the park, Jerusalem St. becomes the midraḥov. The **midraḥov** (pedestrian mall) is the strip of Jerusalem St. running southwest of the park area, up the hill from the artists' and synagogue quarters. **Ha-Palmaḥ St.** begins off Jerusalem St. near the central bus station and crosses the main street over a stone bridge. **Ha-Ari St.** also begins off Jerusalem St. near the bus station and circles around the western edge of the city, descending down to the cemetery grounds. Tzfat is a compact walking city, and getting around in the old city with a car is nearly impossible.

Tourist Information: Visitors' Center (☎692 74 84 or 692 74 85), Kikkar Ha-Atzma'ut. At the intersection of Aliya Bet and Ha-Palmaḥ. Inside the Wolfson Community Center, through the main entrance on the right. Has a small exhibit on the history of Tzfat, updated maps (NIS5), and free brochures about sights. Open Su-Th 10am-3pm.

Currency Exchange: There are several banks on Jerusalem St. on and near the *midraḥov*. **Bank Ha-Poalim** (☎699 48 00), on the *midraḥov,* near the Ha-Palmaḥ bridge. Hefty commission for changing cash and travelers' checks (NIS24). **ATM** outside. Open Su, Tu-W 8:30am-1:15pm; M, Th 8:30am-1pm and 4-6:30pm; F 8:15am-12:30pm.

English Bookstore: Eliezer's House of Books (☎692 22 55), on Meginne Tzfat St. A wide selection of Jewish books in English. Open Su-Th 10am-2pm and 4-7pm, F 9am-2pm.

Laundry: Dry Cleaning, 38 Jerusalem St. (☎697 38 77), also does it wet. Past the post office, away from the *midrahov* and on the left. NIS10 per kg. Open Su-Th 9:30am-2pm and 4-7pm, F 9:30am-1pm.

First Aid: Magen David Adom, next to the central bus station, downhill on the side away from the main intersection.

Police: (☎697 84 44), outside of the main city, up the hill on the road to Rosh Pina.

Pharmacy: Canaan Pharmacy (☎697 24 40), under Ha-Palmaḥ Bridge. Open Su-Th 8am-1pm and 4-7pm, F 8am-1pm. **Golan Pharmacy** (☎692 04 72), on Jerusalem St., opposite the Municipality building. Open Su-Th 9am-1:30pm and 4-7:30pm, F 9am-1:30pm.

Post Office: (☎692 04 05), on Kikkar Ha-Atzma'ut. At the intersection of Ha-Palmaḥ St. and Aliya Bet, through the parking lot on the other side of the Yigal Allon Theater and Cultural Center. **Poste Restante.** Open Su-Tu, Th 8am-12:30pm and 3:30-6pm; W 8am-1:30pm; F 8am-noon. A more convenient branch at 37 Jerusalem St., past the British Police Station at the end of the *midrahov*, has the same hours.

ACCOMMODATIONS

Rooms are plentiful, though finding quality at the right price can take a bit of planning, particularly during weekends in summer (call ahead for stays over Shabbat). In high season, inexpensive **guest rooms** and flats are often available from town residents. The best way to find a rental is to walk around Jerusalem St. and the old city looking for signs. Always inspect potential quarters before paying (blankets are a plus for Tzfat's chilly nights, even in summer), and feel free to bargain.

Shalom Inn, 3 Korchak St. (☎697 04 45 or 691 18 61), at the beginning of the artists' quarter. From the bus station, take a left on Jerusalem St. and a left on Aliya Bet St.; just past the cultural center take the unmarked street on the right with a small wooden sign that says "Artists' Quarter." The inn is on the left, just after the paved road curves left. Fresh and modern rooms were recently redone. Views of the mountain and the artists' quarter. Private bathrooms, cable TV, A/C, and kitchen. Singles NIS75-110; doubles NIS150-200. In Aug. NIS110-120; 200-240. Credit cards accepted.

Beit Binyamin (HI), 1 Loḥamei Ha-Geta'ot St. (☎692 10 86; fax 697 35 14), near the Amal Trade School in South Tzfat. Take bus #6 or 7. From the bus station, take a left on Jerusalem St. and another left on Aliya Bet St. Pass the community and cultural centers and continue on to Ha-Nassi St., which curves down to the right. Stay on this street, through its curves, and look for the hostel sign on the left. Exceptionally clean, recently renovated rooms have private baths and refrigerators. Breakfast included. Check-out 9am. Wheelchair accessible. 4- to 6-bed dorms NIS78 per person; singles NIS162; doubles NIS224. Credit cards accepted.

Hotel Hadar (☎692 00 68), on Ridbaz St., in an alley off Jerusalem St.; take a right onto Jerusalem St. when coming from the bus station and look for the sign on the right that points down the alley. Comfortable, homey atmosphere. Rooms have bath and A/C or fans. Rooftop lounge has a great view of the city. Check-out 11am. Ring after the midnight curfew. Singles NIS100/US$25; doubles NIS200/US$50. In Aug. and on Jewish holidays NIS10 more per person; in winter NIS10 less.

Ascent Institute of Tzfat, 2 Ha-Ari St. (☎692 13 64 or 800 304 070; fax 692 19 42; email seminars@ascent.org.il; www.ascent.org.il). Take a right on Jerusalem St. from the bus station, then the first right off Jerusalem St. Run by Lubavitch Ḥasidim, many of whom are cheerful, New-Agey American expats. Reactions from secular Jews range from personal revelation to annoyance. Internet access, English library, walking tours of the city, and guided day-hikes free for guests. Breakfast, F dinner, Sa lunch included; NIS10 rebate for each class attended on Judaism. Reception open Su-Th 9am-9pm, F 9am-4pm. Check-out 11am. Flexible midnight curfew. Call ahead for Shabbat stays. Airy 4 to 6-bed dorms with private bath NIS50; private rooms NIS150/US$32. Accepts credit cards, personal checks, traveler's checks, and cash.

Shoshana's Rooms (☎697 39 39 or 050 995 623). Will pick up travelers at the bus station. By foot from the bus station, turn left on Jerusalem St. and go up the stairs to the right at the beginning of the *midraḥov.* Cross the Ha-Palmaḥ bridge and take the cobblestone ramp down to the right after the "Trabulsy Hagay Law Office" sign. Go left down the small alley to the sign labeled with Shoshana's name and phone number. Friendly and helpful, with some of the least expensive rooms in Tzfat. Shared bathroom and kitchen. Sound carries between rooms. Dorms NIS35-45; singles NIS90-110.

Livshitz Hostel (☎052 472 360 or 697 47 10), just across from Shoshana's Rooms in the same small alleyway. Dorm rooms in an old stone building with high ceilings and concrete floors tucked away in a flowering courtyard. Shared bathroom and kitchen access. Dorms NIS35; private room NIS80-100.

FOOD

The stretch of Jerusalem St. north of the bridge along the *midraḥov* is lined with both falafel joints and fairly expensive restaurants. A fruit and vegetable **market** is open Wednesdays 6am-2pm next to the bus station. There are **supermarkets** throughout town, including a **Glatt Market** in the basement of the mall on the *midraḥov*, just past Bank Ha-Poalim. (The main entrance is at the back of the building on Arlozorov St. Open Su-Th 8am-8pm, F 8am-2pm.) Almost all restaurants in Tzfat are kosher, and they close for Shabbat.

Mountain View, 70 Jerusalem St. (☎102 04 04), in the middle of the *midraḥov*. Specializes in vegetarian dishes. A trendy cafe with a terrific window view down the mountain. Particularly impressive at sunset. Huge salads (NIS34-38), stir-fry dishes (NIS34), pasta (NIS32-36), sandwiches (NIS20), and smoothies (NIS14-20) all fancily garnished. Open Su-Th 8am-midnight. Credit cards accepted.

Pita Ha-Mama, Jerusalem St., at the top of the Ma'alot Olei Ha-Gardom stairs. This popular bakery is a great place for a quick snack. Baked pitas stuffed with potato or spinach and onions (NIS5) are perfect for munching while strolling through the old city. Try the *lafah* bread with *za'tar* (NIS8). Open Su-Th 7am-8pm, F 7am-2pm.

Pinati (☎692 03 30), on the *midraḥov,* near the Ha-Palmaḥ bridge. Elvis plays the role of the Messiah here, and all await his coming. The walls are plastered with memorabilia from the tumultuous life of the swivel-hipped dreamboat. No peanut butter and banana sandwiches, but the fun keeps going. Kebabs and spaghetti NIS30-40. Open Su-Th 9am-midnight, F 9am-4pm, Sa after sundown-midnight.

Ha-Mifgash Restaurant, 75 Jerusalem St. (☎692 05 10), at the lower end of the *midraḥov.* The restaurant is inside a 150-year-old stone-vaulted room that used to be part of a large underground well. Chicken soup connoisseurs must try the velvety brew (NIS12). Veggie options include stuffed pepper (NIS14) and eggplant (NIS16). Open Su-Th 8am-midnight, F 8am-4pm, Sa sundown-midnight. Credit cards accepted.

Falafel and Shawarma California (☎692 06 78), on Jerusalem St. just before the Ha-Palmaḥ bridge, on the left when coming from the bus station. Falafel NIS8; *shawarma* NIS13. Open Su-Th 8am-11pm, F 8am-3pm.

Cafe Baghdad, 61 Jerusalem St. (☎697 40 65), in the middle of the *midraḥov,* with outdoor seating and a mountain view. Vegetarian restaurant with salads (NIS32-44), pizza (NIS30-35), potatoes with toppings (NIS20-24), cakes (NIS15-17), and shakes (NIS14). Open Su-Th 8am-midnight, F 8am-3:30pm, Sa after sundown-2am.

Golden Mountain Cheese (☎692 30 20), in Ha-Meginim Sq. The friendly proprietors of the small cafe and shop manufacture their own gourmet kosher cheeses from goat milk (NIS90 per kg.). Try the cheese melted on a Yemenite pita (NIS10) or sample from a platter (NIS15, large NIS30). Open Su-Th 11am usually until 7pm.

Leḥem Ha-Panim, in the middle of the *midraḥov* on Jerusalem St., next to Pizza Garden. This bakery has delicious cookies and pastries for NIS20-25 per kg. Open Su-Th 7:45am-8pm, F 7:45am-3pm.

SIGHTS

The best—and inevitably, the only—way to see Tzfat is to get lost in its circuitous sidestreets. Fortunately, there are a few **tour guides** on hand to inject some order into the chaos of navigating the city. **Aviva Minoff** (☎692 09 01, mobile 050 409 187) gives entertaining tours starting from the Rimonim Hotel (M-F 10:30am; 2hr. tour NIS40/US$10, minimum 5 people, reserve in advance). **Yosi Reis** (☎692 28 03 or 051 603 606) gives good but expensive tours with advance notice (2hr. tour NIS200/US$50). Otherwise, try Yisrael Shalem's helpful *Six Self-Guided Tours to Tzfat* (NIS25), available at the candle shop and at Ascent (see **Accommodations,** p. 237).

A WALKING TOUR OF THE SYNAGOGUE QUARTER

Navigating the gnarled synagogue quarter, also called the Old City, is a matter of luck—note landmarks carefully. Only Caro, Ha-Ari, and Abuhav are open to the public; dress modestly and don't take pictures on Shabbat. The following **walking tour** encompasses the major sights:

ASHKENAZI HA-ARI SYNAGOGUE. Across from the post office on Jerusalem St. is a small cobblestone terrace; head down the steps and turn right to reach **Ha-Meginim Square** ("Square of the Defenders"), which was the Jewish city center until the earthquake of 1837. Through the square, under the stone archway, and down the stairs by the "Synagogue Ha-Ari" sign is the Ashkenazi Ha-Ari Synagogue, built in 1580, three years after the death of its namesake, **Rabbi Isaac Luria** (*Ha-Ari* is the acronym of the Hebrew for "our master Rabbi Isaac" and also means "lion"). It was to this site that the famous mystic and founder led congregants to welcome Shabbat. He is most famous for penning the *Kabbalat Shabbat*, an arrangement of prayers in preparation for the Sabbath; Alkabetz, his student, wrote the now standard hymn, *Lekha Dodi*.

The altarpiece was modified by locals, who were concerned that it was idolatrous. They smeared the paintings, replacing the lion's head with a human face. The synagogue features two notable curiosities. One is the fertility chair, more formally used as a ceremonial circumcision chair. It is rumored to bless women who sit in it with miraculous pregnancies. The other is a small hole in the central pulpit, where visitors place notes for wishes and good luck. The hole was made during the War of Independence, when a grenade flew into the synagogue and exploded while worshipers were bowed in prayer, allowing the shrapnel to sail over their heads and leave a mark only in the pulpit's side.

ABUHAV SYNAGOGUE. Exiting the Ha-Ari synagogue, take a left down the stairs, a left at the bottom, a right on Simtat Abuhav St., and then a quick left after going down more stairs; the Abuhav Synagogue will be on the left. Rabbi Isaac Abuhav was a 15th-century Spanish mystic who never actually made it to Tzfat. His 550-year-old Torah scroll, however, is contained in the first ark to the right, inside the entrance. The second ark contains Rabbi Luria's four-century-old Torah scroll. The scroll inside the blue ark is rumored to have been the only object left intact in Tzfat following the 1837 earthquake that leveled the town. Hanging below the mural in the middle of the synagogue is a chandelier brought over from Europe as a reminder of those who suffered in the Holocaust. The chair at the back of the synagogue has been used to circumcise 8-day-old Jewish boys for 213 years, making it perhaps the single most unpleasant piece of furniture in the world.

ALSHEIKH SYNAGOGUE. Exiting this synagogue, continue straight down the same alleyway. On the left will be the Alsheikh Synagogue, named for a student of Rabbi Yosef said to have been escorted to his grave by 12 doves that attended his Saturday afternoon lectures.

TOUCH NO EVIL Above doorways all over the old city of Tzfat, as well as on keychains, in windows, and behind picture frames throughout Israel, is the likeness of a hand. The hand has special significance in Jewish mysticism because of the Kabbalistic meaning of the numbers: a hand (generally) has five fingers, and people have two hands for a total of ten, a number that represents God in mystic texts. Some noteworthy variations on the hand symbol are the hand with an eye in its palm, which represents the evil eye, and the six-fingered hand above the doorway on the right after exiting left from Abuhav Synagogue. One of the builders had six rather than five fingers on one hand and left his mark after finishing the construction project.

CARO SYNAGOGUE. Up the stairs on the left and through the door in the purple walls is the back entrance to the Caro Synagogue, one of the most famous in Tzfat. It was here that Yosef Caro, chief rabbi of Tzfat and author of the vast *Shulḥan Arukh* ("The Set Table," a standard guide to daily life according to Jewish law), studied and taught in the 16th century. Caro was well-known as a philanthropist who served simultaneously as rabbi, counselor, shelter-provider, and soup kitchen coordinator. Notice the glass cabinet in the sanctuary full of Jewish books dating back to the 17th century. Caro Synagogue is also accessible by taking Ma'alot Oleh Ha-Gardom St. off Jerusalem St. and turning right at Beit Yosef St.

CHERNOBYL AND CHERTKOFF SYNAGOGUES. Back at Ha-Meginim Sq., down the narrow Bar-Yochai St., is the Chernobyl Synagogue, marked by a blue box, window grates, and a small English sign on the door. The modest Bar-Yochai St. is believed to be the alley down which the Messiah will make his way on his journey from the nearby mountains to Jerusalem. Off of Ha-Meginim Sq., on Ha-Ḥasadim St., one street past Najara St. and the Ha-Ari Synagogue, is the Chertkoff Synagogue, whose chief rabbi predicted in 1840 that the messianic redemption would begin when 600,000 Jews inhabited the Land of Israel. Both of these synagogues are closed to the public.

CEMETERIES. Three adjoining **cemeteries** sprawl on the western outskirts of the old city, off Ha-Ari St. at the bottom of the hill. Follow the steps all the way down, past the new stone buildings on the left. The small building on the left when the path turns into the cemetery is Ha-Ari *mikveh*, or ritual bath. This natural spring was the bathing place of Ha-Ari himself, and its vibes have attracted the interest of mystics the world over, including the Dalai Lama. The local rabbinical court has ruled that women may not enter the *mikveh*'s icy waters, but renegade females have been known to take a dip late at night while a male friend guards the door.

The oldest cemetery contains the 16th-century graves of the most famous Tzfat Kabbalists. Most prominent is Ha-Ari's blue tomb, where religious Jews come at all hours to pray, light candles, and seek inspiration. Also notice the domed tomb built by the Karaites of Damascus to mark the grave of the prophet Hosea. Legend has it that hidden under this same hill are Hannah and her seven sons, whose martyrdom at the hands of the Syrians is recorded in the Book of Maccabees. This cemetery is the domain of eighth-generation Tzfat resident Mordekhai Shebabo, who left his position as a pedicurist to single-handedly restore the graves. Every visible grave is the result of his efforts.

OTHER SIGHTS

ARTISTS' QUARTER AND GENERAL EXHIBITION. These alleys and galleries display a wide range of art inspired by the local colors. The quality varies, but a keen eye might discern a few real jewels. Gallery highlights include **microcalligraphy** (creating pictures out of verses from traditional Jewish texts) and Ruth Shany's silk artwork. A number of artists, including Avraham Loewenthal and

David Friedman, create mystical art inspired by the Kabbalah. Not to be missed is Mike Leaf's studio, full of satirical paper mache sculptures. The General Exhibition is a collection of works by local artists. The art is displayed in the town's former mosque, which has been empty of worshipers since the 1948 War. *(The artists' quarter is just below the Jerusalem-Arlozorov intersection. Most shops open 10am-1pm and 4-7pm. The General exhibition, well-marked by English signs, is on Arlozorov St., at the bottom of the hill south of Ma'alot Oleh Ha-Gardom St. ☎692 00 87. Open Su-Th 9am-6pm, F 9am-2pm, Sa 10am-2pm.)*

SHEM VA'EVER CAVE. This site is said to be the burial grounds of Noah's son Shem and grandson Ever. Muslims call it the "Cave of Mourning" because they believe that it was here that Jacob learned of the death of his son Joseph. *(The cave is near the top of Ha-Palmaḥ bridge, at the intersection of Jerusalem and Arlozorov St. If the shrine around the cave is locked, knock at the small, domed synagogue nearby.)*

DAVIDKA MONUMENT. This monument memorializes the weapon responsible for the Palmaḥ's victory in Tzfat—the duds that were launched made such a loud noise that Arab forces believed that Palmaḥ had atomic bombs, prompting them to flee. *(Across from the bullet-ridden British Police station on Jerusalem St.)*

CITADEL PARK. Above the town, the 12th-century Crusader fortress that once controlled the main route to Damascus now lies scattered in meager ruins in Gan Ha-Metzuda, a wooded, picnic-friendly park. The phenomenal view makes the short climb to the sight worthwhile. *(Cross over Jerusalem St. from the municipality building to where the street signs point to Metzuda. Climb the stairs behind the old police station. At the top, follow the road to the park's entrance.)*

MUSEUMS

BEIT HA-MEIRI MUSEUM. The 150-year-old stone building is as interesting as the exhibits on display. Its restored three floors tell Tzfat's history through colorful biographies of its elders—including the town matchmaker and the resident man-with-the-evil eye—and exhibits on how they worked and lived. *(From the midraḥov on Jerusalem St. take the Ma'alot Olei Ha-Gardom stairs all the way down to the bottom and make a right. ☎697 13 07. Open Su-Th 9am-2pm, F 9am-1pm. NIS10, students NIS7.)*

MEMORIAL MUSEUM OF HUNGARIAN-SPEAKING JEWRY. This small museum is dedicated to preserving the heritage of Jewish life in Hungary. Personal items on display (including prayer books, diaries, clothing, and paintings) illustrate the vibrancy of a culture that was virtually destroyed by the Holocaust. *(From Jerusalem St. walk down Aliyah Bet St. and turn left at the Wolfson center. The museum is through the parking lot on the left. ☎692 58 81; www.hungjewmus.org.il. Open M-F 9am-1pm. NIS10.)*

ISRAEL BIBLE MUSEUM. American artist Phillip Ratner has filled three floors of an old stone mansion with entertaining sculptures and canvas depictions of famous figures from the Bible. Particularly eye-catching is the *menorah* (Hanukkah lamp) with nine Bible figures serving as candle holders. Check out the 3-D wall hanging of Joseph and his coat of many colors. Ratner's prominent work is housed in permanent collections at the Statue of Liberty, the White House, and the US Supreme Court. *(Just north of the Gan Ha-Metzuda park, take a left at the top of the stairway leading up from Jerusalem St. The entrance is in back. ☎699 99 72; www.israelbiblemuseum.com. Open May-Sept. Su-Th 10am-4pm, F 10am-1pm; Oct.-Apr. Su-Th 10am-2pm. Free.)*

YITZḤAK FRENEL MUSEUM. This museum contains vibrant and colorful paintings by Yitzḥak Frenel, a Parisian modernist artist who moved to Tzfat in 1934 to become one of Israel's most influential painters. Paintings are mostly inspired by Jewish themes, and many depict life in Tzfat. *(The museum is located in Frenel's home in the artists' colony. ☎692 02 35. Open Su-Th 10am-6pm, F-Sa 10am-2pm. Free.)*

CRAFTS

One of the must-see sights in the old city is the **Tzfat Candle Factory.** From Ha-Meginim Sq., head down to Najara St. and take a right past the Ha-Ari Synagogue; the factory is on the right. All of the imaginatively colored and shaped candles on display are produced by the workers at the back of the shop, busily bent over blocks and sheets of beeswax. Make your own for NIS10-40. (☎682 20 68. Open Apr.-Sept. Su-Th 9am-6pm, F 9am-1pm; Oct.-Mar. Su-Th 9am-6pm, F 9am-1pm. Candles start at NIS12.) In Ha-Meginim Sq. is **Torah scribe** Zalmon Bear Halevy Tornek, who can be observed hand-copying Jewish religious texts. (☎692 42 77. Open Su-Tu, Th noon-6pm; F 11am-2pm.) Take note of the sentence stenciled onto many of the Old City's buildings: נ נח נחמ נחמן מאומן, or "Na-Naḥ-Naḥma-Naḥman from Uman." The words refer to the late *Rebbe* Naḥman of Breslev, leader of the Breslever Ḥasidic sect, whose followers chant his name in this fashion to bring good fortune. The lucky charm can be spotted throughout Galilee.

ENTERTAINMENT

Having a wild night in Tzfat takes some creative thinking. The most prominent bar is **Adios,** 73 Jerusalem St.on the *midraḥov,* in a hip, two-story seating area, which serves beer (NIS10-15) and cocktails (NIS15) to that unbelievably bluesy beat of classic American rock. (☎682 12 62. Open Su-Th 8am-1am, F 8am-4pm, Sa 9pm-2am.) Movies, often in English with Hebrew subtitles, are screened at the **Yigal Allon Theater and Cultural Center** a couple nights a week. Call ahead or stop by around 8pm to see if one is showing. The cultural center is next to the main post office, near the traffic circle where Ha-Palmaḥ St. and Aliyah Bet St. meet. (☎697 19 90. NIS20. Movies begin around 8:30pm.)

A late-night walk through the old cemetery can be truly beautiful. Stars twinkle with the cemetery's *yahrzeit* (memorial) candles, and Ḥasidim pass by on their way to Ha-Ari's grave late into the night. The nearby *mikveh* is open 24hr.; nocturnal bathers are greeted by the echoes of their own voices and the icy trickle of spring water flowing from the wall (see **Synagogue Quarter,** p. 239; women technically prohibited). Hanging out in the Synagogue Quarter is perhaps the best way to experience the mystical atmosphere of Tzfat.

Travelers planning a visit to Tzfat well in advance should consider arriving in time for the annual **Klezmer festival** in late July or early August, a three-night extravaganza during which the city sways to the strains of everything from old-world Yiddish tunes to modern Ḥasidic rock. Outdoor concerts are plentiful and free, as is the spontaneous dancing that seems to erupt in front of each stage. Call the tourist office for details. Ascent also throws **wild Ḥasidic parties** every Saturday night; visitors are invited to come for dinner, music, and dancing with a religious theme (see p. 237; donations requested if not staying at Ascent).

NA NAḤ NAḤMA NAḤMAN ME'UMAN It's a typical evening in Jerusalem. You're loitering in Zion Sq., watching groups of American teenagers awkwardly kick around a hackeysack while smooth Israeli soldiers flirt with disinterested English tourists. Suddenly, a large van pulls up, covered in bumper stickers with Hebrew letters. Six or seven men jump out of the back, a crowd of onlookers begins to form, and before you realize what's happening, they're blasting religious Hebrew music from a boombox and dancing excitedly in a big circle. The joy-makers belong to a sect of Hasidim that follows the teachings of Naḥman of Bratslav. Born in the Ukraine in 1772, he became a *tzadik* (righteous man), made a momentous pilgrimage to Israel in 1798, and then finally settled with his followers in the Ukranian village of Bratslav. He and his followers used dance to ward off depression and achieve a higher religious state. Today, the Bratslaver Ḥasidim continue to share the joy of Rabbi Naḥman by dancing and celebrating all over Israel.

NEAR TZFAT

MERON AND MT. MERON הר מירון

For two days every spring, the tranquil hillside surrounding Rabbi Shimon Bar-Yoḥai's tomb at Meron transforms into the scene of a frenzied religious carnival. Some believe that the 2nd-century Talmudic scholar **Bar-Yoḥai** authored the *Zohar*, the central work of the Kabbalah. Thousands of Jews converge upon the town to commemorate the date of his death (the holiday of **Lag Ba'Omer,** May 11 in 2001). The square outside the tomb becomes a Ḥasidic mosh-pit as crowds of over 100,000 dance, shove, and chant Bar-Yoḥai's name. The festivities begin when Tzfat's Ḥasidim parade to the tomb carrying an ancient Torah scroll from the Bana'a Synagogue in the Spanish Quarter. During the celebration, the roads and fields surrounding the tomb are covered with tents and makeshift shops sell a wide assortment of rabbinic and messianic paraphernalia. Tzfat's Visitors' Center (☎692 74 85) has more details on the festival.

Near the tomb stand the ruins of an aesthetically unimpressive but historically noteworthy synagogue dating from the 3rd century CE, when Meron was important in the booming olive oil trade. From Bar Yoḥai's grave, go past the *yeshiva* and follow the uphill path on the left. The **lintel,** an engraved stone slab that once decorated the entrance to the synagogue, is virtually all that remains of the edifice. Legend holds that this lintel's fall will herald the coming of the Messiah. The Israeli Department of Antiquities has nervously buttressed the artifact with reinforced concrete, but every Lag Ba'Omer, pious Jews from Tzfat, enthusiastically dance and stomp in an effort to accelerate their salvation. To reach Meron from Jerusalem, take any one of hundreds of buses running all night from Malaḥi St. in Geulah.

Just west of the village is **Ḥar Meron** (Mt. Meron), the highest mountain in the Galilee (1208m). A good trail affords tremendous vistas of Tzfat and the surrounding countryside—on clear days Lebanon and Syria to the north, the Mediterranean to the west, and the Sea of Galilee to the southeast are all visible. The **information office** offers limited hiking advice. (☎06 698 00 23. Trail map NIS62. Open Sa-Th 8am-7pm, F 8am-2pm.) To reach the trail, continue past the field school turn-off, past the army base on the right, and a small parking lot on the left. The **trail** begins at the back of the lot and follows striped black-and-white, as well as orange, blue, and white trail markers. A one-hour walk uphill through sweet-smelling, wonderfully wooded surroundings leads to an observation area with striking views of the area. Continue along the red-and-white marked trail skirting the summit and follow the trail to the left when it reaches a rocky area near the army radio towers. Twenty minutes farther along the path leads to a picnic site and a traffic circle; make a quick left back into the forest to where the trail begins again. An hour-long, easy descent, again marked with black-and-white, ends at a paved road just above the village of Meron. A 15-minute walk to the right leads to the tomb of Shimon Bar-Yohai. To get to the village, turn left onto the road, follow it into the town, and take a left at the grocery store on the right. After reaching the main gate, turn right down the highway and go left and across the highway at the major intersection to reach the bus stop. Bus #361 returns to Tzfat (every 20min. 6am-8pm, NIS8).

A gorgeous, thickly wooded, 3½-hour **hike** starts from Naḥal Amud at the bottom of the Tzfat cemeteries. The hike continues up a rocky *wadi* and emerges next to an old, bullet-ridden British police station by the road to Bar-Yoḥai's tomb. Interested travelers should get directions from SPNI or the tourist office or consult the rough map on file at Ascent (see **Accommodations,** p. 237).

Buses #43 or 367 from Tzfat go to Kibbutz Sasa, northwest of the mountain (25min.; 6:45, 9, 11:40am, 12:30, 5:30pm; NIS11.50). In summer, catch the early bus to avoid the midday heat. From the kibbutz, continue 1km along the main highway to the turn-off on the left marked with a green highway sign that indicates "Meron Field School." After 1km, there is a brown sign for the SPNI Field School, which is up the small hill to the right. To get to the tomb from the bus stop, walk to the intersection with a sign for Meron and follow the road up for about five minutes.

ALMA CAVE מערת עלמה

Legend has it that the maze-like tunnels of Alma Cave form an underground bridge between the holy cities of Tzfat and Jerusalem and contain the corpses of 900,000 "righteous men." There is no guarantee that a daytrip to the Alma Cave will end up at the Dome of the Rock or yield encounters with long-deceased rabbis, but for those anxious to spelunk despite mud, sweat, and claustrophobic conditions, the Alma Cave is a tailor-made adventure.

CAVING IN. Bring water and one reliable flashlight per person as well as candles and matches for backup, and prepare to get covered with mud. Alma Cave should be tried only by those who feel they can remain up to 108m beneath the earth for several hours. Keep in mind that it is slippery in and around the cave, and large packs will not fit through the tighter spots. It is safest to go during daylight hours with a group of people and to let someone know where you're headed.

The entrance to the cave is hidden in a gorge, behind clusters of large trees; from the green nature reserve sign on the hillside of gray stones, go right and uphill toward the metal poles—the gorge and cave entrance are just beyond this. Notice the black ropes hooked into the stone to aid in climbing down into the gorge and toward the cave entrance. Climb (or slide) down the hole, keeping to the right. At a depth of approximately 60m (one-half to three-quarters of the way down), there are two phallic rocks near the right-hand wall. Behind those lies a small hole leading to the "inner chambers" of the cave. There are markers indicating the correct path: white for the way in, red for the way out. Once inside the large room with a ridge and a steep slope, veer to the far right along the ridge instead of continuing down the slope. Near the end of the trail, the rocks become slippery and the caverns start dripping **stalagmites** and **stalactites.** (Impress your friends by reminding them that stalactites are the ones above—they grip "tight" to the ceiling—hanging like a "T.") Getting out of the cave is a true physical challenge, involving steep climbs and tricky maneuvers.

Bus #45 leaves Tzfat for Reḥania (20min.; Su-Th 8:45am and 1:30pm; F 8:45am, noon, and 3:30pm; NIS11.50). The bus goes all the way to the settlement of Alma, but get off at Reḥania. Bus #45 also makes the return trip to Reḥania to Tzfat (Su-Th 9:15am and 2pm; F (:15am, 12:30, and 4pm). By car, drive north along the Tzfat-Meron highway and continue past the Zeition Junction to Reḥania. Across the street from the entrance to Reḥania village is the dirt path to Alma cave. The path is marked by red and white stripes painted on the light pole beside the main highway; from there, red-and-white trail markers are infrequent. Stay on this path for about 30 minutes, steering close to Alma (left), and away from the hilly, tree-lined area to the right (don't make any sharp turns). The walk goes past farmers' fenced off fields, to the hill covered with tree clusters and stones toward the left. The marked trail leads to the cave entrance.

TEL ḤAZOR תל חזור

Buses #501 and 511 from Tzfat (35min., NIS13) and all buses that run between Rosh Pina and Kiryat Shmona stop near the site. Don't get off at Ḥazor Ha-Gelilit; continue north to Kibbutz Ayelet Ha-Shaḥor. The kibbutz houses a small museum (☎693 48 55) displaying Canaanite and Israelite artifacts and explaining some of the tel's layers. From there, the site's entrance (☎693 72 90) is 250m up the main road. Museum and site open Sa-Th 8am-5pm, F and holidays 8am-4pm. NIS14, students NIS12, children NIS6.

The *tel* at Ḥazor is the largest archaeological dig in northern Israel. Excavations in the 1960s revealed 21 layers of settlements at the site, the oldest dating from the 3rd millennium BCE. Like Megiddo (see p. 222), Ḥazor was once a fortified city situated on the main trading route that linked Egypt to Syria and Mesopotamia. Ḥazor served as a major commercial center in the Fertile Crescent, and the Bible calls it "the head of all those [northern Canaanite] kingdoms" (Joshua 11:10). Ferocious Joshua sacked Ḥazor after winning a battle against a north Canaanite alliance at the Merom River. Following God's command, he slaughtered the entire population and burnt the city to the ground; archaeologists have found evidence of a conflagration during the 13th century BCE. King Solomon in the 10th century BCE and King Ahab in the 9th century BCE rebuilt and expanded Ḥazor; Assyria's Tiglath-Pileser III laid waste to the city during his army's march through the Galilee (732 BCE). At the *tel's* northern foot lies a vast, thick-walled lower city built in the 9th century BCE. The most impressive of the *tel's* ruins is the 38m-deep tunnel, engineered during Ahab's reign to bring water into the city in case of a siege. Today, archaeologists are still searching for the city's archives.

Kibbutz Ayelet Ha-Shaḥar, with its peaceful, palm-tree lined streets and proximity to sights and hikes in the northern Galilee and Golan, offers accommodations in addition to its archaeological museum. The white stucco **country lodge** is on the kibbutz's main road, past the hotel on the left, and has rooms with bathroom, air-conditioning, TV, and fridge. (☎686 86 66. Check-in 2pm. Check-out 10am. Breakfast included. Singles US$55; doubles US$62; US$16 each additional person. Rates increase 25% in July, Aug. and Jewish holidays. Credit cards accepted.)

Bazelet Shooting Range will let you shoot at pigeons and clay targets after a brief training. Inside the entrance of the kibbutz, take the first left before the museum and follow the road to the "T." Turn left and follow the wooden sign (1½km from the gate). Bazelet also offers archery (NIS40) as well as a package deal for NIS150 per person (minimum 12 person group), which includes shooting time, a two-hour jeep tour of the area, and a full barbecue in the palm grove. (☎693 27 21; www.bazelet.co.il. Range open Sa-Th 10am-6pm, F 10am-5pm. Call ahead.)

BAR'AM בר עם

Bus #43 from Tzfat goes to Bar'am (6:45am, 12:30, and 5pm return 7:45am, 1:45pm, 5:45pm; NIS13). Ask the driver for the synagogue ruins, marked by a small brown sign that says Bar'am and points right, not the Bar'am Kibbutz a few kilometers down the road. Open Sa-Th 8am-5pm, F 8am-4pm. NIS9, students NIS8, children NIS4.

These 3rd-century ruins constitute one of the best-preserved synagogues in Israel. Archaeological evidence shows that Bar'am was home to a prosperous Jewish community in the middle centuries of the first millennium. The ruins of two synagogues have been uncovered here. The larger of the two is intact, but only the foundation of the second remains. An inscribed stone from the large synagogue has even made its way into the Louvre in Paris. Tradition labels Bar'am the burial site of the biblical Queen Esther, but the claim has no archaeological support. Bar'am was a Maronite Christian village until the 1948 War of Independence. A few steps up the hill on the left beyond the old synagogue ruins is a beautiful stone Maronite Church that is still used by the Maronites on holidays and special occasions. In front of the church is an observation point with a view of Mt. Meron to the south. On clear days, it's possible to catch a glimpse of the snow-capped peak of **Mt. Hermon** to the northeast, emerging from the clouds.

ROSH PINA ראש פינה

Buses #401, 459, 461, 501, and 511 go to Tzfat (every 30min., NIS10), and buses #480, 500, 842, 845, and 909 go to Kiryat Shmona (every 30min., NIS13).

Because many buses heading north pass through, the town serves as a gateway to the Upper Galilee and Golan. There's not much to do in quaint and quiet Rosh Pina except visit the **Rothschild Garden,** on Ha-Ḥalutzim St., a beautifully maintained park with shady poplars and dozens of varieties of roses lining its terraces or **Drora's Herb Farm,** 25 Ha-Ḥalutzim St., up the hill on the way to the hostel, one block past the post office, a sweet-smelling shop that sells everything organic. (☎693 43 49. Herb teas NIS5-20. Open Su-Th 10am-7pm, F 10am-6pm, Sa 7-10pm.) The **Nature Friends Youth Hostel** has two tidy rooms with fridge, air-conditioning, and shared bath, as well as a small camping area. (☎693 17 64 or 051 572 141. Dorms NIS5; singles NIS15, shower and bath available. Guests must pay at the Beit Binyamin Hostel in Tzfat, and call ahead.) The rest of the rooms in the hostel are occupied by **SPNI field offices** (☎693 70 86; fax 693 43 12). To reach the hostel walk straight up the hill from the main bus stop and look for a sign on the left.

KIRYAT SHMONA קרית שמונה ☎06

Kiryat Shmona ("Town of Eight") commemorates Yosef Trumpeldor and seven others who were murdered in nearby Tel Ḥai in 1920. Situated atop the ruins of the Arab village al-Khalsa, which was destroyed in the 1948 War, the city received its new name in 1949. Due to its location on the Ḥula plain near the Lebanese border, Kiryat Shmona was the target of bombings and terrorist attacks until Israel invaded Lebanon in 1982 to create the nine-mile-wide security zone. Since then, it has been subject to shelling by the militant Islamic group Hizbullah. The town thus graduated from its grim name to an even grimmer nickname: Kiryat Katyusha, referring to the type of rockets used.

GETTING THERE AND GETTING AROUND

Buses: Central bus station (☎681 82 22), on Tel Ḥai Blvd., near the north end of the city. To: **Jerusalem** (#963; 3½hr.; Su every 1½hr., M-Th every 3hr., 5:30am-4pm; NIS50); **Kfar Blum,** (#31 and 32, 3 per day 6:15am-5:20pm, NIS7); **Metulla** (#20 or 21, 8 per day 6:45am-7:15pm, NIS8); **Rosh Pina** (#480, 500, 842, 845, and 969; 30min.; NIS13); **Tel Aviv** (#840, 841, 842, or 845; every 30min. 5:20am-8pm; NIS47); (#840, 841, and 963; 1hr.; every 30min. 5:30am-8pm; NIS21.50); and **Tzfat** (#501 and 511; 45min., every hr. 5:50am-8:40pm; NIS18).

Taxis: Moniot Ha-Tzafon (☎694 333 or 694 23 77), in a stand on Arlozorov St., behind the bus station.

Car Rental: Thrifty at **Shlomo Rent-a-Car** (☎694 16 31), down Henrietta Szold St. from Tel Ḥai Blvd. Take a right into the industrial area; the office is in the first row of offices on the left under a small Thrifty sign. 3-day min. Cheapest manual US$45 per day; cheapest automatic US$57 per day. Under 24 US$12 extra per day; min. age 21. Open Su-Th 8am-5pm, F 8am-2pm. **Eldan Rent-a-Car** (☎690 31 86), on Tel Ḥai St. behind the Sonol gas station, on the right at the southern end of town. Cars start at US$40 per day. Min. age 24.

GALILEE

ORIENTATION AND PRACTICAL INFORMATION

There is little of interest to see and do in the town itself. However, Kiryat Shmona's location makes it a convenient base for travel to the Upper Galilee, Golan Heights, River Jordan, and Mount Hermon. **Tel Ḥai,** a small strip of Rte. 90 north from Tiberias, is the main street. There is a *kenyon* on the north end of Tel Ḥai St. at the junction with **route 99,** the highway that goes across the Hula Valley to the Golan Heights. On the southern end are the Manara Cliff **cable cars.** The **bus station** is in the middle of Tel Ḥai St., next to another *kenyon.*

Tourist Office: Municipality building (☎690 84 44), on Kikkar Zahal St., up the steps to the left of the post office. Free maps of Kiryat Shmona. Open Su-Th 8am-3:30pm. **ISSTA** budget travel office (☎690 32 49), 2 floors up in the mall. Good resource for international airline ticket issues. Open Su-Tu, Th 9am-7pm; W, F 9am-2pm.

ATM: Bank Leumi, to the right on Tel Ḥai when exiting the bus station, has ATMs that take Visa and Plus cards. **Mishkan Bank,** to the left behind the bus station, takes all cards.

Bookstore: Steimatzky (☎690 50 72), in the other mall, north of the bus station at the intersection of Rte. 90 and Rte. 99. Carries a few travel and hiking books in English as well as the 1:50,000 hiking map for the northern Galilee and Golan (NIS62). Open Su-Th 9am-10pm, F 9am-4pm, Sa 6-10pm.

Emergency: Magen David Adom (☎694 43 34), behind the bus station, up Tchernikovsky St. on the left.

Police (☎694 34 44); on Selinger St. From the bus station one block past the mall on Tel Ḥai St. on the left.

Pharmacy: Gaby Pharmacy (☎690 47 76), one floor up in the central mall across Tchernikovsky St. from the bus station. Open Su-Th 9am-9pm, F 9am-2pm, Sa after sundown-10pm. After-hours emergency info on the door.

Post Office: 110 Kikkar Zahal St. (☎694 02 20). From behind the bus station, take a left onto Kikkar Zahal where it branches off Arlozorov St. Post office is on the right near the large plaza with the Granovsky Family Auditorium. Exchanges cash and traveler's checks for no commission and has **international telephone** and **Poste Restante** services. Open Su-Tu, Th 8am-12:30pm and 3:30-6pm; W 8am-1:30pm; F 8am-noon.

ACCOMMODATIONS AND FOOD

Kiryat Shmona is a good place to make necessary shopping excursions or to catch the bus to accommodations in outlying areas, but its **Hotel Hatira** makes it possible to use the city as an overnight base. Located in a castle-like building, the big rooms are less than royal, but come with TV, air-conditioning, fridge, and a location on Tel Ḥai Blvd., a 15-minute walk to the right out of the bus station; look for a sign for the El Gaucho restaurant. (☎694 49 44; fax 690 30 36. Singles NIS100; doubles NIS180; less for longer stays. Credit cards accepted.) There are plenty of falafel places along Tel Ḥai Blvd., as well as some fast food places in the mall. (Open Su-Th 9am-10pm, F 9am-3pm, Sa noon-11pm.) **Club Market,** in the mall by the bus station, is well-stocked with everything from fresh produce to packaged sweets. (☎690 47 76. Open Su-Th 8am-9pm, F 7am-3pm.) On Thursday morning there is an outdoor market past the mall on Tel Ḥai Blvd.

SIGHTS

The most noteworthy attraction is **Manara Cliff,** offering the longest aerial cable ride in Israel. Glassed-in sky gondolas carry people to two stations located midway up and at the top of the 900m cliff. In addition to the bird's-eye view of Galilee and the Golan, the middle station offers cliff rapelling (NIS155). From the top, the trip down can be hiked or biked (3-4km depending on the path followed), as well as traveled by gondola. (Just off Tel Ḥai St., at the southern end of town, on the right driving south from the bus station. ☎690 58 30; email m-cliff@inter.net.il. One-way gondola ride NIS35; round-trip NIS49. Children NIS55. Bike rental NIS67; 2½-3hr. ride down; bikes can be returned at the middle or lower station. Open daily 9:30am-6:30pm.) The big red apple on Rte. 90 at the southern edge of the city is home to the production facilities of all-natural **Galilee Cider.** Twenty-seven workers at the site fill between 120,000 and 150,000 cans of juice every day, and welcome visitors to see how they do it and to taste the fruits of their labor. (☎694 45 54. Tour and tasting NIS15, students NIS13.50. Su-Th 9am-6:30pm, in winter 9am-5pm; F 9am-2pm; Sa 10am-5pm.)

In town, there are two museums interesting enough to ease a few minutes of boredom. The **Museum of Kiryat Shmona,** 16 Jordan St., presents the history of Kiryat Shmona and the surrounding area. From the bus station, walk south on Tel Ḥai St., and turn left on Uri Ilan St.; the museum is at the corner of Ha-Yarden St. Housed in a former mosque, it displays exhibits on nearby archaeological excavations. (☎694 01 35. Open Su-Th 8am-noon. Free.) The park surrounding the museum has green lawns and large trees to lounge under, as well as pieces of old vehicles for kids to romp around in. Across Ya-Harden St., behind the museum and park, is the **Bible Museum,** with a diorama collection of characters and catastrophes from the Bible. Before leaving town, briefly stop by the **Beit Ha-Khan,** the former home of Kamal Afundy, the sheikh of the region responsible for the 1920 Tel Ḥai attack (see below). The restored house now serves as an art exhibition center. From the bus station go two blocks up Tchernikovsky St. and turn right. The house is two blocks up on the right. (Open Su-Th 8am-1pm and 4-7pm.)

NO SUCH THING AS A BAD APPLE In the beginning, there were apples. The climate and soil of the Upper Galilee are perfect for apples, and the region once overflowed with orchards. Soon, however, there were too many apples for the local apple-eating population to swallow. Twenty years ago, in a brilliant effort to alleviate the fruit glut, Galilee Cider was born. The production facility began taking in apples—green and red, tart and ripe, shiny and bruised—mashing them to a pulp, and standardizing their juice into a uniformly smooth, naturally-sweet flavor. The Galilee Cider factory now uses over one hundred tons of apples a day, packing at least six apples into every can of cider, and even has to import crops from Europe.

DAYTRIPS FROM KIRYAT SHMONA

KFAR BLUM קפר בלום

To reach Kfar Blum by car, take Rte. 9779 toward Shamir out of Kiryat Shmona and go right onto road 9778 to Kfar Blum. An orange sign points left to the kayaking off the main road, just before the kibbutz. Take bus #31 or 32 from Kiryat Shmona. NIS 7.20, 5 per day).

At Kfar Blum, each summer during the last week of July, a classical music festival draws huge crowds (info ☎681 6818). The kibbutz's hotel is pricey, but its youth hostel (☎053 79 7440 or 694 8409), to the right of the bright yellow-orange building straight past the gate inside the kibbutz, provides affordable beds in a basic building with shared bathroom, TV room, kitchen, and A/C. Breakfast NIS20. 4-bed dorms NIS70; call ahead or inquire at the pool as the hostel is often full of tour groups in the summer. The kibbutz premises also house a swimming pool. (NIS40, students NIS30; Sa NIS40, students NIS25. Open M-Th 8am-7pm, F-Sa 9am-6pm, Su 10am-7pm.)

Many of the music festival performances are held in the two-story auditorium beyond the parking lot and to the left (main entrance in back); a pool is down the paved path to the left of the auditorium. The kibbutz's other draw is Jordan River kayaking (☎694 8755). A gushing 2½hr. trip is NIS84, students NIS76, while a 1¼hr. ride is NIS52, students NIS47. Try the climbing wall or rappel up the banks and slide down ropes into the river water for NIS25. The long route is run 10am-3pm daily, the shorter one 9am-5pm; both from April to October.

GALILEE

GADOT AND THE JORDAN RIVER גדות

Kibbutz Gadot is off highway 91, near the Jordan River Park. From Kiryat Shmona, head south on highway 90 toward Rosh Pina, and then left on highway 91 at the Mahanayim Junction. Gadot is on the left, and the river park and hike are a bit further on the right.

The bed and breakfast (☎693 91 88; email gadot@gadot-lodging.co.il; www.gadot-lodging.co.il) offers comfort as well as a good location. Clean, quiet rooms come with bathrooms, kitchenettes, TV, A/C, and free use of the pool and zoo (doubles US$70, July, Aug., and holidays US$94). A few minutes past Gadot on highway 91, at a sharp turn in the road just before the Benot Ya'aqov Bridge, a sign points to the red trail in the Jordan River Park to the right. Drive along the gravel red trail to the black trail on the left, where there is a small dirt parking circle. The black trail leads down from the small parking area to a hike that goes south along Jordan River. The easy-going trail runs between the river's banks and hillsides, and is dotted with wandering cattle. The trail follows the Jordan for about 6 kilometers; hikers can turn back towards the parking lot whenever they wish. Hikers are instructed not to enter the Jordan and should be wary of fenced-off areas that indicate mine fields in the area. Kibbutz Gadot also offers **white-water rafting** on the Jordan River. A two hour trip costs NIS220 while a 4 hour trip costs NIS295. Call 1 800 302302 or 06 6934622 ahead of time for more info or check out www.rafting.co.il.

NEAR KIRYAT SHMONA

TEL ḤAI תל חי

Tel Ḥai, or "living hill," sits 3km north of Kiryat Shmona, on a promontory overlooking the Ḥula Valley. Established in 1918 as a military outpost after the withdrawal of British forces from the Upper Galilee, the town has become a symbol of Israel's early pioneer movement and the struggle for "the finger of the Galilee," the narrow mountain range west of the Ḥula Valley region.

GETTING THERE. Buses #20 and 21 from Kiryat Shmona go to Tel Ḥai and continue on to Metulla (8 per day 6:45am-7:15pm, F last bus at 4:30pm; NIS5). Plan ahead and double check bus return times to avoid getting stranded.

ACCOMMODATION. Tel Ḥai's one budget accommodation is the recently built **Tel Ḥai Hostel (HI).** All rooms have air-conditioning and bathrooms with showers. The hostel offers a basketball court as well as discounts to the Metulla Canada Center sports complex and discounted kayaking on the Jordan River. (☎94 00 43; fax 694 17 43. Packaged meal NIS20; dinner NIS35. Reception 24hr. Check-out 10am. 5-7 bed dorms NIS47/US$11.50, July-Aug. and holidays NIS53/US$13; singles US$37; doubles NIS180/US$44, NIS200/US$50; additional person NIS41/US$10, NIS45/US$11. Credit cards accepted.)

SIGHTS. The first armed conflicts between Jews and Arabs within the current borders of the State of Israel occurred at Tel Ḥai. In 1920, a group of Arabs gathered around the settlements of Tel Ḥai, Kfar Giladi, and Metulla (then part of French-administered Syria and Lebanon) and accused the Jewish settlers of protecting French soldiers who had been charged with encroachment on Arab lands. Yosef Trumpeldor, who had years earlier lost an arm fighting a war for the Czar of Russia, led Tel Ḥai at the time. He fell for the trap and allowed four Arabs inside the settlement to search for the French agents. Once inside, the Arabs killed Trumpeldor and five others. The deaths of these six along with those of two Jewish defenders who had died earlier, prompted the Jewish settlers to flee Tel Ḥai. The six men and two women were buried in nearby Kfar Giladi. Trumpeldor's alleged last words—"No matter, it is good to die for our country"—epitomized Zionist convictions for years. Soon after the attack, Jewish settlers returned to these Upper Galilee settlements, and, today, the land from Kiryat Shmona north to Metulla is a part of Israel as a result of their efforts. The site offers a spectacular view of the Galilee and Golan Heights. A monument to Trumpeldor stands on the outskirts of the compound.

The original watchtower and stockade settlement has been reconstructed in the **Tel Ḥai Museum,** which tells the history of the Tel Ḥai settlement through an exhibit of everyday items used by the settlers. From the bus stop, cross the highway and walk to the left through the gate of the regional college; the museum is across the parking lot to the left. (☎695 13 33. NIS15, students NIS12. Open Su-Th 8am-4pm, F 8am-1pm, Sa 10am-5pm.) A statue of a roaring lion marks the graves of the Tel Ḥai Eight at the **Military Cemetery,** a few hundred meters uphill from Tel Ḥai toward Kibbutz Kfar Giladi. Look for the sign pointing to the "Roaring Lion." The Israeli Defense Forces museum, **Beit Ha-Shomer,** meaning "House of the Guardian," documents the history of the Ha-Shomer fighters who defended Jewish settlements in the Galilee during the early years of the 20th century. The museum is located 100-meters up from the cemetery, inside the gates of Kibbutz Kfar Giladi to the left. The exhibits also relate the story of the Jewish regiments during World War I and of the Tel Ḥai Eight. (☎694 15 65. NIS10, students NIS5. Open Su-Th 8am-3:30pm, F 8:30am-12:30pm.) The **Museum of Photography** is in the industrial park on the right side of the main highway, just before the Tel Ḥai Museum and Kibbutz Kfar Giladi. It houses a rotating display of work by international modern photographers, including special theme exhibits, as well as some wonderful photos of early Jewish settlers in Israel. (☎695 07 69. Open Su-Th 9am-4pm, Sa 10am-5pm.)

ḤULA VALLEY NATURE RESERVES

The Ḥula Valley ranks as one of the most beautiful areas in all of Israel. Two thousand years ago, Josephus described the valley as "wonderful in its characteristics of beauty...there is not a plant that does not flourish there, and...the air is so temperate that it suits the most diverse species." At the turn of the 20th century, the entire valley was covered by a knee-deep swamp, until Jewish pioneers arrived and drained the swamps in order to farm the fertile soil beneath. Eventually, the altered land became so dry that its diverse wildlife left the Ḥula Valley and in some instances died out entirely. Out of concern for the area's ecological diversity, Israel's first nature reserve was established in the Ḥula Valley in 1964. Since then, parts of the Ḥula Valley have been refilled with water and are carefully maintained; ecologists hope to lure amphibians, water buffalo, and birds migrating between Europe and Africa to take up increased residence in the area. The five reserves of the Ḥula Valley showcase Israel's forested north, ice-cold streams, swamplands, and their inhabitants.

ḤULA NATURE RESERVE

Between Rosh Pina and Kiryat Shmona, off Rte. 90. From the south, the turn-off is on the right, 8km north of Tel Ḥazor. Look for a brown sign on the right that says "Ha-Ḥula." Buses #501, 511, 840, and 841 (NIS13) leave Kiryat Shmona frequently and go to a junction 2½km from the entrance to the reserve. ☎693 70 69. Open Sa-Th 8am-4pm, F and holiday eves 8am-3pm. NIS18, students NIS15, under 18 NIS9.

This reserve is only really worth visiting between November and March, when it is swarming with animals and birds. Most of the original wildlife from the Ḥula swamplands has returned to the park thanks to the efforts of conservationists. The parking and picnic areas are populated with huge trees, from which a path leads to the **visitors' center,** a small, wood-roofed house. The center gives details on the history of the swamp, the varieties of plant and animal wildlife it contains, and a video presentation. The the 1.5-kilometer-long yellow duck-marked trail is mostly paved except for wood-planked observation bridges and an observation tower. The trail circles through papyrus swamps and thickets populated by ducks, black-winged (and long-legged) stilt birds, turtles, mongeese, waterbuffalo, and other creatures. The visitors' center rents binoculars for bird enthusiasts (NIS10; Sept.-Mar. is the best season for bird-watching). Arrive early in the morning to see the wildlife and to avoid crowded family time in the forest.

GALILEE

ḤORSHAT TAL NATURE RESERVE

Located off Route 99, between Kiryat Shmona and Banyas. From Kiryat Shmona, bus #36 goes to Ḥorshat Tal (6:10am and 2pm, but call ahead to check times; NIS7). Ask to be let off at Ḥorshat Tal, then walk 100m down the hill on the right, toward the brown sign. ☎694 23 60. Park open for swimming Sa-F 8am-5pm, F 8am-4pm. NIS27, children under 14 NIS16.

There are two reasons to visit this reserve: to go swimming or to go camping. The biggest draw is the ice-cold **swimming pool,** a man-made lake that is fed by the Dan river. The **Camping Ground** with a snack bar and shared bathrooms is nearby on the banks of the Dan River. (Tent sites NIS35 per person, children under 14 NIS25; enclosed 4-person bungalows NIS180/US$38; prices rise 50% on F night and holidays.) Stock up on groceries at **Alonit Market** (☎06 690 21 81), on Highway 99, a 15 minute walk from Ḥorshat Tal. Go west toward Kiryat Shmona; it's on the left. (Open daily 7am-11pm.) Scattered around the grounds of the reserve are 100-year-old oak trees. According to a Muslim legend, the trees, which grow nowhere else in Israel, sprang into being because of the 10 warriors of Muhammad who once rested here. Finding no shade or hitching post for their horses, they pounded their staffs into the earth to fasten their mounts, and the sticks sprouted overnight.

TEL DAN תל דן

A few kilometers past Ḥorshat Tal on Route 99. From the main road, take a left at the brown sign and walk a winding 1½km to the site. Take bus #36 from Kiryat Shmona (Su-F 6:10am and 2pm; call ahead to check times). ☎06 695 15 79. Open Sa-Th 8am-5pm, F 8am-4pm; gates close 1hr. before closing time. NIS18, students NIS15, children NIS9; ticket includes a 25% discount at the Beit Usishkin Museum.

Tel Dan is the Ḥula Valley's most thickly forested nature reserve and contains some of the most beautiful scenery in northern Israel. Several short walks loop under a canopy of willow trees and follow the gushing Dan River, the largest tributary of the Jordan. Swimming in the river is prohibited but there is a **wading pool** where hot hikers splash around. The 45-minute circle trail is mostly paved for **wheelchair access;** the one-and-a-half hour trail is rockier but passes by all the ancient ruins. Ongoing excavations at the *tel* have revealed the ancient Canaanite city of Laish, conquered and settled by the Israelite tribe of Dan around 1200 BCE. Interesting remains lie in the ritual site, where King Jeroboam Ben-Nebat of the breakaway Kingdom of Israel placed a golden calf, attempting to draw attention away from the Kingdom of Judah's Temple in Jerusalem (I Kings 12:28-29).

In 1983, archaeologists made a remarkable find at Tel Dan: a broken stele, inscribed with the words "House of David" in 9th-century BCE Aramaic. The earth-shattering piece of rock provided the first known reference to the biblical King David and his climactic expulsion of the Philistines, aside from the Good Book itself. The **Beit Usishkin Museum,** a gray stone building on the left on the way to Tel Dan, displays a replica of the stele. Take a left at the sign. (Open Su-Th 8:30am-4:30pm, F 8:30am-3:30pm, Sa 9:30am-4:30pm. NIS13, students and children NIS11; ticket includes a discount at the Tel Dan Reserve.)

METULLA מטולה

Metulla, 9km north of Kiryat Shmona, is Israel's largest village on the Lebanese border. For many years its main attraction was **Ha-Gader Ha-Tova** (The Good Fence), the only opening in the border between Lebanon and Israel. Israel began passing aid and supplies through this point to Lebanese Christians in 1971, and in June 1976 the Good Fence officially opened, allowing Lebanese Christians and Druze free passage into Israel to obtain medical treatment, visit relatives, and work. When Israel withdrew from southern Lebanon in June 2000, the Good Fence finally closed and has been renamed the Fatmah Gate, its name before 1976. At press time, the future of the gate remains in doubt, and as long as Hizbullah remains a serious threat to the region's security, many southern Lebanese will be left without jobs.

WHOSE LINE IS IT ANYWAY? When The British and French drew the border between their respective mandates in the Middle East, the thick pencil line went just north of Tel Dan. The land covered by the pencil line included the Ein Dan Spring, the most important source of the Dan River, which feeds into the Jordan River and the Sea of Galilee. In the 1960s, the Syrians claimed sovereignty over the Ein Dan Spring and diverted it. Over a number of years Israel and Syria fought for control of the water source. Eventually Israeli soldiers succeeded in keeping the water in Israeli hands. The command-post lookout uphill from the Ritual Site at Tel Dan contains the remnants of a bunker which the Israelis used during the "Water War."

ORIENTATION AND PRACTICAL INFORMATION. Buses #20 and 21 run between Kiryat Shmona and Metulla (15min., 5 per day 6:45am-2:10pm, NIS8). **Ha-Rishonim St.** runs through the center of town, with the community center and municipality building at one end and the Lebanese Border at the other. To reach the main street, walk up the steep paved road into Metulla and continue left, past the Canada Center sports complex and a small playground. The **municipality building** on the right, near the beginning of the street with flags waving in front, has free maps of the town on the ground floor. (☎694 13 64. Open Su-Th 8am-5pm, F 8am-noon.) **First aid** is next door. Further down on the left is the small **post office,** 29 Ha-Rishonim St. (Open Su-Tu, Th 8am-12:30pm and 3:30-6pm; W 8am-1:30pm; F 8am-noon.) In the commercial complex (two compact floors of tiny offices) past the post office is a tiny **Bank Leumi** branch (open Su-Th 9am-noon). A convenient **ATM** is outside the Canada Center sports complex.

ACCOMMODATIONS AND FOOD. The number of buildings that serve as hotels, bed and breakfasts, and restaurants is astounding. Signs throughout town point to private homes that have converted rooms into guest suites. On entering town and before reaching the Canada Center, head right and follow the sign to the pottery studio and lovely guest house **Herut Tamari,** 6 Ha-Goren St. With fish pond in front, pottery studio above, and barbecue garden in back, these apartment-style rooms come equipped with amenities inside and out, including refrigerators, A/C, TV, and private bathrooms. (☎694 05 52; www.zimmer.co.il/herut; email herutdov@barak-online.net. Doubles NIS270/US$56; July and Aug. NIS300/US$62; additional person NIS70, July and Aug. NIS60. Credit cards accepted.) **Motel Bet Shalom,** 28 Ha-Rishonim St., offers kitchenettes, air-conditioning, TV, and private bathrooms. Breakfast included. (☎694 07 67. Singles NIS200/US$47; doubles NIS300/US$72. Cash only.) For more of a budget range, the Tel Ḥai hostel is only a NIS15 taxi ride away. **Anis Restaurant,** on Ha-Rishonim St. near the Canada Center, serves great pizza (NIS22 and NIS39) and pasta (NIS25-29), overlooking the Golan and upper Galilee. (☎690 28 85. Open Su-Th 10am-12:30am, Sa 9pm-1am. Credit cards accepted.) The **Farmer's Daughter,** on Ha-Rishonim across from Bet Shalom, offers tasty pasta (NIS33-41), salads (NIS33-37), and Lebanese omelettes (NIS29). The country breakfast (NIS28) is served until noon. (☎699 71 77. Open daily 9:30am-11pm. Credit cards accepted.) For a picnic lunch, stock up at **Sam's Neighborhood** (☎699 79 92) at the northern end of Ha-Rishonim St.

ENTERTAINMENT. A block to the right of the main street sits the imposing **Canada Center,** perhaps the best sports complex in all of Israel. The price of entry for the day (NIS50, students NIS30) includes use of the two pools, jacuzzi, basketball courts, and ice skating rink, while squash is NIS10 (including racquets), bowling NIS20, weight room NIS10, and lockers NIS5. (☎695 03 70. Open daily 10am-10pm. Most area accommodations including the Tel Ḥai hostel and Metulla's Motel Bet Shalom and Herut Tamari offer 50% discounts to the center.)

HIKING. Curving around town is the **Iyun Nature Reserve,** full of waterfalls in the winter and early spring. There is a large picnic area and space for free camping (Bring your own tent. There are toilets, no showers). Enter the park by the road that branches off the main highway just south of the town. Just a few minutes up the trail from the parking lot is the 30m **Tanur (Oven) Waterfall,** named for the chimney-like structure it forms with the cliff. The path continues uphill for another 45 minutes past two more waterfalls. At press time, the upper entrance to the park was closed due to its proximity to the Lebanese border; the only way back to the parking lot is to retrace the path. Metulla and the bus stop to Tel Ḥai and Kiryat Shmona are a short walk to the right up the highway. Further up the highway toward the Fatmah gate, up the hill on the left, is the **Dado observation point,** with a superb view of the Upper Galilee and southern Lebanon. (☎695 15 19. Open Su-Th 8am-5pm, F 8am-4pm. NIS9, student NIS8, children NIS4.)

GOLAN HEIGHTS

רמת הגולן ☎06

This formerly volcanic plateau overlooking the Ḥula Valley has a sparse population of 35,000 equally divided between recent Jewish settlers and longtime Druze inhabitants, many of which strongly identify with Syria and have relatives across the border. To Israelis, the region is a major source of water as well as the home of ski slopes, apple orchards, wineries, and cattle pastures. The region's natural borders include the Jordan River and Sea of Galilee to the west, Mt. Ḥermon and the Lebanese mountains to the north, and the Syrian plains to the east.

The first recorded mention of the Golan is the Biblical "Golan in Bashan," a city established by Moses as a refuge for Israelites guilty of manslaughter (Deuteronomy 4:43). The Golan was an important holdout in the Jewish Revolt of 66-73 CE, when its steep hills sheltered the city of Gamla, called the Masada of the north (see **Gamla,** p. 259). During the next two centuries, the Golan became a center of the Jewish population, as evidenced by excavations of ancient synagogues. As time passed, however, it degenerated into a backwater Ottoman province, until Turkish officials planted Circassian settlers here to stop Bedouin highwaymen in the 1880s. When the British and French carved up their mandates following WWI, the Golan was given to the French, while Britain maintained control of the rest of Palestine. After WWII the Golan became part of Syria.

Recent history has cast the Golan Heights back into the jaws of political controversy. Throughout the 1950s and 1960s, Israeli towns in Galilee were assailed by artillery fire from Syrian gunposts atop the mountains. Israel captured the Golan in the 1967 Six-Day War but was pushed back by Syria's surprise attack in the 1973 war. Israeli forces quickly recovered and launched a counter-attack, capturing even more territory. As part of the 1974 disengagement accord, Israel returned both the newly conquered territory and part of the land captured in 1967. Israel officially annexed the remaining 768 square kilometers of territory in 1981, arousing international protest. Today, Jewish settlements are scattered among Israeli army bases, Druze villages, live minefields, and destroyed bunkers.

HIGHLIGHTS OF THE GOLAN

Visit **Nimrod's Fortress** (p. 261) for a priceless view of Northern Israel.

Golan hikes are some of the most beautiful in Israel, and the **Yehudiyya Trail** (p. 255) is the best of the best. Spend an afternoon wallowing behind waterfalls.

Kosher wine has come a long way since the days when Manishevitz reigned supreme. Stop by the Golan Winery in **Katzrin** (see p. 257) to see how Israel's finest wines are produced, taste the gourmet products, and walk out with your very own souvenir glass.

The future status of the Golan is currently under negotiation. Syria claims that the land was seized unfairly and demands its return. Israeli officials had always invoked the issue of security in their refusal to budge from the Golan Heights, until the Rabin and Peres administrations announced their willingness to cede all or part of the Golan in exchange for peace and Syrian recognition of Israel, but Syrian President Hafez al-Assad rejected the offer. The reality is that whoever commands the elevated plateau enjoys strategic views of Damascus and all of northern Israel.

The political necessity of compromise became apparent with the election of Ehud Barak in May of 1999, when it was revealed that even Benyamin Netanyahu had been close to making an agreement with the Syrians. The recent death of Hafez al-Assad and his son's rise to power have added an additional twist to the story. The international community awaits to see how the younger Assad will handle negotiations with Israel. Barak's goal is to reach an agreement with Syria that will not leave Israel dependent on the US for its security, as it was during the withdrawal from Sinai.

PRACTICAL INFORMATION

When wandering the Golan in summer, bring a hat, sunscreen, and water bottles. The cool pools of water often found on hikes reward weary walkers ready to take a dip, but don't drink the water. Try to avoid the cold, damp, foggy, and often snowy winter. The best time to visit the Golan is spring, when the temperature is mild, the hills are green, and the streams and waterfalls are satiated with icy-cold water from the melting snow on Mt. Ḥermon. The best way to see the Golan is to **rent a car** in Tiberias or Kiryat Shmona. Those who don't plan to hike can hit the major sights in two days. Don't be afraid to lean on your horn (passing other cars in the Golan is as common as passing breathtaking views), but take care when navigating the narrow, curving roads.

Egged buses reach some sights in the Golan, but infrequent service along remote roads necessitates careful planning. Double-check all schedules, and anticipate some walking. Buses to sights near the Sea of Galilee generally leave from Tiberias. The Upper Galilee, Ḥula Valley, and northern Golan are served by buses from Kiryat Shmona and Hatzor Ha-Galilit. It is nearly impossible to get to Gamla and many hiking trails by bus. Relatively few cars traverse the Golan, and hitchhiking is inadvisable. If you decide to set out on your own, take a good map. (See **Golan Hikes,** below.)

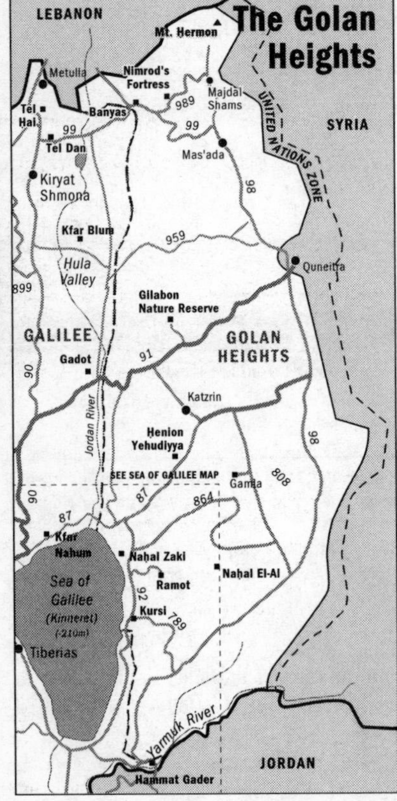

There is a rarely-open **tourist information office** for the Golan Heights at the Maḥanayim Junction between Rosh Pina and Kiryat Shmona, where Rte. 91 branches off of Rte. 90 (look for the gas station on the right and turn right; the information office is in the strip of shops on the left). The office sells maps and has brochures, mostly in Hebrew, on activities, restaurants, and accommodations in the region. (☎693 69 45. Open F 8:30am-3:30pm, Sa 9am-2pm.) There is a **24-hour grocery** next door to the tourist office; bring several bottles of water and at least a day's worth of food on any hike.

Organized **tours** are faster, more convenient, and sometimes less expensive than other forms of transportation; they also go at a quicker pace than many would like. **Matan Tours,** in Tiberias, attracts a young backpacker crowd with one-day professionally guided tours of the Golan and Upper Galilee that include sightseeing and light hiking. (☎06 672 4574 or 05 461 61 48. NIS160/US$38 per person.) **Egged** also offers professionally guided full-day tours of the region from Tel Aviv every Thursday. (☎03 527 12 12. NIS290/US$68; 10% ISIC discount.) **Moshe Cohen** makes military-history-oriented rounds in a van. (☎672 16 08. NIS140 per person; min. 4 people.) **SPNI** offers a three-day hiking tour of the Golan and Upper Galilee that includes kayaking on the Jordan River. (☎03 638 86 88. US$298. Leaves from the SPNI office in Tel Aviv.) For those who'd rather skip all the touristy kitsch and just get outside and hike, **Devorah Leah Rice** leads hikes in the Upper Galilee and Golan. (☎06 682 00 83. Half day NIS80, whole day NIS200.)

Jeep Plus in Moshav Ramot, on the east bank of the Sea of Galilee, runs guided jeep trips. (☎673 23 17. 2hr. trip for 7-8 people NIS540/US$145.) **Tractoron B'Rama** (☎05 053 17 84), also in Ramot, rents one-person ATVs to tourists with valid driver's licenses for NIS120 per hour. **Jimmy Jeep,** at Giv'at Yoav, southeast of Kursi on Rte. 789, runs 2-hour jeep trips for NIS550. (☎676 34 05. Jeep seats 8 people.)

GOLAN HIKES

The Golan offers some of the most beautiful hikes in all of Israel. Although the region gets very hot from late spring to early fall, most hikes go through streams, pools, and waterfalls, offering natural refreshment from the summer sun. Those who wish to hike in the Golan should purchase the 1:50,000 trail map available at SPNI offices and in Steimatzky's (NIS62). SPNI offices also have useful booklets with descriptions and directions for hiking routes in the area, such as the *Israeli Landscapes Vol. 1: Guide to the Golan Heights* (NIS55) and a more general map of the upper Galilee and Golan Heights, with roads and popular sights marked (NIS20). For more detailed directions and alternative trail options in the Golan, check out a copy of Joel Roskin's *A Guide to Hiking in Israel*, on sale at Steimatzky bookstores (NIS39). Consult the SPNI field schools in Katzrin or Ḥermon for up-to-date advice and information; the information desk at **Yehudiyya Reserve** (☎696 28 17) also offers helpful hiking advice. Bus service to the trails, where it exists, is very irregular; call Egged and plan carefully. Be aware that many trails do not loop back to where they started and may leave you far away from your car. Start hiking early in the morning to avoid the busloads of Israeli children and remember that it is not safe to drink water from Golan streams.

DANGER! MINES! The Golan Heights still contain active **landmine fields.** they are marked off by barbed-wire fences with square yellow signs that have red triangles and say, Danger! Mines! in English, as well as in Hebrew and Arabic. In some areas the fences are marked only with red triangles. Mine fields line roads as well as hiking routes, so be sure to stay on paved roads and clearly marked hiking trails. As a rule, avoid fenced-off areas whether or not you see the yellow-and-red warning signs.

YA'AR YEHUDIYYA NATURE RESERVE

By car from Tiberias, drive north along the lake, head east toward Katzrin, pass the Yehudiyya Junction, and continue along Rte. 87 until you reach the orange sign. By car from Kiryat Shmona, head toward Katzrin and the junction with Rte. 87, take a right, and look for the sign and parking lot on the right. Open Sa-Th 7am-5pm, F and holidays 7am-4pm; leave no later than 1hr. after closing time. NIS10, students NIS8, children NIS7. Most trails begin in ***Ḥenion Yehudiyya*** *(☎696 28 17), a parking lot with an SPNI information booth, snack stand (1½L water NIS9, sandwiches NIS12), toilets, phones, and camping facilities accessible by bus from Katzrin. At the Ḥenion, bags can be stored for NIS12 per locker.* ***Camping*** *next to the Henion parking lot costs NIS10 per person; facilities include showers and bathrooms. Before beginning a hike, check in with the information desk and get a map.*

The most exciting and challenging hiking in the Golan is in the Ya'ar Yehudiyya Nature Reserve, southeast of Katzrin. The highlight of the reserve, and one of the best hikes in Israel, is the action-packed **Naḥal Yehudiyya** trail, which consists of an upper and a lower section. From the Ḥenion parking lot follow the red-and-white markers across the street, past the 1800-year-old Jewish and Byzantine town ruins, and into the valley. Upon completion of the **upper trail,** ascend the green-and-white trail to return to Ḥenion (3hr. round-trip) or continue along the red-and-white marked lower trail for a longer hike (5-6hr. round-trip). The lower trail ends with an extremely difficult climb up a boulder-strewn hill (be careful: the rocks are hot during summer), a peaceful stroll through a beautiful yellow field, and a 1.5km walk to the right along the highway back to the Ḥenion. Both trails feature enticing waterfalls and pools, some of which you must swim across to complete your hike (bring a bathing suit and plastic bags to protect food and valuables because everything will unavoidably get soaked). Rocks are slippery when climbing from dry parts of the trail into the water, so look for the strategically placed metal foot- and hand-holds in the cliffs. Jumping off the nine-meter cliff at the second waterfall is dangerous—people have died at this spot. A much safer option is to climb down the slippery ladder into the water to enjoy the swim.

The reserve also harbors the slightly drier but equally beautiful **Naḥal Zavitan;** most of its trail options also start at the Ḥenion Yehudiyya parking lot. Start on the green-and-white marked Lower Zavitan trail. A left turn on the red-and-white trail leads to the **Ein Netef** spring, which purportedly contains the only drinkable water in the reserve. From the spring, backtrack along the red-and-white trail and turn left on the black-and-white trail to reach a pleasant pool and waterfall. This trek eventually crosses the red-and-white one and returns to Ḥenion Yehudiyya (3hr.). Alternatively, turn left and continue on the red-and-white trail for 45 minutes to reach the spectacular **Brekhat Ha-Meshushim** (Hexagon Pool), where hundreds of hexagonal rock columns skirt the water's edge in a wonderful geological phenomenon. From here, backtrack to Ḥenion (total 6hr.). The **Upper Zavitan** (black-and-white trail) tends to be good for all seasons. It begins near the field school in Katzrin and leads to less impressive hexagonal pools; after becoming a purple-and-white trail, it ends in Ḥenion Yehudiyya (3hr.). The more difficult **Lower Zavitan** should be avoided in the winter due to occasional flash floods. The dangerous **Black Canyon** is near the Lower Zavitan trail, and can only be negotiated by rapelling. Many hikers have died here. Do not attempt to hike the Black Canyon unless with an experienced guide.

NAḤAL EL-AL

By car from Tiberias, head south on Rte. 90. At Zemaḥ Junction, turn onto Rte. 98 and follow it to Kibbutz Eli-Al. The site is fairly close to Yehudiyya: turn left out of Ḥenion Yehudiyya, take Rte. 87 to Rte. 808 on the right, turn right onto Rte. 98, and look for the kibbutz sign. Without a car, this hike is impossible to do in a day; the first bus arrives at 12:30pm and the last one leaves at 1pm.

This beautiful hike (no relation to Israel's major airline) lies southeast of the Zavitan and Yehudiyya Rivers. In winter and spring, enough water flows through to allow swimming beneath the falls. The red-and-white trail begins at the northeast end of the kibbutz. Follow the markers to **Mapal Ha-Lavan** (white waterfall) and continue on to **Mapal Ha-Shaḥor** (black waterfall). The trail ends at Kibbutz Avnei-Eitan. From there, take a right on Rte. 98 and walk 2km to return to Kibbutz Eli-Al.

SPIES LIKE US In the early 1960s, Israeli spy **Eli Cohen,** posing as an Arab businessman, infiltrated the Syrian government. Rising through the ranks, he virtually became the president's right-hand man. Cohen suggested that the Syrian army plant tall eucalyptus trees to camouflage their Golan Heights bunkers; he then tipped off the IDF, and the air force began targeting the eucalyptus clusters. The Syrian government eventually caught and hanged the Israeli spy, but the destroyed Syrian bunkers sprinkled over the Golan stand as a testimony to his espionage.

NAḤAL DEVORAH AND NAḤAL GILABON

Naḥal Devorah and Naḥal Gilabon (JEEL-ah-bone) lie north of Katzrin. From Tiberias, take Rte. 90 north and the turn-off for Rte. 91 east. Continue 30min. on Rte. 91. Watch for a brown sign and red-and-white trail marker 3-4km after the turn-off for Road 9088. Turn left onto the dirt road and make a right further up to reach a parking lot surrounded by destroyed Syrian bunkers.

From the main parking lot, red-and-white markings lead to the left around a building and down into the canyon. Join the hundreds who have left their mark by sticking a masticated glob of gum onto the **Even Ha-Mastik** ("The Gum Rock"). The first waterfall on the trail is the Devorah Waterfall. Continuing on the red-and-white path another hour leads to the 21-meter Gilabon Waterfall; wonderful views of the lush Ḥula Valley await at its top. The trail continues another two hours to the Jordan River and Rte. 918, but getting back to the parking lot may be difficult if you don't have a car waiting. Otherwise just retrace your steps to return to the parking lot. To save time, drive to a second parking lot near the top of the Gilabon fall.

NAḤAL ZAKI

Off of Rte. 92, just south of the Yehudiyya Junction on the left. Drive along the green trail to a lot, then park and begin the hike.

Naḥal Zaki makes for a viewless but extremely refreshing hike. In August or September, ripe grapes hang overhead and the sweltering heat makes the cool stream a godsend. Wear a bathing suit and bring plastic bags to protect valuables—half the hike is spent wading in knee-deep water. In winter, the current is strong and this trail could be dangerous. Hike in the stream following the green-and-white trail for three kilometers; at the pipe that stretches across the river, get out of the water on the left side and return by way of a dirt path.

KATZRIN קצרין

Katzrin is the largest Jewish settlement in the Golan. The town was founded immediately after the 1967 War with the express purpose of creating an Israeli presence in the Golan Heights. This quiet residential community of houses with orange tiled roofs has grown rapidly over the past 33 years and is now home to a successful winery and a bottled water manufacturing plant. Katzrin enjoys a high standard of living for a young settlement, but its economic growth has slowed with the possibility of an Israeli withdrawal from the Golan. A visit to the winery and museums in Katzrin takes only a few hours, but the town's central location in the Golan also makes it a convenient base for exploring the region.

GETTING THERE AND GETTING AROUND

By car from **Tiberias,** head north on Rte. 90 and turn off on Rte. 87 toward the east. Drive 20km past Tzomet Yehudiya and turn onto Rte. 9088. From **Kiryat Shmona,** head south on Rte. 90 toward Rosh Pina and take a left on Rte. 91; a right onto Rte. 9088 leads to the town. Buses go to Katzrin from **Ḥatzor Ha-Galilit,** just north of **Rosh Pina** (#55, 56, and 57; 25min., 6 per day 6:15am-7:55pm, NIS10.50); **Kiryat Shmona,** (#58; 30min., 4:40pm, NIS26); and **Tiberias** (#15, 16, and 19; 45min., 4 per day noon-6:30pm, NIS18). **Moniot Ha-Golan** (☎696 11 11), a left out of the tourist office in an office on the right, has *special* taxis to **Rosh Pina** (NIS75) and **Tiberias** (NIS120).

ORIENTATION AND PRACTICAL INFORMATION

There are three points of entry into Katzrin on the right from the highway, all marked by brown signs. The second one leads to the main Daliyot St., at the beginning of which is a mall on the left and on the right a commercial center with the bank, tourist office, and two museums clustered together.

The **tourist information** office in Katzrin, in the shopping strip past the bank on the left, has a bus schedule and information on sights, as well as a list of bed-and-breakfasts in the Golan. (☎696 28 85. Open Su-Th 8:30am-4:30pm, F 8:30am-1pm.) The **Municipality,** in back of the bank, has free Hebrew maps of Katzrin. (Open Su-Th 8am-4pm, F 8am-noon.) **Bank Leumi,** in front of the shopping strip with the tourist office, has an **ATM** outside that takes Visa, Plus, and Diners' Club cards. (☎696 16 01. Open Su, T-W 8:30am-1pm; M, Th 8:30am-1pm and 4:30-7pm; F 8:30am-noon.) Across the street in the mall is a **supermarket** (☎696 13 35; open Su-Th 8am-8pm, F 8am-3pm) and **post office** that exchanges cash and traveler's checks for no commission (☎696 12 02; open Su-Tu, Th 8am-12:30pm and 3:30-6pm, W 8am-1:30pm, F 8am-noon). **Emek Pharmacy** is just past the entrance to the tourist office. (☎696 25 78. Open Su, Tu, Th 8:30am-1pm and 4-7pm; M, F 8:30am-1pm; W 8:30am-1pm and 5-7pm.) **Mayaan Laundry,** in the industrial area past the winery, just after lot #4, washes clothes for NIS6 per kilo. (☎696 44 22. Open Su-Th 8am-5pm, F 8am-1pm.) Those intrigued by the *"Ha-Am Im Ha-Golan"* (the nation with the Golan) bumper stickers all around Israel may want to stop by the **Golan Residents Committee** (☎696 2977), in the shopping center across Dolyot St. from the mall. Look for the flags on the right next to the jewelery store. The committee is dedicated to keeping the Golan in Israeli hands and gives out free bumper stickers and banners and sells shirts for NIS13. (Open Su-Th 8am-6pm, F 8am-3pm.) For a refreshing break from the summer humidity, take a dip at Katzrin's **public swimming pool,** off Daliyot St., next to the Archaeological Museum. (☎696 00 66. Outdoor pool NIS20, students and children NIS15. Use of sauna, jacuzzi, indoor pool and tennis court NIS35, students and children NIS20. Outdoor pool only open from May 15- Oct. 21; indoor facilities open year round. Open M-Th 9am-8pm, F-Sa 9am-5pm.)

GOLAN HEIGHTS

ACCOMMODATIONS AND FOOD

Unfortunately, Katzrin does not offer much in the way of budget accommodations. There are numerous **bed-and-breakfasts** in the town; call ☎696 28 85 or stop by the tourist office for a list. The **SPNI Golan Field School,** on Zavitan St., rents out clean six-bed rooms with A/C and bath, when it isn't full of school groups. Go down Daliyot St. away from the shopping area, make a left at the intersection, and look for a sign for the field school on the right. (☎696 12 34. Dorm rooms NIS60 per bed; doubles with breakfast NIS305, NIS95 for each additional person; prices higher in August. Call the central SPNI office (☎03 638 86 88) to book a room during Jewish holidays and in August.)

For the best budget food in town head to **Chicken Thai,** across from the tourist office, and order a mouth-watering chicken-veggie stir fry on a baguette for NIS16. (☎696 18 71. Open Su-Th 11am-midnight, F 11am-4pm, Sa 8:30-11pm.) For a more extensive feast **Mifgash Ha-Aish,** at the end of the parking lot farthest from Daliyot St., cooks up all sorts of meat on its flaming outdoor grill and serves it with salads, hot pita, and hummus. (Steaks NIS40-55; chicken kebab NIS35. Open Su-Th 10am-midnight, F 10am-3pm, Sa 9pm-midnight.) Katzrin also has one of the most unique pubs in all of Israel. The **Safta Pub,** inside the Ancient Katzrin Park, is located inside a 1400 year old stone building from Talmudic times. During the summer, the pub has an outdoor seating area and features theme nights: M karaoke, Tu cocktail specials, W movie night, Th Israeli music. (☎696 25 21. Beer NIS12-18; cocktails NIS22-35; pizza NIS22; *malaweh* NIS12. Open Sa-Th 9pm-3am.)

SIGHTS

The **Field School** sells 1:50,000 maps of the Golan (NIS62), and staff members are generally helpful in suggesting hikes in the area.

GOLAN ARCHAEOLOGICAL MUSEUM. This museum has an excellent, bilingual exhibit on ancient settlements in the Golan. It displays the remnants of 2000-year-old synagogues, including a lintel inscribed with the Talmudic sage Eliezer Ha-Kappar's name, and sculptures from a Chalcolithic settlement dating back to 4000 BCE. It also shows an amazing 17-minute audio-visual presentation on the Great Revolt battle in Gamla. *(Across the plaza behind the shopping strip off of Daliyot St. ☎696 13 50. Open Su-Th 8am-5pm, F 8am-3pm, Sa 10am-4pm. NIS15, seniors NIS13, students NIS12. Joint admission to museum and Ancient Katzrin Park NIS27, seniors NIS23, students and children NIS19.)*

ANCIENT KATZRIN PARK. The excavations at this site have unearthed a richly ornamented synagogue in use from the 4th through 8th centuries CE. Don't miss the six-screen audio-visual presentation shown in a reconstructed synagogue or the two reconstructed houses with furnishings based on finds from the excavations. *(Just outside of modern Katzrin, to the right down Rte. 9088; look for a brown sign pointing to the left. ☎696 24 12. NIS22, seniors NIS18, students and children NIS14. Save money with a combo ticket that includes the Archaeological museum as well. Ticket allows 10% discount at Gamla and the Golan Winery.)*

SHA'AR HA-GOLAN (GATE OF THE GOLAN). This newly opened information center shows on a giant screen an informative 17-minute movie that covers the history and geography of the Golan Heights. In another pavilion is an enormous, continually updated, 1:5000 three-dimensional map of the Golan that includes every house, road, stream, hill, and radio tower in the entire region. *(Next to the Ancient Katzrin Park; turn into the Ancient Katzrin parking lot and follow the road to the right. ☎696 20 96. Open Su-Th 10am-5pm, F 10am-4pm, Sa map only 10am-5pm. Movie NIS6. 20min. tour of map with explanations from a guide NIS10. Combined ticket NIS15.)*

GOLAN HEIGHTS WINERY. For those who find Katzrin's museums and Talmudic village too sobering, the Golan Heights Winery is a great alternative. The winery produces the world-renowned Yarden, Gamla, and Golan labels. A one-hour tour includes a video explanation, a look at the production process, a souvenir glass, and a taste of grapey bliss along with a demonstration on how to taste wine. The shop sells bottles of their wine beginning at NIS25. *(From the center of Katzrin, turn right onto Rte. 9088; the winery is in an industrial area on the left. ☎696 84 09. Open Su-Th 8:30am-5pm, July-Aug. until 6:30pm, F 8:30am-1:30pm. The last tour begins about 1hr. before closing. Tours NIS17, students NIS14, children NIS12. Call ahead for tours in English.)*

KATZRIN DOLL MUSEUM. Rows of glass cases feature woolly-headed dolls, all wearing looks of blank astonishment. A separate children's room displays episodes from the likes of Peter Pan and Alice in Wonderland, seminal works in the Jewish tradition. *(Across the plaza from the Archaeological Museum, behind the shopping strip with the tourist office. ☎696 29 82. Open Su-Th 10am-4pm, F 10am-2pm, Sa 10am-4pm. NIS15, students NIS13.50, children NIS8.)*

DAYTRIP FROM KATZRIN

GAMLA גמלא

Take a right out of modern Katzrin, a left onto Rte. 87 at the junction, and a right onto Rte. 808. The road to Gamla is on the right, labeled with a sign. Gamla is not accessible by public transportation; those without cars often ask for rides from Katzrin and walk the 1km to the ridge overlooking the ruins. The descent to the ruins along the Roman route takes about 20min. Allot 1-2hr. for the site itself. ☎676 20 46. Open Su-Th 8am-5pm, F 8am-4pm; closes 1hr. earlier in winter. NIS18, students NIS15.

For years the lost city of Gamla existed as no more than a legend from the pages of *The Jewish War* (Book IV, Ch. 1), written by first-century Jewish historian Josephus Flavius After the 1967 War, archaeologists scoured the region for a spot corresponding to the ancient description until archaeologist Shmaryahu Gutman finally uncovered the site. It is called Gamla (meaning "Camel" in Hebrew) because the hill's peak protrudes from the surrounding area like a camel's hump. The film at Katzrin's archaeological museum (see p. 259) is a great introduction.

In 67 CE, the Romans laid siege to this hilltop fortress, which had become a haven for 9000 Jewish refugees. As the siege wore on, Roman commanders became impatient and decided to storm down the corridor of land leading to the town from nearby hills. As the legion penetrated Gamla's walls, hordes of Jews fled to the upper part of the city, where slopes were so steep that one house's rooftop touched the floor of the house above it. The Romans followed, but so many soldiers crowded on the rooftops that the houses collapsed; the Jews quickly turned and killed their pursuers. Some weeks later, three Roman soldiers sneaked into Gamla in the middle of the night and pulled out foundation stones from the watchtower, causing it to collapse. In the ensuing confusion, the Roman army burst into the city and began to slaughter the inhabitants, many of whom hurled themselves into the deep ravine next to the citadel rather than die by enemy hands. Two women survived to tell the tale. (Some archaeologists take issue with Josephus's proclivity for over-dramatization and claim that Gamla's inhabitants were pushed over the cliff in the mayhem of battle.) Inside the city lie remnants of what some archaeologists call the oldest synagogue ever found in Israel, dating from around the 2nd century BCE.

There are three **light hiking** trails at Gamla. The two-hour trail through the ancient city is marked in black and begins at the upper left corner of the parking lot (when facing away from the ticket booth). The climb back up from the ruins to the parking lot can be brutal on a hot summer day; there is a shuttle bus that runs every hour down to the ancient city and returns to the parking lot on the half hour (NIS15). Gamla is also known as a favorite roosting place for the **Griffin Vulture;** for a good glimpse of the bird, try the vultures lookout trail, which arcs from the start of the ancient city trail to the other side of the parking lot (the ticket booth rents out binoculars for NIS10). There is a video screen at the vultures lookout point that shows a live close-up of the vultures. The **Mapal Gamla,** or Gamla waterfall, is the highest in the Golan (51 meters). The trail to the waterfall leads past another fall, usually dry in summer, as well as ancient **Dolmens,** table-like stone graves built 4000 years ago during the middle Bronze Age. The trail is marked in red, takes about an hour, and begins out of the upper right corner of the parking lot, near the water spigots and bathrooms. The two-hour **Daliyot trail,** marked red and white, starts out of the left corner of the parking lot nearest the ticket booth and runs through fields and along a river canyon. While hot and less interesting during the summer, it boasts a seasonal waterfall and vultures soaring overhead.

NORTHERN GOLAN

BANYAS בניס

Buses #55 and 58 each leave Kiryat Shmona once a day on their way through the Golan and stop by Banyas (1:30 and 4:40pm; NIS11.50). *By car, Banyas lies just off Rte. 99, which runs between Kiryat Shmona and the north-south Rte. 98.* ☎ *695 02 72. Park open Sa-Th 8am-5pm, F 8am-4pm. NIS18, students NIS15, children NIS9.*

The most popular site in the Upper Galilee-Golan area, Banyas lies only a few minutes down the road from Dan and Ḥorshat Tal at the foot of Mt. Hermon. The Banyas springs in the Naḥal Ḥermon Nature Reserve have witnessed an odd religious mix: Jesus gave the keys to heaven and earth to St. Peter here, Muslims built a shrine over the Prophet Elijah's (Nebi Khadar) supposed grave in the adjacent hill, and an ancient sanctuary dedicated to the Greek God Pan remains carved into the cliffside. King Herod built a temple in honor of Augustus Caesar

and called the place Caesarea Philippi, after his son Philippus. Because of its ancient association with Pan, however, the area became known as *Paneas* (Pan's Place), rendered in Arabic as Banyas. Arabs settled the town in the 7th century, though possession was passed between the Muslims and the Crusaders many times during the 12th and 13th centuries. Banyas remained an Arab village until the 1967 War. Today, families flock to the reserve for afternoons of light hiking and swimming.

The first brown sign on the road that points to Banyas leads to a parking lot and the entrance closest to the 10m **Banyas waterfall,** the largest falls in the region. From the waterfall, an hour-long trail winds through woods toward the springs, which contain small pools of rare fish. Swimming is forbidden in the pool's icy-cold water, but some visitors wade in to refresh themselves anyway. Along the trail is an old flour mill where Druze sell fresh pita with za'tar (NIS8). From here, head toward the parking lot where the ruins of **Pan's temple** are up and to the left. Those short on time can drive from the waterfall to Pan's Temple by making a right on the main road and following the signs.

NIMROD'S FORTRESS קלעת נמרוד

The trail to the fortress begins just off bus route #55 between Kiryat Shmona and Katzrin. The road to the castle sits across from the bus stop (NIS16.50). The 1hr., uphill approach leads to a view into the Druze village of Ein Qinya. The castle is also accessible by a footpath from Banyas beginning directly above the springs and Pan's temple. This shadeless walk takes about 45min. each way. By car, continue on Rte. 99 past Banyas to Rte. 989; the fortress is up a curvy road on the left. Open daily 8am-5pm. NIS14, students NIS12, under 18 NIS6.

Nimrod's Fortress (Qal'at Nemrud) stands 1.5 kilometers northeast of Banyas on an isolated hill. According to the biblical list of Noah's descendants, Nimrod claims the title, "the first on earth to be a mighty man" (Genesis 10:8). Legend holds that besides building the Tower of Babel, he erected this gigantic fortress high enough to shoot arrows up to God. According to tradition, Nimrod was so large he could sit atop this castle and reach down to take water from the Banyas stream. A plaque above one gate reads in Arabic: "God gave him the power to build this castle with his own strength." Historians like to poke holes in the myth by pointing out that the Ismailia sect of Muslims built the fortress, originally called Qal'at Subeiba, in a strategic location that controlled the road from the Ḥula Valley to Damascus during the 13th century. The extensive fortress has two main sections; the one farther away from the entrance was built earlier. A look around the grounds reveals a secret passageway and game boards carved into the stone sidewalks by bored guards. The 815-meter-high view from the top of the fortress to the region below remains unrivaled anywhere in the Upper Galilee or Golan.

Up the road about 1km past Nimrod's Fortress is a Muslim tomb and hiking route at **Nebi Hazuri.** The location is marked on the left by a brown sign in Hebrew. A white gravel road begins in the parking lot and winds around picnic areas, trees, and monuments. The hiking route, marked in blue and white, heads right and downhill from beside the large wooden sign in the parking area (rocks are marked a bit further down). The trail descends to the riverbed and curves around toward the bottom of the hill upon which Nimrod's Fortress stands. After two hours, the trail ends outside the entrance to the road leading up to Nimrod's Fortress; take a left and head up the main highway to return to the Nebi Hazuri parking area.

MAS'ADA AND MAJDAL SHAMS مسعدة و مجدل شمس

The Druze of these two villages at the foot of Mt. Ḥermon differ from the Galilee's Druze in one major respect: most have remained loyal to Syria and many refuse to accept Israeli citizenship. Many of them have close relatives on the other side of the Syrian border and do not want to fight against them in the event of a war. In 1982, they staged a protest against Israeli rule, and the Israeli Defense Forces were sent in to restore control. Since then, the villages have been quiet.

Mas'ada (pronounced MA-sa-da; ma-SA-da refers to the fortress near the Dead Sea) and Majdal Shams are unprepared for tourism, focusing more on tradition than on commercialism. Women swathe themselves in black and men wear black *shirwal* (low-hanging baggy pants) which date from Ottoman times. Both genders wear flowing white head-coverings.

Mas'ada is located at the foot of Mt. Ḥermon, at the intersection of Rte. 99 (leading west to Kiryat Shmona) and Rte. 98 (leading south to Katzrin). Mas'ada's farmers cultivate the valley and terrace the low-lying ridges around the mountain. Two kilometers north on Rte. 98 rests the locally famous lake **Breiḥat Ram** (Hebrew for "High Lake"). The perfectly round body of water fills the crater of a volcano that has not erupted in over 1000 years. The lake is on the right, past large green gates with a big white sign in Hebrew. In the lake's parking lot is the excellent, two-story **Breiḥat Ram Restaurant.** Dig into their specialty, "Lamb in the Oven." The restaurant's roof boasts a postcard-worthy view of a Druze mosque beneath sometimes-snowy Mt. Ḥermon. (☎698 16 38. Open daily 9am-7pm, sometimes later on weekends.) A small hut in the parking lot sells delicious Druze pita with *labaneh* and *za'tar* (NIS14). A lakefront swimming and picnic area costs NIS10 (free for restaurant patrons; inquire at the shop downstairs).

Majdal Shams (Arabic for "Tower of the Sun"), the largest town in the Golan (pop. 8000), is 5 kilometers north of Mas'ada through a pleasant valley. The town abuts the border with Syria; an Israeli lookout tower that looms above the village sees eye-to-eye with its Syrian counterpart on the opposite peak, while a white UN base spans the neutral valley in between. Because the electric-fence border is closed and pocked with land mines, the lookout area on the outskirts of town provides the setting for a sad, but fascinating, daily ritual. Majdal's Druze line up on the hillside (aptly dubbed *Givat Ha-Tza'akot* or "Shouting Mountain"). Armed with bullhorns, they make small-talk with their relatives on the Syrian side; the best time to communicate seems to be Friday and Saturday afternoons.

DRIVING TOUR

One of the most interesting ways to see the Golan is to drive along Rte. 98 which runs north-south on the eastern end of the Golan near the Syrian border. Starting in Katzrin or Tiberias, drive east along Rte. 87, and turn left onto Rte. 98 northbound, or start in Kiryat Shmona, drive east on Rte. 99 and do the tour in the reverse order from which it is listed here. Along the way are scenic lookouts with views of Mt. Ḥermon to the north and Syria to the east. North of the junction of Rte. 87 and Rte. 98 is the *moshav* Aloney Ha-Bashan, which offers **horseback riding** along the beautiful eastern hills of the Golan. (☎696 0019. NIS85 for a 30min. ride, NIS120 for 1½hr. Open daily 9am-6pm. Call ahead.) A few kilometers north of the *moshav* are the **wind turbines** of Mt. Benei-Rasan. These ten turbines generate an average of 15 million kilowatts per hour—enough for the annual needs of 20,000 people. At the top of the hill near the turbines is an abandoned Israeli bunker with a great view of Syria. Look for the turn-off on the right side of the road. Further north along Rte. 98 are two kibbutzim, **Ein Zivan** and **Merom Golan.** These were the first Israeli settlements in the Golan, founded a few months after the 1967 Six-Day War. There is an observation point at Mt. Bental, near Kibbutz Merom Golan, that has a description of the volcanic layers in the area. Follow the signs to Merom Golan and look for the uphill road just south of the kibbutz. The observation point looks out over the Syrian ghost-town of **Quneitra.** Although Israel returned the conquered city to Syria after the 1973 war, it remained abandoned; some say Syria was just being prudent, while others claim the abandoned village works as political propaganda. The buildings in the valley just south of Quneitra are part of a U.N. border-monitoring base. Damascus lies only 64km to the east of Mt. Bental. From here continue north through the Druze villages Mas'ada and Majdal Shams to the end of Rte. 98 at the base of **Mt. Ḥermon.**

TANK YOU VERY MUCH When most countries choose colors for their tanks, camouflage is the height of concern: The Egyptians pick a sandy tan to match their deserts and the Syrians paint theirs a lush green to blend into the forests. The Lebanese, however, paint their tanks a cool blue. According to superstition, making their tanks the color of the sea and sky will bring their army good luck. In reality, the conspicuous color brings swift bombs. Unfortunately, the world is not yet color-blind.

MT. ḤERMON

The 2800-meter high peaks of the majestic Ḥermon mountain range tower over the rest of the Golan. In the wintertime there is skiing, which can be challenging; it has no trees, and steep dips in the wide expanses are easy to miss. Beginners should not fret, however—gentle runs descend from the top of each lift. On clear days, skiers can see Galilee stretch out beneath them. In summer the same chairlift brings tourists up to a panoramic lookout atop Mt. Ḥermon. The mountain is particularly striking in late spring and early summer when it is covered in brightly colored wildflowers. (Call ☎06 698 13 37 or 03 565 60 40 for ski conditions, lodging information; in summer for chairlift.)

Ten kilometers south of Mt. Ḥermon lies **Moshav Neveh Ativ** (☎698 13 33), founded after Israel captured the Golan. The moshav has developed an expensive resort village to take advantage of the ski slopes. Bus #55 goes from Kiryat Shmona to the moshav twice a day (1:30 and 4:40pm, NIS13). A *sherut* from Mas'ada to Kiryat Shmona in the late afternoon is usually the same price. The road from Mas'ada to Kiryat Shmona runs west along a gorge and past the hilltop village of Ein Qinya and Nimrod's Fortress. For information on outdoor activities in the area or in the Golan in general, try the **Ḥermon SPNI field school,** located near Kibbutz Senir, to the right off Rte. 99 on the way from Kiryat Shmona to Banyas and just beyond Tel Dan. The field school is down a turnoff marked by a wooden sign on the right, then through the gates. In addition to patient and friendly advice, the field school has air-conditioned double rooms with private bathrooms. (☎694 10 91. NIS245/US$60; additional person NIS70; July-Aug. and holidays NIS25 extra per person. Breakfast included.) The field school office is open daily 8am-8pm.

THE DEAD SEA

ים המלח_البحر الميت

HIGHLIGHTS OF THE DEAD SEA

Head to **Siesta Beach** to dodge the tourist crowds, roll around in the black mud, and get a Thai massage after floating too hard (p. 266).

When in **Masada,** do as the Romans do: climb the mountain at sunrise via the Roman Ramp, but don't slaughter anyone (p. 271).

Hike **Naḥal David** at Ein Gedi and glimpse some of the world's rarest wildlife (p. 268).

How low can you go? At 412m below sea level, this is it—the Dead Sea is the lowest point on Earth. If that factoid doesn't sound impressive, wait until you're driving on the highway, pass a SEA LEVEL signpost, and then round a bend to see entire mountains whose *peaks* lie below you.

The morbid "dead" moniker was coined by Christian monks astonished by the apparent absence of any form of life in the sea's waters, however, kill-joy scientists have recently discovered 11 types of hardy bacteria in the water. The sea's Hebrew name, Yam Ha-Melaḥ (The Sea of Salt), is more appropriate: the water has a salt concentration eight times that of the ocean , making it so heavy and dense that even fish would have to walk. This comes as good news to those who can't swim: everyone floats in this sea, without so much as moving a muscle. Besides the much-acclaimed floating effect, the high concentration of minerals is responsible for the gorgeous salt formations that adorn the seaside rocks and postcards. Businesses have capitalized upon this natural resources, building a vast series of evaporation ponds at the southernmost tip, which suck select salts from the water.

The Dead Sea is actually a large lake—65km long, 18km wide, and 412m deep. Its coasts are shared by Israel and Jordan, with the peaceful border drawn smack down the sea's middle. The sea's formation is the result of a geological phenomenon called the "Syrian-African Rift," essentially a mega-valley between shifting tectonic plates extending from southern Africa to Turkey. The resulting image of hollowness has led some to nickname the Dead Sea area "the navel of the world."

Water flows into the sea from the Jordan River and underground water sources from the surrounding desert. But with no outlet for the lake's water, the intense sun evaporates it faster than you can say "Ra." Inadequate rainfall, coupled with Israeli, Jordanian, and Syrian reliance on the sea's freshwater sources for drinking and irrigation, has begun to take its toll. The sun now evaporates more water than flows in; the sea is shrinking so severely that the southern tip has been cut off by a sand bar, and the northern part now recedes at the frightening rate of 80cm a year. Emergency measures to save the Dead Sea, driven by both ecological and economic incentives, are in the planning stages.

From its northern tip, 25 minutes from Jerusalem, to the southern-most Sodom area, the Dead Sea and its surroundings are replete with sights and activities to please even the pickiest of travelers. Many visitors take a quick dip at the tourist-trappy Ein Bokek beach, snap the famous floating-while-reading-a-magazine and caked-in-mud photos, and go along their merry ways. This is an area of great beauty, but the ruggedness can be marred by postcard racks and the hum of international tour buses. Not far from these oft-visited spectacles, shy-horned ibex, camouflaged by their light brown hues, prance vivaciously around the supposedly "dead" sea. Nestled above apparently barren wasteland lie lush nature reserves, and below-ground, the desert dust hides bottomless mineral springs. A trek to the region's more secluded spots, such as Metzokei Dragot or Naḥal Arugot, often yields the most rewarding Dead Sea experience.

GETTING THERE

The Egged buses that serve the rest of the country do so poorly in this region. Fares are outrageous (up to NIS10 for a 10min. ride), and the routes don't cover every destination. These difficulties, in conjunction with the nasty heat and the distance between the main roads and sights, make renting a car an excellent idea. Most companies offer a daily rental rate of US$40-50 for single-day rentals, US$35-45 per day for longer-term rentals. Driving in the Dead Sea region provides spectacular vistas, but be careful—steep, windy roads mean nothing to speed-demon Israeli drivers. The best place to rent is Jerusalem, since cut-throat competition drives prices down (see **Rental Cars** under **Transportation** p. 85). In the Dead Sea, try **Hertz** (☎658 44 33 or 658 45 30) in Ein Bokek.

The few Egged lines that travel along the Dead Sea coast have erratic schedules with waits often lasting 45 to 90 minutes, so check times (call the Central Bus Station in Jerusalem ☎02 530 47 04) and plan ahead. Buses #421, 444, and 486 between Jerusalem and Eilat stop at Qumran, Ein Feshkha, Ein Gedi, and Masada. Bus #487, also from Jerusalem, runs only to Qumran, Ein Feshkha, and Ein Gedi. Buses #384 and 385 combined make about four trips per day (Su-F) between Be'er Sheva and Ein Gedi via Arad, Ein Bokek, and Masada. Buses will stop at many stations only upon request, so **confirm destinations** with the driver. Several sites listed, including Metzokei Dragot and Neot Hakikar, are **not accessible by public transportation**. On Saturdays, none of the buses head to or from the Dead Sea until the evening; to get there earlier, find a *service* across from Damascus Gate (NIS30-45 depending how far south you want to go). Locals claim hitchhiking is relatively safe in this part of the country, but Let's Go doesn't recommend hitchhiking under any circumstances.

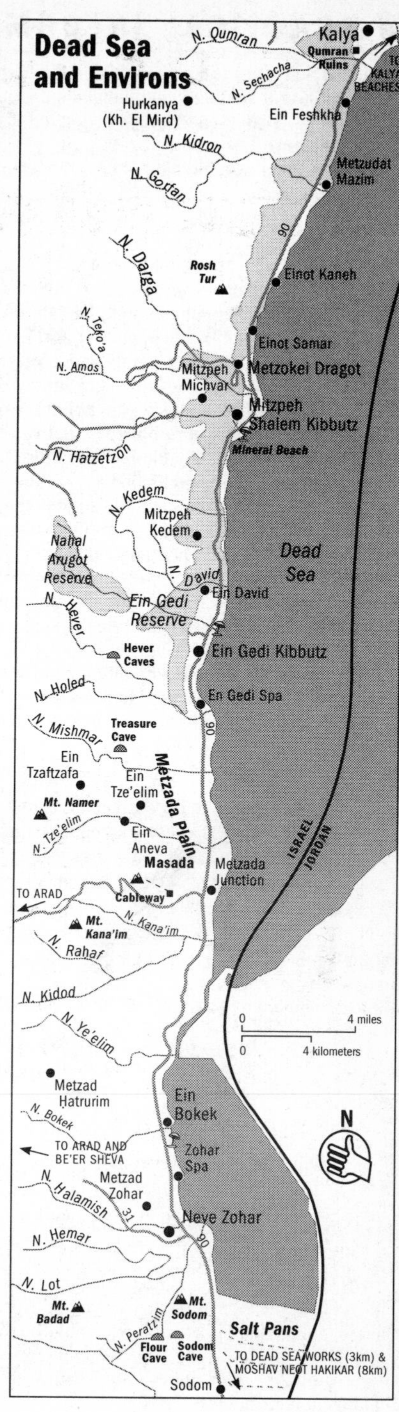

PRACTICAL INFORMATION

The Dead Sea coast is 65km long, and for easy reference may be divided into **northern, central,** and **southern** regions. This section is organized from north to south. Remember—if the sea is on your left, you're going south, if it's on your right, you're going north.

The Dead Sea does not have an ordinary desert climate—instead of being hot and dry, it's hot and humid. The sticky air, the very high temperatures, and 330 days a year of cloudless, steady sun are barely tolerable. While the air does have a 10% higher oxygen concentration, exertion is recommended only in the early morning. The steamroom-like weather has been known to dehydrate people simply waiting at a shaded bus stop. Keep your head covered, take a **water** bottle wherever you go, and chug liberally at the rate of about 1 liter per hour, more if you're hiking. Bring a large bottle with you and keep refilling at faucets to avoid getting ripped off by the 8-Shekel-a-pop street vendors once you're there. While the tap water is drinkable in most places in Israel, don't assume that shower and faucet water is safe to drink—check for "Drinking Water" signs or ask someone.

The **tourist information** hub for the entire region is in the central Dead Sea, near Ein Gedi (see below). Check in at the kibbutz reception center for information on local sights and events (☎07 658 44 44; fax 07 658 43 67; email eg@mishkei.org.il; www.ein-gedi.co.il). It is possible to join the crowds on the popular one-day tour from Jerusalem that shuttles lemmings—er, tourists to Masada (in time for sunrise), Ein Gedi (Naḥal David and the Dead Sea beach), Qumran (jump out of the bus, take a picture, jump back in), Jericho (in time for a late lunch), and photo stops at the Mount of Temptation, St. George Monastery, and the Mount of Olives. Tours cost NIS90 (doesn't include any entrance fees) and can be booked through most of the hostels in the Old City.

There is **no money changing office or ATM** anywhere in the Dead Sea region, so come prepared. The nearest facilities are in Arad and Be'er Sheva.

ADDING INSALT TO INJURY. Dead Sea water is powerful stuff. When it's good, it may cure arthritis, but when it's bad, it's like applying an acid after-shave. If Dead Sea water gets into your eyes, you're in for several minutes of painful blindness. Rinse your eyes immediately in the fresh-water showers, found on all beaches. Don't shave the morning before you go swimming; the water will sear minor scrapes. And, of course, resist the urge to taste it.

NORTHERN DEAD SEA ☎02

KALYA BEACHES

This area in the northern Dead Sea region is only 25 minutes from Jerusalem (Rte. 90), and its shores are the least heavily touristed by foreigners. Take bus #480 or 487 from Jerusalem. From Ein Bokek, take bus #421 or 966 (originating from Tel Aviv and Haifa, respectively). Remember to confirm your destination with the bus driver, and make sure you tell him you're going to the beach or else you'll end up at the Kalya kibbutz by Qumran. All of the Kalya beaches are accessible from the same turn-off and bus stop, but you'll still have to walk at least 1km in the sun. Those who like whooshing and sliding with their sunbathing, can head to **Atraktzia Water Park and Beach** (☎994 23 91), which is closest to the main road. This amusement park is a magnet for Israeli children on vacation (which isn't to say that full-grown kids won't also have a good time) and features waterslides and a wave pool. The restaurant will stuff any order in a pita (hamburger NIS23). Alternatively, there are free BBQ and picnic areas on the premises. Splash all day for NIS67; children under 1m free. The price also includes use of the private Dead Sea beach. Open daily Apr.-Oct. 9am-5pm. While the slides rest in the winter, the beach remains accessible for NIS15.

Farther down the road, two private beaches offer luxuries that might appeal more to the adults. **Siesta Beach** (☎994 41 11) follow a salty float with a Thai massage to calm your sunstroked bod (NIS85 for 10min.). A Jordanian/Palestinian restaurant on the beach serves "authentic" cuisine at unauthentic prices (falafel plate and salad NIS25. Open daily 8:30am-7:30pm, in the winter 8:30am-6:30pm.) in the winter. Next door, **Neve Midbar** (☎994 27 81) complements black mud with Desert's Magic holistic treatments, which include water therapy using the Dead Sea's healing properties (NIS80 for a 30min. "half-treatment"). An outdoor restaurant features pricey drinks and meals. (Schnitzel NIS40. Open daily 8:30am-7:30pm.)

QUMRAN قمران קומרן

About 7km south of Kalya lie the ruins of Qumran, where the **Dead Sea Scrolls** were discovered. In 1947, a young Bedouin looking for a wayward sheep threw a rock into a cliffside cave and heard something break. Upon further inspection, he found a collection of earthenware jars containing 2000-year-old parchment manuscripts. These famed scrolls are an important source for understanding the development of the Bible. The largest, now displayed in the Shrine of the Book at the Israel Museum in Jerusalem, is a 7m-long ancient Hebrew text of the Book of Isaiah. Encouraged by the discovery, French archaeologists searched the caves and excavated the foot of the cliffs. By 1956 they had unearthed an entire village of the sect that wrote the Dead Sea Scrolls.

Archaeological evidence suggests that the site was settled as long ago as the 8th century BCE, re-inhabited in the 2nd century BCE, temporarily abandoned following an earthquake during the reign of Herod, and completely deserted after the Roman defeat of the Jewish revolt in 70 CE. Historians conclude that the authors of the scrolls were the **Essenes,** a Jewish sect whose members, disillusioned by the corruption and Hellenization of fellow Jerusalemites, sought refuge in the sands, arriving in Qumran around the end of the **Hasmonean Dynasty.** The strict and devout Essenes believed that a great struggle would ensue between the Sons of Light (themselves and the angels) and the Sons of Darkness (everyone else). Excavations at Masada suggest that the members of the Qumran sect joined with the Zealots there in the struggle against the Romans.

The Essenes had a serious problem—they were obsessed with ritual cleansing, but they settled in one of the driest spots on the planet. Look for the cisterns and channels that were used for storage and water transport in the arid climate.

Buses #421, 444, 486, or 487 from either Ein Gedi or Jerusalem will stop upon request at the Essene Compound. A marker right outside the bus stop points toward Qumran, up the steep road on the right. Although the peak is nowhere in sight, the winding road is actually only a 100m hike. At the top is a welcome air-conditioned five-minute dramatization of life as an ancient Essene, narrated in the first person and shown in 7 different languages. Following the film, enter the museum through the chamber revealed by the rising screen; the museum in turn leads to the start of the path through the ruins. The cave where the scrolls were found is visible from a lookout 100 steps to the left of the site map. Humbly hidden between the water cisterns is the **scriptorium** (writing room), where archaeologists believe the scrolls were written (several desks and inkstands were found there intact and are now on display at the Rockefeller Museum in Jerusalem). The path leads through a small museum and then outside to the ruins themselves. Renovations are now underway to build a series of lookout bridges above the ruins to make them handicapped accessible. (☎994 22 35. Open daily 8am-5pm, in winter 8am-4pm. NIS14, students NIS12, children (age 5-18) NIS6.)

Qumran's upscale **gift shop** sells the usual tourist fare (replica scroll jars NIS69). The adjoining cafeteria (☎054 992 93 80; serves hot lunches from 11am-3:30pm. Salad and soup NIS26. Open daily 8am-6pm.)

EIN FESHKHA عين فشخه עין פשח'ה

Relief from the heat is nearby: 3km south is the fresh-water bathing spot at **Ein Feshkha** (also called Einot Zukim), where springs wind through the *wadi*'s reeds and tumble into small pools. Ein Feshkha is the only Dead Sea resort with fresh-water ponds adjacent to the sea area. Because of very slick mud, however, swimming is only permitted in the fresh water pools. It remains the favorite spot of nearby Jericho residents and other Palestinians. There are many more men than women, and the females who do show up don't show much. Women will probably be uncomfortable (and make others uncomfortable) without modest covering. There are showers, drinking water, a picnic area, and plenty of Dead Sea mud. (☎994 23 55. Open daily 8am-5pm. NIS22, children NIS8.)

METZOKEI DRAGOT (WADI DARJA) מצוקי דרגות

This **nature reserve,** with its soaring cliffs, is for serious hikers only. About 20km south of Qumran and Ein Feshkha, a steep, winding road branches off on the right. Buses will go no farther than the turn-off; the only ways to reach the reserve and the hostel are by car or a 5km hike. The ascent culminates in a view of soaring cliffs and ravines on one side, the Dead Sea and not-so-distant hills of Jordan on the other. Heed the warnings on the green welcome-board—be sure to carry a trail map and a 20m security rope, both of which are usually available at the office. Climbers and rapellers with their own equipment may wish to take advantage of the excellent conditions in the reserve; unfortunately, there are no longer any organized trips or equipment rental. You may not begin hiking the *wadi* after **9am,** so it is a good idea to stay at the hostel the night before, and be on your feet at the crack of dawn. There is no place to refill water bottles; carry enough for the hike.

Owned and managed by the Mitzpeh Shalem Kibbutz a few kilometers away, the **youth hostel** (☎994 47 77; fax 994 41 10), a great alternative to often-booked Ein Gedi accommodations, lies at the top of the winding road. Air-conditioned 6-8 bed dorms (NIS32) and bed and breakfast doubles (Check-in after 2pm, check-out Su-F 10am, Sa noon. NIS230, singles NIS149). Dinner (NIS45) with advance notice.

CENTRAL DEAD SEA ☎07

EIN GEDI עין גדי

After a hot morning hike or a muggy bus ride, the only thing better than drinking cold water is sitting in it. The Ein Gedi oasis, the epicenter of the Dead Sea region, has a long history of providing shelter and romantic getaway. David fled here to escape the wrath of King Saul (1 Samuel 24), and it was here that he forsook the choice opportunity to slay his pursuing father-in-law. In *Song of Songs* (1:13) the lover declares that her beloved is "a cluster of camphor in the vineyards of Ein Gedi." During the second Jewish revolt (132-135 CE), rebel leader Simon Bar Kokhba sought refuge here.

The cascading waterfalls of the Ein Gedi oasis thrive just a few minutes' hike from the lifeless shores of the Dead Sea. Rare desert wildlife, including ibex, fox, and hyrax, and rare species of birds and flowers in this verdant **nature reserve.** In 1994, the land in and around the Ein Gedi kibbutz was officially recognized as an **International Botanical Garden,** boasting over 800 species of trees, shrubs, and flowers from all over the world, plus about 1000 species of cacti and desert plants. Tired hikers can relax in the afternoons at the **free beach.**

GETTING THERE AND GETTING AROUND

From Ein Gedi, buses go to: **Be'er Sheva** (#384 and 385; 2½hr.; Su-Th 4 per day 8am-6pm, F 8am-3:30pm, Sa 3:30pm; NIS35) via **Masada** (20min.), **Ein Bokek** (30min., NIS18), and **Arad** (1½hr.); **Eilat** (#444; 3hr.; Su-Th 4 per day 7:50am-5:50pm, F 7:50am-2:50pm; NIS50); **Ein Bokek** (#486; Su-Th 4 per day 10am-2:05pm, F 9:50am and 2:05pm); and **Jerusalem** (#421, 444, 486, and 487; 1¼hr.; Su-Th 11 per day 5:45am-6pm, F 5:45am-5pm, Sa 6:25pm-10:30pm; NIS32). **Masada** and the hotels and beach. Students with ISIC cards can receive discounted fares on all bus routes. Departure times are erratic; get a bus schedule from the central bus station in Jerusalem or check with your hostel.

ORIENTATION AND PRACTICAL INFORMATION

Ein Gedi's 6750 acre nature reserve is the heart of this desert attraction. Around it, a kibbutz, several accommodations, a field school, a public bathing area, and a luxury spa have been built. There are four **bus stops** in the area. The first one serves the **nature reserve** and the two youth **hostels.** Farther south is the beach stop, which is convenient for the public beach, food, a gas station, a first-aid station, and the yellow-roofed **tourist information** booth, which covers the entire Dead Sea region (☎658 44 44; fax 658 43 67; email eg@kibbutz.co.il; www.ein-gedi.co.il; open daily 9am-4pm). The third stop, by advance request only, serves the kibbutz and its guest house. At the fourth stop are the thermal baths and spa. The hostels and public beach are a mere 10-15 minute walk apart, but the spas are 6km south of the beach. Food kiosks and public telephone booths crowd the entrances to and exits from all tourist attractions, beaches, and hikes.

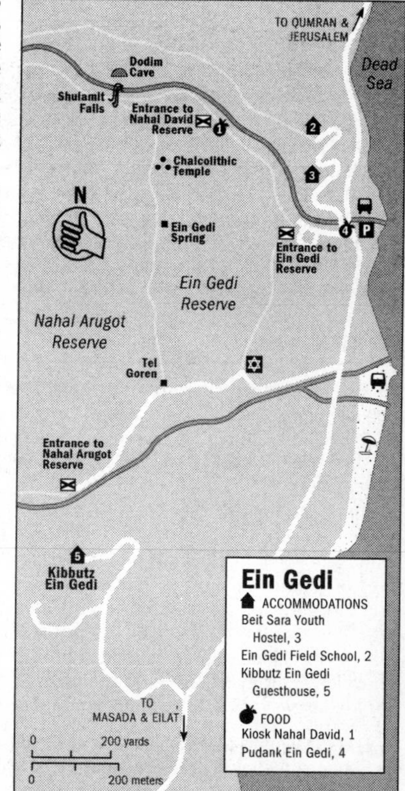

ACCOMMODATIONS

The sweltering weather hardly abates at night, so air-conditioning is a must.

Beit Sara Youth Hostel (HI) (☎658 41 65; fax 658 44 44), uphill at the turnoff for Naḥal David. Clean and uncrowded rooms with A/C and private baths. Ask about discount tickets (15%) for the nature reserve, Ein Gedi Spa, and Atraktzia water park. Office open 7am-9pm; 24hr. phone reception. Check-in 3-7pm. Check-out 9am, Sa 10am. Dorms NIS72/US$17.50; doubles US$56. HI US$1.50 discount on dorms. Breakfast included; dinner US$8.50, child US$7.50, packed lunch available on request (NIS22). Credit cards accepted.

THE DEAD SEA

Ein Gedi Field School (☎658 43 50; fax 658 42 57). A steep 10min. climb up the road behind the more accessible youth hostel yields a less touristed, more scenic spot. Run by the Society for the Protection of Nature in Israel (SPNI), which offers free sound and light shows on the Judean Desert every night. Common kitchen and TV room. This peak is the only place on Earth to get a glimpse of a rare species of bird called *Leilit Hamidbar* (Hume's Tawny Owl). Special bird-shrine and lookout point a few feet from the TV room. Each spartan room equipped with a coffee station and towels for the shared showers. Small grocery store open daily 6-7pm. breakfast included; lunch and dinner can be ordered. Office open Su-F 8am-7pm. Check-in 3pm. Check-out 10am. Call ahead. Dorms NIS75. Students and SPNI members 20% discount; membership available at check-in for NIS82, family membership NIS108. Credit cards accepted.

Kibbutz Ein Gedi Guest House (☎659 42 22; fax 658 43 28; email eg@kibbutz.co.il; www.ein-gedi.co.il), 5km south of the beach. This full-service hotel is a good alternative if other places are booked, as they frequently are. All guests enjoy full use of the large kibbutz's facilities, including swimming pool, cactus garden, and zoo. The Guest House runs inexpensive and convenient **tours** of the region on their own buses. Spacious B&B rooms feature kitchenettes with free tea and coffee, fridge and gas-range, bathrooms, A/C, and color TVs, US$72-92 per person; includes entrance to the spa. **Tzimmers** or "country lodging" (discounted rooms), also with kitchenettes, US$40 per person.

FOOD

Quick snacks are available at kiosks throughout Ein Gedi, including near the entrance to the nature reserve at **Kiosk Naḥal David.** (Beer NIS10. Open 8am-5pm.) A few sandwiches and some juice can provide a relatively cheap alternative to expensive tourist joints, although prices are still higher than in the cities. The cafeteria-style **Pundak Ein Gedi**, in the parking lot of the beach bus stop, serves hungry beach-goers (☎659 47 61. Open daily 10am-6pm; chicken with two side dishes NIS30; kosher). The kiosk next door is open later. (Sandwiches NIS12. Open 7:30am-8pm.) Another dining possibility in the central Dead Sea region is **Gofrit Restaurant** at the Ein Gedi Spa (main course NIS20, with side dishes NIS35; ☎659 48 13. Open daily 11am-4pm.) Hostels in the area will provide an inexpensive **packed lunch** if ordered the previous night.

HIKING

Of the two entrances to the huge **Ein Gedi Nature Reserve,** only the **Naḥal David** entrance (☎658 42 85), just below the youth hostels, is accessible by bus. (Open daily 8am-4pm. note that several hikes may not be started after 1:30pm. Admission NIS18). **Naḥal Arugot** (☎652 0224), 3km past the Naḥal David entrance accessible only by car.

Some sections of the Ein Gedi trails are steep, but well-placed railings and steps have been built into the rock. Once noon rolls around, high temperatures can make even inhaling strenuous, so get going by **8am.** Always bring at least one liter of water per hour of hiking (there are faucets just outside the gate), and don't forget your **swimsuit** for dipping in the occasional freshwater pool or waterfall. The names of the different pools and springs repeat frequently and are almost interchangeable (David this, Ein Gedi that), so get a free map at the entrance and pay attention to the fine print to prevent confusion. Possible hikes vary from easygoing to double diamond difficult. Some suggested trails follow:

1. For a short hike of 45min. each way, enter from the Naḥal David entrance and follow the path straight until **Shulamit Falls,** a delicious, slender pillar of water dropping into a shallow pool. Turning left at the falls leads to a trail that climbs up the cliffside to **Shulamit Spring** (an additional 30min. each way).

2. For a longer hike, continue from Shulamit spring along the cliff and down a ladder to **Dudaim Cave** (Lover's Cave), a mossy niche at the top of the fall (30min. from the spring). Proceed left, passing the 3000-year-old remains of a **Chalcolithic Temple** once dedicated to worship of the moon, on the way to **Ein Gedi Spring** (20min. from the Temple), whose cool water is perfect for a refreshing dip. Resist the urge to dive from the high niches into the pool—it's not deep enough in some places. Next to the spring is a sugar or flour mill from the Islamic period which was powered by water from the spring.
3. The second entrance to the reserve is at **Naḥal Arugot** (no bus; parking lot 3km inland from Rte. 90, between the beach and Naḥal David entrance). A somewhat challenging hour's hike along the river leads to a hidden waterfall and a beautiful, deep blue pool.
4. One long but highly recommended trail connects the David and Arugot entrances, with the Ein Gedi Spring smack in the middle. The trail passes the newly restored ancient **synagogue** and leads directly to the beachfront in time for an afternoon of sunbathing. The trail begins at the **SPNI Field School** and follows the "Zafit Trail" until Ein David. At Ein David, turn left and follow the main marked trail to Shulamit Falls. For a shorter hike, bear left and follow the main trail out; for the full hike, bear right and continue toward Shulamit Spring and the Chalcolithic temple. **Ein Gedi Spring** is a few hundred meters further. Continue straight, due south, until **Tel Goren.** Turn left toward the sea, passing the ancient **synagogue** after a few hundred meters. The light blue building near the end is the Ein Gedi mineral water bottling plant, a refreshing stop.

BEACH

For good ol' Dead Sea floating and mud, Ein Gedi has its own crowded **beach.** Use of the beach and umbrellas is free, but bathrooms and lockers cost NIS1 and NIS5 respectively. **Lot's Wife,** a boat touring around the Dead Sea area, departs from the small dock to the left (when facing the water) of the Ein Gedi beach. (☎054 915 004. Call ahead. 70min.; NIS40, children NIS30; regular trips depart Tu and Sa at 2:30pm, but private tours can be arranged for groups. Call ahead). About 5km south of the beach is the **Ein Gedi Spa,** with indoor sulfur pools, therapeutic mud, and a restaurant. (NIS50, Sa NIS55; children NIS44. ☎659 48 13. Spa open Sa-Th 7am-6pm, F 7am-5:30pm.) Local hostels provide tickets for a 15% discount.

MASADA מצדה

"Masada shall not fall again," swear members of the **Israel Defense Forces** each year at this site. Jewish Zealots' tenacious defense of Masada in the first century CE has been fashioned into a heroic symbol of the defense of modern Israel. Political significance aside, legions of tourists from around the world continue to storm this mountain fortress to catch the spectacular view of the Dead Sea, visit the extensive ruins, and envision the martyrdom of Masada's rebels.

The first fortress (metzuda) on the mountain was built as a refuge from marauding Greeks and Syrians by the Jewish High Priest Jonathan Maccabeus around 150 BCE, and it was expanded a few decades later by John Hyrcanus I. It was chiefly under Herod, however, that Masada became an enormous mountaintop citadel: the Great Builder installed two palaces, baths, villas, storerooms, an intricate system of cisterns and aqueducts, and a defensive wall studded with over 30 guard towers. At the outset of the Jewish rebellion against Rome in 66 CE, a small band of Zealot rebels, members of a small Jewish sect, captured the prize fortress from its unsuspecting garrison. As the Romans gradually crushed the revolt, taking Jerusalem in 70 CE and destroying the Second Temple, Masada became a refuge for surviving Zealots, and the last Jewish holdout in all of Israel. With years' worth of food, water, and military supplies, the 967 men, women, and children held off 15,000 Roman legionnaires through a five-month siege. The Romans called in their best engineers to construct a wall and camps in a ring around the mount. Capitalizing on their superior force, they built an enormous stone and gravel ramp up the side of the cliff, using Jewish slaves as laborers in order to prevent the Zealots from shooting them down as the ramp was built.

When the defenders realized that the Romans would break through their walls the next morning, the community leaders decided that it would be better to die, as their leader Elazar Ben-Yair said, "unenslaved by enemies, and leave this world as free men in company with wives and children" rather than be captured by the Romans. Because Jewish law forbids suicide, ten men were chosen to slay the others, and one chosen to kill the other nine before falling on his own sword. Before burning the fortress and all their possessions, the Jews placed stores of wheat and water in the citadel's courtyard to prove to the Romans that they did not perish from hunger. The following morning, when the triumphant Romans burst in, they encountered only smoking ruins and deathly silence. The only survivors, two women and five children, told the story of the Zealots' last days to Josephus Flavius, a Jewish-Roman general and chronicler. Flavius, always eager to embellish a good tale, never actually visited Masada. He based his dramatic history on the survivors' accounts, later describing the two to be "of exceptional intelligence for women." Although strong corroborating evidence for the story has been found at the site, such as the murder-lottery slips Josephus describes, archaeologists have yet to unearth the Zealots' actual remains. Where the bones of almost 1000 people have gone is still a mystery.

GETTING AROUND

Masada lies 20km south of Ein Gedi, a few kilometers inland from the Jerusalem-Eilat road (Rte. 90). Buses leaving Masada generally start around 8:30am; only a few leave after 4pm. Check at the Taylor Youth hostel for a current schedule, and make sure you are heading in the right direction. Buses go to: **Be'er Sheva** (#384 and 385; Su-Th 4 per day 8:15am-6:15pm, F no 6:15pm bus, Sa 3:45pm; NIS35.50, students NIS31) via **Ein Bokek** (NIS11.50); **Eilat** (#444; Su-Th 4 per day 8am-6pm, F 3 per day 8am-3pm; NIS50, students NIS45); **Jerusalem** (#444 and 486; Su-Th 8 per day 8:35am-7:20pm, F 5 per day 8:35am-3:20pm, Sa 6:50 and 9:20pm; NIS37.50, students NIS34) via **Ein Gedi** (NIS14); Bus #384 and 385 also go to Ein Gedi; **Tel Aviv** (#421; Su-F 2:25pm; NIS47, students NIS42).

By car, Rte. 3199 runs from Arad to the base of the Roman Ramp, and Rte. 90 leads to the Snake Path, the eastern cable car entrance, the bus stop, and the youth hostel. The walk around the base from one path to the other is extremely arduous and time-consuming. Those who decide to do it should follow the SPNI trail, not the incline with the water pipe.

There are three ways to ascend the mountain: by either of two foot paths or by cable car. The more popular, scenic, and difficult of the two is the **Snake Path** (45min. hike), named for its tortuous bends. The **Roman Ramp,** on the western side of the mountain, is an easier hike than the Snake Path and the original path. Even the most grumpy of un-early birds will appreciate a dawn hike to catch the legendary sunrise over the Dead Sea and avoid tour group insanity and blazing heat. Today many warriors opt to take the Snake Path up and cable car down; due to the steepness, the hike down is just as strenuous as the hike up. Another option is to take the cable car up in the afternoon and hike down when the sun is less fierce.

ACCOMMODATIONS AND FOOD

The **Taylor Youth Hostel (HI),** straight ahead and to the left of the bus stop, is surrounded by grass and shady trees. Run by a superfriendly Israeli couple and their two adorable children, the hostel has air-conditioning and a full bath in every impeccable room. A TV lounge and barbecue area are provided for guests. (☎658 43 49; fax 658 46 50. Breakfast included. Lockers NIS6. Reception Su-F 8am-1pm and 3-7pm, Sa 4-7pm. Check-out Su-F 9am, Sa 10am. 10-bed dorms NIS70/US$17.50; singles NIS152/US$38; doubles NIS224/US$56; additional person NIS64/US$16. Members get NIS6 discount. Credit cards accepted.)

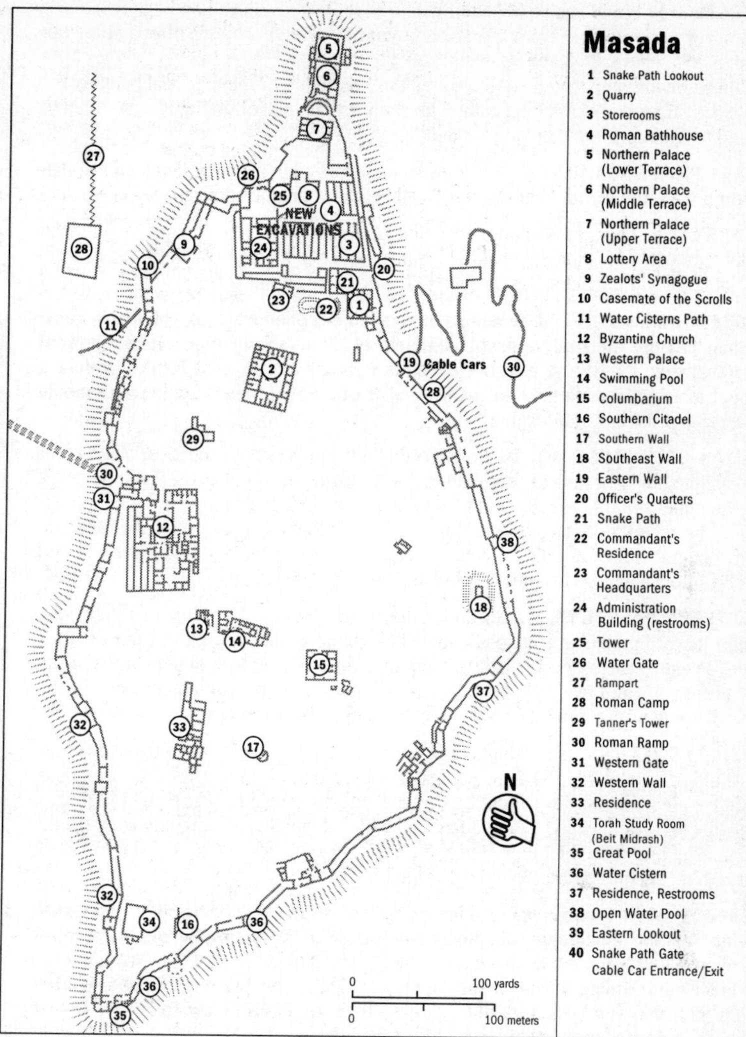

The **food** situation at Masada is cheerless. The Zealots had the right idea—bring a few years' supply. The Taylor Hostel serves kosher meat dinners (Sa-Th NIS34, F NIS40). The other options, which exist only to feed the tour-bus crowds, shut down after 5pm. When it's open, the glossy Masada gift shop camouflages the **Masada Oasis restaurant,** which serves a full lunch including a side dish and dessert for NIS48. (☎658 40 86. Open 8am-5pm; hot lunch served 11am-4pm.)

THE FORTRESS

The ruins at Masada were unearthed from 1963 to 1964; thousands of volunteers excavated in 11 months what would normally have taken 26 years. About one-third of the ruins are actually reconstructed—a black line indicates the extent of the original findings. The re-excavation of the Northern Palace by a group of expert Italian archaeologists has unearthed new mosaic floors and hundreds of coins near the bathhouses.

The **Masada Sound and Light Show** lights up the fortress like a Las Vegas marquee. The show is not visible from the Masada youth hostel. For more information, see **Arad,** p. 287. (☎995 93 33 or 995 89 93; fax 995 50 52)

The following suggested route covers the highlights of Masada and roughly follows the sign-posted walking tour. The numbers listed following the sites correspond to the numbers labeled on the map on p. 267.

SNAKE PATH LOOKOUT (1). This lookout offers views of the Snake Path, the earthen wall, the Roman camps, the Dead Sea, and the Mountains of Moab.

QUARRY (2). This quarry supplied much of the stone for the extensive construction throughout Masada. Between the quarry and the Western Wall, there is a large pile of large round rocks, too perfectly shaped to be anything but catapults' ammo.

STOREROOMS (3). Food, weapons, and other supplies were stored within these rooms. Though the Zealots destroyed most of their valuable possessions and the fortress, they left the storeroom containing mass amounts of food untouched. Josephus explains that the Zealots wanted to prove that their suicide was a means of escaping slavery, not famine.

ROMAN BATHHOUSE (4). Bathers would leave their clothes in the *apodyterium* (dressing room) before proceeding to the *calidarium* (hot room), recognizable by the small pillars, which used to support a secondary floor. A stove channeled hot air between these two floors. Bathers then cooled off in the *tepidarium* (lukewarm room) before a quick dip in the *frigidarium* (cold pool). Built by Herod, the bathhouse served no purpose for the austere Zealots.

NORTHERN PALACE (5-7). Go down the nearby stairwell to Herod's thrice-terraced private pad. The frescoes and fluted columns, still intact on the lower terrace, attest to the splendor Herod enjoyed even on a remote desert butte. In the bathhouse of the lowest section, the skeletons of a man, woman, and child were found, along with a *tallit* (prayer shawl), *ostraca* (lots), and arrowheads.

LOTTERY AREA (8). Climb back up from the Palace to the Lottery Area, to the left of the bathhouses as you face the Palace. The Zealots used this area as a ritual bath for cleansing and purification, but it is most notable for the dramatic discovery of eleven *ostraca*. The uniform shards of pottery inscribed with names (including one with the name Ben-Yair, Zealot commander of Masada) most likely served as lots that decided who would kill the others.

ZEALOTS' SYNAGOGUE (9). Following the western edge of the mountain leads to the Zealots' synagogue, the oldest synagogue in the world. Scrolls were found here containing texts from several books of the Torah; most are now on display at the Israel Museum in Jerusalem, (see p. 132). The scrolls and discoveries, such as a *mikveh* (ritual bath), indicate that the community followed Jewish strictures despite mountainous isolation and the siege.

CASEMATE OF THE SCROLLS (10). A number of important archaeological relics were found within the casemate, including scrolls, papyrus, silver shekels, a *tallit*, a wooden shield, arrows, sandals, keys, baskets, and other items.

WATER CISTERNS PATH (11). The huge cisterns can still be seen dotting the mountaintop from the western wall; they are lined with a near-perfect water-repellent plaster that still won't absorb a single drop. Rainfall used to drain from the surrounding mountains into Masada's reservoirs, filling the entire cistern within a few hours on the one annual day of rain. The Zealots were able to store up to eight years' worth of precious water in these cavernous structures.

BYZANTINE CHURCH (12). Remote Masada, with caves and buildings for shelter, made an ideal hideout for Christian hermits in the 5th and 6th centuries. The chapel with preserved mosaic floors is the most impressive of their remains.

WESTERN PALACE (13). Farther along the edge stands the site of Herod's throne room and offices of state. A system of water cisterns underlies the western wing; the northern wing surrounds a large central courtyard; the southern wing was the royal wing, and includes a waiting room, courtyard, dining hall, kitchen, and throne room. Though just as sumptuous as the Northern Palace, this was Herod's "working palace." He went to his northern "country residence" to relax.

SWIMMING POOL (14). Although water was a rare commodity in the fortress, Herod insisted on maintaining a swimming pool in the backyard of the Western Palace. The Zealots used this as a ritual bath.

COLUMBARIUM (15). The small niches in the walls of this round building, farther back and slightly to the left, sparked an archaeological debate. One team contended that it was a *columbarium*, where the ashes of the non-Jewish members of Herod's garrison were placed, while others thought the niches housed pigeons. After highly scientific tests the former opinion emerged victorious since small pigeons could not even fit inside the niches.

SOUTHERN CITADEL (16). At the southern tip of the mountain, the Southern Citadel looks out at the Masada *Wadi*, Dead Sea, and Roman encampments.

SOUTHERN WALL (17). Along the southern wall lie a tower with a Zealot installation (the building might have been a bakery), a ritual bath, a dressing room (the narrow niches held clothes), and a courtyard. The path is no longer in use.

SOUTHEAST WALL (18). There is a memorial inscription for "Lucius" (possibly a soldier in the Roman Garrison) engraved in the wall of the tower. On the plaster of the southern wall, there are four impressions of the name "Justus" in Latin and Greek. There is also a lookout from which the outer wall is visible.

EASTERN WALL (19). The outer wall and inner wall are joined by partitions, forming casemates. The higher and thicker sections of the inner wall are the sole remains of a series of towers that lined the wall. A channel under the floor of the Zealot additions is older than the wall itself. A small grove of fir trees toward the Snake Path Gate was the site of a 1988 interpretive reenactment of the battle.

SOUTHERN DEAD SEA ☎07

EIN BOKEK עין בוקק

About 15km south of Masada, Ein Bokek, hemmed in by hordes of luxury hotels, international tour-groups, and racks upon racks of postcards, is the gaudy cubic zirconia in the tiara of Dead Sea beaches. For all the glitzy tourist-wooing of this most crowded of Dead Sea beaches, it is still a good spot for some old fashioned fun: floating and coating. Use of the beach and outdoor showers is **free** (8am-5pm), and a package of mineral-rich mud from beachside vendors costs NIS10.

Beachside eateries include the **Hordus Beach Kiosk,** with plastic chairs and tables outside. (☎658 46 36. Falafel NIS10. Open Sa-Th 8am-8pm, F 8am-4:50pm.) For air-conditioned dining, the Hordus storefront houses a more elaborate **cafeteria** (hot entrees NIS35; side dishes NIS15), hidden among the souvenirs, Ahava cosmetics counter (moisturizer NIS99), and swarms of people (free—usually). The crowds are just a few steps away. With your back to the beach and your face to Hordus, turn right and walk about 50m to the building next door, where **Cafe Kapulsky** serves desserts and dairy fare. (☎658 43 82. Huge salads NIS39; chocolate cheesecake NIS19. Open daily 8am-midnight.)

Further to the right is a small **mall,** featuring a **grocery store,** Hertz office, and several restaurants, including the 24-hour **Peace and Love BBQ.** (☎658 43 71. Fruit shake NIS15; hamburger NIS12; fries NIS12.) To the left of the beach, **Me'al Hahof** (☎652 04 04), a bar on the beach, features a great view, French pop music, and a variety of beer (NIS10-16) and baguettes (NIS17). **Hertz** car rental is located inside the Amiel Tours office in the mall. (☎658 45 30. About NIS350/US$55 per day. Open Su-Th 8:30am-4pm, F 8:30am-1:30pm. 21+.)

Ein Bokek sits 30 minutes east of Arad and 10 minutes south of Masada. **Buses** on the Masada/Dead Sea route pass through Ein Bokek and stop at each hotel along the strip. For the public beach, get off at **Ḥof Ein Bokek.** Minivans operating as *sherut* go to Arad (NIS10). **Hassan Taxi** (☎05 276 62 46) goes to Masada (NIS60) and Ein Gedi (NIS100).

MOSHAV NEOT HA-KIKKAR מושב נאות הככר

About 20km south of rowdy Ein Bokek, Moshav Neot Ha-Kikkar is a desert of serenity and desolation. Take Rte. 90 toward Sodom until the Arava junction, passing the Dead Sea Works plant on the left and the southern edge of the sea. The Eilat-bound bus from Jerusalem or Tel Aviv will stop at the junction upon request. Make a left and follow the road for about 10km, until the entrance to the moshav. The ominous "Dead Sea Fish" signs along the way refer to high-tech pools managed by the moshav, which specializes in state-of-the-art desert agricultural technology and experimentation.

Taking the road to the end of the moshav leads to **Fata Morgana** (☎655 79 92, cellular 050 691 585; ask for Koreen or Ya'akov), an amazing oasis featuring large, clean and comfortable Bedouin-style guest-tents, (NIS40; with your own tent NIS30; ask for a *Let's Go* discount), a coffee-bar and a restaurant. Fata Morgana arranges hiking tours of the region (including the famous Sodom flour caves), meeting individual requests whenever possible. It also offers **Shiatsu** massages and lessons in a special shrine tent every Friday, and pick-your-own cherry-tomatoes or flowers. Work four hours in the field and sleep free. Cold beer NIS9; hot fish meals NIS60; vegetarian meals NIS40. Free use of spotless bathrooms and showers, fridge, and BBQ grills.

MT. SODOM AND THE FLOUR CAVE

About 74km to the southeast of Be'er Sheva, near the shores of the Dead Sea, is the glaringly white salt mountain, Ḥar Sodom. This is the Biblical site of Sodom and Gomorah, the two cities so wicked and sexually promiscuous that God resolved to strike them down. God decided to save Lot and his family, but ordered them not to look back at the carnage as they left. Lot's wife took a peek and turned into a pillar of salt (Genesis 19:26).

The **Flour Cave** is tucked out of direct view from Mt. Sodom. Within the site, the unpaved road forks. Go left and continue on the red-marked "Flour Cave" path that eventually leads to a parking lot (marked by a green sign) near the cave. The cave is at the end of a curving trail of high, smooth walls of light-colored sediment left behind by the lake that was a precursor to the Dead Sea. Be forewarned that these white rocks are unyieldingly bright in the sunlight and magnify the merciless daytime heat, so bring along water, sunglasses, sunscreen, head covering. It is a 10-minute walk through the white-walled trail to the cave itself (marked by a sign), where the dark, cool, and heavy air provides an escape from the dead-on rays of the sun. Bring a flashlight for the pitch-black cave. The short, steep ascent at the end of the cave will leave you about a mile to the right as you face the parking lot.

To reach **Sodom Mountain,** take a right onto the blue road from the first fork and another right onto the black road. It is possible to drive all the way up to the lookout point on **Sodom Mountain,** which has a captivating view of the Dead Sea Works and the seemingly frozen blue water below. Alternatively, continue past the Flour Cave entrance for about 1.5hr. From the lookout point, hike the steep and winding "Stairway Trail" downwards, starting at the blue-marked steps to the left.

The site can be reached only by car. From Be'er Sheva, head southeast on Rte. #25 (toward Dimona) then north (toward Jerusalem) on Rte. #90, past the industrial complex of the Dead Sea Works. From Arad, head southeast on Rte. #31 (toward Neve Zohar) then south (toward Eilat) on Rte. #90. From either direction, a small orange sign points to the Flour Cave and Sodom Mountain.

THE NEGEV הנגב

"Wisdom goes with south. It is written: Whoever seeks wisdom, south he shall go."
—David Ben-Gurion

The Bible says that Abraham began his spiritual journey by leaving his home and heading south to the Negev (Genesis 21:32-33). The imposing mountains, majestic canyons, and barren flatlands of the region are just as awe-inspiring today as they were in biblical times. Long considered a wasteland of Bedouin tents and dusty archaeologists, the Negev is entering mainstream Israeli life as new building projects absorb waves of immigrants and high-tech agriculture fulfills the biblical prophecy of making the desert bloom. Visionaries like David Ben-Gurion cherished the Negev's rugged beauty and dreamed of developing the region into one of the most prosperous parts of Israel. Today, hikers, meditators, and adventurous travelers are discovering this beauty, while drip-irrigated citrus groves, flower farms, and instant boom towns are coaxing its resources into fruition. The ruins of Nabatean grandeur glowing on the hilltops along the ancient spice route are today seen less as relics than as inspiration.

The Negev covers roughly half of Israel's territory, but for many years the region received only a small fraction of Israel's tourists. In recent years, tourism has skyrocketed, but these 12,000 sq. km of desert have become no more accommodating. Temperatures soar at midday—those caught without a hat and water will see vultures circling overhead in a matter of minutes. Desert outfitters recommend that hikers drink one liter of water for every hour in the sun.

It's possible to tour the desert on Egged seats; air-conditioned lines run through all major towns and past several important sites. However, buses may be infrequent and late, and some sites and trailheads are only accessible by car. Renting a car or taking a guided tour are excellent options for those who can afford it. However, a more exciting way to see the Negev is on a **camel** or **jeep** tour.

HIGHLIGHTS OF THE NEGEV

Whether explored on foot or hooves, the pastel deserts of **Mitzpeh Ramon** (p. 293) and **Sdeh Boker** (p. 290) are the country's most pristine refuges.

The Hebrew Israelite community in **Dimona** (p. 285) brings a taste of Chicago to the Negev's dunes—and it's vegan.

The multicolored hues of **Har Ardon** (p. 296) make for an astounding hike.

BE'ER SHEVA באר שבע ☎07

Be'er Sheva has a long-standing tradition of serving as a point of replenishment and departure for people traversing the Negev. In recent years, however, increasing numbers of immigrants have decided to settle down in the city rather than just pass through, and the pre-fab apartments are as unavoidable and constricting as the spandex in Eilat discotheques. Despite the din of constant traffic and the overpowering presence of a glassed-in monster mall in the center of town, Be'er Sheva still has a few pockets of romance left, including the old city and the famous Thursday morning Bedouin market. The old city, museums in the surrounding area, and Be'er Sheva's hopping nightlife make it both a convenient base for short forays into the Negev and a destination in-and-of-itself.

"Be'er Sheva" can be read as "well of seven" or "well of the oath" in Hebrew; the Bible (Genesis 21:25-31) supports both etymologies. The Arabic name, Bir al-Saba, also means "well of seven." As the story goes, the servants of King Abimelekh

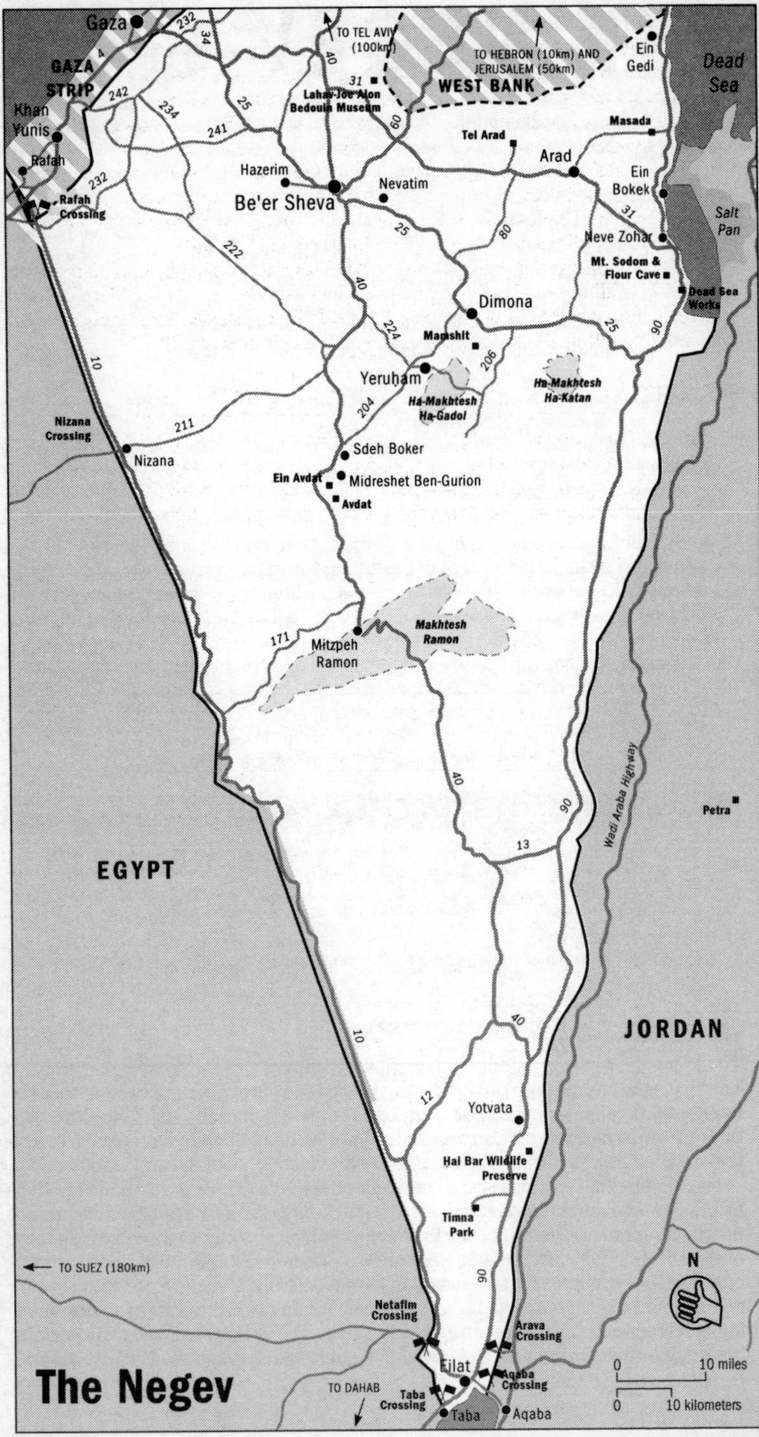

The Negev

Gaza
GAZA STRIP
Khan Yunis
Rafah
Rafah Crossing
TO TEL AVIV (100km)
TO HEBRON (10km) AND JERUSALEM (50km)
WEST BANK
Ein Gedi
Dead Sea
Lahav-Joe Alon Bedouin Museum
Masada
Tel Arad
Arad
Hazerim
Be'er Sheva
Nevatim
Ein Bokek
Salt Pan
Neve Zohar
Mt. Sodom & Flour Cave
Dead Sea Works
Dimona
Mamshit
Yeruham
Ha-Makhtesh Ha-Gadol
Ha-Makhtesh Ha-Katan
Nizana Crossing
Nizana
Sdeh Boker
Ein Avdat
Midreshet Ben-Gurion
Avdat
Mitzpeh Ramon
Makhtesh Ramon
Wadi Araba Highway
Petra
EGYPT
JORDAN
Yotvata
Hai Bar Wildlife Preserve
Timna Park
TO SUEZ (180km)
Netafim Crossing
Arava Crossing
Eilat
Aqaba Crossing
TO DAHAB
Taba Crossing
Taba
Aqaba
N
0 10 miles
0 10 kilometers

seized a well that Abraham claimed to have dug. The dispute ended with an oath of peace between the warring parties, in which Abraham offered seven ewes to Abimelekh in exchange for recognition as the well's rightful owner. The supposed site of Abraham's well now houses the city's main tourist office.

The Ottomans proclaimed modern Be'er Sheva a city in 1906 and established a seat of government, a mosque, a school, and the governor's residence. They hoped the city would function as a political, commercial, and administrative magnet for the nomadic Negev Bedouin, who continue to dwell in tents and makeshift huts outside the city. The Israeli government would prefer it if they settled in towns, but inter-tribal politics prevent most from agreeing to do so.

The streets of the old city, dotted with Ottoman buildings, shops, and restaurants, offer a glimpse of the city's crowded mosaic. Today, Be'er Sheva's 160,000-plus residents, who hail from Morocco, Syria, Poland, Russia, Argentina, and Ethiopia, are doing their best to welcome the streams of newcomers.

GETTING THERE AND GETTING AROUND

Intercity Buses: Egged (☎629 43 11) to: **Dimona** (#48, 56, or 375; 45min.; every 20min. 6:30am-11pm; NIS13.50); **Eilat** (#392, 393, or 394; 3½hr.; every 1½hr. 7:30am-11:45pm; NIS52); **Jerusalem** (#470 (direct) or #446; 2hr.; every 40min. 6am-8pm; NIS33); and **Tel Aviv** (#369 or 370; 1½hr.; every 20min. 5:45am-9:45pm; NIS20.50).

Local Buses: Central bus station (☎627 73 81), on Eilat St., next to the *kenyon*. Buses #2, 3, 7, 8, 9, 11, 12, 18, 21, and 22 all go to the *shuk* and old city (5:20am-11pm), and bus #13 follows Ha-Atzma'ut St. to the Negev Museum and Beit Yatziv Youth Hostel (every 20min. 5:20am-11pm). Buses #7 and 8 go north on Yitzḥak Rager Blvd., passing the hospital and Ben-Gurion University. All local rides NIS3.10.

Sherut Taxis: Moniot Ayil (☎623 53 33), in back of the central bus station, in the kiosk with the blue awning. *Sherut* to **Dimona** (NIS10) and **Tel Aviv** (NIS20) are slightly cheaper than buses, but don't leave until they fill up.

Taxis: Moniot Gan Zvi (☎623 93 32 or 623 93 33), next to the bus station, or **Moniyot Ha-Ḥalutz** (☎627 33 33 or 627 07 07), across from Bank Ha-Poalim.

Car Rental: Avis, 8 Henrietta Szold (☎627 17 77), just before the Paradise Hotel. The #5 bus passes by. From the *kenyon* walk two blocks up Yitzḥak Rager Blvd. and turn right through the parking lot behind the New York Cafe. Red Avis sign in the shopping strip across the street. Min. age 23. Cars start at NIS195/US$42 per day. Open Su-Th 8am-6pm, F 8am-2pm. **Traffic Rent-a-Car,** 5 Ben-Zvi St. (☎627 38 78), behind the bus station, in the shopping strip on Ben-Zvi. Rents to people ages 21-23 for an additional US$12. Rates increase in July and August. Open Su-Th 8am-7pm, F 8am-2pm.

ORIENTATION

The city's **central bus station** is located on **Eilat St.,** across the road from **Kenyon Ha-Negev** (Negev shopping mall; ask for the *kenyon*), whose glass facade faces the three-way intersection of **Tuviyahu Blvd.,** Eilat St., and **Yitzḥak Rager Blvd.** The **Ben-Gurion University** Be'er Sheva campus is a few minutes from the city center.

The old **Muslim Cemetery,** sitting in a wasteland of fenced-in sand, is across Eilat St. behind the central bus station. Just on the other side of that lies the neat grid of the **old city.** This pedestrian haven holds most of the city's attractions. In the center of the Old City is **Keren Kayemet L'Yisrael St.** (**Kakal** or **KKL** for short), a pedestrian-only street between **Herzl** and **Mordei Ha-Geta'ot St.** that is lined with shops, kiosks, and restaurants. The old city streets are reassuringly close together, so miscounting blocks or making a wrong turn isn't disastrous. To reach the old city from the bus station, walk in front of the *kenyon* to Eli Cohen Sq., cross Eilat St., and take Herzl St. or Ha-Ḥalutz St.

PRACTICAL INFORMATION

Tourist Office: 1 Derekh Hevron (☎623 46 13), at Abraham's Well. From Herzl St. in the old city, walk down from the top to the end of the pedestrian KKL. The office is on the left-side corner across from the intersection. Helpful staff sells an excellent English map that lists information about sights and buses (NIS5). Office arranges bus tours of the city's historical sights. Call ahead for English screening of the brief movie on Be'er Sheva. Open Su-Th 8:30am-4pm.

Currency Exchange: The main **post office** on the corner of Yitzḥak Rager and Ben-Zvi St. exchanges cash and traveler's checks at excellent rates without commission. **Bank Ha-Poalim,** 40 Ha-Atzma'ut St. (☎629 26 62), on the corner of Ha-Ḥalutz St. Open Su, Tu-W 8:30am-1:15pm; M, Th 8:30am-1pm and 4-6:30pm; F 8:15am-12:30pm. Minimum charge $6. **Bank Leumi** (☎623 92 22), just past the post office on Ha-Nesi'im Blvd. Open Su, Tu-W 8:30am-1pm; M, Th 8:30am-1pm and 4:30-7pm; F 8:30am-noon. Its **ATM** accepts Visa and Diner's Club.

English Bookstores: The *kenyon* has a **Steimatzky** on the ground floor that carries an extensive collection of books. Open Su-Th 9am-9:30pm, F 9am-3pm, Sa 8:30-11pm. **Memsi** (☎627 06 95), in the bus station, sells maps and travel guides in English, as well as the 1:50,000 hiking map series (in Hebrew only). Open Su-Th 8:30am-6:30pm, F 8:30am-noon. **Mini Book** (☎643 33 96), opposite Israel Discount Bank, in the passageway filled with shops between Hadassah and Ha-Histadrut St. Sells used English and Hebrew books. Open Su-M 8:30am-1pm; W-Th 4-7pm; Tu, F 8:30am-1:30pm.

Emergency: First Aid: Magen David Adom, 40 Bialik St. (☎627 83 33). **Police:** 30 Herzl St. (☎646 27 44), at the corner of KKL St. **Fire:** (☎627 96 91).

Pharmacies: Super Pharm (☎628 13 71), in the *kenyon*. Open Su-Th 8:30am-midnight, F 8:30am-5pm, Sa 10am-midnight. **Pharmacy Ha-Negev,** 94 KKL St. (☎627 70 16), on the corner of Mordei Ha Geta'ot St. Open Su, M, W, Th, 8am-7pm; Tu 8am-1:30pm and 4-7pm; F 8am-1:30pm.

Hospital: Soroka Medical Center (☎640 01 11), on Yitzḥak Rager Blvd., with a green walkway and a blue and green sign in Hebrew. Take bus #7 or 8. Open 5:20am-11pm.

Internet: The **Paradise Hotel** on Henrietta Szold St. has Internet access at a computer on the mezzanine level for US$0.50 per minute. Credit cards only.

Post Office: (☎629 58 32), at the corner of Yitzḥak Rager Blvd., just across the street from the back entrance of the mall and Ben-Zvi St. This main branch has **Poste Restante, Western Union, EMS** services, **international calling, fax, phone cards,** and **commission-free cash and traveler's check exchange.** Smaller branches on Hadassa St. and in the City Hall building. All branches open Su-Tu, Th 8am-12:30pm and 4-6:30pm; W 8am-1pm; F 8am-12:30pm.

ACCOMMODATIONS

Be'er Sheva has several options for budget accommodations, including one youth hostel and a few reasonably-priced hotels. Conveniently, the following accommodations are all within a 5-10 minute walk from the *midraḥov* in the old city.

Beit Yatziv Youth Hostel (HI), 79 Ha-Atzma'ut St. (☎627 74 44), in the old city. Three blocks up from Herzl St., on the left behind the HI sign (walk or take bus #13). Clean rooms with bath, closet, A/C, and table. Pool in back. Full breakfast. Check-out 9am. Reception 24hr. 4-bed dorms US$22; 3-bed dorms US$24. The **Guest House** next-door is run by the same reception desk. Singles US$38-42.50; doubles US$56-59. NIS5/US$1.50 discount for HI members. Credit cards accepted.

Aviv Hotel, 48 Mordei Ha-Geta'ot St. (☎627 80 59 or 627 82 58). Walk down Herzl St. and turn right on KKL St. Run by a sweet Bulgarian woman. All rooms have private baths and high-powered A/C, some have balconies. Breakfast NIS20. Laundry available. Reception 24hr. Check-out 11am. Singles NIS160/US$35; doubles NIS215/US$47. 15% student discount. Cash only.

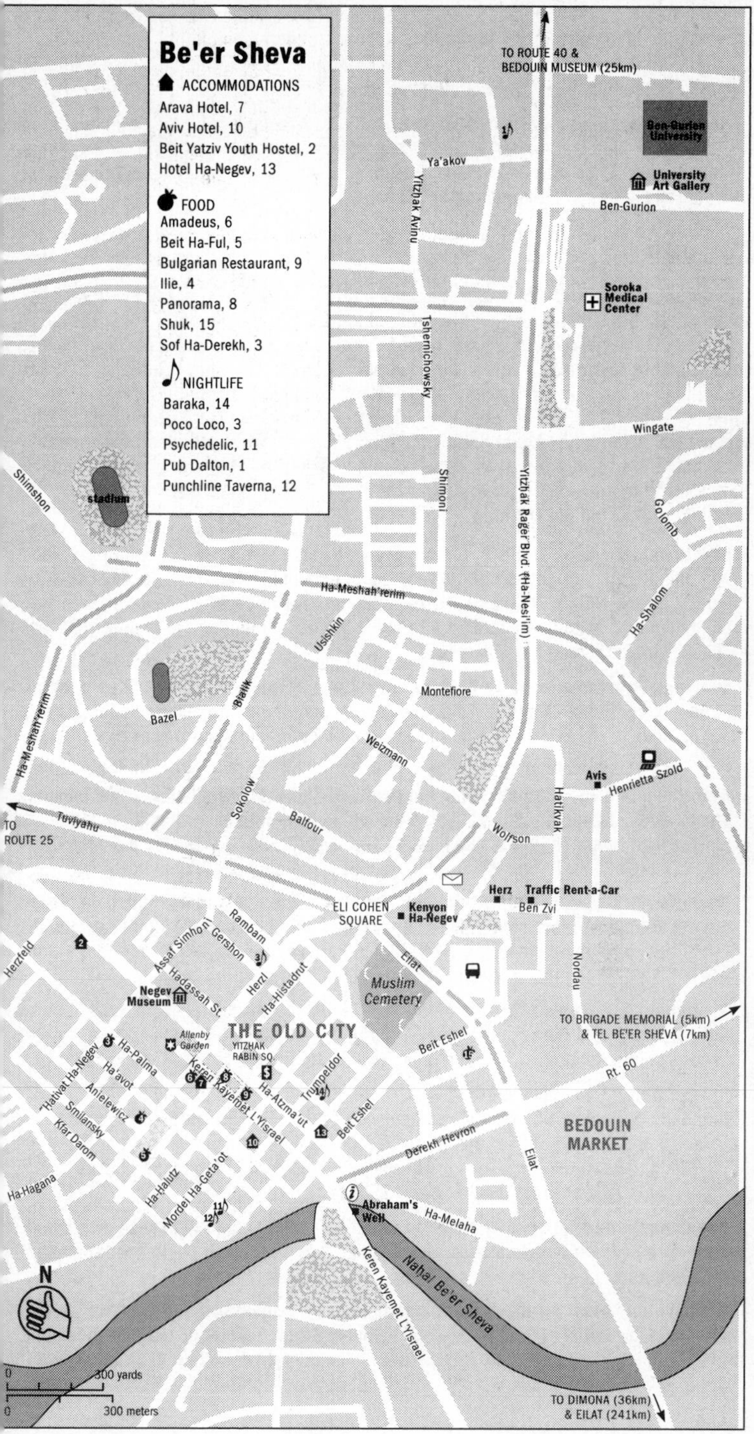

Be'er Sheva

ACCOMMODATIONS
Arava Hotel, 7
Aviv Hotel, 10
Beit Yatziv Youth Hostel, 2
Hotel Ha-Negev, 13

FOOD
Amadeus, 6
Beit Ha-Ful, 5
Bulgarian Restaurant, 9
Ilie, 4
Panorama, 8
Shuk, 15
Sof Ha-Derekh, 3

NIGHTLIFE
Baraka, 14
Poco Loco, 3
Psychedelic, 11
Pub Dalton, 1
Punchline Taverna, 12

TO ROUTE 40 & BEDOUIN MUSEUM (25km)
Ben-Gurion University
University Art Gallery
Ya'akov
Yitzhak Avinu
Ben-Gurion
Soroka Medical Center
Tshernichowsky
Wingate
Shimoni
Yitzhak Rager Blvd. (Ha-Nesi'im)
Golomb
Shimshon
stadium
Ha-Meshah'rerim
Ha-Shalom
Ussishkin
Montefiore
Bazel
Bialik
Ha-Meshah'rerim
Weizmann
Avis
Henrietta Szold
Hatikvak
Sokolow
Balfour
Wolfson
Tuviyahu
TO ROUTE 25
Herz
Traffic Rent-a-Car
Ben Zvi
ELI COHEN SQUARE
Kenyon Ha-Negev
Rambam
Assaf Simhoni
Gershon
Herzfeld
Eilat
Nordau
Hadassah St.
Herzl
Ha-Histadrut
Negev Museum
Muslim Cemetery
THE OLD CITY
TO BRIGADE MEMORIAL (5km) & TEL BE'ER SHEVA (7km)
Allenby Garden
YITZHAK RABIN SQ.
Beit Eshel
Ha-Palma
Hativat Ha-Negev
Ha'avot
Keren Kayemet L'Yisrael
Trumpeldor
Rt. 60
Ha-Atzma'ut
Anielewicz
Smilansky
Beit Eshel
Kfar Darom
BEDOUIN MARKET
Derekh Hevron
Eilat
Ha-Hagana
Ha-Halutz
Mordei Ha-Geta'ot
Abraham's Well
Ha-Melaha
Keren Kayemet L'Yisrael
Nahal Be'er Sheva
N
300 yards
300 meters
0
TO DIMONA (36km) & EILAT (241km)

THE NEGEV

Arava Hotel, 37 Ha-Histadrut St. (☎627 87 92). Turn right off KKL from Herzl St. Close to the popular cafes at the top of KKL. Rooms are fairly comfortable, with small bathrooms and A/C. Reception 24hr. Check-in 1pm. Check-out noon. Singles NIS80/US$25; doubles NIS100/US$35. Cash only.

Hotel Ha-Negev, 26 Ha-Atzma'ut St. (☎627 70 26), a couple of blocks down from Bank Ha-Poalim, after Trumpeldor St. This breezy hideaway has concrete walls, creaky stairs, and simple rooms. Check-out noon. Reception 24hr. Singles NIS120/US$25, with private shower and A/C NIS190/US$40. Cash only.

FOOD

Lined with falafel, *shawarma*, pizza, and sandwich store fronts, the **Keren Kayemet LeYisrael St. (KKL)** *midraḥov* is the best place for affordable eats. For a fast food fix, head to the food court on the lower floor of the *kenyon* across from the bus station. Most restaurants in the *kenyon* are open Su-Th 10am-midnight, F 10am-3pm, Sa after sundown-midnight. A **Hypershuk supermarket** inhabits the supermall. There is a small grocery store in the old city on Mordei Ha-Geta'ot, just off of KKL toward Ha-Palmah St. (Open daily 7am-7pm.) The cheapest place to buy fresh produce, meat, and fish is the **shuk,** located just south of the Muslim burial ground on Beit Eshel St. and easily identifiable by its arched metal rooftops. The listings below are all in the **old city area.**

Sof Ha-Derekh, (☎627 91 55), at the corner of Ha-Palmah and Ha-Tivat Ha-Negev. Feast on one of 22 spicy salads with homemade *lafah* bread (NIS7), or order meat from the grill. Chicken NIS15; steaks NIS55-70. Complimentary dessert of *baklava*, fresh fruit, and mint tea. Open Su-Th 11:30am-1am, F 11:30am-an hour before sundown, Sa after sundown-1am. Credit cards accepted.

Cafeteria Panorama (☎623 52 49), at the corner of Ha-Histadrut and KKL St., on the 2nd floor. Entrance near Rabin Square. Francophone owner serves vegetarian blintzes, pizza, and pasta (NIS11-22) in spartan simplicity. Juice stand downstairs (NIS12). Open Su-Th 10am-3pm and 6pm-1am, Sa after sundown-2am.

Beit Ha-Ful, 15 Ha-Histadrut St., at the corner of Smilansky St. Walk past the park; the restaurant's outdoor seating will be on the left. Popular with locals. *Ful* (Egyptian beans in pita with salads NIS11) or in a bowl with garnish (NIS25). Eat *al fresco* or in A/C dining room. Open Su-Th 8am-midnight, F 8am-3pm, Sa after sunset-midnight.

Bulgarian Restaurant, 112 KKL St. (☎623 85 04), near the corner of Ḥalutz St. Claims to be the oldest restaurant in Be'er Sheva and serves traditional Bulgarian goulash (NIS35), chicken shish kebab (NIS38), and steaks (NIS35-60). Open Su-Th 9am-11pm, Sa 10am-8pm. Reservations recommended for Saturday dinners.

Restaurant Ilie, 21 Herzl St. (☎627 86 85). Facing the police station on Herzl St., walk left 3 blocks and the restaurant is on the right near Negba St. Quiet Romanian grill serves soups, kebab (NIS30), and broiled brains (NIS50). Open Su-Th noon-midnight, F noon-4pm. Credit cards accepted.

Amadeus (☎665 00 85), on KKL, at the corner of Herzl St. This restaurant/cafe has airy outdoor and upstairs seating and a psychedelic spiraling staircase. Breakfast until noon NIS34; salads NIS28-49; a long list of specialty crepes NIS23; and milkshakes NIS19. Open Su-Th 8:30am-1am, F-Sa 8:30am-2:30am.

Bagel Bash, next to the Aviv Hotel on Mordei Ha-Geta'ot St. This bakery has a wide selection of breads and pastries. Open Su-M, W-Th 6:30am-7pm; Tu 6:30am-3pm; F 6:30am-2pm.

Glida Be'er Sheva, on the corner of Ha-Ḥalutz and Hadassah St. Site of the best ice cream in town (NIS5-10.50). Open Su-Th 9am-midnight, F 9am-5pm, Sa 8pm-midnight.

SIGHTS

A good way to begin your visit is to take a self-guided walking tour of the 3000 year old city, which offers some of the finest examples of Ottoman architecture in Israel. Start at the tourist office, which lies on the site of Abraham's Well, at the corner of Derekh Hevron and Keren Kayemet L'Yisrael St. Here, you can pick up maps of Be'er Sheva (NIS5) and other tourist information (see p. 280).

BEDOUIN MARKET. Established in 1905, the famous Thursday market is a nirvana for bargain hunters. Amid the clamor of screaming vendors are cheap Bedouin food and excellent garments. Years ago, the Bedouin hawked camels, sheep, and other wares at the end of agricultural seasons and during winter—now year-round they've added snow globes and t-shirts to the much-ballyhooed wares. Farther south, the quantity of rusty cans, scraps of paper, and dust increases, along with the smell of dung from the live animals for sale. The southern part of the market, however, houses the real gems: beaten copperware, Bedouin robes, fabrics, rugs, and ceramic items. Get there early to see the trading at its peak and to get more of a selection of genuine Bedouin goods. Many Bedouin here speak English, and some may compliment your beautiful eyes while charging six times the going rate for olive wood camels. *(The market is located on the south side of the city, off Eilat St., south of the intersection with Derekh Hevron. Most local buses will stop at the market upon request. By foot, walk to Eilat St. from the central bus station and cross over to the market. Open Th, all day.)*

ABRAHAM'S WELL. The well dates back to at least the 12th century CE, and many believe it to be the original well dug by Abraham. A free, five-minute guided tour of the site illuminates Be'er Sheva's biblical history, the well's archaeological significance, and its camel-powered hydrotechnology. From June to September, the well also serves as an occasional nighttime entertainment venue, with folk songs, stories, live music, and dance performances. *(On the corner of Derekh Hevron and Keren Kayemet LeYisrael St. ☎623 46 13. Call ahead.)*

NEGEV MUSEUM. The residence next to the mosque was built by the Ottomans in 1906 and named Be'er Sheva's City Hall in 1949. Diagonally facing the Governor's House is another Ottoman building, which was used as a boarding school for Bedouin children during the British mandate and then as a Red Crescent hospital during WWI. Together, the buildings now house the Negev Museum. Both the mosque and museum were closed in 1999 for renovations but are scheduled to reopen by winter 2000. *(On Ha-Atzma'ut St., north of Herzl St. ☎623 43 38 or 646 36 63.)*

Israel's largest cemetery of British WWI soldiers, with its rows of uniform, white headstones, is just up Ha-Atzma'ut St. from the museum, on the left.

JOE ALON BEDOUIN MUSEUM. At a time when approximately half of the Negev's Bedouins live in urban "settlements," this museum showcases all facets of the nomads' traditional lives, including tools, embroidery, medicine, and customary desert garb. An audio-visual presentation describes Bedouin culture and their famous hospitality. Outside the indoor exhibit are two Bedouin tents. In one, a Bedouin woman serves traditional pita and tea; in the other, Bedouin men converse with guests and serve bitter coffee. The museum also has an observation tower with a 360 degree view of the northern Negev. *(Several km north of the tel, on the outskirts of Kibbutz Lahav. Drive 15km north on Rte. 40 to the Lahav junction or take bus #369 and ask to be let off at the junction: 20min., every 30min., NIS12. An orange sign behind the bus stop points down the road in the direction of the kibbutz and museum, which are 8km away. Numbered vehicles from the kibbutz drive by frequently and may offer a lift. After arriving, walk along the asphalt road and follow it to where it curves to the right, up to the gate of the museum. Taxi NIS75. ☎991 33 22 or 991 85 97. Open Sa-Th 9am-5pm, F 9am-2pm. NIS15, students NIS13.)*

PARK YOUR OWN ASS when approaching a Bedouin tent, it is customary to cough so as to let your host know that he has a visitor. If you have arrived on a horse or a camel, your host will graciously take your animal and tie it to his tent. However, if you rode in on a donkey, he will refuse his tie-down services, and you must tether it yourself.

ISRAELI AIR FORCE MUSEUM. This museum displays over 100 airplanes from several generations of Israeli aerial combat, including airplanes captured from and shot down by neighboring countries. Free guided tours by Israeli soldiers relate the history behind each of the displays. *(At the Haterim air force base 8km west of town on the Be'er Sheva-Haterim Rd. City bus #31 stops directly in front of the entrance. Walk up Ha-Atzma'ut St. from the youth hostel and cross over the Derekh Joe Alon Highway at the major intersection to reach the bus stop headed away from town. ☎990 68 55. Open Su-Th 8am-5pm, F 8am-1pm. NIS23, ages 3-13 NIS15, senior citizens NIS18. Call ahead for free tours.)*

TEL BE'ER SHEVA. Five kilometers northeast of the city are the ruins of a 3000-year old planned city, recently upgraded to a national park. One pile of unearthed rubble is a 2nd-century Roman fortress, another an 8th-century BCE house, and a third a 12th-century BCE well. The view from the top of the tower in the back right corner of the site is fantastic. Fashionable Israelis flock to conduct their marriages in trendy Bedouin style at nearby marriage hall **Ohalei Kidar.** *(By car, take Rte. 60 out of the city, and turn right at the set of lights after the gas stations. Taxi NIS28 each way. Buses to Arad and Omer run by the road that leads to the site: #388, every 35min. 6:45am-10:30pm, NIS6.20. The walk from the turn-off takes about 30min. There is a roundabout approximately halfway down the road; keep straight to get to the ruins, which are through a parking lot on the right; an orange sign leads the way. Park open Su-Th and Sa 8am-5pm, F 8am-4pm; entrance closes 1hr. earlier. NIS9, students NIS8, children NIS4.50.)*

OTHER SIGHTS. The **Allenby Garden**, the city's first public garden, was commissioned by the Ottomans in the early 1900s. It was renamed after General Allenby, who led the British forces that captured the city from the Ottomans in WWI. Today, the garden serves as a pleasant little resting place, secluded from the streets. *(On Ha-Atzma'ut St., stroll up the midrahov from Abraham's Well. On the left, beyond Herzl St.)* Designed by Israeli artist Dani Karavan, the **Hanegev Palmaḥ Brigade Monument** honors IDF soldiers who died defending Be'er Sheva and other Negev settlements. The eight symbolic structures overlook the city from 5km northeast of the city. *(On Be'er Sheva-Omer Rd. The most practical way to reach the sight is by an NIS20 taxi. Free.)* The **Gan Remez** is a ceramic sculpture garden next to Ha-Jama, an elegant Turkish mosque. *(Between Hadassah St. and Ha-Atzma'ut St.)*

ENTERTAINMENT

Entertainment venues are centered around Trumpeldor St. and Smilansky St. in the old city, with some lying a short distance out of town near the university and industrial areas. Most bars and clubs open at 9 or 10pm but remain quiet until about 11pm. Movie theaters (☎623 52 79) are housed downstairs in the *kenyon*. Shows run Su-Th 5-10pm; F 7:30, 10pm, and midnight; Sa 7:30 and 10pm. Movies are usually in English with Hebrew subtitles (NIS27.50).

Forum, 232 Kiryat Yehudit, in the old industrial area of town, a short drive out of Be'er Sheva's old city (taxi NIS15). Includes multiple dance floors, the largest bar in Israel, and a swimming pool. Open on Friday nights from mid-June through August. Call ahead to find out about theme nights like karaoke and techno. Beer NIS15-20. Cover NIS30-70. Open Tu, Th-Sa 10:15pm-5am; F after-party until noon on Sa.

Baraka, 16 Hadassah St., on the corner of B'nei Ein Harod St. This historic stone building once served as an Ottoman hospital and now serves beer (NIS15-22) outside in a desert-motif courtyard and inside to the beat of pop music. Line forms outside on weekends. No cover. Open nightly 10pm-early morning.

Pub Dalton, near Ben-Gurion University. Take bus #7 or 8 to a stop near the main entrance of the university's dorms. From there, walk along Yitzḥak Rager Blvd., down Ya'akov Ave., and turn right at the pizza place. Look behind a dirt parking lot to the right for a small, white building. Continue down the stairs into a small beach/Bedouin-themed haven for mellow drinking. Beer NIS10-16; coffee NIS8. Open Sa-Th 10pm-2am, F 10pm-4am.

Psychedelic, 6 Trumpeldor St., on the corner of Smilansky. Hanging nets and palm trees bring the desert into this pub's pit dance floor. Upstairs people relax on Turkish rugs. Cover F NIS13, Sa NIS15, no cover other nights. Open daily 11pm-4am.

Poco Loco, 97 Herzl St., near Rambam St. This hip joint plays the latest American pop music and caters to a twenty-something crowd. Breakfast until noon NIS32; Yemenite pancakes NIS26-32; large salads NIS38-44; and gourmet pizza NIS34-38. Fancy cocktails. Ask for the American Gigolo (NIS 28-29). Open daily 10am-4am.

Punchline, 4 Smilansky St., below the Trumpeldor St. intersection. How many beers (NIS20) does it take to get a bunch of Israeli twenty-somethings drunk? Come here for the *punchline*. Salsa dancing on W and F. Cover charge for salsa nights and special performances NIS19, students NIS15. Open M-Sa 10:30pm-late.

NEAR BE'ER SHEVA

DIMONA דימונה

Since immigrating in 1969, the **Hebrew Israelite Community,** referred to as the **Black Hebrews** by non-members, has been working to combine the ideals of religious and communal living. A unique sect of English-speaking immigrants, the Hebrew Israelites trace their roots to ancient Israel. The community, which bases its religion on the revelations of spiritual leader Ben-Ami Ben Israel (formerly Ben Carter), believes that the ancestors of black slaves in antebellum America lived in Israel until they were forced to migrate to Western Africa after the Roman onslaught in 70 CE. Ben Israel's vision included a return to the Holy Land; the group's vanguard left Chicago in 1967 and spent two and a half years in Liberia before coming to Israel. Another group from Chicago followed in 1970 and a third exodus took place from Detroit in 1973. The Israeli government at first refused to grant them citizenship unless they converted to Judaism, but the Hebrew Israelites insisted they were already Jews. The government and the sect came to an agreement in 1990 on a process for normalizing the community's legal status.

The original community of about 100 pilgrims has blossomed into a 1200-person village; branches of the community in other areas in Israel bring the total population of Hebrew Israelites to over 2000. Children are born under the care of community midwives, several families live together in one home and take turns with household responsibilities, and community members come together to make their own clothes and food. Their religious beliefs require them to wear only natural fabrics and prohibit them from eating animal parts or products, white sugar, or white flour. Their speech alternates between equally fluent Hebrew and English. The grace and peacefulness of their small village has to be seen to be believed.

GETTING THERE. Buses to Dimona leave from: **Be'er Sheva** (#48, 56, and 375; 45min.; every 20min. 6:30am-11pm; NIS13); **Eilat** (#393 and 394; 3hr.; every 1½hr. 5am-5pm; NIS43, students NIS39); and **Tel Aviv** (#375, 393, and 394; NIS30, students NIS27). To get to the village from Dimona's bus station, turn left on Herzl St., pass the tall red monument on the right, and continue for about 10 minutes. The village is on the left, past a school.

SIGHTS AND ENTERTAINMENT. Though the village welcomes solo wanderers, a tour can be much more informative. Call ahead to schedule a free tour. (☎07 655 54 00, 657 32 86, or 657 32 87; donations accepted.)

At **Boutique Africa,** leave an imprint of your foot, and the full-time **Sole Brother** will custom design a pair of shoes to be picked up in about two weeks. (Rush orders available. Open Su-M, W-Th 10am-2pm and 4-7pm; Tu and F 9am-2pm.) **Toflé** sells beautifully colored garments and cloth direct from Ghana (NIS80-550; same hours as the boutique). The community restaurant, **Soul Food Eats,** is a blessing for protein-starved vegans, who can take the opportunity to stock up on delicious tofu sandwiches (NIS10) or sit down for a full three-dish lunch meal (NIS12). (Open Su-Th 9am-11pm, F 9am-noon and after sundown-midnight.) The boutiques and restaurant keep to their posted schedules only loosely; if they're closed, it probably won't be long before they open up. The village also has a three-room **guest house.** (Rooms NIS80, breakfast and dinner included. Call ahead.)

Every summer, the Hebrew Israelites host the two-day **Naisik Ha-Shalom Music Festival,** which highlights community entertainment, Hebrew Israelite singers, and Israeli bands. (Call Elisheva Eli-El ☎05 199 63 17 for information.) Other concerts and festivals are scattered throughout the summer. Singing groups from Dimona tour the country when they're not performing at home. Their music is a unique rendition of traditional Jewish and other religious texts in gospel and hip-hop style.

Dimona's other claim to fame lies in the mysterious factory a few kilometers to the east. Any tour guide will say that the ominous barbed wire fences and signs forbidding photography are hiding a "nuclear weapons site? What nuclear weapons site?" Officially, the place is a basketball court, but then again, officially the US military isn't hiding alien ships in New Mexico.

MAMSHIT ממשית

The sunbleached sandstone ruins of ancient Mamshit, the only city in the Negev that was walled-in on all sides, lie 15km east of Dimona. Built in the first century CE, Mamshit reached its height as a garrison town in the Roman and Byzantine periods. From Mamshit, one of the six Nabatean cities in Israel, the Nabateans ruled the Petra-Gaza spice route stretching from India to Rome. On one side is a vast desert plain; on the other, the precipitous canyon of **Naḥal Mamshit** (Mamshit River). Following attacks by desert nomads in the 6th century CE, the city was destroyed and abandoned. Particularly impressive among the ruins are the Eastern Church, with its altar remains at the top of the market area, the 2nd-century CE tower which once guarded the dams of the river below, and the mansion, or "House of the Affluent." Also be sure to take a look down into the canyon from the observation point. (Open Su-Th 8am-5pm, F 8am-4pm. NIS9, student NIS8, youth NIS4; brochure of the site including small map and descriptions free.)

To view the canyon from a camel's back and with a Bedouin guide, contact the **Mamshit Camel Ranch,** 1km east of the ruins. (☎665 10 54; 2hr. tour NIS100.) Bedouin tea, coffee, and overnight stays available for groups of 20 or more.

Buses running between Be'er Sheva and the Dead Sea will stop 1km outside Mamshit, along the main highway, as will bus #394 to Eilat (1¼hr., every 1½hr., NIS19). Call **Mayam Taxi** to get here from Dimona (☎07 655 66 88; 10min., NIS33). Be sure to tell the bus or cab driver to stop at Atar Mamshit, the Nabatean ruins, not the new cinderblock city several kilometers to the west.

ḤA-MAKHTESH HA-KATAN AND HA-MAKHTESH HA-GADOL המכתש הקטן והמכתש הגדול

About a 40-minute drive southeast of Be'er Sheva in the direction of Dimona is the magnificent geological coupling of the Small (Ha-Katan) and Big (Ha-Gadol) Craters, which offers several steep but rewarding hikes. Ha-Makhtesh Ha-Gadol offers mostly large-scale scenery to drive by and admire from a distance, while Ha-Makhtesh Ha-Katan has more places to park and explore on foot. The best way to reach both is by renting a car and driving from Be'er Sheva (see **Car Rental,** p. 279).

THE NEGEV

Before hiking, contact the tourist office in Arad (see p. 287) to ask about specific hiking route suggestions for both craters. Also pick up **1:50,000 Hiking in Israel maps** of the Small and Big Craters (numbers 14 and 15 in the series; NIS70) at Memsi in the Be'er Sheva bus station or at Steimatzky in the mall. These maps are only in Hebrew, but the tourist office in Arad can help identify specific points of interest and routes in English. As always when hiking in the desert, bring plenty of water, as well as sunglasses and head covering, even if you plan on spending most of your time in an air-conditioned car. It is also advisable to hike with at least one other person and to leave a note on your car indicating where you are hiking and how long you plan to be gone.

To hit both places on one trip, begin by heading toward Ha-Makhtesh Ha-Gadol. Take Rte. #25 southeast out of Be'er Sheva, toward Dimona and Eilat. Just before Dimona, turn right onto Rte. #204, heading toward the town **Yeroḥam.** Once in Yeroḥam, take a left and follow the signs to the "Great Crater." There are several places along the way to pull over and admire the multi-colored slopes of the crater. Driving straight through the crater takes about 10 minutes and leads to Rte. #206, which runs to Oron and Dimona. Follow Rte. #206 toward Dimona and turn left onto Rte. #25 after the sign to "Little Makhtesh," the Small Crater.

To get to the Small Crater from Be'er Sheva, take Rte. #25 to Dimona and turn right onto Rte. #206 at the Rotem Junction. Look for the small orange sign on the left that points to a paved road labeled "Small Makhtesh" and leads uphill. At the top of the first bit of road is a park sign with trails and lookouts marked. Notice on the map that double black lines indicate trails for 4x4 vehicles only. The main road, the "Old Road to Eilat," is represented by a solid black line. It was first paved by the British in 1949 and used until 1953 when the road to Eilat via Mitzpeh Ramon was built. The road becomes semi-paved after this point and crosses back over train tracks; signs will point to the Little Makhtesh **observation point.** Park the car and follow the red trail about 20 minutes to an edge of the crater with a breathtaking view. A **free camping area,** marked with a green sign, is on the way. Past the observation point is a dangerous hike.

Backtrack by car to the paved road on the left, marked **"Ha'rava Highway/ Aqrabim Ascent."** The Ma'ale Aqrabim, or scorpion ascent, was a Roman road built around 2 CE and used by troops in 1948 and 1949. A five-minute drive leads to a trail of green stone steps on the right. Up the steps is a view of the area, including a power plant and quarry. A sign at the bottom of the steps shows hikes in the area and gives their difficulty ratings. After this, the road begins its winding and brake-burning descent toward a small collection of 3rd-4th century CE Roman ruins on a flat, open area at the bottom. This site was on the 2nd-3rd century BCE Nabatean spice route and later served as a fort and hostel. A left at the end of the road leads to the town Hazeva. From here Rte. #90 heads north toward the Dead Sea, where it intersects with Rte. #25 heading back west to Dimona and Be'er Sheva.

ARAD ערד ☎07

Built near the ancient Canaanite ruins of Tel Arad, the modern city of Arad lies equidistant from all the major Dead Sea attractions. Besides the resulting pleasant climate from this elevation, the air here is so clean and dry that doctors literally prescribe it worldwide for those suffering from asthma and other respiratory problems. Though considered a less than exciting place by many Israelis, this oasis of civilization is probably what David Ben-Gurion, Israel's first prime minister, envisioned when he spoke of Israel's desert blooming. In 1960, a governmental committee drew up a master plan, and the first residents moved in two years later. The city is a convenient place for Dead Sea floaters to hang their towels and Negev trekkers to replenish supplies, but other travelers may find the town a bit sterile.

GETTING THERE

Buses: Central bus station (☎995 73 93), a small office on Yehuda St. Open Su-Th 5:30am-2pm, F 5:30am-1:30pm. There is no direct service to or from Eilat or Jerusalem; in general it's easiest to go to Be'er Sheva and connect there. To: **Be'er Sheva:** #385 and 388, make a few local stops (40 min., every 30min.-1hr, Su-Th 5:40am-9:30pm, F 5:40am-4:30pm, Sa 5:30-9:30pm; NIS18), #384 (9:30, 11:30am, 2, and 5pm) and #386 (frequent, 6:40-7:45am) are direct; **Ein Bokek** (#384 and 385; 30min.; Su-Th 10:15am, 1, and 3:45pm; F 10:15am, 12:45pm; Sa 2pm; NIS18) via **Masada** (50min., NIS22.50, students NIS20) and **Ein Gedi** (1¼ hr., NIS25, students NIS22.50); **Tel Aviv** (#389; 2hr.; Su-Th 6, 8:30am, 2 and 5pm; F 4 per day 6am-1:30pm; Sa 5 and 9pm; NIS37.50, students NIS34).

Taxis: *Sherut* run from the central bus station between Arad and Ein Bokek (NIS10). **Kenyon Arad** (☎997 44 44) has *special* taxis.

Car Rental: The big rental car companies are in Be'er Sheva; locally try **Yoel Tours** (☎05 256 25 63), a Dead Sea company that can arrange rentals in Arad.

ORIENTATION AND PRACTICAL INFORMATION

Arad rests on the border between the Judean and Negev deserts, about 25km from Masada and Ein Bokek and 60km east of Be'er Sheva. The central bus station is on **Yehuda St.** Across the street and to the left between **Yerushalayim St.** and **Ḥevron St.)** is the central promenade, chock full of late-night restaurants and kiosks. A large *kenyon* is at the end of the promenade, across **Elazar Ben-Yair St.**

Tourist office: 28 Elazer Ben-Yair St. (☎995 44 09), across the street at the end of the promenade. Offers maps and information for Arad, surrounding sights, and events. Also the SPNI map for **hiking** in the Negev. Open Sa-Th 8am-5pm, F 8am-4pm.

Banks: In the town center are three **ATM**-equipped banks, including **Bank Ha-Poalim** (☎997 06 66). Open Su, Tu, W 8:30am-1:15pm; M and Th 8:30am-1pm and 4-6:30pm; F 8:15am-12:30pm.

Police (☎995 70 44), to the right of the bus station. Magen David Adom **First Aid** (☎995 72 22), next to the police station.

Pharmacy: Superpharm (☎997 16 21), in the mall. Open Su-Th 9am-10pm, F 9am-3pm, Sa 11am-11pm.

Post Office: The main branch (☎995 70 88), under the red awning on the promenade, near Elazar Ben-Yair St., has **international phone calls, Western Union,** no-commission currency exchange, and **Poste Restante.** Open Su-Tu, Th 8am-12:30pm and 4-6:30pm; W 8am-1pm; F 8am-12:30pm. There is a branch with better hours in the mall. Open Su-Th 9am-2pm and 4-7pm.

ACCOMMODATIONS

Arad has only one youth hostel. Though large enough to accommodate the usual crowds, it may be full during peak season and packed with Israeli teens during the Arad Music Festival. Alternatively, the tourist office keeps a list of "Zimmers," or rooms to rent within Arad.

Blau-Weiss Youth Hostel (HI), 4 Atad St. (☎995 71 50; fax 995 50 78). From the bus stop facing Yehuda St., turn right on Palmaḥ St. after a block. After the soccer field, make a left onto Arad St., and follow the signs. This complex has a whistle-clean duplex and individual cottages with A/C. Cable TV room and a free coffee bar. Breakfast included. Reception Su-Th 7:30am-1:30pm and 4-7:30pm, F 7:30am-noon and 4:30-7pm, Sa 4:30-7:30pm. Check-in 4-8pm, Check-out 10am. Dorms NIS70/US$17.50; singles NIS152/US$38; doubles NIS224/US$56. NIS20/US$5 extra on Sa. Members get NIS6/US$1.50 discount.

Arad Hotel (☎995 70 40), just up the stairs behind the police station on Yehuda St. You only get closer to the central bus station by sleeping on a bench. *Let's Go* does not recommend sleeping on benches. Rooms show some age but are the cheapest in town. Private bath and A/C. Some rooms have TV. Breakfast NIS20. Reception 7am-10pm. Check-out 10am. Singles NIS130/US$32.50; doubles NIS180/US$45.

Hotel Inbar, 38 Yehuda St. (☎997 33 03; fax 997 33 22), is the pastel-orange compound across the street from the central bus station. Bathe yourself in luxury (and their salt-water pool) in this ritzy and delightfully inexpensive hotel. Private baths, A/C, and TV. Breakfast included. Reception 24hr. Check-in 2pm. Check-out noon. Singles NIS428/US$107; doubles NIS540/US$135. Prices drop NIS80/US$20 from Nov.-Feb. and rise NIS60/US$15 from July-Aug. 10% *Let's Go* discount; ask for Ronit.

FOOD

The usual mess of *shawarma*, as well as American and Italian joints, awaits on the *midrahov.* There is also a large **Hyperneto Supermarket** in the mall. (☎995 27 75. Open Su-W 8am-10pm, Th 8:30am-11pm, F 7:30am-3pm.) On Mondays, there is a surprisingly large and lively **shuk,** with kilos of fresh produce and hot Bedouin pita. To get there from the bus station, make a left on Yehuda, and another left on Ha-Ta'asiya. The market is just past the large intersection.

SIGHTS

Some swear that four-wheel drive is the only way to see the desert. For Negev **jeep tours,** contact Allan Levine (☎997 12 35, mobile phone 050 284 301; fax 997 14 23; email jeepers@netvision.net.il; www.jeeptours-israel.com). These wind-in-your-hair tours are a fast-paced romance with the desert, hitting highlights that are difficult to reach by bus. (Half-day NIS140/US$35; full-day NIS220/US$55; lunch included.) Allan offers a jeep tour and Masada Sound and Light Show combo (NIS260/US$65 dinner included). A night tour (NIS160/US$40) is also available, with wine, live music, and coffee. Allan's tours are a bargain compared with other jeep tours. (10% *Let's Go* discount. The seventh person rides free.)

Those desperate to see something in Arad itself may enjoy the **Arad Museum,** in the same building as the tourist office, with displays on the archaeological findings from Tel Arad and a model of the surrounding Negev region. (Open Sa-Th 8am-5pm, F 8am-4pm. NIS18, students NIS15.) The amazing air quality in Arad can be best appreciated on a walk to the town's **observation points,** which look out over the desert landscape. To reach the observation points from the bus station, continue right on Yehuda St. to Moav St., near an iron sculpture of a woman and child. Turn right on Moav St. and follow the road as it passes quiet residential neighborhoods on the right and desert views on the left. The elevated section of sidewalk with benches on the right serves as the observation deck.

ENTERTAINMENT

The annual **Arad Music Festival** is held every July. This popular four-day jam hosts artists and musicians from all over Israel; Egged runs all-day extra bus service to and from Arad for its duration. Contact the tourist office (☎995 44 09; fax 995 58 66) for information and dates of the 2001 festival.

The dramatic **Masada Sound and Light Show** can only be reached via Arad (take Rte. 3199). The show is visible only from the Roman Ramp side of Masada, not from the side with the youth hostel and cable cars. Currently, there is no public transportation to the show. Travel time from Arad is about a half hour; the road closes at the beginning of the show. Shows are in Hebrew, but simultaneous-translation earphones are available in English, French, German, and Spanish for NIS13. (☎995 93 33 or 995 89 93. NIS33, students NIS27. 50min. shows Mar.-Aug. Tu, Th 9pm; Sept.-Oct. Tu, Th 7pm; arrive a half hour early. Contact the organizers for reservations.) **Yoel Tours** can arrange transportation. (☎658 44 32. NIS85, transportation and admission.)

When night falls, Arad's young and restless gather at **Muza,** an old-fashioned beer-and-darts bar in the Artists' Quarter. From the bus station, make a right (with your back to the information booth) and walk two blocks out Yehuda St. to HaMaccabim (in front of the fields). The ramp on the corner leads down to Muza. Sample dozens of beers (NIS12-14 for local brews; NIS15-22 for imports) at the raucous booths or at the mellow picnic benches outside. On Shabbat, this may the only option for a good hot meal. (Omelettes NIS27; grilled baguettes NIS23-32; hamburgers NIS18. ☎995 87 64. Open daily 5pm-2am.)

CENTRAL NEGEV

SDEH BOKER שדה בוקר ☎07

When experts advised that developing the Negev was a waste of time and money, first prime minister and Zionist visionary David Ben-Gurion insisted on searching for unconventional methods of "making the desert bloom," asking, "If the Nabateans could do it, why can't we?" When he visited the fledgling Sdeh Boker at the age of 67, he was so moved by the young pioneers that he decided to resign from office and settle on the kibbutz. Soon after, he founded the *Midresha* (institute) of Sdeh Boker, which houses laboratories and a field school devoted to the management of desert resources. Established in 1952, the kibbutz raises olives, kiwis, and other fruit, as well as wheat, corn, and livestock (though few cows).

Steeped in Ben-Gurion tributes, sights, and memorabilia, Sdeh Boker now serves as a base for desert exploration in the nearby **Ein Avdat National Park** and **Zin Valley.** There are a tremendous number of truly astounding hikes in this area, traversing jagged desert cliffs, natural springs, canyons, and monk's caves.

ORIENTATION AND PRACTICAL INFORMATION

The only public transportation to or from Sdeh Boker is Egged bus #60, which runs between **Be'er Sheva** and **Mitzpeh Ramon** (35min.; 6:35am-9:30pm; NIS19, students NIS17.50). The bus stops along the highway at three different points a few kilometers apart: the gate of Kibbutz Sdeh Boker, the turn-off to Ben-Gurion's Hut (at the edge of the kibbutz), and the roundabout outside the gate of the Ben-Gurion Institute. To reach the SPNI Field School, accommodations, Ein Avdat National Park, Ben-Gurion's grave, and the Ben-Gurion Heritage Institute, get off outside the gate. From the roundabout, the road on the right with the orange sign leads to the grave, Heritage Institute, and down the canyon to Ein Avdat. The road straight ahead leads to the SPNI office and accommodations. The institute buildings are arranged around a central square, inside of which are the restaurant, supermarket, and **post office.** (☎653 27 19. Open Su-M, W-Th 8:30am-noon and 1-2pm; Tu 8:30-11am; F 8:30-10:30am.) To reach the **SPNI Field School,** turn right at the end of the road inside the main gate and then left at the large parking lot. The helpful staff answers questions about hiking routes and desert flora, sells maps of nearby trails (NIS62), and stores bags during day hikes. (☎653 20 16; fax 653 27 21; www.boker.org.il/betsadeh. Open Su-Th 8am-4:30pm, F 8am-1pm and 5-7pm.)

HONK IF YOU'RE HORNED If the only sorts of horns you've seen close-up involve four doors and rush-hour traffic, passing gazelles and ibex while hiking in Israel can be an experience in and of itself. Males have large, curved horns; females have short horns. Listen for the loud, high-pitched whistle issued by these animals when they sense a nearby threat, usually another animal. Also keep an eye out for Asiatic wild asses, the nature reserve's pride and joy. The world's smallest miniature horses, they're a cross between an Iranian and a Turkish species.

ACCOMMODATIONS

The **SPNI Hostel** (☎653 20 16 or 05 393 04 59; fax 653 2721; email orders@boker.org.il), on the edge of the canyon, has modern rooms with A/C and private baths. The six-bed dorm rooms, Sdeh Boker's only budget lodgings, are reserved for students. (Dorms NIS60; singles NIS195; doubles NIS245. Breakfast included. Call ahead.) The field school also runs the **Hamburg Guest House** next door; the reception is in the SPNI field school's office. The rooms include A/C, TV, refrigerator, and bathroom. (Singles NIS225; doubles NIS295. Credit cards accepted. Prices increase during Passover, Sukkot, and Ḥanukkah.) Both accommodations include discounted use of the community swimming pool (NIS10). Guests are entitled to **Internet** access in the field school office. Camping is free at designated locations within the Zin Valley; contact the **SPNI Field School** for information about facilities and transportation.

FOOD

Food options are slim. The **Super Zin** supermarket in the institute's center is the place to stock up on food before hitting the trail. (Open Su-Th 8am-7pm, F 8am-2pm.) The **Zin Restaurant,** on the other side of the post office, serves tasty breakfasts. (NIS10-32. Open Su-Th 8am-11pm, F 8am-2pm, Sa 10am-6pm. Credit cards accepted.) The **Sdeh Boker Inn,** next-door to Ben-Gurion's Hut, serves cafeteria-style meals, including excellent baked zucchini and goulash. (☎656 03 79. Open daily 8am-3pm. Credit cards accepted.) For Shabbat stays in Sdeh Boker, stock up before Friday night, when stores close.

SIGHTS

From the Ben-Gurion Institute, a walk along the canyon rim leads to the **Ben-Gurion Tombs,** which overlook the Negev. **The Ben-Gurion Heritage Institute** is worth a visit. Scientists and university students work here year-round; their findings on desert irrigation and development are applied in Africa and in much of the world. The nearby **National Solar Energy Center** is a pioneer in solar power development. Those black panels and metal contraptions on every rooftop are solar-powered water heaters, required for households by Israeli law. The center gives tours and shows an audio-visual presentation by appointment (☎659 69 34). The institute's **Desert Sculpture Museum** displays art created from natural desert materials. The SPNI Field School also has a **Desert Wildlife House** where visitors can see live slimy things (inquire at the Field School office).

Ben-Gurion's Hut (☎655 84 44) is 2.5km north of the institute (a 45min. walk to the right along the highway; the road leading to the hut is on the right after a large memorial grove of pistachio trees) and one bus stop in the direction of Be'er Sheva. Ben-Gurion lived in this modest kibbutz house for the last 20 years of his life, and the residence has been kept as he left it. There is a small museum next door. (Open Su-Th 8:30am-4pm, F 8:30am-2pm, Sa and holidays 9am-3pm. Free.)

HIKING

Although many tourists come to Sdeh Boker to see its Ben-Gurion memorials, Ben-Gurion was attracted to the kibbutz because of its majestic setting. The best way to appreciate the natural beauty of the region is to try some of its spectacular hikes. These, however, require careful preparation. Trails may be poorly marked, distances deceptive, and the Negev sun unforgiving. Detailed maps and explanations for all of these hikes are available at the SPNI field office, which you should visit before attempting any hike. With advance notice, SPNI offers guided hikes across the Avdat Plateau or Zin Valley; call ahead for more information. Wear a hat, get an early start, and drink 1L of water every hour.

EIN AVDAT NATIONAL PARK. This easily accessibly park is located in the Zin Canyon. From the institute gate, the steep road to the park's lower, main entrance snakes down the canyon (1hr. on foot, 15min. by car). From the entrance, the hike to **Ein Avdat** (Avdat Spring; the lower pools) is 15 minutes. Allot about one hour for the full hike to the upper gate. Getting to the upper gate requires climbing one-way ladders; unless there's a car waiting at the end of the hike, you'll either need to make a U-turn at the base of the ladders and miss the view or extend your hike a few hours by walking along the rim of the canyon after reaching the top.

Gleaming white walls tower over the green, puddled path that runs through the canyon to the lower pools of the Avdat Spring. The eerie echoes of wildlife resound through the high caves carved in the sides of the canyon, which once served as homes to **Byzantine monks.** A small dam pools water that flows down the rocks from the Avdat Spring; just before the dam an easy-to-miss small set of stairs in the rock leads up to the rest of the hike and the one-way ladders. The foliage becomes denser along the upper part of the trail, where a grove of **Mesopotamian poplar trees** sits below a series of ladders that lead to a dazzling view at the top of the canyon. From the end of the trail on the canyon's rim, a trek along the riverbed to the nearby Nabatean ruins in Avdat takes about two hours (see **Avdat,** p. 293); the trail markings are difficult to follow so consult SPNI for details before going. To either return to Sdeh Boker or head on to Avdat on wheels, exit the park through the parking lot near the upper pools and walk down the road to the highway where there are stops for bus #60 headed in both directions. *(☎655 56 84. Park open daily May-Sept. 8am-5pm; Oct.-Apr. 8am-4pm. Entry permitted until 1hr. before closing. NIS14, seniors and students NIS12, children NIS6; free brochure).*

KARAKASH WADI. This magnificent three-hour hike passes an inviting pond and waterfall (water flows 1-2 times a year in the winter). The Karakash Wadi eventually runs into the **Ḥavarim Wadi.** A one-hour hike along the Ḥavarim Wadi passes a Nabatean cistern and slopes of smooth, white rock that are striking (and slippery) in moonlight. The cistern is below ground, down a flight of stairs from the beginning of the Ḥavarim Wadi hike. Part of the spice traders' efforts to squeeze water out of the desert, the cistern was used to catch and hold water from rain storms. A one-hour hike along the trail leads to the bottom of the road and park entrance. The brush and rocky hills are popular spots for idling ibex. Turn right on the road to reach Ein Avdat or left to make the uphill haul back to Sdeh Boker. *(To begin the hike, turn left on the Be'er Sheva-Eilat highway from the end of the entrance road to the midresha and walk approximately 1km; the trailhead is to the left. For the entrance to the Havarim cistern and Wadi hike, continue along the highway past the Karakash trailhead to an orange sign on the left, a 20min. walk from the institute. The sign points into the parking lot, where a blue-and-white marked trail descends on the left. Free.)*

EIN AKEV. This 5½-hour hike offers magnificent views from above the Zin Canyon and leads to an oasis where chilly spring water provides a refreshing respite from the desert sun. From the SPNI field school walk down the winding road toward Ein Avdat. From the bottom of the canyon, walk for 20 minutes and look on the left for a trail with green and white markers that ascends the canyon. This trail goes southeast across a desert plateau for several kilometers and reaches a green pool surrounded by lush green vegetation. After a swim in the pool head north along a trail with blue markers. Turn left at the junction and return to Sdeh Boker on the trail marked by orange, blue, and white, which leads from Lebanon to Eilat. *(This hike winds along the edge of cliffs at times. Be very careful and walk slowly in these areas. The return from Ein Akev is along the floor of the canyon and gets very hot during the middle of the day. It's best to start hiking as soon after sunrise as possible.)*

DAYTRIP FROM SDEH BOKER: AVDAT עבדת

The magnificently preserved ruins of a 4th-century BCE **Nabatean city** are perched upon a hill 11km south of Sdeh Boker. Avdat once thrived as a pit stop for caravans along the spice route from the Far East to Gaza (via Petra) that continued on to Europe. Nabateans used their strategic perch at Avdat to spy on caravans as far away as present-day Mitzpeh Ramon or Sdeh Boker. After the Romans captured the city in 106 CE, it continued to flourish, reaching its economic peak during the Byzantine period (see p. 9). Most of the ruins date from this time. The most important Nabatean remains are a handsome esplanade on top of the hill, a winding staircase that led to a Nabatean temple, and a potter's workshop, all dating from the first century CE. When the Nabateans converted to Christianity around 300 CE, the temple became a church. The best of the 6th-century Byzantine remains include a 7m surrounding wall, a monastery, two churches, and a baptistry. In this century, the site was resurrected on film as the setting for the movie *Jesus Christ Superstar*. The small grove of crops just below the ruins is irrigated through ancient Nabatean techniques.

Bus #60 (40min., 6:35am-10pm; NIS20, students NIS18) runs from Be'er Sheva to Mitzpeh Ramon, stopping in Avdat. Tell the driver you're going to the Nabatean archaeological site and not Ein Avdat (the oasis). The site can also be reached by hiking from Sdeh Boker via Ein Avdat (3-4hr.); consult the SPNI guides in Sdeh Boker for information. Bus #60 runs to Avdat from Sdeh Boker (NIS11) and from the highway near the end of the Ein Avdat trail (NIS5). ☎658 63 91; fax 655 09 54. Drinking water and bathrooms are across from the ticket booth; bring water for the 20min. uphill hike to the entrance. Open in summer Su-Th 8am-5pm, F 8am-4pm; in winter Su-Th 8am-4pm, F 8am-3pm. NIS18, students NIS15, children NIS9.

MITZPEH RAMON מצפה רמון ☎07

Mitzpeh Ramon sits on the rim of **Makhtesh Ramon** (Ramon Crater), the largest natural crater in the world. At 40km long, 9km wide, and 400m deep, its sheer size is mind-boggling. The crater makes visitors feel small in every respect: its rock formations are millions of years old, its 1200 different kinds of vegetation span four distinct climatic zones, and evidence of human life in the area predates written history. Since some of the geological formations are found nowhere else in the world, hikes pass through what seem to be landscapes of desolate, far-away planets. Uphill treks wind toward phenomenal views of the desert expanse, a rainbow of multi-colored sand.

In the 1920s and 30s, Makhtesh Ramon was not on British maps of Palestine. The young Israeli government came upon the crater while exploring the potential of the Negev. Until a direct route to Eilat was built from the Dead Sea in the 1970s, Mitzpeh Ramon (Ramon Observation Point) was the stop-off for those heading south. Today, the crater is a 250,000-acre national park with well-marked trails through mazes of geological stunners. From campsites in the crater, the lack of artificial light offers a spectacular view of the starry sky.

ORIENTATION AND PRACTICAL INFORMATION

From the main stop at the Delek gas station, buses #60 and 392 run to **Be'er Sheva** (1hr., Su-Th 5:30am-9:30pm, F 5:30am-2:15pm; NIS22.50, students NIS20). Bus #392 uses Mitzpeh Ramon as a waystation between Be'er Sheva and **Eilat;** it stops for 15 minutes at the gas station and will pick people up if there are empty seats. Drivers are instructed to take 10-minute breaks if they feel drowsy on long desert treks; don't panic if the bus is 10 to 40 minutes late. From the gas station, the tan, flat-roofed **Visitors Center** is visible on the left edge of the crater. Clustered around it are the **youth hostel, Bio-Ramon,** and the crater-rim **promenade.** Cross the street, turn left at the gas station, and then take a right to get to the Visitors Center.

A commercial center containing a **Bank Ha-Poalim** branch is a bit downhill to the right from the gas station, across **Ben-Gurion Blvd.** (open Su, Tu-W 8:30am-12:45pm; M, Th 8:30am-12:30pm and 4-6:30pm; F 8:30am-12:30pm). The **post office** is upstairs behind the bank and across the parking lot. It houses Western Union and offers fax and telegram services, EMS, and Poste Restante. (Emergency ☎630 73 30. Open Su-Tu, Th 8am-12:30pm and 4-6:30pm; W 8am-1pm; F 8am-12:30pm.) **Police** (☎100), **first aid** (☎101 or 658 83 33), and **fire** (☎102) offices are located up the walkway through the small park across Ben-Gurion Blvd. from the commercial center.

ACCOMMODATIONS

Staking out a **campsite** in the middle of the *makhtesh* is **forbidden** and environmentally destructive. Though campers have been known to do it, they run the risk of being awakened by an angry ranger or an even angrier **Asiatic wild ass.** There are inexpensive accommodations both in the town and in the crater, as well as interesting alternatives to hosteling and camping. There are campgrounds in town at the municipal park next to the gas station and at the SPNI field school.

SPNI Field School (☎658 86 15 or 658 86 16; fax 658 83 85) is located directly on the crater's rim and has a trail leading down it. From Camel Observation Point, turn right at the Har Gamal dirt road at the crater's rim, and walk along the black-marked cliffside trail toward the tall antennae. To get to the Observation Point take bus #60 through town or turn left from the Visitors Center and follow the crater-rim promenade about 15min. A/C and private bath. No showers. Reception Su-Th 8am-6pm, F 8am-noon, Sa call ahead. Check-in 3pm. Check-out 8:30am. 6-bed student dorm NIS83; doubles NIS275/US$58; each additional person NIS110; children NIS65. Sleep outside under the bedouin tent (NIS20) or pitch your own (NIS20). MC, V.

Mitzpeh Ramon Youth Hostel (HI) (☎658 84 43; fax 658 80 74; email mitzpe@iyha.org.il), on the canyon's rim, across from the Visitors Center, next to the promenade. Lounge, TV room, dining hall, and spacious rooms. A/C and private baths. Breakfast included. Reception 24hr. Check-in 3pm. Store bags for early arrivals. Check-out 10am. 6-bed dorms NIS89/US$19.50; singles NIS190/US$43.50; doubles NIS260/$US63. HI discount US$1.50. Credit cards accepted.

Be'erot Camping Site, 16km south of Mitzpeh Ramon and nearly impossible to reach without a car. Follow the orange signs after the turn-off on the main highway. This is the only site with bathrooms. Pitch-your-own-tent NIS10; mattress in a Bedouin tent NIS20. Pay the attendant at the Bedouin tent or the Visitors Center.

Desert Eco Lodge by Desert Shade (☎575 68 85 or 658 62 29; 800 222 211; fax 658 62 08) is 10min. past the gas station along the road to Be'er Sheva and marked by an orange sign on the right. Rustic, Bedouin-inspired tents with comfortable beds and excellent views of the crater. Full bathrooms. Vegetarian, Bedouin-style dinner and breakfast included. Dorm tents with your own sleeping bag NIS60. Private room in tent NIS90-120. Cash only.

Succah in the Desert (☎658 62 80; fax 658 64 64; email succah@netvision.net.il; www.succah.co.il), 7km outside town (accessible by foot or car only). Take Ben-Gurion Blvd. past the bank and post office, and turn right onto the road with the alpaca ranch sign. The premises, a haven for artists and hard-core meditators, consists of eight elaborate *succah* structures that generate electricity from solar energy. Vegetarian dinner and breakfast included. Reservations required. Free pick up with advance notice. *Succah* NIS210/US$50, F NIS310/US$65; couples NIS470/US$100, F NIS580/US$125; additional adult US$45 weeknight, US$60 weekend.

FOOD

Before hiking, stock up on fruits and vegetables at the **Hyperneto supermarket** on Ben-Gurion St., in the shopping plaza near the post office (open Su-Th 8am-8pm, F 8am-2pm). While you're there, grab a fresh baguette (NIS3) at the **Bonjour bakery** (open Su-Th 5am-9pm, F 5am-2pm). Most restaurants are closed during Shabbat so stock up on food ahead of time.

Ha-Makhtesh Restaurant, 2 Naḥal Tzihor St. (☎658 84 90), one block below the youth hostel in the green-arched arcade; look for the signs. Offers a profusion of complimentary salads. Kebab, spicy *shishlik,* steak, or schnitzel (NIS25-35) comes with rice or fries. Open Su-Th 10am-10pm, Sa after sundown-10pm.

Ha-Tzukit Restaurant (☎658 60 79), next to the Visitors Center. A/C, a stunning view, and often a lazy family of ibex outside. Sandwiches NIS16; vegetarian meals NIS32; hot meat lunch NIS35. Open daily 9am-5:30pm.

Chana's Restaurant (☎658 81 58), connected to the Delek station. A hangout for locals and soldiers on bus layovers. Baguette sandwiches (NIS10) and meals (NIS25-35) are better than the location suggests. Open Su-Th 5:30am-8pm, F 5:30am-3pm.

SIGHTS AND ENTERTAINMENT

Although Mitzpeh Ramon's center of gravity solidly sits within the fabulous crater, several quirky attractions have sprung up in and around town. There are two spectacular **promenades** on the rim of the crater, one extending in each direction from the Visitors Center. The nighttime desert sky is an amazing sight, as are the desert sculpture gardens along both paths, inspired by the terrain. Sunrises are awe-inspiring; for the best view head to the small building on the left of the highway before the golden orb descends into the crater.

Bio-Ramon (☎658 87 55), downhill from the Visitors Center. Desert lizards, scorpions, and snakes for some pre-hike viewing. NIS8, children and seniors NIS5; ticket with Visitors Center NIS21, children and seniors NIS11. Open Sa-Th 8am-5pm, F 8am-4pm.

Desert Archery (☎658 72 74), a 20min. walk 500m west of the city center. Golf-based bow and arrow game sprawls on a 45-acre course. Equipment, explanation, and limitless playing time NIS35. Call ahead. Cash only.

Alpaca and Llama Ranch (☎658 80 47), 3km west of Mitzpeh Ramon, past Desert Archery. Follow Ben-Gurion Blvd. west to Naḥal Tsiya and turn right on the road toward the field school. 45min. walk until the sign is visible. The largest alpaca and llama ranch outside of South America. Extended horseback riding and camel tours are available with reservations (2hr. horseback or camel ride NIS110); Overnight tours for groups of over 20 people NIS20 per person; students, children, and seniors NIS17. Open daily in summer 8:30am-6:30pm; in winter 8:30am-4:30pm.

Municipal Swimming Pool, behind the bank, near the post office. Sauna and water slide. Non-residents NIS36. Open May-June, Sept.-Oct.: Su 2-8pm, M-Th 2-8pm and 8:30-10:30pm, F 10am-5pm, Sa 9am-5pm. July-Aug.: M-Th 8am-10:30pm, F-Sa 9am-5pm, Su 8am-8:30pm.

Pub Ha-Ḥaveet (☎658 82 26), in the commercial center next door to Bank Ha-Poalim. Astral patterns on the ceiling, blacklight, and mellow Israeli rock make this a popular hangout for soldiers, backpackers, and locals. Beer NIS11-13; drinks NIS17-26; sandwiches NIS15. 18+. Open Su-M, W-Th 8am-midnight; Tu dance party with DJ 8am-4am. Cover Tu NIS20, one drink minimum.

Jeep Tours (☎658 89 58). Peter Bischel masterminds tours of the crater and Negev Desert. Offset the staggering price by squeezing eight people into a car. Half day US$250, full day US$350.

HIKING

Far-flung trailheads are best reached by car or 4x4 vehicle. For trailheads off of the main highway, bus #392 to Eilat travels through the crater and can stop at the turn-off for the Be'erot Camping Site. Locals say hitchhiking on the highway is a safe option, though the highway is not heavily trafficked. However, Let's Go does not recommend hitchhiking.

> **!** Makhtesh Ramon is a spectacular park, but it should not be taken lightly. Always consult with Nature Reserve or SPNI personnel before setting out. Wear a hat, hike as early as possible in the morning, and carry food and 1L of water per person per hour. Heatstroke and dehydration can be deadly in the Negev.

VISITORS CENTER. The Park Ramon Visitors Center, one of two hiking resources in Mitzpeh Ramon, is housed in the round building with the flat top overlooking the crater. Nature Reserve Authority staffers help plan hikes and provide an excellent map of the crater (if only Hebrew maps are available, ask the guides to write English names). It also has a first-rate film, audio-visual presentations, and a rooftop observation deck. The gift shop across the plaza sells detailed 1:50,000 topographical maps (NIS70; Hebrew only) and other information about the crater and the Negev. *(☎658 86 91 or 658 86 98; fax 658 86 20. Open Su-Th, Sa 8am-5pm; F 8am-4pm. NIS18, child NIS9; combo ticket with Bio-Ramon NIS21, children NIS11.)*

SPNI FIELD SCHOOL. The school, located near the edge of the crater, 500m southwest of Camel Observation Point, occasionally offers organized tours (call ahead to schedule). Although the trails are well marked, a pre-hike stop at the Visitors Center for maps is a prudent idea for an unguided expedition. Leave your route description and estimated trip duration at the field school before hiking—they have an on-site rescue team and are in direct communication with army units in the area. While hiking, keep a fix on the main highway or Be'erot Campsite. *(☎658 86 15 or 658 86 16; fax 658 83 85. Open Su-Th 8am-6pm, F 8am-noon.)*

DESERT SHADE. This agency leads excellent tours by foot, mountain bike, and camel (bikes US$50 per day; 1hr. camel ride NIS60). The two-day camel ride along the Nabatean spice route includes food and accommodation (US$99, cash only; min. 6 people, call ahead). The Desert Shade office and ranch (see **Accommodations,** p. 295) is a 15min. walk north from the Delek station on Rte. 40/KKL Blvd.; buses #60 and 392 to Be'er Sheva run past it, but it's faster to walk. (☎58 62 29; fax 658 62 08; 800 222 211. Office open Su-Th 9am-5pm, F 9am-noon.)

HAR ARDON. Har Ardon (Mt. Ardon) is a full-day hike, combining challenging terrain with unbeatable views. To climb Har Ardon, turn left out of the Be'erot campsite and follow the black markers north for 3km to the sign marked Mt. Ardon. From here, follow the blue path on the right to a parking area, where the mountain ascent begins. The steep climb up follows a narrow, white rock trail that changes about halfway up into a smoother and wider trail lined with hills of red and tan rocks. The top of Har Ardon is the heart of the crater; the mountain gives the crater its heart-shaped appearance. From the top, a rainbow of sand colors the crater floor. The descent from the mountain can be quite a physical feat; take it slow since the narrow, white-rock-and-sand trail is steep and slippery. Down the mountain and along the trail in the crater are the remarkable sand and hills of the **Red Valley,** which range in color from yellow to crimson. After passing the black hill of Givat Harut, turn right on the black trail and follow the signs back to the campsite to complete the hike.

WADI ARDON. South of Mt. Ardon, this hike leads past unique geological formations and Nabatean ruins. From the campsite walk along the black-marked trail for half a kilometer, and turn right on a dirt road marked in red. After about 1km take the dirt road on the left marked in black. From the parking lot continue south through Wadi Ardon. Along the colorful borders of Wadi Ardon are a pair of vertical magma intrusions, one big and one small, known as the Father and Son Dikes. To continue on, take the blue path. It points toward **Parsat Nekarot** (the Horseshoe of Crevices), which includes **Sha'ar Ramon** (the Ramon Gate), where water exits the crater. The Parsat Nekarot river bed is flanked by soaring cliffs and cave-like enclaves that make welcome shady stops.

From Parsat Nekarot, follow the blue markings to **Ein Saharonim.** The vegetation lasts all year, but the water evaporates to mere puddles in summer. The remains of a **Nabatean caravanserai** stand at the end of the spring on the right. This is also the spot where animals are most likely to be seen wandering around in search of water sources. To return to the campsite from here, take the orange trail away from Parsat Nekarot. To start hiking from Ein Saharonim, go left from the campsite, and follow the orange trail next to a sign on the right.

HAR SAHARONIM. Along the southern edge of the crater rises **Har Saharonim** (literally, Mountain of the Crescent-Shaped Ornaments). Start the climb from the western side, closest to the main road. Take a right from the campsite and turn left onto the "Oil Pipeline Route" black trail. After about 40min., follow the steep incline past the green trail to Ein Saharonim and the Naḥal Gevanim turn-off. Turn left at the green markers at the top, which lead to "Mt. Saharonim." The green-trail descent from Har Saharonim goes to Ein Saharonim. From there, follow the blue path through Parsat Nekarot in reverse, or return to the road or campsite.

OTHER HIKES. Trailheads for the most interesting hikes are outside of town; two beautiful trails that pass by significant points of geological interest originate in Mitzpeh Ramon. An excellent three-hour hike begins at the end of the western promenade, near the mini-amphitheater, and leads to **Ha-Minsarah** (Carpentry), where piles of prism-like rocks, configured and baked by volcanic heat, resemble carpenters' supplies. Follow the promenade from the Visitors Center. After passing two iron ball sculptures, a green-marked trail makes a rocky descent from the cliff. At the bottom of the crater follow the green trail left to Ha-Minsarah. A dirt road leads east toward the highway.

A turn-off point marked in red along the green Carpentry trail leads south to a five-hour hike along **Ramon's Tooth,** a dark rock formation of cooled magma that was exposed during the crater's creation. The hike also goes past the **Ammonite Wall,** an impressive collection of crustacean fossils embedded in rock. From the red Ammonite Wall path, a black path eventually leads off to the left and to the highway. Bus #392 from Eilat generally comes by on its way to Mitzpeh Ramon (Su-Th around 3 and 5pm).

EILAT
אילת

☎07

Eilat has two goals—to get you tan and to make you poor. The city is soaked with the sweat of rowdy Israelis, international backpackers, and European tourists; the air is abuzz with jet skis and cell phones. Some swear by Eilat's sun, coral, and nightlife, while others see the city as a huge tourist trap attached to a nice beach. In between the cocktails and Coppertone, stick your head in the ocean and you may notice some of the most spectacular underwater life the world's seas have to offer. Above the waves, the wildlife is bikini-clad and muscle-bound.

The busiest times of the year are Passover (Apr. 8-14 in 2001), Sukkot (Oct. 2-9 in 2001), and Israel's summer vacation (July and Aug.), when nearly 100,000 Israelis descend upon the city. Don't fool yourself into thinking that this is a good time to visit. True, there are more parties and crowded pubs, but hostels and restaurants charge double their normal rates, petty theft runs rampant, and every inch of beach crawls with human flesh.

GETTING THERE AND AWAY

Flights: The **airport** (☎636 38 38) is on the corner of Ha-Tmarim Blvd. and Ha-Arava Rd. **Arkia Airlines** (☎638 48 88) flies to: **Haifa** (2 per day, NIS370); **Jerusalem** (2 per day, NIS370); and **Tel Aviv** (every hr., NIS370). **Israir Airlines** (☎634 06 66) flies to Tel Aviv (every hr., NIS268-298).

Buses: Central bus station (☎636 51 20) on Ha-Tmarim Blvd. Reserve tickets at least one day in advance, 3 days during high season. Buses to: **Haifa** (#991; 6hr.; Su, Th 8:30am, 2:30, and 11:30pm; M-W 2:30 and 11:30pm; F 8:30am; Sa 5 and 11:30pm; NIS68); **Jerusalem** (#444; 4½hr.; Su-Th 7, 10am, 2, 5pm; F 7, 10am, 1pm; Sa 4:30 and 7pm; NIS58); and **Tel Aviv** (#394; 5hr.; Su-Th 10 per day, F 7 per day, Sa 8 per day; NIS58). If these are full, it is possible to take a bus to **Be'er Sheva** and transfer. ISIC discounts. Bus schedules change frequently.

GETTING AROUND

City Buses: Bus #15 runs down Ha-Tmarim Blvd. and Ha-Arava Rd., through the hotel area, and past the HI hostel and Coral Beach to **Egypt** (every 20-30min. Su-Th 4:45am-8:30pm, F 4:45am-5pm, Sa 8:30am-8:30pm; NIS2.10-3.20). Buses #1 and 2 run from downtown to the hotel area (every 30min. Su-Th 7am-8pm, F 7am-2:15pm, Sa every 2hr. 10am-6pm; NIS3).

Taxis: King Solomon (☎633 33 38). City rides NIS10; to observatory NIS20; to Egyptian border NIS25-30; to Jordanian border NIS20. Taxi sharing is common. In winter, *sherut* run along the #1, 2, and 15 bus routes.

Car Rental: Hertz (☎637 50 50 or 637 66 82), in Red Canyon Center. 23+. **Budget** (☎637 41 25), in Shalom Center. **Avis** (☎637 31 64), next to the tourist office. All offer similar plans. NIS45/US$11 plus NIS1 per km. or unlimited mileage NIS160-200/US$40-50 per day. Insurance starts at NIS50/US$12 per day; NIS50/US$12 extra per day in high season. Rentals cannot go to Egypt or Jordan. All open 8am-6pm.

Bike Rental: Red Sea Sports (☎633 08 66) in the marina. NIS90 per day. Open Su-Th 8am-9pm, F-Sa 8am-6pm. Rental recommended for winter only.

Scooter Rental: Doobie Scooter (☎633 65 57), in the Dalia Hotel. Just off the promenade, behind the airport. NIS75 for 3hr.; NIS140 per day. Open Su-Th 9am-2pm and 5-7pm, F 9am-3pm.

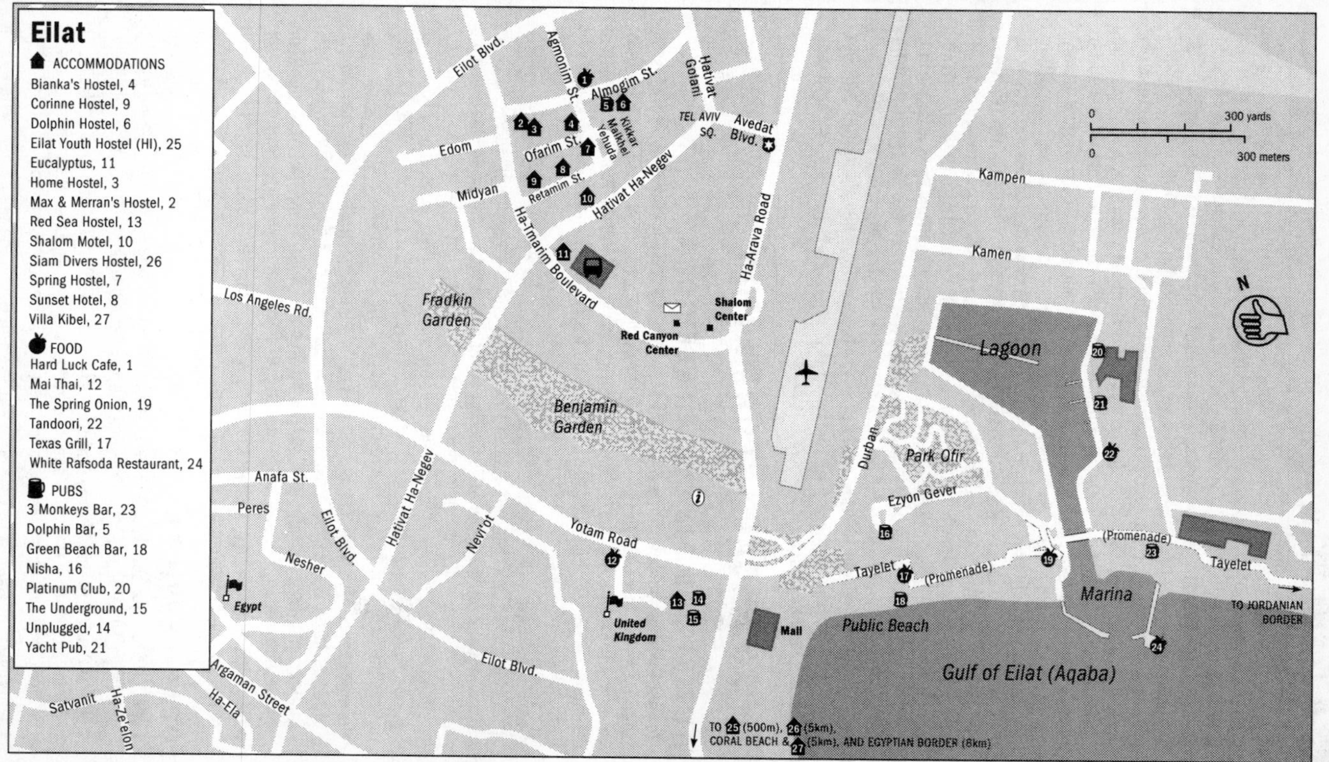
Eilat
ACCOMMODATIONS
Bianka's Hostel, 4
Corinne Hostel, 9
Dolphin Hostel, 6
Eilat Youth Hostel (HI), 25
Eucalyptus, 11
Home Hostel, 3
Max & Merran's Hostel, 2
Red Sea Hostel, 13
Shalom Motel, 10
Siam Divers Hostel, 26
Spring Hostel, 7
Sunset Hotel, 8
Villa Kibel, 27
FOOD
Hard Luck Cafe, 1
Mai Thai, 12
The Spring Onion, 19
Tandoori, 22
Texas Grill, 17
White Rafsoda Restaurant, 24
PUBS
3 Monkeys Bar, 23
Dolphin Bar, 5
Green Beach Bar, 18
Nisha, 16
Platinum Club, 20
The Underground, 15
Unplugged, 14
Yacht Pub, 21
Eilot Blvd.
Agmonim St.
Almogim St.
Hativat Golani
TEL AVIV SQ.
Avedat Blvd.
Kikkar Malkhei Yehuda
Edom
Ofarim St.
Retamim St.
Midyan
Hativat Ha-Negev
Ha-Tmarim Boulevard
Ha-Arava Road
Shalom Center
Red Canyon Center
Los Angeles Rd.
Fradkin Garden
Benjamin Garden
Anafa St.
Peres
Nesher
Egypt
Nevi'ot
Yotam Road
United Kingdom
Argaman Street
Ha-Ela
Satvanit
Ha-Ze'elon
0
300 yards
300 meters
Kampen
Kamen
N
Lagoon
Durban
Park Ofir
Ezyon Gever
Tayelet
(Promenade)
Marina
TO JORDANIAN BORDER
Mall
Public Beach
Gulf of Eilat (Aqaba)
TO 25 (500m), 26 (5km), CORAL BEACH & 27 (5km), AND EGYPTIAN BORDER (8km)

ORIENTATION

Eilat is a 5km strip of coastline on the Negev's sandy bottom, the precarious intersection of Israel, Jordan, Egypt, and Saudi Arabia; at night the lights of all four are visible on the horizon. The city is divided into three sections: the town itself on the hills, the hotel area and Lagoon Beach to the east, and the port to the south.

The main entrance to the central bus station is on **Ha-Tmarim Blvd.,** which crosses the center of the city from the southeast (downhill) to the northwest (uphill). Across the street from the bus station is the **Commercial Center,** with restaurants and cafes. Uphill and to the right are most hostels and cheap restaurants. Walking downhill along the bus station side of Ha-Tmarim Blvd. leads to the **Red Canyon Center,** which resembles a futuristic Bedouin tent and houses the post office, supermarket, and cinema. Farther downhill is the **Shalom Center,** a mall. Ha-Tmarim Blvd. ends here, perpendicular to **Ha-Arava Rd.** If you turn right onto Ha-Arava Rd., you will soon find the main entrance to the Eilat airport on your left. A block past the airport, to the right of the intersection with **Yotam Rd.,** a three-level conglomeration of cheap restaurants and shops calls itself the **New Tourist Center.** On the other side of Yotam Rd. is the tourist office. Ha-Arava Rd. leads to Dolphin Reef, the Coral Beach reserve, the Underwater Observatory, and finally Taba Beach and the Egyptian Border. Bus #15 runs this route (every 15-20min., NIS2-3). Turning left at the intersection of Ha-Arava Rd. and Yotam St. leads to the **promenade** and the **public beach.**

PRACTICAL INFORMATION

TOURIST AND FINANCIAL SERVICES

Tourist Information Center: (☎637 21 11; fax 632 58 67), at the corner of Yotam Rd. and Ha-Arava Rd. Maps and brochures. Will help find accommodations for no commission. Open Su-Th 8am-6pm, F 8am-2pm. **SPNI,** the Society for the Protection of Nature in Israel (☎637 20 21), opposite Coral Beach. Maps and info about local hiking. Open Su-Th 8am-8pm.

Consulates: Egypt, 68 Ha-Efroni St. (☎637 68 82). From the bus station, turn right on Ha-Tmarim Blvd. and left onto Ḥativat Ha-Negev. Continue 900m until Sderot Argaman St., and turn right. Ha-Efroni St. is the first street on the right; look for the flag. Submit a visa application in the morning; pick it up at noon. Visas must be paid for in NIS (US nationals NIS50; South Africans free; all others NIS70). Bring a passport photo. Free Sinai-only visas are available at the border. Open Su-Th 9-11am. **UK** (☎637 23 44), above the New Tourist Center (next to the Adi Hotel). By appointment only.

Currency Exchange: Bank Leumi (☎636 41 11). Open Su, Tu, Th 8:30am-noon and 5-6:30pm; M, W, F 8:30am-noon. **Bank Ha-Poalim** (☎637 61 57). Open Su, Tu, Th 8:30am-noon and 4:30-6pm; M, W, F 8:30am-noon. Both banks are across from the central bus station. The post office exchanges traveler's checks with no commission.

ATM: 24hr. machines (V, MC, Plus, Cirrus) outside Bank Ha-Poalim, next to the post office, and in the marina.

LOCAL SERVICES

Luggage Storage: Left Luggage (☎632 67 73), at the bus station. NIS15 per bag per day. Open Su-Th 6am-12:30am, F 6am-10pm, Sa and holidays 10am-12:30am.

Cultural Center: Phillip Murray Cultural Center (☎637 22 57), on Ḥativat Ha-Negev St. near the bus station. Has a TV, a reading room, and rotating art exhibits. The jazz, classical, rock, film, and theater seasons run Sept.-May. Open daily 8am-8pm.

Laundromat: Kuiskal (☎637 48 38), at the Razin Center, on the corner of Ha-Tmarim Blvd. and Edom St. NIS36 for 6kg full service; NIS25 for self-service. Open Sa-Th 8am-8pm, F 8am-4pm. Hostel services are cheaper.

Camping Equipment: Azimut, The National Center for Hiking Equipment (☎634 11 12), on the bottom floor of the mall at the corner of Yotam Rd. and Ha-Arava Rd. Good selection of pricey gear. Open Su-Th 9:30am-midnight, F 9am-4pm.

EMERGENCY AND COMMUNICATIONS

Emergency: First Aid: (☎637 23 33). **Magen David Adom** first aid stations are located on some beaches. **Police:** (☎633 24 44), on Avdat Blvd. at the eastern end of Ḥativat Ha-Negev. "Lost and found" for packs stolen from the beach.

Pharmacy: Super-Pharm (☎634 08 80), in the mall. Best selection in town. Open Su-Th 9am-midnight, F 9am-4pm, Sa 11am-midnight. **Eilat Pharmacy,** 25 Eilat St. (☎637 50 02). Open Su-Th 8:15am-1:15pm and 4:15-8pm, F 8:15am-2pm. **Michlin Pharmacy** (☎637 24 34), in the Rechter Center, next to Bank Leumi. Open Su-Th 8:30am-2pm and 4-8pm, F-Sa 8:30am-3pm. Delivery services available.

Hospital: Yoseftal Hospital (☎635 80 11), on Yotam Rd. **Maccabee Healthcare Services** (☎676 49 00; emergency ☎633 31 01), on the corner of Eilat St. and Ha-Tmarim Blvd. Modern facility that offers services for dental emergencies.

Telephones: Starcom Gold (☎632 65 27; fax 632 64 94), at the New Tourist Center. Cheaper than the post office or public phones. Offers phone, fax (NIS13), and voice-mail. Open daily 4-11pm.

Internet Access: Internet access in Eilat is easy to find, and prices are standard. **BJ's Books** (☎634 09 05; email bjsbooks@eilatcity.co.il), in the New Tourist Center. NIS30 per hr. Open Su-Th 9:30am-10pm, F 9am-6pm. **Unplugged Internet Bar** (☎632 62 99), next to the Unplugged Bar, in the New Tourist Center. Fast but oddly old-fashioned coin-operated machines accept NIS5 coins for 15min. per coin. Open 24hr.

Post Office: (☎637 44 40), in the Red Canyon Center. Traveler's check cashing, Western Union, Poste Restante. Open Su-Tu and Th 8am-12:30pm and 4-6:30pm, W 8am-1pm, F and holidays 8am-12:30pm.

ACCOMMODATIONS

Finding a cheap room in Eilat is easy. Finding a safe, comfortable, convenient, and cheap room is another story. New arrivals to the bus station are attacked by a gaggle of apartment hawkers. Just say, "lo." Don't get into a cab with a stranger or commit to a room before seeing it. Most hostels are located less than three blocks from the bus station—walk up the hill on Ḥa-Tmarim Blvd. and take a right on Retamim St. The atmosphere of a smaller hostel can add tremendously to the enjoyment of Eilat. Some of the bigger hostels have been known to turn out backpackers in favor of large groups or to have patrons switch rooms in the middle of the night. The tourist office can assist if hostels are full. Vague pricing is easily deciphered; low prices apply during winter, high ones in summer. Always bargain.

There are two camping options in Eilat: expensive and legal or free and illegal. For the latest and greatest info on the former, stop by the SPNI Field School (☎637 20 21), across the street from Coral Beach. SPNI's campsite (NIS20 per person) offers showers and toilets; huts on the campground cost NIS300, but you have to call the Tel Aviv office to reserve ahead (☎(03) 638 86 88). Most hostels allow camping on their roof or in their backyard for NIS15-20. During July and August, hundreds of people ignore the "No Camping" signs on the public beach or in the park; year after year, many are victims of theft. Aside from burglars and sexual harassers, there are also rats at these camps. If sleeping on the ground and taking communal showers sounds appealing, take bus #15 to **Coral Beach Campground,** the municipal campground opposite the beach of the same name. The site's small huts have only their prime location to the reefs to recommend them. (☎637 19 11 or 637 50 63. Breakfast included. Refrigerator NIS10 per day. Pitch-your-own-tent NIS30; huts NIS300.)

Proprietors at resorts, hostels, cafes, discos, and bars are often looking to employ newcomers. Jobs with hotels and hostels generally include lodging and should offer a pittance as well. Unfortunately, most work is under the table, with long hours and miserable wages (about US$400 per month). Workers report that the corner next to the Hard Luck Cafe is a good place to begin the job search. In the marina on the gate leading to the boats there are lists of tourist boats looking for workers. The pay is low, but comes with free room, board, and social life.

Red Sea Hostel (☎637 60 60), in the New Tourist Center directly above the Unplugged and Underground Bars. Location, location, location! These small, crowded rooms are just a beer bottle's throw from the rest of Eilat's hot spots on the promenade. A/C; free safe. Mattress on the roof NIS15; dorms NIS25-30; singles NIS100; doubles NIS120; triples NIS150. Prices double during high season, but bargain anyway, especially for multiple night stays.

Siam Divers Hostel (☎637 05 81), right on Coral Beach. Priority goes to divers, but the location and atmosphere make this a great pick for any traveler. Oddly shaped rooms are simple, with common bath. Only 10min. by bus from Eilat. Dorms NIS60; doubles NIS150; triples NIS180.

Villa Kibel, P.O. Box 8304 (☎/fax 637 69 11; cell 050 345 366; email russell@eliat.ardom.co.il). Fully furnished, upscale apartment-style rooms with TV, mini-fridge, fresh linen, and cooking facilities. Within 1km of the beach; some rooms have ocean view. Two are wheelchair accessible. Call for bus station pick up. Doubles NIS150-220. Larger rooms also available. Prices negotiable, especially for longer stays.

Spring Hostel, P.O. Box 1278 (☎637 46 60; fax 637 46 60), halfway down Retamim St., around the corner. Immaculate but basic rooms. Billiards, pub, a pool, and very tight security. Dorms NIS30-60; singles NIS100-160; doubles NIS120-200.

Max & Merran's Hostel, P.O. Box 83 (☎637 13 33; fax 637 35 13), off Almogim St. Under new ownership and in a new location next to the Home Hostel (they share a courtyard), this hostel has lost none of its friendly atmosphere. Clean and newly built rooms with kitchen and common bathrooms. Dorms NIS25.

Eilat Youth Hostel (HI), P.O. Box 152 (☎637 23 58; fax 637 58 35), on Ha-Arava Rd., one block from the New Tourist Center. This sterile behemoth hosts many Israeli teens. Refrigerators NIS20; TV rental NIS28. Breakfast included; extra meals NIS30. Lockers NIS6 per use. Laundry NIS24 for 6kg. Internet NIS12 for 15min. 7-bed A/C dorms NIS78-89; singles NIS162-190; doubles NIS224-260. Members subtract NIS5.

Sunset Motel (☎637 38 17; cell 052 708 795), halfway down Retamim St. Slightly upscale rooms with small kitchens and bathrooms. All rooms include cable TV, kitchen, fridge, and showers. Check-out 9am. Doubles NIS100-300.

Corinne Hostel, 127/1 Retamim St. (☎637 14 72), just off Ha-Tmarim Blvd. Large, clean, dorm rooms with private bath and A/C. Billiards/game room. Check-out 9am. Dorms NIS25-60; singles NIS60-120; 2-person cabins NIS80-200. AmEx, MC, V.

Bianka's Lodge (☎632 63 35), at the end of Retamim St. One large dorm room with a mock-Bedouin outdoor TV room and plenty of pets. Bianka is a great resource for deals, but some may feel smothered by her love. A/C. Check-out noon (flexible). Dorms NIS25; pitch-your-own-tent NIS20; doubles NIS100; triples NIS120; quads NIS150.

Home Hostel (☎637 24 03; fax 637 35 13), just off Almogim St. behind the Family Bakery. Looks like a backyard shed, but friendly staff and feel-good vibe makes it seem like home. Cheap beer and TV room. Check-out 1pm. Dorms NIS22.

Eucalyptus (☎637 05 92, cell 052 915 867), 100m up Ha-Tmarim Blvd. from the bus station, next to a park. Outdoor sitting area with cable TV becomes spot for late-night drinking. Basic rooms with A/C. Check-out 10am. Dorms NIS25; doubles NIS80-120.

Shalom Motel (☎637 65 44; fax 637 46 83), halfway down Retamim St. Friendly manager is willing to bargain. Clean rooms have mini-furniture and private baths. Check-out 9am. Dorm beds NIS30-60; singles NIS80-160; doubles NIS100-200.

Dolphin Hostel (☎637 04 19, cell 053 753 847), on Almogim St. Attached to the cheapest bar in town. Dorm beds with common bath NIS20.

FOOD

Many falafel stands, pizzerias, and sandwich vendors crowd Ha-Tmarim Blvd. near the bus station and on Retamim St. by the hostels. Burger-lovers rejoice: McDonald's is in the waterfront mall, and Burger King shares the tourist office building. Over the past few years, ethnic food in Eilat has boomed: the streets are now lined with inexpensive Chinese, Thai, Mediterranean, and Italian restaurants.

Since many accommodations in Eilat provide cooking facilities, backpackers can eat inexpensive food from the supermarket at Eilat St. and Ha-Tmarim Blvd. (Look for the blue and white squares on the building. Open Su-Th 7:30am-10pm, F 7:30am-2pm.) Closer to the center of town is **SuperKolbo Supermarket** in the Rekhter Commercial Center. (Open Sa-Th 7am-midnight, F 7am-9pm.) **Shekem Supermarket** is in the Red Canyon Center. (Open Su-Th 8:30am-midnight, F 8:30am-2:30pm.) There are three great bakeries on Ha-Tmarim St. north of the bus station.

Pedro's Steak House, 14 Ye'elim St. (☎637 95 04). Moderately expensive, but unbelievable food. A local favorite. Steak NIS63; ostrich NIS75; vegetarian options NIS38. Don't miss the freshly baked bread (NIS2) or the divine creme brulee. Open daily 5-11:30pm.

Tandoori (☎633 38 79), in the Lagoon Hotel on the King's Wharf. Excellent Indian food. Very friendly waitstaff will help arrange a menu to meet a lower budget. Filling 3-course lunch special (NIS49). Great curry (NIS30-50) and *naan* (NIS5-16). Open daily noon-3:30pm and 7pm-1am.

The Spring Onion (☎637 74 34), at the marina. This popular vegetarian and dairy restaurant serves fresh salads and pasta (NIS30-40) and offers a wide selection of tea and coffee. Large breakfast NIS32; fish NIS50. Open daily 8am-3am. AmEx, MC, Visa.

Malibu Restaurant (☎634 19 90), adjacent to Siam Divers, near the end of Coral Beach. A great place to get a sandwich (NIS16) on the beach or dinner on the dock. Dinner specials NIS60; pizzas NIS28-35. Open daily 10am-midnight.

Mai Thai (☎637 25 17), on Yotam Rd. just uphill from the New Tourist Center, overlooking the city. A bit expensive, but a treat. Try the egg rolls (NIS15) or get a set menu for two (NIS78). Main course NIS40-47. Open daily 1-3:30pm and 6:30-11pm.

Texas Grille (☎633 88 80), on the Promenade near the Neptune Hotel. Americans will find themselves at home with the Texas-sized portions of ribs, steak, and chicken (NIS49-59). Salads and sandwiches NIS40. Open 1pm-1am.

Tiramisu (☎637 00 03), in the Hotel "La Coquille" near the airport. Small, relatively inexpensive Italian restaurant with a large bar and fair selection of wines. Pizzas start at NIS30 and pastas at NIS36. Special tourist 3-course meal (NIS50).

The White Rafsoda (☎633 91 99 or 633 91 11), on the pier next to the marina. Massive new restaurant caters to those who can't decide what to eat: it's divided into Thai, Japanese, Italian, and Mediterranean quarters. Beautiful view of the sea. Full meal NIS40-80. After 11pm, music in the Upper Deck Club upstairs turns from mellow to techno. Restaurant open Su-F 5pm-midnight, Sa opens at 1pm, club open all night.

Mandy's (☎637 22 38), in the Coral Reef next to Aqua Sport. Chinese restaurant with simple bamboo interior. Large selection of meat and vegetarian dishes. Entrees NIS20-40. Open Su-F noon-3pm and 6:30pm-midnight, Sa noon-midnight. AmEx, MC, V.

Hummus Assli (☎632 66 10), across Eilot St. on Ha-Tmarim Blvd., the first restaurant on the left. Four varieties of the best hummus in town (NIS15-20). Dine in or take-out. Open daily 8am-2am.

Sultan Restaurant (☎637 10 15), across the street and 150m uphill from the bus station. With a view overlooking the gulf, this open-air Middle Eastern diner serves *shawarma* (NIS15-18), falafel (NIS9-15), full meals (NIS9-22), and Guinness (NIS12).

SIGHTS

UNDERWATER

Eilat's brilliant underwater world is filled with marine creatures: from undignified blubberfish to regal emperorfish, which frolic in a psychedelic coral paradise. The city has long served as the center of Red Sea diving—with its warm waters and a wide variety of unusual marine life, it's not surprising that it has continued to thrive as a major dive resort. Although dive sites in Eilat are less pristine than many in Sinai, they are the most technically advanced and safest areas to dive in the Red Sea. All dive centers provide modern equipment and multilingual guides and instructors. Eilat also offers a fully equipped and professionally operated recompression chamber at the local hospital, which is within 12 minutes of all dive sites. All of the following sites are accessible by a short snorkel or truck ride from the major dive centers along Coral Beach. For an up-to-date list of dive sites and activities, try www.Eilat.net.

JAPANESE GARDENS. Arguably the finest in Eilat, this dive site gets its name from the placid, "manicured" look of the coral, which almost completely covers the sandy bottom. Sushi and *sashimi*-lovers will be glad to know that the Japanese Gardens are home to the most plentiful fish life in Eilat. *(Take bus #15; 10min. from the central bus station. Entrance is on the right by the underwater observatory. Diving available only through established dive clubs (see below); snorkeling is free and open to the public.)*

CORAL BEACH NATURE RESERVE. This national reserve (which includes Moses' and Joshua's Rocks) offers a wealth of coral species and fish life, making the entry fee well worthwhile. Five water trails marked by buoys go through the reef, and two bridges into the water protect coral from human feet and vice versa. *(Take bus #15 from the central bus station toward the sea. ☎637 68 29. Open Sa-Th 9am-6pm, F 9am-5pm. NIS18, children NIS9. Lockers NIS6.)*

DOLPHIN REEF. The commercially operated scuba and snorkeling center at Dolphin Reef allows divers to observe semi-wild dolphins in a somewhat natural environment. Although the project has raised some ethical eyebrows, the dolphins are free to swim away at any time (although it would be difficult for any mammal to refuse a free feeding, as most budget travelers will agree). The dolphins perform a variety of tricks daily at the four "interaction" sessions, but observing them underwater is a more rewarding experience. The four original dolphins brought from the Black Sea have added seven new babies to the group. *(Beyond the port on bus #15. ☎637 18 46. Open daily 9am-5pm. NIS29, children NIS22. Interaction sessions every 2hr. 10am-4pm. Snorkeling NIS202, children NIS193. Beach open and free after 5pm.)*

SCUBA RENTAL AND TOURS

Siam Divers (☎637 05 81; fax 637 10 33; email siamdive@netvision.net.il; www.siam.co.il), at the end of Coral Beach next to the Nature Reserve. While many may initially be attracted to the high-gloss finish of the larger dive clubs, this is the friendliest, safest, and most experienced dive center in Eilat. For more info, email or write to: P.O. Box 1020, Eilat 88000, Israel. Introductory dives (no certificate necessary) NIS160; 2 guided dives with full equipment NIS170; 5-day open water course NIS790/US$190. Extremely convenient dorms NIS60, with course NIS40. Unforgettable 3- to 5-day dive safaris to Sinai start at NIS1600/US$340. 10% student discount.

Red Sea Sports Club (☎637 65 69 or 637 00 68; fax 637 06 55; email manta1@netvision.net.il), in the Ambassador Hotel; also has an office at the King Solomon Hotel. PADI open-water courses NIS1164/US$291; dives with dolphins NIS265/US$56. Office on North Beach near the lagoon offers windsurfing (NIS68 per hr.), water-skiing (NIS120 for 15min.), and parasailing (NIS150 for 10min.). Also arranges horseback riding lessons at the nearby **Texas Ranch.** (☎632 65 02. 1hr. NIS150; 2hr. NIS170; 4hr. NIS235.)

Aquasport, P.O. Box 300 (☎633 44 04; fax 633 37 71; email info@aqua-sport.com; www.aqua-sport.com), on Coral Beach next to Siam Divers. This large and active beachfront houses a PADI-certified diving center (open water beginner course NIS1100/ US$275) and windsurfing rentals (NIS75 per hr.).

UNDERWATER OBSERVATORIES

The **Coral World Underwater Observatory and Aquarium** features shark and turtle tanks and an underwater observation room. Though interesting, it is best for those who won't be snorkeling. (☎637 66 66. Open Sa-Th 8:30am-5pm, F and holiday eves 8:30am-3pm. NIS63, children NIS145.) Live a life of ease beneath the sea of green in the observatory's **Yellow Submarine,** which goes 60m below the surface. (☎637 66 66. Admission to observatory and submarine NIS255, children NIS145.) The **Galaxy** is one of the city's many glass-bottomed boats. (☎631 63 60. 1½hr. NIS60.) The **Jules Verne Explorer** may not venture 20,000 leagues down, but full glass walls make it a true underwater observatory. (☎633 36 66. 2hr. cruise to the Japanese Gardens NIS80.) Both the Galaxy and the Jules Verne Explorer can be found at the marina.

IN THE AIR

Some say that the best of Eilat's wildlife is in the air. Avid birdwatchers flock to the salt ponds north of the lagoon mid-February through May and mid-September through November, when 30 species fly overhead on their way to or from Africa. The **International Birdwatching Center (IBC),** P.O. Box 774, Eilat 88106, near the northern end of the airport on Eilat St., runs walking tours (US$5) and jeep tours (US$50). There's a bird watching festival in March. Contact the IBC for more information. (☎633 53 39. Open Su-Th 9am-1pm and 5-7pm, F 9am-1pm.)

Visitors pretend to be birds at the skydiving simulator **Airodium** (☎637 27 45), behind the Riviera Hotel. An air-vent contraption makes for an expensive but fun 10 minutes (NIS120). For stimulation beyond simulation, jump with **Skydive Red Sea** (☎633 23 86), P.O. Box 4139, Eilat 88150.

ENTERTAINMENT

Eilat's nightlife offers a little bit of everything: beer swilling with hard-core backpackers, dancing with greased-up Israelis, and hobnobbing with affluent yuppies. Most bars open at lunchtime, though drinking often starts earlier. Nightclubs open at 10:30-11pm, get going around midnight, and don't close until 5 or 6am. The discos are expensive (NIS25-30) and centered in the lagoon area; shorts and sandals are a bad idea, and Day-Glo bras are the norm. The best parties are hosted by the elusive Red Sea Productions. The free and mellow **promenade** along the water offers some of Israel's most efficient people-watching—the visible-flesh-per-capita index is the highest in the country. Street vendors sell cheap jewelry and 5-minute portraits, and Israeli studs try in vain to pick up the ladies. People start arriving at about 9:30pm and stay for most of the night.

Eilat's entertainment is not exclusively limited to bars and clubs. The tourist office has information on events at the **Phillip Murray Cultural Center** (see p. 300). Kids of all ages like **Luna Park** (☎(05) 031 50 49), in front of the Queen of Sheba Hotel. Bumper cars and pirate ships cost NIS10; kiddie thrills are NIS5. (Open M-Sa 6pm-midnight.) The end-of-August international **Red Sea Jazz Festival,** with ten daily performances on four stages, is Eilat's most popular annual event. Ask the tourist office for information.

Unplugged (☎632 62 99), in the New Tourist Center. Loud music and big TVs. Free Sony Play Station, Sa karaoke, and foosball attract the masses. Cheap coin-operated Internet (NIS5 for 15min.). Happy hour 4-9pm: NIS7 for ½L local beer; daiquiris NIS9. Heineken NIS12; local beers NIS7-15. Open 24hr.

Green Beach (☎637 70 32), on the promenade close to the shopping mall. A sprawling beach bar frequented by beautiful people at all hours. During the day, scantily clad waiters shoot water guns to cool the crowd, and at night they keep the liquor and coffee coming–whatever you need to stay until the sun rises over the Red Sea. Half liter drafts NIS11 and up; cocktails NIS26 and up; coffee NIS8. Open 24hr.

Nisha (☎631 55 55), in the basement of the Neptune Hotel. This dance bar is Eilat's trendiest and craziest night spot. Reserved for the chic and beautiful. Travelers are advised to pull out their best duds for this place. Beer NIS12 and up; cocktails NIS26 and up. Cover NIS20-40. Open daily 11:30pm-4:30am.

Dolphin Reef (☎637 18 46), just before Coral Beach. The place to be on Th once the dolphins have gone to sleep. Beach parties are known as the kinkiest in Eilat. Open daily until sunset and Th 11:30pm-4:30am. Th cover NIS50-80.

Dolphin Bar (☎637 04 19), on Algomim St., across the street from the Hard Luck Cafe, conveniently close to most hostels. Escape Eilat's exorbitant prices in this hole-in-the-wall pub, which serves the cheapest beer in town. Half liter bottles of Tuborg NIS2.50. Billiards and Internet (NIS5 for 15min.) available. Open 24hr.

3 Monkeys (☎636 88 88), in the Royal Beach Hotel toward the end of the promenade. Features nightly live British band. Packed with tourists. Local brews start at NIS13, but imported beers go for as high as NIS28; cocktails around NIS30. Open 9pm-3:30am.

Yacht Pub (☎636 34 44), on the marina by King Solomon's Wharf. Huge, with a fancy bar. Upscale Israeli clientele and prices to match. Platinum blondes and platinum disco records. Huge 1L Carlsberg NIS23; cocktails around NIS25. Happy hour 10-11pm: 2 for 1 drinks. Open daily 10pm-4am. No cover, but must spend at least NIS20 at the bar.

Hemingway's Hard Luck Cafe, 15 Almogim St. (☎634 33 22). Its proximity to the hostels has made the Hard Luck a place for travelers, both transient and resident, to eat, drink, and compare how broke they are. Beer and wonderfully greasy pub food, but no rock memorabilia. Carnivores can devour the mixed grill and chips, but veggies are stuck with spaghetti. Most meals go for NIS15. Carlsberg NIS4. Single women might appreciate a companion (male or female). Open daily 8am-3am.

The Underground (☎637 02 39), in the New Tourist Center under the Red Sea Hotel. Terrific freebie specials: free food at 6pm with the purchase of any drink; every 4th beer is free. Pint of Carlsberg NIS9, pitcher NIS27. Spaghetti or eggs and beans NIS18. Internet NIS7 for 15 min. Daily videos and live football at 4:30pm. Open daily 11am-6am.

Platinum (☎636 34 44), in the King Solomon Hotel. Upscale, ultra-modern club where the laser show enhances the disco, pop, and new wave dance experience. Energetic bartenders and strong drinks, but dance space is dominated by scantily clad Israeli teenagers. Cover NIS45, F NIS65; includes one drink. Open daily 11pm-5am. 18+.

Tarabin Pub, across from the airport. Bedouin-tent meets rave atmosphere somewhat successfully. Local beer NIS10; imported NIS15; mixed drinks NIS20. Cover NIS20; includes one drink. Open 9pm-5am.

HIKING

The beauty of the red granite mountains towering over Eilat matches that of the coral reefs thriving beneath it. The **SPNI Field School,** across from Coral Beach (bus #15), is an essential stop for independent hikers. It sells extensive trail maps and provides good advice on hikes. (☎637 20 21. Open Su-Th 8am-4pm.) Many of the sites are accessible by northbound bus #393, 394, or 397. Buses fill up fast during high season and on Sundays and Fridays—make reservations at the central bus station two days in advance.

There are countless safari companies, which offer jeep tours. These include **Egged Tours** (☎636 51 23), in the bus station, **Johnny Tours** (☎632 52 65), in the Marine Bridge House, and **Red Sea Sports** (☎633 08 66), also in the Bridge House. Half-day tours cost NIS80-190. **Camel Ranch** (☎637 00 22), inland from Coral beach, offers half-day camel excursions (NIS155; book one day in advance).

MT. TZFAḤOT. The hike to Mt. Tzfaḥot is convenient and offers great views. The green-and-white trail begins at the left end of the fence separating the highway from the field school complex. The climb to the summit takes 45 minutes. From here, the blue trail heads north, ending at the Club Inn Hotel near Aqua Sport beach. The round-trip takes about two hours and makes a good evening outing. If you wander too far on paths leading south, you may end up in Egypt.

RED CANYON. The most exciting and accessible terrain north of Eilat includes **Ein Netafim, Mt. Shlomo,** and **Ha-Kanyon Ha-Adom** (Red Canyon). Buses will stop nearby upon request. From Red Canyon, hike to the lookout above **Moon Valley,** a pocked canyon in Egypt, and to the unusual **Amram's Pillars.** These hikes are not advisable in summer; October through April is the best hiking season. Before attempting any of these hikes, consult SPNI (see **Tourist Offices,** p. 300). SPNI also runs guided hikes to Moon Valley; call its Tel Aviv office for details (☎(03) 638 86 75).

TIMNA NATIONAL PARK. Timna National Park is another hiking destination. The 6000-year-old Timna copper mines remain a fascinating destination. Some people believe the Israelites passed through here on their way out of Egypt. The park houses remains of workers' camps and cisterns dating from the 11th century BCE. The sandstone **King Solomon's Pillars** dominate the desert at a height of 50m near the 14th-century BCE Egyptian Temple of Hathor. The park's lake offers **camping** facilities (including showers) and a restaurant on its artificially created shores. *(Most buses that go to Tel Aviv or Jerusalem will stop at the sign for Alipaz. Don't get off at the Timna Mines signpost; the entrance is 2km away, which is too far to walk in summer.* ☎*635 62 15; fax 637 25 42. Open daily 7:30am-6pm. NIS27, ages 5-18 NIS21.)*

ḤAI BAR BIBLICAL NATURE RESERVE. Most northbound buses will stop at the Ḥai Bar Biblical Nature Reserve, a wildlife park designed to breed animals indigenous in Biblical times, many of which have become rare in the region. The reserve has an impressive predator center, where 11 native predators can be seen in their habitats. There is also a nocturnal room, where night-time animalia can be viewed. The bulk of the preserve is a game park, home to ostriches, wild asses, antelopes, addaxes, and oryxes. *(The center is a 20min. walk (very hot in summer) from the bus stop. The entrance to Ḥai Bar is opposite Kibbutz Samir, 2km south of Yotvata. (*☎*637 60 18. Open Su-Th 8:30am-5pm, F-Sa 8:30am-3pm. NIS30, children NIS14, plus NIS5 for a mandatory guide. Those without cars can only see the predator center and nocturnal room. NIS18, children NIS5.)*

KIBBUTZ YOTVATA. One of Israel's oldest kibbutzim is Kibbutz Yotvata, producer of the most delicious chocolate milk *(shoko)* in the world. At Kibbutz Yotvata, the **Ye'elim Desert Holiday Village** has tent space for NIS100. A **swimming pool** is free for guests. Munch on Yotvata's famous cheese and yogurt at the **cafeteria.** *(*☎*637 43 62. Check-in 10pm.)*

WEST BANK

الضفة

For the first time in history, the Palestinian flag flies over many towns in the West Bank, but the process by which self-rule was established has been long and arduous, the struggle is far from over, and the outcome is unpredictable. Daily fluctuations in Israeli-Palestinian relations and extremist actions on both sides frequently disrupt daily life, but well-informed and cautious travelers will have no problem visiting the area's major sites. Tourists may be invited into Palestinian homes, where hot spiced tea and muddily delicious coffee are accompanied by discussions of the *intifada* and occupation. Modest dress will make both men and women's experiences more enjoyable. The Israeli **settlements** are close to many Palestinian towns, but don't expect transportation between the two. The best way to visit a settlement is to go back to Jerusalem and catch a bus from there.

HIGHLIGHTS OF THE WEST BANK

Sip coffee at one of **Ramallah's** (p. 311) hip cafes and groove to live Arab music.

The city of **Jericho** (p. 306) shines as a center of Palestinian renewal and houses the ancient ruins of **Hisham's palace,** a stunning example of early Islamic architecture.

Near Jericho, the **Wadi Qelt** (p. 310) offers a brilliant hike and is the closest place to Jerusalem to enjoy the striking beauty of the desert landscape.

GETTING THERE

Visiting the West Bank from Israel is possible with a private car; expect numerous Israeli checkpoints and bring your passport. Most public transportation connections are from Jerusalem, with Ramallah serving as a major hub for the northern West Bank. Check with the Israeli tourist office before going; they'll probably issue a standard governmental warning worthy of serious consideration, but some may find the warning heavy-handed and decide to go anyway.

SAFETY WARNING. In the recent past, the West Bank has seen considerable conflict between Palestinian residents and Israeli settlers and security forces. Carry your passport at all times. Be aware of the situation in each town before visiting. Avoid visiting on the anniversaries of uprisings or terrorist attacks. Do not travel if Israel has just announced a new building program or territorial acquisition. Visibly Jewish travelers may be in danger and should cover *kippot* with a baseball cap.

When visiting cities in the West Bank or Gaza be sure to pick up the colorful **"This Week in Palestine,"** available in hotel lobbies and restaurants in the West Bank and East Jerusalem. Published monthly, it has an extensive listing of events and resources throughout the Palestinian Territories. The pamphlet is published by Jerusalem Media and Communication Center, 7 Nablus Rd. (☎581 97 77; fax 582 95 34; email ptw@jmcc.org; www.jmcc.org), in East Jerusalem.

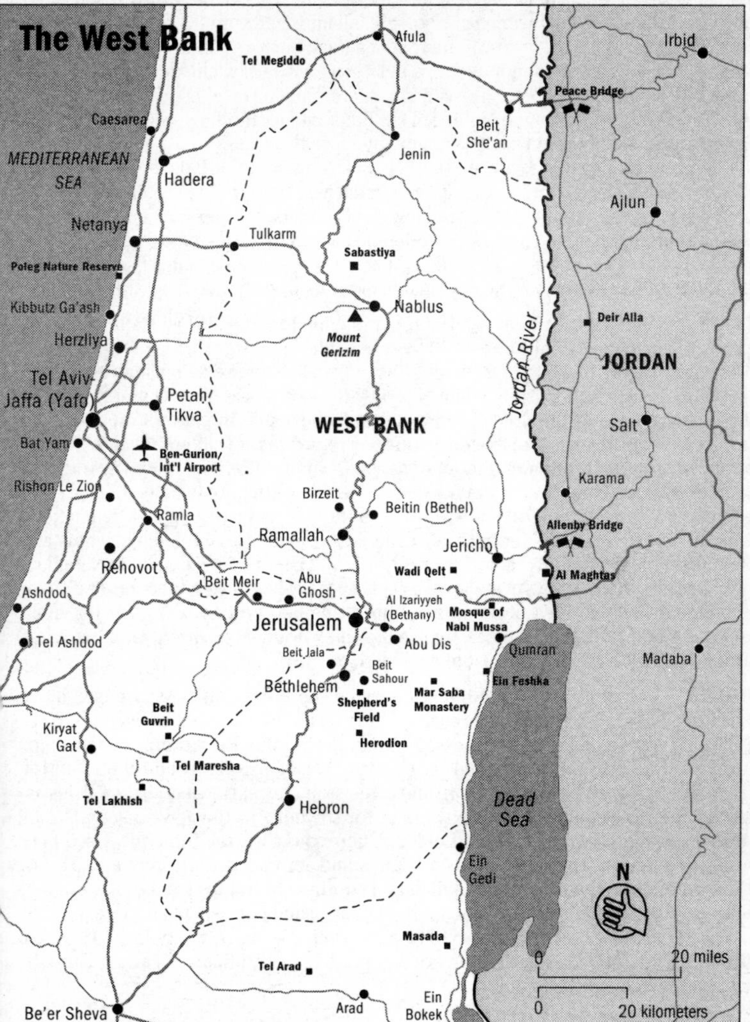

GETTING AROUND

A system of colored **license plates** differentiates vehicles. Those registered in Israel, Jerusalem, and Jewish settlements have yellow plates. White plates with green numbers belong to vehicles registered with the Palestinian Authority. Blue plates are a remnant from the days when the Palestinian territories were the Occupied Territories; they signify Arab cars not registered with Israel. Others are black-on-white (UN or diplomatic), red (police), white on green (Palestinian taxis and buses), and black (army). It's probably safer to travel with white or blue plates here (the opposite is true in Israel), but many Arab-owned cars that are registered in Israel proper (thus with yellow plates) travel hassle-free in the West Bank.

East Jerusalem is the transportation hub for the West Bank, but travel restrictions have made it impossible for non-Jerusalemite Palestinians to use Jerusalem as a transit terminal. As a result, many lines have been re-routed to Ramallah; its Manara Circle is a hub for connections between East Jerusalem and northern West Bank cities. When possible, however, it is preferable to travel from Jerusalem into the West Bank rather than from one West Bank city to another, since direct roads from Jerusalem can often cut travel time by more than half.

One great and easy way to see the West Bank is to hire a Palestinian guide for the day. Alternative Tourism Group (see **Bethlehem Tours,** p. 313) is a reliable company with excellent guides. Alternatively, look for a taxi driver who speaks decent English (there are many) and ask whether he can drive by the major sights. Specify how many hours you wish to spend and agree on a price in advance; something in the range of NIS45 per hour is reasonable for transportation and waiting time.

TAXIS. Shared *service* taxis are the recommended mode of West Bank transportation (*"service,"* pronounced ser-veece, the equivalent of Israeli *sherut*). Although slightly more expensive than Arab buses, they are faster, more reliable, and more frequent, departing whenever they fill with passengers. If you get lost or disoriented, consult the drivers; they are knowledgeable in matters ranging from politics to the location of obscure ruins. Private taxis (called *"special,"* pronounced spay-shal) are much more expensive but are often the only way to get to remote sites. Be sure to bargain for a price before getting in; usually, they are not equipped with a meter. Drivers will drive to the site and (for a few extra shekels) wait around to make the return trip. Some West Bank cities, including Nablus and Ramallah, have adopted a color convention for taxis: yellow cabs are private, and orange cabs are *service.* As always, insist that the driver turn on the meter if there is one and have an idea of an appropriate price beforehand. Even for the most remote sites, do not pay more than NIS50 per hour. Most local rides average around NIS10; none should cost any more than NIS15.

BUSES. Both Arab and Egged buses service the West Bank. Arab buses leave from two bus stations in East Jerusalem: the Suleiman St. Station between Herod's Gate and Damascus Gate for the south; and the Nablus Rd. Station (a few steps away) for the north. Catch Egged buses at the West Jerusalem central bus station on Jaffa Rd. Egged buses cost more and often stop only at the outskirts of Palestinian towns. However, they are convenient for traveling to the Jewish settlements. Arab bus schedules to the West Bank are unpredictable; the intervals listed here are approximate. Transportation to Nablus and Jericho is especially erratic. For the former, take a *service* to Ramallah and continue to Nablus from there. For Jericho, go first to Abu Dis or al-Izariyyeh (Bethany) and connect from there.

To: **Bethlehem** (every 15min., NIS2); **al-Izariyyeh** (Bethany; every hr., NIS2); **Abu Dis** (every hr., NIS2); **Ramallah** (every 30min., NIS3); and **Nablus** (Tamini Bus Co., every hr., NIS6).

MONEY

The **new Israeli shekel (NIS)** is the currency most frequently used (see p. 38), although **Jordanian dinars (JD)** and **U.S. dollars (US$)** are also sometimes accepted. Expect prices to increase when paying in foreign currency. ATMs are not nearly as common as in Israel, though most cities have at least one equipped bank. Traveler's checks and credit cards are also less recognized, so carry enough cash.

KEEPING IN TOUCH

The **postal service** in the West Bank is, for now at least, a part of the Israeli mail system. All major towns in the West Bank have at least one post office with **Poste Restante.** Letters should be addressed, for example, "Angela KUO, Poste Restante, Main Post Office, Town, West Bank, via Israel" (see p. 55). The Palestinian Authority in Jericho has its own postal system, with Palestinian stamps that are currently good only for sending letters between Jericho and Gaza.

The **telephone** system is also part of the Israeli telephone network. All services, including collect and calling-card calls, are available from any private or public telephone. Shekel-operated phones are available in the West Bank, but public phones can be difficult to find. Blue-colored **Telecard-operated phones** are conveniently located in most post offices, where cards can also be purchased, but these new telecard phones do not accept Israeli Bezeq cards.

The international phone code for the West Bank is the same as that of Israel (972), although it's rumored it will change to 970. Relevant area codes are 02 for Bethlehem, Ramallah, and the south, and 09 for Nablus and the north.

POLITICAL HISTORY

For those who seek the truth, discussing West Bank politics is likely to be disappointing and confusing—everyone has his own opinion. Nevertheless, no one wants to talk about anything else, and eliminating personal ideology and emotion from the conversation is inevitably difficult. Historically, the West Bank represents the most complex facet of the Arab-Israeli conflict, due to its relevance to three major groups: Palestinian Arabs, Israelis, and Jordanians. Palestinian Arabs form the region's largest indigenous group and have resided throughout Israel and the West Bank for hundreds of years. Jews lived in the West Bank long before the 1967 and even the 1948 wars. For the most part, Jews were drawn to the holy city of **Hebron** (see p. 332), but in 1929 they fled the city after an Arab massacre claimed 80 Jewish lives. Over 70% of the Jordanian population is of Palestinian origin.

The political region now called the West Bank was created in the 1948 Arab-Israeli War, when Jordan conquered the "west bank" of the Jordan River (see p. 13). The Jordanian government subsequently did little to develop the West Bank and discriminated against its Palestinian residents. Overall, Palestinians in the West Bank fared slightly better than those in the Egyptian-occupied Gaza Strip, since the fertile West Bank was economically vital to Jordan.

In the 1967 Six-Day War (see p. 14), Israel captured the West Bank, placing the area under temporary military administration (except for East Jerusalem, which was annexed). Arab mayors and police kept their offices, Jordanian school curriculums continued to be taught, public welfare programs were established, National Social Security payments made, and Israeli medical treatment instituted.

Israeli occupation was not all benevolent, however. Because the area was administered under martial law, basic rights granted to Jews and Israeli Arabs were denied the Palestinians, who suffered curfews and mass arrests. Houses were destroyed in retaliation for the terrorist actions of one family member. There was no freedom of assembly—Palestinians could not have weddings without permits from Israeli authorities. Flying the Palestinian flag was illegal, and the infrastructure, schools, and public works of the West Bank were neglected in comparison with those of Israel proper. Palestinian attempts at establishing economic independence were thwarted. **Birzeit University** (see p. 330) was denied a building permit for years and shut down frequently.

Israeli settlements in the West Bank were, and continue to be, a source of constant controversy. Some 160,000 Israeli Jews have settled in the West Bank since 1967. Launched by Labor governments eager to establish an Israeli presence in areas of strategic importance such as the Jordan Valley, the settlement project has been an ideological cornerstone of right-wing Likud governments since 1977. The settlements are motivated primarily by strategic considerations, but also by the desire to maintain the historical boundaries of *Eretz Yisrael* (the biblical land of Israel), an area including Israel, the West Bank, the Gaza Strip, and a bit beyond. Often strategically situated on hilltops overlooking Palestinian towns, some settlements resemble military installations more than housing developments.

In December 1987, the Palestinians of the occupied territories launched the **intifada;** two decades of occupation, economic stagnation, and increasing Israeli settlement erupted into stone-throwing, demonstrations, the unfurling of the Palestinian flag, and other expressions of nationalism. The *intifada* (see p. 16) led to major changes in the nature of the Palestinian-Israeli conflict. The populist nature of the uprising and the televised suppression by the Israeli army managed to draw more international attention than decades of PLO terrorism.

After about six years of continued struggle, many Palestinians were worn out. The *intifada* had stopped making headlines by the time the **Gulf Crisis** began in 1991. In contrast to most Arab governments in the region, which joined a US-led coalition opposing Saddam Hussein, the PLO and most Palestinians supported Iraq. Palestinians cheered from rooftops when dozens of Iraq's SCUD missiles landed on Israel, which wasn't involved in the war. Saudi Arabia and other oil-rich Gulf states, whose financial support had been trickling through the PLO into the territories, suspended their aid.

In the aftermath of the Gulf War, Middle Eastern governments became convinced that it was high time for a regional peace conference. Since the historic Madrid conference in October 1991, negotiations have gone on intermittently. Most recently, Israel's twenty-year occupation of southern Lebanon came to a close. Current prime minister Ehud Barak hoped the pullout would indicate Israeli good will and encourage peace-talks with neighboring Syria. For more information, see **The Peace Process,** p. 17.

ECONOMY

The economy of the West Bank has depended on that of Israel since the 1967 occupation. The West Bank felt Israel's economic crises even more sharply than did Israelis, since Palestinians were the first to be laid off in times of hardship. Many West Bank Palestinians continue to work in Israel with no health insurance, job security, or workers' rights.

The West Bank economy was a major battleground of the *intifada*. Palestinians boycotted Israeli products in an attempt to rid themselves of crippling economic dependence, and in return, the Israeli government imposed economic sanctions on the Palestinian community. The Palestinian Authority has inherited a stagnant economy and an undeveloped and outdated infrastructure. Support from foreign nations including Sweden and Japan in recent years has helped Palestinian development get on its feet. Today, perhaps the most common sight in cities like Bethlehem and Ramallah is the construction of new buildings to house growing businesses, as well as residences.

LITERATURE

Much recent Palestinian literature concerns the agony of foreign occupation and exile, touching also on the themes of reconciliation with the Israelis. Ghassan Kanafani, perhaps the greatest contemporary Palestinian fiction writer, recreates the desperation and aimlessness of the refugee in his short stories *All That Remains: Palestine's Children* and *Men in the Sun and Other Palestinian Stories*, which portrays the struggle through adult eyes. His *Return to Haifa* is an electrifying account of a face-to-face encounter between an exiled Palestinian family and an elderly Jewish couple who are Holocaust survivors. The poetry of Mahmoud Darwish depicts Palestinians' attachment to the land. The poems of Fouzi al-Asmar, collected in *The Wind-Driven Reed and Other Poems*, share the longing for a homeland. Jabra Ibrahim Jabra's novel *The Ship* is engrossing, as is his autobiography *The First Well*, an idyllic account of his Christian upbringing in Bethlehem. In his *Wild Thorns*, Sahar Khalifeh describes an expatriate's return to Palestine and his conversion from an intellectual to an ideologically committed terrorist. Israeli Arab Anton Shammas's *Arabesques* documents Palestinian identity crises; Fawaz Turki's autobiographical tomes discuss life in exile. The works of Liyana Badr, Raymonda Tawil, and Samih al-Qassem all deserve note; most of these authors and others are translated in Salma Khadra Jayyusi's behemoth *Modern Palestinian Literature*.

BETHLEHEM בית לחם بيت لحم ☎02

Bethlehem and its environs were the backdrop for some of history's quieter religious moments: Rachel's death, the love between Ruth and Boaz, the discovery of the shepherd-poet-king David, and of course, the pastoral birth of Jesus. Bethlehem, which is almost entirely Christian, and the surrounding villages of Beit Sahour and Beit Jala are home to most of the Palestinian Christian minority.

The three Wise Men followed a star to a peaceful manger, and today's pilgrims can follow Star St. to bustling Manger Sq., where fleets of tourist buses and armies of postcard-sellers swarm around the stocky Basilica of the Nativity. The glow-in-the-dark Virgin Marys and plastic crowns of thorns may take crass commercialism to a new level, but some visitors still manage to see past the blinding flashbulbs to a site of true religious significance.

Besides being home to one of Christianity's most important sites, Bethlehem is a prime example of what independence can achieve. In 1995, Bethlehem celebrated Christmas for the first time under Palestinian rule. The changing of the guard has breathed new life into this town; grants from other countries have been pouring in and have been put to good use. In preparation for the throngs of visitors expected for the millennium, Bethlehem was given a much-needed face lift: Manger Sq. was cleaned up and modernized; the abandoned Israeli police station, where Palestinian youth used to throw rocks at soldiers, was replaced with a Peace Center; and English-language street signs were installed all over town (though street numbers on buildings have yet to come). The *Bethlehem 2000 Project*, launched by the PNA in 1996, features cultural, religious, and artistic events that began in November 1999 and will conclude at the end of Easter 2001 (pick up a schedule of events at the tourist office).

The most crowded and interesting time to visit Bethlehem is during a Christian holiday, especially Easter 2001, for which you should make hotel reservations well in advance (i.e. it might already be too late). Other times allow more personal space to explore and a more accurate portrait of life in Bethlehem.

GETTING THERE AND GETTING AROUND

Buses make the 8km trip from the Suleiman St. station in East Jerusalem, right outside Damascus Gate (30min., daily every 15-30min. until 5pm, NIS2.50). **Service** leave from Damascus and Jaffa Gates and are slightly faster than the bus (20 min., NIS3). Both will stop at **Rachel's Tomb** on the outskirts of Bethlehem (or at the checkpoint 200m from the tomb) and at **Bab al-Zaqaq,** the intersection of **Hebron Rd.** and **Paul VI Rd.** From Rachel's Tomb, it's a 30-minute walk (or NIS2 *service*) to **Manger Sq.,** where most of the Christian sites are clustered. To walk, continue along Manger St. until it forks into Star St.; then walk along Star St. until Paul VI Rd. A left turn leads into the square. From Bab al-Zaqaq, take Paul VI Rd. away from Beit Jala all the way to Manger Sq., about 15min. away. A new bus station closer to Manger Sq. is under construction; for now, only tour buses stop there, but there may be regular service to Jerusalem and other locations in the future.

Taxis are the *only* local transportation; you can find them on Beit Sahour Rd. behind the Peace Center. To get back to Jerusalem, take a local taxi to the pick-up for Jerusalem-bound taxis (tell the driver you're going to Jerusalem), or ask to go to Rachel's Tomb. A ride to the checkpoint or Rachel's Tomb in a shared taxi should cost NIS1.50; NIS5 in a private taxi. Try to leave earlier in the day; buses stop running after dark, and *service* become dramatically more expensive after the afternoon rush hour. A private cab from the checkpoint to Jerusalem should cost NIS25-30; set a price before you leave. **Orabi Rent-a-Car** (☎050 372 687), down the hill in Beit Sahour, rents cars with Palestinian plates.

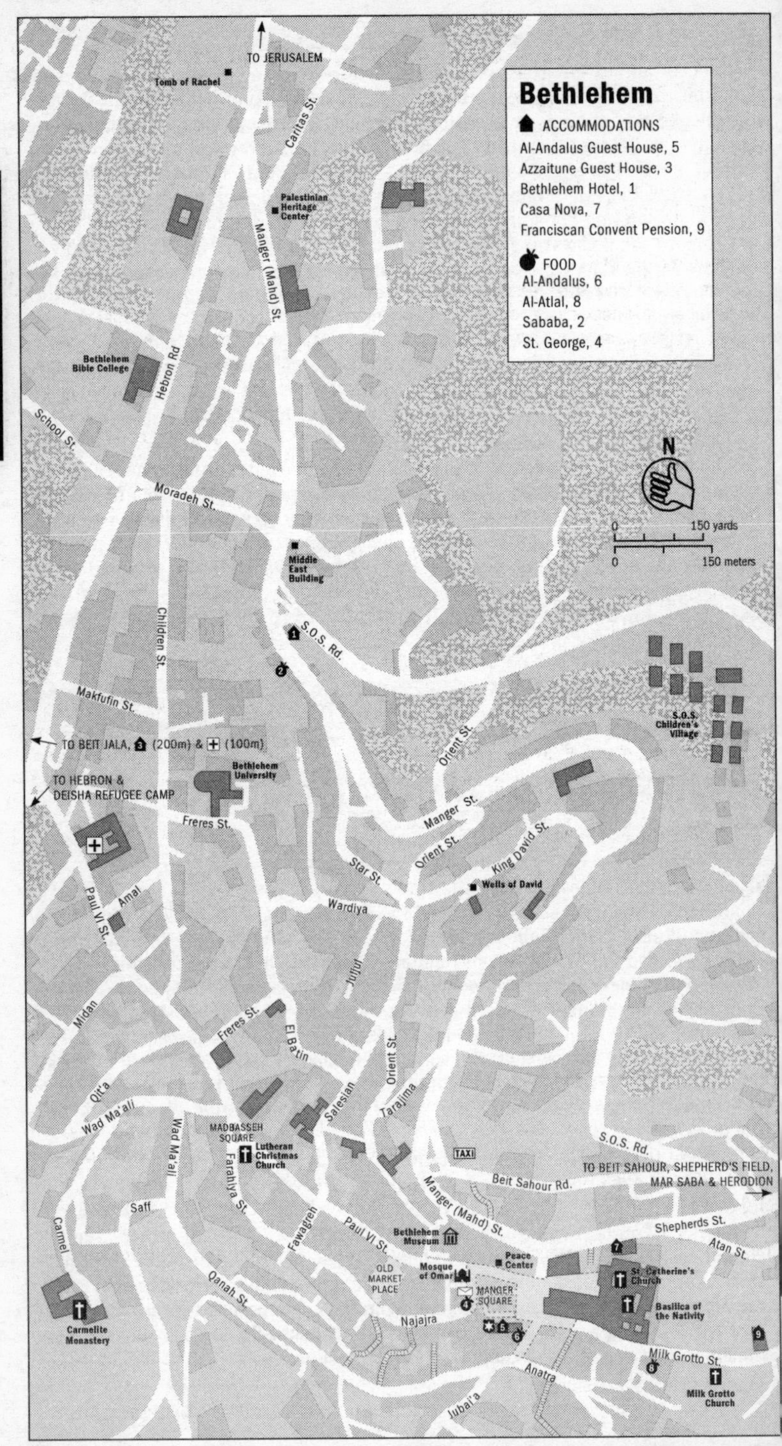
Bethlehem
ACCOMMODATIONS
Al-Andalus Guest House, 5
Azzaitune Guest House, 3
Bethlehem Hotel, 1
Casa Nova, 7
Franciscan Convent Pension, 9
FOOD
Al-Andalus, 6
Al-Atlal, 8
Sababa, 2
St. George, 4
N
0
150 yards
0
150 meters
TO JERUSALEM
Tomb of Rachel
Caritas St.
Palestinian Heritage Center
Manger (Mahd) St.
Bethlehem Bible College
Hebron Rd
School St.
Moradeh St.
Middle East Building
S.O.S. Rd.
Children St.
Makfufin St.
TO BEIT JALA, (200m) & (100m)
TO HEBRON & DEISHA REFUGEE CAMP
Bethlehem University
Freres St.
S.O.S. Children's Village
Orient St.
Manger St.
King David St.
Star St.
Wells of David
Wardiya
Paul VI St.
Amal
Juljul
Midan
Freres St.
El Batin
Orient St.
Qit'a
Wad Ma'ali
Wad Ma'ali
Salesian
Tarajima
MADBASSEH SQUARE
Lutheran Christmas Church
Farahiya St.
S.O.S. Rd.
TAXI
TO BEIT SAHOUR, SHEPHERD'S FIELD, MAR SABA & HERODION
Beit Sahour Rd.
Manger (Mahd) St.
Shepherds St.
Saff
Carmel
Fawagreh
Paul VI St.
Bethlehem Museum
Peace Center
Atan St.
St. Catherine's Church
OLD MARKET PLACE
Mosque of Omar
MANGER SQUARE
Basilica of the Nativity
Qanah St.
Najajra
Carmelite Monastery
Milk Grotto St.
Anatra
Milk Grotto Church
Jubai'a

ORIENTATION AND PRACTICAL INFORMATION

Religious sights center around **Manger Sq.**, across from the Basilica of the Nativity. **Najajreh St.**, **Paul VI Rd.**, and **Star St.** are home to the town's shopping district and open-air market and lead into the square.

Tourist Office: PNA Ministry of Tourism (☎276 66 77, fax 274 10 57), in the Peace Center in Manger Sq. Distributes a free PNA **town map** with a glossy pamphlet of major sights, details about special events during Christmas and Easter, and transportation information. Open M-Sa 8am-6pm.

Tours: Alternative Tourism Group (ATG) in Beit Sahour (☎277 21 51; fax 277 22 11; email atg@p-ol.com; www.patg.org). High-quality, inexpensive tours of Palestinian cities and refugee camps throughout the West Bank, ranging from half-day trips to 2-week volunteer programs. Multi-day tours involve staying overnight with local families in Beit Sahour. This politically motivated organization adds a non-objective slant in their otherwise wonderful tours. Prices range depending on the size of group, length of tour, or towns visited, but are quite reasonable—in the vicinity of $16 per day.

Currency Exchange: Mercantile Discount Bank (☎274 25 95), in Manger Sq. Open M-Th and Sa 8:30am-12:30pm, F 8:30am-noon. Surprisingly, there are **no ATMs** for foreign bank cards in Bethlehem. However, most services accept US dollars and many take credit cards as well.

Police Station: (☎274 49 35), but try the **tourist police** first (☎277 07 50 or 51), in Manger Sq. beneath the Andalus Hotel; another branch in the new bus station.

Hospital: Beit Jala Government Hospital (☎274 11 61), on Main St. (the continuation of Paul VI Rd.) on the Beit Jala side of Hebron Rd.

Internet Access: ICC Internet Center (☎276 58 48), on Manger St. just past the new bus station, has the fastest connection in the Manger Sq. area. NIS7 per 30min. Open M-Sa 9am-10:30pm, Su 10am-1pm. Further up Manger St., **Speed Net** (☎276 48 47), in the Middle East Building, opposite Moradeh St., complements speedy computers with an espresso and cappucino maker. (Open daily 10am-10pm.)

Post Office: (☎274 27 92). In Manger Sq., beneath the Municipality Building. Open Sa-Th 8am-2:30pm. Send and receive mail via Israel and buy PA telecards and stamps.

ACCOMMODATIONS

While Bethlehem's accommodations are a little expensive, the few extra shekels provide serene comfort foreign to Jerusalem's hostels. Hotels are usually less-than-packed during non-peak times. Ask for a discount if business seems slow.

One attractive addition to Bethlehem's (almost) hostel-less options is a **Bed and Breakfast** program instituted for the millennium celebration and intended to give individuals a taste of life with a local Palestinian family for very reasonable costs. Families are typically extraordinarily hospitable and talkative. Under a project overseen by ATG (see above) and made possible by a grant from Japan, 27 double rooms have been renovated in Bethlehem, Beit Jala, and Beit Sahour homes, all with clean private bathrooms and some with telephones. Rates are approximately NIS95 per person with breakfast. Lunch or dinner is available for NIS25.

Another accommodation arrangement is a new "tourist Bedouin village" in Beit Sahour's biblical Shepherd's Valley. Tents with modern bath facilities and breakfast are US$12 per person. The village also offers occasional storytelling and Bedouin dinners, mostly for groups. (☎277 38 75; fax 277 38 76. Open Apr.-Oct.)

Franciscan Convent Pension (Franciscaines de Marie) (☎274 24 41), on Milk Grotto St. On the left past the Grotto. Look for a set-back gray gate with small "White Sisters" plaque. Welcoming French nuns rent 3 sparkling flower- and Bible-bedecked rooms. Breakfast NIS20. Check-out 9am. Curfew 9pm, in winter 8:30pm. Reservations recommended. "Dorms" (for two or three people) NIS50; singles NIS100. No credit cards.

Azzaitune Guest House (☎/fax 274 20 16; mobile 052 360 769), a 20min. walk from Manger Sq. Follow Paul VI Rd. away from Manger Sq. until it becomes Main St. on the other side of Hebron Rd.; after the intersection take the second right. The closest thing Bethlehem has to a youth hostel, complete with clean, carpeted rooms and a kitchen for guests. Dorms NIS50/US$12; singles US$22; doubles US$35. No credit cards.

Casa Nova (☎274 39 80; fax 274 35 40), off Manger Sq., in a corner to the left of the Basilica entrance. Caters primarily to Franciscan pilgrims, but even agnostics are welcome. Modern rooms and plenty of hot water. Heated in winter. Reception 24hr. Check-out 8am. Flexible midnight curfew. Faxed reservations recommended. For Christmas stays, reserve up to 1 year in advance. Bed and breakfast US$22 per person, half-board US$27, full board US$33; single supplement US$15. 5% service charge.

Al-Andalus Guest House (☎274 35 19; fax 276 56 74; email andalus@p-ol.com), in Manger Sq. across from the Peace Center. Basic rooms, all with fans, private baths, and views of Jerusalem or Manger Sq. Guests can use the kitchen. Bed and breakfast rooms US$25 per person, US$30 during peak times.

Bethlehem Hotel (☎277 07 02; fax 277 07 06; email bhotel@p-ol.com; www.bethlehem-hotel.com), at the corner of Manger St. and S.O.S. Rd. Halfway between Rachel's Tomb and Manger Sq.; main entrance is downhill on S.O.S Rd. A modern hotel built especially for heavy 2000 tourism. Nice but antiseptic rooms, all with carpeting, TV, and A/C; some are handicapped accessible. Breakfast included; other meals US$10. Check-out noon. Singles US$50; doubles US$75; triples US$90. Children ages 2-6 50% discount, age 7-12 30% discount.

FOOD

Greasy fast food establishments among the souvenir shops and tourist-priced falafel and *shawarma* stands in Manger Sq. and on Manger St. provide fuel for church-hopping excursions. When no prices are marked, tourists are charged slightly more than locals, but bargaining helps.

Balloons (☎274 10 36), on Hebron Rd. near Rachel's Tomb (closer to Jerusalem). Bethlehem's one-and-only nightspot dishes up renowned pizza. Soft drinks only; alcohol served at **Memories,** the pub upstairs. Open Sa-Th 1pm-1am.

St. George (☎274 37 80), in Manger Sq., next door to the post office. Gets most of the tourist traffic from the Basilica. Sit outside and watch the activity in the square. Salads NIS18; omelettes NIS20; meat plates NIS35-50. Open daily 8am-6pm, later during peak times.

Sababa (☎274 40 06), on Manger St., near the junction of Star St. One of Bethlehem's nicer lunch options. Set daily menu includes salad, traditional main dishes, coffee, and dessert for NIS55. Open daily 11am-4pm.

Al-Andalus Restaurant (☎274 35 19; fax 276 56 74), just off Manger Sq., around the corner from the affiliated guest house. Affordable meals are disguised as "snacks." Hot dogs, hamburgers, and cheeseburgers (NIS12-20) come with salad and fries. Large variety of Middle Eastern foods NIS28-45. Ask for a free, excellent map of Bethlehem (edited by the owner). Open daily 8am-midnight.

Al-Atlal (The Ruins) Restaurant (☎274 11 04), 1 block from Manger Sq. on Milk Grotto St. Provides neo-Crusader arches and needed respite from the hordes. Lamb *me'orav* (mixed grill) NIS35; cheese toast NIS16. Open daily noon-4pm and 8pm-midnight.

SIGHTS

There are two ways to "do" Bethlehem. Traditionally, tourists arrive from Jerusalem, hop from one Christian holy place to another in several hours, and are back in Jerusalem before dinner. Bejeweled with dozens of flagship churches at every turn, Bethehem, Beit Sahour, and Beit Jala offer non-stop sights. However, spending a night or two (or at least an evening) in the area gives visitors a more memorable, behind-the-scenes peek into the window of Palestinian life. There are numerous opportunities to interact with the locals, who are generally very friendly and speak excellent English. The must-see sights, which can be seen in 2-3 hours, are listed first. After that are some highlights for a more in-depth sojourn.

Because no reliable public transportation is available, the best way to see the more distant sights (including Shepherd's Field, Mar Saba, and Herodion) is to rent a car (see above) or hire a guide with a vehicle for an afternoon. Guides gather in Manger Sq.; be sure to choose someone wearing a PA-issued ID tag. Tours should cost no more than US$10-12 per hour, including transportation. Guides will ask for double that, so be sure to bargain. To explore the villages and other West Bank cities from Bethlehem, contact ATG (see **Tours,** p. 315).

BASILICA OF THE NATIVITY. Masquerading as a fortress, this massive basilica is the oldest continuously used church in the world and honors the spot generally considered to be Jesus' birthplace. A far cry from any previous incarnation as a reflective, quiet sanctuary, today's church bursts with pilgrims and tourists. Begun in 326 CE by Queen Helena, mother of Constantine, the first basilica was completed in 339. It was partially destroyed in the Samaritan uprising of 525 and then rebuilt by Justinian. During the 614 Persian invasion, when virtually every Christian shrine in the Holy Land was demolished, the basilica was reputedly spared because it contained a mosaic of the three (Persian) Wise Men that had special anti-artillery powers. Tancred, the brat of the First Crusade, claimed Bethlehem as a fief and extensively renovated the church. After the Crusader kingdom fell, the church lapsed into disrepair. By the 15th century it had become undeniably decrepit, but its importance as a holy shrine never waned. During the ensuing centuries, struggle for its control among Roman Catholic, Greek, and Armenian Christians led to bloodshed. In the 1840s, the church was restored to its former dignity, but squabbles between the various denominations over the division of the edifice continue. An elaborate system of worship schedules, established in 1751, has worked through competing claims, but the confusion resulting from the Greek Orthodox Church's rejection of summer daylight savings time demonstrates the teetering balance of this arrangement. As of summer 2000, Catholic mass was held M-Sa at 6am, Armenian at 1:30pm, and Greek Orthodox at 4pm; Su has a schedule of its own. Check at the entrance to St. Catherine's Church for the exact times.

Despite its impressive history, the Basilica of the Nativity is not particularly attractive from the outside. The main entrance and windows were blocked up as a safety precaution during medieval times, rendering the facade awkward. To enter, assume a kneeling position and step through the narrow **Door of Humility**—a remnant of Christian attempts to prevent Muslims from entering on horseback.

Fragments of beautiful mosaic floors are all that remain of Helena's original church. View them beneath the huge wooden trap doors in the center of the marble Crusader floor. The four rows of reddish limestone Corinthian columns and the mosaic atoms along the walls date from Justinian's reconstruction. England's King Edward IV offered the oak ceiling as a gift. The Russian royal family bequeathed the handsome icons adorning the altar in 1764.

The underground sanctuary beneath the church is the **Grotto of the Nativity.** Crosses are etched into the columns on both sides of the cramped doorway—religious graffiti from centuries of pilgrims. The focus of the hubbub is a silver star bearing the Latin inscription: *Hic De Virgine Maria Jesus Christus Natus Est* (Here, of the Virgin Mary, Jesus Christ was born). The fourteen points represent the fourteen stations of the Via Dolorosa (see p. 116). The star, added by Catholics in 1717, was removed by Greeks in 1847 and restored by the Ottoman government in 1853. Quarrels over the star are said to have contributed to the outbreak of the Crimean War. *(In Manger Sq., tour guides often roam the square and nave; a reasonable fee is NIS15 for an hour-long tour with a licensed guide. Modest dress required. Basilica complex open daily 5:30am-7pm; in winter 5am-5pm. Free, though donations are encouraged.)*

ST. CATHERINE'S CHURCH. Built by the Franciscans in 1881, this simple and airy church is a welcome contrast to the grim interior of the adjacent basilica. Superbly detailed wood carvings of the 14 stations of the cross line the walls. Down the stairs, near the main entrance are a series of crypt rooms. The first, the **Chapel of St. Joseph,** commemorates the carpenter's vision of an angel that advised him to flee with his family to Egypt to avoid Herod's wrath. The burial cave of children slaughtered by King Herod (Matthew 2:16) lies below the altar and through the grille in the **Chapel of the Innocents.** Beyond the altar, a narrow hallway leads to the Grotto of the Nativity. The way is blocked by a thick wood door with a peephole. During times of greater hostility between Christian sects, this glimpse was as close as Catholics could get to the Greek Orthodox shrine. To the right of the altar, a series of rooms contain the tombs of St. Jerome, St. Paula, and St. Paula's daughter Eustochia. These lead to the spartan cell where St. Jerome produced the **Vulgate,** the 4th-century translation of the Hebrew Bible into Latin.

The Franciscan Fathers conduct a solemn procession to the basilica and underground chapels every day. To join in the 20 minutes of Gregorian cantillation and Latin prayer, arrive at St. Catherine's by noon. Saint Catherine's also broadcasts a **midnight mass** to a worldwide audience every Christmas Eve. *(Adjoins the basilica. Use the separate entrance to the left of the basilica entrance, or face the altar in the basilica and pass through one of the doorways in the wall on the left. Open daily 6:30am-8pm.)*

MILK GROTTO CHURCH. The cellar of this church is thought to be the cave in which the Holy Family hid when fleeing from Herod into Egypt. The cave and church take their names from the original milky white color of the rocks, most of which have now either been blackened by candle smoke or painted blue. According to legend, some of Mary's milk fell while she was nursing the infant Jesus, whitewashing the rocks. Today, women with fertility problems can request small packets of white dust as a charm. Male visitors may be slightly uncomfortable amid the women who come here to pray for fertility and the photo-diorama of suckling babies born to those whose prayers were rewarded. *(A 5min. walk down Milk Grotto St. from the Basilica of the Nativity. Facing the line of stores in Manger Sq., tum left and take the narrow alleyway to the Franciscan flag; the grotto is on the right. ☎274 38 67. Open daily 8am–6pm; in winter 8am-5pm. If the door is locked, ring the bell.)*

TOMB OF RACHEL. *Kever Raḥel* is a sacred site for Jews, a spot where synagogues have been built and destroyed throughout history. When Rachel died giving birth to Benjamin, Jacob is said to have erected a pillar upon her grave (Gen 35:19-20). In Crusader times, the site was marked with a small square structure; the Turks constructed a larger building over the tomb in 1620; a new dome was added in 1841; and the current fortress was completed around the Ottoman sanctuary only in 1997. On one side are fervently praying Ḥasidic men, and on the other, weeping Yemenite women. The tomb, a timeless symbol of maternal devotion and suffering, is now revered as a place to pray for a child or a safe delivery. There are separate entries for women and men. Women should dress modestly; men must don a paper *kippah,* available at the entrance.

While the IDF has left Bethlehem, the Israeli government retains control of the Tomb of Rachel. The PA insists that the tomb is the property of the Islamic *waqf,* though the status quo leaves the tomb in the hands of the IDF. *(The tomb is on the northern edge of town on the road to Jerusalem, at the intersection of Manger St. and Hebron Rd., a30min. walk from the Basilica of the Nativity. All buses between Jerusalem and Bethlehem or Hebron pass the tomb. ☎654 11 42. Open Su-Th 7:30am-4pm, F 7:30am-1:30pm.)*

PALESTINIAN HERITAGE CENTER. The new showroom displays and sells traditional Palestinian crafts. The small but interesting exhibit features a "traditional Palestinian sitting room," complete with handwoven carpets and teapots. The stores sell inexpensive needlework and other crafts, most of which are made by women from the Bethlehem area and nearby refugee camps. *(On Manger St. near the intersection with Hebron Rd. ☎274 23 81. Open M-Sa 9am-7pm.)*

BETHLEHEM MUSEUM. Also known as "Baituna at Talhami," this small museum showcases a 19th-century Palestinian home, furnished with authentic antiques. It is run by the Arab Women's Union, a group of local women who sell embroidered placemats, tablecloths, and traditional clothing at the museum and other Bethlehem and Jerusalem locations. *(Off Star St. between the market and Manger Sq. ☎274 25 89. Open M-W and F-Sa 8am-5pm, Th 8am-noon. NIS8.)*

MARKET. Bethlehem means "House of Meat" in Arabic (*Beit Lahm*) and "House of Bread" in Hebrew (*Beit Leḥem*). The sprawling market that clings to the town's steep streets lives up to both names. Recently re-paved, it has lost some of its hectic charm, but remains the one-stop shopping center for natives and tourists alike. *(Up the stairs from Paul VI Rd., across from the Syrian Church, 2 blocks west of Manger Sq.)*

DAYTRIPS FROM BETHLEHEM

BEIT SAHOUR

Most of the time, a bus (NIS1) from the parking lot below Manger Sq. runs to Beit Sahour; from the drop-off, it's still a 20min. walk to the site. Otherwise, you can follow signs and walk the 1.5km from Bethlehem. A cab should cost NIS15.

Home to some 15,000 inhabitants, Beit Sahour lies on the eastern edge of Bethlehem. Its open stretches of grazing land include the **Fields of Ruth,** believed to be the setting for the biblical Book of Ruth, in which a wealthy local farmer falls in love with a poor young widow, a new convert to Judaism. The name of the village in Hebrew is "House of the Shepherds," and Christian tradition holds that this is **Shepherd's Field,** where those tending their flocks were greeted by the angel who pronounced the birth of Jesus (Luke 2:8-12).

A sign points left toward an alternate Shepherd's Field, believed by Franciscans to be the actual field. The Franciscan site, or **Latin Shepherd's Field,** features recent excavations of religious buildings dating back to the 4th or 5th century, as well as a modern chapel built in 1954 by Antonio Barluzzi. (☎277 24 13. Church and excavations open daily 6am-6pm.) Staying to the right leads to the **Greek Orthodox Shepherd's Field,** a more impressive and less-touristed site. The Byzantine basilica here was thrice destroyed and repaired, in the 5th, 6th, and 7th centuries. The Holy Cave (325 CE) features mosaic crosses on the floor. In the baptistry are 1300-year-old bones belonging to victims of the Persian invasion (open daily 8am-12:30pm and 2-5pm). The newest addition to the field is the incredible red-domed, Byzantine-style church, opened in 1989. Inside are strikingly colored frescoes of starving local saints and an imported Greek marble floor.

The main street within the residential part of the village is Star St., dominated by the Greek Orthodox church. Along Star St. is the main office of the **Alternative Tourism Group** (see **Bethlehem Tours,** p. 315). Past the post office, Omar al-Khattab mosque is one of the city's few mosques. Accommodations in Beit Sahour can be found in local homes or at the Bedouin tourist village; alternatively, the new **Golden Park Resort** (☎277 43 81) should be offering luxurious accommodations near Shepherd's Field by 2001. Non-guests are welcome to relax in the resort's inviting **swimming pool** (NIS30).

HERODION

From Jerusalem, take Egged bus #166, which stops at the bottom of the hill, a 5-10min. walk from the entrance. Round-trip private taxi from Bethlehem NIS30, includes waiting time. ☎050 505 007. Free site-maps available at entrance; guided tours in English by prior arrangement only. Open daily 8am-5pm; in winter 8am-4pm. NIS18; with ISIC NIS15.

Eleven kilometers east of Bethlehem, the man-made, flat-topped mountain of Herodion arrests the eye with its startling silhouette. Much of the road between Herodion and Bethlehem crosses over the "Valley of Fire," a continuation of Jerusalem's Kidron Valley. In biblical times it was the site of *Molekh* worship, where fathers sacrificed their first-born sons by fire. It was also the site of the suicide of Judas, betrayer of Jesus. On a clear day, the Mt. of Olives is visible from the road. Although located in the West Bank, Herodion is an Israeli National Park.

Herodion is one of the world's finest examples of well-preserved early Roman architecture. Built as a summer palace by King Herod, it contained swimming pools and bathhouses, all of which have been carefully dug up. Herod's body is believed to be buried here, although his bones haven't been found. Excavators have found bones dating back to 2000 BCE, some of the oldest ever discovered, buried under the western tower in what is called the **Kroutoon Cave.**

There are two ways to ascend the mountain: the excruciating outdoor steps or the naturally air-conditioned 200 steps inside the mountain, carved into the cisterns. Begun in Herod's time and later expanded by rebels in the Bar Kokhba revolt, who used the site as a base around 132 CE (see **the Romans,** p. 9), the network of tunnels and steps leads directly into the former palace's central courtyard. At the top, the western defense tower is directly above the Kroutoon Cave. The vista from this point is breathtaking on a clear day, when the Dead Sea is visible (right of the cistern exit). The red roofs below are those of the politically sensitive Jewish settlements of **Teqoa, Noqedim,** and **Ma'ale Amos,** where the prophet Amos is buried. Take the outside steps to get back down. The bridge was recently built directly over what used to be the palace's main gate, which is prominently visible.

If you've come by taxi, ask to be driven through the villages of Beit Ta'amar and Irtas on the way back to Bethlehem. A tiny mosque along the road, named after the conqueror Omar ibn Khattab, is thought to be the oldest in the country. Irtas village (Irtam of the Bible) is divided by a valley that cuts across it. Look for the beautiful red-roofed and gold-trimmed Catholic monastery on the left-hand side below the road. Near Irtas are **Solomon's Pools;** these three man-made reservoirs are a miracle of pre-modern technology. Originally designed to hold 40 million gallons of water, the pools now serve as concert halls with great acoustics for events such as the popular annual **Irtas Arabic Music Festival,** held in midsummer. Opposite the pools is a fortress which guarded them, behind which is St. George's gate, the ancient doorway to the village.

DEHEISHA REFUGEE CAMP

Service transportation is readily available between Deheisha and Bethlehem, along Manger St. or at Bab al-Zaqaq (NIS2). For an organized tour, contact Alternative Tours in Jerusalem (☎05 286 42 05; see p. 132) or ATG in Beit Sahour (☎277 21 51).

The largest of the three refugee camps in Bethlehem's environs, Deheisha has been and continues to be a symbol of the depressed quality of life Palestinians have suffered during the period of Israeli occupation. Once guarded and completely fenced in, Deheisha has ripped down its walls since the Palestinian Authority gained control of the city, although the remains of turnstiles are still visible near the main road. Although poverty and crowding continue to reign here, the atmosphere is optimistic and forward-looking.

Besides learning first-hand about life in a refugee camp, there is not much to do in Deheisha. Along the main entrance to the camp (which today can be accessed freely) near where the fences used to be, is **Martyr's Monument,** a sculpture recently erected by the residents as a memorial to "martyrs of the Palestinian cause." A complex of arches standing about five meters high, the Jerusalem stone sculpture is a three-dimensional map of the hoped-for Palestine. The monument is striking, particularly because of the rarity of public art displays in places like Deheisha. The other interesting stop is at the **Ibda'a Cultural Center** (☎277 64 44; email moh_sayed3@hotmail.com). The center serves the youth of the camp and has recently established a dance-troupe, which has performed traditional Palestinian dance in festivals in several countries. Photo albums and videos are on hand. Admire the display of Palestinian handcrafts on the ground floor, donated by local women. Youth leaders offer tours and invite visitors to their homes for tea even without advance notice. A donation to the center is appreciated.

MAR SABA MONASTERY

Drive through Beit Sahour, following the signs past Shepherd's Field, or take a private taxi from Bethlehem (16km; NIS76 round-trip). Open daily 7-11am and 1:30-6pm; in winter 7-11am and 1:30-5pm. Donation expected.

The Mar Saba Monastery stands in complete isolation in the middle of the desert. Literally carved into the walls of a remote canyon, the extensive monastery complex perches above the nasty-looking Kidron River. The monastery is built opposite the cave and marked by a cross. St. Saba began his ascetic life here in 478 CE, and his bones are on display in the main church. Women may not enter and can only view the buildings from a nearby tower; men must wear long pants and sleeves. To get inside, pull the chain on the large blue door. The monks occasionally ignore the doorbell, especially on Sundays and late afternoons. If they're feeling social, the monks might lead five-minute tours in broken English.

JERICHO יריחו أريحا ☎02

The first city to fly the Palestinian flag and the headquarters of the Palestinian Authority, Jericho vibrates with ground-breaking activity. Streets strewn with banners, flags, and portraits of Yassir Arafat convey Palestinian pride and optimism, which shines through in the hospitality and openness of the city's residents. Settled 10,000 years ago, Jericho is believed to be the world's oldest city. At 250m below sea level, it's also the world's lowest. Its location in the middle of the Judean Desert leaves Jericho brutally hot in the summer and pleasantly hot in the winter, making it a winter resort for vacationers as far back as the 8th century, when Syrian King Hisham built a magnificent winter palace here. Excavations at several sites around Jericho have been extensive, but besides several beautiful mosaic floors, the ruins themselves aren't that spectacular—after all, the city walls are famous for having tumbled down. After Joshua destroyed the city with a blast of his trumpet (Joshua 6:20), Jericho remained in shambles for centuries. The oasis town was partially rebuilt in the days of King Ahab in the early 9th century BCE (I Kings 16:34), embellished by King Herod during the Hasmonean Dynasty, and further strengthened under Roman, Crusader, and Mamluk rule.

The population skyrocketed after 1967, when thousands of Palestinian refugees fled here from Israel. Free from Jordanian control, the refugee camps were replaced by apartment buildings, and the standard of living drastically improved. Today Jericho is the site of several noteworthy million-dollar investment projects, including a new luxury resort popular with wealthy Palestinians, a cable-car/hotel complex at the foot of the Mount of Temptation, and the Oasis Casino, the region's very own mini-yet-majestic sin city. Jericho is under the custodianship of the Palestinian Authority and can be visited without difficulty. All travelers should dress modestly, and women travelers may feel safer with a male companion.

GETTING THERE AND GETTING AROUND

Forty kilometers east of Jerusalem, Jericho is on the road to Amman, at the junction of the highway to Galilee (for information on crossing to **Jordan,** see p. 344). The quickest and most reliable way to get to Jericho is by **service** taxi. Direct transportation from Jerusalem (across the street from Damascus Gate) is possible, but expensive (NIS15) and infrequent. Take a *service* to Abu Dis instead (NIS 2.50; coming out of Damascus Gate turn right and head toward the end of the line of taxis), get out at the gas station, and switch to a Jericho-bound *service* (NIS6), which will stop in the central square or at the Oasis Casino. There is no schedule—*service* taxis leave when full, and they fill most quickly during morning and afternoon rush hours. Repeat this process backwards to return to Jerusalem; from the casino, however, you might be better off going into Jericho first because *service* taxis usually only depart for Abu Dis or Jerusalem when full. On Fridays, almost all shops and services close for the day. Mosques broadcast prayers and sermons over loudspeakers and are generally open to worshipers only. There is no public transportation within the city, but there are a multitude of yellow taxis. Hiring a taxi for several hours is the recommended way of seeing the sights, since the blistering heat most of the year makes even walkable distances unbearable. Pay no more than NIS30-40 per hour. A great way to see the sights on cooler days is by bike. **Zaki Sale and Rent Bicycle** (☎232 40 70), in the main square by the corner of al-Kastal, rents functional 21-speed mountain bikes with locks (NIS3 per hr. or NIS12 per day). Open daily 8am-10pm. Bring water and watch out for cars.

PRACTICAL INFORMATION

Tourist Information Office: No official tourist office, but you can get free maps and info at the municipality building in the main square (☎232 24 17; email info@jericho-city.org) or at the Elisha's Spring complex, across the parking lot from the old city.

Currency Exchange: Cairo Amman Bank (☎232 36 27), in the main square. Cash only. Open Sa-Th 8:30am-12:30pm. **Kamel al-Issawi Money Changer** (☎232 28 49 or 052 263 200), in the main square next to the municipality building, has better hours and changes traveler's checks as well as foreign cash. Open daily 8am-9pm.

Police: (☎232 21 00 or 232 14 26). In the main square, next to the bank. Open 24hr.

Tourist Police (☎232 40 11), next to the old city office, across from Elisha's Spring. Open daily 8am-6pm.

Pharmacy: Arabi, 74 Ein al-Sultan St. (☎232 23 25), by Hisham's Palace Hotel. Open Sa-Th 8am-11pm.

Hospital: Palestinian National Authority Ministry of Health Clinic, 51 Jerusalem Rd. (☎232 24 06), just off the square. Open Sa-Th 8am-2:30pm. The **New Jericho Hospital** (☎232 19 66), farther down Jerusalem Rd., is open 24hr.

Telephones: The blue public phones in the West Bank take non-Bezeq telecards. Storekeepers may accept a few shekels for use of their phone.

Post Office: (☎232 25 74; fax 232 36 09), down Amman St. from the police station. Beautiful Palestinian National Authority (PNA) stamps starting at NIS1. For the time being, they're good only for West Bank- and Gaza-bound mail, but they make great souvenirs. The post office also has regular Israeli stamps for sending mail anywhere in the world. Open Sa-Th 8am-2pm.

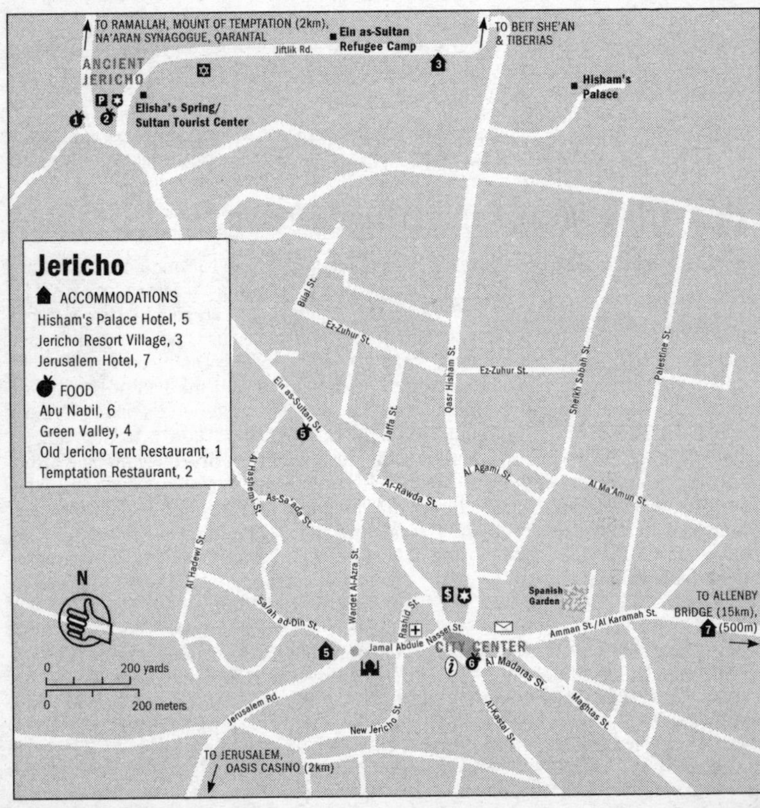

ACCOMMODATIONS

With only a few sights to see and a relatively easy commute to Jerusalem, there isn't much reason to sleep here; accommodations are often expensive or unappealing. Nevertheless, there are several options.

Jerusalem Hotel (☎232 24 44; fax 232 13 29), also known as al-Quds Hotel. Down Amman St., about 1.5km east of the city center, on the right. Comfortable, almost elegant lobby and large dining room set the hotel apart from its budget counterparts, making this the best value in town. "Dorms" (no more than 4 beds per room) are airy (fan, no A/C) and have shared baths. Upstairs, medium-sized rooms have A/C, satellite TV, and phone; most have balconies. Breakfast included. Check-out noon. Dorms US$25 per person. Singles US$60; doubles US$80; triples US$100.

Jericho Resort Village (☎232 12 55; fax 232 21 89; email reservation@jericho-resort.com; www.jericho-resort.com), off Qasr Hisham St. near Hisham's Palace. Full-fledged resort complex with swimming pools, restaurants, cafés, bars, and luxurious lounge areas. A magnet for wealthy Palestinian families. While definitely not cheap, the prices are about one-half the price of comparable accommodations in Jerusalem or the US. Breakfast included. Check-out noon. Singles US$100-120; doubles US$120-140. 4-person bungalows including kitchenette and sitting room US$140-150.

Hisham's Palace Hotel (☎052 483 808), on Ein al-Sultan St., close to the city center. The once-grand lobby and hallways aren't quite palace-like anymore. Rooms, hallways, and bathrooms are time-ravaged to the extreme and only borderline clean. Rooms have either A/C or fans; some have balconies and private baths. Flexible check-in and check-out. NIS30-80 per person, depending on season, type of room, and bargaining skills. No credit cards.

FOOD

Many cheap and tasty restaurants cluster around the city center. Falafel should be about NIS3, *shawarma* NIS6. Cheap fruit and vegetable bins are crowded in the southeastern corner of the square (near al-Kastal St.).

Abu Nabil (☎232 21 60), under the red awning in the city's main square. The city's best "locals" restaurant, catering to native tastes and pockets. Full lunch or dinner including grilled meat, salad, pita, and hummus NIS25. Open daily 6am-midnight.

Green Valley (☎232 23 49), on Ein al-Sultan St., on the way to Hisham's Palace. Excellent local specialties in a well-touristed and spacious indoor-outdoor restaurant. Ask about the *musakhan*, a huge bedouin chicken dish that serves two, served with nuts, vegetables, and bread (NIS40), and wash it down with a glass of *'araq*, a strong *anise* drink (like ouzo) that turns cloudy when you add ice (NIS8 per glass). Live music on F and Sa nights in winter. Open daily 8am-midnight.

The Old Jericho Tent Restaurant (☎232 38 20), near the Mount of Temptation. In the style of a large Bedouin tent, with desert life scenes painted on the walls. Dishes up the best of traditional Arabic cuisine. *Fukhara*, a lamb and rice dish slowly cooked in clay pots, is one of their specialties (NIS40). Open daily 8am-midnight.

Temptation Restaurant (☎232 26 14), underneath the Mount of Temptation (Qarantal) in the monstrous Elisha's Spring complex. With about 2000 seats, this restaurant can easily feed the mouth of every tourist and pilgrim who comes to see the mountain. Huge buffet for US$9 (daily 11am-5pm). Open daily 6am-9pm.

SIGHTS

The best way to see the sights is to hire a taxi for several hours from the city center at the relatively inexpensive rate of NIS30-40 per hour (be sure to set a price in advance). Another option is to rent a car for the day—much more convenient, and for a group of three or four, this might even be less expensive than relying on taxis. Jericho's most popular sights, Hisham's Palace and ancient Jericho, lie on the outskirts of town and make for an excruciating walk, even in the winter. It's best to visit Hisham's Palace first, since a cluster of restaurants and a cooling spring near the ancient city provide a pleasant post-tour rest stop.

HISHAM'S PALACE. Begun in 724 CE and completed in 743, Hisham's Palace was ravaged only four years later by an earthquake. Known as Khirbet al-Mafjar in Arabic, the palace was designed for the Umayyad Caliph Hisham as a winter retreat from Damascus—although there is no evidence that the caliph ever actually spent any time here. The most renowned feature is a courtyard window in the shape of the six-pointed Umayyad star. In the "guest house," a beautifully preserved mosaic depicts a sinister tableau in which a lion devours a gazelle as its naive playmates frolic beneath the Tree of Life. Get a guide from the entrance to show you around (tip NIS5-10). *(To reach the palace from the square, head 3km north from Qasr Hisham St., following the signs to the turnoff at a guard post. Coming from ancient Jericho, head east on Jiftlik Rd., past the synagogue and the Ein al-Sultan refugee camp. After 1.5km, turn right on the road back to Jericho; the turn-off to Hisham's Palace appears on the left. ☎232 25 22. Open daily 8am-6pm. NIS10, students NIS7, children NIS5.)*

ANCIENT JERICHO. Thought to be the oldest city in the world (as opposed to Damascus, the oldest continually inhabited city), ancient Jericho is now a heap of ruined walls. Called **Tel al-Sultan,** the mound contains layer upon layer of garbage from ancient (and modern) cities. Some of the finds date from the early Neolithic period, leading archaeologists to suspect that Jericho was inhabited as early as the 8th millennium BCE. The oldest fortifications are 7000 years old. A limited amount of excavation has exposed many levels of ancient walls, some of them 3.5m thick and 5.5m high. Imagination will have to substitute for visible splendor at this site, which is distinctly unimpressive. *(To get to ancient Jericho from the city center, follow Ein al-Sultan St. to its end. The entrance is through a parking lot around the corner, opposite the Elisha's Spring complex. From Hisham's Palace, 2km away, turn right onto the road that runs past the Palace (away from the city center), cross a narrow bridge, then take a left at the next junction, following the "Tel Jericho" signs. ☎232 29 35. Open daily 8am-6pm, in winter 8am-5pm. NIS10, students with ISIC NIS7, children NIS5.)*

MONASTERY. An imposing Greek Orthodox monastery stands on the edge of a cliff among the mountains west of Jericho; the peak is believed to be the New Testament's **Mount of Temptation,** where the Devil tried to tempt Jesus. The complex of buildings stands before a grotto, said to be the spot where Jesus fasted for 40 days and 40 nights at the end of his ministry (Matthew 4:1-11). Three Greek monks now live in the monastery, built in 1895. They can point out the rock where Jesus was tempted by the devil and served by angels. The summit of the mountain, named **Qarantal** after the Latin word for "forty," is also a pedestal for the Maccabean **Castle of Dok,** beside which lie the remains of a 4th-century Christian chapel. *(The monastery can be reached by climbing up the mountain from the base, not far from the ancient city; the hike takes under an hour, but bring plenty of water. A much easier way up is to take the téléphérique (see below), which still requires a short hike to reach the monastery. Open M-F 9am-1pm and 2-5pm, Sa 9am-2pm, Su 10am-2pm. Modest dress required.)*

JERICHO SYNAGOGUE. This 6th-century synagogue, one of the oldest in the world, features an expansive mosaic floor with a *menorah*, a *shofar* (ram's horn), a *lulav* (palm branch), and the inscription *Shalom al Yisrael:* "Peace Be Upon Israel." Discovered by accident in 1936 while a British family was digging foundations for a winter house, the entire floor is remarkably preserved. As part of extensive preliminary peace agreements, the PA promised to watch over this synagogue, which is now a functioning *yeshiva* by day. Ask the caretaker to sprinkle some water over the tiles to reveal the mosaic more clearly. *(From Ancient Jericho, go 0.5km up the road past the Sultan Tourist Center and turn right at the sign. ☎052 694 568. Open daily 8am-6pm; in winter 8am-4pm. NIS10, students NIS7, children NIS5.)*

SULTAN TOURIST CENTER AND ELISHA'S SPRING. Papayas, grapes, oranges, bananas, and mint thrive behind the spring. A new US$10 million project for attracting tourism includes a hotel (not yet completed as of summer 2000), souvenir shops, restaurants, and a **cable car** ("téléphérique") that saves tourists the difficult, albeit scenic, 45-minute hike up the Mount of Temptation. The 5-minute ride

ALPS ASPEN

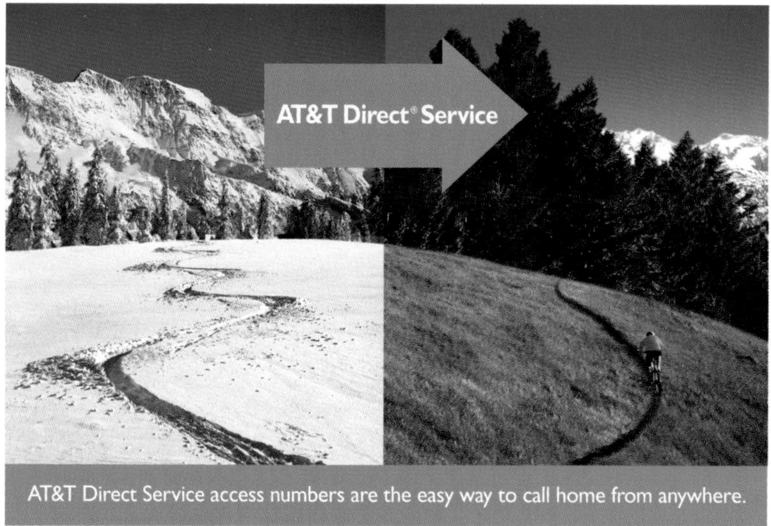

Global connection with the AT&T Network | **AT&T** direct service

AT&T

www.att.com/traveler

AT&T Direct® Service

The easy way to call home from anywhere.

AT&T Access Numbers

Austria ● 0800-200-288	France 0800-99-00-11
Belarus ✖ ....8 ◆ 800-101	Gambia ● 00111
Belgium ● 0-800-100-10	Germany 0800-2255-288
Bosnia ▲ 00-800-0010	Ghana 0191
Bulgaria ▲ 00-800-0010	Gibraltar 8800
Cyprus ● 080-900-10	Greece ● 00-800-1311
Czech Rep. ▲ 00-42-000-101	Hungary ● 06-800-01111
Denmark 8001-0010	Iceland ● 800-9001
Egypt ● (Cairo) ‡....510-0200	Ireland ✓......1-800-550-000
Finland ● 0800-110-015	Israel 1-800-94-94-949

AT&T Direct® Service

The easy way to call home from anywhere.

AT&T Access Numbers

Austria ● 0800-200-288	France 0800-99-00-11
Belarus ✖ ....8 ◆ 800-101	Gambia ● 00111
Belgium ● 0-800-100-10	Germany 0800-2255-288
Bosnia ▲ 00-800-0010	Ghana 0191
Bulgaria ▲ 00-800-0010	Gibraltar 8800
Cyprus ● 080-900-10	Greece ● 00-800-1311
Czech Rep. ▲ 00-42-000-101	Hungary ● 06-800-01111
Denmark 8001-0010	Iceland ● 800-9001
Egypt ● (Cairo) ‡....510-0200	Ireland ✓......1-800-550-000
Finland ● 0800-110-015	Israel 1-800-94-94-949

Italy● **172-1011**	**Russia (Moscow)▶▲●755-5042**
Luxembourg✚..800-2-0111	**(St. Petersbg.)▶▲● ..325-5042**
Macedonia● ..99-800-4288	**Slovakia▲ ..00-42-100-101**
Malta.......... 0800-890-110	**South Africa ..0800-99-0123**
Monaco●........800-90-288	**Spain 900-99-00-11**
Morocco........002-11-0011	**Sweden 020-799-111**
Netherlands●...0800-022-9111	**Switzerland● 0800-89-0011**
Norway 800-190-11	**Turkey● 00-800-12277**
Poland▲● ..00-800-111-1111	**Ukraine▲..........8◆100-11**
Portugal▲ 800-800-128	U.A. Emirates●......800-121
Romania●......01-800-4288	**U.K.............0800-89-0011**

FOR EASY CALLING WORLDWIDE

1. Just dial the AT&T Access Number for the country you are calling from. *2.* Dial the phone number you're calling. *3.* Dial your card number.

For access numbers not listed ask any operator for **AT&T Direct®** Service.
In the U.S. call 1-800-331-1140 for a wallet guide listing all worldwide AT&T Access Numbers.
Visit our Web site at: **www.att.com/traveler**
Bold-faced countries permit country-to-country calling outside the U.S.

- ● Public phones require coin or card deposit to place call.
- ▲ May not be available from every phone/payphone.
- ✚ Public phones and select hotels.
- ◆ Await second dial tone.
- ▶ Additional charges apply when calling from outside the city.
- † Outside of Cairo, dial "02" first.
- ✖ Not available from public phones or all areas.
- ✔ Use U.K. access number in N. Ireland.

When placing an international call *from* the U.S., dial 1 800 CALL ATT.

EMEA © 8/00 AT&T

goes over the old city ruins and provides stunning views of the valley and mountains; the view can be further enjoyed from the **Sultan Coffee Shop** at the top. *(Opposite the entrance to Ancient Jericho. ☎232 15 90. Open daily 8am-7pm. Cable car round-trip ticket US$8, students US$6, children US$5; one-way ticket US$5.)*

ENTERTAINMENT

Spanish Garden (☎232 39 31 or 050 515 518), on Amman St. near the center of town. Built recently through the contributions of the Spanish government. Beautiful public garden reminiscent of a medieval Andalusian *hadeeqa,* with 2 large fountains illuminated by colored lights. Livens up every evening after sunset, when families, small children, and teenagers show up to enjoy Arabic music, coffee, and *nargilah* (NIS8). A small cafe serves inexpensive snacks next to a game-room. Open daily sunset-1am, in winter sunset-9pm. NIS2, children NIS1.

Oasis Casino (☎231 11 11 or 1 800 511 555), several kilometers before the city center, toward Jerusalem. State-of-the art casino, with the full array of slot machines. All gambling is in US$, which can be exchanged from any currency at the door. Minimum bids for some tables US$5, though most are US$10-25. Restaurant upstairs serves light meals and snacks. No T-shirts. Passports required for entrance. At press time, the adjacent hotel was still under construction but expected to open by 2001. Open 24hr.

Al-Shalal Swimming Pool (☎232 39 30), near the old synagogue. Sparkling blue, clean waters for leisure swimming and small water slides for kids. Separate men's and women's pools. NIS20, children NIS10. Snack bar serves a variety of sandwiches and drinks (NIS3-10). Open daily 9am-9pm.

DAYTRIPS FROM JERICHO

MOSQUE OF NABI MUSA

The only way to visit is by car or taxi (NIS40 taxi ride from Jericho). To get to the mosque, head toward Jerusalem about 5km, then turn left at the sign, and follow the road for another 5km. Open daily 8am-sunset. Free but donations welcome.

The road from Jerusalem to Jericho slices through harsh desert landscape. About 8km from Jericho, the huge Mosque of Nabi Mussa, topped with a complex of white domes, stands on a hill in a sea of sand. The mosque was built in 1269 CE, on a spot revered throughout the Muslim world as the grave of the prophet Moses. Islamic tradition holds that the 13th-century Ottoman sultan Salah al-Din had a dream, revealing the spot to which God carried the bones of Moses so that the faithful could pay their respects. Devout pilgrims continue to pay their respects, traveling to the mosque during the week preceding Easter for the annual **Nabi Mussa Festival.** The tomb is said to have special powers—run your hands over the velvet cloth of Mussa's Tomb while making a wish and see for yourself. Across from the tomb, stairs lead upward into a minaret with incredible views of the surrounding Judean desert. Ask the souvenir vendors to unlock the gate if it is wired shut. The shrine is surrounded by naturally flammable bituminous rocks—the unique property is scientifically explained by the high content of *qatraan*, or tar, but, science aside, it's yet another feature that adds to the site's mystique.

WADI QELT

Threading 28km between imperious limestone cliffs and undulating ridges of bone-white chalk, the three fresh-water springs of Wadi Qelt nourish wildlife and lush greenery, 20min. outside of Jerusalem. A string of murders, presumably political, took place here in the mid-90s, but fortunately the last few years have been peaceful and problem-free; nevertheless, it's not a good idea to hike in the *wadi* alone or after dark. SPNI (☎03 638 86 36 or 02 624 46 05) offers one-day tours focusing on both natural and artificial attractions in the *wadi* (departs Monday from Tel Aviv at 8am, Jerusalem at 9am. US$59). Bring 4-5L of water per person.

The most interesting and accessible section of the *wadi* extends from the spring of Ein Qelt, past the 6th-century St. George's Monastery, and down into Jericho, 10km east. The trek takes about four hours. The best place to start is at the turn-off from the Jerusalem-Jericho highway about 9km west of Jericho, marked by the orange sign for "St. George's Monastery." *Service* taxis to Jericho, Ein Gedi, and Allenby Bridge stop here on request. By car, it is possible to skip the hike and drive most of the way to St. George's Monastery.

St. George's Monastery dates from the 5th or 6th century CE. Byzantine mosaics decorate the floor of the church; look for the likeness of a two-headed eagle, the Byzantine symbol of power. According to tradition, the monastery occupies the site of the cave where St. Joachim took refuge to lament the infertility of his wife Hannah. An angel told him to return to Hannah, who then gave birth to the Virgin Mary. The neighboring **St. John's Church** houses a spooky collection of skulls and bones of monks slaughtered when the Persians swept through in 614 CE. The Greek Orthodox monks who maintain the monastery can refill canteens for a journey into Jericho. (Open M-Sa 8am-1pm and 3-5pm; in winter 8am-1pm and 3-4pm. Modest dress required; modest donation desired.)

On the way to Jericho from St. George's, the ruins of **Tel Abu Alaya** (also called **Herodian Jericho**) are on the right. The palaces here, used by the Hasmoneans and later by King Herod, boast decorated walls, nearby bath houses, and pools. Though not as extensive as the ruins at Hisham's Palace, this *tel* is still more impressive than the remains of Ancient Jericho.

RAMALLAH رام الله ☎02

Perched 900m above sea level, Ramallah, along with its smaller sister city al-Bireh, is famous for its cool, pleasant mountain air. Before 1967, the then-prosperous town was a summer haven for Arabs from Jordan, Lebanon, and the Gulf region. With vacationers long gone by the time of the *intifada*, Ramallah and the energetic young intellectuals at nearby Birzeit University joined Nablus as leaders of West Bank resistance. Now under PA control, the city has become a transportation hub and will replace Gaza as the administrative hub of the PA when Palestinian self-rule expands. It already houses several important Palestinian Authority offices, including the Ministries of Transportation and Education.

Ramallah is known for its religiously relaxed atmosphere (alcohol flows freely and movie theaters are well attended) and the cafes along its main streets. Ramallah is, without question, the cultural capital of the West Bank, with a highly educated and fashionable population. It is also the hub of Palestinian feminist activity; the city's women frequently attend university rather than marry early, and several women-run cafes are used to fund local feminist organizations.

GETTING THERE AND GETTING AROUND

Life moves at a faster pace here, and fewer people go out of their way to help bewildered tourists than in other West Bank cities. Due to its location 16km north of Jerusalem and the frequent closures of East Jerusalem roads, the city has become a transportation hub. It is possible to get from Ramallah to most northern West Bank towns by direct *service;* from Jerusalem, they leave outside Damascus Gate, at the corner of Nablus Rd. (20min., NIS3.50). Arab buses leave from the station on Nablus Rd., just north of Damascus Gate, but they're not on a schedule and not worth the frustration (40min., NIS2). From Ramallah, buses and *service* to Jerusalem leave from the second floor of the parking-garage-turned-bus-station on al-Nahda St., just off **Manara Circle** ("al-Manara"), the town's epicenter. *Service* run to **Nablus** (1hr., NIS9). The last bus to Jerusalem leaves at about 5pm; the last *service* leaves around 8pm. Private taxis leave later (NIS40). **Orabi Rent-A-Car** (☎240 35 21), starts at US$50-60 per day for cars with Israeli plates and US$40 per day for Palestinian plates. **Goodluck** (☎234 21 60), start at US$46 per day.

PRACTICAL INFORMATION

Tours: The Palestinian Association for Cultural Exchange (PACE) (☎295 88 25; fax 298 68 54; email pace@palnet.edu), on Nablus Rd. in al-Bireh, organizes full and half day tours throughout the West Bank and Gaza Strip. Full day in Ramallah and vicinity NIS120. Serves as an unofficial tourist office.

Currency exchange: Money changers and banks can be found on all major streets and at Manara Circle. The only bank that accepts foreign ATM cards is **HSBC,** at the corner of Jaffa St. and al-Rasheed St., downhill from al-Bardoni's Restaurant.

Police: (☎295 70 20) on al-Nahda St., past the al-Wehdeh Hotel from Manara Circle.

Hospital: The **Ramallah General Hospital** (☎995 65 61 or 995 65 62) is more accessible than Ramallah's **pharmacies,** which close at 8pm or earlier.

Internet Access: Carma Cyber Club (☎298 48 54), on the 6th floor of the Lo'lo'at al-Manara building, near Manara Circle on Main St. NIS4 per hr. Open Sa-Th 8am-1am, F 3pm-1am. **Leader Net** (☎296 52 31), on the 6th floor of the Burj al-Sa'a Building in Mughtarbin Sq. NIS5 per hr. Open Sa-Th 9am-midnight, F noon-midnight.

Post office: (☎295 66 04), on Park St., off Main St., downhill from Rukab's Ice Cream, sells beautiful Palestinian stamps and serves the rest of the world with Israeli stamps. Open Sa-Th 8am-2:30pm.

WEST BANK

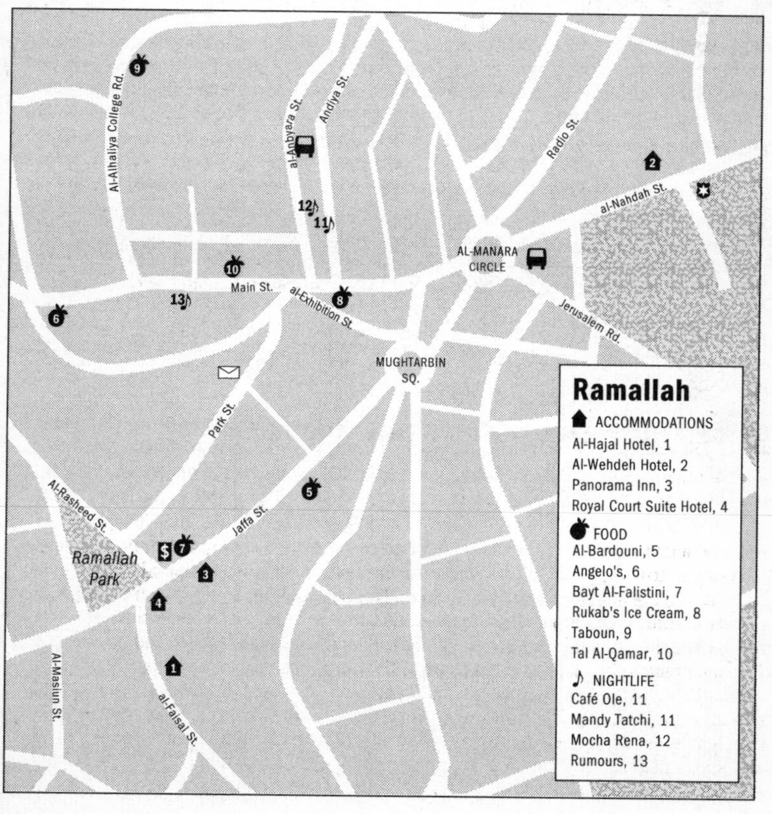

ACCOMMODATIONS

Although a night in Ramallah is very worthwhile, accommodations are expensive compared with nearby Jerusalem. There are no true hostels in Ramallah.

Panorama Inn (☎/fax 295 68 08), on Jaffa St., downhill from Al-Bardouni Restaurant near the Faisal St. intersection. Not too far from the center of town but surprisingly quiet with a sunny patio. Rooms with private bath, TV, and phone. Some with balcony and/or small fridge; large balcony in the hall on both floors. Knowledgeable and helpful staff. Breakfast included. Check-out noon. Singles NIS120; doubles NIS150.

Al-Wehdeh Hotel (☎298 04 12; fax 295 48 72), on al-Nahdah St. one block from Manara Circle. Ramallah's cheapest accommodation and also the most central, if you don't mind the noise from the street (it does quiet down eventually). Recently renovated. Rooms with TV, fans, and private bath; some with balconies. Breakfast included. Check-out flexible. Singles NIS100; doubles NIS150; long-term discounts available.

Al-Hajal Hotel (☎/fax 298 67 59), off Jaffa Rd. opposite the Ramallah park. Spacious rooms with satellite TV, fan, phone, and private bath, but not worth the price for just one person. Breakfast included. Check-out noon. Singles US$40; doubles US$55.

Royal Court Suite Hotel (☎296 40 40; fax 296 40 47; email rcshotel@rcshotel.com; www.rcshotel.com), on the corner of Jaffa St. and Faisal St., next to the Panorama Inn. Snazzy new luxury hotel. All rooms have kitchenettes, balconies, A/C, cable TV, phones, internet access lines (you supply the laptop), minibars, safe boxes, and even hair dryers. Breakfast included. 24hr. reception. Single US$69; double US$99.

FOOD

Ramallah's streets are lined with falafel and *shawarma* stands. The quality inexpensive restaurants look down on the city from the tops of the buildings all around Manara Circle, especially along Main Street. Most restaurants serve international dishes as well as traditional Palestinian cuisine. Ramallah's hip cafes attract Arabs from all over the West Bank and even Israelis from across the green line.

Rukab's Ice Cream (☎295 64 67), at the corner of Main St. and al-Exhibition St., one block from Manara Circle. Possibly the best ice cream in the hemisphere; their gum-thickened, gooey goodness comes in a rainbow of blissful flavors. Try the popular pistachio (tiny cones NIS3; large, multi-flavored cones NIS9. Open daily 8am-1am.

Angelo's (☎295 64 08), a left turn off Main St. one block after Rukab's; the restaurant is on the corner. Flings pizza into the air and onto the plates of plucky budget travelers (small cheese NIS20; large "Angelo's Supreme" NIS55. The garlic bread (NIS8 per basket) is a local favorite. Open daily 11am-midnight.

Al-Bardouni (☎295 14 10), on Jaffa St., several blocks from Manara Circle. A stone's throw from the city center, but in a quiet part of town. Flowers and lattices cover the outdoor terrace of the comparatively fancy (but not overly pricey) restaurant. Especially beautiful (and packed) on sunny afternoons. Salads NIS8-12; BBQ dishes NIS38-50; *musakhan* (traditional dish with half a chicken) NIS35. Open daily 11am-midnight.

Bayt al-Falistini (☎298 71 88), on Jaffa Street, 3rd floor of the British Bank Building, opposite Al-Bardouni. Lively music and a family atmosphere. Palestinian specialties NIS28. The attached **Black Horse Bar** has an English pub feel—decidedly *not* a family atmosphere. Open daily 9am-1am.

Tal Al-Qamar (☎298 79 05), on the 5th floor of the Nasser Building on Main St., on the right, one block past Rukab's. Beautiful Arabic cafe with a terrific view serves well-priced sandwiches (NIS15) and grilled meats (NIS25-50). Su-W live *oud* after 9pm. Th nights live Arabic singing. Open daily noon-1am.

Taboun (☎298 05 05), 6th floor of Cairo-Amman Bank Building, at the end of al-Ahaliya College St., 2 blocks past Rukab's. Traditional Middle Eastern dishes with emphasis placed on natural ingredients and cleanliness. Full meal with drink approximately NIS40. Funds support a local women's science initiative. Open Sa-Th 9am-9pm.

SIGHTS AND ENTERTAINMENT

The main attraction is the city itself; on Saturdays, Manara Circle is a crammed jungle. For a more historical view, the **Palestinian Folklore Museum,** in the town of al-Bireh a few blocks away, exhibits traditional costumes, handicrafts, and rooms of a Palestinian house. (☎240 28 76. Open Sa-Th 9am-2:30pm.)

There's always something interesting going on in Ramallah's theaters and cultural centers. *This Week in Palestine*, actually a monthly publication, can be found at most hotels (or on the web at www.jmcc.org); it features a detailed listing of events. Ramallah and Birzeit University (☎998 20 59) sponsor frequent cultural events. Their website (www.birzeit.edu/ramallah) lists information on Ramallah's present and past, including an online travel guide, a performance schedule for university-sponsored events, and links to many of the establishments listed below.

The **al-Siraj Theatre** (☎995 70 37) near Clock Circle, the **Ashtar Theatre** (☎82 72 18 or 050 512 285) on Radio St., and the **Popular Arts Cinema** (☎995 38 91) on al-Bireh St. produce performing arts and dance: call or ask around town for details. **Al-Walid Cinema,** on al-Nahda St., a movie theater with three screenings daily, caters to a predominantly male clientele. There's a **swimming pool** at Ramallah First Sarriyeh. It is in lower Ramallah; walk about 25 minutes along Main St. or take a taxi. (☎995 20 91. Tu women only. NIS15.)

WEST BANK

NIGHTLIFE

On weekends, many restaurants offer live music (in particular the *oud*, a bassy Middle Eastern stringed instrument). As comparatively liberal as Ramallah may be, local single women rarely congregate in the evenings unchaperoned; nevertheless, it is perfectly acceptable for foreign women to go out.

Rumours (☎295 37 70), in the basement of a building on Main St., on the left, one block past Rukab's. Stylish cafe/bar/restaurant, with an extensive alcohol menu. Sex on the Beach NIS18. International cuisine NIS25-60. Tables are cleared Saturday nights for one of Ramallah's only weekly dance parties; DJ mixes European and Arabic pop. Occasional live performances. Open Su-F noon-midnight, Sa noon-3am.

Mocha Rena (☎298 14 60), on Mafad St., off Main St., to the right before Rukab's. The funky, modern atmosphere in this French-Italian cafe attracts a suave, young crowd—it's a good place to start the nightlife circuit. One of the few places in Ramallah where you can get a breakfast that doesn't involve salad (pancakes NIS10-18; omelettes NIS18; crepes NIS18-20). Lunches and dinners run about NIS15-35; a slice of delicious NY-style cheesecake for dessert is NIS15. Open daily 9am-midnight.

Cafe Ole (☎298 41 35), on the second floor of a building on al-Anbyara St., off Main St., a block from Manara Circle. There is no food here. One of Ramallah's most popular bars, with Th night disco parties (cover NIS25, includes 1 beer) and general drunken revelry all other nights (no cover). Open daily 4pm-midnight, Th until 2am or later.

Mandy Tatchi (☎298 70 27), on al-Anbyara St., opposite Café Ole. The Arabic music doesn't exactly match the Chinese decor, but you'll forgive the incongruities as soon as you taste the scrumptious food. Very reasonable prices for your favorite Chinese dishes (NIS20-40). Stay to eat or get take-out. Open daily 11am-11pm.

DAYTRIPS FROM RAMALLAH

TAYBEH. This predominantly Christian farming village several kilometers from Ramallah is the site of **Taybeh Beer Brewing Co.,** the only beer brewery in the West Bank. Owner Nadim Khoury gives free tours and tastes. Taybeh means "delicious" in Arabic; their three brews happily live up to the name. *(Take a Taybeh Village-bound service from Jamal Abdel Nasser mosque in Ramallah's center. ☎289 88 68; fax 289 80 22; email taybeh@palnet.com; www.taybehbeer.com. Call a day in advance. Open M-Sa 8am-4pm.)*

BIRZEIT بير زيت. Twelve kilometers northwest of Ramallah is the extensive, impressive campus of **Birzeit University,** the largest university in the West Bank. Birzeit's 2500 students have a history of vocal opposition to the Israeli occupation; the university was often shut down by the Israeli Army during the 1980s and was closed altogether from the first years of the *intifada* until April 1992.

Today, Birzeit remains a vital presence. The university takes pride in its history and its strong leadership position in the West Bank, and it has even developed an Internet training program and an extensive website (www.birzeit.edu). Foreign students can study at the university through the Palestinian and Arab Studies (PAS) Program (for details, see **Alternatives to Tourism,** p. 68). *(To get here from Ramallah, take a Birzeit-bound service from Manara Circle for NIS3.)*

NABLUS نابلس ☎09

Serene mountains surround the city of Nablus, founded in 72CE by Titus near the site of Biblical Shechem as the "New City" of Flavia Neapolis. Enjoy the serenity if you can; the city is not called *Jabal al-Nar* (Hill of Fire) for nothing. Home to some of Palestine's oldest and wealthiest families, Nablus has a tradition of impassioned resistance to foreign occupation. Its citizens fought the Turks, the British, and the Jordanians and were wholly consumed by the *intifada*. Nablus, one of the largest Palestinian cities, is home to the West Bank's second-largest university, al-Najah. Since 1996, its new, wealthy neighborhood of Rafiddiyah has also housed the first Palestinian **stock market.** Tourists looking for eye-catching sights will find few, but those searching for an uncensored glimpse of the Palestinian present will find it. Nablus is a very conservative town—dress modestly. Because so few travelers make their way here, residents of Nablus tend to be curious and friendly; accepting invitations of hospitality can be very rewarding.

GETTING THERE. Nablus lies 63km north of Jerusalem, 46km north of Ramallah, and 50km south of Nazareth—in the middle of nowhere. Direct transportation to and from Jerusalem is practically non-existent; go through Ramallah. *Service* taxis from the parking lot in Ramallah's bus station by Manara Circle make the trip frequently throughout the day (1hr., NIS9) and are more reliable than buses. In Nablus, taxis and *service* gather in the main square. Nablus's main thoroughfare is called **Faisal Rd.'**; on it are the **post office** and, next door, the **police** (☎238 30 40).

ORIENTATION AND PRACTICAL INFORMATION. There is a small **Tourist Information Center** next to the New Clocktower between Faisal Rd. and al-Shuhada Sq. with not-very-helpful maps for sale (☎239 87 70. Open Sa-Th 8am-7pm). A more useful (and free!) map can be found at the Al-Yasmeen hotel.

ACCOMMODATIONS. Unlike most of the other cities in the West Bank, which can easily be done as daytrips from Jerusalem, Nablus is far enough that an overnight is more convenient, especially if the city is being used as a stepping stone to Nazareth, Tiberias, or other northern locations in Israel. Unfortunately, however, there are no budget accommodations in the city—the options are either expensive or more expensive. **Al-Yasmeen Hotel** is in the heart of the city, at the end of Tetouan St., by the market. While small, its stylish and luxurious rooms are well worth the price. Each has satellite TV, phone, Internet line, air-conditioning, private bath, and sound-proof double-glass windows. (☎233 35 55; fax 233 36 66; email yasmeen@palnet.com; www.alyasmeen.com. Singles US$50; doubles US$70. 15% service charge. Breakfast included.) **Al-Qasr Hotel,** in a quiet neighborhood 25 minutes from the center of town, offers well-furnished rooms. Take Gharnatah St. away from al-Shuhada Sq. and turn left up al-Fataimia St. (☎238 54 44; fax 238 59 44; email antaribasem@hotmail.com. Singles US$70; doubles US$90; negotiable during slow seasons. Breakfast included.)

FOOD. Food options are plentiful; from the center of Nablus, wander into the crowded streets and passageways of the *souq* (market), which overflows with meat stores, clothing merchants, and produce stalls. Try a piece of the extraordinarily rich *kinafeh nablusiyya*, a warm cheese concoction topped with sweet orange flakes and syrup (one sticky, wonderful slab NIS2). Cheap food stands abound; the **Silawi Restaurant,** on Gharnatah St. near al-Shuhada Sq. (identifiable by the red-and-yellow awning) is a local favorite with an impressive array of fresh salads and toppings (NIS2) or *shawarma* (NIS5) sandwiches. (☎237 01 70. Open daily 5am-11pm.) **Zeit Ou Za'ater,** in the Al-Yasmeen hotel, features traditional food made in their olive-wood oven. Try the *fukhara* (NIS20-30), a meat or vegetarian dish cooked in a clay pot. (☎233 35 55. Open daily 8am-11pm.)

SIGHTS. The **al-Qasaba Museum,** on a side street in the market near the Great Mosque, was built over the remains of a colonnaded street from the first century CE. The original cardo had 110 columns; few remain today. A tunnel, accessed by a steep staircase, leads to an aqueduct that still flows from a spring at the ancient city of Shechem. (☎238 06 09. Open Sa-Th 9am-4pm; NIS5, children NIS1.)

A few kilometers from the town center lie two famous but unspectacular pilgrimage sites. **Jacob's Well,** now enclosed within a subterranean Greek Orthodox shrine, is believed to date from the time when Jacob bought the surrounding land to pitch his tents (Genesis 33:18-19). The church over the crypt, begun in 1908, was badly damaged in an earthquake in 1927, but is finally being repaired and restored. The well is on Zut Rd. across from the **Balata refugee camp;** the road is unmarked, but anyone can point out the direction to Balata. (Open daily 7-10am and 2-5pm or simply ring the bell. Modest dress required.) The **Tomb of Joseph** lies closer to town off Zut Rd. According to the Book of Joshua, the bones of Joseph were carried out of Egypt and buried in Shechem (Joshua 24:32). The site of clashes between Jews and Palestinians as recently as August 1998, the tomb is now closed to the public and is surrounded by barbed wire and armed guards. Special permits to enter may be obtained through the Israeli government.

NEAR NABLUS

MOUNT GERIZIM

This tree-covered slope southeast of Nablus features a terrific view of the Shomron Valley. Since the 4th century BCE, it has been the holy mountain of the Samaritans, who believe it is the spot where Abraham prepared to sacrifice his son Isaac and where the original Ten Commandments are buried. They built a rival temple here to the one in Jerusalem, but it was destroyed by Hercanus in 128 BCE. The Samaritans, an Israelite sect excommunicated in biblical times, are distinguished by their literal interpretation of certain scriptures and acceptance of only Mosaic law (see **Other Faiths,** p. 24). About 300 of them live in Nablus today, representing two-thirds of the world's Samaritans. Their synagogue houses what they believe to be the world's oldest *Torah* scroll. The Samaritan observance of Passover includes the sacrifice of a sheep atop Mt. Gerizim on the evening before the full moon.

Tourist buses from Jerusalem and Tel Aviv bring visitors to witness the bloody rite. Taxis make the arduous drive up the mountain for about NIS20.

SABASTIYA סבסתיה سبستية

An array of Israelite, Hellenistic, and Roman ruins crown an unassuming hill 11km northwest of Nablus. The ruins lie on a peak first settled by Omri, King of Israel, in the 9th century BCE as the city of **Shomron** (Samaria). Shomron served as the capital of the Israelite kingdom until the Assyrian invasion of the 8th century BCE. Over the next several centuries, it served as the seat of Assyrian, Persian, and Greek governments. Under Herod, the city was made into the showpiece of the Holy Land to win the favor of the Roman emperors.

The ruins, under the control of the Israel National Parks Authority, are above the present-day Arab village of **Sabastiya.** Unfortunately, most of the ancient splendor is long gone, although the weed-covered ruins and beautiful 360-degree views may make it easier to imagine the city in ancient times. At the top of the hill lie the remnants of Israelite and Hellenistic walls, a Roman acropolis and amphitheater, and the bases of columns built for the **Temple of Augustus.** Watch your step—the narrow 1.5km path (a 30min. walk) encircling the ruins is slippery. Just before the site on the main road, **Rajab's Holy Land Sun Restaurant** offers *musakhan* (NIS50), a Palestinian dish with chicken, onions, and spices served on a large flat bread. (☎239 74 20. Open daily 8am-8pm; in winter 8am-6pm.)

Service taxis to Sabastiya are available from Nablus (NIS3.50); hire a cab on Fridays or if the wait is too long (NIS30). Open daily 8am-4pm. NIS14, students NIS12, children NIS6.

AL-IZARIYYEH (BETHANY) العزرية

A relatively prosperous Palestinian village, Bethany is sacred to Christians as the home of Lazarus and his sisters Mary Magdalene and Martha. Jesus performed one of his best-known miracles here, raising Lazarus from the dead (John 11:1-44). Churches and archaeological sites commemorate the event on the hillside. Signs and souvenir vendors point tourists left up a small road to the Franciscan **New Church of St. Lazarus.** Built in 1954, it marks a spot where Jesus was supposed to have slept. Excavations near the church have unearthed shrines dating back to the 4th century. South of the church lie the remains of an **abbey** built in 1143 by Queen Melisende of Jerusalem. The excavations are unlit—bring a light and try to find someone to show you around. Women should dress modestly. (☎674 92 91. Church and excavations open daily Apr.-Sept. 8-11:30am and 2-6pm; Oct.-Mar. 8-11:30am and 2-5pm. Donations accepted.)

Signs from the Franciscan Church point uphill to the first-century **Tomb of Lazarus.** When the Crusaders arrived, they built a church over Lazarus's tomb, a monastery over Mary and Martha's house, and a tower over Simon the Leper's abode (Simon was another resident of Bethany cured by Jesus). In the 16th century, Muslims erected a mosque over the shrine, and in the following century, Christians dug another entrance to the tomb so they too could worship there. The tomb does not contain Lazarus's body—although some believe that he was re-buried in the same spot when he died again 30 years later. Descend the steps and stoop down to observe. (Tomb open daily 8am-7pm. When approaching, a person will come and ask for a donation; NIS2 is appropriate.)

Five minutes further along the main road, the beautiful silver domes of the **Greek Orthodox Convent** shelter the boulder upon which Jesus sat while awaiting Martha. Twelve friendly nuns live here now but don't speak much English. (☎279 97 08. Use the resounding door knocker to summon a nun. Open daily; early mornings or evenings are best. Free.)

Bethany lies on the road between Jerusalem and Jericho and blends into its sister city, Abu Dis, which lies just to the west. Take a *service* from either Damascus Gate in Jerusalem (NIS2.50) or from Jericho's central square (NIS7). No one (other than tour guides) knows where "Bethany" is; use the Arabic name, al-Izariyyeh (ih-zar-EE-yeh). *Service* stop by request at the gas station in town, next to the road to al-Quds University. To reach the sights, walk away from Jerusalem on the main road. Alternately, stay in the *service* and ask the driver to stop where the road makes a bend to the right.

HEBRON חברון الخليل

Today, Hebron is the most important industrial center in the West Bank. With a population of about 190,000 in the city proper and 418,300 in the district, it is the largest West Bank city. Since 1997, the city (and the mosque) has been divided into two parts; H1 (about 80% of the city) is under PA (Palestinian Authority) control and H2 (the remaining 20%) is under Israeli control. While promised security as part of the redeployment agreements, the enclave of about 500 Israelis who live here engenders strong feelings of resentment from the Palestinian population of 130,000. As of summer 2000, relations were relatively peaceful; nevertheless, all visitors to Hebron should make their tourist status as obvious as possible and take into account that even native Palestinians sometimes regard the city as unsafe.

While the city lags behind other West Bank destinations in terms of Western influences and infrastructure, it is not without tourist appeal. For the intrepid traveler, this is *terra incognita*, just waiting to be explored and appreciated. A handful of tour agencies in Jerusalem, Bethlehem, and Ramallah also lead excellent, informative daytrips (see below). From its lively Old City market and taxi-filled New City streets to the quieter Jewish settlement and venerated burial ground of Abraham, Hebron provides visitors with a strikingly multi-faceted, non-commercialized taste of reality.

GETTING THERE. Transportation to Hebron from Jerusalem is simple; *service* taxis leave frequently from the parking lot across the street from Damascus Gate (45min., NIS7). From Bethlehem, *service* taxis leave from Bab al-Zaqaq, at the corner of Hebron Rd. and Paul VI Rd. (30min., NIS6). To find a *service* back to Jerusalem or Bethlehem, take the right fork uphill from the center of town.

PRACTICAL INFORMATION. Because Hebron has never been a big tourist destination, commodities that have become prevalent in towns such as Bethlehem and Jericho (such as maps or English street signs) are non-existent. The main street in Hebron is **Bab al-Zawiyeh,** which leads down into the maze of **Old City** arches and alleys. The Jewish area, south of Bab al-Zawiyeh, is easily identified by the dozens of Israeli flags strung over the roads. The **Tomb of the Patriarchs** is at the eastern end of the city; walk through (or around) the Old City to get there.

Although there is no real tourist office, the **Ministry of Tourism and Antiquities** (☎222 96 33), in the Ministry of Local Government building ten minutes outside of town (take a taxi, NIS6), will do their best to answer questions. Tour agencies that offer full or half-day trips to Hebron (sometimes combined with Bethlehem) include **Alternative Tours,** leaving from the Jerusalem Hotel in East Jerusalem (☎628 32 82 or 052 864 205; 6hr., NIS70); **PACE,** leaving from their office in Ramallah (☎298 68 54; 10hr., NIS170); and **ATG,** leaving from Beit Sahour (☎277 22 11; full or half day, price and length depend on group size and length of trip). Call for updated schedules.

ACCOMMODATIONS AND FOOD. In terms of accommodations, there's really only one option: the **Hebron Tourist Hotel** (☎/fax 222 67 60), on King Fossel St. Breakfast included. Clean rooms have TV, fans, and private baths. (Take the right fork uphill from the center of town; about 20m past the municipality building, go up the stairs on the left; the hotel is to your right. (Singles US$35; doubles US$45; triples US$55.) For cheap **food,** there's no beating the fresh produce and falafel stands found throughout the market.

SIGHTS. The primary tourist site in Hebron, the half-synagogue, half-mosque **Tomb of the Patriarchs** is thought to lie directly above the underground tombs of Abraham, Isaac, Rebecca, Jacob, and Leah. The tomb of Abraham is visible through bars from both sides; the tombs of Isaac and Rebecca, however, are entirely within the mosque. The cave itself may not be visited but can be seen through an opening in the floor of the mosque, in front of Abraham's tomb. While in the same room, note the huge, oak lectern from which the *imam* delivers the Friday sermon. Added by Salah al-Din in the 12th century, it is one of the few in the world carved from a single block of wood. In the same room, the longest Herodian cut stone ever discovered forms part of the walls. More than 4m in length, it lies in the southeast corner of the room. Lift the carpet to get a glimpse or ask someone to point it out. Since 1994, when an American-born Jewish extremist entered the mosque and opened fire, killing 48 muslims and injuring 200, Jews have been officially barred from entering the mosque. All entrants are required to present a passport (without a Jewish-sounding last name) and pass through several metal detectors. Security at the Jewish and Muslim entrances is extremely tight, and modest dress is required. (Mosque closed F; Synagogue open M-F, Jews only Sa.)

Formerly a Jewish hospital and currently a small museum on King David St., **Beit Hadassah** commemorates the massacre of 1929. The museum has no regular hours; knock at the door upstairs on the left.

For sights of a less political nature, the **al-Salam Glass Factory** is located on the road between Hebron and Bethlehem. Watch the famous Hebron glass being handmade and blown from recycled materials, or shop at the adjacent wholesale store. (☎222 91 27. Open Sa-Th 8am-8pm, F 8am-noon.)

GAZA غزة

The distance separating Israel from the Gaza Strip is covered in a one-minute car ride from one side of the border checkpoint to the other. Once in Gaza City, however, it becomes apparent that the short distance from Israel's booming industrial centers to Gaza City's Palestine Square sets the two regions worlds apart. A 46km long and 6-10km wide sliver along the Mediterranean coast, the Gaza Strip contains some of the most densely populated areas of the world. Population has increased dramatically in recent years, swelling to more than 1 million people with an influx of over 570,000 Palestinian refugees since 1951.

Gaza's history stretches back to 3000 BCE, when it was inhabited by Arab Canaanites. It grew as a stopping point for traders traveling from Africa and the Sinai to the southwest and from parts of the Middle East and Asia to the east. The Prophet Muhammad's grandfather, Hashem Bin Abd Manaf, is said to have been one such trader. He died when passing through Gaza City and is purportedly buried in one of the city's mosques (see p. 341).

Gaza is perhaps most well-known for its history of occupation and uprising under Israel. The region was administered by Egypt from 1948 until the 1967 Six-Day War. Refugees flooded into the area after the Israeli occupation of that year, and of the 770,000 refugees living in Gaza today, over 420,000 continue to live in the overcrowded United Nations-sponsored camps. The *Intifada* (see p. 16) began in 1987 in Gaza in the Jabalya camp near Gaza City. The peace process intensified with the onset of the intifada, and the Oslo and Cairo agreements of 1994 placed the Palestine Authority in control of the Gaza Strip.

Gaza now seeks to reinvigorate its long history as an intercontinental crossroads, as evidenced by widespread construction and the growing numbers of international trade and investment signs that line Gaza City's streets. Renewed attempts are being made to rehabilitate refugee camps with the help of the U.N., the European Community, and other international resources. Tourist officials hope that the sea and beaches will entice crowds of visitors. However, it is the disorderly everyday life of Gaza's present—the mosques, churches, and unearthed archaeological finds that blend haphazardly into side-streets and vending stalls—that makes for the most fascinating and affordable random wandering for travelers. Gaza throbs with the activity of its capital's outdoor markets, chokes in the dust and cramped quarters of the refugee camps, and embraces its visitors with hospitality and an eagerness to communicate the experience of life in Gaza.

SAFETY WARNING. Since 1994, the Gaza Strip has been governed by the autonomous Palestinian National Authority (PNA). While Israeli citizens cannot travel into Gaza without special permission, foreign tourists can generally visit without problems. Travel in the Gaza Strip is usually perfectly **safe,** though tourists should register with their respective consulates in Israel before going and should keep abreast of current events in the region so as to avoid visiting during times of unrest or tension. Women must dress modestly–long sleeves and a long skirt–and men should not wear shorts. Have your passport on hand at all times.

BORDER CROSSINGS

At press time, **Erez** was the only border checkpoint open for crossing from Israel into Gaza. Passing through the checkpoint is relatively easy for foreign tourists. There are several ways to get to the Erez checkpoint. From **Tel Aviv,** catch a bus to **Ashkelon** (see p. 169). Bus #037 from Ashkelon's bus station will stop at the Erez checkpoint—be sure to specify the checkpoint and not the town (30min.; Su-Th

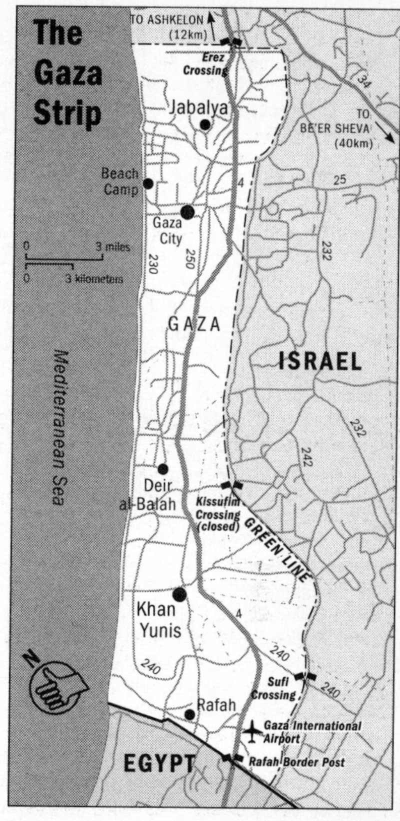

9:15am, 2:15, 6:10pm, F 12:45pm; return Su-Th 6:35, 10:30am, 3:40pm, F 6:35am and 1:45pm; NIS10). From the bus stop, follow the highway as it curves left into the checkpoint parking lot, beyond which are the covered walkway and Israeli and Gazan checkpoints. Buses from Ashkelon to the **Yad Mordechai Junction,** about 4km from the checkpoint, run more frequently (#36, 364, 365; 7-8 per day 8:30am-6pm; NIS8). There may be taxis at the junction or running along the highway that will take passengers to the checkpoint, but don't count on it. From **Jerusalem,** *service* taxis meet across from Damascus Gate and go directly to the checkpoint (1hr.; infrequent, depart when full; NIS30). Though it is not possible to enter Gaza by car, it is helpful to understand the system of colored **license plates** that differentiates vehicles. Those registered in Israel or in Jewish settlements have yellow plates, white plates with green numbers belong to vehicles registered with the Palestinian Authority. Blue plates are a remnant from the days when the Palestinian territories were the Occupied Territories; they signify Arab cars not registered with Israel. Others are black-on-white (UN or diplomatic), red (police), and black (army).

There are three steps to crossing the checkpoint. First, Israeli soldiers will inspect your passport and record the reason for and proposed length of your stay in Gaza. They will then give you a slip of paper for presentation when entering Gaza. Taxis cross the border for NIS10, but the walk is very short. After crossing into Gaza, your information will once again be entered into a ledger. On the return trip to Israel, luggage is passed through an X-ray machine.

On the Gaza side of the checkpoint are taxis heading into Gaza City. A *service* taxi should cost NIS5 to Palestine Square on the main street, **Omar al-Mukhtar.** A *special* taxi, with a single passenger or party, can cost anywhere from NIS20-50.

GETTING AROUND

The bus system in Gaza Strip tends to be erratic, slow, and uncomfortably warm. Taxis are far more convenient and almost as cheap. Within Gaza City, where there is no intracity bus service, seemingly half of all cars serve as taxis. *Special* taxis are more expensive than *service* (group) taxis. Rides anywhere along Omar al-Mukhtar St., which runs from the Palestine Sq. market to the hotel strip along the beach, cost NIS1. Destinations off the main road will cost more; pay NIS1 and negotiate an additional fare upon entering the taxi. Buses and taxis to destinations in the Gaza Strip outside of Gaza City, such as Khan Yunis and Rafah, leave from a parking lot in Palestine Square, just beyond the Gaza City municipality building. Long yellow *service* taxis depart whenever they fill with passengers.

JEWISH SETTLEMENTS. It is not possible to travel from within Palestinian Authority areas of the Gaza Strip directly to the Jewish settlements, which are under Israeli jurisdiction. However, Egged buses run from Israel to the settlements (see **Israeli Settlements,** p. 342).

MONEY

New Israeli shekels (NIS) are the most frequently used currency in the Gaza Strip, though **dollars (US$)** are often accepted as well and can be changed to shekels for little or no commission at many places in Gaza City. Credit cards are not widely accepted, and travelers' checks are very difficult to cash. Western Union is available, but it is advisable to **bring sufficient cash** for your stay. Keep in mind that many of the places to change or spend money are closed on Fridays.

LANGUAGE AND KEEPING IN TOUCH

Do not exercise any newly-gained knowledge of Hebrew during your stay; counter any taunting "*shalom*" with an Arabic "*marhaba.*" Many people, especially children, are eager to practice their English on a native speaker. For some basic Arabic words and phrases, see the **Arabic Phrasebook,** p. 376.

The blue public phones in the Gaza Strip operate on phone cards that can be purchased in small shops and groceries throughout Gaza (NIS15-60). Phone calls can be made from hotels as well, but are more expensive. There are less expensive privately run phone offices in Gaza City (see **Telephones,** p. 56).

GAZA CITY ☎07

Despite an initial assault on the senses, visitors soon settle into the remarkably laid-back rhythm of life in the city. Roaming around Gaza City's centers of activity brings a glimpse of present-day life—of women peering through the slits of full-body dark clothing and of men sucking on large, feathered *sheeshas*—but it also offers encounters with the city's centuries-old architectural and cultural treasures. The key to Gaza City is exploration of the ancient sights and thriving culture.

GETTING THERE AND GETTING AROUND

Flights: Gaza Airport (☎213 56 96 and 213 42 28), near Rafah. **EgyptAir** (☎282 51 80), on Jala'a St. at the corner with al-Wihda St., to the right off of Omar al-Mukhtar St. when coming from Palestine Sq., flies to **Cairo (**NIS240/US$80, round-trip NIS668/ US$167. Cash only. **Royal Jordanian** (☎282 54 03) flies to Amman (US$120, round-trip US$190). **Palestinian Airlines** (☎282 28 00) also flies to Cairo (US$142 one-way) and other destinations.

Buses: In Palestine Sq., in front of where the taxis leave. **Gaza Bus Company** (☎282 26 16) sends non-A/C buses to **Khan Yunis** (1hr., NIS2) and **Rafah** (1½hr., NIS2.50).

Taxis: Long yellow *service* taxis leave when full to **Khan Yunis** (30min., NIS3.50) and **Rafah** (45min., NIS4.50). *Special* taxis will go to either location for much higher prices. In Gaza City taxis honk for passengers (NIS1 along Omar al-Mukhtar St.). For *special* taxis, **Imad** will pick up passengers at pre-arranged locations (☎286 40 00).

Car Rental: Yafa Rent-a-Car (☎282 51 27), on Omar al-Mukhtar St., one block toward Palestine Sq. from Ahmed Orabi St. Look for the blue sign on the left. One day rentals NIS120-200/US$30-50. 24+. Open Sa-Th 8am-10pm.

ORIENTATION

Taxis from the Erez checkpoint stop in **Palestine Sq.** (*Midan Filisteen*), the site of the main market, the Gaza City municipal building, taxis and buses to destinations in the Gaza Strip, and many of the historical sights. The main street, **Omar al-Mukhtar St.,** runs from Palestine Sq. to the coast. Almost all of the hotels are in the **Remal** (beach) district of the city, lined up along the coastal road **Ahmed Orabi,** which forms a T-junction at the end of Omar al-Mukhtar St.

Money-changing facilities and small shops cluster around Palestine Sq. Another commercial center is built around the **Unknown Soldier Garden,** a grassy and flowered walkway median that divides the lanes of Omar al-Mukhtar. The Garden is about 1.5km toward the beach from Palestine Square. Restaurants lie along the main street, on streets near the main street, and in the hotel district on the coastal road. Only the major streets in Gaza City have both English and Arabic street signs, and establishments are rarely numbered, making directions a matter of finding landmarks and approximating distances from there.

PRACTICAL INFORMATION

TOURIST AND FINANCIAL SERVICES

Tourist Offices: Gaza City's **public relations and information office** (☎282 47 00), at the beginning of Palestine Sq., near the Arab Bank and under an English sign. Enter from Omar al-Mukhtar through the gate for the Municipality and walk through the parking lot and under the overhang to the door on the left. Friendly staff gives out a free brochure with a map of Gaza City, a list of important phone numbers, and a description of sights. Open Su-Th 8am-2:30pm.

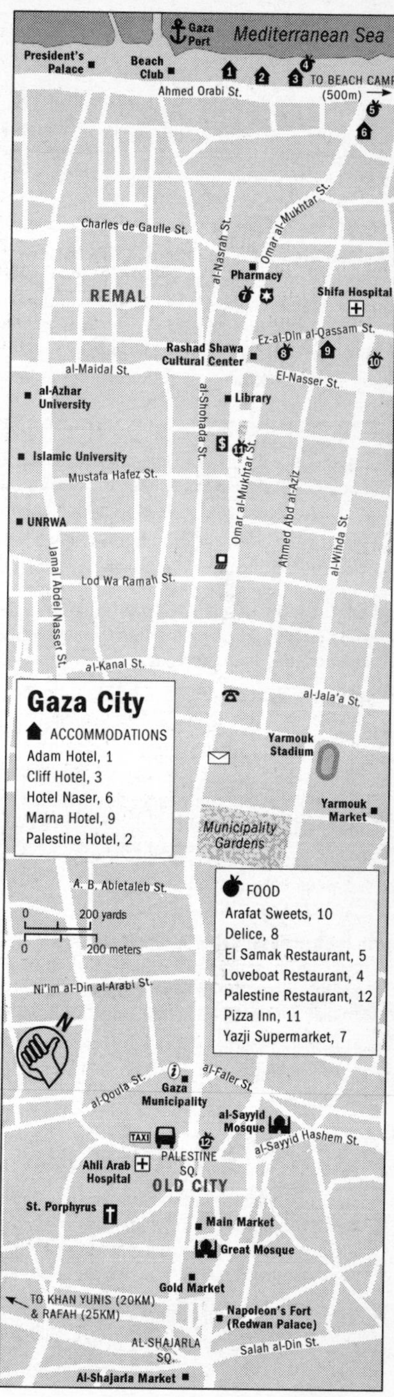

GAZA

Currency Exchange: Private agencies along Omar al-Mukhtar St. and near Palestine Square change money for no commission: look for the dollar signs. Open Sa-Th 9am-9pm. **Bank of Palestine** (☎284 30 39), on Omar al-Mukhtar St. on the right when walking away from the beach. No commission. Offers Moneygram. Open Sa-W 8:30am-12:30pm and 3-5pm, Th 8:30am-12:30pm. **Western Union** (☎282 10 77), on Omar al-Mukhtar St., 20m past the Bank of Palestine toward Palestine Sq. Open Sa-W 8:30am-12:30pm and 2-4pm, Th 8:30am-12:30pm.

LOCAL SERVICES

Human Rights Organizations: UNRWA (☎677 74 88), on Jamal Abdel Nasser St. Take a taxi to the "UN." Once there, go to the public information office. Offers tours to **Jabalya refugee camp,** a 15min. ride from the city. Call in advance to arrange a tour–the office has limited personnel and finances. Donations requested. Open Su-Th 7:30am-3pm. **Palestinian Center for Human Rights,** 29 Omar al-Mukhtar St. (☎282 47 76; www.pchrgaza.com), one block from the beach on the left next to the Al-Amal Hotel. Has a public library on Gaza, focusing on refugees and Jewish settlements. Call ahead. Open Sa-Th 8am-2:30pm.

Library: Public library, 84 Omar al-Mukhtar St. (☎286 58 96), at the end of the Unknown Soldier park closest to the Rashad Shawwa Cultural Center under a sign reading "Center of Culture and Light." Has English books and West Bank newspapers. Open M-Th, Sa 9am-5pm; F 9am-1pm. There is also a library on the second floor of the **Rashad Shawwa Cultural Center** (☎282 11 04.) Open Sa-Th 8am-6pm.

EMERGENCY AND COMMUNICATIONS

Police (☎286 34 00), on Omar al-Mukhtar St., one block up from Charles De Gaulle St. when coming from the beach.

Pharmacy: Masoud (☎286 18 79), at the corner of Charles de Gaulle St. and Omar al-Mukhtar St. Open daily 7:30am-midnight. Call 24hr. for emergency.

Hospitals: Ahli Arab Hospital (☎282 03 25), on the first street to the right just beyond the bus and taxi stand in Palestine Sq. **Shifa Hospital** (☎286 55 20), on Ez al-Din al-Qassam St. From the beach, turn left on Omar al-Mukhtar St. just before the Rashad Shawwa Cultural Center.

Telephones: El-Baz (☎286 01 20), on Omar al-Mukhtar St. just after Canal St., on the left when coming from the beach. Open Sa-Th 9am-10pm. International calls NIS4 per min., local calls NIS1 per min.

Internet Access: Cyber Internet Cafe (☎282 23 37), on Omar al-Mukhtar St., one block past the Unknown Soldier Garden when coming from the beach. Enter under the green sign that reads "Arab Islamic Bank." Go upstairs and take the elevator to the fifth floor. Internet access NIS7 per hr. Open Sa-Th 9am-11pm, F 4-11pm.

Post Office: 183 Omar al-Mukhtar St., next to the Municipal garden, halfway between the Unknown Soldiers' Park and Palestine Sq., Open Su-Th 8am-2:30pm. Palestinian (not Israeli) stamps are issued here.

PUFF THE MAGIC SHEESHA In Gaza, relaxation has become synonymous with gurgling and puffing noises accompanied by the smell of sugary tobacco. The *sheesha* consists of a snake-like tube and a small bowl filled with burning coals, tobacco, and spices. Water vapor carries the tobacco smoke through the .3-1m tube and into the mouth. The instrument of pleasure is a popular smoking apparatus known in Gaza, like in Egypt, as a *sheesha* (elsewhere as a *nargilah*), and is thought to have been introduced by the Turks and popularized by the Egyptian elite during the late 17th century. Though smoking a *sheesha* seems to come as second nature to Gazans, the trend has only recently been borrowed from Egyptian Arabs.

ACCOMMODATIONS

Gaza City offers a number of non-budget accommodations. Rooms start at around NIS120 and include breakfast. Most of the hotels are in the Remal district on the strip along the coastal road Ahmed Orabi, a short walk from the end of Omar al-Mukhtar St. Proprietors generally speak English and are eager to offer insights into Gaza, as well as suggestions for sights and places to eat.

Marna House (☎282 26 24 or 282 33 22), on Ahmed Abd al-Aziz St. From Palestine Sq., walk along Omar al-Mukhtar St. and turn right on Ez al-Din al-Qassam St., just past the Rashad Shawwa Cultural Center. Ahmed Abd is on the right and the hotel is on the left. Lounge downstairs has English books on Gaza, maps of Gaza City, and the infamous talking bird. Rooms are tastefully decorated, with bath, satellite TV, and A/C. Singles NIS200/US$50; doubles NIS240/US$60. Traveler's checks accepted.

Adam Hotel (☎286 69 76), on Ahmed Orabi St., 120m past Cliff Hotel. Plexi-glass elevator on outside of building offers views of the city. Small rooms with red decor, abundant mirrors, private bath, TV, and A/C. Reception 24hr. Singles NIS160/US$40; doubles NIS220/US$55. NIS20/US$5 student discount. Cash only.

Palestine Hotel (☎282 33 55; fax 282 68 13), on Ahmed Orabi St., 100m past the Cliff Hotel. All rooms behind the glitzy facade have balconies with a seaside view, as well as satellite TV, fridge, bath, and A/C. Beds are especially large. Check-out noon. Singles NIS220/US$55; doubles NIS260/US$65. Additional person NIS60/US$15. 15% student discount. MC, V, and traveler's checks accepted.

Hotel Naser (☎283 73 09), on Omar al-Mukhtar, on the right one block before the beach. Cheapest singles in Gaza City. Clean rooms have floral carpets, balconies (with no view), and very comfortable chairs. Spotless shared bathrooms with tiled floors and bathtubs. Singles NIS100; doubles NIS200; triples NIS250. Cash only.

Cliff Hotel (☎286 13 53), on Ahmed Orabi St. Take a left at the end of Omar al-Mukhtar St., where it forms a T-junction with Ahmed Orabi St., the coastal road. The hotel is on the right. Claims to be the first hotel in the Gaza Strip, though its beautiful airy rooms don't betray their age. Ocean-view rooms with full bath, A/C, TV, fridge, and phone. Breakfast included. Adjoining seaside restaurant. Reception 24hr. Check-out noon. Singles NIS200/US$50; doubles NIS240/US$60. MC accepted.

FOOD

Gaza City's fare ranges from typical Middle Eastern falafel to multi-course traditional Palestinian meals, though the city's speciality is seafood, served in restaurants along the coastal road. These seafood restaurants offer the most after-dark activity in the city. Prices are affordable enough for the thrifty traveler to indulge, and the market near Palestine Sq. offers fresh fruits and veggies for even less. Drinking water is of inconsistent quality: for bottled water, as well as other basics, try the **Yazji Supermarket** on Omar al-Mukhtar. When coming from the beach, look for the red awning on the right side of the street, one block past Charles De Gaulle St. (Open daily 8am-11pm. MC accepted.) Keep in mind that the Islamic prohibition of alcohol makes asking for or consuming alcohol in Gaza a bad idea.

Palestine Restaurant (☎284 85 83), on Omar al-Mukhtar St. Look for the large sign on the building overlooking Palestine Sq. Offers affordable food high above the city. Extensive menu includes hamburgers (NIS10), kebabs (NIS20), and pizza (NIS20-45). Relax with a *sheesha* (NIS5-6). Open Sa-Th 8am-1am, F noon-midnight.

El Samak Restaurant (☎286 43 85), on Ahmed Orabi St., on the corner of Omar al-Mukhtar St. Inviting seafood restaurant with a beautiful ocean view. Wide variety of fish and shrimp dishes (NIS40-60) are complemented by a large salad (NIS30) and soup (NIS10) selection. Cash only. Open daily 9am-midnight.

Loveboat Restaurant, through the courtyard in the Cliff Hotel on Ahmed Orabi St. Full meat (NIS40) or fish (NIS50) meal includes salad and coffee or tea, served in room shaped like the hull of a boat. Come aboard daily 7am-10pm.

Pizza Inn (☎284 04 25), on Omar al-Mukhtar St., in the middle of the Unknown Soldier Garden. Specialty pizzas (small NIS25, medium NIS35, large NIS48), all-you-can-eat salad bar (NIS15), hamburgers (NIS10), and spicy chicken wings (NIS12) served in this monolithic glass building. Open daily 9:30am-midnight.

SWEETS

Pastries play an important role in the lives of Palestinians. During weddings it is customary for male members of the family to present sweets to the guests. Those who do not have the opportunity to attend a Palestinian wedding can sample delicious pastries at one of the many stores around Gaza City.

Arafat Sweets (☎286 37 14). From the beach on Omar al-Mukhtar St., take a left on al-Nasser St., walk 3 long blocks to al-Wihda St., and take another left. On the right, with a large sign in English. The Arafats have been churning out pastries since 1912. Ask to see the factory in back where workers grind out and hand-mold loads of cookies (NIS18 for 0.5kg), cakes, and traditional Palestinian desserts (NIS10-36 per kg) Another location on Famey Buuk St., next to Palestine Sq. Open M-Sa 7:30am-11:30pm.

Delice (☎282 25 69), 4 Ez al-Din al-Qassam St. From the beach on Omar al-Mukhtar St., take a left on Ez al-Din al-Qassam St. The cafe is one block down on the right. Small meals, warm drinks, and a delectable selection of sweets and cheese-filled croissants (NIS2) in a chic patio. Pastries NIS4. For sweet-tooth overload, sample from the wide variety of cakes. Fruit NIS5. Open daily 8am-midnight.

SIGHTS

Gaza City's sights are concentrated in the area immediately surrounding Palestine Sq. Though they are in varying states of disrepair and are not really maintained for tourists, Gaza has a wide range of cultural, religious, and archaeological sights that are well worth the hunt.

MARKET. The central *souq* is a whirlwind of bagged spices, slabs of raw meat, and heaps of fruits and vegetables. The market operates from early morning to dusk, but it is most lively in the morning. The food can be a great deal, but only if properly bargained. See **The Fine Art of Haggling**, p. 120. *(Along the narrow street running parallel to Omar al-Mukhtar St., on the opposite side of the Bank Jordan in Palestine Sq.)*

GREAT MOSQUE. The Great Mosque, or al-Omari Mosque, is Gaza's most impressive archaeological structure. Representative of Gaza's eclectic history, it stands on the site of a 12th-century Crusader church, which was built over an ancient temple. The mosque is still used today by local Muslims. *(Directly off Market St. Often open to visitors between prayer times.)*

GOLD MARKET. Gaza City's glimmering gold market is what remains of a large Mamluk market. Sidewalk vendors and small shops along the street display ropes and bangles of bright, yellow gold. *(The market is off Market St., under a vaulted walkway that runs alongside the Great Mosque.)*

AL-REDWAN CASTLE. This 17th-century fortress was built from the remains of a 13th-century Mamluk Palace. Napoleon spent three nights here in 1799 while waging a war against Egypt and Syria. During Ottoman rule the building served as the governor's residence, and during the British mandate, it was a prison. Today, the dilapidated fort is hidden behind an overgrown garden on the grounds of a girls' school. *(Streets branching off to the left from the souq and the gold market lead to*

REFUGEE CAMPS There are eight Palestinian refugee camps scattered throughout the Gaza Strip. Most are clustered in the north, in the vicinity of Gaza City: Jabalya is a 15-minute car ride and Beach camp a mere five-minute walk from the city. There also are sizable camps in the Strip's other two major cities to the south, Khan Yunis and Rafah. From Gaza City, visitors can walk into Beach camp, though the most meaningful way to understand a camp is to set up a tour to Jabalya with Gaza City's United Nations Relief and Works Agency (UNRWA; see practical information below). UNRWA guides visitors through the camp to the educational, health, and community facilities it has helped establish to aid refugees.

al-Wihda St. and the fort. Look for an opening in the gate. Caretakers usually let visitors see the fort 7am-7pm.)

AL-SAYYID HASHEM MOSQUE. The great-grandfather of the Prophet Muhammad, a merchant who died while traveling through Gaza City, is said to be buried under one of the four porticos of the courtyard, built in 1850 by an Ottoman Sultan. *(From Palestine Sq. take the side street on the right when facing the Palestine Restaurant. At the intersection bear left, and the minaret and mosque walls will come into view.)*

GREEK ORTHODOX CHURCH OF SAINT PORPHYRUS. Gaza's major historical church abuts the minaret of a small mosque to the right. The church was first built on the site in the beginning of the 5th century and was named after Saint Porphyrus, who laid its cornerstone. St. Porphyrus, who hailed from northern Greece, was charged with spreading Christendom in Gaza at a time when many of the city's residents prayed to multiple gods and literally threw stones at the idea of monotheism. Upon prophesying the birth of the empress' child, St. Porphyrus won a mandate for the city's polytheistic temples to be torn down and for a Christian church to be built. March 10, the day of the saint's death, is still celebrated by Gazan Christians. There is an impressive collection of dark Orthodox icons along the walls. *(Across Palestine Sq., on the 2nd street that curves down to the right beyond the bus station. To see the inside of the chapel go to the 2nd floor of the modern church building to the left and ask to see the church. ☎282 68 06. Open daily 9am-1:30pm).*

BEACH CAMP. For those unable to plan a tour of the Jabalya camp with UNRWA, the Beach camp is a five-minute walk from Gaza City. Seafood restaurants gradually give way to the small cinder-block constructions and mostly unpaved roads of the refugee camp. *(Turn right on Ahmed Orabi St. from the end of Omar al-Mukhtar St.)*

ENTERTAINMENT

A 15-minute walk past Palestine Sq. back toward the beach is the **Municipality Garden** on the right at 185 Omar al-Mukhtar St. The park stands out along the dry city street as an oasis of lush green lawns, prettily-planned walkways, and a variety of palms and flowers.

Gaza City's **beaches,** while nice to look at out of hotel and restaurant windows, are dishearteningly dirty along Ahmed Orabi St. Farther away from the city and the Beach camp the beaches begin to look more appealing, though swimming is still discouraged due to dangerously strong undertows, a lack of lifeguards, and the requirement of full-body coverage for females. However, this does not stop hundreds of Palestinian youngsters from romping around on hot summer days.

For all of your flag desires, head to the **PLO Flag Shop** on Wihda St. To get to the shop, take a left on al-Nasser St. when coming up Omar St. from the beach, and then turn right onto al-Wihda St. (☎286 04 01. Open daily 7am-11pm.)

DAYTRIPS FROM GAZA CITY

KHAN YUNIS

Take a bus (1hr., NIS2) or a service taxi (30min., NIS3.50) from Gaza City's Palestine Sq.

Khan Yunis's primary points of interest are its dilapidated *khan* (an ancient road-stop for caravans) and the active agricultural market nearby. Once in Khan Yunis, ask to be let off at the city center, a bustling street with a small park and the ruins of the *khan* stretching across toward the market at the far end. The two-story *khan* was built in the late 14th century. The **Restaurant Bolevar** (☎206 79 88) opposite the garden from the *khan*, to the left of the mosque, serves *shawarma* (NIS5), hamburgers (NIS6), salads (NIS2) and steaks (NIS20) in a cozy two-story seating area. (Open daily 10am-midnight.) There's also a hotel in Khan Yunis, run by the **El Amal City Red Crescent Society** (☎205 45 43; fax 205 46 21). Rooms have old-fashioned curtains, fans, bath, and satellite TV. Go to the tenth floor of the hotel for a birds-eye view. (Breakfast included. Free use of indoor swimming pool. Singles NIS120/US$30; doubles NIS200/US$50. Visa accepted.) The contrast with Gaza City is evident in the number of people crowded into considerably smaller streets and in the prevalence of women covered from head to toe in dark cloth.

GAZA

RAFAH

From Gaza City, take a bus (1½hr., NIS2.50) or service taxi (45min., NIS5). From Khan Yunis, backtrack along the main street from the khan toward the fruit and vegetable market, until reaching the corner with two-way traffic. Take a taxi from the khan (NIS2).

Rafah, the Strip's third-largest town and its border crossing point with Egypt, is 45 minutes south of Gaza City and a mere 15-minute drive from Khan Yunis. Rafah has been on the lips of ancient Egyptians, Assyrians, Greeks, Romans, and Arabs in the region for thousands of years. Today, it is known as the town that was divided between Egypt and Gaza in 1979. Part of its population remained in Egypt, while the remaining Palestinians fell under Israeli and ultimately PNA jurisdiction. To see the border with Egypt where Palestinians stand on boxes to talk to their relatives on the other side of the fence, walk on the main street with the market on your right for half a kilometer, then turn left.

JEWISH SETTLEMENTS: ḤOF TEMMARIM

Scattered across the Gaza Strip are 18 Jewish settlements, which are divided into two large groups: those in the north near Erez and those in the south near the coast. The Jewish settlements are under Israeli governance and are connected to Israel by roads traversed by Egged buses and heavily guarded by Israeli soldiers. They have little to offer in the way of tourist attractions, but some have begun to lure tourists with the attractive and uncrowded beaches on their territory. In Gush Katif in the very southern corner of the Strip, the **Hof Temmarim** settlement has a hotel complex and **Youth Hostel,** which is located to the right of where the bus lets off. The hostel has a private pool and is a close walk to the beach. All rooms have private bath and A/C. There is no restaurant within walking distance so bring your own food. (☎684 75 96 or 684 75 96. Call before 4pm to make reservations. Check-out 10am. NIS70 per bed. Cash only.)

The journey into **Ḥof Temmarim** is a sight in and of itself. Buses from Ashkelon stop at the **border checkpoint** and run to **Gush Katif** (#036; 2hr., Su-Th 5 per day 8:30am-6:30pm, F 3 per day 8:30am-2:15pm, Sa 10:45pm; return Su-Th 5 per day 6:34am-4:49pm, F 6:34am and 12:04pm, Sa 9:18pm; NIS23.50). All schedules are erratic; check ahead. With a military escort, the bus then drives into Gush Katif.

PETRA & SINAI

The two most popular sidetrip destinations from Israel are Jordan's Nabatean stone city, Petra, and Egypt's desert playground, the Sinai Peninsula. Petra makes an ideal two-day foray from Eilat; another option is to cross at the Allenby Bridge and follow the King's Highway southward from Amman (see **Border Crossings,** p. 344). Sinai, significantly bigger than Israel, is difficult to cover in less than a week, but its diving, hiking, mellow atmosphere, and religious sites are worth the trek.

PETRA البتراء ☎03

Match me such marvel save in Eastern clime,
a rose-red city 'half as old as Time'!
—Dean Burgon, *Petra*

As one approaches the once-lost city of Petra, towering sculptures peek out from the walls of a natural three-meter-wide fissure to reveal raw mountains that were fashioned by human hands into impossibly delicate structures. Petra ("stone" in Ancient Greek) is perhaps the most astounding ancient city left to the modern world, and certainly a must-see for visitors to the Middle East.

For 700 years, Petra was lost to all but the few hundred members of a Bedouin tribe who guarded their treasure from outsiders. In the 19th century, Swiss explorer Johann Burkhardt heard Bedouin speaking of a "lost city" and vowed to find it. Though initially unable to find a guide willing to disclose the city's location, he guessed that the city he sought was the Petra of legend, the biblical Sela, which should have been near Mt. Hor, the site of Aaron's tomb. Impersonating a Christian pilgrim, Burkhardt hired a guide, and on August 22, 1812, he became the first non-Bedouin in thousands of years to have walked between the cliffs of Petra's *siq* (the mile-long rift that was the only entrance to Petra). In the nearly two centuries since Burkhardt's discovery, Petra has become a feature tourist attraction, admired by visitors from all over the world, including the film crew of *Indiana Jones and the Last Crusade.*

Humans first set foot in the area back in the 8th millennium BCE. By the 6th century BCE, the Nabateans, a nomadic Arab tribe, had quietly moved onto land controlled by the Edomites and had begun to profit from the trade between lower Arabia and the Fertile Crescent. Over the next three centuries, the Nabatean Kingdom flourished, secure in its easily defended capital. The Nabateans carved their monumental temples out of the mountains, looking to Egyptian, Greek, and Roman styles for inspiration. Unique to the Nabateans are the crow-step patterns that grace the crowns of many of the memorials. The crow-steps so resemble inverted stairways that the people of Meda'in Salih (in Saudi Arabia) claimed that God threw Petra upside down and turned it to stone to punish its people for their wickedness. More historically verifiable evidence suggests that the Nabatean King Aretes defeated Pompey's Roman legions in 63 BCE. The Romans controlled the entire area around Nabatea, however, prompting the later King Rabel III to strike a deal: as long as the Romans did not attack during his lifetime, they would be permitted to move in after he died. In 106 CE, the Romans claimed the Nabatean Kingdom and inhabited this city of rosy Nubian sandstone. In its heyday, Petra housed as many as 30,000 people, but after the earthquake in 363 CE, a shift in trade routes to Palmyra, Syria, expansion of the sea trade around Arabia, and another earthquake in 747, much of Petra had deteriorated to rubble.

For decades after Burkhardt made his discovery public, the Bedouin adapted to the influx of tourists by providing them with food and accommodations inside Petra, a practice outlawed in 1984-85 out of concern for the monuments. While many of Petra's Bedouin have been relocated to a housing project near Wadi Musa, a large portion still make their homes in the more remote caves and hills of the city (spanning 50km, most of which the average tourist never sees). Many Bedouin sell souvenirs and drinks amidst the ruins; others tend goats—don't be surprised at the barnyard smells emanating from inside the tombs.

BORDER CROSSINGS

THE OLD IN AND OUT. The Israelis, Palestinians, and Jordanians are still trying to figure this one out for themselves. Much of the information listed here is erratic, though in summer 2000 border crossings were generally smooth.

There are three possible border crossings into Jordan: one in Jericho in the West Bank, one in Beit She'an in the North of Israel, and one in Eilat. Travelers to Petra usually cross at Eilat, which is only a few hours away. The border crossing from Eilat to Aqaba is surprisingly simple and should take less than an hour. Everyone must pay an NIS57 exit tax (for up-to-date info call ☎(07) 633 68 12) and walk the 1km no man's land between the two countries—there is no transportation. Jordanian visas can be obtained at the border; prices vary greatly according to nationality (Australia JD16, Canada JD36, Ireland JD11, New Zealand JD16, South Africa free, UK JD23, US JD33). Visas are valid up to one month. Taxis from Eilat to the border cost NIS15-20; from the border to Aqaba JD4. (Border open Su-Th 6:30am-10pm, F-Sa 8am-8pm; closed Yom Kippur and 'Eid al-Adha.)

Tourists crossing through Jericho's King Hussein/Allenby Bridge must obtain visas in advance (available in Tel Aviv, at the crossing between Eilat and Aqaba, and from Jordanian embassies and consulates). Everything remains unpredictable; get thorough, up-to-date information from your embassy or consulate before trying to cross. (NIS126. Border open Su-Th 8am-midnight, F-Sa 8am-3pm.) Buses and *service* frequently leave Amman's Abdali Station for the bridge. To get from Amman to Petra, it is necessary to drive or take public transportation. **JETT buses** depart to Petra (3½hr.; Su, Tu, F 6:30am; JD5.5, round-trip JD11, round-trip including admission to Petra JD33). Reserve one day in advance. You can catch a **service** to Petra from Abdali Station for JD4. *Service* depart when full.

PRACTICAL INFORMATION

CURRENCY

US$1 = JD0.71 (JORDANIAN DINARS)	JD1 = US$1.41
CDN$1 = JD0.48	JD1 = CDN$2.09
IR£1 = JD0.82	JD1 = IR£1.22
UK£1 = JD1.07	JD1 = UK£0.94
AUS$1 = JD0.41	JD1 = AUS$2.45
NZ$1 = JD0.32	JD1 = NZ$3.13
SAR1 = JD0.10	JD1 = SAR9.78
EUR€1 = JD0.66	JD1 = EUR€1.51
E£1 (EGYPTIAN POUND) = JD0.21	JD1 = E£4.83
NIS1 = JD0.17	JD1 = NIS5.83

The **Petra Visitors Center** offers a variety of services. (☎215 60 20. Open daily 7am-6pm.) For a "low-tour" of the city center, hire an official guide (2½hr., JD8). More comprehensive tours go to al-Madbah (JD8), al-Deir (JD15), and Jabal Harun (JD35-60). You can rent a horse for JD7 (you're also responsible for renting the guide's horse), but it's more interesting to remain on foot. It's easy to tag along with a guided group or form your own.

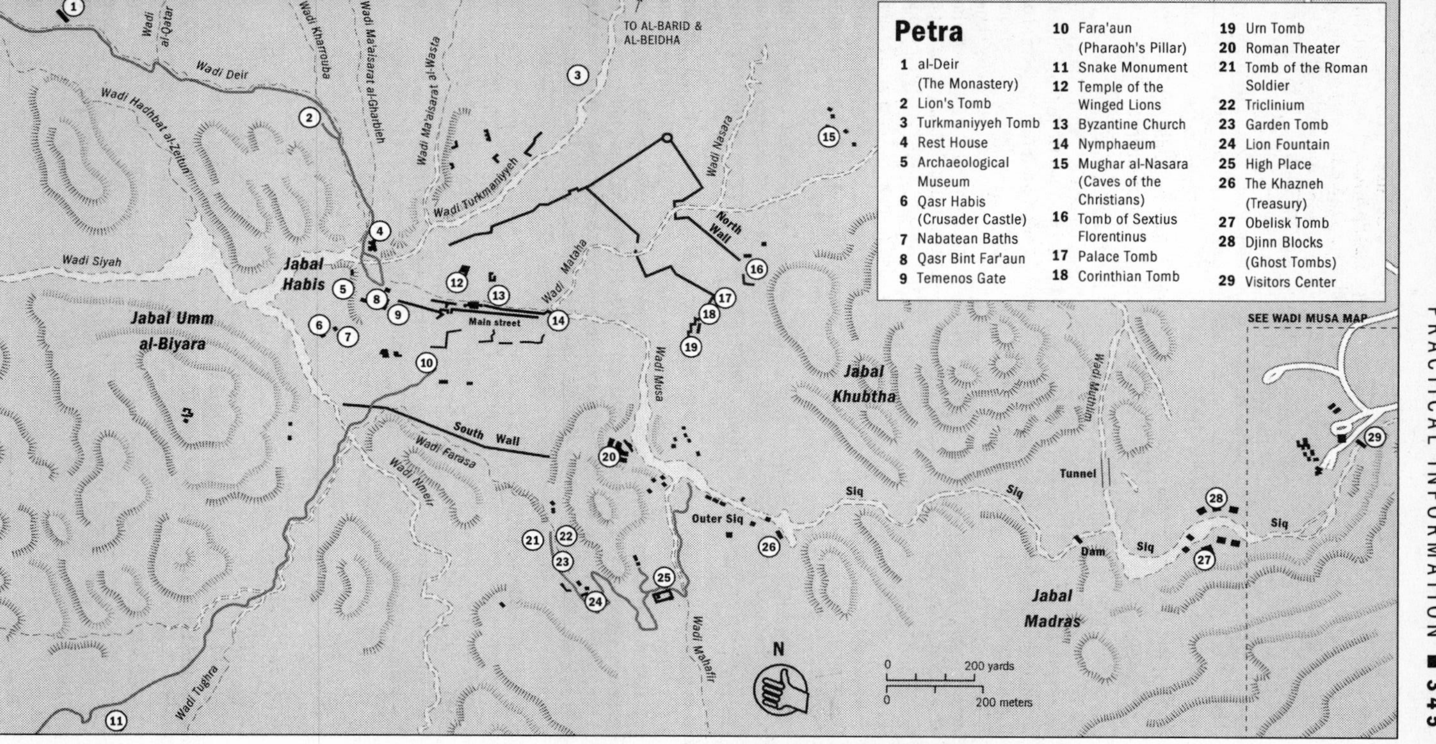
Petra
1 al-Deir (The Monastery)
2 Lion's Tomb
3 Turkmaniyyeh Tomb
4 Rest House
5 Archaeological Museum
6 Qasr Habis (Crusader Castle)
7 Nabatean Baths
8 Qasr Bint Far'aun
9 Temenos Gate
10 Fara'aun (Pharaoh's Pillar)
11 Snake Monument
12 Temple of the Winged Lions
13 Byzantine Church
14 Nymphaeum
15 Mughar al-Nasara (Caves of the Christians)
16 Tomb of Sextius Florentinus
17 Palace Tomb
18 Corinthian Tomb
19 Urn Tomb
20 Roman Theater
21 Tomb of the Roman Soldier
22 Triclinium
23 Garden Tomb
24 Lion Fountain
25 High Place
26 The Khazneh (Treasury)
27 Obelisk Tomb
28 Djinn Blocks (Ghost Tombs)
29 Visitors Center
TO AL-BARID & AL-BEIDHA
Wadi al-Qatar
Wadi Deir
Wadi Kharrouba
Wadi Ma'aisarat al-Gharbieh
Wadi Ma'aisarat al-Wasta
Wadi Hadhbat al-Zeitun
Wadi Turkmaniyyeh
Wadi Nasara
Wadi Siyah
Jabal Habis
Jabal Umm al-Biyara
Wadi Mataha
Main street
North Wall
South Wall
Wadi Musa
Wadi Farasa
Wadi Nmeir
Wadi Tughra
Outer Siq
Wadi Mahafir
Jabal Khubtha
Wadi Muthlim
Tunnel
Siq
Dam
Jabal Madras
SEE WADI MUSA MAP
N
0 200 yards
0 200 meters

Next to the Visitors Center are the rest house and the swinging gate that mark the beginning of the trail down to the *siq*. There are almost as many banks and money exchanges in Wadi Musa as there were Nabateans in Petra. The two largest, the **Arab Bank** (☎215 68 02) and the **Housing Bank** (☎215 60 82), are next to the main traffic circle. (Both open Sa-Th 8:30am-12:30pm.) **Cairo Amman Bank** is in the Mövenpick Hotel, just outside the entrance to Petra. (Open daily 8:30am-3pm.) All banks extract exorbitant commissions. Visa **cash advances** are available from any bank. If you need to contact the **tourist police** (☎215 64 41), they can be found munching on cigar ends outside the Visitors Center. The **Wadi Musa Pharmacy** is on the main traffic circle. (☎215 64 44. Open 24hr.) The **government health center** is a 15-minute walk uphill from the main traffic circle. (☎215 60 25. Open 24hr.) The **Petra Polyclinic** (☎215 66 94), at the traffic circle, costs more but has modern equipment. Plug in at the **Rum Internet Cafe** just downhill from the main circle. (☎215 72 64. JD3 per hr.) Of the many **post offices** in Wadi Musa, one with **Poste Restante** service lies next to the Musa Spring Hotel. (☎215 62 24. Open Sa-Th 7:30am-7pm, F 7:30am-12:30pm.) A second branch is behind the Visitors Center, by the entrance to the *siq*. (☎215 66 94. Open daily 8am-7pm.)

ACCOMMODATIONS

Since Jordan and Israel signed a peace treaty, visitors from all over the world have flooded the Jordanian hillside, and construction has boomed in Wadi Musa. Most of the development revolves around luxury resorts, but there are plenty of cheapies to go around, and budget travelers should have little trouble finding a suitable place to sleep (prices also become negotiable in the off-season, May-July and Dec.-Feb.). **Camping** inside Petra is illegal, but lingering explorers (especially women) may receive invitations for overnight stays from Bedouin. Others pick off-the-beaten-path caves for the night. Camping is available in Wadi Musa at some of the hotels.

Al-Anbat 1 Hotel (☎215 62 65 or 215 79 65; fax 215 68 88). Follow the trough down from the spring. Has the best views around. Free and frequent buses to Petra. Witness the most beautiful sunset in Wadi Musa from mattresses in the "greenhouse" (JD2). Buffet dinner JD4; breakfast JD2. Camping facilities (tents, communal baths; JD2). The basement of this two-star hotel (soon to be three-star, after the addition of a swimming pool and Turkish bath) offers cavernous student rooms with private baths. Student rooms JD4 per bed; singles JD9; doubles JD15; triples JD18.

Petra Gate Hotel, P.O. Box 120, Wadi Musa (☎215 69 08; email petra-gate-hotel@hotmail.com). 40m up the hill from the main circle in Wadi Musa, on the right, overlooking the valley. A homey atmosphere with smallish rooms and home-cooked dinners. Cordial, helpful employees live up to the "funky and friendly staff" slogan. Free billiards, so you can bet all the money you're saving by staying here. Breakfast JD1.5. Rooftop mattresses JD1; dorm beds JD2; singles JD5; doubles JD8; triples JD10.5.

Orient Gate Hotel and Restaurant, P.O. Box 185, Wadi Musa (☎/fax 215 70 20). Left of traffic circle, facing downhill. Small, cozy rooms, some with downhill view and balcony, house backpacker clientele. Two neighboring mosques and their competing *muezzins* create an interesting aural experience. Breakfast JD1-2; dinner buffet JD2.5-3. Rooftop mattresses JD2; singles JD6, with bath JD8; doubles JD8-10; triples JD15.

Sunset Hotel, P.O. Box 59 (☎215 65 79; fax 215 69 50). 200m uphill from Visitors Center. If your feet are sore and your bottom hurts from a Petra camel ride, this is the place for you—the first inexpensive and clean option outside the mega-hotel complex. Breakfast JD2. Singles JD7, with bath JD15; doubles JD10, with bath JD18. V.

Cleopetra Hotel, P.O. Box 125 (☎/fax 215 70 90). 50m uphill from the main traffic circle, on the left. Colorful rooms with relatively clean private baths. Friendly manager gives maps and info. Breakfast included. Rooftop mattresses JD3; singles JD10; doubles JD15; triples JD18-21.

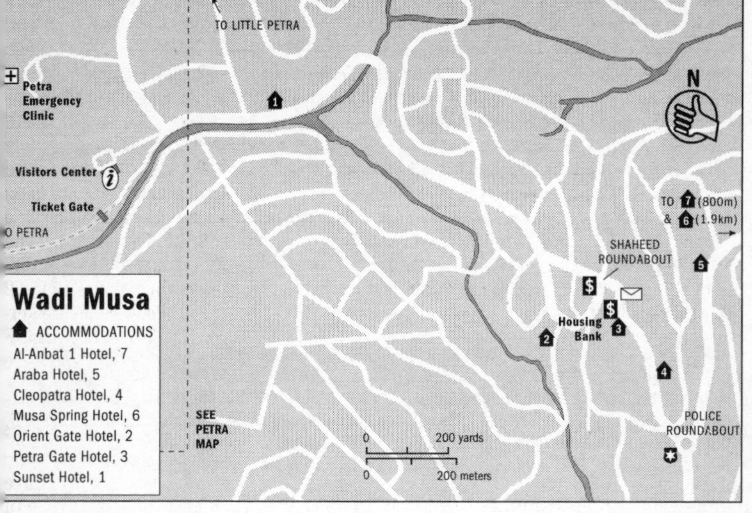

Musa Spring Hotel and Restaurant, Wadi Musa Gate (☎215 63 10; fax 215 69 10). The first hotel as you enter from Amman, but a trek from Petra proper. Plenty of budget traveler companionship. Free shuttle to Petra (leaves 7, 8am; returns 6pm). Free use of kitchen. Breakfast JD1.5; salad lunch 500fils per salad; all-you-can-eat dinner buffet JD3. Rooftop mattresses with hot showers JD2; dorm beds JD4; singles JD7, with bath JD10; doubles JD10, with bath JD12; triples JD15.

Araba Hotel (☎/fax 215 61 07), 200m uphill from the main circle in Wadi Musa. Pastel-hued rooms have soft, colorful mattresses. Some rooms come with private bath. Breakfast JD2. Rooftop mattresses JD2; rooms JD6 per person.

FOOD

Wadi Musa boasts the best bargains, especially in the streets to the right of its main circle as you approach from Petra. Many hotels have all-you-can-eat buffets at reasonable prices; others offer filling meals with pasta, rice, chicken, salad, and bread (JD2-3; open 6-9pm). The **Star Supermarket,** on the left and uphill from the traffic circle, has the cheapest water (300fils) and the most reasonably priced basics for bagged lunches. **Pizza Hut** and **Papazzi** (☎215 70 87), next to each other uphill from the Visitors Center, can satisfy your post-Petra pizza cravings (medium pizza at both JD5-7). Even if you can't afford to eat there, the **Mövenpick** offers affordable ice cream (JD1 per scoop), an excellent salad lunch buffet (JD4.5), and a deliciously air-conditioned interior. The Mövenpick and its rival, the **Petra Forum Hotel,** also house the most pleasant bars in town. The former rests in a tea garden on the roof of the hotel, and the latter sits on a terrace at the base of the Petra hills, offering the best (and closest) view of the sunset over Petra (drinks JD3-5).

Al-Wadi Restaurant (☎215 71 63), in the city center on the main circle. Climb the steep staircase for delectable omelettes (JD1.5) and filling *mezze*. Soups and salads 500fils; main meals JD1-3. Ask about student deals. Open daily 6:30am-midnight.

Al-Janoub Restaurant (☎215 75 65), on the first street on the right before reaching the main circle from Petra. Modest kebabs are the cheapest in town (JD1). Hummus 500fils; falafel 500fils; soda bottles 200fils. Open daily 6am-1am.

Cleopetra Restaurant, to the left of the main circle when facing downhill. Friendly Egyptian cooks serve rice, salad, bird, and bread (JD2.5). Arabic breakfast JD1.5; kebab or mixed grill JD2.5; buffet JD4; soda 75fils. Open daily 5am-midnight.

Rose City Restaurant (☎215 73 40), just uphill from the site. Pick up a sandwich lunch for the park at this diner-cum-souvenir shop. Hummus 600fils; sandwiches 400fils-JD1; grills JD3; soda 300fils. Open daily 6:30am-1pm and 6:30-11pm.

Red Cave Restaurant (☎215 77 99; fax 215 69 31), up the street from Petra. Well-decorated and bamboo-covered restaurant. Delicious food matches elegant setting. Daily specials and *mensaf* (JD5). Pasta JD3-3.5; appetizers JD1. Open daily 11am-midnight.

The Petra Pearl (☎215 50 60), across the street and 10m uphill from Cleopetra. Serves up a chicken buffet (JD3) and *ad hoc* Arabic lessons. Open daily 6am-midnight.

SIGHTS

Many spectacular monuments are close enough to be viewed in a day, but a few require multi-day expeditions. Guides are expensive but recommended for four of the remoter hikes. Bring water bottles from outside; Bedouin sell water throughout the park, but at JD1-1.5 per bottle, you'll need to empty the Treasury to stay hydrated. Open daily 6am-6pm; in winter 6am-5pm, but hours are loosely enforced. If you stay to see the sunset, you should have no problem getting out. One day JD20; two days JD25, children JD12.5; three days JD30, children JD15.

Although the Nabateans worshiped only two deities—Dushara (the god of strength) and al-Uzza (or Atargatis, the goddess of water and fertility)—the number of temples and tombs in Petra seems infinite. Climbing will allow you to escape the tour groups crowding the inner valley. Paths beyond the standard one-day itinerary are marked by stones piled into neat columns.

OBELISK TOMB. If you head toward the canyon-like *siq*, large *djinn* monuments (ghost tombs) and caves will stare down at you from distant mountain faces. The Obelisk Tomb is built high into the cliff on the left. Closer to the entrance of the *siq*, rock-cut channels once cradled the ceramic pipes that brought 'Ain Musa's waters to the city and the surrounding country. A nearby dam burst in 1963, and the resulting flood killed 28 tourists in the *siq*. While designing the new dam, the Nabateans' ancient dam was uncovered and used as a model.

KHAZNEH. As you enter the *siq*, 200m walls on either side begin to block out the sunlight, casting enormous shadows on the niches that once held icons meant to hex unwelcome visitors. The *siq* winds around for 1½km, then slowly emits a faint pink glow at the first peek of the Khazneh (Treasury). The Khazneh is the best preserved of Petra's monuments, though bullet holes are clearly visible on the upper urn. Believing the urn to be hollow and filled with ancient pharaonic treasures, Bedouin periodically fired at it, hoping to burst this petrified *piñata*. Actually, the Treasury is a royal tomb and quite solid. The Khazneh's rock face changes color as the day progresses: in the morning, the sun's rays give the monument a rich peach hue; in late afternoon it glistens rose; and by sunset it drips blood red.

ROMAN THEATER. Down the road to the right as you face the Khazneh, Wadi Musa opens up to the 7000-seat Roman Theater. The long row of Royal Tombs on the face of Jabal Khubtha stands to the right. The Romans built their theater under the red stone Nabatean necropolis, and the ancient carved caves still yawn above it. The theater has been restored to its 2nd-century appearance, and audiences are returning after a 1500-year intermission. A marble Hercules (now in the museum) was discovered just a few years ago in the curtained chambers beneath the stage.

ROYAL TOMBS. Across the Wadi are the Royal Tombs. The **Urn Tomb,** with its unmistakable recessed facade, commands a soul-scorching view of the still-widening valley. The two-tiered vault beneath the pillared facade is known as the **prison,** or *sijin*. A Greek inscription on an inner wall describes how the tomb, originally dedicated to the Nabatean King Malichus II in the first century CE, was converted to a church 400 years later. Nearby sits the **Corinthian Tomb** (allegedly a replica of Nero's Golden Palace in Rome) and the **Palace Tomb** (or the Tomb in Two Stories), which juts out from the mountainside. Laborers completed the tomb by attaching preassembled stones to its upper left-hand corner. Around the corner to the right is the **Tomb of Sextus Florentinus,** who was so enamored of these hewn heights that he asked his son to bury him in this ultimate outpost of the Roman Empire.

MAIN STREET. Around the bend to the left, a few restored columns are all that remain of the paved Roman main street. Two thousand years ago, columns lined the full length of the street, shielding markets and residences. At the beginning of the street on the right, the **Nymphaeum** ruins outline the ancient public fountain near its base. On a rise to the right, before the triple-arched gate, recent excavations have uncovered the Temple of al-Uzza (Atargatis), also called the **Temple of the Winged Lions.** In the spring you can watch the progress of US-sponsored excavations that have already uncovered several workshops and some cracked crocks.

BYZANTINE CHURCH. A joint Jordanian-American team has recently excavated an immense Byzantine church with a wealth of mosaics. The site lies several hundred meters to the right of the Roman street, near the Temple of the Winged Lions. Each of the church's side aisles is paved with 70 square meters of remarkably preserved mosaic, depicting humans of various professions, representations of the four seasons, and indigenous, exotic, and even mythological animals. Recent studies attest that the church was the seat of an important Byzantine bishopric in the 5th and 6th centuries, an assertion that challenges the belief that Petra was in decline by 600 CE. The archaeologists on the site constantly dig, scrape, and sniff. They also protect their site quite zealously—entrance may require charm and luck.

SOUTHERN TEMPLE AND ENVIRONS. A team from Brown University in the US is in the process of unearthing the Southern Temple. White hexagonal paving stones cover an extensive tunnel system that marks the importance of this holy site. Farther along, the triple-arched **Temenos Gate** was once the front gate of the **Qasr Bint Fara'un** (Palace of the Pharaoh's Daughter), a Nabatean temple built to honor the god Dushara. On the left before the gate are the **Nabatean Baths.** On a trail leading behind the temple to the left, a single standing column, **Amoud Fara'un** (Pharaoh's Pillar), gloats beside its two fallen comrades.

MUSEUMS. To the right of the Nabatean temple, a rock-hewn staircase leads to a small **archaeological museum** holding the spoils of the Winged Lions dig as well as carved stone figures from elsewhere in Petra. On the way to the monastery, the **Nabatean Museum** has good artifacts and air-conditioned restrooms with what is probably the **world's best toilet seat view.** *(Both museums open daily 9am-4pm. Free.)*

HIKES: AROUND PETRA

Many people rave about Petra's most accessible ten percent, content with what they can see in one day. The Bedouin say, however, that in order to appreciate Petra, you must stay long enough to watch your nails grow long. **Jabal Harun** requires a guide (officially JD35, but good luck finding one who charges less than JD50). It's unwise to hike the remote hills alone. If you feel lost, keep a sharp eye out for remnants of donkey visits, which can serve as a trail of crumbs.

WADI TURKIMANIYYEH وادى تركمانية

The shortest and easiest of the hikes leads down the *wadi* to the left of and behind the Temple of the Winged Lions. Fifteen minutes of strolling down the road running through the rich green gardens of Wadi Turkimaniyyeh leads to the only tomb at Petra with a Nabatean inscription. The lengthy invocation above the entrance beseeches the god Dushara to protect the tomb from violation. Unfortunately, Dushara took a permanent sabbatical and the chamber has been stripped bare.

AL-HABIS الحا بس

A second, more interesting climb begins at the end of the road that descends from the Pharaoh's Pillar to the cliff face, a few hundred meters left of the museum. The trail dribbles up to al-Habis, the prison. While the steps have been restored recently, they do not lead up to much. A path winds all the way around the mountain, however, revealing gorgeous canyons and (you guessed it) more tombs on the western side. The climb to the top and back takes less than an hour.

JABAL HARUN جبل هارون

This climb begins just to the right of Jabal Habis, below the museum. A sign points to **al-Deir** (the Monastery) and leads northwest across Wadi Siyah, past the Forum Restaurant and on to Wadi Deir and its fragrant oleander. Squeeze through the narrowing canyon along an endless, twisting stairway to confront a human-shaped hole in the facade of the **Lion's Tomb.** A hidden tomb awaits daredevils who try to climb the cleft to the right; less intrepid wanderers can backtrack to the right and spot the tomb a few minutes later. Back on the path, veer left to reach Petra's largest monument. Larger but less ornate than the Khazneh, al-Deir has a single inner chamber that dates back to the first century CE. Most scholars believe that al-Deir was originally either a Nabatean temple or an unfinished tomb dedicated to one of the later Nabatean kings. It picked up its orthodox appellation in the Byzantine period. On the left, a lone tree popping through a crack in the rock marks more ancient steps, which continue all the way up to the rim of the urn atop the monastery. Those with more courage than caution may actually step out onto the ancient urn. Straight across the *wadi* looms the highest peak in the area, **Jabal Harun** (Aaron's Mountain or Mt. Hor). On top of the mountain, a white church reportedly houses the **Tomb of Aaron.** The hike straight up to al-Deir takes 30 minutes, but the whole trip takes a few hours. Expect to spend a couple more hours if you detour into **Wadi Siyah** and visit its seasonal waterfall on the way back.

THE HIGH PLACE OF SACRIFICE المكا ن العالى

One of the most popular hikes is the circular route to the **High Place of Sacrifice** on **Jabal al-Madhbah,** a site of sacrifice with a full view of Petra. A staircase sliced into the rock leads to the left just as the Roman Theater comes into view. Follow the right prong when the trail levels and forks at the top of the stairs. On the left, **Obelisk Ridge** presents one obelisk to Dushara and another to al-Uzza. On the peak to the right, the High Place supports a string of grisly sights: two altars, an ablution cistern, gutters for draining away sacrificial blood, and cliff-hewn bleachers for an unobstructed view of animal sacrifices. Head downhill past the Pepsi stand, leaving the obelisks behind you, and backtrack under the western face of the High Place. A hard-to-find staircase leads down to a sculptured **Lion Fountain.** The first grotto complex beyond it is the **Garden Tomb.** Below it is the **Tomb of the Roman Soldier** and across from it a rock **triclinium** (feast hall), which has the only decorated interior in Petra. The trail then leads into Wadi Farasa and ends near the Pillar. The circle, followed either way, takes about 1.5 hours.

SINAI السيناء

The Sinai is the collision point of two continents, an enormous tectonic summit. A handful of small towns and a major road artery occupy the sandy shelf where the mountains meet the sea, but only the Bedouin brave the rest of the Sinai's dry, rough landscape. The greatest profusion of life in the area thrives below the sea: The Gulf of Aqaba's warm waters support a carnival of brilliantly colored coral reefs and subaquatic life. In sharp contrast to the bland browns and earthy hues of the rest of the Middle East, the underwater environs explode with color—the reds and greens of coral broken by the flashes of yellow, blue, and orange fins, set against the sparkling turquoise backdrop of the Red Sea.

The Sinai has had a surprisingly long history of war. Since the pharaohs' troops first trampled the broad plains of the northern Sinai on their march to Syria and Canaan, the favor has been returned by marauding Hyksos, Assyrians, Persians, Greeks, Arabs, and Turks. In 1903, the British drew the borders of the Sinai from Rafah to Eilat in an attempt to keep Turkey and Germany safely distanced from the Suez Canal. On the fourth day of the Six Day War of 1967, Israel took control of the Sinai Peninsula from Egypt and began to capitalize upon the region's tourism potential. The Israelis established most of the original hotels and dive centers, including those in Dahab and Sharm al-Sheikh. The new development altered the lives of many Bedouin, who began to give camel tours and work in hotels.

In the 1973 Yom Kippur War, Egyptian forces crossed the canal in a surprise offensive to recapture the Sinai. The Egyptian army broke through the Israeli defense line, but later Israeli counterattacks recaptured most of the peninsula. Israel retained the Sinai until it was returned to Egypt under the terms of the Camp David Accords: the first half in 1979, the second in 1982. The Sinai never regained its politically strategic status but remains a highly touristed vacation spot.

HIGHLIGHTS OF THE SINAI PENINSULA

Secluded **al-Arish** (p. 354) is the jewel of Egypt's most inviting shore, while **Sharm al-Sheikh** (p. 366) is world-renowned for the beauty beneath its waves.

Even if Dopey's not your favorite of the Seven Dwarfs, visit the Bedouin camps of **Dahab** (p. 360) and you'll put on a Happy face.

Moses made the hike up **Mount Sinai** (p. 355); now thou shalt too.

BORDER CROSSING

Crossing from Eilat to Taba takes a while and costs a few pounds. Passports must be valid for at least three months; Israeli visas must be valid for the day of travel. For travel outside Sinai, get a visa at the Egyptian consulate. The border is open 24 hours but is closed on Yom Kippur and 'Eid al-Adha (border info ☎637 31 10).

The border-crossing process unfolds in an orderly way, but involves a surprisingly long hike. Allow at least an hour, longer on a busy day. Take the #15 bus from Eilat, and keep your passport handy; it will be checked frequently throughout the 1km obstacle course to the bus depot on the other side. There are 11 exciting steps: (1) Bus drop-off. (2) Little Taba snack bar ("last beer before Sinai"). (3) Passport pre-check. (4) Passport control booth (pay NIS57 exit tax). (5) Israeli last passport check; they automatically stamp your passport at this point unless you ask them not to. (6) Stroll through no-man's-land. (7) Egyptian passport control—fill out entry form, get stamp. (8) Egyptian security (X-ray machine). (9) Post-border passport check. (10) Passport check and E£17/US$6 Egyptian border tax. The Taba Hilton is the best place to **change money** (open 24hr., no commission for foreign currency converted to Egyptian pounds). (11) Welcome to Egypt! The bus station is a ten-minute walk from the border.

For Sinai stays of 14 days or less, get a **Sinai-only visa** stamp on the Egyptian side of the border. This visa limits travel to the Gulf of Aqaba coast as far south as Sharm al-Sheikh (but not the area around Sharm al-Sheikh, including Ras Muhammad) and to St. Catherine's monastery and Mt. Sinai (but not sites in the vicinity of St. Catherine's). Unlike ordinary one-month Egyptian visas, the Sinai-only visa has no grace period; you'll pay a hefty fine if you overextend your stay.

From Taba there are buses to: **Cairo** (7hr., E£70); **Nuweiba** (1½hr., E£12); **Dahab** (2½hr., E£15-17); and **Sharm al-Sheikh** (3-4hr., E£25). There are always taxis waiting to take people to Dahab, Cairo, Nuweiba, or anywhere. There may be a long wait until they fill up, but the fare is only slightly more expensive than the bus. After the last bus, taxi prices rise dramatically.

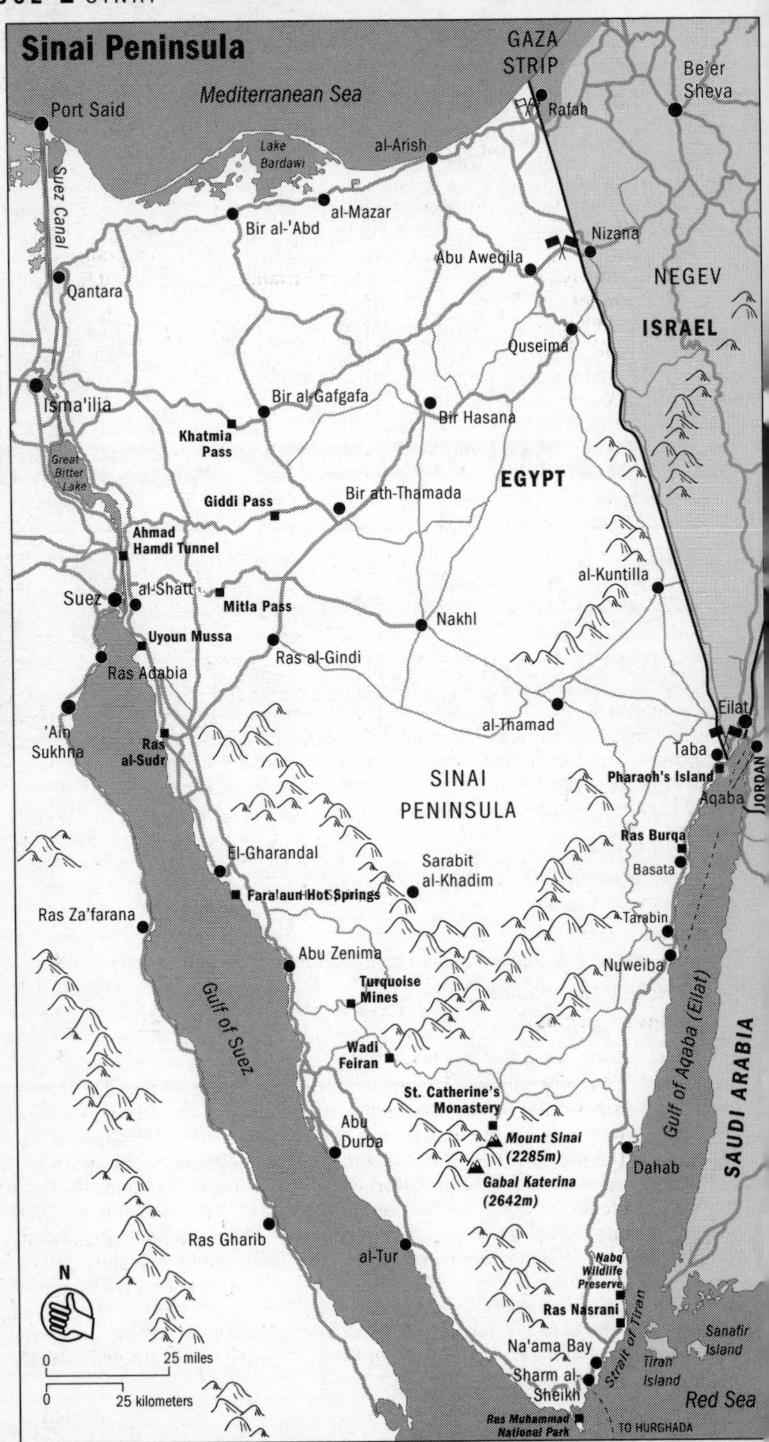
Sinai Peninsula
Mediterranean Sea
GAZA STRIP
Port Said
Rafah
Be'er Sheva
Lake Bardawi
al-Arish
Suez Canal
al-Mazar
Bir al-'Abd
Nizana
Abu Aweqila
NEGEV
Qantara
ISRAEL
Quseima
Isma'ilia
Bir al-Gafgafa
Bir Hasana
Khatmia Pass
Great Bitter Lake
EGYPT
Giddi Pass
Bir ath-Thamada
Ahmad Hamdi Tunnel
al-Kuntilla
Suez
al-Shatt
Mitla Pass
Nakhl
Uyoun Mussa
Ras Adabia
Ras al-Gindi
Eilat
al-Thamad
'Ain Sukhna
Ras al-Sudr
Taba
Pharaoh's Island
SINAI PENINSULA
Aqaba
JORDAN
Ras Burqa
El-Gharandal
Sarabit al-Khadim
Basata
Fara'aun Hot Springs
Ras Za'farana
Tarabin
Abu Zenima
Nuweiba
Turquoise Mines
Gulf of Suez
Gulf of Aqaba (Eilat)
SAUDI ARABIA
Wadi Feiran
St. Catherine's Monastery
Mount Sinai (2285m)
Abu Durba
Gabal Katerina (2642m)
Dahab
Ras Gharib
al-Tur
Nabq Wildlife Preserve
N
Ras Nasrani
Sanafir Island
Strait of Tiran
Na'ama Bay
Tiran Island
Sharm al-Sheikh
0
25 miles
0
25 kilometers
Red Sea
Ras Muhammad National Park
TO HURGHADA

GETTING AROUND

Travel in the Sinai Peninsula is far easier than in the rest of Egypt. Women can comfortably wear shorts and sleeveless shirts in most places, and professional con artists are rare. Many Bedouin have given up their camels for Camaros, but there are still places where travelers can get a sense of their nomadic lifestyle.

The noble machines of the **East Delta Bus Company,** battered cruelly by the rocks, ruts, and dust of Sinai roads, heroically tread the scorched highway. With towns few and far between, buses and taxis are the only means of transportation. Timetables are really no more than an administrator's pipe dream. At bus stations, patience is more a necessity than a virtue.

A reasonably priced and convenient alternative to buses is the *service* taxi. Weathered old Peugeot 504s piloted by Bedouin cabbies are ubiquitous. Hop in with other passengers or negotiate with a driver and wait while he recruits more travelers. Women should avoid riding alone with a driver. *Service* are comparable in price to the bus under ideal circumstances, but only with a full load of seven. Consistent with the laws of supply and demand, taxi prices will drop immediately before the arrival of a bus, then skyrocket after the bus has departed.

The Sinai can be divided into four major regions: the **Northern Sinai** governate has its capital at **al-Arish** (p. 354); the rugged terrain and industrial belching of the **Western Sinai** is not for the faint-of-heart; the **High Sinai** (p. 355) makes for great hiking and biblical sightseeing; and the **Gulf of Aqaba coast** (p. 360), Sinai's major hotspot, is known the world over as a scuba diver's paradise.

PRACTICAL INFORMATION

CURRENCY		
	US$1 = E£3.47 (EGYPTIAN POUNDS)	E£1 = US$0.29
	CDN$1 = E£2.31	E£1 = CDN$0.43
	IR£1 = E£4.09	E£1 = IR£0.25
	UK£1 = E£5.15	E£1 = UK£0.19
	AUS$1 = E£1.97	E£1 = AUS$0.51
	NZ$1 = E£1.58	E£1 = NZ$0.63
	SAR1 = E£0.49	E£1 = SAR2.02
	EUR€1 = E£3.21	E£1 = EUR€0.31
	JD1 (JORDANIAN DINAR) = E£4.86	E£1 = JD0.21
	NIS1 = E£0.83	E£1 = NIS1.21

A number of **regulations** govern travelers to the Sinai. Unguided travel is restricted to main roads and settlements, though parts of the desert interior are accessible with a Bedouin guide. Sleeping on the beach is prohibited in some areas, and the police often harass dozing backpackers. Since these areas are not always marked, ask around before settling down for the night. Nude sunbathing is illegal, as is the oft-hawked **marijuana.** It is not possible to bring a rented car into the Sinai from Israel. **Prices** in the Sinai are fairly high. In winter, warm clothes and a sleeping bag are advisable. **Bug season** descends upon the Sinai in the spring and early summer. Dahab is periodically clouded by mosquitoes with killer munchies. Some travelers rig mosquito nets; others advise sleeping by the beach. In summer, no one wears or carries much, and it only takes a few days before travelers begin to reexamine conventions of hygiene and appearance.

NORTHERN SINAI

AL-ARISH العريش ☎068

Al-Arish is caught in the cultural vortex between the *sheesha*-smoking Mediterranean and the who-knows-what-smoking Sinai—and manages to avoid the worst of both. Al-Arish is a favorite spot for vacationing Egyptian families, and Western tourists will find themselves a bit of a curiosity, but less hassled here than in many parts of Egypt. Currently the capital of the North Sinai Governorate, al-Arish was once an important stopover on what was perhaps the oldest military route in history. It has since given up military mottos and has settled down with a more mellow one: life's a beach. Al-Arish is much less touristed than the High Sinai and the beach here is clean and inviting (some say the best on Egypt's Mediterranean coast)—the only shore in Egypt spotted with palm trees.

GETTING THERE AND GETTING AWAY. There are only two roads to know in al-Arish: **Fouad Zekry St.,** which runs along the beach, and **Tahrir St.,** perpendicular to Fouad Zekry. The **bus station** (☎34 01 08) is at the south end of Tahrir St., 2km from the beach. Buses run daily to **Cairo** (5hr.; 8am E£25, 4pm E£35) and **Isma'ilia** (3hr., every 30min. 7am-5pm, E£10). Rafah and the Israeli border can be reached by **service** (E£5). Getting around the downtown area by foot is easy, but a walk to the beach is a bit far—catch a *tut-tut* bus or one of the brightly colored Mercedes that serve as shared taxis (50pt). City minibuses constantly run along the beach on Fouad Zekry St. (50pt) and a private taxi within al-Arish should never cost more than E£5.

PRACTICAL INFORMATION. The ETA **tourist office,** on Fouad Zekry St., is just off the beach. (☎34 05 69. Open daily 9am-2pm and 4-8pm.) Coming from the downtown/Tahrir St. area, bear left at the intersection with Fouad Zekry St. The **tourist office** and **tourist police** (open 24hr.) are in the same building on the right. There are banks along Tahrir St., including the **National Bank of Egypt** (☎35 18 81) and the **Bank of Cairo** (☎35 30 32), which exchanges traveler's checks and cash or gives cash advances on credit cards. (Both open Su-Th 9am-2:30pm.) The **police station** is at the northern end of Tahrir Sq., but you're better off paying a visit to the tourist police. **Pharmacies:** in the downtown area. (Generally open daily 8am-1am.) **Government Hospital:** on al-Geish St., just off Tahrir St. (☎34 00 11. Open 24hr.) **Telephone office:** three blocks north and two blocks east of Tahrir Sq. (Open 24hr.) **Post office:** across the street from the telephone office. Sends **faxes** for E£5.50 plus the cost of the call. (☎35 15 03; fax 35 15 01. Open Sa-Th 8:30am-2:30pm.)

ACCOMMODATIONS AND FOOD. Most of al-Arish's beachfront hotels are reasonably priced. The **Moonlight Hotel** is on the beach, just west of the tourist office, off Fouad Zekry St. Moonlit or not, the hallways are a bit dark, but the rosy-fingered (okay, bright pink) rooms with bath are like a cheerful vision of the dawn. Reservations are advised. (☎34 13 62. Singles E£20; doubles E£35.) The **Green Land Beach Hotel** is east of the tourist office, a little off Fouad Zekry St. Walk toward the beach on the road that angles behind William's Restaurant; the Green Land is on the beach side of the road. (☎34 06 01. Doubles and triples with fan, balcony, bath, breakfast, and the occasional TV E£30.) The airy **El-Salaam Hotel** is on Tahrir St., off the square and near the bus station. Ask for a room away from the street. (☎35 42 19. Doubles E£18.50; triples E£25; with private bath.)

Food consists mostly of standard Arab fare, with the exception of **William's,** on Fouad Zekry St. near the Green Land Beach Hotel. Minimalist decor does not detract from the fish and meat entrees, complete with french fries and salad (Entrees E£10-20. Open daily 8am-2am.) At the far western end of al-Arish is the pleasant **Basata.** (Full meals E£10-20. Open daily 11am-1am.) In town, the best budget meal award goes to **'Aziz,** located next to El-Salaam Hotel on Tahrir St. 'Aziz has a variety of grilled foods (E£5-15) and rice or noodle side dishes. (Side dishes E£1-3. ☎35 43 45. Open daily 9am-1am.)

SIGHTS AND ENTERTAINMENT. Life in al-Arish revolves around the Mediterranean. The entire length of the **beach** is pristine and, except for brief sections in front of the Semiramis and Egoth Oberoi Hotels, there is no difference between public and private shoreline. There are a few **Bedouin craft stores** at the north end of Tahrir St. Every Thursday, Tahrir Sq. comes alive when local Bedouin sell silver, rugs, garments, and camel accessories at the weekly **souq.** A few kilometers east of town on the road to Rafah is the **Sinai Heritage Museum,** which details traditional Bedouin life on the Peninsula and has an excellent collection of clothes and jewelry. (Open Sa-Th 9:30am-2pm. E£2; camera privileges E£5, video E£25.) In the evenings, many locals take to the *sheesha* parlors of Tahrir Sq., while the coffee shops along the promenade attract tourists. The expensive drinks (Stella E£12) outnumber the people at the **bars** of the Semiramis and Oberoi hotels.

HIGH SINAI

The central region of the Sinai Peninsula, known as the High Sinai, is worlds away from the lazy daze of Dahab. Cosmopolitan coastal life may cause you to forget that you're on the outskirts of over 60,000 square kilometers of arid desert, but savvy hikers know that high times can be had in the High Sinai. Nestled in this rugged desertscape are the biblical locales of **Mount Sinai,** the mountain on which Moses received the Ten Commandments, and **St. Catherine's Monastery,** near the Burning Bush. The **High Sinai desert** is an ideal place for unforgettable hikes.

MOUNT SINAI

The holy peak of Mount Sinai, or as locals call it, Mount Moses (Gabal Mussa), stands 2285m above sea level. The Bible describes a mountain engulfed in fire and smoke that Moses ascended to receive the Ten Commandments while the Israelites built a golden calf at its base. Mount Sinai is one of only two places in the Old Testament where God revealed himself to the people, making the desolate peak sacred for both Christians and Muslims (Jews have not universally identified the modern Mount Sinai as the promontory made famous by the Bible). In the Book of Exodus, God warned the people, "Take heed that you do not go up into the mountain or touch the border of it; whoever touches the mountain shall be put to death" (Exodus 19:12). This prohibition seems to have been long forgotten—busloads of tourists climb the peak each day. Despite the Baraka bottles, the view from the summit is awe-inspiring.

HIKING: MOUNT SINAI

You don't necessarily need a guide, but for safety, neither men nor women should hike alone, especially at night. Most people hook up with **organized groups** from Dahab and begin their climb (via the camel path) around 2am in order to enjoy the cool night and catch the sunrise at the top. Bring a flashlight. If you're hiking **alone,** hike in the early afternoon when it's still light, watch the sunset, and sleep on the summit. Neither hiking shoes nor sneakers are necessary for the climb, but considering the amount of camel dung you'll walk over (especially at night), you probably don't want to expose your bare feet. Socialites can stake out a spot directly on the summit platform by the tea and refreshment stands. More secluded spots are available just beyond the boulders and human feces on the sloping shoulder to the west. Walk about 40m until you cross a ravine; the small summit ahead has several campsites protected by stone windbreaks. If you explore this area during the daylight hours, you'll discover an ancient Bedouin **cistern** where water was stored during the summers. You can also beat the crowds by sleeping in Elijah's Hollow (see p. 356) or by climbing at midday (not recommended in summer).

Overnighters should bring ample **food,** and everyone should bring at least two or three bottles of **water** for the ascent. The cheapest place to buy these amenities is the supermarkets in St. Catherine's town. The monastery **rest house** also sells snacks and water at reasonable prices. There are refreshment stands on the way up, but prices increase with altitude. A stand on the summit sells tea (E£2), water (E£4), and various snacks (E£3-6). If you plan to spend the night on the mountain, bring a **sleeping bag** and **warm clothes.** Even in the summer, it's often only 8-10°C at night, and the breeze makes it feel much colder. Those without the necessary gear can rent blankets (E£2.50) and mattresses (E£5) at the top. Hikers should bring a warm change of clothing—sweaty shirts quickly turn to shirtsicles. There are also "toilets" at the summit (holes in the ground with more flies than privacy).

The hike to the top is not that challenging, but you should still leave all but the bare essentials behind. The monks of St. Catherine's will allow you to leave your bags in a room (E£5 per piece per day). There are two paths up the mountain: the **Steps of Repentance** and a **camel path.** To find either path, walk up the hill to the monastery, bear left at the fork, and continue to the back of the monastery. From here the camel path continues down the valley while the Steps start to the right, at the southeast corner of the monastery. There is one juncture that confuses hikers: near the top, the camel path intersects the Steps after passing through a narrow, steeply walled stone corridor. Turn left to reach the summit; the camel path stops here. Riders will have to get off their high humps and huff up the rest of the way.

STEPS OF REPENTANCE. Of the two paths up the mountain, this is shorter and more difficult, but you probably deserve it. It is said that the 3750 steps were built by a single monk in order to fulfill his pledge of penitence. The monk cut corners here and there and made many of the steps the height of two or three mortal ones. The steps are treacherous by night; after dark they are difficult to follow even with a flashlight. Save them for the descent in the morning. *(About 2hr.)*

CAMEL PATH. The longer route was built in the 19th century and begins directly behind the monastery. **Camel rides** up the mountain usually cost E£30 during peak hours, but if you can stand the sun and the heat, you can get a ride up in the middle of the day for the low price of E£10. Unfortunately, the camels are not always available when you need them—you may arrive at the dispatch area and find only dung. *(At night about 2½hr. by toed foot, 1½hr. by cloven.)*

ELIJAH'S HOLLOW. Turn right at the juncture about two-thirds of the way up and you'll arrive at a 500-year-old cypress tree dominating the depressional plain known as Elijah's Hollow. This is where the prophet Elijah is said to have heard the voice of God after fleeing Jezebel (I Kings 19:8-18). Two small **chapels** now occupy the site, one dedicated to Elijah and the other to his successor Elisha. Moses supposedly hid in the **cave** below when he first came face-to-face with God: "While my glory passes by, I will put you in a cleft of the rock, and I will cover you with my hand until I have passed by" (Exodus 33:22). You can still see the watering hole used by the prophet. *(The chapel is almost always closed in afternoons, but usually open immediately after sunrise for 1-2hr.)*

HOLY MOUNT SERBAL? In some religious circles, the debate still rages over whether Mount Sinai is actually the site where Moses received the Ten Commandments. Though most believe that Mount Sinai is the real McCoy, some maintain that the actual mountain referred to in the Bible is Mount Serbal, 20 miles to the west. According to most biblical scholars, however, the Mount Serbalists are fighting a losing battle. The Bible mentions three characteristics of the mountain in question: it is surrounded by a vast plain, the summit is visible to all below, and it is accessible to all who surround it. All three describe Sinai, none Serbal. It is also doubtful that the Israelites would have chosen to camp for a year in the valley beneath Mount Serbal, the site of fierce floods, little drinking water, and hordes of mosquitoes. Besides, who wants to tell 18 generations of pilgrims they've been climbing the wrong mountain?

ST. CATHERINE'S ☎069

St. Catherine's rich history of monasticism started in the 3rd century CE when Christian hermits, attracted by the tradition designating the valley below as the site of the Burning Bush, migrated here in a quest for holiness and freedom from Roman persecution. Living in complete poverty and isolation (except on holy days, when they gathered at the Burning Bush), these hermits often fell victim to harsh weather and raiding nomads. In 313 CE, Constantine the Great officially recognized Christianity, and soon afterwards the monastery was founded by Constantine's mother, Empress Helena. The monastery thrived under the continual protection of the incumbent rulers (including Prophet Muhammad and Napoleon) during the ensuing 1600 years. As a tribute to the monks' tradition of hospitality to Christians and Muslims alike, it has never been conquered. Modern pilgrims and curious tourists of all faiths visit St. Catherine's throughout the year. Though much of the monastery is closed to the public, its beautiful architecture and mountainous setting ensure an unforgettable visit.

TRANSPORTATION AND PRACTICAL INFORMATION. At an elevation of about 1600m, **St. Catherine's Monastery** is hidden away in the mountainous interior of the southern Sinai. Excellent roads run west to the Gulf of Suez and east to the Gulf of Aqaba, both about 100km away. Tiny **St. Catherine's town** lies about 3km east of the monastery.

Buses serving St. Catherine's are notorious for their scarcity, but they do run to Cairo (9hr., 6am, E£35) via Suez (6hr., E£25), and seasonally to Sharm al-Sheikh (3hr., 1pm, E£25). Posted times at the tourist office and hotel owners are often wrong; ask the bus driver who brings you, but be aware that leaving St. Catherine's often takes patience and perseverance. **Taxis** are always available, but prices are entirely dependent on the number of passengers and the bus schedule. Popular destinations are Cairo (E£500), Dahab (E£120-150 per car), Nuweiba (E£200), and Sharm al-Sheikh (E£200). Taxis hover around the central square in the daytime; ask at the market if you don't see any. Lone women should avoid taxis.

Taxi drivers will drop you in St. Catherine's town, which boasts a number of modern conveniences despite its size. The **bus station** is at the main square; it's not a "station" per se, but a point in space where the bus is assumed to stop. Note that there are no more buses to or from Dahab. On one side of the square is an arcade with a **Bank Misr,** where you can exchange money or traveler's checks and withdraw cash (Visa only). (☎47 04 63. Open daily 8:30am-1:30pm and 6:30-8:30pm.) The local **police station** (☎47 03 13) is farther up the hill near the mosque. The **tourist police** (☎47 00 46) and the **hospital** (☎47 03 68) are both opposite the bus station and open 24hr. The 24-hour **telecommunications office** (☎47 00 10) has international phone service. The nearby **post office** (☎47 03 01) is open daily 8am-3pm.

ACCOMMODATIONS AND FOOD. The cheapest and most popular choice is the free **camping** on Mount Sinai's chilly peak. The nearest budget alternative is the monastery's **St. Catherine's Auberge.** To get there, turn right at the fork just before the monastery. The clean but cramped rooms are within earshot of the monks, so keep blasphemous thoughts to yourself. The location alone is worth the price. A delectable dinner and breakfast are included. Reservations are recommended if you intend to arrive after 11pm or in August or April. (☎47 03 53. 4-5-bed dorms E£70; singles E£122; doubles E£174; triples E£231.) A cheaper option, though farther from the monastery, is the **El-Fairouz Hotel.** To reach El-Fairouz, walk out of town toward the monastery and take your first left. The hotel, encircling a giant sandy lot, is a five-minute walk away and has an incredible view of the surrounding mountains. Pitch your tent in the sand courtyard (E£5) or join the other sardines in one of the 10-bed dorms (E£12). Some rooms have private baths. (☎47 03 33 or 47 03 23. Singles E£50; doubles E£60; triples E£70.)

Gift shops, supermarkets, and **restaurants** surround the bus station. The restaurants are virtually identical, offering hearty food (usually E£5-8 dishes of spaghetti or rice and chicken) with a side order of flies. Some of them will even cook food you've purchased from a supermarket. (Markets open daily 8am-11pm.) Opposite the mosque is a brick-oven **bakery,** where the price of pita is hotly negotiated.

ST. CATHERINE'S MONASTERY

To get to the monastery from the access road, go straight past the tourist police for about 5min. until the fork in the road, then bear left; the monastery is on the right. Spend the night on the mountaintop, watch the sunrise; hike down at 7am and reach the monastery just as the doors open at 9am (to avoid crowds). Modest dress required. Open M-Th and Sa 9-11:45am, F 11am-noon; closed Orthodox holidays (Nov. 14; Jan. 6; Feb. 26-28; Apr. 7, 12, 14, 16; May 24; June 4; Aug. 28; Sept. 27; Nov. 14; Dec. 8). Free. For more information, contact Father John (☎ 47 03 43) or the monastery's Cairo office, 18 Midan al-Dahr, 11271 Cairo (☎ (02) 482 85 13; fax 482 58 06).

St. Catherine's is believed to be the oldest example of unrestored Byzantine architecture in the world. The complex was named after the martyred Alexandrian evangelist, Catherine, whose body was found on top of Gabal Katerina to the south. About to be tortured on a wheel of knives for converting members of the Roman emperor's family, Catherine was miraculously saved by a malfunction in the wheel (but they slit her throat anyway). Her body showed up centuries later on top of the isolated mountain. Once home to hundreds of monks, the monastery now houses only a handful. These ascetics are members of one of the strictest orders; they never eat meat or drink wine, and they wake up at 4am each morning when the bell of the Church of the Transfiguration is rung 33 times.

ICONS. The monastery has many treasures, including over 2000 exquisite 5th-century icons. The icons with brushed gold halos have a holographic effect, an artistic style unique to the Sinai. In the 7th century, Prophet Muhammad dictated a document granting protection to the monastery and exempting it from taxes; a copy of this still hangs in the icon gallery, near a similar letter penned by Napoleon in 1798.

LIBRARY. The monastery's impressive library contains over 8000 books and manuscripts, said to be second only to the Vatican library in the number and value of religious texts. The collection is currently being copied onto microfiche to make it available to scholars everywhere.

CHURCH OF THE TRANSFIGURATION. The first permanent structure in the monastery was erected in 330 CE, when Helena built a small church and tower at the site of the Burning Bush. Around 530, Emperor Justinian ordered a splendid basilica within a walled fortress to be constructed on the top of Mount Sinai. When Justinian's trusted architect Stephanos found the mountain's peak too narrow, he built the **Church of the Transformation** next to St. Eleni's chapel instead. This structure became known as the Church of the Transfiguration, owing to its spectacular almond-shaped mosaic depicting this event in Jesus' life. The peeved emperor ordered Stephanos's execution, but the builder lived out his days in the safety of the monastery and eventually achieved sainthood (his bones are in the **ossuary**). Both St. Helena and Justinian dedicated their structures to the Virgin Mary, since Christian tradition asserts that the Burning Bush foreshadowed the Annunciation, when the archangel Gabriel heralded the birth of Christ. *(Closed F, Su, and holidays. A gift shop sells books on the area's history for E£8.)*

CHAPEL OF THE BURNING BUSH. Only the central nave of the Church of the Transfiguration is open to the public. On tiptoe you can see mosaics of a barefoot Moses in the Chapel of the Burning Bush, behind the altar. Should you manage to visit the icons back there, you'll have to remove your shoes, as the roots of the sacred shrub extend under the floor (a living descendant resides just outside). Such privileges are only accorded to true pilgrims, who are traditionally allowed to ask God for one favor. The monks themselves, with the help of the local Gabaliyya Bedouin (descended from Byzantine slaves), built a **mosque** within the fortress to convince advancing Ottoman armies that the complex was partly Muslim.

MOSES' WELL. Outside the main entrance of the Church of the Transfiguration is Moses' Well, where the savior of the Israelites reportedly freshened up after his holy ascent. The gruesome **ossuary,** a separate building outside the walls, houses the remains of former monks.

HIKING: SINAI DESERT

WHEN TO GO

Spring and fall are the most temperate seasons for hikes. In summer you'll spend most of the day resting in the shade with the Bedouin until the sun calms down, and in winter you'll freeze. The nights are frigid year-round. You may be able to rent blankets from the Bedouin, but don't count on it; bring a warm sleeping bag.

HOW TO GO

Organized tours can be arranged in Israel through **SPNI.** The Israeli travel outfitter **Neot Ha-Kikar** specializes in Sinai tours (offices in Tel Aviv, Jerusalem, and Eilat), with trips beginning in Eilat and Cairo (6-day high range circuit US$360). No matter where in Israel you book your tour, however, you'll eventually end up at Sheikh Moussa's office. You'll save a lot of money by starting there, too.

To venture into any of the mountains other than Mount Sinai, you must be accompanied by a **Bedouin guide** and have a regular **Egyptian tourist visa**—the Sinai-only visa won't do. **Sheikh Moussa** (☎(069) 47 04 57), head of Mountain Tours, has a monopoly on all the mountains, and trips must be arranged through him (reservations accepted). You are required by law to leave your passport with Mr. Moussa; he will notify the army of your whereabouts. To get to his office in St. Catherine's town, walk uphill from the town square, past the petrol station. Take the first right and walk for three minutes; Mr. Moussa will be lounging outside.

Sheikh Moussa will procure both a guide and a permit for you. The price, which includes guide, food, and camels, is US$20-30 per person per day, and fluctuates depending on the size of your party and where you go. Surplus gear can be stored in Sheikh Moussa's house. You'll leave for your hike within an hour of arriving at his office. You and your guide will camp with the Bedouin, so be prepared for long nights by the fire smoking "Bedouin tobacco," drinking tea, and learning a great deal about a little-known culture. Tell Sheikh Moussa what you want to see and how quickly, and he'll tailor an itinerary. Routes include the following possibilities (estimated length of trip in days noted in parentheses):

HIKING ROUTES:

Gabal Banat: A mountain north of St. Catherine's town overlooking a vast desert. (2).

Gabal Bab: From this peak you can see west all the way to the Gulf of Suez. (2)

Gabal Katerina: The highest mountain in Egypt (2642m), 6km south of Mount Sinai. The path to the top is more difficult, secluded, and beautiful than Mount Sinai's highway. A chapel replenishes you with shade at the summit. (11hr. round-trip)

Gabal 'Abbas Pasha: A rock with a ruined palace and excellent views. (2)

Gulat al-Agrod: A deep, crystal-clear mountain pool where you can swim in the shade of overhanging trees and dive off the surrounding rocks. (3)

Wadi Talla: There are two, a big one and a small one. Go to the big wadi for some swimming in spring-fed pools. (3)

Wadi Nogra: A rocky valley with a natural dam (Nogra Dam). The water trickles off moss-covered boulders to form a natural shower. (3)

Sheikh Owat: A picturesque oasis with palm trees, a deep well, and a lot of goats. (3).

Farsh Romana: A campground equipped with showers on the way to Gabal Banat. (2)

Wadi Feiran: An lush oasis 50km west of St. Catherine's Monastery; Islamic tradition holds that Hagar fled here when banished from Abraham and Sarah's camp. Today there is a nunnery in the center of the valley. The best way to get here is by taxi from St. Catherine's (E£70 round-trip). though buses to and from Cairo pass by, the schedules are unpredictable, and you might get stranded.

GULF OF AQABA COAST

The Gulf of Aqaba coast offers underwater splendor, with some of the world's best scuba diving, particularly in Sharm al-Sheikh. It is also home to Dahab, a yesteryear hippie haven known for its relaxed atmosphere and good times. Above water and below, the Gulf of Aqaba coast offers its travelers beauty and excitement.

UNDERWATER TIPS

Without question, the Red Sea has some of the greatest coral reefs and marine life in the world. Diving was not very big in the Middle East until Jacques-Yves Cousteau made his voyage through the Red Sea aboard *Calypso* (as chronicled in his famous book and movie *The Silent World*). Now that diving is a major part of many trips to the Sinai Peninsula, the regional administration has begun to face the serious problem of **irresponsible ecotourism.** All coral reefs from Dahab to Ras Muhammad are under the jurisdiction of the Ras Muhammad National Park. Regulations forbid the removal or defacement of any animal, plant, or shell, living or dead, from the sea. The park is fighting a difficult battle with developers waiting to exploit the region. You can do your part to preserve the reefs by observing a simple rule: look, but don't touch. Ras Muhammad, like most James Bond movies, has underwater police who will chase you out of the water if they see you breaking this rule. Even accidentally bumping the coral can damage it (and damage you).

Diving is very expensive, but you're paying for safety. The sites along the Gulf of Aqaba coast listed below emphasize safety above all else. **Snorkeling gear** can be rented all over, while **dive shops** are concentrated mainly in Dahab and Sharm al-Sheikh. Divers must be certified to rent equipment; most five-day courses provide certification and cost around US$300. The only decompression chamber in the area is in Sharm al-Sheikh. If you're rusty, take a check-out dive for US$35.

Beginning divers should make sure their instructors speak their language flawlessly, as small misunderstandings can have a big significance underwater ("Tanks!" "You're welcome!"). The instructor must also be certified to teach your particular course, whether it's PADI or SSI—ask to see his or her card. Some clubs are active in protecting the reefs, participating in annual clean-up dives, and making sure their operations have minimal impact on the marine ecosystems. The size of the club also matters: larger centers often have more scheduled dives and more extensive facilities, whereas smaller ones give you personal attention and will usually run a course for just one or two people rather than waiting for six to sign up. Quality of equipment and safety records are important. Ask divers for advice.

DAHAB دهب ☎069

Like Goa or Amsterdam, Dahab (meaning "gold" in Arabic) is one of those places that has grown larger than life in the minds of travelers. For most, it conjures up images of glossy-eyed, tie-dyed hippies lounging on the shore, blissfully asphyxiating themselves in blue clouds of marijuana smoke. While this scene is still a significant part of the Dahab experience, Dahabitants no longer think of Jamaica with the reverence that Mecca inspires in the rest of the Arab world. The hippies are slowly being outnumbered by cleaner-cut travelers and dive instructors. Dahab die-hards of yesteryear may lament its relative cleanliness, but the town is becoming more like paradise, not less.

ORIENTATION AND PRACTICAL INFORMATION

Dahab city is of almost no significance to the budget traveler, who only glimpses it between climbing off the bus and getting into a taxi headed for the Bedouin village. **Buses** leave daily from the station (☎64 02 50) in Dahab city to: Cairo (8hr.; 8:30am, 1, 10:30pm; E£55-70); Nuweiba (1½hr., 10:30am and 6:30pm, E£10); Sharm

SCU-BETTER WATCH OUT... Scu-better not die! Hidden among the crevices in the coral reefs around the Sinai Peninsula are creatures capable of inflicting serious injury and even death. If you see something that looks like an aquatic pin cushion, it's probably a **sea urchin** or a **blowfish**, both of which should be touched only in sushi form. Avoid the feathery **lionfish** as well—its harmless-looking spines can deliver a paralyzing sting. The well-named **fire coral** can bloat a leg to mammoth proportions, leaving welts the size of croquet balls. The **stonefish** is camouflaged flawlessly to resemble a mossy lump of coral or rock; if you step on one, you'll puff up and may die within hours. Reach into a hole and a two-meter-long **moray eel** may lock its jaws onto your hand. The list goes on. Before plunging in, ask at any dive shop for a look at one of the picture cards that identifies these underwater uglies.

When snorkeling, try to enter the water in a sandy area to avoid damaging underwater plants and animals. If you have no choice but to enter where sea creatures and coral may dwell, wear foot protection. **Sharks** are attracted by blood, so never enter the water with an open wound or if menstruating. Panicking and thrashing tends to excite sharks. If you see one, calmly climb out of the water and casually share the news. Most sharks, however, are not aggressive; most marine animals get aggressive only if *you* have done something threatening or irritating. If you see an animal getting defensive, simply back away slowly. *Let's Go* does not recommend dying.

al-Sheikh (1hr.; 8:30am, 10, 1, 2:30, 5:30, 10:30pm; E£10); and Taba (3hr., 10:30am, E£20). Prices fluctuate depending on departure time—the last bus of the day is always the most expensive. If you get a group together, you can convince a **taxi** driver to go to any destination. **Service** end up being more expensive, but the rides are much faster. From the bus stop, you can catch a taxi to the **village** (E£5 per car, E£1 per person for a crowded pickup).

The **National Bank of Egypt** is located in Dahab city. (☎64 02 42. Open daily 8:30am-2pm and 6-9pm.) Other services in the city are: the **supermarket** (open daily 6am-2am); **police station** (☎64 02 15); **telephone office,** where you can make calls within Egypt or through Cairo to an international operator (open 24hr.); and **post office** with **Poste Restante.** (☎64 02 23. Open Sa-Th 8am-3pm.) In the Bedouin village, the **Banque du Caire** allows you to withdraw money with a Visa or MC or change traveler's checks with an outrageous commission. (☎64 04 44. Open Sa-Th 9am-2pm and 6-9pm.) Above the Ghazala supermarket at the village's southern end, the **Dahab Polyclinic** treats patients. (☎64 04 44. Open 24hr.) A few supermarkets have **telephones** connecting to Cairo.

ACCOMMODATIONS

There are over two dozen **camps** in the Bedouin village, and the number grows weekly. Dahab camps are an unfortunate bastardization of the thatched beach hut; someone came up with the brilliant idea of casting the huts in concrete, connecting them in rows around a central courtyard, and creating bare cells with minimal ventilation. Fortunately, the huts mostly serve as storage space for your belongings while you lounge outside in one of the restaurants. Rooms with only a mattress are cheapest (E£5-10); those with private bath are a bit pricier (E£10-30). A tangle of hotels and camps crowds the main part of the strip near the restaurants. The coolest and most comfortable are the thatched-hut quarters slightly off the main strip (the first three accommodations listed below fit into this category).

Oasis Fighting Kangaroo (☎64 00 11; email bedouinn@yahoo.com), down a small alleyway across from Napoleon's Restaurant (don't confuse it with the Fighting Kangaroo Camp). Generally regarded as the best place to stay in Dahab, the O.F.K. has a super-friendly atmosphere and two Bedouin-style TV rooms outside. Cell-like singles E£10; doubles E£15. Nicer rooms cost up to E£60.

Bedouin Moon Hotel (☎64 00 87; email reef2000@intouch.com), about 2km north of the Bedouin village. Owned and operated by 2 Bedouin brothers, the Bedouin Moon is a beautiful hotel with a sandy beach and the dive center Reef 2000. Dorm rooms E£35 (breakfast included); doubles E£110-140. Ask about 10-15% *Let's Go* discount.

Cleopatra's (email cleopatra140@hotmail.com). A Bedouin camp whose thatched huts are hot commodities in the Dahab market. Many visitors fall asleep in the lounge or on the roof as they sit on their asps waiting for huts to open up. Rooms with shower and toilet E£25-30; 2-person huts E£14; 4-person huts E£24.

Muhammad 'Ali Camp (☎64 02 68). Clean, cheap, and right in the middle of the action. The camp has its own supermarket, coffee shop, dive club, and laundry facilities. Breakfast E£10; dinner E£20. Doubles E£40.

Auski Camp (☎64 04 74), on the beach south of the Bedouin village, near the Sphinx Hotel. Friendly owner keeps rooms spic-and-span and smelling fresh. Doubles E£15.

FOOD

If you find yourself with the munchies, fear not: Dahab is home to some of the best food in Egypt, but quality varies in the extreme. The local hospital has taken exception to the hygiene of many local restaurants and advises against consuming fish (except at Tarabouche's). Be wary of ordering anything slightly undercooked, especially meat. For more information on how to minimize the risks of food poisoning, see **Food- and Water-borne Diseases,** p. 47. If you want complete control over food preparation, try **Ghazala Market** at the southern end of town.

PETRA & SINAI

Tota (☎64 92 71), next to the Crazy House. A *Let's Go* favorite for 16 years. Despite the tugboat architecture and the waiters' sailor costumes, Tota specializes in pasta (E£6.50-9.50), not seafood, but you can drink like a fish—the restaurant possesses a hard-to-come-by liquor license. Cocktails E£7.50-8.50; Stella E£7.50. Open 8am-1am.

Jay's Restaurant (☎335 33 77; email julie_jays@yahoo.com), on the main street near Fantasea Dive Club. You must step out of the Dahab daze and think ahead to eat at this excellent inexpensive restaurant. Stop by before 6pm to order dinner for that night (the menu changes daily), and Jay's will have the food ready when you come back. It may test your short-term planning and memory skills, but not your math: full meals around E£10. Open for dinner 7-10:30pm; in winter 6-10pm. Open for reservations at 10am.

Tarabouche's (☎(012) 235 63 38), on the pathway past the Banque du Caire and the Sunrise Camp, across the small parking lot. Three-course, home-cooked Egyptian meals (E£25-50) include salad, choice of fish or meat, and dessert. Food is hygienically prepared, so indulge in anything on the menu. Reservations are necessary.

Shark Club, features shakes that will leave you speechless. The owner speaks perfect English, and the dive instructors practically live here. The gigantic portions may cause feeding frenzies among patrons. Half-order pasta E£3-4; shakes E£3-5.

Crazy House Pub (☎64 02 81), near the southern end of the bay. The best place to go stir-crazy. Beer E£7.5; mixed drinks E£7-8. Open noon-4am.

SHAKE 'N' BAKE

SHAKE. The Helnan Hotel (20km north of town) has recently opened the **Zanzibar Disco.** A free shuttle runs from town around midnight, and on a good night the disco draws quite a crowd. On Monday and Wednesday nights, rock out to a live local band at the **Hilton Hotel** until dawn. Free *hors d'œuvres* ease the pain of pricey Stellas (E£10).

BAKE. In order to get an **alcohol license** in the Sinai, an establishment must first possess a building license (obliging the owner to keep his building above certain standards) and pay a property tax. There are six main sources of booze in Dahab: the restaurant at the Nesima Dive Club, the Crazy House Pub, Tota, the Sphinx Hotel, Green Valley, and Neptune Billiards, where pool sharks can also rack up a game. (E£10 per hr. Open 10am-2am.) This lack of liquor is one of the reasons Dahab grew notorious for its **dope scene.** Though the scene is less noticeable nowadays, marijuana is still available for those who want it. People generally do not actively advertise what type of smoke is coming out of their *sheesha*. Remember that the possession of drugs is illegal in Egypt, and Egyptian jails rate low on the Michelin system. Dealers may win an all-expenses-paid trip to the hereafter via firing squad. *Let's Go* just says no.

SIGHTS

OVERLAND DAYTRIPS. Daytrips to nearby natural wonders are great ways to escape the haze of Dahab. Four-by-four trips to the **Colored Canyon** cost E£50 per person for a group of six. You can travel by camel or truck to the brackish oasis of **Wadi Gnay** (E£30 per person). A one-day camel trip to **Nabq** (E£35-50) is also an option. Hamed the Lobster Man runs **Crazy Camel Camp** (☎64 02 73) and organizes jeep and camel safaris. He also takes people on night **lobster hunting** trips that culminate in lobster feasts on the beach. **Blue Hole Travel** (☎64 02 36; email bluehole-travel@n2mail.com), across the street from the Sphinx Hotel, runs camel safaris, trips to St. Catherine's, and daily snorkeling excursions to their namesake. If you want to go anywhere nearby, ask around the Bedouin community. The Bedouin know these hills better than anyone and will often be happy to organize a trip.

SNORKELING. The snorkeling in Dahab is excellent; enter the **Blue Hole** at either end of the bay where the waves break on the reefs (just be sure to wear shoes or flippers, because if the sea urchins don't get you, the coral will). Trips to Blue Hole and **Canyon** are arranged every morning by most camps, and you can rent snorkel gear at camps or on the beach (E£5-10). Make sure the flippers fit, the mask is airtight, and the snorkel unobstructed before paying. **Paddleboats** are available for rental near the northern part of the village; use them to trek to some of the more secluded spots (E£15 per hr.).

BEDOUIN VILLAGE. The Bedouin village is no longer that. It's so loaded with tourists that the Bedouin themselves have moved north to 'Aslah. These days, the bay is lined with restaurants, camps, and gift shops that peddle the famous "Dahab pants" (E£15). Meanwhile, camels and horses trot up and down the beach road carrying Dutch women or pink-hued Brits (camels E£5, horses E£10 for 30min.). Pillowed courtyards hug the beach; at night, they are cheerfully illuminated by electric lights and Baraka bottle lanterns.

SCUBA DIVING

DIVE SITES

Dahab offers some of the best dives reachable by land. The dive sites, on the Red Sea, are all accessible by car (usually 4x4 vehicles) and cover the areas both north and south of the main lighthouse region.

THE ISLANDS. The most plentiful and beautiful supply of coral and aquatic life in Dahab are here. The labyrinth of pathways, valleys, and coral peaks can make it a difficult but rewarding site to visit, as divers often navigate new and different routes while weaving through delicate cities of coral. Many guides believe that this is the best-preserved coral in the entire Sinai area.

CANYON. Most of the corals have now died due to over-tourism, but the long, narrow canyon ranging from 18m to 50m deep still thrills divers looking for deep adventure. At the end of the canyon, divers move through a man-sized crack into the "fish bowl," an enclosure almost completely filled with schools of glass fish.

BLUE HOLE. The most famous site in Dahab is well-known for all the wrong reasons. Every year, some of Dahab's best (and craziest) divers try unsuccessfully to swim through the arched passage (52m below sea level) or even touch the bottom (160m) of this Hole on Earth. The site is recognized for the incredibly blue dive, starting at The Bells and continuing along the cliff of coral to the Blue Hole.

A TAIL OF TWO DOLPHINS Uleen is one of 12 dolphins in the world that have chosen to live and play with humans. While the exact details of her decision remain mysterious, the competing versions of this fish tale are like fatuous episodes of *Flipper*. One story is that in 1994, Awda, a Bedouin fisherman, noticed that Uleen's mother was beached on the shore. Attempting to save her, Awda pulled the dolphin back into the water; but she didn't survive the transition. The next day, Uleen followed Awda and his deaf-mute brother, 'Abdullah, (who could only make one sound: "Uleen") on their daily fishing trip. 'Abdullah jumped into the water to swim with her, forging a bond that neither would soon forget. Another version has it that Uleen's companion (who is male in this tale) was caught in a net and shot by soldiers who mistook him for a shark. Grief-stricken, the lovelorn female lay crying in the water while 'Abdullah stroked her silvery skin to calm her—again forging that special interspecies bond. Scientists assign more, well, scientific reasons to her behavior: she was ejected from her pod (perhaps due to some illness or weakness) and sought social interaction, which she eventually found with humans. Whatever the explanation, Uleen has not left the vicinity of the beach, where visitors swim with her every day. It became clear, however, that humans were not meeting her every need: in 1996, Uleen became the mother of a bouncing baby, whom she lost to natural causes. Though the mother entertains visitors everyday with smiles that would make any delphine dentist proud, her second calf, Ramadan, has mysteriously disappeared, leading many to ask exactly what price Uleen has had to pay for human interaction.

DIVE FACILITIES

The Dahab diving scene has unfortunately turned into a cut-throat operation in which inexperienced and ill-equipped dive centers cut corners on services and prices. There are very few dive centers in Dahab aside from Reef 2000 that offer safe and first-rate services at relatively inexpensive rates.

Reef 2000 (☎64 00 87; email reef2000@intouch.com), at the Bedouin Moon Hotel in its own bay, just north of the Bedouin village. Run by Dave and Rachelle, a British couple who offer low prices and a safe atmosphere where even the most inexperienced will feel comfortable (especially since most of the guides and instructors are English-speaking expats). One guided dive with full equipment US$40; PADI courses US$310. **Camel safaris** to Ras 'Abd Galum and Gabr al-Bint include full equipment, lunch, water, and two dives (US$90-95). 15% *Let's Go* discount.

Fantasea (☎64 04 83; ☎/fax 64 00 43; email fdc@intouch.com), at the northern end. Offers everything from open water dives to assistant instructor courses. The lowest prices for individual dives around.

NUWEIBA نويبع ☎069

One of Sinai's natural oases, Nuweiba lies at the mouth of an enormous *wadi* that is filled with drifting sand for 10 months of the year. About the only excitement in town occurs in winter, when sudden, rampaging walls of water 3m high charge down the *wadi*. Nuweiba resembles a younger version of Dahab: a town with no inherent appeal or style that happens to be blessed with a cheap, carefree Bedouin camp and a great beach (complete with friendly dolphin). Nuweiba's importance rests primarily on its role in interstate travel: a ferry shuttles tourists and workers to Aqaba, Jordan.

GETTING THERE AND GETTING AROUND

Nuweiba, named after the Bedouin tribe whose territory reaches Taba, is divided into a **port** and a **city.** The city lies 10km to the north of the port; a taxi between the two costs E£10. **Ferries** to Aqaba leave from the port. The **bus stop** is in the port, in front of the post office. **Buses** leave daily to: Cairo (6hr., 10am and 3pm, E£50);

Sharm al-Sheikh (2½hr., 6:30am and 4:30pm, E£15) via Dahab (1½hr., E£10); St. Catherine's (6:30am, E£15); Suez (7hr., 7am and 3:30pm, E£25); and Taba (1hr., 6am and noon, E£10). To get to Tarabin from the city, either walk north along the beach (1½hr.) or take a taxi (E£20).

ORIENTATION AND PRACTICAL INFORMATION

For credit card cash advances, use the **Banque du Caire** in the Hilton Hotel. (Open Su-Th 9:30am-noon and 6-9pm.) Across the street and near the port is **Bank Misr,** with a Visa/MC **ATM.** Most stores are in either the new or the old commercial center, both in the city. The new center is near the Helnan; the old is north, closer to Tarabin. Both have **supermarkets,** but the old center keeps longer hours. A **newsstand** in the old center has English-language newspapers, international telephone service, and bus schedule information. The old center also houses a **24-hour pharmacy** (☎50 06 05). Next to the Helnan stands the **tourist police** (☎50 02 31). Farther north past the communications antenna are: the **police station** (☎50 02 42; open 24hr.); the **hospital** (☎50 03 02; open 24hr.; higher quality Israeli health care is just over the border); the **telephone office** (open 24hr.); and a **post office** with **Poste Restante** and **EMS.** (☎50 02 44. Open daily 8am-3pm.)

ACCOMMODATIONS AND FOOD

Budget travelers are better off staying in nearby Tarabin. The camps are cheaper and more plentiful, the restaurants are closer to the beach, and the nightlife is livelier. The only budget accommodation in Nuweiba City is **El-Waha Village,** 500m south of the Helnan, which sports garden shed-style bungalows. (☎/fax 50 04 20 or 50 04 21. Breakfast E£10. Singles E£25; doubles E£35; triples E£45; camping E£8 per person.) The **Helnan International Hotel,** located next to El-Waha Village, also offers relatively inexpensive rooms with access to a private beach and facilities. (☎50 04 01. Single huts E£46; double huts E£62; triple huts E£78; includes breakfast. Pitch your own tent for E£15.) Everything else you need lies north of El-Waha Village and the Helnan, along Nuweiba City's one road.

Dr. Shishkebab (☎50 02 73), in the old commercial center, offers sandwiches (E£3-4), meat entrees (E£15-25), and vegetarian dishes (E£3-5). **'Ali Baba,** around the corner from Dr. Shishkebab, serves meat dishes (E£12).

SIGHTS AND SAFARIS

Nuweiba's most rewarding sight is **Dolphin Beach,** named for the friendly dolphin, Uleen, who lives there (see **A Tail of Two Dolphins,** p. 364). Dolphin Beach is a 20-minute walk south of Nuweiba Port or a E£5 taxi ride. Tell your driver, "Dolphin." Bedouin will charge you E£10 to swim, and another E£10 for mask, snorkel, and fins. The beach is open until 6pm.

Nuweiba is an excellent starting point for **camel** or **jeep safaris** through the desert terrain. Ask about trips at **Explore Sinai,** in the commercial center (☎50 01 41; open 9am-4pm and 7:30-11pm), or at the slightly cheaper **Moonland Camp** in Tarabin. (☎50 06 10. Colored Canyon trips E£50 per person.) You may save E£10-15 per day by dealing directly with a guide. Look for one at Tarabin if none approach you. Guides here are generally trustworthy. Desert trips require a **permit,** achieved by some mysterious passport fermentation process at your friendly neighborhood police station (your guide will take care of it for you). Tour prices always include food, but often exclude water. The price of bottled water rises dramatically during the safari, so start off with a large supply.

SCUBA DIVING

Like all towns on the Sinai coast, Nuweiba is surrounded by beautiful coral reefs, but unlike Dahab, Na'ama Bay, and Sharm al-Sheikh, Nuweiba's shores are not teeming with dive clubs. There are only three in town. **Emperor Divers,** in the Hilton Hotel, opened in 2000. (☎52 03 20 or 52 03 21, ext. 900. Two suited dives with full equipment and transport US$70. PADI open water training and certification for around US$325. Open daily 8am-6pm.) **Diving Camp Nuweiba** is in the Helnan Hotel. (☎50 04 02. Two dives with vehicular transport US$60, with boat US$65; introductory dives US$45. Open water training US$325. Open 8am-6pm.) Divers can arrange trips to Ras Abu Galum through either center. Both diving centers are open from 8am to 6pm. **Sinai Dolphin Divers,** in the Nakim Inn, offers snorkeling with the dolphin Uleen for US$20. (☎50 08 79; email sinaidolphin@yahoo.com. Full equipment dives US$40, includes transport.)

FROM NUWEIBA TO TABA

The 70km stretch between Nuweiba and Taba is undoubtedly the most magnificent part of the Sinai: mountains come down to the sea, reefs and sand turn the water a magnificent shade of turquoise, and the mountains of Saudi Arabia tower in the distance. Unfortunately, the view will soon be ruined by the five-star resorts that are popping up like weeds along this beautiful stretch. The coastline is dotted with **Bedouin camps,** which are accessible by bus or *service* from Taba or Nuweiba. East Delta buses leave from Taba for Nuweiba at 9am and 3pm, and from Nuweiba for Taba at noon (1hr., E£10). Drivers may not know the names of some camps; keep your eyes peeled for signs. The camps follow a standard layout: a couple of huts, a central lounge, and a restaurant. Most huts do not have electricity (and those that are electrified rely on shaky generators), so bring a flashlight. It's quiet out here: people spend the days reading and swimming, while nighttime brings on backgammon, stargazing, shagging like a rabbit, and all that good stuff.

SHARM AL-SHEIKH شرم الشيخ ☎069

No one goes to Sharm al-Sheikh for the sights, though with its dozens of wrecking balls, cranes, and half-finished buildings, there is ample opportunity to view ruins-in-progress. Sharm, like the rest of the Sinai coast, is in the midst of a building boom. Sharm and nearby Na'ama Bay are often called twin resorts, but they're far from identical. Na'ama inherited the good looks and good-looking travelers, while Sharm got the big boats and bigger buildings. Wealthy Europeans fill Sharm's four- and five-star hotels, leaving little room for budget backpackers to enjoy the already crowded beach. The tiny bay is crammed with dive boats attracted by the calmness of the water, further adding to the congested, over trafficked feel. For more excitement and breathing space, head north to Na'ama.

GETTING THERE AND GETTING AROUND

Flights: The **Egypt Air** office (☎66 10 58) is south of the bus station. Open Sa-Th 9am-2pm and 6-9pm. The airport branch (☎60 06 40) is far more helpful.

Ferries: The ferry to **Hurghada** (☎66 01 66) leaves three times weekly from the port just south of Sharm al-Sheikh (6hr.; M, W-Th 9am; E£125). From the Sharm Marina, keep walking around the harbor and over the hill at the southern end. Book tickets a day ahead, either through a hotel or at **Thomas Cook** (☎60 18 08), 50m south of the Pigeon House Hotel.

Buses: Buses leave daily to: **Cairo** (7-10hr., 10 per day 7:30am-midnight, E£65); **Dahab** (1½hr., 6 per day 6:30am-11:30pm, E£10); **Nuweiba** (2½hr.; 9am, 2, 5pm; E£15); **St. Catherine's** (2½hr., 7:30am, E£15); **Suez** (7hr.; 9am and 2pm; E£25); and **Taba** (3hr., 9am, E£25). Most buses leave from behind the Mobil station between Na'ama and Sharm al-Sheikh, though some leave from Sharm itself—call ahead as schedules change frequently (☎60 06 00 or 60 06 66).

Taxis: For taxis, call ☎66 03 57.

PRACTICAL INFORMATION

At the top of the hill, next to the post office, is the **Bank of Alexandria,** which allows money withdrawal with Visa and MC. (☎66 03 55. Open 8:30am-2pm and 6-9pm.) The **tourist police** (☎60 03 11, 60 05 54; open 24hr.) and **police station** (☎66 04 15) are 300m from the banks. The 24-hour **hospital** (☎66 04 25; **ambulance** ☎60 05 54) is just north of the bus station. The **new hospital** (☎66 08 93) is halfway between Sharm al-Sheikh and Na'ama Bay. The **telephone office** is 300m from the banks, near the tourist police. (☎66 04 00. Open 24hr.) At the top of the hill to the right, the **post office** has **Poste Restante** and **EMS.** (☎66 05 18. Open Sa-Th 8am-3pm.) **Pharmacy Sharm al-Sheikh** is in the same complex. (☎66 03 88. Open daily 9am-1am.)

ACCOMMODATIONS AND FOOD

If there is room at Na'ama Bay, there is absolutely no reason to stay in Sharm. The cheapest place is the **Youth Hostel,** at the top of the hill and to the left. From the bus station, follow the signs for the Cliff Top Hotel. Breakfast is included, and the preteen angst is free. (☎66 03 17. Beds E£20.) Another option is the somewhat dingy **El-Kheima Hotel,** next to the Diving World Dive Club. Be sure to tell them that you *only* want bed and breakfast, or else they'll charge double and include dinner. (☎/fax 66 01 66. Bungalow singles E£40; doubles with portable fans E£60.) A last resort (and the only hotel on the beach) is **Safetyland,** at the bottom of the hill at the intersection of the road leading to Na'ama Bay and the road to the Sharm bus station. Stuffy thatched bungalows are situated in what looks like a construction site. (☎66 34 63. Open tent sites E£20 per person; singles E£40; doubles E£80; breakfast included.)

The food situation in Sharm is pretty dismal. The **Sharm Express Supermarket** is next to the Pharmacy Nada'a. (☎60 09 24. Open daily 9am-2am.) A row of cheap **restaurants** hugging the hill south of the bus station offers an opportunity to chow down on everything from pizza to Asian food. (Most open daily 11am-midnight.)

SCUBA DIVING

The Sharm al-Sheikh and Na'ama Bay area is undoubtedly the mecca of Red Sea diving and the growth spot for most of the Sinai's tourism. Despite the large number of wealthy Germans and Italians in five-star hotels, Sharm al-Sheikh still has several undiscovered sites and unexplored gems in and around the Straits of Tiran, Ras Muhammad National Park, and the wreck of the *Thistlegorm.*

DIVE SITES

RAS MUHAMMAD NATIONAL PARK. This area encompasses most of the southern tip of the Sinai and has eclipsed almost all other dive sites in international acclaim. The most famous sites in the park are the **Shark** and **Yolanda Reefs.** The latter includes a swim through the wreckage of the freighter *Yolanda* (the actual ship has slipped off the continental shelf and lies 220m below the surface). This surreal sight is possibly the only place in the world where you can swim with sharks among broken toilets and containers. For more information, see below.

THISTLEGORM. The World War II cargo ship *Thistlegorm* was sunk in 1941 by long-range German bombers off the southern coast of the Sinai. Discovered years later by Jacques-Yves Cousteau (who kept the location secret until it was rediscovered in the early 90s), the *Thistlegorm* has become legendary among divers and is widely considered the best wreck dive in the world. Located quite far off shore, the *Thistlegorm* requires at least a day and two dives to explore. The cargo bays are crammed full of tires, rifles, motorcycles, aircraft wings, tanks, trucks, and railway carriages. The commander's deck and outer shell is downright eerie. Although a more expensive dive (US$120-150), it is unforgettable.

JACKSON'S REEF. Of the four reefs extending down the center of the spectacular **Straits of Tiran,** this is the best and northernmost dive. The strong current is particularly challenging, but also encourages the growth of some of the most beautiful and plentiful coral in the entire Sinai. Not only does the current bring enough nutrients to feed the coral and schools of fish that congregate on the reef, but it also attracts a variety of sharks and turtles. Schools of hammerheads are seen frequently during July and August.

RAS GHOZLANI. In the area just north of the famous Ras Muhammad National Park lie many peaceful and often overlooked local dive sites. Many of the sites are incredibly beautiful and tranquil; Ras Ghozlani is the most superb. Divers here are less likely to see the big predators found prowling the deep at other sites, but this location is rarely crowded, uniquely preserved, and full of colorful fish.

DIVE FACILITIES

Camel Dive Center, P.O. Box 10, Na'ama Bay, Sharm al-Sheikh, South Sinai, Egypt (☎60 07 00; fax 60 06 01; email reservations1@cameldive.com; www.cameldive.com), across from the Cataract Resort. One of the oldest dive centers in the area, and probably the friendliest. Offers over six daily boats, state-of-the-art equipment, and highly trained multilingual guides, as well as inexpensive accommodations by Na'ama's standards (dorm rooms US$30). One guided dive US$30; full equipment US$20; O/W course US$360. Call for a 10% discount on all services.

Oonas Dive Club (☎60 05 81; fax 60 05 82), at the northern end of the bay. Slightly cheaper rates and much better after-hours camaraderie than the other centers. Five-day PADI course US$295-330; certification US$30. Intro dives US$65 including equipment. Full gear rental US$24. Full day with two dives US$50.

NEAR SHARM

RAS MUHAMMAD NATIONAL PARK

*The park is accessible by boat and taxi (E£100). Since it is beyond the jurisdiction of a Sinai-only visa, you need your passport and a full **Egyptian tourist visa.** Dive shops run trips to the park, and you may not need a full visa if you stick with their boats and hotels. Park open daily 8am-5pm (strict closing time). US$5 per person, additional US$5 per car. For information on **scuba diving** at Ras Muhammad, see **Dive Sites,** above.*

Sticking out into the Red Sea at the tip of the Sinai peninsula, **Ras Muhammad National Park** is the most famous dive site in Egypt and one of the most spectacular in the world. The tiny neck of land is bordered on the west by the Gulf of Suez and on the east by the Gulf of Aqaba. The waters of Ras Muhammad contain over 1000 species of fish, many of which are unique to the Red Sea. The aquatic wonders found here far outweigh the time and expense of the trip, making it by far the best daytrip from Sharm al-Sheikh or Na'ama Bay.

In the early 1980s, it became clear that tourist and fishing traffic was destroying the underwater treasures of Ras Muhammad, so the Egyptian government declared the area a national park in 1983. Most of the fragile underwater habitat is now closed to the public, and it is against Egyptian law to remove any material, living or dead, from the park. Diving, snorkeling, and swimming are only permitted in specified areas, mostly around the very tip of the peninsula. On rough days, snorkeling at Ras Muhammad can be difficult. For underwater advice and warnings, see **Scu-better Watch Out,** p. 361. Camping is permitted in designated sites; check with the park's Visitors Center for details. Further information about Ras Muhammad is available from the Sharm al-Sheikh info office (☎66 06 68 or 66 05 59).

NA'AMA BAY ☎069

This five-star hotel nexus is the center of Egypt's anti-backpacker sentiment. The budget traveler is about as welcome in Na'ama as the narcotics agent is in Dahab; however, if you look clean-cut (and act like you own the place), you can freely roam the waterfront shops and hotels. As soon as you don your hip new tie-dye from Dahab, however, you invite stares along the promenade and may be barred from certain areas. Many budget travelers do flock here each year, drawn by the world-class diving and snorkeling as well as the most active nightlife in the Sinai. It is sometimes possible to get a job at a hotel or dive center; the pay is just enough for food and entertainment. If you work for a hotel, you usually get free accommodations; if you work at a dive club, you get free diving lessons or courses. Knowledge of Arabic is not necessary, but French and Italian are helpful.

GETTING THERE AND GETTING AROUND

The **bus stop** is officially in front of the Helnan Marina Hotel, but the driver will drop you off at any hotel along the road. **Intercity buses** leave from behind the Mobil station at the southern end of town and from the Sharm al-Sheikh bus station. Southbound, open-sided **minibuses** (E£1) and **taxis** (E£10) go to **Sharm al-Sheikh,** and northbound minibuses (E£10) and taxis (E£20) pass **Shark's Bay.**

ORIENTATION AND PRACTICAL INFORMATION

Na'ama Bay is a long strip of hotels on the water side of the highway, the town's only street. Most of the beach is owned by five-star resorts. Between the beach and hotels is a **promenade,** where most restaurants, bars, and diving clubs cluster.

The **National Bank of Egypt** has branches in the Marina Sharm, Gazala, and Mövenpick Hotels and usually exchanges money. (Open Sa-Th 9am-1pm and 6-9pm, F 9-11am and 6-9pm.) **Bank Misr,** at the Marriott Hotel, will give cash advances on Visa or MC. (☎60 16 67. Open Sa-Th 9am-2pm and 7-10pm, F 10am-12:30pm and 7-10pm.) The **Commercial International Bank** has two locations, one next to the Camel Dive Center and one across from the Mövenpick Hotel. (Both open daily 9am-2pm and 6-9pm.) There is an **ATM** that accepts Visa and MC in the Mövenpick Hotel lobby, as well as a branch of **EgyptAir.** (☎66 06 67; fax 66 03 37. Open daily 9:30am-2pm and 6:30-9pm.) The **tourist police** (☎64 03 01) are just north of the Helnan Marina Hotel. Call ☎60 05 54 for an **ambulance.** The **Towa Pharmacy** is in the bazaar south of the Mövenpick. (☎60 07 79. Open daily 10am-1am.) The **Lifeline Clinic** (☎(012) 212 4292), between Sharm al-Sheikh and Na'ama Bay, has American- and German-trained doctors who take drop-ins (daily 5-7pm). **Internet access** is available at **CyberDisco,** next to the Crazy Daisy nightclub. (Open daily 9pm-1am.) The **post office** is in Sharm al-Sheikh, but most hotels will drop off mail.

ACCOMMODATIONS

If there is room, opt for accommodations in Na'ama rather than in Sharm. Hotels are nicer, and you won't have to take expensive taxis to and from the beach.

Pigeon House (☎60 09 96; fax 60 09 95), at the northern end of the bay. The only relatively cheap place to roost in Na'ama. After you've flocked together with birds of a feather in the happening courtyard (*the* place for a Stella or *sheesha*), nestle down in one of their thatched huts with fans. Middle-quality rooms without A/C or the cool breeze of the huts become stifling ovens in the summer; not recommended unless you want your goose cooked. Breakfast included. Huts: singles E£38; doubles E£56. Rooms: singles E£65; doubles E£85; with A/C E£190; extra bed E£20.

Oonas Dive Club (☎60 05 81), at the northern end of the promenade. Look for the red neon sign at the top of the building. With beach access, swimming pool, A/C, and a lively bar, this dive hotel offers everything the slightly over-budget traveler could want. Singles US$40; doubles US$60.

PETRA & SINAI

Camel Dive Club (☎60 07 00), in the center of the small bazaar, close to the beach. This slightly pricey option is worth it for the location as well as the beautiful rooms, pool, A/C, and private bath. Breakfast included. Dorm rooms US$30; doubles US$104.

Shark's Bay Camp (☎60 09 42; fax 60 09 44), 4km north of town. A ship-shape Bedouin camp that overlooks a quiet bay. Features a breathtaking view of Tiran Island, an excellent restaurant, and a dive club, but the cost of a *service* (E£10) or taxi (E£20) to Na'ama makes these clean bungalows an expensive choice. Bedouin tent on the beach E£125. Singles E£50-60; doubles E£65-75; triples E£90-100.

FOOD

Food in Na'ama Bay is high in quality, at least along the main hotel strip. **Tam Tam Oriental Corner** (☎60 01 50 or 60 01 51), on Ghazala Hotel beach next to the Hilton beach, is the cheapest place in town. An enormous bowl of *kushari* goes for E£7.70, and salads cost E£3.50. (Open daily noon-1am.) The **Pigeon House** dishes out excellent pork, meat, and fish. (Pasta E£10.50-16.75; kebab E£19.75-22.75. Open daily until 11pm.) **Viva Restaurant,** opposite the Red Sea Diving College in Kanabesh beach, serves up tasty pizzas (E£18-22. ☎60 09 64. Open daily 10am-midnight.) Live it up a little at the **Hard Rock Cafe,** around the corner from the Camel Dive Center. Indulge in the Caesar Salad for E£21 or the Club Sandwich for E£25. (☎60 26 65 or 60 26 66. Open daily 1pm-3am.)

SURF...

CORAL REEFS. Na'ama Bay itself has no spectacular reefs, but a veritable colossus of coral lies just outside the bay to the north and south. Dive centers have maps of the reefscape; pick one up and put on your flippers. The closest free site is **Near Gardens** at the northern tip of Na'ama Bay, a moderate walk down the beach. The nearby **Tower** and **Sodfa** are a decent walk south of Na'ama Bay, but both require a E£10 fee, payable at the Tower Hotel. Ask at a dive center which sites are accessible by land; some are tricky to reach.

SNORKELING. Many swear that boat-based snorkeling is the best. For US$15-25, spend a day on a boat and explore spectacular waters. Arrange trips through the dive clubs. The legendary reefs of the **Straits of Tiran** are distant and accessible by boat only. **Ras Nasrani** and **Ras Umm Sidd** are good sites a little closer to town.

AQUATIC SPORTS. Water activities are not restricted to diving. **Sun-n-Fun** booths (☎60 16 23; open 9am-11pm) at the Hilton and Aquamarine beaches rent equipment for **windsurfing** (E£50 per hr.; lessons E£65 per hr.), **water skiing** (E£40 per 15min.), **jet skiing** (one-person jet E£60 per 15min., two-person E£70), and **sailing** (E£40 per hr.; lessons E£55). Try a **glass bottom boat** ride (every hr. 10am-4pm; E£25 per person) or the big **Discovery** (every 2hr. 11am-5pm, E£55). Frolic for free at the tiny **public beach** just south of Gafy Land Hotel.

...AND TURF

Landlubbers can strap on some plaid pants and tee off in a game of **miniature golf** at the Hilton. (E£10 per game, E£55 deposit on clubs.) **Horseback riding** is available across from the Novotel Hotel. (E£55 per hr.) **Safari Tours,** next to the Pigeon House, offers **ATV** trips out in the desert. Most leave before sunset. (US$35 per hr.)

WADI KID. Here's looking at you, Kid: this *wadi*, 40km north of Na'ama Bay, is a deep, fertile canyon where you can hike among rock formations and fruit trees. Most hotels are affiliated with a tour company that goes once a week. *(Mövenpick Hotel organizes half-day trips to Nabq and Wadi Kid for US$30, with a 4-person minimum.)*

NABQ WILDLIFE RESERVE. On the coast 20km north of Na'ama Bay, Nabq's most notable site is a strip of coastline where the largest **mangrove forest** in the Sinai flourishes, attracting herons, ospreys, foxes, and hard-to-spot gazelles. The mangroves sprout in a few feet of warm, clear water with a sandy bottom, marking ideal swimming and relaxation spots. The problem of maintaining traditional Bedouin lifestyles in the modern world is being actively addressed in Nabq: a Bedouin "reservation" attempts to preserve the culture and openly welcomes visitors. *(Most hotels organize daytrips to Nabq. Wandering off the path in the park is extremely dangerous, as there are still a number of landmines in the area.)*

LIBATIONS 'N' GYRATIONS

LIBATIONS. Nights in Na'ama are most often spent tossing back Stellas and swapping diving stories. One of the best places to do this is the **Pigeon House,** where the brew flows and the *sheesha* smoke billows. (Open daily 5:30pm-12:30am.) Slip on your eye patch and head for the **Pirate's Bar,** a popular watering hole in the Hilton. With cutlasses and rigging hanging from the wall, the bar attracts an appropriately ridiculous mix of swashbucklingly tan diving instructors and suave Europeans. They serve Stella (E£9.50), import draught beer (E£18-20), and free bar munchies. (☎60 01 36, ext. 850. Open daily 11am-1am.) Most of the local dive masters and tourists congregate at the **Camel Dive Club,** upstairs from the dive center of the same name. The first floor is packed and often features live music; the low-key rooftop patio overlooks the main street. (Stellas E£12, E£9 for divers.)

GYRATIONS. Top off the evening at the **Bus Stop Disco,** between McDonald's and the Camel Dive Club. (☎60 01 97 or 60 01 98. Open daily noon-3:30am.) Give the roulette wheel a spin at the Las Vegas-style **Casino Royale,** across from the Mövenpick Hotel. (☎60 17 31. Open daily 8pm-4am. 18+. No shorts.) The **Crazy Daisy,** next to Tam Tam, offers techno dancing. (Open daily 9pm-4am. E£10 cover after midnight.) Across the street from the Mövenpick Hotel, **Jolie Disco** spins a mix of American, Arabic, and Euro pop/disco beats. (☎60 01 00. Open daily 9pm-4am.)

APPENDIX

Avg. Temp. (lo/hi), Precipitation	January			April			July			October		
	°C	°F	mm	°C	°F	mm	°C	°F	mm	°C	°F	mm
Jerusalem	5/13	41/55	132	10/23	50/73	28	17/31	63/88	0	15/27	59/81	13
Tel Aviv	8/17	46/62	202	12/25	54/77	30	21/31	69/87	0	17/28	63/83	20
Haifa	9/18	48/64	13	14/25	57/77	4	24/31	75/88	0	20/29	68/84	2
Eilat	10/21	50/70	0	18/31	64/88	5	26/39	79/102	0	21/33	70/91	0

TIME ZONE

Israel and the Palestinian territories are exactly two hours ahead of Greenwich Mean Time (GMT). During standard time, they are normally eight hours behind Sydney, two hours ahead of London, seven hours ahead of New York and Toronto, and ten hours ahead of California and Vancouver. During Daylight Savings time, however, such calculations are easily confused.

MEASUREMENTS

The metric system is used throughout the Middle East.

MEASUREMENT CONVERSIONS

1 inch (in.) = 25.4 millimeters (mm)	1 millimeter (mm) = 0.039 in.
1 foot (ft.) = 0.30m	1 meter (m) = 3.28 ft.
1 yard (yd.) = 0.914m	1 meter (m) = 1.09 yd.
1 mile = 1.61km	1 kilometer (km) = 0.62 mi.
1 ounce (oz.) = 28.35g	1 gram (g) = 0.035 oz.
1 pound (lb.) = 0.454kg	1 kilogram (kg) = 2.202 lb.
1 fluid ounce (fl. oz.) = 29.57ml	1 milliliter (ml) = 0.034 fl. oz.
1 gallon (gal.) = 3.785L	1 liter (L) = 0.264 gal.
1 acre = 0.405ha	1 hectare (ha) = 2.47 acres
1 square mile (sq. mi.) = 2.59km^2	1 square kilometer (km^2) = 0.386 sq. mi.

TELEPHONE CODES

ISRAEL	
Akko/Haifa	04
Be'er Sheva	07
Eilat	07
Golan	06
Jerusalem	02
Nazareth	06
Tel Aviv	03
Tiberias	06
Tzfat	06
West Bank	02

WEST BANK & GAZA	
Bethlehem	02
Gaza	07
Jericho	03
Nablus	09
Ramallah	02
JORDAN & EGYPT	
Petra (Jordan)	03
Amman	06
Sinai (Egypt)	062
Cairo	02

HEBREW (IVRIT) עברית

See **Language,** on p. 29, for historical background. The transliterations *ḥ* (ח) and *kh* (כ) are both guttural, as in the German word *ach.* The Hebrew *r* is close to the French *r*, although an Arabic (or even English) *r* is also understood. Hebrew vowels are shorter than English ones, which leads to discrepancies in transliteration. The definite article is the prefix *ha.* Feminine adjectives add an "-ah" at the end; feminine verbs usually add an "-at" or an "-et." Verbs and adjectives are inflected by gender. Below, the self-referential masculine form is listed as "m," while the female form is indicated by an "f." The gender of the person addressed is indicated by a "To m" or "To f."

Although Hebrew is read from right to left, numerals are read from left to right.

HEBREW NUMERALS										
0	1	2	3	4	5	6	7	8	9	10
efes	eḥad	shtayim	shalosh	arba	ḥamesh	shesh	sheva	shmoneh	teisha	eser

PHRASEBOOK

GENERAL

ENGLISH	HEBREW
Hello/Good-bye	Shalom
Could you help me?	Atah yaḥol la'azor lee (To m)/At yeḥola la'azor lee (To f)?
Good morning	Boker tov
Good evening	Erev tov
See you later	L'hitra'ot
How are you?	Ma nishma?
Okay/fine	Be-seder
Not good	Lo tov
Excellent	Metzuyan
I'm tired	Anee ayef (m)/Anee ayefa (f)
Yes	Ken
No	Lo
Thank you	Todah
Maybe	Oolai
Excuse me/I'm sorry	Sliḥa
Please/You're welcome	Bevakasha
I don't know	Anee lo yodeah (m)/Anee lo yoda'at (f)
What is your name?	Eikh korim lekhah? (To m) Eikh korim lakh? (To f)
My name is...	Shmee...
I'm a student	Anee student (m)/Anee studentit (f)
Who	Mee
How do you say...?	Eikh omrim...
I don't understand	Anee lo mevin (m)/Anee lo mevinah (f)
I don't speak Hebrew	Anee lo medaber ivrit (m)/Anee lo medaberet ivrit (f)
I'd like to make a call to the U.S.	Anee rotzeh letalfen le'america (m)/Anee rotzah letal-fen le'america (f)
Do you speak English?	Ata medaber anglit? (m)/At medaberet anglit? (f)
Please repeat	Tagid od pa'am, bevakasha (To m)/Tageedi od pa'am, bevakasha (To f)
Please speak slowly	Tedaber le'at bevakasha (To m)/tedabri le'at bev-akasha (To f)
Telephone	Telephon
What do you call this in Hebrew?	Eikh korim le'zeh be'ivrit?

APPENDIX

DIRECTIONS

ENGLISH	HEBREW
Where is... ?	Eyfoh... ?
straight	Yashar
Right (direction)	Yameen
Left	Smol
How far...?	Kama raḥok...?
North/South/East/West	Tzafon/Darom/Mizraḥ/Ma'arav
I'm lost	Ne'ebadetee
When	Matai
Why	Lamah
I'm going to...	Ani nose'a le... (m)/Ani nosa'at le...(f)
There is...	Yesh...
There is no...	Ein...
Do you know where... is?	Ata yodeah eifoh nimtzah... ?(To m)/At yodahat eifoh nimtzah. . . ?(To f)
Wait (for authenticity, bring fingertips together and gesture as you say this)	Regah

PLACES

ENGLISH	HEBREW
Bathroom	Sherutim
Beach/Ocean/Mountain	Ḥof/Yam/Har
Boulevard	Sderot
Building	Binyan
Center of town	Merkaz ha'ir
Church	Knessia
Hostel	Akhsaniya
Hotel	Malon
Market	Shuk
Museum	Muzaion
Mosque	Misgad
Pharmacy	Beit Markaḥat
Post office	Do'ar
Restaurant	Mees'adah
Room	Ḥeder
Street	Reḥov
Synagogue	Beit knesset
University	Universitah

TRANSPORTATION

ENGLISH	HEBREW
Central bus station	Taḥanat merkazit
Bus stop	Taḥanat otoboos
Do you stop at...?	Ata otzer be-...?
From where does the bus leave?	Mi'eifo ha-otoboos ozev?
I would like a ticket for...	Anee rotzeh (f: rotzah) kartees le...
One-way	Keevoon eḥad
Round-trip	Haloḥ ve'ḥazor
Please stop	Atzor, bevakasha
Take the bus from ___ to ___	Kaḥ (to m)/ Kḥi (to f) et ha-otoboos me___ le___
What time does the ___ leave?	Matai ha___ ozev?
Bus	Otoboos

APPENDIX

ENGLISH	HEBREW
Taxi	Monit/Taxi
Automobile	Mekhonit
Train	Rakevet
Where are you going?	L'an ata nosayah?

MONEY/BARGAINING

ENGLISH	HEBREW
Do you have... ?	Yesh lekha... ? (m) Yesh lakh... ? (f)
How much is this?	Kama zeh oleh?
I want...	Anee rotzeh... (m)/Anee rotzah... (f)
I don't want... (male/female)	Lo rotzeh... (male) Lo rotzah... (female)
Is there a student discount?	Yesh hanaḥa le'studentim?
Cheap/Expensive	Zol/Yakar
Do you accept credit cards/traveler's checks?	Atem mekablim kartisei ashrai/hamḥaot nos'im
Money	Kesef
Change (literally "leftovers")	Odef
Discount	Hanaḥa
Go away	Tistalek
Go to hell	Lekh l'azazel

DATE AND TIME

ENGLISH	HEBREW
What time is it?	Ma hasha'ah?
At what time...?	Be'eizeh sha'ah...?
Hour, Time	Sha'ah
Day/Week/Month/Year	Yom/Shavuah/Ḥodesh/Shanah
Early	Mookdam
Late	Me'ooḥar
Morning/Afternoon/Evening/Night	Boker/Tzohora'im/Erev/Lyla
Open/Closed	Patoo'aḥ/Sagoor
What time do you open/close?	Matai atem potḥim/sogrim?
Today/Yesterday/Tomorrow	Ha-yom/Etmol/Maḥar
Sunday	Yom rishon
Monday	Yom shaini
Tuesday	Yom shlishi
Wednesday	Yom revi'i
Thursday	Yom ḥamishi
Friday	Yom shishi
Sabbath (Saturday)	Shabbat

ACCOMMODATIONS

ENGLISH	HEBREW
Do you have a single/double room?	Yesh laḥem ḥeder le'yaḥeed/kafool?
Do you know of a cheap hotel?	Ata makeer malon zol? (To m)/At makeera malon zol? (To f)
Hotel/Hostel	Malon/Aḥsania
How much is the room?	Kama oleh Ha-ḥeder?
I'd like a room	Anee rotzeh ḥeder (m)/Anee rotzah (f) ḥeder
I'd like to reserve a room	Anee rotzeh le'hazmeen ḥeder (m)/Anee rotzah le'hazmeen ḥeder (f)
L'malah	upstairs

ENGLISH	HEBREW
L'matah	downstairs

FOOD

ENGLISH	HEBREW
Restaurant	Mees' ada
Waiter	Meltzar (m)/Meltzarit (f)
Water	Mahyim
Bread	Leḥem
Grocery store	Makolet
Breakfast/Lunch/Dinner	Aruḥat boker/Aruḥat tzohora'im/Aruḥat erev
Chicken	Oaf
Beef	Basar
Vegetables	Yerakot
Do you have vegetarian food?	Yesh laḥem oḥel tzimḥonee?
I am vegetarian	Ani tzimḥonee/tzimḥoneet
Coffee	Kafeh
Tea	Teh
Milk	Ḥalav
Eggs	Beitzim
Candy	Soocariah
Chocolate	Shokolad
Ice cream	Glida
Cake/cookies	Oogah/oogiot

EMERGENCY

ENGLISH	HEBREW
Hospital	Beit-ḥolim
Doctor	Rofeh
I need a doctor	Anee tzariḥ rofeh (m)/Ani tzriḥa rofeh (f)
Don't touch me	Al teegah bee
Help!	Hatzeeloo
I'm calling the police	Anee kore lamishtara (m)/Anee koret lamishtara (f)
Leave me alone	Azov otee
Police/Fire fighters/Ambulance	Mishtara/Meḥabei esh/Ahmboolance
I'm ill	Anee ḥoleh (m)/Anee ḥolah (f)
I'm hurt	Anee patzoo'ah (m)/Anee ptzoo'ah (f)
Stop!	Tafseek (m)/Tafseekee (f)
Passport	Darkon
Magen David Adom	Israeli Red Cross
Miklat	Bomb shelter

ARABIC (AL-'ARABI) العربى

Arabic uses eight sounds not heard in English. *Kh* (خ) is like the Scottish or German *ch*; *gh* (غ) is like the French *r*. There are two "h" sounds; one (هـ) sounds like an English "h" and the other (ح, in Muhammad) is somewhere between *kh* and plain *h*. The letter *'ayn* (ع) comes from the throat; it is indicated by ' in transliteration. *R* is pronounced as a trill, similar to Spanish. Finally, *s*, *d*, *t*, *dh* (as in **th**is), and *k* have two sounds each, one heavier than the other.

The heavy *k* (ق), represented by a "q" in transliteration, is not commonly pronounced (one exception is in the word Qur'an). Instead, city people replace it with a glottal stop (a sound similar to that of the middle syllable of the word "butter" pronounced with a cockney accent), indicated by ' in transliteration. Vowels and consonants can be either long or short, often an important distinction (it means the difference between a *hammam*, bathroom, and a *hamam*, pigeon).

The definite article is the prefix *al*. When *al* comes before the sounds t, th, j, d, dh, r, z, s, sh, or n, the *l* is not pronounced. Never say "*ihna fee al-nar*" (we are in Hell); a more correct pronunciation is "*ihna feen-nar.*"

Although Arabic is read from right to left, numerals are read from left to right.

ARABIC NUMERALS										
0	1	2	3	4	5	6	7	8	9	10
٠	١	٢	٣	٤	٥	٦	٧	٨	٩	١٠
sifr	waahid	itnein	talaata	arba'a	khamsa	sitta	sab'a	tamanya	tis'a	'ashara

PHRASEBOOK

GREETINGS, ETC.

ENGLISH	ARABIC
Hello	Marhaba
Hello (formal)/response	As-Salammu aleikum/Wa Aleikum as–salaam
Welcome	Ahlan/Ahlein/Ahlan wa sahlan
(response)	Shukran/Ahlein beek (m)/Ahlein beekee (f)
Good morning /response	Sabah al-kheir/Sabah an-nour *or* Sabah al-ful
Good evening /response	Masa' al-kheir/Masa' an-nour
Good-bye	Ma' as-salaama
Yes	Eeh/Na'am (formal)
No	La/La-a (for emphasis)
Thank you	Shukran
Please	Min fadlak (m)/Min fadlik (f)
I'm sorry	Ana aasif (m)/Ana aasfa (f)
Excuse me (to get attention)	'An iznak (m)/'An iznik (f), 'Afwan
God willing	In sha allah (shortened to inshaala)
Praise God (also: "OK")	Al hamdu lillah
What is your name?	Shoo ismak? (m)/Shoo ismik? (f)
My name is...	Ismee...
Who?	Meen?
How are you?	Keefak? (m)/Keefik? (f)
Fine	Mnih (m)/Mniha (f)
I'm fine (lit. thank God)	Al-ḥamdu lillah
I'm tired	Ana ta'baan (m)/Ana ta'baana (f)
I don't understand	Ma bafham
Student	Talib (m)/Taliba (f)
Never mind, No big deal	Ma'alesh

DIRECTIONS

ENGLISH	ARABIC
Let's Go!	Yalla! or Yalla beena!
Where? or Where is ...?	Wayn?
Right (direction)	Yameen
Left	Shimal or yasaar
Straight	Dughree
What? (Also as in "Excuse me?")	Shoo?
When?	Imta?
Why?	Leish?
I'm going to ...	Ana rayih (m)/Ana rayha (f) ila...

ENGLISH	ARABIC
There is ... or Is there ... ?	Fee ... ?
There is no ... or Isn't there any ... ?	Mafeesh ... ?
Restaurant	Mat'am
Post office	Maktab al-bareed
Street	Shaari'a
Market	Souq or sou'
Museum	Mat-haf
Mosque	Masjed/Jaame'
Church	Kineesa
University	Jaami'a
Hotel	Funduq or (h)otel
Room	Ghurfa
Airport	Mataar
Station	Mahatta
Bus	Bas
Automobile	Sayyaara
Tourist	Saayih (m)/Saayiha (f)/Suwwaah (pl)

BARGAINING

ENGLISH	ARABIC
How much?	Addeish
No way!	Mish mumkin!
Will you take half?	Taakhud nuss? (m)/Taakhdee nuss? (f)
money	Masaari
change	Fraata
I want...	Biddee

DATE AND TIME

ENGLISH	ARABIC
What time is it?	Addeish as-saa'a?
Hour, time	Saa'a
Day/Week/Month/Year	Yom/Usbuu'/Shahr/Sana
Today/Yesterday/Tomorrow	Al-yom/Imbaareh/Bukra
Sunday	Yom al-ahad
Monday	Yom al-itnein
Tuesday	Yom at-talaat
Wednesday	Yom al-arba'
Thursday	Yom al-khamees
Friday	Yom aj-juma'a
Saturday	Yom as-sabt

EMERGENCY

ENGLISH	ARABIC
Do you speak English?	Bitihkee inglizi?
I feel like I'm about to die.	Hamoot
I don't speak Arabic.	Ma bahki 'arabi
Tourist police	Bolees as-siyaaha
Hospital	Mustashfa
Doctor	Duktoor
Passport	Basbor/jawaz

ENGLISH	ARABIC
Embassy	Safaarah
Water	Mayya

GLOSSARY

HEBREW=(HEB) ARABIC=(AR)
Achshav: (HEB) now
Agorot: (HEB) worthless coins that clog your pockets
Aḥlah: (AR) totally cool
Ain lee coaḥ: (HEB) I don't have any strength/I don't want to do that
Aish: (HEB) fire (note: use as "ten lee/tenee lee (To f) et ha-aish," can I have a light?)
Aliyah: (HEB) literally translated, "moving up"; denotes non-Israeli Jews making permanent residence in Israel
Ars: (HEB) sleazy, lecherous male, usually with slicked back hair and skin-tight garb
Ahsoor l. . .: (HEB) it is forbidden to. . .
Assimon: (HEB) old phone token
Atzma'ut: (HEB) independence
Avodah: (HEB) work
Ain bayah: (HEB) I have no problem with that
Balagan: (HEB) craziness; confusion
Beerah: (HEB) beer
Beetaḥon: (HEB) security
Beit: (HEB) house of. . .
Betaḥ: (HEB) of course
Bevadai: (HEB) certainly
Betay Avon: (HEB) Bon appetit!
Bo!: (HEB) come here!
Caḥa-caḥa: (HEB) so-so
Caliph: (AR) Muslim ruler
Chik-chak: (HEB) finished right away
Dafka: (HEB) ironically
Dafuk: (HEB) a cruder way to say "messed-up"
Eser: (HEB) very cool
Falafel: (HEB) fried chickpea balls
Freiḥa: (HEB) female version of ars; generally promiscous
Fuul: (AR) cooked, mashed fava beans with garlic, lemon, olive oil and salt.
Gever (m)/geveret (f): sir/madam
Ha-Aretz: (HEB) "the land," Israel
Ḥadashot: (HEB) breaking news
Hafsakah: (HEB) break; also refers to the10min. break half-way through movies
Hajj: (AR) pilgrimage to Mecca and Medina
Hakol yiyeh beseder: (HEB) Everything will be o.k. Israeli mantra
Ḥam lee: (HEB) I'm hot (note: NOT ani ḥam, "I'm *feeling* hot")
Ḥamud: (HEB) cutie
Haredi: (HEB) Ultra-Orthodox (black hat) Jews
Hateeḥ (m)/hateeḥah (f): (HEB) extremely good-looking member of opposite gender
Ḥaval al Ha-Zman: (HEB) too bad there's not enough time
Ḥefetz ḥashood: (HEB) suspicious package; bomb threat
Ḥofesh: (HEB) free time
Ḥootzpan (m)/Ḥootzpaneet (f): (HEB) Someone possessing a lot of nerve
Ḥummus: (AR) mashed chickpeas with tahini
Ḥurva: (HEB) ruin
Ich zeh!: (HEB) expresses extreme disgust
Imam: (AR) Muslim leader
Kabbalah: (HEB) mystical branch of Judaism
Kav yarok: (HEB) green line
Keelu: (HEB) like, in the valley-girl sense of the word, e.g. "he was like. . ., and then she was like. . ., and then I was like, oh my gosh!"
Kef: (HEB) fun
Kefyeh: (AR) traditional black-and white checkered headscarf
Khan: (AR) caravanserai (inn for travelers)
Kfar: (HEB) Village
Kikkar: (HEB) town square
Kippah: (HEB) head covering worn by observant Jews as a sign of respect before G-d
Kol-kaḥ: (HEB) dramatic way of stating: "altogether" or "everything"
Lafah: (AR) soft bread used to wrap shawarma
Laf-laf/laf-lafeet (f): (HEB) nerd
Macabee/Goldstar: (HEB) Israeli brand beers

Mah koreh?: (HEB) what happened?; used to express extreme concern
Makhtesh: (HEB) crater
Masteek: (HEB) chewing gum
Mazgan: (HEB) air conditioner
Meaḥuz: (HEB) Alright! (one hundred percent)
Midraḥov: (HEB) main pedestrian walkway
Milḥamah: (HEB) war
Minaret: (AR) a tall, slender tower of a mosque, stood on by the Muezzin
Motek: (HEB) sweetie
Muezzin: (AR) person who summons Muslims to prayer five times a day
Naḥal: (HEB) valley
Naḥon: (HEB) I agree
Nargilah: (AR) water pipe, used to smoke fruit-flavored tobaccos
Neeflah: (HEB) awesome
Neḥmad: (HEB) nice
Nu?: (HEB) So?
Oi vei!: (HEB) yiddish phrase expressing exasperation
Oleem: (HEB) immigrants
OO/WC: symbol that denotes bathrooms
Pashoot: (HEB) simple
Patooaḥ: (HEB) open
Pelephon: (HEB) cell phone, owned by absolutely everyone
ptza-tzah: (HEB) bomb or hot girl
Rikud Ha-am: (HEB) Israeli dance
Rooaḥ: (HEB) spirit; gusto; energy
Roogelaḥ: (HEB) cinnamon-y rolled pastry
Sababa: (HEB) cool
Sagoor: (HEB) closed
Shacor (m)/Shacorah (f): (HEB) drunk
Shawarma: (HEB) roasted lamb
Shkadeh marak: (HEB) soup-nuts
Sheesha: see nargilah.
Sheket: (HEB) quiet
Sherut (HEB)/**Service** (AR): cheaper, van-like taxi that carries up to eight passengers
Sheshbesh: (HEB) the game "Backgammon"
Shev!: (HEB) sit down!
Shil-shool: (HEB) disastrous diarrhea
Shitaḥeem: (HEB) territories
Sof-sof: (HEB) finally
Special: (AR) private taxi
Stam: (HEB) Just kidding; whatever
Taeem: (HEB) tasty
Tamar: (HEB) date (the fruity sort)
Teepesh: (HEB) stupid
Tel: (HEB) hill or mound
Telecart: (HEB) telecard
Tiyool: (HEB) short trip
Tzaḥal: (HEB) the Israeli Defense Forces
Ulpan: (HEB) intensive hebrew classes
Wadi: (HEB) riverbed
Yafeh: (HEB) great!
Yayin: (HEB) wine
Yeshiva: (HEB) Religious Jewish day school
Yotvatah: (HEB) famous brand of milk
Za'tar: (AR) thyme mixed with sesame seeds
Zeh ooh: (HEB) That's all!
Zooz!: (HEB) move it, buddy!

INDEX

INDEX

INDEX

INDEX

MAPS